Bottom Line's
HEALTH
BREAKTHROUGHS
2004

Bottom Line
Books
www.BottomLineSecrets.com

ISBN 0-88723-299-X

Articles in this book were written by reporters for HealthDay, an award-winning international daily consumer health news service, headquartered in Norwalk, Connecticut.

The articles were selected and edited by HealthDay Editor-in-Chief Barry Hoffman and Managing Editor Jean Patman. The staff at Bottom Line Books reviewed and edited all content.

The editors would like to acknowledge and thank the following veteran journalists who crafted the articles specifically for this book:
Craig N. Berke; Jennifer Udall Berke; Steven Jusczyk; Shirley Mathews

Bottom Line® Books publishes the opinions of expert authorities in many fields. The use of this book is not a substitute for health or other professional service. Consult a physician or other health-care practitioner for answers to your specific questions and before you make any decision regarding your health.

Addresses, telephone numbers and Web sites listed in this book are accurate at the time of publication, but they are subject to frequent change.

Bottom Line® Books is a registered trademark of Boardroom® Inc.
281 Tresser Boulevard, Stamford, CT 06901

Printed in the United States of America

Contents

8 • EMOTIONAL WELL-BEING

9 • FAMILY HEALTH

10 • HEART DISEASE

11 • NATURAL REMEDIES

12 • NUTRITION, DIET & FITNESS

13 • PAIN TREATMENTS

14 • RESEARCH NEWS

15 • STROKE PREVENTION

16 • WOMEN'S HEALTH

1

Aging & Senior Health

A Positive Attitude Adds 7.5 Years to Your Life

A Yale University study has found that a positive attitude about aging may actually help you live longer. If you have a tarnished view of your Golden Years, however, that negative attitude may shorten your life by affecting your will to live, says lead author Becca R. Levy, an assistant professor of epidemiology and public health at Yale.

Levy's study, published in the *Journal of Personality and Social Psychology*, found that older people with positive perceptions of aging lived 7.5 years longer than people with negative perceptions.

Levy says she hadn't expected to find that attitude has such a big impact on longevity.

The study included 660 people (338 men and 322 women) from a small Ohio town who in 1975 gave responses to questions asked as part of a study on aging and retirement. At the time they gave their responses, all were 50 years or older. They were asked to agree or disagree with statements such as, "As you get older, you are less useful."

"In this study, we did a snapshot of their perception of aging," Levy says.

She and her coauthors compared the participants' responses to their death rates in the ensuing years and found that people with more positive attitudes toward aging lived 7.5 years longer.

The study accounted for other factors such as age, gender, overall health, loneliness, and socioeconomic status.

Although the effect of negative attitudes about aging on the will to live does have an impact on longevity, it isn't the only influence, Levy says. Her research indicates that those

Becca R. Levy, PhD, Assistant Professor, Department of Epidemiology and Public Health, Yale University, New Haven, CT.

Michael Brickey, PhD, Psychologist, Bexley, OH.

August 2002, *Journal of Personality and Social Psychology.*

negative stereotypes of aging may also have an adverse effect on older people's cardiovascular response to everyday stress.

Where do people get these pessimistic thoughts about growing old? Levy says we pick them up from society and we may not even be aware it's happening.

"I think older adults can think about ways to question some of the negative stereotypes they encounter in everyday life. I think there is reason to believe that that may have a positive impact over time," Levy says.

■ ■ ■ ■

A Sense of Purpose

Michael Brickey, a psychologist and author of *Defy Aging*, says that 50 years ago, it was easier for the typical American to have a sense of purpose in life. He could grow up and live his entire life in the same town, stay married to one person, and work for the same company until he retired.

"There weren't as many choices and options. Now, we have so much change and so much choice that it's easy to lose your footing," Brickey says.

His book gives an overview of 36 age-defying beliefs. *He also lists some secrets to longevity…*

- **Refuse to hold onto feelings of resentment** and loss.
- **Refuse to conform to conventional thinking** or engage in pessimistic thinking.
- **Continue to learn and grow.**
- **Stay physically active.**
- **Be self-reliant.**
- **Place an inordinate emphasis on humor.**

■ ■ ■ ■

A Healthy Lifestyle

The United States government has decided to measure how well we're taking care of ourselves. And, in doing so, the researchers may be able to come up with some recommendations to help people live longer.

Healthy People 2010, coordinated by the National Institutes of Health, will measure 10 health indicators through the year 2010. *In the meantime, make a personal assessment of the following influences in your life…*

- **Physical activity.**
- **Overweight and obesity.**
- **Tobacco use.**
- **Substance abuse.**
- **Responsible sexual behavior.**
- **Mental health.**
- **Injury and violence.**
- **Environmental quality.**
- **Immunization.**
- **Access to health care.**

Do Hormones Help You Live Longer?

Paula Bickford, PhD, Professor, Neurosurgery, University of South Florida Center for Aging and Brain Repair, Tampa, and Past President, American Aging Association, Media, PA.

Valter D. Longo, PhD, Assistant Professor and Chairman, Biogerontology, University of Southern California, Los Angeles.

Nir Barzilai, MD, Director, Institute for Aging Research, Albert Einstein College of Medicine, Bronx, NY.

February 28, 2003, *Science.*

Scientists already know that very low-calorie diets lengthen the life spans of many living creatures, but for humans, it could be that manipulating the levels of certain hormones can lead to longer life.

People with excess amounts of 2 hormones —one produced by the pituitary gland and one produced by the liver—tend to have shorter life spans. They also have a higher incidence of diseases associated with old age, even when they're relatively young.

Long life may come from biological aberrations, namely mutations that cause low levels of *insulin-like growth factor* (IGF-1), a hormone produced by the liver, and of *growth hormone* (GH), a hormone manufactured by the pituitary gland that stimulates growth in children.

POSSIBLE APPROACHES

One theory is based on the fact that dwarf mice lack GH and live 50% longer than normal-stature mice.

"This is a powerful issue that has not just been demonstrated in one organism, but in all major model systems, so there is a good chance that it is going to work in humans also, at least to a certain degree," says Valter D. Longo, assistant professor and chairman of biogerontology at the University of Southern California, Los Angeles.

Scientists are hoping to create a drug that would act on the mechanisms that control the release of GH. The key would be to get the long life without the dwarfism or its associated side effects, such as obesity.

A second possibility would be to prevent the liver from secreting as much insulin-like growth factor (IGF-1). It may also be possible to find a way to manipulate the effects of IGF-1 on the cellular structure. In this case, the IGF-1 would still be present in normal or close-to-normal levels in the blood, it just wouldn't be able to hit home as well.

NOT ALL AGREE

Dr. Nir Barzilai, director of the Institute for Aging Research at Albert Einstein School of Medicine in New York City, is not so sure of the theory.

Many antiaging centers actually give their clients more GH, he said, presumably to stop or reverse aging.

For another thing, Barzilai found slightly elevated IGF-1 levels in a group of 250 centenarians he is studying.

"It's possible that IGF-1 has some role in the longevity of rodents, but whether it has a role in the longevity of humans is not really well-established," he says.

Research on these hormones is already under way by a group at the University of Southern California and other groups, but it isn't likely to come to fruition any time soon, says Paula Bickford, a professor of neurosurgery at the University of South Florida Center for Aging and Brain Repair in Tampa.

New Web Site Lowers Prescription Drug Costs For Seniors

Eileen Zenker, MSW, Assistant Director, Social Work, New York University Medical Center, NY.

Scott Parkin, spokesman, National Council on the Aging, Washington, DC.

The National Council on the Aging has developed a program called Benefits-CheckUpRx that is a fast, easy-to-use online database to help low- and middle-income seniors find cost-saving programs for prescription drugs.

"The goal was to bring together all the various public and private discount drug programs for seniors and centralize the information," says Scott Parkin, spokesman for the National Council. It's a fast and easy way to find out if seniors are eligible and to supply them with the information needed to contact the various programs.

The site supplies information on more than 240 public and private prescription savings programs, including state and federal initiatives along with those sponsored by individual drug companies. Included in the database is discount information on nearly 800 of the most commonly used prescription medications.

HOW IT WORKS

To see if they qualify, all seniors need to do is complete a brief and secure online questionnaire. The computer program does the rest.

"In a matter of a few minutes, the service displays a personalized report that specifies which programs the person is eligible for, plus offers detailed instructions on how to enroll," Parkin says.

Once enrolled in a discount program, seniors receive all the necessary information to purchase prescriptions at the discounted price at a local pharmacy. Although not all pharmacies honor all prescription discount plans, most major chain drugstores and many smaller independent pharmacies do, Parkin says.

On 2 common blood pressure medications used together—Norvasc and Atacand—the normal cost for a 30-day supply of both can range from $80 to $130, depending on where they are purchased. Using 2 options suggested by BenefitsCheckUpRx, the total cost for a 30-day supply of both drugs was just $25.

"Programs like these allow seniors to not only get their much-needed medication, but to keep their much-needed sense of pride and independence," says Eileen Zenker, assistant director of social work at New York University Medical Center. That can go a long way toward improving their mental and physical health.

For those who don't have a computer or are unfamiliar with navigating Web sites, the National Council on the Aging suggests asking a close family friend or relative to log on and help out. And many senior centers, libraries, and even doctors' offices and clinics offer Internet access and may be able to help, Zenker says.

info To learn more about BenefitsCheckUpRx, visit the Web site at *www.benefitscheckuprx.com.*

■ ■ ■ ■

High Costs for the Elderly

Many Americans struggle with the high cost of health care, but seniors often take the brunt of the beating.

• **According to a recent *Wall Street Journal* report,** up to 80% of all retirees take a prescription drug every day. Yet, the Kaiser Foundation reports that 40% of Medicare beneficiaries have no drug coverage of any kind.

• **Another report by the Kaiser Foundation** revealed that nearly one-quarter of all seniors don't even fill their much-needed prescriptions because they can't afford to—or they try to save money by taking fewer pills.

The Real Risk of Cholesterol Drugs Is Not Taking Them

Cynthia A. Jackevicius, BScPharm, MSc, Adjunct Scientist, University Health Network–Toronto General Hospital, Toronto, Ontario, Canada.

Joshua S. Benner, PharmD, ScD, Director, Health Economics, Epinomics Research, Alexandria, VA.

William B. Applegate, MD, Dean, Wake Forest University Baptist Medical Center, Winston–Salem, NC.

July 24, 2002, *Journal of the American Medical Association.*

Most seniors eventually stop taking the cholesterol-lowering drugs that help prevent heart attacks and stroke because they do not understand the dangers associated with not taking their medicine.

Money is not an issue, because the seniors could get the drugs at little or no cost, say 2 reports in the *Journal of the American Medical Association.* Researchers don't have the whole answer to the high dropout rate, but part of the problem seems to be that it takes a clear and present danger to make people of any age swallow their medicine.

"People who had a heart attack the previous year were more likely to take the medication," explains Cynthia A. Jackevicius. She is an adjunct scientist in the health policy management and evaluation department of Toronto General Hospital. Her study looked at people 66 years and older who were in the Ontario province drug plan.

Her results were similar to those of a second study that included people in the New Jersey Medicaid program.

"It's striking how alike they are. We must have it right," says Joshua S. Benner, who led the New Jersey study when he was at Brigham and Women's Hospital in Boston.

DROPPING OUT

In the New Jersey study, 40% of people who were given a prescription for a cholesterol-lowering statin stopped taking the recommended dosage within 3 months. That number rose to 61% after 1 year.

In the Canadian study, 25% of patients stopped taking their prescribed drugs within the first 3 months. Nearly 75% of those who had dangerously high cholesterol levels but no active heart disease stopped taking the medications after 2 years. Approximately 60% of people with active heart disease stopped taking their drugs after 2 years.

"If I had to guess why people stop taking their medication, I would say that they don't understand that their condition requires long-term treatment," Benner says.

"Other studies have postulated that having high cholesterol levels is like having high blood pressure," Jackevicius says. "You can't feel it, so it is not obvious that you need to treat it."

HOW TO IMPROVE THE SITUATION

"Education is a big first step," Benner says. Compliance seems to improve when there are published reports showing the benefits of statins, he says. Both doctors and pharmacists should try to get the message across.

"Because there is a high early dropout rate, the important thing is that when a patient comes in to fill the first prescription, the pharmacist should spend some time explaining the benefits," Benner says.

THE EXTRA STEP

The reports can help by publicizing the issue, says Dr. William B. Applegate, dean of the Wake Forest University School of Medicine and author of an accompanying editorial, but just reporting is not enough.

"We need to do a better job in terms of health management, in general," he says. "Second, it has been shown that nurse-run health plans, where they go over information with patients, show higher rates of compliance with preventive medications."

info For more on high cholesterol, visit the Web sites of the American Heart Association at *www.americanheart.org* or the National Heart, Lung, and Blood Institute at *www.nhlbi.nih.gov.*

Warning: Hormone Therapy Doubles Dementia Risk

Sally A. Shumaker, PhD, Professor, Public Health Sciences, Wake Forest University School of Medicine, Winston–Salem, NC.

Sylvia Wassertheil–Smoller, PhD, Professor, Epidemiology and Public Health, Albert Einstein School of Medicine, Bronx, NY.

May 28, 2003, *Journal of the American Medical Association.*

Combined hormone therapy for women doubles the risk of dementias, such as Alzheimer's disease. It also does not protect against mild cognitive impairment, a less severe loss of mental function, and it increases the risk of stroke.

That alarming news comes from data extracted from the Women's Health Initiative (WHI) study, which was stopped in 2002 when combined hormone therapy was found to increase the risk of breast cancer and heart disease.

The reports are based on studies of subsets of the more than 100,000 women who enrolled in the study. Two studies of mental function done by researchers at Wake Forest University School of Medicine reported data on more than 4500 women who were taking daily doses of estrogen and progestin.

When the study began, combined hormone therapy was thought to prevent dementia, says Sally A. Shumaker, a professor of public health sciences at Wake Forest University and lead author of the paper on dementia.

The data show a dementia rate of 45 per 10,000 women taking the hormones, compared with 22 per 10,000 in women taking a placebo, Shumaker says.

Although the risk was small, the result reinforces the finding that the risks of combined hormone therapy outweigh the benefits, especially for older women, she says.

Other researchers at Wake Forest looked at the incidence of mild cognitive impairment in the women in the study. Periodic tests of mental function showed no significant benefit and a possible harmful effect of hormone therapy, another report says.

Combined hormone therapy now is recommended only for short-term use in women suffering extremely uncomfortable symptoms during menopause, such as hot flashes, vaginal dryness, and insomnia. The problem with the short-term approach is that the medical community doesn't know how short that term should be, according to Sylvia Wassertheil–Smoller, a professor of epidemiology and public health at Albert Einstein College of Medicine and lead author of the stroke report.

There are indications that the risk of both dementia and stroke increases rather quickly, possibly within a year or 2, Wassertheil–Smoller says.

Women in the dementia study are still being followed up to see whether the risk decreases when they stop hormone therapy, Shumaker says.

info A detailed overview of the Women's Health Initiative is available at *www.nhl bi.nih.gov/whi*.

■ ■ ■ ■

Early Warning Signs of Dementia

The Veterans Administration Healthcare Network provides a list of the early warning signs of dementia. *They are...*

● **Recent memory loss** that affects performance at work.

● **Difficulty performing familiar tasks.**

● **Difficulty finding the right word** when speaking.

● **Difficulty remembering the date.**

● **Feeling lost.**

● **Loss of judgment.**

● **Misplacing things.**

● **Difficulty with abstract thinking.**

● **Changes in mood or behavior.**

● **Changes in personality.**

● **Loss of "get-up-and-go."**

The 'Walking Test' That May Prevent Dementia

Joe Verghese, MD, Assistant Professor of Neurology, and Richard Lipton, MD, Lead Investigator, Einstein Aging Study, Albert Einstein College of Medicine, Bronx, NY.

November 28, 2002, *New England Journal of Medicine*.

Peculiar kinds of walking in the elderly can be warning signs of dementia. Although this might sound scary to an older person who is unsteady on his/her feet, it's actually good news, researchers say.

Lots of people have problems walking when they get older, and most of the time the problem is caused by something like arthritis or back trouble, says Dr. Joe Verghese, assistant professor of neurology at Albert Einstein College of Medicine and lead author of the study. But some kinds of abnormal gaits are warning signs of vascular dementia, which is not as well known as Alzheimer's disease— the major type of dementia in older people— but does account for approximately 1 in 3 cases, Verghese says.

SIGNS OF TROUBLE

Gait problems that may indicate vascular dementia include noticeable swaying, balance trouble, the inability to walk heel-to-toe, short steps, shuffling, not swinging the arms, and difficulty making turns.

Verghese was surprised by how strongly abnormal gait predicted vascular dementia. "It predicted the future—at least 10 years into the future," he says.

And this is actually good news, because vascular dementia is preventable. It results when blood flow to the brain is restricted. Taking measures to control blood pressure and cholesterol can keep blood flow at a normal level, Verghese says.

THE STUDY

Verghese looked at more than 400 people between the ages of 75 and 85, whose gait had been evaluated as a part of a long-term study. After almost 7 years, 70 of them developed Alzheimer's disease and 47 developed vascular dementia. The people with abnormal gaits were more than 3 times as likely to have vascular dementia as those with normal gaits, although their risk of Alzheimer's disease was not affected.

It was known when the study began more than 20 years ago that an older person with dementia who had difficulty walking was more likely to have the vascular form, says Dr. Richard Lipton, the Lotti and Bernard Benson Faculty Scholar in Alzheimer's Disease at the Albert Einstein College of Medicine, who heads the long-term aging study.

"What wasn't known previously was that this predicted the future development of vascular dementia, even a decade before diagnosis," he says.

TREATABLE DISEASE

Today, 3 drugs are approved for treating Alzheimer's disease, and some drugs are also effective in treating vascular dementia. "Already, the condition has shifted from being rarely treatable to being almost always treatable," Lipton adds. The next transition, he says, is to prevent these conditions.

Several preventive trials are presently under way. Lipton believes that the key to finding something to prevent these diseases is to figure out ways of pinpointing which people are at the highest risk.

The finding that an abnormal walking pattern can be a long-term warning sign of dementia can help doctors start preventive therapy early, he says.

info You can get insight into dementia from the National Library of Medicine at *www. nlm.nih.gov* or the National Institute on Aging at *www.nia.nih.gov.*

Sweeten Your Memory With Apples!

Paula Bickford, PhD, Research Career Scientist, James A. Haley Veterans Hospital, and Professor, University of South Florida Center for Aging and Brain Repair, Tampa, FL.

July 15, 2002, *Journal of Neuroscience.*

Eating more fruits and vegetables has always been smart, but new research shows just how smart it really is. Antioxidants in fruits and vegetables can improve learning and memory, as well as minimize the effect of aging on the brain, say 2 new studies. Antioxidants can also undo cell damage caused by renegade molecules (called *free radicals*). Previous studies have shown antioxidants can prevent disease and improve mental functioning.

"What we have done is focus on the fruits and vegetables high on the US Department of Agriculture [USDA] list of antioxidants," says Paula Bickford, a senior career scientist at the James A. Haley Veterans Hospital in Tampa and lead author of both new studies, published in the *Journal of Neuroscience.*

The USDA ranks foods by their antioxidant content. Spinach, spirulina (an algae often sold in capsule form in health food stores), and apples were particularly good for learning and memory, Bickford says.

In the first study, the researchers fed a group of rats a diet rich in spinach, while another group got regular rat chow for 6 weeks. The rats were then tested for how well they learned using the following technique: The rats heard a tone, then they got a puff of air to the eye. The researchers studied how long it took rats in each group to learn to blink to avoid the air puff.

"The ones on spinach learned to make the association with fewer trials," Bickford says. "By the third day, they were at their learning maximum. It took the [other] rats 5 or 6 days to learn." The nerve cells in the spinach-fed rats work better, making it easier for them to learn, she speculates.

AN APPLE A DAY

In the second study, the researchers compared 3 types of diets. One group of rats got a diet enriched with spirulina (high in antioxidants), another group got apples (moderate in antioxidant activity), and a third group got cucumber (low in antioxidants).

"We were seeing effects within 2 weeks with the apple and spirulina diets," Bickford says.

The rats eating the apple and spirulina diets had reversed the age-typical accumulation of inflammatory substances in the brain. These rats also had better neuron functioning.

The amount of apple in the rats' apple-enriched diet translates to approximately an apple a day in humans, Bickford says.

info For information on antioxidant levels in fruits and vegetables, see the US Department of Agriculture Web site at *www. usda.gov.*

Why the Simple Sandwich Could Save Your Life!

Stephen A. Siegel, MD, Clinical Assistant Professor, Medicine, New York University School of Medicine.

April 2, 2003, *Journal of the American Medical Association.*

As the nation ages, rates of cardiovascular disease are expected to skyrocket. Right now, there are 35 million people 65 years or older in the United States, and that number is expected to reach 70 million by 2030, say researchers. Cardiovascular disease is the leading cause of death and disability in this age group.

Dietary fiber has been shown to reduce incidence of ischemic heart disease and stroke in middle-aged people, and experts have worried the same eating habits may not be as effective among older people, in whom disease has theoretically already set in. In fact, that seems not to be the case.

People 65 and older who added as few as 2 slices of whole grain bread per day to their diets had a lower risk of new cardiovascular disease, researchers say. That's a whole lot cheaper and less complicated than most medical interventions.

COMPLEX FIBERS MAKE A DIFFERENCE

"It's always nice to have another group specifically targeted. It helps to give more scientific support for the general recommendation that's been in place for quite a while in terms of increasing the amount of dietary fiber, and in particular the more complex fibers," says Dr. Stephen Siegel, a clinical assistant professor of medicine at New York University School of Medicine who was not associated with the study.

Researchers from the University of Washington in Seattle analyzed data from 3588 men and women 65 years or older. None of the participants had cardiovascular disease at the beginning of the study.

After factoring in age, sex, diabetes, smoking status, exercise, alcohol intake, and fruit and vegetable consumption, it became clear that intake of cereal fiber reduced the incidence of newly developed cardiovascular disease. Those who consumed the highest amounts of this type of dietary fiber had a 21% lower risk than those who consumed the least amount.

DARK BREAD IS BEST

The trend was especially strong among people who ate dark breads such as wheat, rye, or pumpernickel. They had a 24% lower risk of cardiovascular disease.

Neither fruit nor vegetable fiber intake was associated with new cardiovascular disease, but it didn't seem to be protective, either, the study found.

info For more on dietary fiber, visit the Johns Hopkins Bayview Medical Center Web site at *www.jhbmc.jhu.edu/healthy/ stayinghealthy.*

A Drink a Day May Ward Off Dementia

Kenneth J. Mukamal, MD, MPH, Internist, Beth Israel Deaconess Medical Center, Boston, MA.

Antonio Convit, MD, Associate Professor, Psychiatry and Medical Director, Center for Brain Health, New York University School of Medicine.

March 19, 2003, *Journal of the American Medical Association.*

Older adults who allow themselves 1 to 6 alcoholic drinks weekly have a lower risk of dementia than those who completely abstained, according to a Boston study.

Although there have been several studies on alcohol and cognitive functioning, the results have been mixed, says the study's author, Dr. Kenneth J. Mukamal, an internist at Beth Israel Deaconess Medical Center in Boston.

Mukamal said the study included repeated assessments of how much people were drinking before signing up with the researchers.

The exact biological mechanisms are still unclear, although there are theories. Previous work has shown that light and moderate drinkers had fewer white matter lesions, which scientists think might be linked to blood vessel blockages. Such blockages are implicated in heart attacks and in dementia.

"Much like alcohol consumption is supposed to prevent heart attacks by preventing blockages in blood vessels, the same thing might be happening in dementia," Mukamal says. "By preserving blood flow to the brain, we could hold off dementia."

Mukamal does point out, however, that in the 65 years and older age group, alcohol could interact with medications and that current guidelines recommend no more than 1 drink a day for older adults.

THE STUDY

Mukamal and his colleagues looked at 373 people with a recent onset of dementia and 373 control patients who were among the 5888 participants in the Cardiovascular Health Study. All were 65 years or older.

Those who consumed 1 to 6 drinks per week had the lowest odds of developing dementia—a 54% lower risk than those who abstained. Those who had between zero and 1 drink per week had a 35% lower risk; those who consumed 7 to 13 drinks a week showed a 31% lower risk. But, importantly, those who consumed 14 to 21 drinks per week had a 22% greater risk.

The association between moderate drinking and dementia was similar for men and women, but the risks of heavier drinking seemed to be more apparent among the men, Mukamal says.

QUESTIONS FINDINGS

"It's very difficult to conclude whether alcohol has any impact on your risk for dementia," says Dr. Antonio Convit, an associate professor of psychiatry and medical director of the Center for Brain Health at New York University School of Medicine in New York City.

"Because of the known cardiovascular benefits, I would tell them moderate amounts of alcohol—1 drink a day—certainly doesn't seem like it's going to harm you," he says.

Routine Dementia Screening May Be Dangerous

Alfred O. Berg, MD, MPH, Chairman, US Preventive Task Force, Professor and Chairman, Department of Family Medicine, University of Washington, Seattle.

Malaz Boustani, MD, MPH, Assistant Professor, Medicine, Indiana University School of Medicine, Indianapolis.

Sharon Inouye, MD, MPH, Professor, Medicine, Yale University, New Haven, CT.

June 3, 2003, *Annals of Internal Medicine.*

There is no evidence to support the screening for dementia in older patients who do not show signs of the disease, according to a federal government advisory panel called The Preventive Task Force.

The Preventive Task Force is an independent panel of private-sector experts who assess evidence for a wide range of preventive services. The panel's recommendations are considered the standard of care.

Routine screening of patients with no signs of dementia can be risky, says Dr. Alfred O. Berg, task force chairman. Patients might have a positive test result for dementia but not actually have the problem, which could have a devastating psychological effect. And patients with dementia could have normal test results.

The medical evidence for the task force recommendation comes from a report from a team led by Dr. Malaz Boustani, an assistant professor of medicine at the Indiana University School of Medicine.

Boustani's team, after reviewing all the literature on dementia screening from 1994, found there was not enough data to decide whether the benefit of screening outweighed the potential harm.

Patients with no signs of dementia but who are diagnosed with dementia might suffer consequences, such as canceled health insurance or revoked driver's licenses.

The only benefit that Boustani sees from screening is that patients and their families can begin to make health care arrangements and decisions about finances and other personal matters.

He stresses that if family members or your doctor notes signs of memory loss or other cognitive problems, the patient should be tested for dementia.

TAKES ISSUE WITH RECOMMENDATIONS

The panel's recommendations are not unanimously applauded. Dr. Sharon Inouye, a Yale University professor of medicine specializing in dementia, said the recommendations are disappointing. She would like to see more screening done in the older population because dementia is so often missed, particularly in its early stages.

"Geriatric investigators need to concentrate on getting better evidence so we can document the need for more widespread screening," Inouye says.

She also says there is need to document the value of early treatment. There is some good evidence, Inouye notes, that medications can slow the progression of dementia for several months and if patients are not diagnosed early they lose out on this benefit altogether.

Moderate Drinking Is Even Healthier As We Age

Ian R. White, Statistician, British Medical Research Council Biostatistics Unit, Cambridge, England.

July 27, 2002, *British Medical Journal.*

The older you get, the more likely it is that an alcoholic drink (or 2) a day will help protect you against heart disease, says a British study published in the *British Medical Journal.*

"People have long believed this to be the case. But nobody has really quantified it," says Ian R. White, the statistician in the British Medical Research Council Biostatistics Unit who led the study. "Our contribution is to point out the effects of age on the U-shaped curve."

That U-shaped curve is on a chart showing the association between alcohol intake and death rate.

Using death statistics for England and Wales and information on drinking habits from a national survey in the United Kingdom, White and his colleagues found the low point of that curve shifts as people grow older. The measure of intake they use is a British standard—9 grams of alcohol. That's a half-pint of beer, a smallish glass of wine, or a shot of whiskey, White says. Americans use a different standard of 13 grams of alcohol.

Here's how it works: Imagine the lowest point of the letter U. That would be the best combination of age and number of drinks a person should have—the lowest mortality rate. For example, for women older than 65 years, the lowest point of the U-shaped curve is an intake of 3 standard drinks a week; for men in the same age category, it's 8 standard drinks a week.

Here's the rule of thumb: If you're a little younger, drink a little less. If you're older than 65, a little more is probably beneficial.

■ ■ ■ ■

When the Risk Outweighs The Benefit

If you're wondering how much is too much, the following numbers are for you. *The amount of alcohol that provides the most benefit for women's hearts is…*

- **1 standard drink per day up to age 44.**
- **2 per day up to age 74.**
- **3 per day after age 74.**

The amount of alcohol that provides the most benefit for men's hearts is…

- **1 standard drink per day up to age 34.**
- **2 per day up to age 44.**
- **3 per day up to age 54.**
- **4 per day up to age 84.**
- **5 per day after age 84.**

Anything over those numbers increases the risk of death by more than 5%, White says.

Those numbers yield practical guidelines for health-conscious drinkers, White says.

In the United States, the American Heart Association cautiously says moderate alcohol intake is associated with lower risk of death—with the emphasis on "moderate." The Association's guidelines call for a daily limit of 1 alcoholic drink a day for women, 2 for men. One drink means 12 ounces of beer, 4 ounces of wine, 1.5 ounces of 80-proof whiskey, or 1 ounce of 100-proof whiskey, with no changes for age. Saving up the allowance for a binge is not advisable, the AHA says.

White also adds a caution that is being taken into account by American authorities who are lowering the level of blood alcohol in the definition of drunk driving. For younger people, he says, alcohol-related accidents are a significant cause of death, and so "a greater focus could be placed on avoiding risky patterns of drinking, rather than on reducing average alcohol consumption."

MRIs Proved Safer Than Stress Tests

Sidney Smith, MD, former President, American Heart Association, and Professor, Medicine, University of North Carolina, Chapel Hill.
John Mazur, MD, Cardiologist, Scripps Mercy Hospital, San Diego, CA.
March 5, 2003, *Journal of the American College of Cardiology.*

Stress tests are a helpful tool to find out whether someone has clogged arteries. Just ask talk-show host David Letterman, whose doctors discovered he needed an immediate quintuple bypass operation after reviewing the results of his stress test. However, the tests require that someone either exert himself or take a drug that simulates physical stress—both difficult propositions for the most fragile patients.

However, there is a small study that suggests doctors could order less-invasive magnetic resonance imaging (MRI) scans instead.

"The interesting aspect is that you may be able to detect significant blockages in the arteries without having to stress the heart," says Dr. Sidney Smith, former president of the American Heart Association and a professor of medicine at the University of North Carolina at Chapel Hill.

Stress tests are common, especially among older patients. Typically, a patient will walk on a treadmill or ride a stationary bicycle to increase the heart rate. The doctor will track the progress of radioactive dye that's been injected into the patient's bloodstream.

As the dye reaches the heart, doctors can use scanning technology to watch what it does. "If a portion of the heart wall isn't receiving enough oxygen, it can't generate the energy it needs to contract and it usually bulbs out," says Dr. John Mazur, a cardiologist at Scripps Mercy Hospital in San Diego. Doctors can then figure out where a blockage is by determining which artery supplies blood to that part of the heart.

Some patients, such as those with arthritis or neurological damage, can't exert themselves through heavy exercise and need to take a drug similar to adrenaline to make their hearts work hard, Mazur says.

But while studying the use of MRI scans, researchers in Germany discovered they could detect which parts of the heart aren't receiving enough oxygen without requiring a stress test or a dye injection.

MAGNETIC SIGNALS IN THE BLOOD

The MRI scans picked up magnetic signals from the blood that was coming back to the heart to be refilled with oxygen. If there was less deoxygenated blood coming into the heart, the scans showed a darker area, suggesting an artery was blocked down the line.

Experts who reviewed the study findings say it's much too early to tell whether the MRI scans will supplement or even replace stress tests. However, they say the research deserves further study.

info Learn more about stress tests from HeartSite.com at *www.heartsite.com.* Click on "Cardiac Tests" at the bottom of the Web page.

Pulmonary Artery Catheter Doesn't Benefit Older Patients

James Dean Sandham, MD, Professor, Department of Critical Care Medicine, University of Calgary, Alberta, Canada.
January 2, 2003, *New England Journal of Medicine.*

The pulmonary artery catheters implanted in more than 1 million surgical patients in the United States every year do no good—but also no harm—in older, high-risk patients, according to Canadian researchers.

It's too early to tell whether the results apply to all surgical patients, says Dr. James Dean Sandham, a professor in the University of Calgary's department of critical care and the lead author of a paper reporting the results. But the good news is that the study found no evidence that the catheter increased the death rate of surgical patients. The patients in the

study had undergone major abdominal, thoracic, vascular, or hip-fracture surgery.

A pulmonary artery catheter is a balloon-tipped tube that is placed into that blood vessel to obtain measurements that can help refine treatment.

BOLSTERING DOUBTS

There have been doubts about the catheter's use since a 1996 study found that more patients died if they had one implanted during surgery than if they hadn't. The latest research offsets the 1996 report. Almost 2000 patients in the newer study were all 60 years or older.

The in-hospital death rate was virtually the same for those who got the catheter and those who did not. The 6-month survival rate was also virtually identical for both groups at almost 90%.

The only significant difference was that 8 of the catheter patients had *pulmonary embolisms* (blood clots or air bubbles), while none of the other patients did.

The study results can only be applied to patients who are similar to those studied—aged 60 or older, having major surgery, and whose associated medical conditions put them at high risk, Sandham says. But the results open the door for studies in a wider group of patients, such as those who are younger and have severe trauma or shock, he adds.

At least one study looking at a broader group of patients is under way, he adds.

info You can learn more about pulmonary artery catheters from Cardiovascular Consultants Medical Group at *www.cardiac consultants.com.*

Best Way to Prevent Deadly Drug Errors

Zane Robinson Wolf, RN, PhD, Dean and Professor of Nursing, LaSalle University, Philadelphia, PA.
March 5, 2003, *Journal of the American Medical Association.*

Elderly people fall victim to a large number of medication-related mistakes, more than 25% of which are preventable.

If these findings are extended to the total Medicare population of approximately 38 million people, that would mean more than 1.9 million adverse drug events occur each year, including 180,000 that are life-threatening or fatal.

That's not surprising when you look at the amount of medications that are prescribed to senior citizens, says Zane Robinson Wolf, dean and professor of nursing at LaSalle University in Philadelphia. A national survey found that more than 90% of people 65 years and older take at least 1 medication per week, more than 40% take 5 or more each week, and 12% take 10 or more.

A University of Massachusetts research team looked at 27,617 Medicare enrollees who received care at a group practice in a New England–based health maintenance organization over the course of 1 year.

In all, the researchers pinpointed 1523 adverse drug events, of which 27.6% were considered preventable. An adverse event referred to medication errors involving prescribing, dispensing, patient adherence or monitoring, or an adverse reaction not involving an error.

The preventable errors occurred most often at the time of prescribing and monitoring; the study participants had a 1-in-18 chance of something going wrong with their medication, and a 1-in-67 possibility that it could have been prevented.

Vitamin D Lowers Risk of Broken Bones

Kay Tee Khaw, Professor, Clinical Gerontology, University of Cambridge School of Clinical Medicine, United Kingdom.

Khaled Imam, MD, Geriatric Medicine Specialist, William Beaumont Hospital, Royal Oak, MI.

March 1, 2003, *British Medical Journal.*

Y ou can cut your risk of bone fractures as you age by taking vitamin D supplements, even if it's only 4 times a year in high-dose, slow-release capsules.

So say British researchers who found that quarterly supplements of vitamin D could reduce the overall risk of fractures by 22% in people older than 65 years. The risk of fracture at common sites such as the hip, wrist, forearms, or back was reduced by 33% with vitamin D supplementation.

Vitamin D is known as the "sunshine vitamin" because your body manufactures it when exposed to the sun. Vitamin D is also found in enriched dairy products, fatty fish, and fish oils, as well as supplements. A lack of vitamin D can cause weak bones and contribute to the development of osteoporosis.

Older people are more at risk for vitamin D deficiencies because the body doesn't produce vitamin D as efficiently with age, and the elderly often spend more time indoors, away from the sun.

However, too much vitamin D can be toxic and no one should take more than 800 international units (IU) of vitamin D a day without consulting their physician first, says study author Kay Tee Khaw, a professor of clinical gerontology at the University of Cambridge School of Clinical Medicine.

HEAVY EMPHASIS ON MEN

Khaw and his colleagues recruited 2686 people between the ages of 65 and 85 years for this study. Slightly more than 2000 of the participants were men. All were still living in a community, not in a nursing home.

For 5 years, the researchers sent half the volunteers 1 slow-release vitamin D capsule by mail every 4 months. The other half of the group received a placebo capsule every 4 months. They were told to take the capsule immediately and to complete a short survey about their health that included questions about any fractures that may have occurred.

The researchers also took a blood sample from 235 of the participants after 4 years to measure vitamin D levels.

Dr. Khaled Imam, a geriatric medicine specialist at William Beaumont Hospital in Royal Oak, Michigan, says the study is interesting because it included more men than women and because of the high doses of vitamin D given. Most studies on osteoporosis focus on women, but the condition is a serious problem for elderly men, as well, he says.

Although the dose of vitamin D given was in a slow-release form, Imam says he is concerned about what effect such a high dose might have on people with medical problems, such as kidney disease. One limitation of the study, according to Imam, is that the researchers didn't take more frequent blood samples to measure the concentrations of vitamin D.

info To learn more about vitamins and dietary supplements, visit the National Institutes of Health's Office of Dietary Supplements at *www.cc.nih.gov/ccc/supplements/vitd.html*.

■ ■ ■ ■

What Foods Contain Vitamin D?

The National Institutes of Health provides the Daily Value (DV) of vitamin D for many foods. The DVs are reference numbers based on the Recommended Dietary Allowance (RDA), and were developed to help consumers determine how much of a particular nutrient is in a food item. The DV for vitamin D is 400 international units (IU). The percent DV (%DV) tells adults what percentage of the DV is provided by 1 serving.

Percentages of DV are based on a 2000-calorie per day diet. Individual requirements may be higher or lower depending on your calorie needs.

Food/Amount	Daily Value
Cod liver oil, 1 tbsp=1360 IU	340%
Salmon, cooked, 3½ oz=360 IU	90%
Mackerel, cooked, 3½ oz=360 IU	90%
Milk, 1 c=98 IU	25%
Margarine, 1 tbsp=60 IU	15%
Liver, beef, cooked, 3½ oz=30 IU	8%
Egg, 1 whole (vitamin D in yolk)=25 IU	6%

Secret to Staying Steady On Your Feet

Lesley Day, PhD, Senior Research Fellow, Accident Research Center, Monash University, Victoria, Australia.

July 20, 2002, *British Medical Journal*.

One of the best ways to prevent falls for people older than 65 years is a targeted program of exercise, an Australian study has found. This is no trivial finding. Injuries are the fifth-leading cause of death among people 65 years and older, and two-thirds of injuries are caused by falls. When you're older than 65, your chances of suffering a fall are approximately 30% in any given year. The risk increases to 50% by age 80.

The Australian study by the Accident Research Center of Monash University looked at 3 different approaches to preventing falls. Results were published in the *British Medical Journal*.

One method was to do exercises designed to improve flexibility and balance. Participants worked out in 1-hour sessions every week with ankle weights, balanced themselves on rocker boards, and performed exercises that "challenged some normal systems we use to maintain balance, such as walking in opposite directions to 2 lines of people walking past you," says Lesley Day, a senior research fellow at Monash.

A second approach was to look for hazards in the home—steps and stairs, handrails or the absence thereof, lighting, slippery or uneven surfaces, and kitchen cupboards that were too high or too low.

A final focus was on vision—whether people had the early, undetected signs of vision loss from glaucoma, how well they did on a variety of tests of visual acuity, with referrals to specialists if needed.

A total of 1090 people between the ages of 70 and 84 years took part in the study. The study participants were divided into 8 groups. Three groups got 1 intervention, 3 groups got all possible combinations of 2 interventions, 1 group got all 3 interventions and 1 group acted as the control group, and were given no intervention at all. They sent in postcards monthly to report any falls.

"When we looked at all 3 interventions, exercise was the only one that showed a significant effect on its own," Day says. "All the combinations that included exercise showed a positive effect."

The best result, a 14% reduction in falls, was in the group that had the benefit of all 3 interventions. Neither home hazard management nor treatment of poor vision had positive results when used alone.

Hidden Dangers of Anemia Can 'Unbalance' Elderly Women

Bimal Ashar, MD, Assistant Professor, Department of Medicine, Johns Hopkins University School of Medicine, Baltimore, MD.

Loren G. Lipson, MD, Associate Professor, Medicine, and Chief, Division of Geriatric Medicine, University of Southern California Keck School of Medicine, Los Angeles.

July 2002, *Journal of the American Geriatrics Society.*

Even mildly low levels of iron in the blood may mean older women will have trouble walking, balancing, or moving around in general. Further, it might be time to lower the bar for defining anemia in older adults, says Dr. Bimal Ashar, a Johns Hopkins assistant professor of medicine and a coauthor of a recent study, published in the *Journal of the American Geriatrics Society.*

A person with anemia doesn't have enough red blood cells. These cells contain hemoglobin, a protein that carries oxygen from the lungs to the organs and muscles of the body. If there's not enough oxygen carried around the body, the person gets tired.

Anemia affects about 3.4 million Americans, according to the National Anemia Action Council. It can occur after blood loss or as a side effect of medication. It can also accompany many serious illnesses. At greatest risk

are those with chronic kidney disease, heart disease, or diabetes—all diseases that tend to become more prevalent with age.

The research team looked at 633 Baltimore-area women, aged 70 to 80 years. In the study, the women had to show their mobility by walking, rising quickly from a chair several times, and keeping their balance. Those with levels of hemoglobin on the low side of normal had twice the risk of mobility problems as those with higher levels.

A NORMAL LEVEL

Typically, in older adults, "12 [grams per deciliter of blood] is considered normal for women and 14 for men," Ashar says. However, women who had levels between 13 and 14 did best on the mobility tests, and those with levels lower than 12 did the worst. Those with hemoglobin levels between 12 and 13 performed in the mid-range. The risk of problems with movement when the woman's hemoglobin level was 12 was more than twice as high as for those with higher levels, the researchers say.

The research is applauded by a geriatric specialist from the University of Southern California. "This is something I know anecdotally, but this study is scientifically sound," Dr. Loren G. Lipson says. In his own practice, he has noticed older adults with lower hemoglobin levels do have problems moving.

"It's easy to say to an older person, 'You're out of shape,' or 'You're old,' but there might be another problem," he says.

Older adults should ask their doctor about their hemoglobin levels when they get their blood work done, he adds.

Treatment for anemia linked to poor nutrition includes supplements of iron, folate, and vitamin B-12. However, anemia associated with chronic disease has no specific treatment, the researchers say.

info For information on anemia, visit the National Anemia Action Council at *www. anemia.org/about_anemia/anemia_overview.jsp.*

Easy Fixes Make Homes Safe for Seniors

Mary Becker–Omvig, MS, Occupational Therapist, Aging in Place Coordinator, Office on Aging, Howard County, MD, and Aging in Place spokeswoman, American Occupational Therapy Association (AOTA), Bethesda, MD.

December 4, 2002, Housing Options for Older Americans, Administration on Aging, US Department of Health and Human Services, Washington, DC.

Sturdy bars you can grab to help you get in and out of the tub. Wide doorways to allow easy wheelchair access to bedrooms and bathrooms. Lever door handles that replace hard-to-turn round knobs.

Such simple modifications to homes can make all the difference for elderly people who prefer to keep living in their own homes.

Senior advocacy groups call it "aging in place"—staying in comfortable and familiar surroundings, even if aging diminishes your ability to perform the daily routines that once came so easily.

Predictably, most seniors want to stay where they are. An AARP survey, for example, found that 83% of older Americans want to stay in their current homes the rest of their lives.

"What people want is to be able to live in their house as long as possible, but today, houses aren't really designed to allow people to age in place," says Mary Becker–Omvig, an occupational therapist and spokeswoman for the American Occupational Therapy Association (AOTA).

As America rapidly grays (there are 76 million baby boomers), Becker–Omvig offers advice to those living at home and approaching their senior years.

"Don't wait for the crisis to start thinking about planning," says Becker–Omvig, who is also the home modification/fall prevention coordinator for the Aging in Place program in Howard County, Maryland.

SUGGESTIONS

AOTA says the 3 most common problems for seniors at home are getting in and out of the house, accessing the bathroom, and going up and down stairs.

Becker–Omvig says one-third of all home accidents involving people 65 years and older could be prevented through simple modifications.

■ ■ ■ ■

Make Your Home Senior-Friendly

Houses can be adapted to be more senior-friendly, according to the AOTA and Rebuilding Together, a volunteer organization that repairs and builds homes for low-income people. *Here are their suggestions...*

●**Make sure there's access to a first-floor bathroom,** if possible.

●**Use bathmats and rugs that have non-skid backings,** and secure the rugs with double-sided tape.

●**Install an adjustable-height or hand-held shower head** and an adjustable-height shower seat, if needed.

●**Turn down the hot water temperature** to 120 degrees to avoid scalding.

●**Widen or clear pathways into rooms.**

●**Post emergency numbers and a list of current medications near the phone,** and make sure a phone with a cord is near the bed.

●**Make sure railings are secure,** and stairwells have railings on both sides.

●**Increase lighting** at entranceways.

●**Make sure at least one outside entrance has no steps;** use a ramp if necessary.

Of course, modifications will depend on individual needs. And it's a good idea to assess which routines or tasks prove difficult, what the resident used to do but no longer can, and which modifications would provide solutions.

"Despite the infirmities that accompany increased longevity, the majority of seniors can —and do—remain in their own homes," says a report from the Administration on Aging of the US Department of Health and Human Services.

info For more information, visit the Administration on Aging at *www.aoa.dhhs. gov* or the National Council on the Aging at *www.ncoa.org.*

The Flu Is Not Under Control, Especially in the Elderly

David M. Morens, MD, Epidemiologist, National Institute of Allergy and Infectious Diseases, Bethesda, MD.

January 8, 2003, *Journal of the American Medical Association*.

Deaths caused by influenza and other respiratory infections have increased substantially over the past 2 decades, hitting the oldest Americans the hardest, federal epidemiologists report. The study also singles out *respiratory syncytial virus* (RSV), generally regarded as a threat primarily to children, as a serious cause of death for older people, as well.

And the toll will continue to rise, because the number of Americans 85 years and older is rising steadily, says the report.

Year-to-year comparisons are difficult, because the number of deaths vary considerably. For instance, there were more than twice the deaths in the 1977–1978 flu season (32,000+) than in the previous season. However, both numbers pale in comparison to the more than 70,000 deaths in the 1997–1998 season and the almost 65,000 deaths in the following season, says the report by William W. Thompson and other epidemiologists at the Centers for Disease Control and Prevention (CDC).

CHILDREN AND ELDERLY AT RISK

These numbers indicate that the problem is bigger than we once thought, CDC director Dr. Julie Gerberding says in a statement.

Thompson and his colleagues used a new mathematical model to estimate the number of deaths caused by influenza and other respiratory illnesses. Estimating that number has been difficult since the exact cause of death in people with severe medical conditions, such as heart disease, can be difficult to determine.

An editorial by Dr. David M. Morens, an epidemiologist at the National Institute of Allergy and Infectious Diseases, says these estimated yearly deaths are surprising.

A SIGNIFICANT NUMBER OF DEATHS

Each year these numbers may approach or exceed the total number of US lives lost during the entire decade-long Vietnam War, surely placing influenza in the forefront of public health priorities, according to Morens.

Doctors and older Americans can do a lot to reduce the toll, Morens adds. Older people should be aware that someone aged 85 years or older is far more likely to die an influenza-related death than someone aged 65 to 69, he says.

Protection starts with the flu vaccine, Morens says. "The problem is partly that the public doesn't accept the flu vaccine and doesn't think the problem is as serious as these numbers show." Today's flu vaccine is not perfect, Morens acknowledges, but it considerably reduces the risk of infection.

Doctors should also practice more preventive medicine, he says. Preventive medicine focuses on the health of individuals and defined populations to protect, promote, and maintain health and well-being and prevent disease, disability, and premature death.

Some common-sense rules can reduce the risk for older people, Morens says. Be careful when you're around people with serious illnesses and think twice before going to crowded places, for example, he says.

info You can learn more about influenza from the Centers for Disease Control and Prevention at *www.cdc.gov* or the American Lung Association at *www.lungusa.org*.

Sleep: The Key to a Longer Life

Mary Amanda Dew, PhD, Professor, Psychiatry, Psychology and Epidemiology, University of Pittsburgh School of Medicine, PA.

January/February 2003, *Psychosomatic Medicine*.

Elderly people who don't sleep well may have more than mental alertness to worry about. They are also more likely to die sooner than their sound-slumbering counterparts, say the authors of a recent study.

Sleep difficulties, such as having trouble falling asleep or middle-of-the-night waking, significantly increased the risk of death in seemingly healthy older individuals, the researchers say.

"We were surprised because the people we studied were so healthy at the time we looked at them," says study author Mary Amanda Dew, a professor of psychiatry, psychology and epidemiology at the University of Pittsburgh School of Medicine.

Of 185 people, most from 60 to 80 years old, who began the study, 66 had died in the follow-up period that averaged about 12 years.

None of the participants had major health problems when they entered the study and none thought they had sleep problems, Dew says. People with sleep apnea or serious medical problems were excluded. The participants each spent 3 nights in the sleep laboratory where their quality of sleep was recorded.

Taking a long time to fall asleep was found to be the deadliest sleep-related problem. Those who required more than 30 minutes to nod off had a 2.14 greater risk of death than those who needed less time to do so. People who slept for less than 80% of the time they spent in bed were also almost twice as likely to die as sound sleepers. Participants with too much or too little *rapid eye movement* (REM)—the dream portion of sleep—also faced greater risk for death, although to a lesser degree.

A VARIETY OF CAUSES

There were a variety of causes for the deaths, Dew says. "We thought maybe they'd die of brain-related problems," but this was not necessarily so, she notes.

Although the connection between the numerous deaths and poor sleepers could be chance, she doesn't think that's the case. "The sleep was a very subtle indicator that they were on the verge of developing other medical problems not yet evident," she says. "This could be reflecting degenerative diseases that didn't become obvious until later."

The researchers did not look at the amount of sleep the study participants received each night, although they reported sleeping an average of 7 to 8.5 hours.

Many people don't know how well they sleep, Dew says. She suggests that people who think they are having sleep problems see their doctor, but adds that even those who seem to sleep well should work on improving their sleep habits. "Don't do work in bed for example, and no napping during the day," she says. Dew also suggests limiting caffeine intake and avoiding the use of sleeping pills.

Being elderly is not a prescription for sleeping poorly, Dew stresses. "There's this myth that older people need less sleep or shouldn't be concerned if they have sleep problems. That's incorrect."

New 'Underwear' That May Stop Hip Fractures

Natasja M. van Schoor, MSc, Vrije Universiteit Medical Center, Amsterdam, the Netherlands.

Gerard T. Varlotta, MD, New York University School of Medicine's Rusk Institute of Rehabilitation Medicine, New York, NY.

April 16, 2003, *Journal of the American Medical Association.*

Debate continues over the effectiveness of the shock-absorbing underwear called hip protectors in preventing hip fractures in the elderly.

More than 300,000 Americans suffer hip fractures each year, most of them aged 65 and older. And 15% to 30% of those people will die within 1 year from complications due to surgery or prolonged immobility.

The hip protectors are usually plastic shields or foam pads that are held in place with specially designed underwear.

A Dutch study that found the devices ineffective was immediately criticized by an American bone expert who says the study was flawed and that the protectors are beneficial.

Lead author Natasja M. van Schoor, a researcher at the Vrije Universiteit Medical Center in Amsterdam, said most studies have shown the protectors can help prevent fractures, but she does not think they are as effective as the studies suggest.

The Dutch researchers studied 561 older Amsterdam residents who had a high risk of hip fractures; 276 wearing the protectors and 285 going without. Over 70 weeks, 18 of the people assigned to the hip-protector group suffered fractures, compared with 20 of those assigned to the other group, which is a negligible difference.

Dr. Gerard T. Varlotta, an associate professor of medicine at New York University School of Medicine's Rusk Institute of Rehabilitation Medicine, says the findings are meaningless because the study had a very high noncompliance rate, meaning that patients often did not wear the hip protectors as advised.

"Of the 18 people who had fractures, only 4 were wearing hip protectors at the time," he said. And the type of hip protector used in the study was not the best, Varlotta adds. It was designed to absorb shock, while most fractures are caused by sudden stress on the hip from an unexpected movement.

■ ■ ■ ■

Preventing Hip Fractures

If you have a hip protector, wear it 24 hours a day, says van Schoor, because 4 fractures in the study's protector-wearing group occurred during the night. She also recommends prescription drugs that build bone strength, as well as a combination of calcium and vitamin D.

Eliminating smoking and limiting alcohol consumption to modest levels are also important, Varlotta says. An exercise program, even a moderate one, can help prevent fractures. So can paying attention to your living arrangements. Avoid small throw rugs, electric cords, and newly waxed floors. Wear sensible shoes.

Have a support system of people you can call if an accident happens, and consider a device that can alert others. Some people who fall end up lying on the floor for hours or days because they can't reach a phone.

info For information on osteoporosis and hip protectors, visit Johns Hopkins Health After 50 Web site at *www.hopkins after50.com.*

Oxygen Damage May Trigger Age-Related Blindness

John Crabb, PhD, Professor, Ophthalmology and Cell Biology, The Cleveland Clinic Foundation, OH.

Researchers think they can slow the onset of *age-related macular degeneration* (AMD) by preventing the formation of oxidized proteins called *drusen* that build up in the retina.

AMD affects more than 10 million Americans older than 55 years, and is the leading cause of blindness in adults.

A study found signs of oxidative stress in the drusen, which accumulate in the eyes of patients early in age-related blindness. Researchers think they can slow the progression of AMD by preventing the formation of these clumps.

Dr. John Crabb, a Cleveland Clinic ophthalmologist and leader of the study, says drusen may be the strongest risk factor for AMD. The link is circumstantial but also fairly strong.

Some eye doctors are convinced that eradicating drusen can improve AMD symptoms, and they've taken to vaporizing the clumps with lasers. The jury is still out on that procedure.

THE STUDY

In their study, Crabb and his colleagues saw structural signs of oxidative damage in some of 129 molecules shared by the study subjects. This discovery hints that what makes good drusen go bad may be exposure to oxygen radicals.

The retina's tissue is rich in a fatty acid and is especially vulnerable to the ravages of oxygen radicals. Evidence has also found that smokers are more prone to the condition, and in some people, high doses of antioxidants—like zinc and vitamins C and E—can slow its advance.

The researchers found damaged proteins were more abundant in an area of the eye called Bruch's membrane in AMD patients than in those with healthy retinas.

■ ■ ■ ■

Reducing the Risk of Macular Degeneration

It is possible to reduce the risk of developing macular degeneration. *The American Macular Degeneration Foundation (www. macular.org) recommends the following...*

•**Eat large quantities of dark green leafy vegetables rich in carotenoids.** Spinach and collard greens are possibly the most beneficial vegetables in this respect.

•**Protect your eyes** from potentially harmful ultraviolet (UV) light and blue light.

•**Take antioxidant vitamin and zinc supplements.**

•**Don't smoke.**

•**Eat a low-fat diet.** Avoid junk food.

•**Exercise regularly.**

info To learn more about age-related macular degeneration, visit the AMD Alliance International at *www.amdalliance.org.*

New Wrinkle in Botox Treatments

Frederic S. Brandt, MD, Clinical Associate Professor, Dermatology, University of Miami School of Medicine, FL.
Franklin L. DiSpaltro, MD, President, American Society for Aesthetic Plastic Surgery, Los Alamitos, CA.

Botox injections may be all the rage since being approved for cosmetic use by the US Food and Drug Administration, but if you're not careful, frown lines won't be all you have to worry about.

Doctors are seeing an increase in the number of people suffering complications from Botox injections. Although they have no proof, the dermatologists suspect these problems may be the results of treatments performed by unqualified people.

In the Botox procedure, which takes a few minutes, small doses of *botulinum toxin type A* are injected into the facial muscles responsible for wrinkles. The toxin binds to the nerve endings, then paralyzes the muscles; they remain in this paralyzed position for 3 to 4 months.

"The success of the procedure is very technique-dependent. It depends on who's using the needle," says Dr. Frederic S. Brandt, a professor in the department of dermatology at the University of Miami School of Medicine. He said that whoever performs the procedure must have a thorough knowledge of anatomy so he or she knows exactly where to put the injection.

Dr. Franklin DiSpaltro, president of the American Society for Aesthetic Plastic Surgery, says that most cosmetic procedures have excellent safety records, so people may assume that they are simple to perform and are without risk. But in the hands of untrained practitioners, the results can be disastrous.

"Botox parties" may offer treatments at lower cost than what you'd pay for a private session with a physician. But unless proper measures are in place to ensure both safety and effectiveness of treatments, the Society for Aesthetic Plastic Surgery advises that you wait and get your Botox injections in the doctor's office.

■ ■ ■ ■

Before You Try Botox...

Before you undergo Botox injections anywhere, the American Society for Aesthetic Plastic Surgery (ASAPS) recommends that you take a quiz. *Make sure you can answer "yes" to the following questions...*

•**Have you been asked to provide a complete medical history?** You should never undergo Botox treatment without having provided details of your medical history that may be necessary in the event of an emergency or adverse reaction to the toxin.

• **Have you been advised of the risks and given your informed consent?** A discussion of the benefits and risks of a procedure is required for informed consent, and it should be documented in the medical record.

• **Is a qualified physician administering the treatment?** Although Botox treatment is both safe and effective, every medical procedure has risks and possible complications. Botox must be administered by an experienced physician who understands facial anatomy and proper injection techniques.

• **Is the physical setting appropriate for administering medical treatment,** including handling emergency situations? Any medical procedure requires sanitary conditions. In addition, drugs or equipment that might be necessary to handle an emergency situation must be readily accessible.

• **Are you willing and able to follow post-treatment instructions?** Botox treatment requires that you restrict physical activity for a period following the injections. Failure to follow post-treatment instructions can lead to complications. In a party atmosphere, people may tend to forget such restrictions, particularly if alcohol is being served.

• **Will you receive adequate follow-up care?** Follow-up care is an important part of the doctor–patient relationship, and should not be overlooked, even when treatment is administered outside of the usual medical setting.

Surgical and nonsurgical cosmetic procedures are medical procedures and should be undertaken only under the care of a trained specialist.

info If you'd like to verify a doctor's certification in any recognized medical specialty, you can check with the American Board of Medical Specialties, 866-ASK-ABMS (275-2267) or *www.abms.org.*

■ ■ ■ ■

What Else Can Make Wrinkles Disappear?

The Spanish explorer Ponce de Leon never discovered the mythical Fountain of Youth, but scientists and cosmetics companies haven't stopped searching for new methods to slow the aging process.

The National Institute on Aging provides information about how to make your face appear smoother.

The only products that have been studied for safety and effectiveness and approved by the Food and Drug Administration (FDA) to improve the appearance of sun-damaged or aging skin are tretinoin cream and carbon dioxide (CO_2) and erbium (Er:YAG) lasers.

• **Tretinoin cream (Renova).** This vitamin A derivative, available by prescription, is approved for reducing the appearance of fine wrinkles, mottled darkened spots, and roughness in people whose skin doesn't improve with regular skin care and use of sun protection.

However, Renova does not eliminate wrinkles, repair sun-damaged skin, or restore skin to its healthier, younger structure. Its effects have not been studied in people 50 and older or in people with moderately or darkly pigmented skin.

• **The CO_2 and Er:YAG** lasers are approved to treat wrinkles. The doctor uses the laser to remove skin one layer at a time. Laser therapy is performed under anesthesia in an outpatient surgical setting.

The FDA is currently studying the safety of *alpha hydroxy acids* (AHAs), widely promoted for their ability to reduce wrinkles, spots, and other signs of aging and sun-damaged skin. Some studies suggest that they may work, but there is concern about adverse reactions and the long-term effects of their use.

If you're interested in finding a treatment for wrinkles, discuss all of your options with a dermatologist.

Anti-Aging Cosmetics That Make You Look Older

Darrell Rigel, MD, Professor, Dermatology, New York University School of Medicine.

Ted Daly, MD, Director of Pediatric Dermatology, Nassau University Medical Center, and Dermatologist, Garden City Dermatology, Garden City, NY.

Women who use skin-care treatments and cosmetics containing the popular anti-aging ingredients known as *alpha hydroxy acids* (AHAs) may soon see warning labels on the products.

The US Food and Drug Administration wants manufacturers to print a warning indicating that the ingredients used to reduce the signs of skin aging may also be causing the skin to age, primarily by increasing the risk of sunburn which, in turn, increases the risk of skin cancer.

The label would read: "Sunburn Alert: This product contains an alpha hydroxy acid that may increase your skin's sensitivity to sunburn. Use a sunscreen and limit sun exposure while using this product and for a week afterward."

Alpha hydroxy acids—fruit acids—help the skin maintain a more youthful appearance by increasing the rate of cell turnover, a process that slows down as a person ages and that contributes to more wrinkled, older-looking, skin.

However, the other factor that increases skin aging is sun damage. And the FDA says AHAs contribute to that damage by increasing the rate at which skin burns.

The proposed label change was prompted by studies conducted by the Cosmetic, Toiletry and Fragrance Association on the safety of topically applied AHAs.

Those studies confirmed that applying an AHA to the skin increased ultraviolet (UV) sensitivity by up to 18% after 4 weeks of use. On average, skin sensitivity to UV-induced cellular damage doubled.

SOME DERMATOLOGISTS DISAGREE

Not all dermatologists think the findings are significant, or that they warrant a label warning.

Dermatologists have been using the AHAs in prescription strength for decades with no increased risk of skin cancer and sunburn, says Dr. Ted Daly, an assistant professor of dermatology at Nassau University Medical Center in New York.

"To put this kind of warning on a label seems to me to be alarming women for no reason. I don't really see it as necessary," he says.

Dr. Darrell Rigel, a professor of dermatology at the New York University School of Medicine and past president of the American Academy of Dermatology, says, "I don't think that AHAs are dangerous, and the new label, though an important reminder to use sunscreen, could be very misleading."

Rigel says that although an AHA may, in fact, increase your risk of sunburn, that risk is small and can be avoided with sunscreen protection.

Both do agree, however, that any time attention can be drawn to the need for using sunscreen, the outcome is positive. In this respect, the proposed label change may offer an important public service.

■ ■ ■ ■

Using AHAs

Currently, there are some 1500 different products containing AHAs. This comprises a $6 billion market in the United States alone.

The Cosmetic Ingredient Review Panel—the industry's self-regulating body for reviewing scientific information about cosmetic ingredients—has established safety guidelines. *Products containing AHAs are safe for consumers under the following circumstances…*

●**The concentration of AHA does not exceed 10%.**

●**The acid content (pH) of the product is listed at 3.5 or greater** (the higher the pH number, the lower the acidity).

●**The product either contains ingredients that protect the skin from sun damage,** or directions recommending the use of sunscreens following applications of products containing AHAs.

info For more information on how sun ages the skin, visit the American Academy of Dermatology at *www.aad.org*.

Two Minerals That May Cause Parkinson's Disease

Karen M. Powers, Research Scientist, University of Washington, Seattle.

June 10, 2003, *Neurology*.

People with high levels of iron and manganese in their diets are more likely to develop Parkinson's disease, a University of Washington researcher says.

The minerals are suspected in the development of Parkinson's disease, but it's far from clear whether iron and manganese, found in a variety of healthy foods, actually cause people to become ill.

"We don't know about cause and effect," says study author Karen M. Powers, a research scientist at the University of Washington. "We are not saying that we know what causes Parkinson's, and it's way too soon for us to make any recommendations about diet."

An estimated 1 million to 1.5 million Americans have Parkinson's disease, a brain disorder that can cause tremors, difficulty walking, and rigid muscles. Many patients develop dementia and die from the disease. Parkinson's is largely a disease of the elderly, and is estimated to affect 1 in every 100 Americans older than 60 years.

TOO MUCH OF A GOOD THING

Researchers have suspected a link between iron and Parkinson's disease, but this study is the first to look at the combined effects of both iron and manganese, Powers says.

"These are essential elements in the diet; we absolutely need them," Powers says. But the idea that "if a little is good, a whole lot is better" is simply not true.

Powers and colleagues looked at 2 groups of people—250 who were newly diagnosed with Parkinson's disease and 388 healthy people. The researchers interviewed members of each group about their diets.

The 25% of the subjects with the highest levels of iron intake were 1.7 times more likely to be Parkinson's patients than those in the lowest 25th percentile.

Those who had higher-than-normal intakes of both iron and manganese were 1.9 times more likely to have Parkinson's disease.

INTERACTION WITH BRAIN CHEMICALS

Parkinson's develops when the brain doesn't make enough of a vital brain chemical called *dopamine*. If iron does, in fact, contribute to Parkinson's disease, one theory is that excess amounts of the minerals may interact with dopamine and create new chemicals that hurt brain tissue, Powers says.

More research will be necessary to confirm these findings, Powers says.

■ ■ ■ ■

About Parkinson's

Approximately 2% of the population will develop Parkinson's disease, according to Mayo Clinic estimates.

Parkinson's disease is a progressive disorder of the central nervous system that produces symptoms such as body tremors, slowness of movement, stiffness of limbs, and balance problems.

The disease results from a progressive degeneration of the brain, with a loss of neurons that produce dopamine. Medication to restore dopamine levels is commonly prescribed, but as the disease progresses, the disabilities accumulate. *Following are some facts about Parkinson's disease...*

•**Parkinson's affects approximately 1.5 million people in the United States,** with some 50,000 new cases diagnosed each year.

•**Although Parkinson's can start at any age,** it is most common among adults older than 50 years.

•**A chronic neurological condition,** Parkinson's is characterized by symptoms ranging from tremors on one side of the body to slowness of movement, stiffness of limbs, and balance problems.

Head Injuries May Cause Parkinson's Disease

James H. Bower, MD, Department of Neurology, Mayo Clinic, Rochester, MN.

Miguel A. Hernan, MD, Harvard School of Public Health, Boston, MA.

May 20, 2003, *Neurology.*

People who suffer a severe head injury with a loss of consciousness and memory may be at greater risk of developing Parkinson's disease later in life, research suggests.

Patients who had mild head trauma without loss of consciousness or only a brief episode of memory loss did not have an increased risk for developing the disease, says study author Dr. James H. Bower of the Mayo Clinic.

Those who had moderate or severe head trauma with a loss of consciousness or a prolonged episode of memory loss, a skull fracture, or bruising on the brain appeared to be 11 times more likely to develop Parkinson's, Bower says.

"What was surprising was that these people only had one head trauma and on average this head trauma occurred 20 years before the development of Parkinson's," he notes. But trauma is only one of the many causes for Parkinson's, he said, including genetic predisposition and other factors.

Bower's team came up with 3 possible explanations for their findings. One is that when you suffer head trauma, the blood–brain barrier is disrupted and certain poisons from the bloodstream, such as a virus or toxins, get into the brain, triggering a cascade that leads to cell death. "But it can take 20 years before symptoms develop," Bower speculates.

Another possibility is that the trauma causes brain cells to produce new proteins that can lead to cell death, he says.

The third, and least likely, is that after a head trauma, some cells are lost, and over time normal aging and a normal rate of cell death combine to allow Parkinson's to develop.

Bower notes that some boxers, such as Muhammad Ali, suffer from *dementia pugilistica,* which is similar to Parkinson's. Although the patients in his research did not suffer from dementia pugilistica, "The findings of our study are another reason to emphasize the importance of wearing protective head gear when playing sports," Bower says.

Dr. Miguel A. Hernan, of the Harvard School of Public Health, says the problem with Parkinson's disease is that very few risk factors have been identified in epidemiologic studies. "Adding head injury to the list will definitely open new lines of basic research," he said.

Pesticides May Increase Risk of Parkinson's

Andrew Grandinetti, PhD, Epidemiologist, Pacific Biomedical Research Center, University of Hawaii at Manoa.

Honglei Chen, MD, PhD, Research Associate, Department of Nutrition, Harvard School of Public Health, Boston, MA.

April 1 and 3, 2003, presentations, American Academy of Neurology Annual Meeting, Honolulu, HI.

Although consuming lots of fruits and fruit juices appears to increase the risk of Parkinson's disease, researchers say people should not cut back on their consumption of fruit.

The culprit may be pesticides, plant-borne toxins, or herbicides, not the fruit itself, says researcher Andrew Grandinetti, an epidemiologist at the Pacific Biomedical Research Center at the University of Hawaii at Manoa.

Fruit is an important part of healthy eating and has been linked with cancer prevention, Grandinetti says. The risk may indicate pesticide exposure because there is no increase in cancer with people who have a high vitamin C intake from supplements and other foods in their diets.

"Eating fruit is a healthful thing," he said, but "it's probably a good idea to wash fruit pretty thoroughly."

STUDY SUPPORTS WHAT WE KNOW

Dr. Honglei Chen, a Parkinson's expert and research associate at the Harvard School of Public Health, says the findings reflect those of earlier research.

"There is little doubt that environmental factors, though still to be identified, play important roles in late-onset Parkinson's disease," she says.

In addition to pesticides, living in rural areas and neurotoxins have also been implicated in the development of Parkinson's, Chen says.

Grandinetti's team evaluated more than 8000 study subjects, noting the incidence of Parkinson's disease and taking into account dietary habits. Increased fruit and fruit juice intake boosted the risk of getting the disease. The study began looking at data in 1965, Grandinetti notes, when pesticides were more persistent than the ones currently used.

info To learn more about Parkinson's disease, visit the Mayo Clinic's Web site at *www.mayo.edu.*

■ ■ ■ ■

The Most Dangerous Pesticides

According to the US Environmental Protection Agency (EPA), there are several pesticides that present the greatest threat to humans. *They are...*

●**Atrazine.** First registered in 1958, the bug fighter is estimated to be the most heavily used herbicide in the US. The largest uses are on corn, sugarcane, and residential lawns.

In a study of Missouri men, high levels of exposure to the herbicide were associated with a 30-fold increased risk of diluted or struggling sperm.

Atrazine is the most commonly detected herbicide in US drinking water and has been shown to disrupt the correct sexual development of frogs.

●**Organophosphates and carbamates.** Scientific panels have found that organophosphate and carbamate insecticides may disrupt the central nervous system. Children are particularly vulnerable to the effects of some of these neurotoxins.

●**Dursban (chlorpyrifos).** Until recently dursban was the most widely used household pesticide produced in the US. It was used for a broad range of lawn and home insecticide products, for agricultural purposes, and for termites. The EPA and Dursban's manufacturer have agreed to eliminate its use for nearly all household purposes and to move to significantly reduce its residues on several foods that are popular with children.

Under the agreement, there is a phase-out of all home, lawn, garden, and termite-control uses.

Drinking Alcohol Doesn't Protect Against Parkinson's Disease

Miguel A. Hernan, MD, Harvard School of Public Health, Boston, MA.

Harvey Checkoway, PhD, Professor, Environmental Health, University of Washington, Seattle.

May 15, 2003, *Annals of Neurology.*

Alcohol apparently has no effect on preventing the onset of Parkinson's disease, according to a study at the Harvard School of Public Health. Its effect on the disease has been a hotly debated issue among researchers.

Study author Dr. Miguel A. Hernan said there is no strong association between alcohol consumption and the disease.

Hernan and his colleagues at Harvard collected data from 2 large population-based studies—the Nurses Health Study and the Health Professionals Follow-up Study. Of the 88,722 women and 47,367 men for whom data on drinking were available, 167 of the women and 248 of the men developed Parkinson's.

There was no correlation between moderate to low alcohol consumption and the development of Parkinson's, Hernan says. There was no data available for heavy drinkers, he adds.

Some studies have shown cigarette smoking and coffee have a protective effect, Hernan says. Although his findings show that alcohol drinking is not associated with a lower or higher risk of Parkinson's, Hernan said it's possible that beer is associated with a slightly lower risk. But he is quick to add that these findings and the findings of other studies should not encourage people to drink more beer or start smoking. The risks far outweigh any possible benefits.

Harvey Checkoway, a professor of environmental health at the University of Washington, says the findings are not surprising, but he was intrigued by the idea of reduced risk of Parkinson's for beer drinkers.

"It is possible, as the authors mention, that components of beer other than alcohol may have a protective effect," Checkoway said. "Identifying what the specific protective factors are, and how they act in the brain, could be a valuable area for additional research."

Amazing! Arthritis Drugs That Block Parkinson's

Serge Przedborski, MD, PhD, Professor, Neurobiology and Pathology, Columbia University, New York, NY.
Jay Van Gerpen, MD, Neurologist, Ochsner Clinic Foundation, New Orleans, LA.
April 7–11, 2003, *Proceedings of the National Academy of Sciences.*

Researchers have identified a brain enzyme that might contribute to the progression of Parkinson's disease.

The good news is that arthritis drugs already on the market can block the activity of that enzyme, which means the finding could lead to a new Parkinson's treatment. "It might open up real treatment options for slowing Parkinson's disease," says Dr. Jay Van Gerpen, a neurologist and specialist in movement disorders at the Ochsner Clinic Foundation.

Parkinson's disease is a degenerative disorder of the brain that affects approximately 1 in 100 Americans older than 65 years. Symptoms include tremors, slowness of movement, and muscle stiffness to the point of paralysis.

No one knows what causes Parkinson's. However, doctors do know the disease gradually destroys the nerve cells that transmit the brain chemical called *dopamine.* Dopamine is important in regulating movement.

Certain drugs, including *levodopa,* can reduce symptoms by restoring dopamine levels. But no treatment slows the progressive cell death, Van Gerpen says. As the cells continue to die, levodopa loses its effectiveness.

FINDING A CONNECTION

An enzyme called *cyclooxygenase-2* (cox-2) plays a role in triggering the pain of osteoarthritis. Osteoarthritis can be treated with a class of drugs called cox-2 inhibitors, which include Celebrex and Vioxx.

Previous research had also implicated cox-2 in other neurodegenerative diseases, including Alzheimer's and *amyotropic lateral sclerosis* (ALS, or Lou Gehrig's disease).

"We put 2 and 2 together," says Dr. Serge Przedborski, senior author of the study and a professor of neurobiology and pathology at Columbia University. "We thought it was a natural study to assess what could be the role of cox-2 in Parkinson's."

CHEMISTRY TELLS THE STORY

Researchers found elevated levels of cox-2 in the brains of patients who died of Parkinson's disease and in mice with a disease similar to Parkinson's.

Next, researchers gave the mice cox-2 inhibitors. They found more dopaminergic neurons survived—nearly 90%—in the mice that were taking the drug than in the mice who were not (41%).

Although the cox-2 inhibitors seem very promising, Przedborski said they will not be a cure for Parkinson's.

"We've started to realize that the death of neurons is probably not the result of a single factor, but probably of multiple factors that interact with each other to ultimately kill the cell," he says.

info For more information, visit the Parkinson's Disease Foundation at *www.pdf. org* or the National Institute of Neurological Disorders and Stroke (NINDS) at *http://accessi ble.ninds.nih.gov.*

Cutting-Edge Parkinson's Therapies

Jill Marjama–Lyons, MD, Director, Parkinson's Disease Research, Education and Clinical Center, VA Medical Center, Albuquerque, NM, and coauthor of *What Your Doctor May Not Tell You About Parkinson's Disease: A Holistic Program for Optimal Wellness.*
August 2003, *Bottom Line/Health.*

Until recently, doctors have been only moderately successful at controlling the disabling tremor and motor symptoms that characterize Parkinson's disease.

New development: An advanced surgical technique, known as *deep-brain stimulation,* uses a "brain pacemaker" to reduce tremor and related symptoms so effectively that many Parkinson's patients are able to function almost normally.

During the procedure, doctors implant an electrode inside the brain to stimulate specific areas associated with movement. The electrode is connected to a palm-sized pacemaker implanted underneath the skin below the collarbone.

The pacemaker stimulates a specific area of the brain for optimum control of motor symptoms, such as tremor and slowed movements.

Deep-brain stimulation causes adverse effects, such as stroke or seizure, in fewer than 2% of patients. The procedure costs $30,000 to $60,000.

Other facts about Parkinson's…

SYMPTOMS AND DIAGNOSIS

●**Tremor is not the only symptom.** While tremor—most commonly in an arm or hand—is a hallmark of the condition, up to one-third of Parkinson's patients do *not* suffer from this symptom. When tremor does occur, it usually is noticeable at rest, while sitting, reclining on a bed, or when the extremity is extended to hold a newspaper or book. Typically, tremor is more exaggerated on 1 side of the body and may worsen with stress.

Other Parkinson's symptoms include muscle stiffness, slowed gait, decreased arm swinging, lack of facial expression, and infrequent blinking. Less commonly recognized Parkinson's symptoms may include constipation, blurry vision, and the loss of the sense of smell.

As the disease progresses, some people may experience difficulty swallowing, trouble with balance or falling, and sexual difficulties, such as impotence or decreased libido. Many sufferers' handwriting may also become very small (a condition known as *micrographia*).

If you experience Parkinson's symptoms, see a neurologist who specializes in the disease. To locate a specialist in your area, consult the National Parkinson Foundation at 800-327-4545, *www.parkinson.org.*

●**Environmental toxins may play a role.** Numerous reports suggest that pesticides, including rotenone, herbicides, and heavy metals are associated with an increased risk for Parkinson's.

To protect yourself: Do *not* spray pesticides or herbicides yourself. If you must, wear protective equipment, such as gloves and a mask that covers your eyes, nose, and mouth.

If your drinking water comes from a well, have it tested for heavy metals and pesticide–herbicide residues. If you use municipal water, consider having it tested. If necessary, switch to bottled water or install a filter.

●**Diagnosis is often delayed.** Parkinson's symptoms progress gradually. Most people have had them for 2 to 3 years before seeing a doctor. Because there is no test for Parkinson's, doctors diagnose it by looking at history and the results of a careful physical examination. If standard medication reduces motor symptoms, Parkinson's is confirmed.

Diagnosis typically occurs between the ages of 50 and 79 years. Parkinson's affects 1 person in 100 older than 60 years. However, up to 10% of patients develop symptoms before age 40.

Surprising: Genetics plays a role in fewer than 10% of Parkinson's cases.

TREATMENT

●**Single drugs may not be effective.** The longer a person has Parkinson's, the more likely it is that multiple medications will be needed. It may require real clinical expertise to fine-tune the dosage in a way that keeps symptoms under control most of the time without undue side effects.

Because the nerve cells that malfunction in Parkinson's rely on the neurotransmitter *dopamine,* medications aim to replace it or mimic its effects.

●*Dopamine agonists.* These drugs, including *bromocriptine* (Parlodel), *pergolide* (Permax), *ropinirole* (Requip), and *pramipexole* (Mirapex), stimulate the same brain cells that respond to dopamine.

●*Carbidopa–levodopa* (Sinemet). This precursor to dopamine (*levodopa*) is combined with another chemical (*carbidopa*) that prevents levodopa from breaking down before crossing into the brain.

In newly diagnosed Parkinson's, treatment often begins with a dopamine agonist. These drugs are less likely to cause side effects, such as uncontrolled writhing or twitching, than carbidopa–levodopa.

As the disease progresses, it is usually necessary to add carbidopa–levodopa. Medications called *catecholamine-o-methyltransferase (COMT) inhibitors* may be used as well. These block an enzyme that breaks down dopamine and allow carbidopa–levodopa to work more efficiently.

●**Complementary therapies are worth trying.** Anecdotal findings show that many Parkinson's sufferers are helped by complementary treatments, such as acupuncture, nutritional therapy, and yoga.

Seek the guidance of a qualified professional (a licensed acupuncturist or trained nutritionist who works with Parkinson's patients) to ensure that your entire health history will be taken into account.

Of particular importance for Parkinson's sufferers…

●Exercise minimizes the effects of movement symptoms. Swimming, walking, or using a stationary bicycle raises stamina and energy, and can improve sleep quality. Yoga and tai chi help the body move more smoothly and improve balance.

●Proper nutrition provides general health benefits and helps fight constipation, which is common among Parkinson's patients. Exercise is essential for the same reason. Eat lots of vegetables, fruits, and other sources of fiber, such as whole grains, barley, and oats.

Helpful: Eat smaller meals throughout the day. Eating a large, protein-rich meal around the time you take your medication may hinder the drug's absorption.

●Stress control can reduce the severity of tremor, as well as help you deal with the difficulties of a chronic disease. *Good choices:* Massage, meditation, music, and aromatherapy.

●Supplements may protect the nervous system from damage caused by unstable molecules known as *free radicals.* This damage may accelerate Parkinson's progression.

The theory hasn't been definitively proven, but it's wise to take supplements totaling 1000 milligrams (mg) of vitamin C and 400 to 800 international units (IU) of vitamin E daily.

Coenzyme Q-10, a powerful antioxidant, may reduce Parkinson's symptoms. The recommended daily dose—300 mg, 2 to 4 times a day—costs about $200 per month. Ask your doctor if supplements would be appropriate for you.

●**Older surgeries can cause irreversible side effects.** Before the advent of deep-brain stimulation, only 2 surgeries were available for Parkinson's patients. During these procedures, doctors destroyed tiny areas of the brain, the *globus pallidus internus* (pallidotomy), or part of the *thalamus* (thalamotomy), to help reduce tremors and rigidity.

Adverse effects, such as weakness, partial loss of vision, or speech impediments, may occur after these surgeries and are sometimes permanent. With deep-brain stimulation, side effects are less likely to occur and are usually reversible.

2

Alzheimer's Disease

Is It Really Alzheimer's?

Study results indicate that using *positron emission tomography* (PET) scans to diagnose Alzheimer's disease reduces unnecessary medications and nursing home time. The PET scans measure the brain's metabolic pattern and can help determine whether early Alzheimer's–type damage has set in.

The author of the study, Dr. Daniel Silverman, says more patients would be accurately diagnosed in the early stages of the disease if they have the PET scans.

Not everyone suspected of having Alzheimer's needs a scan, but in appropriate patients it could be a boon, says Silverman, head of the Neuronuclear Imaging Research Group at the University of California at Los Angeles.

Silverman recommends that anyone who suspects he/she has Alzheimer's first find a geriatric psychiatrist or neurologist. He suggests

that the doctor follow the Academy on Alzheimer's guidelines for diagnosis before ordering a PET scan.

THE STUDY

Two approaches to diagnosing Alzheimer's were analyzed by a team from UCLA. One approach used mental status exams, memory impairment screening tests, and other evaluations. The other approach added PET scans to the workup.

The researchers found that the group who had received the PET scans had 47% fewer incorrect diagnoses of Alzheimer's (false-positive results) and 62% fewer false-negative results. "What that converts to in terms of outcome is cutting months of unneeded drug treatment in half and the avoidable months of nursing home care by about 60%," says Silverman.

Daniel Silverman, MD, PhD, head of the Neuronuclear Imaging Research Group, and Assistant Professor of Molecular and Medical Pharmacology, University of California, Los Angeles, School of Medicine.

October 2002, *Molecular Imaging and Biology*.

■ ■ ■ ■

Early Symptoms of Alzheimer's

To help family members and health care professionals recognize the warning signs of Alzheimer's disease, the Alzheimer's Association has developed a checklist of common symptoms. *They are...*

1. Memory loss.

2. Difficulty performing familiar tasks.

3. Problems with language.

4. Disorientation to time and place.

5. Poor or decreased judgment.

6. Problems with abstract thinking.

7. Misplacing things.

8. Changes in mood or behavior.

9. Changes in personality.

10. Loss of initiative.

If you recognize any warning signs in yourself or a loved one, the Alzheimer's Association recommends consulting a physician. Early diagnosis of Alzheimer's disease or other disorders causing dementia is important in getting appropriate treatment, care, and support services.

 For more information, visit the Alzheimer's Association at *www.alz.org.*

Breakthrough Medical Test Spots Alzheimer's While It's Manageable

Trey Sunderland, MD, Chief, Geriatric Psychiatry Branch, National Institute of Mental Health, Bethesda, MD.
David A. Bennett, MD, Director, Rush Alzheimer's Disease Center, Chicago, IL.
October 22, 2002, *Neurology.*
April 23–30, 2003, *Journal of the American Medical Association.*

Two proteins that appear in the spinal fluid may one day help doctors diagnose Alzheimer's disease, a degenerative brain condition that to date can be confirmed only by an autopsy, say researchers.

Their study suggests that doctors could diagnose the disease in the early stages, or even predict it, by looking for abnormal levels of the 2 spinal substances called *beta-amyloid* and *tau.* Early diagnosis of the disease is key because the few treatments now available can slow the progression of symptoms only if they are started early.

AGING POPULATION ADDS URGENCY

Alzheimer's disease, which is believed to be caused by a buildup of these toxic substances in the brain, affects approximately 4 million Americans. The number of patients is expected to quadruple over the next 50 years as the population ages.

In the study, Dr. Trey Sunderland, an Alzheimer's expert at the National Institute of Mental Health, and his colleagues compared tau and beta-amyloid levels in spinal fluid samples from 131 people with suspected Alzheimer's disease with a group of healthy people.

As expected, levels of tau were almost 2.5 times higher in the people with brain disease than in healthy subjects. Beta-amyloid levels were approximately half as high in the sick group.

Tau is released by dying brain cells, so higher concentrations in cerebrospinal fluid reflect increased damage to neurons. Beta-amyloid levels fall in the spinal fluid of Alzheimer's patients, experts say, because more of the protein stays in the brain, where it causes harm.

BOLSTERING THE RESULTS

Sunderland and his colleagues also reviewed 51 previous studies of the link between tau and beta-amyloid in spinal fluid and Alzheimer's. Taken together, these studies included more than 3100 people with the brain disorder, and the overall results echoed his group's own findings.

Sunderland says testing for the 2 proteins is a better gauge of Alzheimer's than a doctor's examination, as it can distinguish diseased brains from normal ones roughly 90% of the time. Today, Alzheimer's is commonly diagnosed through symptoms and by ruling out other diseases.

Researchers must now learn if the protein changes are a result of Alzheimer's brain damage, or whether they precede it.

CAN DRAINING SPINAL FLUID WORK?

In another study, researchers reported that draining spinal fluid from Alzheimer's patients—which some scientists believe draws away toxic proteins that worsen the disease—can be done safely enough to warrant additional trials of the procedure, despite several serious adverse reactions, including seizures, severe headache, and infection.

Dr. David A. Bennett, director of the Rush Alzheimer's Disease Center in Chicago, isn't so sure. "Safe is in the eye of the beholder," he says. For Alzheimer's patients, the gains from the technique—if they exist—might be temporary because of the irreversible nature of the disease.

A QUESTION OF ETHICS

The study taps into a roiling debate in Alzheimer's research over whether people with dementia can truly give informed consent for clinical studies, particularly those studies with the potential for serious side effects. One side is adamant that anything other than the mildest dementia robs volunteers of the necessary understanding of the risks they're facing. Others, equally insistent, believe the trials can be conducted ethically.

"It's making research tough," Bennett says.

Memory Coaching May Be Key for Alzheimer's Patients

Linda Clare, PhD, lecturer, Clinical Psychology, University College, London, England.

October 2002, *Neuropsychology*.

If you care for someone with Alzheimer's, or think you may be seeing early signs of dementia in yourself, you may be interested to know that one British study suggests failing memories can improve—with a little work.

Researchers, led by clinical psychologist Linda Clare, found that the standard face-recognition coaching that is often used to help brain injury patients also works in people with dementia that is linked to Alzheimer's disease.

They studied 12 men and women with early-stage dementia consistent with Alzheimer's. For 1 hour each week for 6 weeks, study volunteers were shown a different picture of a famous person or someone from their social circle. A month after the last session, the volunteers were tested on their recall, then again periodically throughout the following year.

At the start of the study, the volunteers couldn't remember even one face. But after the training sessions, they were able to recall an average of about 3 faces each, the researchers say. Their ability to remember other items was basically unchanged.

One rather surprising outcome, Clare says, was that those taking medication for dementia did no better on the memory recall than those who were not on medication. She says she expected that the drugs would have helped them with their memory tasks. "I think that we need some more research to really see what's going on there," she says.

■ ■ ■ ■

Want to Improve Your Memory? Think 'Mnemonics'

Mnemonics is a technique intended to assist the memory. Mnemonic "tricks" might help you keep your memory sharp. *Here are some mnemonic tricks from the University of Texas…*

●**Acronyms.** You form acronyms by using each first letter from a group of words to form a new word. This is particularly useful when remembering words in a specified order. Some common acronyms are NBA (National Basketball Association), SCUBA (Self-Contained Underwater Breathing Apparatus), BTUs (British Thermal Units), and LASER (Light Amplification by Stimulated Emission of Radiation).

●**Sentences/Acrostics.** Use the first letter of each word you are trying to remember. Instead of making a new word, though, you use the letters to make a sentence. *Here are some examples...*

●My Very Educated Mother Just Served Us Nine Pizzas (Mercury, Venus, Earth, Mars, Jupiter, Saturn, Uranus, Neptune, Pluto).

●King Phil Came Over for the Genes Special (Kingdom, Phylum, Class, Order, Genus, Species).

●**Rhymes and Songs.** Rhythm, repetition, melody, and rhyme can all help memory. Homer's *Odyssey* is a good example. It is remarkable to realize that this epic was told by storytellers who relied solely on their memories.

●**Method of Loci.** First, you must identify a familiar path that you walk and have a vivid visual memory of the path and objects along it. Once you have determined your path, imagine yourself walking along it, and identify specific landmarks that you will pass.

●**Chunking.** A common rule is that a person can remember 7 (plus or minus 2) items in short-term memory. When you use "chunking" to remember, you decrease the number of items you are holding in memory by increasing the size of each item. For example, in remembering the number string 64831996, you could try to remember each number individually, or you could try thinking about the string as 64 83 19 96 (creating 4 chunks of numbers).

●**Practice makes perfect** (or closer to it, anyway). Okay, it may not be a mnemonic, but repeating is still a great memory aid. Remember the children's game "I'm going on a picnic and I'm bringing..." As each new object is added, the old objects are repeated. People can often remember a large number of objects this way. When trying to remember a list of items, you might try a similar concept. Once you are able to remember 5 items on your list without looking, add a 6th, repeat the whole list from the start, and add a 7th, and so on.

Alzheimer's Disease May Be Caused by Lack of Iron

Hani Atamna, PhD, Assistant Scientist, Children's Hospital Oakland Research Institute, Oakland, CA.

David Bennett, MD, Director, Rush Alzheimer's Disease Center, Chicago, IL.

November 4, 2002, *Proceedings of the National Academy of Sciences.*

There may be a link between iron deficiency and Alzheimer's disease. Researchers say that brain cells deprived of a key form of iron become damaged in a way that mimics Alzheimer's and similar destructive brain diseases.

In their study, Oakland, California, researchers examined 2 types of human brain tumor cells, as well as neurons from rats. Normally, the types of cells they looked at would be constantly dividing, but without enough of the "heme" form of iron, those cells died when pushed to multiply.

Hani Atamna, a scientist at Children's Hospital Oakland Research Institute and a co-author of the study, says many of the changes in the cell activity mimic what happens to the brain cells of people with Alzheimer's disease.

Many scientists believe that Alzheimer's is caused by thickets of a specific protein. Atamna's group couldn't determine whether low iron levels promoted these plaques, but they're working on studies that may answer that question, he says. The researchers are also interested in following people over time to see how fluctuations in iron levels may affect brain health.

Dr. David Bennett, director of the Rush Alzheimer's Disease Center in Chicago, is cautious not to overstate the importance of the study, calling it "just another piece of data that would support" looking into a possible role of iron in brain disease.

■ ■ ■ ■

Stages of Alzheimer's

According to the Institute for Brain Aging at the University of California at Irvine, there are several stages of Alzheimer's disease. *They are...*

●**Mild.** Often the person forgets where he/she has put things or has difficulty finding the right word.

●**Moderate.** The patient has difficulty performing more complex tasks, such as balancing the checkbook, grocery shopping, or planning common events like a dinner party. The patient has deficits in intellect and reasoning, becomes apathetic, and gets lost in familiar places. At this stage, the impairments are obvious to family and friends.

●**Severe.** In addition to the problems in the first 2 stages, the patient loses the ability to speak, or may repeat words and phrases over and over. The patient fails to recognize friends and family and may even fail to recognize himself or herself in a mirror.

The 'Fatty Diet' That May Lower Your Risk of Alzheimer's 80%

Martha Clare Morris, ScD, Epidemiologist, Rush–Presbyterian–St. Luke's Medical Center, Chicago, IL.

Marcelle Morrison–Bogorad, PhD, Associate Director, Neuroscience and Neuropsychology of Aging Program, National Institute on Aging, Bethesda, MD.

February 2003, *Archives of Neurology.*

Two studies offer mixed news when it comes to warding off Alzheimer's disease through your diet.

One study says vitamins C and E and carotenes don't alter your chances of developing Alzheimer's disease. But the second study says that eating a diet that's low in saturated and hydrogenated fats and high in unsaturated fats just might help fend off the disease that afflicts 4 million Americans.

In the study on fats and Alzheimer's, researchers found those who ate the least "bad" fats (saturated and hydrogenated) and the most "good" fats (unsaturated) had an 80% lower chance of developing Alzheimer's than those who consumed the opposite.

"What's important is that so many people are under the impression that they should cut fat out of their diets, when in fact the vegetable fats are very good for you, and you should think about getting a little at every meal," says Martha Clare Morris, lead author of the study and an epidemiologist at Rush–Presbyterian–St. Luke's Medical Center in Chicago.

The group with the lowest incidence of Alzheimer's ate approximately 38 grams of unsaturated fats per day, Morris says, while those with the highest incidence of Alzheimer's ate only approximately 19 grams of good fats per day.

THE VITAMIN STUDY

Although the exact cause of Alzheimer's disease is unknown, researchers believe that *free radicals*—tiny particles generated by normal metabolism—can damage neurons in the brain and, over time, contribute to dementia. Antioxidants reduce the damage done by free radicals, so researchers had hoped that eating foods or taking supplements high in antioxidants would help prevent the disease. Unfortunately, this study did not prove that to be true.

Of the people in the study who developed Alzheimer's, researchers found no link between their intake of antioxidant vitamins and the disease.

But you may not want to stop taking your vitamins E and C just yet. Other studies have shown antioxidants can help stave off dementia, and the National Institute on Aging is funding more research on the subject.

Marcelle Morrison–Bogorad, associate director of the Institute's Neuroscience and Neuropsychology of Aging Program, says, "One of the things we're hoping for at the National Institute on Aging is that in our attempts to slow the development of Alzheimer's, we will eventually have a combination of lifestyle changes plus very directed, specific drugs that together will give us a chance of really fighting this dreadful disease."

info For more information on the research and treatment of Alzheimer's disease, you can visit the Alzheimer's Disease Education & Referral Center at *www.alzheimers.org.*

■ ■ ■ ■

All Fats Are Not Created Equal

Unsaturated, saturated, hydrogenated. We see these terms listed on food labels, but what's the real difference?

●**Unsaturated fats** are found in vegetable oils (such as canola, corn, safflower, or olive), in nuts and seeds, in liquid margarine, and in mayonnaise.

●**Saturated fats** are those found in animal products, such as butter, red meat, whole milk, and cheese.

●**Hydrogenated fats** are found in snack foods, such as commercially produced baked goods and potato chips, as well as in hard margarines. Hydrogenation is a chemical alteration of vegetable oils that occurs during the manufacturing process.

Wine, Not Beer, Keeps Memory Clear

Thomas Truelsen, MD, PhD, Institute of Preventive Medicine, Kommunehospitalet, Copenhagen, Denmark.

Bill Thies, PhD, Vice President, Medical and Scientific Affairs, Alzheimer's Association, Chicago, IL.

November 12, 2002, *Neurology*.

Another sign that your favorite red or white wine may be as healthful as fruits and vegetables is research that shows that wine can protect the brain from the ravages of Alzheimer's disease.

However, experts still aren't advising people to run out to the liquor store.

"It is still premature to talk about wine as a 'health food' product," says study coauthor Dr. Thomas Truelsen, a researcher at the Institute of Preventive Medicine at Kommunehospitalet in Copenhagen, Denmark.

And, even if wine does protect the brain, the Danish study suggests beer does exactly the opposite.

FINE WINE

Wine, of course, is gaining a reputation as much more than just a requisite beverage for dinner parties. Researchers in recent years have linked it to lowering the risk of heart disease. And wine drinkers seem to have healthier habits than teetotalers.

The Danish researchers studied reports from the 1970s on the drinking habits of more than 1700 people. Then the researchers checked the subjects again in the 1990s to see how many people developed dementia, a major symptom of Alzheimer's disease. Dementia refers to the loss of memory, concentration, and other brain functions due to disease.

Eighty-three people in the study had developed dementia. But people who drank wine weekly or monthly were more than 2 times less likely to develop dementia than the others.

FEAR BEER

On the other hand, drinking beer monthly actually increased the risk of developing dementia.

Truelsen says the researchers don't know why drinking beer was linked to a higher risk of dementia. "It may be that drinking beer is associated with a poorer diet or trauma, or that the drinking patterns [of beer drinkers] are different," he says.

Previous studies show a link between wine drinking and less dementia, Truelsen says. The Danish researchers think that plant-derived substances in wine known as *flavonoids* may protect the brain. Flavonoids are more common in red wine than white wine, but they are also found in other foods, raising questions about whether they're really the reason for wine's beneficial effects.

Truelsen acknowledges the study didn't account for diet, which could affect overall health. For that reason and others, the findings aren't firm enough to make any recommendation about drinking wine, he says.

Also, he adds, "There may be many good reasons for not drinking—health, family, pregnancy, economy, work, etc."

Bill Thies, vice president for medical and scientific affairs for the Alzheimer's Association, agrees that a blanket endorsement of wine drinking would be a bad idea.

"There are people who are genetically prone to alcoholism who need to avoid alcohol," he says. "Recommending that everyone drink red wine for the health of their brain may expose such people to alcohol with severe health consequences."

info For more information, visit the New York Academy of Sciences Web site at *www.nyas.org.*

Motor Problems Could Be Prelude to Alzheimer's Disease

Robert S. Wilson, PhD, Professor, Neuropsychology, Rush–Presbyterian–St. Luke's Medical Center, Chicago, IL.

Bill Thies, PhD, Vice President, Medical and Scientific Affairs, Alzheimer's Association, Chicago, IL.

April 2003, *Archives of Neurology.*

Symptoms that mimic Parkinson's disease —muscle rigidity, difficulty walking, and other motor problems—could be a prelude to Alzheimer's disease, researchers say.

A study at Rush–Presbyterian–St. Luke's Medical Center in Chicago found that older people who had a rapid progression of these symptoms were 8 times more likely to develop Alzheimer's disease than those with no worsening of such symptoms.

Any progression of the symptoms is a bad sign and suggests that there are degenerative changes occurring in the brain, says study author Robert S. Wilson, a professor of neuropsychology at Rush–Presbyterian.

The symptoms are similar to those seen in people with Parkinson's disease, but, Wilson says, they're not actually caused by Parkinson's.

The findings aren't all that surprising, says Bill Thies, vice president of medical and scientific affairs at the Alzheimer's Association. "Alzheimer's disease is typically worse in people who have more dysfunction."

Perhaps the most significant aspect of the study is the data showing that annual declines in motor ability are paralleled by reductions in cognitive function, Thies says.

Although it isn't necessarily a new concept, this study provides actual evidence of a link between motor and mental skills.

THE STUDY

The researchers studied 824 older Catholic clergymen with an average age of 75.4 years at the start of the study. None had any clinical signs of Parkinson's or Alzheimer's.

The researchers found that motor problems worsened in 79% of the subjects over the course of the study. Among that group, those with the most rapid symptom progression had a more than 8 times greater risk of developing Alzheimer's disease than those whose symptoms did not worsen.

Seniors with a slow to moderate progression of the symptoms had a 2 to 5 times greater risk of developing Alzheimer's.

Depression, Head Injuries Linked to Developing Alzheimer's

Robert C. Green, MD, Associate Professor, Neurology, Boston University School of Medicine, MA.

Jennie Ward–Robinson, PhD, Director, Medical and Scientific Affairs, Alzheimer's Association, Chicago, IL.

May 2003, *Archives of Neurology.*

A recent study found that a bout of depression early in life may be a warning sign that Alzheimer's disease will develop decades later. The study is important, says Dr. Robert C. Green, an associate professor of neurology at Boston University School of Medicine, because it adds to the collection of possible risk factors that could be used to identify people at high risk for Alzheimer's.

"What is exciting is that we are beginning to learn more about Alzheimer's disease and are getting to the point where we can talk in terms of risk factors," said Jennie Ward–Robinson, director of medical and scientific affairs at the Alzheimer's Association.

In addition to depression, head injuries can increase the risk of Alzheimer's, Green explains. Taking antidepressants, vitamin E, or statins (cholesterol-lowering drugs) appears to reduce the risk.

THE RESEARCH

This study included 1953 people with Alzheimer's disease who were matched with 2093 of their close relatives who did not have the disease. The incidence of depression was found by questioning those relatives.

Overall, people with a history of depression were twice as likely to have Alzheimer's, the researchers report.

If the depression began a year before the onset of Alzheimer's, the association was almost 5 times stronger. Even if depression was reported to have begun more than 2 decades earlier, the incidence of Alzheimer's was 70% greater than in those who did not have a history of depression.

Among the still unanswered questions, Green says, are whether the disease starts in a subtle way in a person's 20s and 30s, whether people who are less prone to depression have more resistance to Alzheimer's, and whether depression is toxic to the health of the brain.

■ ■ ■ ■

Diagnosing Alzheimer's

According to the Alzheimer's Research Foundation, diagnosing Alzheimer's usually involves several types of evaluations. *These include...*

●**Medical history.** This is usually an interview or questionnaire to identify past medical problems, difficulties in daily activities, and prescription drug use, among other things. A depression screening should also be done.

●**Physical examination.** This should include evaluations of hearing and sight, as well as blood pressure and pulse readings.

●**Standard laboratory tests.** Lab tests might include blood and urine tests designed to help eliminate other possible conditions.

●**Neuropsychological testing.** Doctors use a variety of tools to assess memory, problem-solving, attention, vision–motor coordination, and abstract thinking, such as performing simple calculations in your head.

Lithium Eyed For Treating Alzheimer's Disease

Peter Klein, MD, PhD, Assistant Professor, Medicine, University of Pennsylvania School of Medicine, Philadelphia, and Assistant Investigator, Howard Hughes Medical Institute, Chevy Chase, MD.

Arnold Licht, MD, Chairman, Psychiatry, Long Island College Hospital, Brooklyn, NY.

Deborah B. Marin, MD, Professor, Psychiatry, and Dean, Clinical Research, Mount Sinai School of Medicine, New York, NY.

May 22, 2003, *Nature.*

A drug that has been a standard treatment for manic depression is being studied for its potential to prevent and treat Alzheimer's disease.

The risk of developing Alzheimer's disease increases dramatically with age. According to the Alzheimer's Association, up to 10% of people older than 65 years, and as many as 50% of people 85 years and older, have the disease. There are also inherited forms of the disease.

Scientists have found that in mice and in cultured cells, *lithium* inhibited an enzyme that is critical to the development of *amyloid plaques,* a distinctive feature of Alzheimer's.

The study's finding that lithium interferes with the suspected pathological process in Alzheimer's is intriguing, says Dr. Deborah B. Marin, a professor of psychiatry and dean of clinical research at the Mount Sinai School of Medicine in New York City.

The brains of people who have died of Alzheimer's disease have 2 types of lesions that normal brains do not have. The first is called an *amyloid plaque,* which is composed of a protein called *beta-amyloid.* This protein accumulates outside the cells. The second type of lesion is called a *neurofibrillary tangle,* which is composed of a different protein that accumulates inside the cells.

"What our paper shows is that if you use lithium in a test tube or in mice it can reduce the amount of beta-amyloid that gets produced," says study author Dr. Peter Klein, an assistant professor of medicine at the University of Pennsylvania School of Medicine in Philadelphia.

SPECIAL ISSUES

There are special concerns about giving lithium to older people. It is used for the elderly, but only with close monitoring.

Because lithium has a narrow dosage range between effective medicine and toxic agent, it is hard to manage, says Dr. Arnold Licht, chairman of psychiatry at Long Island College Hospital in New York.

Lithium has also been known to cause cognitive problems, namely short- and long-term memory deficits, Marin says. Doses would have to be low enough that they would not cause the kinds of side effects seen when lithium is used for bipolar patients.

■ ■ ■ ■

How Is Lithium Used?

According to the New York–Presbyterian Hospital, lithium is a natural type of salt. *It is most commonly used to treat…*

- **Mania.**
- **Manic–depressive illness** (also called bipolar disorder).
- **Depression.**
- **Intermittent explosive disorder.**
- **Mood instability** and/or impulsivity in personality disorders.

3

Asthma & Allergies

Pets May Be Early Allergy Fighters

For many years, pets have been blamed as a significant source of allergens in the home, but a recent Georgia study may give them at least a partial furlough from the proverbial doghouse.

Researchers say some infants exposed to at least 2 pets in the house are less—not more—likely to develop allergies to dogs, cats, and other irritants later in life.

The findings, published in the *Journal of the American Medical Association*, confirm earlier, counterintuitive studies from the United States and abroad showing that pet dander seems to protect children from allergies and asthma.

"For years, I've been telling people concerned about their kids and allergies that they ought to get pets out of the house," says Dr. Dennis Ownby, an allergist at the Medical College of Georgia and leader of the research team. Ownby says he has retracted that statement and has even taken the matter a step further. "If you're going to have a pet," he says, "it's probably better to have 2 than 1."

Ownby says there's a debate about why early exposure to pets is protective. His group feels that animals may track in irritants from the dirty world outside the home, which can beef up a child's immune system. The generally increasing cleanliness in developed countries has been blamed for a surge in allergies and asthma.

"This suggests that there is something we can do that will, in fact, reduce risk. If we could define what it is, maybe we could refine that and give it to kids" as a way to shield them from allergies, Ownby says.

Dennis R. Ownby, MD, Professor of Pediatrics and Medicine, Medical College of Georgia, Augusta.

Thomas A.E. Platts–Mills, MD, PhD, Chief, Division of Allergy and Clinical Immunology, University of Virginia Health System, Charlottesville.

August 28, 2002, *Journal of the American Medical Association.*

BUILDING TOLERANCE

Scientists long believed that pets posed a major source of household allergens—and for some people that's certainly true, says Dr. Thomas Platts–Mills, an allergy expert at the University of Virginia in Charlottesville.

Platts–Mills, author of an editorial accompanying the journal article, estimated that as many as 20% of people may develop tolerance to pet allergens by living with animals.

In the study, Ownby and his colleagues followed 474 Detroit–area children from birth to age 6 or 7 years. By then, 33.6% of those with no cat or dog at home during their first year of life had developed skin sensitivity to 6 common irritants, including dust mites and pollen. That figure was slightly higher for those with 1 cat or dog. But it plunged to 15% among the children with at least 2 pets.

After adjusting for factors that exacerbate allergies—including exposure to cigarette smoke, dust mites, and a parental history of asthma—researchers found that 2 or more cats or dogs in the house reduced an infant's risk of allergies between 67% and 77%, compared with having 1 pet or no pets.

info For more on allergies, visit the Web site of the American Academy of Allergy, Asthma & Immunology at *www.aaaai.org*.

Farms Good Place To Keep Allergies From Cropping Up in Kids

Andy Liu, MD, Pediatric Allergist, National Jewish Medical and Research Center, Denver, CO.

Scott T. Weiss, MD, Professor, Harvard Medical School, Brigham and Women's Hospital, Boston, MA.

Children who grow up on farms, around barns and animals, are much less likely than other children to suffer from allergies and asthma.

A European study offers strong support for the theory that, as developed nations become cleaner—reducing childhood infections that toughen the immune system—their citizens become more vulnerable to allergies.

Cities were once a major source of endotoxins, but that changed with improvements in sewage, plumbing, and other sanitary practices. Endotoxins are the fatty proteins that make up the outer shells of bacteria in animal feces.

Contact with endotoxins at key points in the development of the immune system primes the body's defenses enough so that later exposure to the proteins doesn't spark allergic reactions.

Farms with animal stock have always been rife with bacteria. If farm children are exposed to more endotoxins, according to the theory, they should have fewer allergy problems than those raised in more sterile homes.

Other research has shown that concentrations of endotoxins are as much as 50,000 times higher in barn dust than they are in dust from cities, according to Dr. Andy Liu, an allergy expert at Denver's National Jewish Medical and Research Center. Barns are also far dustier than homes, increasing the volume of exposures.

Another aspect of life on the farm, Liu says, is exposure to endotoxins in unpasteurized dairy products, such as raw milk. Some members of the European research team showed that babies whose mothers had fed them unpasteurized milk had remarkably low rates of asthma as children.

THE STUDY

Led by Dr. Charlotte Braun–Fahrländer, the researchers compared asthma and allergy rates and endotoxin exposure in 812 children, ages 6 to 13 years, growing up in rural communities. Of those, 319 were raised on farms.

Parents were interviewed about their child's history of asthma and hay fever, and blood samples were taken from the children to look for immune system activity.

The researchers also vacuumed the children's mattresses to measure the amount of endotoxins they encountered every day. The level of endotoxins in bedding was higher on the farm, and children exposed to more endotoxins at home were less likely to have hay fever and asthma.

UNANSWERED QUESTIONS

Some exposure to endotoxins appears protective, yet many people suffer from contact with very high levels of the fatty proteins. There seems to be a middle ground that's beneficial, Liu says, but scientists haven't yet found how much is too much.

Dr. Scott Weiss, an immunologist at Harvard Medical School in Boston, agrees the study supports this theory, but says no one is going to feed dirt to a baby or put a crib in a barn to shield infants from allergies later in life. Some other aspect of farm life, he adds, may be protecting the children.

■ ■ ■ ■

Best Ways to Combat Allergies

The University of Kentucky has some suggestions for fighting against sources of allergies. Dust and dust mites are the most common causes of allergies in homes. In fact, more people have allergic reactions to this duo than they do to mold and pollen. Dust-related allergies are a year-round problem, whereas mold and pollen are seasonal.

Dust mites feed on skin flakes and particles shed by people and pets. Since mites inhabit household dust, a big part of the solution is sanitation where shed skin and dust particles collect, mainly, areas where you and your family and pets spend a lot of time.

To make your home as mite unfriendly as possible, regularly vacuum items that trap and hold dust—mattresses, upholstered sofas and chairs, drapes, carpet and even your children's stuffed animals.

For best results, use a vacuum cleaner with a High Efficiency Particulate Arrester (HEPA) filter. A HEPA filter will trap more than 99 percent of particles less than one micron in size. Conversely, using a vacuum cleaner without a HEPA filter will shoot dust and mite particles out the back, allowing them to become airborne and increasing the chance of allergic reactions.

Dust mites also like humidity. The higher the humidity, the more attractive your home becomes to them; so reduce humidity indoors to less than 60 percent.

Additional ways to reduce dust mite problems include laundering your bed linens every week in hot water, and putting a high-efficiency filter in your heating-air conditioning system.

If a member of your family is extremely sensitive to dust or dust mites, here are more suggestions...

●**Use a low-pile carpet.** It's even better to eliminate as much carpet as possible by using hardwood, linoleum, or tile floors.

●**Encase mattresses and box springs** in a plastic cover.

●**Don't allow children to sleep with stuffed animals.**

●**Use a portable air filtration system** to purify the air in an area where the person spends a lot of time such as a bedroom.

●**Install a HEPA-type filter** in the air circulation system.

●**Avoid products that trap dust mites** and increase humidity like thick pile carpet, heavy drapes, and thick woolen blankets.

What Is the Worst Possible Pet for Asthmatics?

Clifford Bassett, MD, Director, Allergy & Asthma Care of New York.

May 20, 2003, presentation, American Thoracic Society Meeting, Seattle, WA.

Your dog may be your best pal, but if you've got asthma, he might be your lungs' worst enemy.

Although more people are allergic to cats than to dogs, one study shows dog allergens are more ferocious irritants to asthmatics than cat dander, cockroaches, mold, and dust mites.

The study included 809 men and women with mild to moderate asthma who were given skin tests for various irritants.

To measure sensitivity to an allergen, the researchers tested subjects in several areas. *They were...*

●**Their ability to exhale** while exposed to an irritant (reduced exhalation indicates an increased sensitivity).

●**The amount of nitric oxide gas in their breath** (more nitric acid signals inflammation).

●**The nature of the phlegm,** if any, they coughed up (cells called *eosinophils* present in mucus suggest an allergic exposure).

Their lungs were also provoked with a drug that constricts airways.

DOG DANDER AFFECTS FEWER, BUT HITS HARDER

Cat allergens were most likely to trigger at least one reaction, doing so in nearly 75% of the volunteers—the most of any irritant. Dog dander, by comparison, did so only approximately half as often. However, dog dander was the irritant most likely to decrease lung function, constrict the airways, and provoke inflammation.

Dr. Clifford Bassett, a New York City allergy specialist, says the findings run counter to what most asthma experts have believed. "Normally we think cat dander is most provocative," says Bassett, who sits on the public education committee of the American Academy of Allergy, Asthma and Immunology. However, this study shows that both dogs and cats are a problem for adults with the breathing problem.

Interestingly, the researchers say, pollens didn't seem to irritate the lungs as much as dog and cat dander and other indoor irritants.

DON'T GIVE UP YOUR PETS YET

Some doctors say pets are a no-go for asthma patients. Bassett says it's possible to keep animals around, as long as you take steps to reduce your exposure to their allergens. Using special air filters to intercept the particles is one way to reduce exposure. Lower-tech measures, such as wearing cotton (wool is a magnet for pet dander) and keeping your animal out of the bedroom, help, too.

Also important, Bassett says, is that everyone with asthma be tested for allergies. "Certain allergies can be modified" with lifestyle changes, prevention, or medication, he says.

■ ■ ■ ■

Keeping Pet Allergens Under Control

Even though they suffer from asthma and other allergies, many people still want to own pets. Dr. Bassett, writing in the *Allergy and Asthma Advocate,* offers many suggestions for keeping pet allergens in your home at a minimum. *They include...*

●**Avoid hugging and kissing pets.**

●**Remove litter boxes from direct contact with allergy sufferers** and place them away from air filtration intake vents in homes with central heating and air-conditioning.

●**Wash hands after handling or touching a pet** to avoid spreading the dander.

●**Consider placing plastic covers on the couch** or other upholstered furniture where the pet sleeps or rests.

●**Wash your pet every week.** Recent studies indicate that this significantly reduces the amount of pet allergens. Pet shampoos that may neutralize or inactivate allergens are available in pet stores.

●**A nonallergic person should brush the pet regularly,** outside of the home.

●**Your veterinarian can recommend a well balanced diet for your pet,** which may help to minimize hair loss and thereby, reduce dander indoors.

●**Use a double or micro-filter vacuum bag** to augment the filtration of the vacuum cleaner. This will reduce the amount of pet allergen present in carpeting.

●**Removing carpeting and rugs** is the best way to reduce exposure. Barring this, there are a number of chemical solutions available that may remove allergens present in carpeting.

●**Ask your physician to consider allergy shots** (*immunotherapy*) to reduce the effects of having a pet in the home.

■ ■ ■ ■

Asthma Triggers

The American Academy of Allergy, Asthma and Immunology says that pet dander is only one irritant that can trigger asthma. *Following are some others...*

●**Allergens or irritants.**

●**Viral or sinus infections.**

●**Exercise.**

●**Reflux disease** (stomach acid flowing back up the esophagus).

●**Medications or foods.**

●**Emotional anxiety.**

info For specifics about pets and asthma, go to the US Environmental Protection Agency's Web site at *www.epa.gov/iaq/asthma* and click on "Asthma Triggers."

Best-Ever Asthma Treatment

Francine Ducharme, MD, Assistant Professor, Pediatrics, Montreal Children's Hospital, McGill University Health Centre, Montreal, Quebec, Canada.
March 22, 2003, *British Medical Journal.*

People with mild to moderate asthma might want to stick with steroids rather than switch to nonsteroidal drugs. That's the suggestion from Canadian researchers who found that nonsteroidal drugs are less effective for this group of people.

Many asthma sufferers who are concerned about the effects of steroids over the long term have switched to nonsteroidal medications to control their symptoms. Like steroids, the nonsteroidal drugs, called *leukotriene receptor antagonists* (LTRAs), aim to reduce swelling and inflammation of the airways.

However, Dr. Francine Ducharme, assistant professor of pediatrics at McGill University Health Centre, found that adults who took the nonsteroidal drugs were 60% more likely to suffer a worsening of symptoms, including more asthma flare-ups, night awakenings, and days with symptoms.

In the United States, common brand names of inhaled steroids are Flovent and Beclovent. Commonly prescribed LTRAs are Singulair and Accolate.

AMERICANS ARE CAUTIOUS WITH STEROIDS

The LTRAs have become very popular in the US, accounting for 30% of the anti-asthmatic drug market, compared with only 10% in Canada and the United Kingdom, says Ducharme. This disparity is due partly to different marketing patterns in these countries, but also because of concern in the US about the effects of long-term steroid use.

"The steroids are pretty safe, but people still have that concern in their minds. The aversion to steroids is much greater in the States than elsewhere," she says.

THE STUDY

For her study, Ducharme and her colleagues reviewed 13 trials involving approximately 5000 people who suffered from mild to moderate asthma. These people received either inhaled steroids or LTRAs, which are taken in pill form

Asthma levels are defined by pulmonary lung function. Mild asthma is defined as a lung function of 80% of full capacity or better. Moderate asthma is a lung function between 50% and 80% of full capacity.

NOT APPLIED TO CHILDREN

Results of one study of children were the same as those of the adult studies. However, Ducharme says the numbers were too small to make statistical conclusions on the effects of the 2 drugs on children.

info A thorough explanation of asthma can be found at the National Institute of Allergy and Infectious Diseases Web site at *www.niaid.nih.gov/publications/asthma.htm.*

■ ■ ■ ■

Safe Uses for Steroids

Corticosteroids are effective anti-inflammatory medications. They are very different from the anabolic steroids that are misused by some athletes to enhance performance.

The American Academy of Allergy, Asthma and Immunology describes corticosteroids and their uses for a variety of allergic conditions.

They are available in several forms—topical creams, ointments, nasal sprays, inhalers, pills, and by injection. Usage should be supervised by a physician.

WHEN THEY ARE INHALED

•**Inhaled corticosteroids** are considered the most effective medications for long-term control over persistent asthma.

•**Minor side effects from using corticosteroid inhalers** include hoarseness and thrush (a fungal infection of the mouth and throat). Both are less likely to occur when the patient rinses and gargles with water after use.

•**Long-term use of inhaled corticosteroids** in children could potentially result in a reduced rate of growth. However, in most situations, the benefit of having the asthma controlled is greater than the potential for a certain side effect.

WHEN YOU TAKE THEM ORALLY

•**Oral corticosteroids** are usually considered as short-term medications for asthma flare-ups, marked nasal congestion, and at times for skin conditions such as poison ivy.

•**Taken orally they** generally have more side effects than inhaled or topical agents. But short-term use (up to several weeks) is usually not a problem for an otherwise healthy person.

•**Side effects of short-term use** include slight weight gain, increased appetite, menstrual irregularities, cramps, heartburn, or indigestion. These symptoms will cease shortly after stopping the corticosteroids.

•**Long-term use** (months to years) of oral corticosteroids is associated with ulcers, weight gain, cataracts, weakened bones and thinner skin, high blood pressure, elevated blood sugar, easy bruising, and decreased growth in children.

Despite the side effects associated with corticosteroids, when taken properly, these drugs can be very effective in treating asthma and allergies.

Good News for Asthmatics! Lower Doses of Steroids Work Just as Well

Neil C. Thomson, MD, Professor of Respiratory Medicine, University of Glasgow, Scotland.
John J. Costa, MD, Assistant Clinical Professor of Medicine, Harvard Medical School, Boston, MA.
May 24, 2003, *British Medical Journal.*

If you're among the 15% of all asthmatics who take high dosages of inhaled steroids, you may not need as much medicine as you think to keep your disease in check.

A Scottish study shows that patients with chronic, severe asthma can sharply reduce their dosages of inhaled steroids (to cut the risk of side effects) and still keep their condition under control.

The study was the first carefully controlled trial to show that this "step-down" approach works in chronic, severe cases of asthma.

Inhaled steroids are the recommended treatment for chronic asthma, but they are accompanied by a number of side effects, including weakened bones and eye problems, such as cataracts and glaucoma. For these reasons, doctors prefer to keep the dosage at a minimum.

The study included 259 adult asthma patients with symptoms severe enough to require an average of 1400 micrograms per day of *beclomethasone*, or equivalent amounts of other steroids.

For the study, 130 patients began taking half of their previous dosage, while 129 continued their old dosage. As is common in such controlled studies, none of the patients were told how much they were taking.

After 1 year, results were as good for the reduced-dosage patients as they were for the higher-dosage patients, according to Dr. Neil C. Thomson, professor of respiratory medicine at the University of Glasgow, and leader of the study.

DOCTORS SHOULD FOLLOW UP ON TREATMENT

"The study is a welcome reminder that doctors treating asthma patients should look toward reducing steroid dosage," says Dr. John J. Costa, assistant clinical professor of medicine at Harvard Medical School, and a spokesman for the American Academy of Allergy, Asthma and Immunology.

Often, asthma patients go to their doctors when the disease flares up, and higher doses are prescribed to bring things back to normal, he says.

"The importance of this is to remind practitioners that often they see asthmatics and decide that a certain amount of medicine is needed to address what is going on at that moment. It may not be the amount of medicine needed when the patient is not in the middle of a flare-up," Costa says. "The doctor should follow up to see if it is possible to reduce the dosage."

Breathe Easy! Heartburn Drug Helps Relieve Severe Asthma

Michael R. Littner, MD, Pulmonary Physician, Veterans Administration Greater Los Angeles Healthcare System, Sepulveda, CA, and Professor, Medicine, David Geffen School of Medicine, University of California, Los Angeles.

Timothy Wang, MD, Chief, Gastroenterology, University of Massachusetts Medical School, Worcester.

In a recent study, patients who took daily acid-reducing medicine along with their asthma medicine had fewer severe asthma attacks and an overall improvement in their quality of life.

Those with asthma and acid reflux symptoms who were taking 2 maintenance medicines, as well as acid-reducing *lansoprazole* (Prevacid), had a significant improvement, according to Dr. Michael Littner, a professor of medicine at the University of California in Los Angeles and the study's lead author.

The benefits, Littner says, were that those on lansoprazole reported fewer severe asthma attacks, called exacerbations, than did those who took a placebo.

The improvements occurred only in patients with severe asthma. Dr. Timothy Wang, chief of gastroenterology at the University of Massachusetts Medical School, says asthma and gastroesophageal reflux disease (GERD) seem to be closely linked.

Littner said the study participants had not been taking acid reflux medicines on a daily basis before the study. "The patients in the study were those who thought their heartburn was being controlled by occasional antacids. When they were having a pizza, they'd take an antacid…but normally did not take daily medications for reflux symptoms," he says.

Sinusitis or Plain Old Cold? The Nose Doctor Knows

Jordan S. Josephson, MD, Ear, Nose and Throat Surgeon, Lenox Hill Hospital, New York, NY.

Erica Thaler, MD, Assistant Professor, Department of Otorhinolaryngology, University of Pennsylvania Medical School, Philadelphia.

Stuffy nose. Headache. A cough that won't quit. These are all the classic signs of a cold, right?

Maybe not, say doctors who warn that those symptoms could also signal sinusitis, a potentially painful condition that, left untreated, can become chronic.

Sinusitis is characterized by inflamed nasal passages that can be caused by a number of factors, including viral infections and allergies. The inflammation shrinks the passages so mucus can't drain properly, leading to discomfort and the growth of microorganisms that are the hallmarks of sinusitis.

The result: Headache; pain in the teeth, jaws, and cheeks; swelling of the eyelids and tissues around the eyes; and pain between the eyes. *Other potential problems:* Stuffy nose, loss of the sense of smell, earaches, neck pain, and deep aching at the top of the head, according to the National Institute of Allergy and Infectious Diseases.

Left untreated, sinusitis can last weeks or even years. It's one of the most common chronic health problems in the United States, affecting approximately 34 million people every year.

KNOW THE SYMPTOMS

The key is to recognize sinusitis early and treat it before it becomes chronic. But how can a person know when to pay attention to their sniffles?

It's tricky, doctors admit. "There's a continuum between a plain old viral infection, a cold, and sinusitis," says Dr. Erica Thaler, a University of Pennsylvania Medical School otorhinolaryngologist (ear, nose, and throat specialist). "It's hard to tell the difference between a cold and sinusitis. A lot of people think they have sinusitis, but they don't. Half the time it's a lousy cold," she adds.

However, there are some clues that differentiate sinusitis from a cold.

If you have what seems to be a cold that won't go away after a week or 2, or seems to get better and then gets worse, it's probably sinusitis.

Another clue to sinusitis is mucus that's thick and yellow–green in color, a sign of a bacterial infection, says Dr. Jordan Josephson, an otorhinolaryngologist at Lenox Hill Hospital in New York City.

"Other signs are having trouble breathing through your nose, congested nasal passages, fatigue, postnasal drip, cough, hoarseness, and headaches," he says. If you have 2 or more of those symptoms, or one that is really uncomfortable, get to a doctor.

GOING FOR TREATMENT

A good internist, Thaler says, can examine you and give you the appropriate drugs to treat sinusitis. They include decongestants, antibiotics to control any bacterial infection, pain relievers, and steroid nasal sprays to reduce inflammation in the nose.

If this still doesn't help, you might have to see an otorhinolaryngologist, who can do a more thorough examination of the nasal passages.

Josephson adds that people can also try to reduce the triggers that cause inflammation of the nasal passages.

For example, during allergy seasons, keep the windows closed, use saline spray for the nose, and shower before bedtime to wash pollen out of your hair.

info The Web site for the American Academy of Family Physicians at *www.family doctor.org* offers information on sinusitis. A description of the sinuses can be found at the American Rhinologic Society's Web site at *www.american-rhinologic.org.*

'Dormant' Peanut Allergies Can Crop Up Later!

Scott H. Sicherer, MD, Assistant Professor, Pediatrics, Jaffe Food Allergy Institute, Mount Sinai School of Medicine, New York, NY.

Anne Munoz–Furlong, Founder and Chief Executive Officer, Food Allergy & Anaphylaxis Network, Fairfax, VA.

November 7, 2002, *New England Journal of Medicine.*

That peanut allergy you thought you outgrew? It may still exist, ready to bounce back without warning. Medical researchers have found that peanut allergies that seem to disappear in young children can return years later, raising concerns that the same may hold true for other food irritants.

An estimated 1 in 150 Americans are allergic to peanuts, some so acutely that even the slightest contact with peanut proteins can trigger severe or fatal reactions. Yet doctors have learned that as many as 20% of toddlers who are allergic to peanuts grow tolerant of them by the time they enter school. Doctors have assumed that once the allergy disappears, it never returns.

However, immune system specialists at the Mount Sinai School of Medicine in New York City found 3 children whose peanut allergies had vanished and then resurfaced. All of the patients were boys aged 6 to 10 years when their allergies returned. Each had first suffered reactions to peanuts when he was 12 to 18 months old.

"No one had ever reported that anyone who outgrew an allergy grew back into it again," says Dr. Scott Sicherer, a pediatrician at Mount Sinai's Jaffe Food Allergy Institute who saw the patients. "The remarkable thing was they not only had symptoms but they developed increased sensitization" to peanut proteins, he adds.

The boys were among 44 children participating in a program to chart the course of peanut allergies. Their reactions began approximately 1 year after a doctor-monitored "challenge" to see how well they tolerated small amounts of peanut foods. Those who didn't react to the foods, including the 3 boys, were told they could safely eat peanuts at home.

STARTING OVER

Sicherer says allergists should be cautious about advising their patients with dormant peanut allergies to dive headfirst into peanut-rich foods.

The rebound phenomenon probably doesn't apply to other foods frequently implicated in allergies, such as milk, eggs, wheat, and soy, he says. Whether it's a factor with allergies to fish and tree nuts isn't clear.

Anne Munoz–Furlong, founder and chief executive officer of the Food Allergy & Anaphylaxis Network, calls the Mount Sinai discovery "surprising."

"When we're talking about a peanut allergy, we have to start from scratch and assume nothing," Munoz–Furlong says. "We always have to be ready that it might come back."

Food allergies account for 30,000 emergency room visits and between 150 and 200 deaths a year in the United States. Many of those are believed to be a reaction to peanuts, Munoz–Furlong says.

info For more on food allergies, including food-safety tips and allergy-free recipes, visit The Food Allergy & Anaphylaxis Network at *www.foodallergy.org.*

■ ■ ■ ■

Watch Out for Hidden Sources Of Peanuts

Peanut derivatives are sometimes used in foods and not properly identified. For those people with peanut allergies, this can be deadly. *The Food Allergy & Anaphylaxis Network offers some information that might be a lifesaver…*

●**"Artificial" nuts can be peanuts** that have been deflavored and reflavored with a nut, such as pecan or walnut. Mandelonas are peanuts soaked in almond flavoring.

●**Arachis oil is peanut oil.**

●**Peanut-allergic patients should avoid chocolate candy** unless they are absolutely certain there is no risk of cross-contact during manufacturing.

●**African, Chinese, Indonesian, Mexican, Thai, and Vietnamese dishes** often contain peanuts, or are contaminated with peanuts during preparation.

●**Foods sold in bakeries and ice cream shops** are often in contact with peanuts.

●**Many brands of sunflower seeds** are produced on equipment shared with peanuts.

●**Studies show that most allergic individuals can safely eat peanut oil** (not cold pressed, expelled, or extruded peanut oil). Patients should ask their doctors whether or not to avoid peanut oil.

●**Most experts recommend peanut-allergic patients to avoid tree nuts** (walnuts and cashews for example).

●**Peanuts can be found in many foods.** Check all labels carefully. Contact the manufacturer if you have questions.

●**Peanuts can cause severe allergic reactions.** If prescribed, carry epinephrine at all times.

New Drug Stops Peanut Allergies Before They Start

News teleconference with Donald Y.M. Leung, MD, PhD, head of Pediatric Allergy–Immunology, National Jewish Medical and Research Center, and Professor of Pediatrics, University of Colorado Health Sciences Center, Denver.

Traci Tavares, spokeswoman, Food Allergy & Anaphylaxis Network, Fairfax, VA.

March 10, 2003, presentation, American Academy of Allergy, Asthma and Immunology Annual Meeting, Denver, CO.

March 14, 2003, *New England Journal of Medicine.*

It's not a cure, but a new drug may ease the worries of the 1.5 million Americans with peanut allergies.

The experimental medication, which is called TNX-901, increases the threshold of an allergic reaction from half a peanut to approximately 9 peanuts. Although that may not seem like much to peanut lovers, it has been estimated that most of the 50 to 100 deaths each year from peanut allergies occur after ingesting only 1 or 2 nuts.

Although a study on the drug was limited to those with peanut allergies, researchers say it could have a much wider impact.

"This drug may well also apply to other nut allergies and other food allergies, so it could affect 6 million to 8 million people," said Dr. Donald Leung, co-lead author of the study.

People with peanut allergies live in a culinary minefield, because their condition forces them to eat defensively. They or their caregivers—the problem is worse among children, who don't always know better—must examine ingredient labels with a fine-tooth comb and study the manufacturing process to determine if there are any peanuts or peanut products in the food. They also must ask detailed questions about restaurant fare. Allergic reactions are possible if even a trace amount of peanut is ingested.

PREVENTION RATHER THAN REACTION

The allergic reaction takes place when the body's immune system tries to protect itself from a substance it mistakenly identifies as harmful. The body creates antibodies against the food. The antibodies can cause something as minor as an itch or as lethal as swelling of the throat, obstructing breathing.

Avoidance has always been the best way to combat the allergy, but that's not always possible. The most common treatment for someone who has an allergic reaction is a shot of a life-saving drug called *epinephrine,* sold under the brand name Epipen. However, studies have found that only a small number of people with allergies carry the remedy with them.

TNX-901 is the first drug that could prevent the allergic reactions in the first place. "It's a buffer that would protect against most reactions from accidentally ingested peanuts," says Traci Tavares, a spokeswoman for the Food Allergy & Anaphylaxis Network in Fairfax, Virginia. "Folks with a peanut allergy have never had that peace of mind. Boosting the tolerance like this staves off what could be a life-threatening reaction and provides the added benefit of safety, so it's very exciting."

Patients would have to get shots regularly and would still need to watch what they eat, say the investigators.

The medication was on fast-track review by the US Food and Drug Administration at the end of 2003, with a decision expected some time in 2004.

Allergies May Transplant Along With Organs

Tri Giang Phan, MBBS, FRACP, FRCPA, Department of Clinical Immunology, Royal Prince Alfred Hospital, Sydney, Australia.

Anne Paschke, spokeswoman, United Network for Organ Sharing, Richmond, VA.

January 27, 2003, *Archives of Internal Medicine.*

Can transplanted organs pass on the allergy problems of the donor? There's evidence to suggest this can happen.

A 60-year-old Australian man who received a liver from a 15-year-old donor with allergies to nuts also got a life-threatening nut allergy, according to researchers.

Less than a month after the man got the liver from the boy (who died after a reaction to peanuts), the recipient had a serious, but not fatal, reaction to cashews. The researchers report that the man had no reported allergy before the transplant.

Although getting such an allergy from an organ donor is rare, Dr. Tri Giang Phan, an immunology expert at Royal Prince Alfred Hospital in Sydney, says the report should alert the transplant community.

He thinks this case is only the second reported case of allergies passed via solid organ transplant. The first case was reported by French doctors 6 years ago.

Both of these transplants involved livers, Phan says. The transfer of an allergy has also been reported for bone marrow transplants, he says, but the mechanism is probably different.

In the Australian case, doctors don't know exactly how the allergy was passed to the recipient, Phan says, but it's likely that the transplanted liver contained antibodies to allergens—in this case, nuts—that sparked the reaction. When tests were done after the reaction, both donor and recipient had antibodies to the same three allergens—peanut, cashew, and sesame seed.

Other people who received the teen's heart, kidney, and pancreas reported no allergies to nuts after their transplants.

REVEALING THE ALLERGY

Organ donors should be tested for allergies, and recipients should be told to avoid certain allergens if their donor was allergic, Phan says.

In the United States, an organ transplant procurement team routinely asks the donor family questions about allergies, says Anne Paschke, a spokeswoman for the United Network for Organ Sharing, an organization that manages the transplant system.

"There have been more than 55,000 liver transplants since we started keeping records in 1988, and this is the second case [of allergy transfer] that we are aware of," she says.

info For more information, go to the United Network for Organ Sharing at *www. unos.org.*

■ ■ ■ ■

Top Food Allergies

Approximately 6 million Americans have true food allergies, according to the Food Allergy & Anaphylaxis Network, with peanuts and tree nuts (walnuts and cashews) among the top 8 food allergens.

The other 6 top food allergens are: Milk, eggs, soy, wheat, fish, and shellfish.

Although an individual could be allergic to any food, these 8 foods account for 90% of all food-allergic reactions.

4

Breast Cancer Treatments

American Cancer Society's New Breast Cancer Screening Guidelines

The American Cancer Society has come up with new breast cancer screening guidelines. These standards loosen the recommendations for self-examination, but encourage women to take a more active role in managing their breast health. Officials envision an ongoing conversation between women and their physicians, says Debbie Saslow, director of breast and gynecological cancer for the American Cancer Society.

"We're talking about women knowing and discussing the benefits and limitations of screening," Saslow says. "We are giving them information so they can be more proactive, if that is what they choose." For example, the guidelines recommend a more thorough review of various technologies—other than mammography—such as ultrasound and magnetic resonance imaging (MRI), Saslow says.

The Society is no longer recommending that all women start breast self-examinations in their 20s. Instead, "we refer to women in their 20s and 30s," Saslow says. "We emphasize that younger women should realize that their risk is very low. Breast self-examination is now an option."

SOME THINGS HAVEN'T CHANGED

Most of the new guidelines are similar to the older ones. *They include...*

●**Annual mammograms starting at age 40** and continuing for as long as a woman is in good health.

●**Clinical breast examinations** as part of a periodic health examination, approximately every 3 years for women in their 20s and 30s, and every year starting at age 40.

Debbie Saslow, PhD, Director, Breast and Gynecological Cancer, American Cancer Society, Atlanta, GA.

D. David Dershaw, MD, Director, Breast Imaging, Memorial Sloan–Kettering Cancer Center, New York, NY.

●**Prompt reporting of any breast change** to a health-care provider.

●**An emphasis on having women who are at increased risk** because of family history, genetic tendency, or a previous breast cancer talk to their doctors about the benefits and risks of different screening methods.

That last recommendation is appropriate because "our experience with this population is evolving and we don't have any clear-cut answers," says Dr. D. David Dershaw, director of breast imaging at Memorial Sloan–Kettering Cancer Center and president of the Society of Breast Imaging. "Our recommendations may change at very short intervals. These guidelines recognize that there is a controversy about which screening technologies should be used and the appropriate schedule for their use for women at high risk."

The new guidelines allow more flexibility in terms of age, Saslow says. They say decisions about screening should be based not only on a woman's age, but also on her general health. "A woman who is 85 and in excellent health has enough years in front of her to benefit from screening, while a woman of the same age with major health problems may not," she says.

info Learn more about the disease from the American Cancer Society at *www.cancer.org*, and about screening techniques from the National Cancer Institute at *www.cancer.gov*.

Soy-Rich Diet Lowers Your Risk of Breast Cancer

September 2002, *Cancer Epidemiology, Biomarkers and Prevention.*
September 2002, American Association for Cancer Research news release.

Tofu and other soy-based foods have been found to reduce levels of a class of estrogens linked with breast cancer in postmenopausal women, says a study in *Cancer Epidemiology, Biomarkers and Prevention.*

"The study results support the idea that you can reduce your risk for breast cancer by consuming a lot of soy," says lead investigator Anna H. Wu, a professor of preventive medicine at the Keck School of Medicine at the University of Southern California in Los Angeles. The reason for that, she says, is that soy lowers certain estrogen levels, particularly that of *estrone.*

In their study of 144 postmenopausal Asian women in Singapore, aged 50 to 74 years, Wu and her colleagues found a link between soy-rich diets and lower levels of estrone, the predominant type of estrogen in postmenopausal women.

Estrone levels in women who consumed the most soy protein were approximately 15% lower than in other women. The researchers could not find any other easily changeable lifestyle factor that could produce that much of an estrone reduction.

■ ■ ■ ■

How to Get Soy Into Your Diet... A List of Soy Foods

John Henkel, a US Food and Drug Administration writer, offers some good definitions of soy products. *They are...*

●**Tofu.** Made from cooked, puréed soybeans processed into a custard–like cake, tofu has a neutral flavor and can be stir-fried, mixed into "smoothies," or blended into a cream cheese texture for use in dips or as a cheese substitute. It comes in firm, soft, and silken textures.

●**Soy milk.** This is the name some marketers use for a soy beverage. It is produced by grinding dehulled soybeans and mixing them with water to form a milk–like liquid. It can be consumed as a beverage or used in recipes as a substitute for cow's milk. Soy milk, sometimes fortified with calcium, comes plain or in flavors such as vanilla, chocolate, and coffee. For lactose-intolerant individuals, it can be a good replacement for dairy products.

●**Soy flour.** Created by grinding roasted soybeans into a fine powder, soy flour adds protein to baked goods. Because it also adds moisture, it can be used as an egg substitute in these products. Soy flour can be found in cereals, pancake mixes, frozen desserts, and other common foods.

●**Textured soy protein.** Made from defatted soy flour, which is compressed and dehydrated, textured soy protein can be used as a meat substitute or as a filler in dishes such as meatloaf.

●**Tempeh.** Made from whole, cooked soybeans formed into a chewy cake, tempeh is used as a meat substitute.

●**Miso.** A fermented soybean paste, miso is used for seasoning and for soup stock.

Tamoxifen May Reduce Benign Breast Disease

Elizabeth Tan–Chiu, MD, Director, Prevention and Early Stage Breast Cancer Program, Cancer Research Network, Plantation, FL.

Carl Kardinal, MD, Associate Section Head, Hematology/Oncology, Ochsner Clinic Foundation, New Orleans, LA.

February 19, 2003, *Journal of the National Cancer Institute.*

Tamoxifen, the drug that has been shown to cut the risk of breast cancer in high-risk women, also appears to reduce the incidence of noncancerous breast disease, research shows.

Tamoxifen interferes with the activity of the hormone estrogen, and is effective in breast cancers that are estrogen-receptor positive. Estrogen receptors also appear in benign breast lesions, leading researchers to believe that tamoxifen might also have an effect on them.

The researchers looked at the incidence of benign breast disease and the number of biopsies performed on 13,203 women who were treated either with tamoxifen or a placebo within the auspices of the Breast Cancer Prevention Trial.

Women who were given tamoxifen had a 28% reduction in their risk of benign breast disease, including *fibrocystic disease* and *hyperplasia*. They also had 29% fewer biopsies compared with women in the placebo group.

Most of the benefit occurred in women younger than 50 years, probably because of hormones, says study author Dr. Elizabeth Tan–Chiu, director of prevention and the early stage breast cancer program at the Cancer Research Network in Plantation, Florida. "Breasts are still very active in premenopausal women, swelling and unswelling," she says. "I think when you're cycling the most is when you see the effect of tamoxifen."

FEWER BIOPSIES

Not all benign lesions evolve into breast cancer, but they do indicate that the risk of developing it is increased, says Tan–Chiu.

Even conditions not associated with increased breast cancer risk often require biopsies because it's not always possible to make a diagnosis by physical exam or even mammography, according to Dr. Carl Kardinal, associate section head of hematology/oncology at the Ochsner Clinic Foundation in New Orleans.

The reduction in biopsies in women taking tamoxifen was significant. "For every intervention that we don't need to perform, that's one less woman suffering the anxiety of waiting for results," Tan–Chiu says.

■ ■ ■ ■

Symptoms of Benign Breast Disease

According to the University of Michigan Health System, symptoms of fibrocystic disease include pain and tenderness, usually in both breasts. However, some women with fibrocystic disease experience no pain, but notice lumps or nodules within the breast.

In some women, one or both breasts may develop lumps and become most tender 7 to 14 days before the start of each menstrual period. Breast pain occurs most often in the upper, outer part of the breast.

Persistent breast pain should be brought to the attention of your health care provider. Most women will experience relief from their breast pain when they get treatment.

info The Susan G. Komen Breast Cancer Foundation at *www.komen.org* has information on tamoxifen.

Gene Discovery May Lead To Better Treatment for Breast Cancer

Ira Pastan, MD, Chief, Laboratory of Molecular Biology, Division of Basic Sciences, and Kristi A. Egland, PhD, postdoctoral fellow, National Institutes of Health, Bethesda, MD.

January 20–24, 2003, *Proceedings of the National Academy of Sciences.*

A breast cancer gene discovered by scientists at the National Institutes of Health (NIH) may help researchers diagnose the disease in its early stages and treat it more effectively.

The gene, found in breast cancer cells and in salivary glands, is named BASE (Breast Cancer and Salivary Gland Expression).

"We have identified the RNA and the gene that encodes the protein for BASE," says senior author Dr. Ira Pastan, chief of the NIH's laboratory of molecular biology. "The next step is to make an antibody to detect the protein."

If an antibody can be developed that could detect the protein in the bloodstream, it could be a way to identify breast cancer in the early stages. Researchers also hope to make a vaccine to kill the cells that make the unique protein, Pastan says.

For several years, scientists have believed that approximately 5% to 10% of breast cancer cases are caused by inherited genetic mutations in 2 breast cancer genes.

The genes code for proteins that have tumor suppressor capabilities, but in women who have mutations in these genes, the protein is abnormal and doesn't suppress the tumors. A blood test can detect these mutations.

Kristi A. Egland, lead author of the NIH report, says the goal is to find genes that make proteins that are only expressed from breast cancer cells. "Then, breast cancer–specific proteins can be used as diagnostic markers [such as in a blood test] and as targets for drugs to kill only breast cancer cells."

■ ■ ■ ■

Why Early Detection Is Important

Each year, doctors diagnose 182,000 cases of breast cancer and 43,300 women die of the disease, according to the Breast Cancer Site (*www.thebreastcancersite.com*).

One woman in 8 either has breast cancer or will develop it in her lifetime. In addition, 1600 men will be given a diagnosis of breast cancer and 400 will die this year.

If breast cancer is detected early, the 5-year survival rate exceeds 95%. Mammograms are among the best early detection methods, yet 13 million women in the US are aged 40 years or older and have never had a mammogram. Medical experts don't agree when a woman should start having regular mammograms, but there is strong consensus that an annual mammogram should take place after a woman turns 50 years.

The National Cancer Institute and the US Department of Health and Human Services recommend that women older than 40 years have mammograms every 1 to 2 years.

Scientists Identify Cells That Generate Breast Cancer Tumors

Michael F. Clarke, MD, Professor, Internal Medicine, University of Michigan Medical School, Ann Arbor.

Calvin Kuo, MD, PhD, Assistant Professor, Medicine, Hematology Division, Stanford University, Palo Alto, CA.

February 25, 2003, *Proceedings of the National Academy of Sciences.*

Michigan researchers have isolated a tiny—but particularly aggressive—group of breast cancer cells that may be responsible for the spread of the disease. The discovery, which took years of study, bodes well for earlier detection and treatment of the cancer found most often in women.

There aren't many breast cancer cells in a tumor—fewer than 100 out of tens of thousands. But these cells are, in effect, stem cells. The researchers found that these cells reproduce the malignancy very rapidly, but they don't convert benign cells into cancerous cells, and that makes it much easier to isolate them, the scientists conclude.

"We're really excited; we're extraordinarily excited," says study author Dr. Michael F. Clarke, a professor of internal medicine at the University of Michigan Medical School. By isolating these cells, we've narrowed the field that therapies may one day target in the overall confusing mix of cells in these tumors, he adds.

Detecting these cells may also let doctors diagnose the disease sooner, says Clarke.

THE NEXT PHASE OF RESEARCH

"We're 3 steps away [from developing a drug to treat breast cancer]," Clarke says. The first step for researchers is to find out what pathways let these cells form tumors. Then they can find out where the pathways are and focus on them. The third step is to develop drugs to attack these pathways.

Other scientists also see potential in this discovery. This is "a very intriguing study, which provides molecular identification of particularly aggressive breast cancer cells and which suggests potential new avenues for diagnosis and therapy," says Dr. Calvin Kuo, an assistant professor of medicine at Stanford University.

BUILDING ON PREVIOUS WORK

The Michigan research builds on a previous study that saw a similar effect in a type of leukemia (blood cancer). But this is the first time these stem cells have been found in a solid cancer, the researchers say.

Because an aggressive subset of cells has been found in both blood and breast cancers, the scientists think other types of cancer might be driven by them, as well.

Breast Cancer Cells Spread Earlier Than Thought

Christoph A. Klein, MD, Institut fur Immunologie, Ludwig–Maximilians Universitat, Munich, Germany.

Christos Patriotis, PhD, Associate Member, Department of Medical Oncology, Fox Chase Cancer Center, Philadelphia, PA.

June 9–13, 2003, *Proceedings of the National Academy of Sciences.*

If all the usual reasons to have regular breast exams aren't enough to get you to a doctor, perhaps this one is—researchers in Germany have found that breast cancer cells appear to move to other parts of the body much earlier than scientists had thought.

This finding could change the way health experts think about approaches to cancer and could affect how doctors find *metastatic* cancer—a cancer that has spread from one part of the body to another.

"It's definitely a new paradigm," says Christos Patriotis, an associate member of the Fox Chase Cancer Center's department of medical oncology in Philadelphia. "There's always been a suspicion among scientists that advanced metastatic disease is not necessarily the same disease as the primary disease."

A commonly accepted explanation of the spread of cancer is that cells in the first tumor go though a series of genetic changes before leaving that tumor and heading off to other parts of the body. The news from the German study has given experts reason to believe that the most advanced cell within the primary tumor may move to another site and establish a metastasis there, the researchers say.

IMPLICATIONS FOR TREATMENT

Ideally, the study authors say, treatment should take into account any differences between primary tumors and malignant cells that have dispersed. Currently, clinicians use drugs to kill cells without really understanding them. That is why they decided to investigate, says study author Dr. Christoph Klein.

Klein and his colleagues at the Institut fur Immunologie, Ludwig–Maximilians Universitat in Munich, took bone marrow from breast cancer patients and analyzed the individual cells that had migrated to the marrow from the primary tumor. "We were quite surprised about the genetic findings," Klein says. "It seems that the cells leave the primary tumor very, very early. We found [the dispersed cells] had even less changes than the primary tumor, meaning they leave at an early stage of genetic development, even before the primary tumor has accumulated certain changes."

The majority of these wandering cells won't develop into a tumor, but there's always that potential.

"That's why time is against us," Patriotis says. "The longer you live and the longer you have those cells around, the higher the risk that cells will accumulate the necessary mutations and really take off to become tumors."

Investigations are under way to see whether the same process is at work in other cancers, Klein says.

Newest Mammography Camera Sees More Than Before

Cahid Civelek, MD, Associate Professor, Johns Hopkins University, Department of Radiology and Radiological Science, Johns Hopkins Institutions, Baltimore, MD.

Lon Slane, President, Dilon Technologies, Newport News, VA.

July 2002, *Journal of Nuclear Medicine.*

A portable device that peers into the biochemical machinery of cells can help identify breast cancers that conventional scanning can't find. Experts say the machine, a *high-resolution breast-specific gamma camera* (HRBGC), is not meant to replace mammography. Rather, it will be able to screen women who have dense breasts and other tissue traits that can cloud a clean mammogram.

"Because it's small, you can bring it much closer to the patient at any angle you want," says Dr. Cahid Civelek, a Johns Hopkins University nuclear medicine specialist and coauthor of the study, which appeared in the *Journal of Nuclear Medicine.*

Conventional X-ray mammography works very well for most women. However, for the 25% of women with dense breasts, the scan's ability to find tumors drops markedly, and as many as 35% of their tumors go undetected. Although mammography can identify lesions, it's not very good at differentiating between harmless masses and cancers. It is successful in identifying lumps approximately 90% of the time in women older than 50 years and 75% of the time in younger women. But only through a biopsy—taking an actual tissue sample—can malignancy be confirmed.

Scientists have been working on ways to sharpen the accuracy of mammography. One promising approach, the original gamma camera, has been available in various forms for decades, but its bulkiness prevents it from easily detecting tumors. As a result, some of the images are blurry. By contrast, the new camera's smaller size can be more easily positioned, and its high resolution can identify lumps in dense breasts.

RESULTS OF THE STUDY

Civelek and his colleagues tested the machine on 50 women who had breast lesions previously discovered by a manual exam or during mammography or ultrasound scanning. Later cell samples showed that 52% of the lesions were harmless and 48% were cancerous.

Both the original gamma camera and the new HRBGC were able to identify the benign lesions most of the time. However, the new high-resolution device successfully identified a much higher percentage of the cancerous tumors, compared with the conventional gamma camera. The newer device was also better at diagnosing tumors that couldn't be felt manually and at finding lumps that were 1 centimeter or smaller in diameter. It also detected 4 masses, with an average size of just 8.5 millimeters, which the other gamma camera missed.

OUTLOOK FOR THE MACHINE

The HRBGC has been approved by the US Food and Drug Administration. Lon Slane, president of Dilon Technologies, which sponsored the research, says the company has received federal approval to market its new 6800 gamma camera. Slane says the most likely candidates for this scan are women with dense breasts—which includes younger women and those taking hormone replacement therapy—as well as those with scars from previous biopsies. "An X-ray simply can't penetrate the breast, and you get a cloudy, washed-out picture," Slane says.

info For more on mammography, visit Radiology Info at *www.radiologyinfo.org* and use the pull-down menu under "Diagnostic Radiology."

The Test That's Better Than Mammograms at Spotting Breast Tumors

Nehmat Houssami, MD, PhD, Senior Lecturer, School of Public Health, University of Sydney, Australia.

Diane Palladino, MD, Breast Surgeon, Exeter Hospital, Exeter, NH.

April 2003, *American Journal of Roentgenology.*

Mammography may be the standard screening test for breast cancer, but if you're a woman younger than 45 years with symptoms of the disease, an ultrasound is more likely to find malignancies.

So says a study by Dr. Nehmat Houssami, a senior lecturer at the School of Public Health at the University of Sydney, Australia. Dr. Houssami was the director of the MBF Sydney–Square Breast Clinic at the time the study was conducted.

THE STUDY

Radiologists examined the mammograms and sonograms of 480 women between the ages of 25 and 55 years. All of the women had symptoms of breast cancer, but only half actually had breast cancer. The 240 women without cancer were age-matched to those in the breast cancer group.

Overall, there was not a statistically significant difference in the detection of cancer between the 2 tests, the researchers found. However, in women younger than 45 years, sonography correctly identified 84.9% of breast cancers, while mammography was only able to pick up 71.7% of the cancers.

The reason for the difference, Houssami says, is that younger women's breasts are generally denser than older women's breasts, and sonography is better than mammography at capturing images through that density.

It's important to note that the study did not look at general-population screening for breast cancer, and the author says he is definitely not suggesting that ultrasound replace mammography for screening.

In most cases, a woman with breast cancer symptoms is referred for both mammography and sonography, regardless of her age, according to the study.

A mammogram is an X-ray of the breast; ultrasound images are generated by sound waves.

BOTH APPROACHES HAVE BENEFITS

Dr. Diane Palladino, a breast surgeon at Exeter Hospital in Exeter, New Hampshire, says she always orders both tests for a woman who has symptoms of cancer, explaining that both tests have their strengths and weaknesses.

"Ultrasound helps us judge the size of the lesion and can give us some idea of whether the tumor is benign or malignant," she says. But, she says, ultrasound can't see microcalcifications, which are signs of very early breast cancer.

Palladino says it's important for women to realize that "mammography is not 100% accurate, especially in younger women. If you have a lump but a negative result on a mammogram, you still need to address that lump in your breast."

The American Cancer Society recommends that every woman older than 40 years has a mammogram annually.

■ ■ ■ ■

Symptoms of Breast Cancer

Every year, nearly 200,000 American women are diagnosed with breast cancer, according to the National Cancer Institute (*www.cancer.gov*). *Symptoms of the disease include...*

- **A lump in the breast.**
- **Nipple discharge.**
- **Pitting or ridges in the breast.**
- **Changes in the size,** shape, or appearance of the breast.

Double Protection— Mammograms May Spot Heart Trouble

Kirk Doerger, MD, Radiology Resident, Mayo Clinic, Rochester, MN.

Susan Orel, MD, Associate Professor, Radiology, University of Pennsylvania, Philadelphia.

December 4, 2002, presentation, Radiological Society of North America Annual Meeting, Chicago, IL.

Mammography makes headlines as a screening test for breast cancer, but the technology may do double duty as a predictor of heart disease.

Women whose mammograms show calcium deposits in their breast arteries are more vulnerable to heart attacks and other cardiovascular diseases than those with clean vessels, researchers say. Although the calcifications in the breast don't harm the heart, they appear to echo the narrowing of the coronary arteries.

Most people don't worry about the deposits because they're not cancer, says Dr. Kirk Doerger, a radiology resident at the Mayo Clinic and a collaborator on the research. "But now we're finding that they do have some importance."

DUTCH STUDY

In 1998, Dutch doctors found that women with calcified breast arteries faced a sharply higher risk of cardiovascular death, especially if they had diabetes. Israeli scientists also found that the deposits, which increase with age, upped the risk of cardiovascular disease in women—enough to lead the researchers to conclude that mammography might be a cheap and effective screening tool for heart and vessel problems.

However, the Mayo study can't make as strong a statement, says Doerger.

Doerger and his colleagues reviewed the records of nearly 2000 women who'd had detailed coronary artery exams. Regardless of the woman's age, the presence of breast artery calcifications on mammograms slightly increased the risk of narrowed blood flow to the heart.

Smoking markedly raised that risk, and diabetes drove it up more than 200%, Doerger says. Considering these figures, the increased risk associated with breast artery calcification is on the modest side. Still, he adds, it's information that radiologists currently ignore.

BREAST CANCER VS. HEART DISEASE

Turning mammography into a tool to detect heart disease underscores a common misperception many women have about their health. Although many women say they're more afraid of breast cancer than cardiovascular disease, heart disease is more dangerous.

Heart disease kills nearly a half million American women each year, more than all cancers combined. And nearly two-thirds of women who suddenly die of heart problems had no previous symptoms.

Still, Dr. Susan Orel, a radiologist at the University of Pennsylvania School of Medicine, says she's not sure what to make of the Mayo research.

Since the women already had signs of artery trouble, the study group may not have represented the average woman, she says. What's more, you see calcification of the breast vessels almost all the time in older women, diluting the potential significance of the marker.

On the other hand, Orel adds, calcifications on the mammograms of women in their 30s and 40s arouse her concern.

info For more on women and heart disease, try the American College of Obstetricians and Gynecologists at *www.acog.org* or the American Heart Association at *www.americanheart.org*.

Genetic Profiling May Revolutionize Breast Cancer Treatment

May 10, 2003, *The Lancet.*

A system known as genetic profiling may help predict the course of breast cancer and determine which patients will require aggressive treatment for long-term survival. It could also revolutionize the treatment of all cancers.

A group of Duke University scientists, working with researchers from the Koo Foundation Sun Yat–Sen Cancer Center in Taipei, China, offer the strongest evidence yet that the system works, showing a 90% accuracy rate.

Genetic profiling is a way of analyzing a breast cancer patient's basic cell information to develop "genetic signatures" that can ultimately be used to define risk levels of disease. Using genetic profiling, researchers could predict the aggressiveness of a breast cancer tumor and whether a cancer was likely to recur with 90% accuracy.

Removing and testing the lymph nodes—cells that surround the breast—provides useful information to assess a woman's long-term cancer profile and her current treatment needs. The condition of the lymph nodes is believed to be critical in determining long-term survival rates, since cancers that spread to these cells are thought to be more aggressive.

However, experts say it's not uncommon to find women with few or no cancerous lymph nodes whose disease recurs in just a few years, or to find women with extremely aggressive lymph node profiles who are effectively cured in just one course of treatment.

The genetic profiling system, the researchers say, will give a far more accurate prognosis and will help doctors know from the start which women are likely to benefit from chemotherapy and radiation, and which women can safely skip these regimens without compromising their future health.

Duke researchers say they won't be satisfied until accuracy is closer to 100%, something they hope to accomplish as their methods of analysis are refined.

Genetic Tests Most Accurate in Predicting Breast Cancer Survival

Clifford Hudis, MD, Chief, Breast Cancer Medicine Service, Memorial Sloan–Kettering Cancer Center, New York, NY.
December 19, 2002, *New England Journal of Medicine.*

A sophisticated genetic test can single out breast cancer patients with the best chance of survival and those who need more aggressive treatment, say Dutch researchers.

Examining 70 specific genes in breast cancer victims, researchers have been able to predict which ones have the best chance of surviving. For example, over a 10-year period almost 95% of those patients who the test said had a good chance of surviving were still alive. But only 54% of those who scored a poor prognosis had survived after 10 years.

In addition to the overall survival rate, there was a clear difference between the 2 groups in the development of *metastases*—cancer colonies that spread to other parts of the body. Metastases are associated with a poor outcome. The poor-prognosis group had more than 3 times the incidence of metastases than the good-prognosis group.

This gene array is a more powerful predictor of the outcome of disease in young patients with breast cancer than standard systems that are based on clinical and cellular criteria, according to the report.

The report came from researchers and physicians at the Netherlands Cancer Institute, who have been following almost 300 women with breast cancer for more than a decade.

The test could have an important impact on breast cancer treatment, but more work is needed before that happens, says Dr. Clifford Hudis, chief of the breast cancer medicine service at Memorial Sloan–Kettering Cancer Center in New York. The test has to be studied in other patients by other investigators, Hudis adds.

Mastectomy Survival Rates No Better Than Alternative Surgeries

Jay Brooks, MD, Chief, Hematology/Oncology, Ochsner Clinic Foundation, Baton Rouge, LA.
October 17, 2002, *New England Journal of Medicine.*

According to research published in the *New England Journal of Medicine,* 2 different breast-conserving surgeries have the same 20-year survival rates as the radical mastectomy, in which a woman loses her breast. As a result of these 2 trials, authors of an Italian study believe that approximately 300,000 women worldwide with early breast cancer will undergo breast-conserving surgery each year, rather than radical mastectomy, the previous gold standard.

"Whether a woman decides to preserve her breast or not, the chances of being alive and free of cancer 20 years from now is the same," says Dr. Jay Brooks, chief of hematology/ oncology at the Ochsner Clinic Foundation in New Orleans.

STUDIES IN ITALY AND PITTSBURGH

The first 20-year study, led by Dr. Umberto Veronesi of the European Institute of Oncology in Milan, Italy, looked at 701 women who had either received a radical mastectomy or a procedure known as a *quadrantectomy,* in which the quadrant of the breast containing the tumor is removed.

The result: There was little difference in the incidence of *metastasis,* or spread, of the cancer. As a result, the overall survival rate

was virtually identical among women in the 2 groups, the researchers say.

Veronesi says the study shows that if breast cancer is diagnosed early enough, there's no need for radical surgery. "I believe that today the treatment of a woman with early breast cancer with a mastectomy must be considered unethical," he maintains.

The second study, conducted by the National Surgical Adjuvant Breast and Bowel Project in Pittsburgh, also used a 20-year follow-up. It compared a radical mastectomy with a *lumpectomy,* in which the tumor and a margin of tissue are removed.

Among 1851 women, those receiving lumpectomy with radiation had the lowest incidence of a recurrence in the same breast.

The authors of the Pittsburgh study say it's unclear which of the 2 breast-conserving surgeries is better. The lumpectomy removed tumors that were no more than 4 centimeters in diameter, while the quadrantectomy excised tumors that were no more than 2 centimeters in diameter.

Brooks believes the lumpectomy is the better of the 2 options because "it gives a better cosmetic result."

More Frequent Chemotherapy Increases Survival Rate

Clifford Hudis, MD, chief, Breast Cancer Medicine Service, and Larry Norton, head, Division of Solid Tumor Oncology, Memorial Sloan–Kettering Cancer Center, New York, NY.
December 12, 2002, presentation, 25th annual San Antonio Breast Cancer Symposium, TX.

Simply increasing the frequency of chemotherapy treatments for breast cancer patients increases survival rates, shortens the treatment time, and reduces side effects, say researchers.

Usually, when a treatment helps patients live longer, they pay a price in toxicity or length of treatment, says Dr. Clifford Hudis, chief of the breast cancer medicine service at Memorial

Sloan–Kettering Cancer Center in New York City, and a leader of the study. "In this case, you get a win, win, win effect."

The study included more than 2000 women whose breast cancer had spread to the lymph nodes. They were all given standard chemotherapy, but at varying frequencies.

After 4 years, 82% of the women who got chemotherapy most often were alive and free of the disease. Of the women who were treated less frequently, 75% were alive and free of disease.

SHORTER TREATMENT

In addition, the treatment time was shorter for the women receiving chemotherapy most often. One notable side effect of chemotherapy—a decline in white blood cell levels—was less common in the "dose-dense" group. However, the women in this group were also given a drug that stimulates the growth of white blood cells.

"This is not some random event," Hudis says. Mathematical models predicted this response. The mathematical model was developed by Dr. Richard Simon of the National Cancer Institute (NCI) and Dr. Larry Norton, then at NCI and now head of the division of solid tumor oncology at Memorial Sloan–Kettering.

MORE OFTEN IS BETTER

Essentially, the model showed that more frequent doses of cancer-killing drugs give the cancer cells less time to grow back again after each treatment, Norton says. His finding prompted the study, which was coordinated by NCI.

The results are already benefiting many women, Hudis says, adding that this was a large trial where hundreds of doctors and dozens of centers participated.

Other centers are expected to adopt the treatment schedule, Norton says.

Breast cancer patients might not be the only ones to benefit, Norton says. "I would love to see it attempted in other [cancers]. There is every reason to believe it will work."

Several studies of the new dosing regimen are starting for other cancers. "We are starting trials on prostate and lung cancer," Norton says.

Vitamin That Kills Breast Cancer Cells Better Than Radiation Alone

David A. Gewirtz, PhD, Professor, Pharmacology and Toxicology, Virginia Commonwealth University, Richmond.
LaMar McGinnis, MD, Medical Consultant, American Cancer Society, Atlanta, GA.
May 2003, *Cancer Chemotherapy and Pharmacology.*

Adding a type of vitamin D to radiation therapy works better at killing breast cancer cells than radiation alone, say the authors of a new study.

Approximately 200,000 American women are given a diagnosis of breast cancer each year and close to 40,000 die. Radiation therapy is often used before surgery to reduce the size of tumors, and following surgery to reduce the chance of tumors coming back.

ENHANCING THE RESPONSE

In this study, the scientists treated breast cancer cells with normal doses of a vitamin D analog (ILX 23-7553) before radiation, and the response to radiation was enhanced.

The addition of vitamin D meant that lower doses of radiation were necessary for treatment, and there was an increase in tumor cell death, says study coauthor David A. Gewirtz, a professor of pharmacology and toxicology at Virginia Commonwealth University. In fact, the vitamin D helped reduce the number of cancer cells by almost 30% more than radiation alone.

After treatment with the vitamin D analog and radiation, tumor cells continued to die for 7 days; cells treated with radiation alone did not. Treatment with the vitamin D analog worked 3 times better than radiation therapy alone at preventing new tumor growth, the study says. The combination didn't hurt normal cells, Gewirtz says.

He cautions these results were produced in cell cultures, and they don't yet apply to treating breast cancer in women. Currently, the vitamin D analog is not being tested in humans in the United States. However, it is being tested in humans in Europe, he says.

In a forthcoming paper, Gewirtz says he and his colleagues show the same effect is found when breast tumors are grown in mice.

"There is also evidence that using a vitamin D analog and radiation prevents cancer cells from growing back," Gewirtz says. "We think that this treatment may also have implications for treating radiation-resistant brain tumors and prostate cancer."

UPPING THE 'KILL RATE'

Dr. LaMar McGinnis, a medical consultant for the American Cancer Society, says that although the effect was only seen in cultured cells, "it appears that this vitamin D compound is a radio-sensitizer for cancer cells and results in a greater kill rate with a sustained effect."

With radiation therapy, there is always a balance between killing cancer cells and protecting normal cells, he adds. If these findings pan out in human trials, controlling cell growth within tumors could be enhanced, he notes.

"It is an interesting observation, and I await the results of clinical trials, particularly since this compound seems to have no significant side effects," McGinnis says.

info For more on breast cancer, visit the National Breast Cancer Coalition at *www.natlbcc.org*. For more on vitamin D, check with the National Institutes of Health at *www.cc.nih.gov.*

Breast Cancer Self-Defense for Women (and Men)

Ruth Lerman, MD, Internist specializing in breast disease and wellness, and contributor to *Cancer* and *Annals of Internal Medicine*.
October 2003, *Bottom Line/Health*.

B reast self-exams can make many people feel a little awkward at first. *Here's what I tell my patients to do…*

1. While standing in front of a mirror under good lighting, press your hands down firmly on your hips and look at your breasts. This position will contract the chest wall muscles, which enhances breast abnormalities. Look for dimpling and subtle changes in size, contour and shape. For large or pendulous breasts, lean forward at the waist and use a hand mirror so you can see the underside of the breast.

2. Lie on your back, and place your right arm behind your head. This position allows breast tissue to spread evenly over the chest wall so you can feel changes more easily. Use the finger pads of the three middle fingers of your left hand to feel the right breast. Use three different levels of pressure—light pressure to feel tissue closest to the skin…medium pressure to feel a little more deeply…and firm pressure to feel the tissue closest to the chest and ribs. Be sure to check the entire breast—up to the collarbone, out to your blouse side seam, down to the bra line and to the middle of the breastbone. Cover the entire breast area in a head-to-toe, toe-to-head direction, also known as vertical strips. Also, carefully check your armpits.

Place your left arm behind your head, and repeat this process using the three middle fingers of the right hand to examine the left breast.

If you discover a possible lump: Change the direction from which you approach it. *Example:* Check it from right to left and left to right. This will help you determine if what you're feeling is actually a lump. Recheck it the next day, in a week or two and, if applicable, after your next period. If it is still there, see your doctor.

Caution: See your doctor immediately if you find a red, firm area of the breast. This could be an infection or inflammatory breast cancer, which is rare but fast-growing.

3. While showering, cover your breasts and armpits with water and soap. This will make it easier for you to perform the vertical strips exam (explained earlier) of both breasts. Also check your armpits. A shower exam allows you to identify lumps you may have missed while lying down.

■ ■ ■ ■

For Men Only…
From Dr. Lerman

Few doctors discuss breast self-exam with their male patients—primarily because the disease is rare among men. But breast cancer strikes up to 1,300 American men each year. As men grow older, they are at increased risk for the disease. The risk is also greater in men who have close relatives with breast cancer, those who have the BRCA2 gene, have undergone radiation to the chest to treat cancer, have the congenital chromosomal disorder Klinefelter's syndrome, have liver disease and/or are obese. Any man who notices a breast lump, or discharge or bleeding from the nipple, should see his doctor.

Fewer Heart Troubles
For Survivors of
Breast Cancer

Elizabeth Lamont, MD, Medical Oncologist, Health Services Researcher and Professor, Medicine, University of Chicago, IL.

Julia Smith, MD, Oncologist and Clinical Assistant Professor, New York University School of Medicine.

July 2003, *Cancer.*

There's some more good news for women who survive breast cancer—your risk of a heart attack may be much lower than women who have always been cancer-free.

There is evidence that either having breast cancer or taking one type of breast-cancer drug—a *selective estrogen receptor modulator* (SERM), such as *tamoxifen*—might have some effect on protecting the heart, says study author Dr. Elizabeth Lamont, an assistant professor of medicine at the University of Chicago.

"Our study has identified a subset of women with a one-third reduction in the risk of heart attack. And with heart disease being the single most significant cause of death in elderly women, this protective effect is definitely important," says Lamont.

Although Lamont believes the link is estrogen—either because of the naturally higher concentrations in women who had breast cancer or as a result of the SERMs that act like estrogens in the body—not all experts agree.

ANOTHER VIEW

Oncologist Dr. Julia Smith is not quick to embrace the idea that either estrogen or SERMs are offering the protective effect.

"What this study tells us is that women who have breast cancer have a reduced risk of heart attack. But it really doesn't offer any solid evidence as to why. And I would not jump to any conclusions about either the protective effects of estrogen or that of SERMs," says Smith, a clinical assistant professor at New York University's School of Medicine.

One reason, she says, is because the research conclusions were drawn using data from a much larger study—one that identified women with breast cancer but did not indicate the type of tumors found.

Because the data does not indicate which women or how many took SERMs, Smith says it is impossible to link cardioprotective effects to this medication or to estrogen.

"Perhaps most important is that other major studies of estrogen and SERMs have not found even a hint that this protection exists. So you have to wonder how this study came to these conclusions," says Smith, who adds that it's certainly worth further investigation to learn more.

Lamont counters that other studies have indeed hinted at some cardioprotective effects of the SERMs, including not only tamoxifen but also *raloxifene,* which is used to treat osteoporosis.

info For more on women and heart disease, check with the National Heart, Lung, and Blood Institute at *www.nhlbi.nih.gov.*

New Breast Cancer Drug Cuts Recurrence in Half

Paul Goss, MD, PhD, Medical Oncologist, Princess Margaret Hospital, Toronto.
October 9, 2003, *New England Journal of Medicine.*

Until very recently, scientists believed the "miracle" anti-cancer drug *tamoxifen* showed the most promise to keep the disease from returning to women who had breast cancer and had undergone surgery and other treatments.

However, tamoxifen not only lost its effectiveness after about 5 years but its side effects have been suspected of promoting the cancer's return. Clinical trials began on a drug called *letrozole* to see if it could be used when tamoxifen treatments end. Letrozole is one of a new class of drugs called *aromatase inhibitors.*

Tamoxifen has been a great boon to women who have estrogen-receptor-positive breast cancer, the largest breast cancer subgroup, Goss says. The drug has reduced the risk of recurrence by 47% and the risk of death by 26% for 5 years after surgery. Unfortunately, tamoxifen stops working after that time and may even reverse its action, promoting the growth of cancer cells.

"What is unrecognized is that over 50% of recurrences unfortunately occur beyond 5 years after diagnosis," Goss says. "Because it continues to relapse almost indefinitely, there is no limit to the disease." Doctors have lacked any appropriate tools for the hundreds of thousands of women worldwide who enter that post-five-year wilderness every year. Until now.

THE NEW STUDY

The letrozole trial started enrolling participants in 1998 and ended up with 5,187 women in Canada, the United States, and Europe who were postmenopausal, had hormone-receptor-positive tumors and had been on tamoxifen for about 5 years. Participants had to be within 3 months of stopping tamoxifen and all were disease-free when enrolled. The trial was coordinated by the National Cancer Institute of Canada.

THE POSITIVE RESULTS

The trial results showed that the letrozole group had about half the rate of cancer recurrences as women taking a placebo. The results were considered so amazing that the clinical trials were halted and letrozole was given to the placebo group. Investigators also recommended accelerating other trials to determine the best candidates for letrozole, either as an addition or as a replacement for tamoxifen.

"The results are absolute, confirmed, and credible," study investigator Dr. Paul Goss says. Goss is also the lead author of a special article detailing the findings that appeared in the *New England Journal of Medicine.*

THE SIDE EFFECTS

Side effects in the placebo and letrozole groups were roughly equivalent, except the rate of bone thinning was slightly higher with letrozole. Tamoxifen, by contrast, provides protection against bone fractures, although it contributes to endometrial cancer and blood clots. Women considering taking letrozole should consult their doctors about ways to offset the risk of osteoporosis.

Current and future studies of aromatase inhibitors will look at many issues, including whether letrozole could be used instead of tamoxifen, whether it could be used if women had been off tamoxifen for longer than 3 months, whether it works in an equivalent fashion, and whether the letrozole's success will continue over longer time frames.

"Waiting for the other shoe to drop really wears people [with breast cancer] down," Goss says. "We're going to fell this tree. We're chopping away at it. This is one big chunk that makes me go to the clinic tomorrow with a lighter step."

The US Food and Drug Administration has already approved letrozole for some forms of breast cancer.

5

Cancer Breakthroughs

Cancer Survival Rates Are Higher Than You Thought

Life expectancies for people with cancer may be longer than previously believed. A study in *The Lancet* figures that 20-year cancer survival estimates are up to 11% higher when they are calculated using an improved statistical method.

"This is really good news, and optimistic. It shows that in recent years more cancer patients are living longer," says Dr. Ruth Oratz, an associate professor of medicine at New York University School of Medicine in New York City.

Dr. Allan Novetsky, director of medical oncology at Maimonides Medical Center in Brooklyn, New York, says, "The more accurately I can tell a patient what the probability is of them living 5, 10, 15, or 20 years, the more I am able to help them accept treatment, understand what the impact is, and make plans for their short-term and long-term needs."

HOW TO FIGURE

In the study, Dr. Hermann Brenner, scientific director of the German Centre for Research on Aging in Heidelberg, Germany, examined survival estimates using the relatively new *period analysis* method instead of the traditional *cohort* method. The cohort method looks at the longevity of patients who were given a diagnosis of cancer many years ago. Period analysis uses more recent data, so it theoretically reflects advances in detection and treatment.

Brenner compared survival estimates obtained with period analysis for 1998 with cohort analysis for patients given a diagnosis between 1978 and 1993. He used data from the US National Cancer Institute's Surveillance, Epidemiology, and End Results program.

Hermann Brenner, MD, Professor and Chair, Department of Epidemiology, and Scientific Director, German Centre for Research on Aging, Heidelberg, Germany.

Allan Novetsky, MD, Director, Medical Oncology, Maimonides Medical Center, Brooklyn, NY.

Ruth Oratz, MD, Associate Professor, Medicine, New York University School of Medicine.

October 12, 2002, *The Lancet.*

Using period analysis, every estimate of surviving for 20 years after a diagnosis was higher for all types of cancer. *The new numbers are...*

- **Testicular cancer**—90%.
- **Thyroid cancer**—90%.
- **Prostate cancer**—80%+.
- **Melanoma**—80%+.
- **Endometrial cancer**—80%.
- **Bladder cancer**—70%.
- **Hodgkins disease**—70%.
- **Breast cancer**—65%.
- **Cervical cancer**—60%.
- **Colorectal cancer**—50%.
- **Kidney cancer**—50%.
- **Ovarian cancer**—50%.

Novetsky says that the study could not only influence the ability to obtain funding for research, but it also helps people focus on where progress has occurred (for example, in prostate cancer) and where more progress still needs to take place (in lung cancer, for instance, which didn't even make the list).

info The National Cancer Institute at *www. cancer.gov* and the American Cancer Society at *www.cancer.org* have a wealth of information on cancer detection, diagnosis, treatment, and survival rates.

The $3.99 Cancer Fighter: Sunscreen

Michael Huncharek, MD, MPH, Radiation Oncologist, Department of Clinical Oncology, Marshfield Clinic Cancer Center, Marshfield, WI.

Kenneth Ellner, MD, Chief of Dermatology, Southeast Permanente Medical Group, and Assistant Clinical Professor, Dermatology, Emory University's School of Medicine, Atlanta, GA.

July 2002, *American Journal of Public Health*.

You've heard the mantra a million times —wear sunscreen and save your skin. However, some researchers have questioned whether sunscreen really protects against the deadliest forms of skin cancer. In seeking the answer to this question, a team of analysts found some good news—sunblock lotions work, and people are not lulled into a false sense of security against skin cancer just because they use sunblock.

"Our data show there is no risk from using sunscreen, and it implies that it probably does what it's supposed to do. The most prudent thing to do is to use it," says study coauthor Dr. Michael Huncharek, a radiation oncologist with the Marshfield Clinic Cancer Center in Wisconsin.

Skin cancer affected more than 1 million people in the United States in 2001. Approximately 54,000 will get melanoma, the most serious of the 3 types of skin cancer and the type that is increasing at the fastest rate in this country, according to the American Cancer Society.

THE DEBATE

Some experts have argued that sunscreens may actually do more harm than good when it comes to melanoma. One argument suggests people use sunscreen incorrectly—mainly by putting on too little—and stay in the sun longer than they would have otherwise.

"It's kind of like no-fat brownies. You're eating them and gaining weight because you're getting rid of the fat but not the calories," says Dr. Kenneth Ellner, chief of dermatology at Southeast Permanente Medical Group in Atlanta.

Also, there is debate over protection from harmful ultraviolet rays. Until recently, many sunscreens provided significant protection only against ultraviolet-B (UVB) radiation, and not against ultraviolet-A (UVA) radiation, Ellner says.

Although researchers know sunscreens with UVB protection work against largely curable skin cancers known as *basal cell* and *squamous cell carcinomas*, melanomas are a different matter, he says. UVA radiation may play a major role in the development of melanomas.

THE STUDY

In his analysis, Huncharek reviewed 11 studies that looked at links between sunscreens and melanoma cases. His findings appeared in the *American Journal of Public Health.* He found no indication that people who use sunscreens are more likely to develop melanoma.

Ellner says researchers have much more to learn about melanoma. Genetics appear to play a role, and the immune system may also affect whether someone gets the cancer, he says. Melanoma is treatable in its early stages, but becomes deadly once it spreads to other parts of the body, Huncharek says.

He says that ironically "the incidence of melanoma is less in roofers and people who work in the sun than in occasional sun worshippers."

Both Huncharek and Ellner agree that people who go outside should slather on sunscreen. It's important to use it liberally and reapply it frequently, Huncharek says.

Ellner suggests the use of sunscreens that include these ingredients: Zinc oxide, titanium dioxide, and avobenzone (also known as Parsol 1789 or 1789). Over the past few years, more sunscreens have added those ingredients, he says.

■ ■ ■ ■

You've Heard It Before, But Always Remember Your Sun Protection

The Skin Cancer Foundation (*www.skincancer.org*) has some good tips for protecting yourself against the sun. *Here are a few suggestions...*

- **Do not sunbathe.**

- **Avoid unnecessary sun exposure,** especially between 10:00 AM and 4:00 PM, the peak hours for harmful ultraviolet (UV) radiation.

- **When outdoors, use sunscreens rated SPF 15 or higher.** Apply them liberally, uniformly, and frequently.

- **When exposed to sunlight, wear protective clothing** such as long pants, long-sleeved shirts, broad-brimmed hats, and UV-protective sunglasses.

- **Do not use artificial tanning devices.**

- **Teach your children good sun protection habits at an early age.** The damage that leads to adult skin cancers starts in childhood.

- **Examine your skin head-to-toe at least once every 3 months.** Look for a new growth or any skin change.

Skin Cancer Is on the Rise for Older Men

Alan Geller, MPH, RN, Associate Professor of Dermatology, Boston University School of Medicine, MA.

Catherine Poole, Executive Director, National Melanoma Foundation, Philadelphia, PA.

October 9, 2002, *Journal of the American Medical Association.*

Death rates from the most severe form of skin cancer more than tripled for older American men during the last 3 decades. This is in contrast to fewer such deaths among the younger crowd, say scientists.

The surge in fatal melanoma cases in older and middle-aged white men was largely responsible for the nation's overall rising death rate from melanoma. Between 1969 and 1999, fatal melanoma cases rose from 2 per 100,000 to 3 per 100,000 people.

Melanoma deaths fell by approximately one-third for Americans aged 20 to 44 years during the same period. The researchers say this decrease was the result of skin cancer education efforts and smarter sunbathing habits.

"People are beginning to reap some of the positive messages from the sun protection campaigns," says Alan Geller, a skin cancer expert at Boston University and lead author of a recent study of cancer death rates.

The study only looked at Caucasian people, who have 10 to 15 times more melanoma than black and Hispanic people.

MEN ARE HIT HARDER

Death rates from melanoma in American women aged 45 to 64 years rose 19% during the study period. Men in the same age group had a 66% increase in deaths. The increase for men 65 years and older was 157%, 3 times the rate for women in the same age group.

65

Geller says it's not entirely clear why seniors are experiencing more melanoma now than they did 30 years ago, but the surge reflects more than simply an increased diagnosis of the disease. One theory, he says, is that increased sun exposure during World War II and the Korean War might be driving the rise. Another theory is that bathing suit styles in the 1950s and 1960s revealed more skin than they ever had before, boosting the risk of cancer.

PREVENTION ATTENTION

Geller and his colleagues stressed the importance of looking for suspicious moles and sores and reporting them to your doctor.

Catherine Poole, executive director of the National Melanoma Foundation in Philadelphia, disputes the notion that Americans are being more cautious about the sun than they were 30 years ago. "Our society still thinks it's pretty healthy to be out there on the beach at noon," she says. "Our kids are playing sports at high noon."

Until the country takes a much dimmer view of the sun, Poole says, public education efforts will continue to fizzle.

info For more information on melanoma, visit the Melanoma Patients' Information Page at *www.mpip.org* or the Melanoma International Foundation at *www.nationalmela noma.org*.

Melanoma Gene Discovery Could Mean Early Screening Tests

Martin A. Weinstock, MD, PhD, Professor, Dermatology, Brown Medical School, Providence, RI.

Suzie Chen, PhD, Associate Professor, Chemical Biology, College of Pharmacy, Rutgers University, Piscataway, NJ.

April 21, 2003, online edition, *Nature Genetics*.

Researchers at Rutgers University think they've discovered a gene that contributes to melanoma, a form of skin cancer that kills 7600 Americans a year.

Although the finding won't immediately translate into a treatment, researchers say, it's possible doctors could eventually develop a test to determine which babies are at highest risk for the disease, says Dr. Martin A. Weinstock, a professor of dermatology at Brown Medical School.

"For those at the greatest risk, we could take a lot of precautions and do lots of surveillance," Weinstock says. "You could protect them from ultraviolet [sun] exposure and screen them when they get to be adults."

Although melanoma accounts for just 4% of skin cancer cases, it is by far the deadliest form of the disease. Melanoma, which often appears in moles, is easily cured if caught early. But the disease often kills if the cancerous moles aren't discovered until the tumors have spread to other parts of the body.

SERENDIPITOUS FIND

Suzie Chen, an associate professor of chemical biology at Rutgers University, stumbled on a melanoma gene accidentally, while she was studying how cells form and make themselves different from others. While working with genetically altered mice to understand how cells turn into fat cells, she noticed that one mouse developed a melanoma on its skin.

After more research, Chen found the cancer appeared to be directly related to a gene that turns itself on only in the brain, where it releases a protein and contributes to learning and memory. Somehow, the gene also turned itself on in the skin of the mouse, contributing to melanoma.

Chen and her colleagues later discovered that the gene had turned itself on in one-third of tissue samples from people who had various types of melanoma. That suggests the gene contributes to the disease in humans and mice.

With more study, it could be possible to design chemotherapy to target melanoma cells by detecting the protein given off by the troublesome gene, Chen says.

SUN PROTECTION IS KEY

Weinstock says genetic research by scientists like Chen is important to gaining a better understanding of melanoma. But the findings don't change the fact that the best way to prevent the disease is to limit sun exposure, he adds.

Melanoma can appear on parts of the body that never see sunlight, but sunburns and exposure to ultraviolet light—especially in childhood and adolescence—are considered risk factors.

Weinstock calls on people to adopt a "slip, slop, and slap" approach: "Slip on a shirt, slop on the sunscreen, and slap on a hat."

info Learn more about melanoma from the American Academy of Dermatology at *www.aad.org.*

Double Trouble For Skin Cancer Found in Families

Johan Hansson, MD, PhD, Director, Melanoma Unit, Department of Oncology, Karolinska Hospital, Stockholm, Sweden.

Vincent DeLeo, MD, Associate Professor, Clinical Dermatology, Columbia University, New York, NY.

June 4, 2003, *Journal of the National Cancer Institute.*

People who have a genetic mutation that makes them susceptible to the deadly melanoma type of skin cancer also may suffer other damage brought about from too much time in the sun. Sun exposure for these people may literally mean the difference between life and death, because it could encourage other types of skin cancer, sun poisoning, and other dangerous conditions.

But there's also a silver lining to this discovery by Swedish scientists. In discovering the genetic similarities, researchers believe they may have found a way to predict when a person is most likely to contract melanoma, which is responsible for more than 95% of all skin cancer deaths.

The mutation is not common, but people who have it need to be told about the research and about how to protect themselves, says study author Dr. Johan Hansson, director of the melanoma unit at Stockholm's Karolinska Hospital.

A tumor-suppressing gene called CDKN2A mutates in approximately 20% of a tiny minority of melanoma patients who have a family history of the disease, Hansson says. There are, however, different types of mutations of the same gene. Here, the researchers looked at only one type of mutation.

Melanoma affects approximately 54,000 Americans annually, but causes 79% of the deaths from skin cancer, according to the American Cancer Society.

FAMILY TIES

The researchers looked at 35 melanoma patients—25 with a family history of the disease who carried the CDKN2A mutation, and 10 with no family history of melanoma. They then tested them to see if any had a gene mutation related to sun exposure, which is also known to be associated with melanoma.

They found that only 10% of those with no family history of the disease had the sun-related mutation, and 95% of those with the genetic mutation of the CDKN2A gene also had the sun-related mutation.

"The results were so striking," Hansson says. A further important finding, Hansson says, is that all but 1 of the skin cancers in the first group were found on parts of the body that are exposed to the sun, suggesting an association between ultraviolet light exposure and the activation of the sun-related gene mutations.

THE LONG SEARCH

"People have been looking for these genes for a long time. Epidemiology studies have shown that one of the most important risks for melanoma is a family history of the disease," says Dr. Vincent DeLeo, an associate professor of clinical dermatology at Columbia University in New York City.

info To find out if you're at risk for melanoma, go to SkinCarePhysicians.com at *www.skincarephysicians.com.*

Prostate Cancer Update: PSAs Important Even *After* Treatments

October 2002, Abstract, *International Journal of Radiation Oncology.*

October 2002, American Society for Therapeutic Radiology and Oncology news release.

A blood test given to men 5 years after receiving radiation treatment for prostate cancer helps predict their chances of surviving for several more years, according to research published in the *International Journal of Radiation Oncology.*

Men who have low levels of the *prostate-specific antigen* (PSA) at the 5-year mark have low odds of suffering a relapse of prostate cancer at 10 years and beyond, the study says.

Researchers identified 328 men whose prostate cancer was treated with external beam radiation and who were biochemically disease-free 5 years after treatment. The median follow-up period was 7.4 years.

The men were divided into 4 groups according to their PSA levels at the 5-year mark. The results showed that the lower the PSA number, the better the chance of survival. Ten years after treatment, there was a 92% survival rate for the group with the lowest PSA numbers. As PSA numbers rose, survival rates declined to 71%, 78%, and 56%, respectively.

"If low PSA levels [can be achieved] early in treatment, and those low levels can be maintained to 5 years and beyond, the long-term outlook for prostate cancer patients treated with radiation therapy will be good," says study coauthor Dr. Anthony L. Zietman, of the department of radiation oncology at Massachusetts General Hospital.

■ ■ ■ ■

What Is PSA?

According to the American Foundation for Urologic Disease, PSA is a protein that is originally found in semen, the fluid that carries sperm. PSA helps keep the semen in its liquid form.

Small amounts of the protein get into the blood and can be measured by a blood test. Certain prostate conditions, including prostate cancer, can cause high levels of PSA in the blood. PSA itself does not have any known effect outside the prostate; even high levels are not directly harmful. In addition to prostate problems, some medical treatments can affect PSA levels. Any treatment that lowers male hormone levels will cause a drop in PSA blood levels.

info Learn more about PSA at the American Foundation for Urologic Disease Web site at *www.afud.org/conditions/psa.html.*

Tall Men Have Elevated Prostate Cancer Risk

J. Michael Gaziano, MD, MPH, Chief, Division on Aging, Brigham and Women's Hospital, affiliate of Harvard Medical School, Boston, MA.

Allan J. Pantuck, MD, Assistant Professor, Urology, University of California, Los Angeles, Jonsson Cancer Center.

February 20, 2003, presentation, Preventive Medicine 2003 meeting, San Diego, CA.

Older men who are tall have a higher risk of getting prostate cancer, a Harvard study suggests.

"These are modestly increased risks," says study author Dr. J. Michael Gaziano, chief of the division on aging at Brigham and Women's Hospital, an affiliate of Harvard Medical School in Boston.

Using data from the Physicians Health Study of 22,071 men in the United States, the researchers zeroed in on 1634 men with prostate cancer, asking about their age, height, weight, and body mass index (BMI), a ratio of height to weight.

They evaluated 3 categories of height: 5'9" or shorter; 5'10" to 5'11"; and taller than 5'11".

•**Among the men who were 50 to 59 years old,** those 5'10" to 5'11" had a 21% greater risk of prostate cancer than those shorter than 5'10". Those taller than 5'11" had a 32% greater risk.

•**For men who were 60 to 84 years old,** those who were 5'10" to 5'11" had a 22% higher risk of prostate cancer than shorter men in the same age bracket. Those taller than 5'11" had a 24% higher risk.

Exactly why this association exists is not known, Gaziano says. "Height may just be a genetic marker for some other genetic reason [the man] might be at risk," he speculates.

The study is not the first to link height with prostate cancer, Gaziano says. Other researchers have studied the association with mixed findings. "Most show an association with obesity," says Dr. Allan J. Pantuck, assistant professor of urology at the University of California, Los Angles, Jonsson Cancer Center. The Harvard researchers did not find an association between weight or BMI and prostate cancer.

Pantuck cautions that the association that was found between height and prostate cancer is based on an observational study and does not prove a cause-and-effect relationship. "The data, in general, are very limited, and this needs to be explored and then duplicated or refuted before we can say something definite," Gaziano says.

Gaziano stresses that men should continue to get screened. Eventually, if more research bears out the association between height and prostate cancer, it will help researchers and physicians take preventative measures with the men most likely to contract the disease, he says.

■ ■ ■ ■

Screening and Diagnosis

The early stages of prostate cancer usually have no symptoms. Risk factors include increasing age, and family history. More than 70% of all prostate cancers are found in men who are older than 65 years. Black men have the highest prostate cancer rates in the world.

An annual *digital rectal exam* (DRE) and a *prostate-specific antigen* (PSA) blood test are recommended by the American Cancer Society for all men beginning at age 50; for those at elevated risk, the recommended age for the tests is 45.

Less of a Gene May Signal Less Troubling Prostate Cancer

Arul M. Chinnaiyan, MD, PhD, Assistant Professor, Pathology and Urology, University of Michigan Medical School, Ann Arbor.
Bruce Zetter, PhD, Professor, Cancer Biology, Harvard Medical School and Children's Hospital, Boston, MA.
October 10, 2002, *Nature*.

The amount of a certain gene in prostate cancer tumors may help doctors decide how aggressively to treat the disease.

EZH2 is the gene in question, and it prevents tumor-blocking proteins from doing their job. The gene is much more active in aggressive prostate tumor cells than in either localized cancer or in healthy prostate tissue. Therefore, men whose tumors have low levels of this gene could be spared unnecessary treatments.

HELPS SET A COURSE OF TREATMENT

"This helps us distinguish between aggressive prostate cancer and slow-growing prostate cancer, and allows us to identify patients appropriate for watchful waiting and those who need radical [prostate removal] surgery or radiation," says Dr. Arul M. Chinnaiyan, a University of Michigan pathologist and leader of the research effort.

WORKING IN THE CELL

Laboratory tests showed that the higher the EZH2 protein levels in prostate cells, the more often cells that fight cancer shut down. When the scientists reversed the process, the rapid growth of cancer cells stopped.

Bruce Zetter, a cancer biologist at Children's Hospital in Boston, says EZH2 seems to behave like the first in a line of dominoes—tipping it sends the whole array into a tumble.

Knowing which genes encourage the spread of cancer is valuable for all tumor types, but especially for prostate cancer, Zetter says, since the disease isn't deadly for most men.

"What we need in prostate cancer is a better prognostic marker. We don't need to improve the diagnosis so much," says Zetter, coauthor of a commentary on the study. "That's what these latest developments are paving the way to do."

The researchers also are experimenting with *alpha-methylacyl-CoA racemase* (AMACR), a gene found in elevated levels in cancer cells. It appears to be a good marker for early cancer detection.

Chinnaiyan is now working on a single test that would measure both AMACR and EZH2, as well as identify the presence of prostate cancer and determine its virulence.

info For more on prostate cancer, visit the University of Michigan Health System's Web site at *www.cancer.med.umich.edu* or the site for the Prostate Cancer Research Institute at *www.prostate-cancer.org*.

Lung Cancer Drug Proves That Sometimes, Older Is Better

Rafael Rosell, MD, Chief, Medical Oncology Service, Hospital Universitari Germans Trias i Pujol, Barcelona, Spain.

October 2002, *Annals of Oncology*.

January 2002, *New England Journal of Medicine*.

A newer drug commonly used in the United States to treat lung cancer may not be as effective as an older one when it comes to survival, says a study of more than 600 European patients. But the difference in life expectancy is not large.

Those patients taking the older chemotherapy drug, called *cisplatin*, lived an average of 1.25 months longer than those who took a newer drug, called *carboplatin*. Both drugs were taken in combination with paclitaxel, a standard part of lung cancer treatment.

"It was interesting to see that perhaps cisplatin is better than carboplatin in terms of survival," says Dr. Rafael Rosell, an oncologist from Barcelona, Spain. He is lead author of the study, which appears in the *Annals of Oncology*.

"This gain in life expectancy is not dramatically significant, but it is still not trivial," Rosell says. "People should be fully aware that the benefits could be small, but they should still know about them."

THE STUDY

For the study, Rosell and his colleagues recruited 618 patients, most of whom had the most advanced form of lung cancer. Over 15 months, approximately half the patients received cisplatin, and the other half took carboplatin to treat their lung cancer. During their treatment, the patients were evaluated every 6 weeks with blood tests, X-rays to measure the size of their tumors, and a quality-of-life survey, which included questions about side effects, as well as questions about their emotional and social functioning. The evaluations were similar between the groups, Rosell says. The difference was in the slightly longer survival rates in the cisplatin group.

Rosell says his findings must be seen in the context of the poor prognosis for lung cancer patients overall, an opinion echoed in an editorial that accompanied the study. The editorial called for new treatment strategies, other than chemotherapy, to treat lung cancer.

info Facts about lung cancer are available at *www.lungcancer.org*. The National Institutes of Health Web site at *www.nih.gov* has information about cisplatin and carboplatin.

Common Plant Compound May Halt Lung Cancer Growth

D. Neil Watkins, MD, PhD, Research Associate, Kimmel Cancer Center, Johns Hopkins University, Baltimore, MD.

Myung K. Shin, PhD, Associate Member, Fox Chase Cancer Center, Philadelphia, PA.

March 5, 2003, *Nature.*

The deadliest form of lung cancer—the one closely linked to smoking—may have an Achilles' heel.

Scientists have found that a naturally occurring plant compound called *cyclopamine* stopped tumor growth in mice with human cancers. The findings may hold promise for small-cell lung cancer, which accounts for approximately 20% of all lung cancers.

Certain cancer tumors appear to proliferate by hijacking a process that is involved in forming and repairing cells. The research aims to determine how to thwart that hijacking.

"Knowing what the key molecules are that cause this process is really exciting," says Myung K. Shin, associate member of the Fox Chase Cancer Center in Philadelphia.

Something seems to go wrong at a fundamental, molecular level.

"In adult organisms, the skin, bone marrow, and gut all have cells that are constantly growing and turning over and replacing lost cells," says study author Dr. D. Neil Watkins, a research associate with the Kimmel Cancer Center at Johns Hopkins University in Baltimore. That's normal. What is not normal is when these pathways start working on behalf of tumor cells.

"In a normal adult lung, everything is quiet," Watkins says. There is no hustle and bustle of repairing and replicating activity unless you're a smoker. In people who smoke, injured airways signal repair crews to patch them up so they'll continue to perform the work of breathing.

REPAIR PROCESS DOESN'T KNOW WHEN TO STOP

This is still a normal process, as long as it stops when the repair is finished. The authors found, however, that when a small-cell lung cancer tumor is present, a signaling molecule called the "Sonic Hedgehog" (after a cartoon character) stays on. Instead of simply repairing the lungs, it can also fuel specific types of cancer.

"The cells are regenerating and they don't know when to stop. They're bypassing the normal process," Shin explains

Although it's not clear exactly why this happens, the authors speculate that the normal cells involved in repair are vulnerable to mutations that cause them to transform into cancer cells.

Though the malignant tumors are aggressive, they are extremely vulnerable to being stopped, Watkins says.

"Cyclopamine is not conventional chemotherapy. It does nothing else [to the body]," Watkins says. "It's potentially a very exciting finding because this may be a way of treating certain types of cancer very specifically without affecting the rest of the body."

Although the compound seems to work in sheep and mice, it will be years before it's ready for human cancer patients.

info Visit the American Lung Association at *www.lungusa.org* for more information on lung cancer, including small-cell lung cancer.

Growth Hormones: Can They Cause Colon Cancer?

Anthony Swerdlow, MD, PhD, Professor, Epidemiology, Institute of Cancer Research, Surrey, England.

Michael Pollak, MD, Professor, Oncology, McGill University, Montreal, Quebec, Canada.

July 27, 2002, *The Lancet.*

Human growth hormone, a substance given to people who lack it, might increase the risk of colon cancer decades later.

The US Food and Drug Administration has approved therapy with human growth hormone only for children and adults whose pituitary glands don't make enough growth hormone. Since the 1950s, more than 100,000 people worldwide have received the growth hormone supplements.

A British study showed a significant increase in colorectal cancer among people who took nonsynthetic pituitary growth hormone between 1959 and 1985, although the actual number of cases was small.

THE STUDY

Dr. Anthony Swerdlow, an epidemiologist at the Institute of Cancer Research in Surrey, England, and his colleagues looked at cancer rates and deaths among 1848 Britons treated with human growth hormone between 1959 and 1985. All but 1% of the patients were younger than 19 years when they began the therapy.

By the end of 2000, people who had received the hormone were nearly 3 times as likely to have died of cancer as those in the general population. The group's risk of dying from colorectal tumors or Hodgkin's disease, which strikes the body's lymph system, was 11 times greater than in the general population, and the incidence of colorectal cancer was roughly 8 times higher.

Before 1985, the growth hormone supplement was obtained from the pituitary glands of cadavers and was prone to contamination. Since then, doctors have used a synthetic growth hormone that is administered in strictly controlled doses.

The synthetic form may have different effects on the body. Doctors administer the drug at doses that do not exceed age-appropriate thresholds, and patients are carefully monitored to make sure their blood levels of the substance stay in the proper range.

No other studies have found a reason to connect growth hormone supplements and cancer. And Swerdlow says the abnormally high rate of Hodgkin's disease could just be a coincidence.

WEIGHING THE RISKS

Experts say the results deserve further investigation, though they do not warrant stopping growth hormone treatments in patients who need it.

The potential link to cancers should give pause to older adults who are considering growth hormone injections to slow the aging process, an increasingly common but scientifically unproven theory. It should also be a strong warning to athletes who take extreme doses of the drug as a workout aid.

"If the dose you take achieves normal levels, you have nothing to worry about," says Dr. Michael Pollak, a cancer specialist at McGill University in Montreal. "But if you're not really growth hormone deficient and your growth hormone therapy is giving you unnaturally high levels, then this may be an important warning for you."

■ ■ ■ ■

Symptoms of Growth Hormone Deficiency in Adults

According to the Hormone Foundation, there are symptoms that may indicate a growth hormone deficiency. *They include...*

● **Increased amount of fat** around the face and abdomen.

● **Lower level of lean body mass.**

● **Osteopenia (bone loss).**

● **Thinning skin** with fine wrinkles.

● **Poor sweating** or impaired temperature regulation.

● **Loss of interest in sex.**

● **Sleep problems.**

● **Decreased muscle strength,** energy, and vitality.

● **Higher cholesterol levels,** especially LDL ("bad") cholesterol.

● **Production of too much insulin,** related to being overweight.

● **Decreased sense of well-being,** increased depression, and emotions that change or seem inappropriate.

info Learn about growth hormone therapy from The Hormone Foundation at *www.hormone.org* or Vanderbilt Medical Center at *www.mc.vanderbilt.edu.*

Simple Test May Soon Predict Colon Cancer

Andrew P. Feinberg, MD, MPH, King Fahd Professor of Medicine, Kimmel Cancer Center, Johns Hopkins University School of Medicine, Baltimore, MD.

Robert C. Kurtz, MD, Chief, Gastroenterology and Nutrition Service, Memorial Sloan–Kettering Cancer Center, New York, NY.

March 14, 2003, *Science*.

March 13, 2003, Centers for Disease Control and Prevention news release.

March 13, 2003, Washington University School of Medicine news release.

A simple blood test may eventually pinpoint individuals who are likely to develop colorectal cancer, and this could significantly increase the number of people who volunteer for early detection.

The test would hunt down a genetic change that causes cells to reproduce wildly, according to scientists from Johns Hopkins University. And this could be extremely timely news.

Even though one-third of colorectal cancer deaths could be avoided by being screened, only about half of American adults 50 and older are tested, says the Centers for Disease Control and Prevention (CDC).

The standard colon cancer test is a colonoscopy, which requires preparation, some anesthesia, time, and considerable cost.

"It's hugely expensive and a tremendous drain on resources. We couldn't do it even if everybody agreed to it," says Dr. Robert C. Kurtz, chief of the gastroenterology and nutrition service at Memorial Sloan–Kettering Cancer Center in New York City.

Colorectal cancer is the second leading cancer killer in the United States, with about 155,000 new cases diagnosed each year. More than 57,000 people die from colon cancer each year.

THE STUDY

Dr. Andrew P. Feinberg, the King Fahd Professor of Medicine at Johns Hopkins' Kimmel Cancer Center in Baltimore, set out to find if some genetic coding existed that would indicate whether a person had a predisposition to colon cancer. The results were originally reported in a story in *Science* magazine.

The genetic change that Feinberg and his team investigated involves a process called *loss of imprinting* (LOI). The gene in question is named the IGF2 gene, which is involved in cell growth.

Normally, humans acquire 1 copy of each gene from each parent. For certain "imprinted genes," only 1 of these genes is actually "turned on," or activated. The other is "silenced" and does not function, which is normal. When both imprinted genes are mistakenly turned on, however, problems can occur.

Feinberg's team had already shown that in up to 40% of colon cancers both IGF2 genes were turned on and were directing cells to multiply.

As they analyzed blood samples, the scientists found that people with a family history of colon cancer were more than 5 times more likely to have both IGF2 genes turned on than individuals with no history of colon cancer in their family. Individuals who had had colon polyps were more than 3 times more likely to have the loss of imprint marker. Those who had already had colon cancer were almost 22 times more likely to have the marker.

Feinberg is not sure the IGF2 gene change happens. But additional testing that involves little more than drawing blood from an individual would certainly reduce cost and expand the reach for colon cancer testing.

"We're guessing that you're not born with this," Feinberg says, adding that the stability of these changes may vary in the population. Some people may preserve their gene structure better than other people, and that may itself be genetically determined, he adds.

info For more on colorectal cancer, visit the Centers for Disease Control and Prevention at *www.cdc.gov* or the Colorectal Cancer Network at *www.colorectal-cancer.net*.

Montezuma's Revenge May Block Colon Cancer

Giovanni Pitari, MD, PhD, Professor, Clinical Pharmacology, Thomas Jefferson University, Philadelphia, PA.

Stephen L. Carrithers, PhD, Assistant Professor, Medicine, University of Kentucky, Lexington.

February 10, 2003, *Proceedings of the National Academy of Sciences.*

You probably never thought there could be an upside to Montezuma's revenge. But it turns out that *Escherichia coli*, the bacteria that causes traveler's diarrhea, may be used to treat colon cancer.

Colorectal cancer is the fourth-leading cause of cancer and cancer-related deaths in the world. Yet most colorectal cancer occurs in industrialized nations, says Dr. Giovanni Pitari, a professor of clinical pharmacology at Thomas Jefferson University in Philadelphia and lead author of a study on the disease.

Because the incidence of colorectal cancer is lowest in developing countries, where *E coli* infections are the most common, Pitari and his colleagues reasoned that something about *E coli* might ward off colorectal cancer.

E coli produces toxic by-products that are resistant to high temperatures. Researchers placed these toxins into colon cancer cells grown in the laboratory. "We found the toxin doesn't cause cell death, but it does reduce the proliferation of colon cancer cells," Pitari says.

Researchers also delved further into the mechanism of how the toxins prevent the growth of colon cancer cells. What they learned might one day lead to the development of new treatments for colon cancer, Pitari says.

Most of the deaths from colorectal cancer occur when it has *metastasized,* or spread, to other organs. Theoretically, doctors could inject the *E coli* intravenously, and the toxins would target the colon cancer cells throughout the body.

FROM THEORY TO PRACTICE

Pitari emphasized that his work was done in the laboratory. The next step is animal and, later, human testing.

"Sometimes, what you see in [the lab] seems really promising, but you don't see the same effects in animals or humans," he says.

Stephen L. Carrithers, an assistant professor of medicine at the University of Kentucky and a colon cancer researcher, says it's important to remember that there is still no direct evidence linking *E coli* to a reduced colon cancer risk in the real world.

"There just hasn't been an epidemiological study that shows people chronically infected with *E coli* really do have lower rates of colon cancer," says Carrithers, who wrote a commentary about the study.

However, Pitari's findings are promising, Carrithers says. "In the laboratory, he's shown that something secreted from *E coli* does prevent the progression of colorectal cancer."

Carrithers says it's possible that some day people could take supplements to prevent colorectal cancer. "You might be able to give people low amounts of *E coli* all the time, which would keep the colorectal cancer from ever forming."

■ ■ ■ ■

Signs and Symptoms of Colon Cancer

Colon cancer usually does not exhibit symptoms in the early stages, so it is important to have periodic screening tests. *As the disease progresses, any of the following may be seen…*

- **Blood in the stool.**
- **Diarrhea.**
- **Constipation.**
- **Bowel obstruction causing nausea,** vomiting, and abdominal distension.
- **Abdominal pain.**
- **Pelvic pain.**
- **Anemia.**

- **Weight loss.**
- **Loss of appetite.**
- **Fatigue.**

info The Colorectal Cancer Network says the disease is highly curable in the early stages, when cancerous polyps can be found and removed. Their Web site, *www.colorectal-cancer.net,* can also help you find a support group.

How Often Do You Need a Sigmoidoscopy?

Jack S. Mandel, PhD, MPH, Chairman, Department of Epidemiology, Rollins School of Public Health, Emory University, Atlanta, GA.

Polly Newcomb, PhD, MPH, Researcher, Fred Hutchinson Cancer Research Center, Seattle, WA.

April 16, 2003, *Journal of the National Cancer Institute.*

Researchers are questioning the recommended guidelines for a common colorectal cancer screening procedure. Some think the current 5-year screening interval for *sigmoidoscopy* may be excessive. The benefits of the procedure, they say, can last as long as 10 or even 15 years.

But doctors do not agree on how often patients older than 50 years should be screened.

Previous studies have shown that precancerous tissue, called *polyps,* can take up to 15 years to progress to cancer, suggesting that screening every 5 years may not be necessary.

Researchers from the Fred Hutchinson Cancer Research Center in Seattle looked at the effectiveness of sigmoidoscopy screening in reducing the incidence of colorectal cancer.

The findings show that those who had received a screening sigmoidoscopy had a fourfold reduction in the incidence of colorectal cancers compared with individuals who had never had the procedure. Moreover, this benefit appeared to be sustained for more than 15 years, indicating the recommended screening interval is too aggressive.

If more adults older than 50 had a sigmoidoscopy every 10 years, the incidence and mortality of colorectal cancer could be substantially reduced, according to the lead author of the study, Polly Newcomb, a researcher at the Fred Hutchinson Cancer Research Center.

Patients typically don't like invasive screening procedures such as sigmoidoscopies, in which a scope is used to examine the lower part of the large bowel. If the screenings were recommended once every 10 years, instead of every 5 years, more patients would be likely to comply. And the reduction in the amount of sigmoidoscopies performed would also translate into significant savings for the healthcare system.

One expert, however, says the number of study participants was so small that the results could easily be distorted by a mistake or classification error. Jack S. Mandel, chairman of epidemiology at Emory University's Rollins School of Public Health says the study looked at self-reported data that was not verified using patient records.

■ ■ ■ ■

Early Detection Is Wise

According to the American Cancer Society, early detection is key for treating and curing colorectal cancer. *Following are some facts about screening...*

- **Screening tests are used to spot the disease early** even if you do not have symptoms or a history of that disease.

- **Screening for colorectal cancer cannot only find it at an early curable stage,** it can also prevent it by identifying and removing polyps that might become cancerous.

- **Cancers can also be found early by reporting symptoms right away to your doctors.** However, being screened before symptoms occur is preferable.

Hormone Replacement Therapy May Still Have Cancer-Fighting Benefits

August 1, 2002, *British Medical Journal.*

Women who take hormones to counter the effects of aging or illness do not have a higher risk of endometrial cancer. In fact, hormone replacement therapy (HRT) may even help prevent this type of cancer by protecting the lining of the uterus, according to a study from the *British Medical Journal.*

The study, conducted by researchers throughout the United Kingdom, included 534 postmenopausal women, one of the largest studies of its kind.

Prior to the start of the study, 360 of the women had taken combination HRT (estrogen and progestin), 164 hadn't taken any HRT, and 10 had taken estrogen-only (ERT). During the study, the women were given continuous combined HRT. The researchers took biopsy samples from the women before they started the combined HRT, at 9 months, between 24 and 36 months, and then again at the end of the 5-year study.

The biopsies showed that 21 of the women had an abnormal endometrium before the study began. When associated with other cellular changes, that can be an early sign of cancer. But after 9 months of the combined HRT, the endometrium in all 21 women had reverted to normal. None of the 534 women developed endometrial cancer during this study.

The authors say the study indicates that women who take daily combined HRT may be better protected against endometrial cancer than women who don't take any kind of HRT.

HRT has been the subject of several recent studies, with controversial results. A national clinical trial in the United States was halted after 5 years when doctors found that the health risks outweighed the benefits. The *Journal of the American Medical Association* has reported that women in this trial who were taking the combination of estrogen and progestin experienced a 29% increased rate of coronary heart disease problems, compared with women taking a placebo.

Does Chemotherapy Affect Your Memory?

Stewart Fleishman, MD, Director, Cancer Supportive Services, Continuum Cancer Centers of New York, Beth Israel Medical Center and St. Luke's–Roosevelt Hospital Center, New York, NY.

Mark Laufer, cancer patient, New York, NY.

Mark Laufer can tell you the exact moment he realized something was wrong.

Laufer, 43, had just exited the subway station at West 72nd Street in Manhattan and was walking home when he noticed a message on his cell phone.

"I could not, for the life of me, remember my password or remember the process for retrieving the message," he says.

Laufer stood in this memory fog for more than 20 minutes before he finally remembered how to complete the process.

In retrospect, Laufer realized many other things had been eluding him in the months after he had undergone chemotherapy for breast cancer. The cell phone incident took place only 2 months after Laufer's last chemotherapy session.

"Everyone is absent-minded at one time or another, but this was a different feeling—as though somebody turned a switch off in my brain right in the middle of my sentence, and the word was kind of left behind the door. And I couldn't open the door. I physically felt the block in my brain. I know that I know it, but I can't touch it; I can't retrieve it," he recalls.

Laufer, along with countless other cancer patients, had been suffering from "chemobrain," a set of changes affecting memory, attention, and concentration that seem to appear after chemotherapy.

Dr. Stewart Fleishman, director of cancer supportive services at Continuum Cancer Centers of New York at Beth Israel Medical Center and St. Luke's–Roosevelt Hospital Center, first heard the term from a patient in the early 1990s.

LOOKING FOR HELP

Fleishman is involved in a trial to investigate if a central nervous system stimulant called Focalin, which is approved to treat attention-deficit hyperactivity disorder, might help chemobrain.

"This has never really been acknowledged by the cancer community because years ago, people didn't live so long with cancer, or they lived and were so appreciative of being alive that they were able to write off cognitive impairment or fatigue as the cost of being alive after cancer," Fleishman explains.

Chemobrain fits in with a host of other postcancer problems, including altered taste and digestion, changes in bowel movements, and fertility and sexual functioning issues, Fleishman says.

THE ESTROGEN FACTOR

Some researchers think estrogen is involved in chemobrain because cancer-free women who are going through menopause or perimenopause complain of many of the same symptoms.

Although, there's little that can be done about chemobrain, sometimes just having a name for your problem helps.

"Patients often say, 'I thought I was the only one. I thought I was going crazy,'" Fleishman says. "Just bringing it out in the open is a great relief."

Although there are no rigorous studies behind his advice, Fleishman advocates mental exercise, such as learning a new skill, as well as various common-sense strategies like good nutrition and exercise.

A Rat Poison That Can Save Your Life!

Peter Maslak, MD, Chief, Hematology Laboratory, Memorial Sloan–Kettering Cancer Center, New York, NY.

Josephine Comeau, leukemia patient, Brooklyn, NY.

Take a dose of poison to battle a form of leukemia? No way, thought Josephine Comeau, a teacher's aide from Brooklyn, New York.

Comeau's doctors at the Memorial Sloan–Kettering Cancer Center in New York City had made a frightening suggestion—perhaps she should take arsenic to combat her disease, *acute promyelocytic leukemia* (APL).

"I went crazy when they told me," she says. "It's poison. They had to call a psychiatrist. I couldn't stop crying, I was so scared."

But it worked.

NEW USE FOR AN OLD REMEDY

Americans may associate arsenic with rat poison, but in China it's a folk remedy that has been around for 2000 years. Doctors there have been using arsenic to treat APL since the 1980s. Sloan–Kettering researchers began testing it in the late 1990s.

Comeau learned she had APL after she stubbed her toe. It turned black and blue. The next day, other parts of her body were dark-colored, too, because of massive internal bleeding. In the hospital, doctors told her she had APL.

This type of cancer works by shutting down the production of red blood cells and healthy, infection-fighting white blood cells, allowing immature white blood cells to take over. Since the cancerous cells don't die naturally, they flood the body, often leading to internal bleeding, explains Dr. Peter Maslak, chief of the hematology laboratory at Sloan–Kettering.

FEW SIDE EFFECTS

Initially, arsenic scared American doctors. But researchers found that, in the right dose, arsenic can kill off the immature white blood cells, causing the remission of APL.

And unlike chemotherapy or bone marrow transplants, which can devastate a body as they fight the cancer, arsenic has limited side effects. However, arsenic isn't good as a first treatment, Maslak says, because the patient's liver can't respond until after it has been treated with other therapies. So doctors combine arsenic with other drugs and lower doses of chemotherapy.

Comeau's leukemia went into remission after she began the arsenic treatment. Within 6 months, she returned to her elementary school job.

"I felt like I walked in from the dead. I looked like I was 100 years old, but I enjoyed seeing the kids again," she says. "I'm grateful I'm here."

The 'Cocktail' That Combats Leukemia

Edward D. Ball, MD, Director, Translational Oncology, Rebecca and John Moores University of California at San Diego Cancer Center.

Stephen Forman, MD, Director, Hematologic Neoplasia Program, City of Hope Cancer Cancer, Duarte, CA.

October 2002, *Biology of Blood and Marrow Transplantation.*

Anew cancer-killing "cocktail" shows promise in laboratory studies as an effective way to attack *acute myeloid leukemia* (AML), a cancer of the blood.

A team led by Dr. Edward D. Ball, director of the Blood and Marrow Transplantation Program at the University of California–San Diego School of Medicine, took blood samples from 12 patients, who were diagnosed with or just relapsed with AML.

The researchers separated out the white cells, which included cells that mount an immune response to infected or cancerous cells.

They added 2 substances to the mix: Growth factors and interleukin-4. Interleukin-4 helps activate the immune system. This "cocktail" was designed to turn the lymphocytes into stronger fighters, creating T-cells.

"At the end of the 40-day culture, we had a pure culture of T-cells," Ball says. "Almost all the leukemia cells were gone."

The work is in the laboratory stage, Ball cautions, and he must prove the mixture works in animals and in humans before it can become available. The long-term hope, of course, is to have the cancer "cocktail" be a cure.

Approximately 10,600 new cases of AML are diagnosed each year, according to the Leukemia and Lymphoma Society. Patients often feel a loss of well-being and complain of fatigue. They may notice bruises after minor injuries and have fever, swollen gums, and slow healing of cuts.

Currently, Ball says, "we're pretty good at getting people into remission. But over 50% [have a] relapse. And when they relapse, they start to develop chemotherapy resistance."

This study extends the possibility that immunotherapy might be effective, says Dr. Stephen Forman, director of the hemotologic neoplasia program at the City of Hope Cancer Center in Duarte, California.

"What Dr. Ball's approach does is take a series of growth factors and stimulate them in culture to generate cells from a patient's own blood that will recognize leukemia and kill it."

info For more information on AML, visit The Leukemia & Lymphoma Society Web site at *www.leukemia-lymphoma.org.*

New 'Miracle' Drug To Fight Leukemia

Alan Kinniburgh, PhD, Vice President, Research, Leukemia & Lymphoma Society, White Plains, NY.

Hagop Kantarjian, MD, Chairman, Leukemia Department, University of Texas, M.D. Anderson Cancer Center, Houston.

Samuel Kopel, MD, Associate Director, Hematology/ Oncology, Maimonides Medical Center, Brooklyn, NY.

March 13, 2003, *New England Journal of Medicine.*

Gleevec, the "miracle" anticancer drug, has swept aside interferon-alpha combination therapy as the drug of choice for newly diagnosed *chronic myeloid leukemia* (CML), say the results of a 16-country trial.

"By all parameters, Gleevec is better," says Dr. Hagop Kantarjian, a coinvestigator on the study and chairman of the leukemia department at the M.D. Anderson Cancer Center in Houston.

It's not a complete fix, but Gleevec is better than interferon therapy and may well cure many patients, says Dr. Samuel Kopel, associate director of hematology/oncology at Maimonides Medical Center.

Currently, the only cure for CML, which affects just under 15,000 Americans, is a bone marrow transplant. But that's only an option for approximately 1 in 4 of the people who develop the disease, and the transplant has considerable risks.

SHORT-CIRCUITING CANCER

CML plays havoc with white blood cells, which normally fight infection, and sends them into reproductive overdrive.

A genetic flaw in the cancer cells makes them produce an abnormal protein, which, in turn, triggers the cells to multiply. Gleevec interacts with the abnormal protein and stops it from sending these "bad" signals.

Previous studies showed that Gleevec worked, but there was no direct comparison with existing treatments so doctors would know when to use it.

Patients were telling their doctors that it was a great therapy and that they felt much better, says Alan Kinniburgh, vice president of research at the Leukemia & Lymphoma Society. "What needed to be shown in a head-to-head comparison was if it was medically better."

RESEARCHING THE DRUG

Researchers studied more than 1100 patients—half received Gleevec and half received interferon alpha plus low-dose cytarabine. The study involved 177 hospitals in 16 countries. Participants were followed up for approximately 19 months.

Gleevec appeared to rank higher in 2 basic and important ways. First, people taking the drug lived longer without progressing to the next phase. And more of the people taking Gleevec had fewer CML genetic flaws in their blood cells.

After 18 months, nearly 90% of those taking Gleevec had a vast reduction in the CML genetic flaw compared with approximately 34% in the other group. And almost none of the patients in the Gleevec group had progressed to the acute phase of the disease, which is often quickly fatal. Approximately 25% of the people in the other group had progressed to the acute stage.

Doctors used to tell CML patients they would survive 3 years. With interferon, that estimate increased to approximately 6 years, Kantarjian says.

"With Gleevec, the average survival will go beyond 10 years, and we may be able to get rid of the disease completely in about half the patients," he adds.

info To learn more about chronic myeloid leukemia, try CML Support at *www.cmlsupport.com*. Read more about Gleevec at the US Food and Drug Administration's Web site at *www.fda.gov*.

Organ Transplants Can Also Transfer Disease

Rona MacKie, MD, Professor of Dermatology, University of Glasgow, Scotland.
Daniel Coit, MD, Chief, Gastric and Mixed Tumor Service, Memorial Sloan–Kettering Cancer Center, New York, NY.
Robert Fisher, MD, Professor, Surgery and Director, Liver Transplantation and Transplantation Research, Virginia Commonwealth University Medical Center, Richmond.
February 6, 2003, *New England Journal of Medicine*.

Sixteen years after a Scottish woman was diagnosed with melanoma, the deadly cancer was transferred to 2 more people via the woman's donated kidneys.

That incident and similar ones have resulted in stricter controls in some hospitals for organ transplants.

"It's very worrisome," says Dr. Rona MacKie, lead author of a letter in the *New England Journal of Medicine*. "The amazing thing about this patient is the gap between having the melanoma diagnosed and giving her kidneys."

The time gap was twice as long as any other case, which testifies to the resilience of tumor cells in the bloodstream, MacKie says.

Although other cancers have been transferred with a transplanted organ, melanoma seems to be particularly dangerous.

"There is a significant risk in patients with melanoma, even after 10 or 15 years. It's not the same with other cancers," says Dr. Robert Fisher, director of liver transplantation and transplantation research at Virginia Commonwealth University Medical Center.

People who have had invasive melanoma should not donate organs. In fact, they are already prohibited from donating blood, according to the American Red Cross.

And although the transplant surgeons should have checked the Scottish woman's background, they were unable to reach her primary care physician.

THE TRANSPLANTS

In May 1998, a woman in Glasgow finally received the kidney that would enable her to go off dialysis. She seemed well until a year and a half later, when a routine mammography turned up a spot on the woman's left breast.

A biopsy uncovered something highly unusual: Secondary melanoma, but no primary site. Secondary cancers are those that have spread from another part of the body. MacKie said there was no evidence of a primary melanoma, which is usually attached to a tumor.

Four months later, a second transplant patient arrived at the same hospital with a lump in his kidney that turned out—again—to be secondary melanoma with no indication of a primary site. His transplant and the woman's transplant were done only 24 hours apart.

The donor in both cases turned out to be the same person, a 62-year-old woman who had been treated for melanoma in 1982. After treatment, her doctors considered her cured of the cancer. She died 16 years later, ostensibly of a hemorrhage.

Both kidney recipients had the organs removed and were treated for melanoma, but only 1 survived.

HOW DID IT HAPPEN?

Although how this happened will never be known because an autopsy was not performed on the donor, 2 scenarios emerge as possibilities, says Dr. Daniel Coit, chief of gastric and mixed tumor service at Memorial Sloan–Kettering Cancer Center in New York City.

One scenario is that the donor actually died of undetected metastatic melanoma. The second is that individual melanoma cells were lurking in her body, waiting for the opportunity to flourish.

MacKie prefers the second scenario, and believes the cancer cells were lying dormant in the kidneys. Because transplant patients take immunosuppressant drugs to minimize the chances that the donated organ will be rejected, the weakened immune system may have encouraged the cancer growth.

New Treatment Lengthens Lives of Myeloma Patients

J. Anthony Child, MD, Professor, Clinical Hematology, General Infirmary at Leeds, Yorkshire, United Kingdom.

Stephen D. Nimer, MD, head, Division of Hematologic Oncology, Memorial Sloan–Kettering Cancer Center, New York, NY.

May 8, 2003, *New England Journal of Medicine*.

A British study has helped establish a standard treatment for the deadly blood cell cancer called *multiple myeloma*. It calls for high-dose chemotherapy, using stem cells from the patient's own bone marrow to help the body withstand the damage done by the cancer drugs.

Multiple myeloma causes the uncontrolled overproduction of white blood cells, resulting in pain and the destruction of bones.

Dr. J. Anthony Child, a British hematology specialist and lead author of a report on the trial says the treatment is far from a cure, but it does buy time—an average of almost 1 extra year of life compared with lower-dose chemotherapy.

"A cure for this disease is what everyone is looking for," Child adds. "The next best thing is long-term control with very low-level symptoms. If you can achieve a low level of disease with therapy, it is perhaps a step toward therapy that can keep patients symptom-free in the very long term."

Dr. Stephen D. Nimer, head of the division of hematologic oncology at Memorial Sloan–Kettering Cancer Center in New York, says the study confirms that patients using the initial high-dose therapy do better than those who don't.

Efforts to improve both survival time and quality of life are continuing, Child and Nimer say.

THE STUDY

The trials included 407 patients, divided into low-dose and high-dose groups. Both groups were given a number of cancer drugs, but the drug regimens differed. In addition, the high-dose group were also given stem cells taken from their own bone marrow to fortify the body.

The initial response rate was almost the same for both groups—the progression of the disease slowed or stopped in 40% of the standard-therapy patients and in 42% of those in the high-dose group.

However, the long-term results were significant: The average survival period was 54.1 months for those getting intensive treatment compared with 44.9 months for those getting the lower doses.

The British physicians are beginning a new trial to see whether stem cells from a patient's close relative can give even better results.

Nimer and his colleagues are also trying 2 stem cell transplants instead of 1, and they are trying a drug called *thalidomide* on patients whose disease comes back after a stem cell transplant.

■ ■ ■ ■

Who's Affected by Myeloma?

The American Cancer Society can provide information on multiple myeloma.

- **Approximately 14,600 new cases of multiple myeloma** (7800 in men and 6800 in women) will be diagnosed during 2003.

- **Approximately 10,900 Americans** (5400 men and 5500 women) are expected to die of multiple myeloma in 2003.

Beta-Carotene Warning: Is It Increasing Your Risk of Cancer?

John A. Baron, MD, Professor, Medicine, Dartmouth Medical School, Hanover, NH.

Bernard Levin, MD, Vice President, Cancer Prevention, University of Texas M.D. Anderson Cancer Center, Houston.

May 21, 2003, *Journal of the National Cancer Institute.*

You may have heard that antioxidants can fight cancer. But one of them—beta-carotene—may actually increase the risk of certain cancers in people who smoke or drink.

Researchers at Dartmouth Medical School found that a combination of smoking, drinking, and using beta-carotene supplements is linked to a possible recurrence of colorectal cancer. Previous studies have found the same connection with lung cancer.

The results of the Dartmouth study were surprising to Dr. Bernard Levin, vice president for cancer prevention at the University of Texas's M.D. Anderson Cancer Center.

"The common wisdom has been that antioxidants might be good for you, or at least do no harm," he says. "That some actually cause an accelerating effect is unexpected."

The study "certainly raises the issue of whether beta-carotene supplements are worthwhile," says Dr. John A. Baron, a professor of medicine at Dartmouth and leader of the team that did the research.

But Baron says the results cannot be extended to all cancers. "Each cancer has unique characteristics; all have their own causative factors," he explains.

His study of 864 people found that intestinal polyps, which can become cancerous, doubled for those who smoked, drank, and took a beta-carotene supplement. But the incidence of polyps dwindled in supplement takers without those habits.

After 4 years of taking beta-carotene supplements, nonsmokers and nondrinkers reduced their recurrence of polyps by 44%, the researchers report.

But the recurrence rate for smokers who took beta-carotene increased by 36%; for nonsmoking drinkers who took beta-carotene, the recurrence rate increased by 11%.

WHAT IS BETA-CAROTENE?

Beta-carotene, found naturally in fruits and vegetables such as carrots, mangos, and oranges, is transformed into vitamin A in the body and has been widely promoted as a natural cancer preventative.

The researchers can't say for sure why coupling beta-carotene supplements with smoking and drinking seems to boost the risk for colorectal cancer. One theory is that in some people beta-carotene can change from an antioxidant to a different type of molecule with damaging effects.

Because beta-carotene cuts the risk of colorectal cancer in nonsmokers and nondrinkers, such supplements may still have a role in cancer prevention, Levin says, but they should not be high on the list.

STRIDES TOWARD PREVENTION

A better—and more obvious—first step in reducing colorectal cancer risk is not to smoke, Levin says. Physical activity also seems to help. For people at high risk for the cancer, aspirin therapy can help, he says.

A low-fat diet that's high in fiber and low in red meat seems to be a good idea, Levin adds. And there's some evidence that multivitamin supplements might be helpful. "The emphasis should be on a varied diet," he says.

info You can learn about colorectal cancer and measures to prevent it from the National Institutes of Health Web site at *www.nih.gov*.

New Technique Zaps Away Kidney Tumors!

Debra Gervais, MD, Director, Interventional Radiology, Massachusetts General Hospital, and Assistant Professor, Radiology, Harvard Medical School, both in Boston, MA.
Bradford Wood, MD, Interventional Radiologist, Diagnostic Radiology Department, Clinical Center, National Institutes of Health, Bethesda, MD.
February 2003, *Radiology*.

Kidney tumors just got a little easier to cure. A treatment called *radiofrequency ablation* zaps kidney cancers with electrical currents, causing the tumors to disintegrate without the need for surgery.

"It's very promising for small tumors and tumors growing outside of the kidney," says Dr. Debra Gervais, director of interventional radiology at Massachusetts General Hospital in Boston. It's more of a problem if the tumors are large or close to a vital structure or organ, she adds.

Gervais and her colleagues tried the technique on small tumors whose cancer hadn't spread to other organs. The researchers were able to eliminate the vast majority of the tumors completely, including all the tumors on the surface of the kidney.

Larger tumors (larger than 1 inch) deep inside the kidney were more difficult to treat. The researchers were able to eliminate approximately half of them.

THE ROAD TO A CURE

After more than 3 years, no one in the study had a recurrence of kidney cancer.

"It's a very promising application of this technology," says Dr. Bradford Wood, an interventional radiologist at the National Institutes of Health who was involved in some of the earliest studies on radiofrequency ablation and cancer.

The American Cancer Society estimates that there will be approximately 31,900 new cases of kidney cancer in the United States in 2003. Using the current standard treatment of surgical removal of the kidney, the 5-year survival rate is near 60%.

In radiofrequency ablation, first a needle is inserted into the tumor. Then an electrical current from the needle burns the cancer tumor, turning it into a mass of dead scar tissue, says Gervais, lead author of the study and an assistant professor of radiology at Harvard Medical School.

NOT FOR EVERYONE

Radiofrequency ablation cannot be used to treat all cancers, Gervais says. Doctors have to be very careful not to damage surrounding organs or tissues. For now, Gervais limits radiofrequency ablation to patients who aren't good candidates for surgery either because of kidney disease or because they have only 1 functioning kidney.

The technique is also used on some liver cancers, lung cancer, and to treat a type of heart arrhythmia.

One newer use of the technique is to relieve pain in people in the terminal stage of cancer, Wood says. Cancerous tumors, as they grow, can push on other structures in the body, causing pain. In some of these cases, physicians can use radiofrequency ablation to reduce the size of the tumor, thereby easing the discomfort.

The $450 Medical Test That's Not Worth The Price!

Parthiv J. Mahadevia, MD, MPH, Research Scientist, MEDTAP International, Bethesda, MD.

Victor Grann, MD, PhD, Clinical Professor, Medicine, Columbia University, New York, NY.

January 15, 2003, *Journal of the American Medical Association.*

Although *computed axial tomography* (CAT) scans are useful in some medical diagnoses, they are apparently not helpful in screening for lung cancer.

A CAT scan allows doctors to see a 3-dimensional view of the inside of your body. The scans—which cost as much as $450 each—can detect tumors smaller than 1 centimeter, and doctors routinely use them on patients who show other symptoms of lung cancer.

If you're not suffering from any symptoms of lung cancer, however, researchers say you should save your money. The cost apparently doesn't justify the findings, and errors could lead to unnecessary surgeries, says Dr. Parthiv J. Mahadevia, a research scientist who studied the potential use of the technology.

THE NUMBERS

Mahadevia and his colleagues designed a computer model to estimate how many lives would be saved if smokers and former smokers got annual CAT scans. Of 100,000 smokers in the hypothetical scenario, the scans would have saved an estimated 553 lives. But an estimated 1100 people would undergo unnecessary biopsies and other types of surgery that pose risks of their own. And the number of people who would develop complications from the procedures is greater than the number of lives saved by early detection, researchers say.

However, Dr. Victor Grann, a clinical professor of medicine at Columbia University says that it may be cost-effective to give the CAT scans to smokers who seem healthy if their level of worry about cancer is so high that it affects their quality of life.

info You can find out more about CAT scans from a patient-friendly publication (*CT Scan: A Guide for Patients*) produced by the department of radiology at Brigham and Women's Hospital in Boston. It is available online, at the hospital's Web site *www.brighamrad.harvard.edu/patient.html.*

6

Diabetes Update

No Insulin Needed?
New Hope for
Type 1 Diabetics

illions of people around the world suffer from diabetes, a condition in which the body's ability to produce the hormone insulin is compromised. Insulin controls blood sugar levels.

If blood sugar levels aren't kept in check, complications can include blindness, heart and blood vessel disease, stroke, kidney failure, amputations, and nerve damage.

Currently, people with diabetes can only manage their disease through diet and insulin. There is no cure. Type 1 diabetics produce no insulin at all, and must give themselves daily insulin shots. Restoring the body's ability to make insulin has long been a goal of many researchers.

Because pancreatic islet cells are involved in insulin production, the transplantation of these cells has become the focus of recent research that is working toward restoring the body's ability to make insulin.

In pancreatic islet transplantation, cells are taken from a donor pancreas and transferred into another person. Once implanted, the new islets begin to make and release insulin.

"There's tremendous progress being made right now with islet cell transplants that has resulted in several centers in the US beginning programs to duplicate that work," says Dr. George Loss, director of the Pancreas Transplant Program at the Ochsner Clinic Foundation in New Orleans.

Transplantation of an entire pancreas has had some success, but there are several

George Loss, MD, PhD, Director, Pancreas Transplant Program, Ochsner Clinic Foundation, New Orleans, LA.

Camillo Ricordi, MD, Professor, Medicine, Scientific Director, Diabetes Research Institute, University of Miami School of Medicine, FL.

August 2002, International Congress of the Transplantation Society, Miami, FL.

problems, not the least of which is the severe shortage of donors.

EXPANDING THE REACH OF TRANSPLANTS

Dr. Camillo Ricordi, scientific director of the Diabetes Research Institute at the University of Miami School of Medicine, and his team are using an organ preservative to enable the shipment of islet cells to distant health centers. Nine patients who received islet cell transplantations at remote sites were able to stop taking insulin for varying periods of time.

"This proves the concept that you could process islets in centralized facilities, and distribute them regionally and even across the ocean," Ricordi explains.

Various other routes to expand the available yield of islet cells are also being studied.

Stem cells—"generic" cells that can grow into specialized cells—are a huge focus of research. Scientists hope they will one day be able to coax stem cells into becoming insulin-producing cells. They have already had some success in doing this in animals.

FIGHTING REJECTION IS CRITICAL

There have also been advances in the ways to counter the rejection of transplanted cells. "A major innovation has been the development of much more effective immune-suppressive drugs," Ricordi says.

Recipients generally have to take immuno-suppression drugs for the rest of their lives to prevent their bodies from rejecting the transplants.

"You cannot really talk about a cure until you perform cellular therapies that eliminate the need for antirejection drugs for life," Ricordi says.

info To learn more about islet cell transplantation, visit the American Diabetes Association on the Web at *www.diabetes.org.*

Scientists Make Cells That Produce Insulin!

Marko Horb, PhD, Postdoctoral Research Officer, Centre for Regenerative Medicine, Department of Biology and Biochemistry, University of Bath, England.

Robert Fisher, MD, Surgical Director, Liver Transplant Program, Virginia Commonwealth University Medical Center, Richmond.

January 21, 2003, *Current Biology.*

British scientists have changed liver cells into pancreatic cells, a feat that holds enormous promise for the 150 million people worldwide who have diabetes.

"This is very important work," says Dr. Robert Fisher, surgical director of the Liver Transplant Program at Virginia Commonwealth University Medical Center in Richmond.

The pancreas, which produces the hormone insulin, holds the key to curing diabetes. In healthy people, insulin is released into the bloodstream after eating in order to control glucose (blood sugar).

People with Type 1 diabetes produce little or no insulin at all and must give themselves shots to balance their sugar load. People with Type 2 diabetes, by far the more prevalent form of the disease, can often keep their condition under control with diet and exercise. In some cases, they need medication and insulin, as well.

Scientists have been trying for years to find a way to boost the functioning of the pancreas, including transplantation of the islet cells that produce insulin.

The British scientists used an approach called *transdifferentiation,* which involves converting one type of cell to another.

GENES AREN'T ENOUGH

"Other people have tried to convert cells with gene therapy, but a lot of times one single protein isn't enough. You need a combination of different factors," explains Marko Horb, lead author of the study and a postdoctoral research officer at the Centre for Regenerative Medicine at the University of Bath in England.

The researchers basically engineered a souped-up version of a certain gene that is necessary for fashioning a pancreas out of stem cells.

The idea was to introduce this super-gene into liver cells to see if they would produce pancreatic cells.

The theory worked in 2 tests, 1 using human cells and the other using tadpoles of the African clawed frog. The cells took on aspects of pancreas cells and some even made insulin.

"They really need to take a mature animal and show that they can get the cells to change," Fisher says.

Jonathan Slack, who led the research team, believes that, if future research goes well, the method could start helping diabetics within the next decade.

info For more information about the treatment of diabetes, visit the National Institute of Diabetes & Digestive & Kidney Diseases at *www.niddk.nih.gov.*

Ladies, Drinking Wine May Prevent Type 2 Diabetes

Goya Wannamethee, PhD, Research Fellow, Epidemiology, Royal Free and University College Medical School, London, England.

June 9, 2003, *Archives of Internal Medicine.*

Women who drink a glass or 2 of wine or beer a day could significantly reduce their risk for Type 2 diabetes, a Harvard study claims.

In a study of the effects of various types and amounts of alcohol, researchers found that light wine and beer drinking seems to have a protective effect on a woman's risk for Type 2 diabetes. Drinking hard liquor was not as beneficial; in fact, more than 2 drinks of hard liquor a day more than doubled their risk for the disease.

For the study, researchers used data from the Nurses' Health Study II, a national study started in 1989 to look at risk factors for major chronic diseases in women. Data from detailed health questionnaires about weight, diet, smoking, physical activity, family history, and alcohol consumption was collected from 101,690 healthy women, aged 25 to 42 years. The questionnaires were analyzed and compared with similar data a decade later.

Over the period of the study, 935 of the women were diagnosed with Type 2 diabetes, a number that reflects the low incidence of the disease in younger women, says study co-author Goya Wannamethee.

LIGHT DRINKERS HAVE LOWER RISK

After adjusting for other health factors, such as smoking and physical activity, researchers found that women who were light to moderate drinkers—classified as consuming 1 or 2 drinks daily—had a lower risk of developing diabetes compared with women who didn't drink. Of interest was that the risk-reduction benefits of wine and beer drinking were higher than that of hard liquor.

In real numbers, the women who drank between 1 and 2 glasses of wine daily had a 40% reduction in their risk of developing Type 2 diabetes, compared with those who drank no wine. Those who drank an equivalent amount of beer had a 30% reduction in risk. Drinking an equivalent amount of hard liquor did not bring a similar benefit—only a 20% reduction of risk.

But Wannamethee says there were differences in lifestyle characteristics that the researchers weren't able to adjust for in their analysis. Wine drinkers reported a healthier lifestyle—they were thinner, nonsmokers, more physically active, and better educated than those who drank beer or hard liquor, she says.

"There are better preventive measures to lower the risk for Type 2 diabetes, like not smoking and increasing physical activity—obesity is the overwhelming risk factor for the disease. But it appears that light to moderate drinking of wine or beer has a protective effect," says Wannamethee.

info For more facts on women and diabetes, you can visit the Centers for Disease Control and Prevention at *www.cdc.gov/dia betes/pubs/women.*

■ ■ ■ ■

Alcohol Still Should Be 'Handled With Care'

Many medical experts still raise the warning flags when it comes to alcohol consumption, despite recent positive research findings. According to the National Institutes of Health MedlinePLUS, alcohol is considered a *macronutrient* in that it provides energy. But the calories obtained from alcohol (about 7 per gram) are considered to be "empty" because alcohol contains no vitamins or minerals.

One-half ounce of pure alcohol, the amount in a 1-ounce shot (2 tablespoons) of liquor, contains approximately 80 to 90 calories. Carbonated beverages and fruit juices add calories when they are mixed with alcohol in various cocktails.

"Proof" is the alcohol content of distilled liquors. It is the percentage of alcohol (by volume) multiplied by 2. *For example...*

- **100-proof alcohol** = 50% alcohol.
- **200-proof alcohol** = 100% alcohol.

The alcohol content of wine is given as a percentage. White wines average 12%, and red wines are approximately 14%.

The alcohol content of beer is between 3% and 8%. "Light" beers have fewer calories and are closer to 3% alcohol content. Liqueurs, such as sherry and dessert liqueurs, contain 40% to 50% alcohol and tend to be higher in calories.

In terms of alcohol content, a 12-oz beer, a 5-oz glass of wine, and 1½ oz of liquor are all equivalent.

SOME DANGEROUS SIDE EFFECTS OF OVERCONSUMPTION

- **Alcohol is a leading cause of traffic accidents** in the United States because it slows reaction times and impairs judgment.

- **Continued excessive alcohol use can damage the liver** in various ways, including the development of a fatty liver. A fatty liver can progress to *cirrhosis* of the liver, a potentially fatal condition.

- **Alcohol is a risk factor for the development of cancer of the esophagus,** throat, larynx, and mouth.

- **The presence of alcohol impairs the absorption of essential nutrients** because it can damage the lining of the small intestine and stomach. Alcohol also requires some vitamins in its metabolism, and it interferes with the absorption and storage of certain vitamins.

- **Alcohol can impair sexual function,** although it may increase interest in sexual activity.

- **Alcohol intake during pregnancy has been identified as the cause of fetal alcohol syndrome.**

If It Isn't Diabetes, It Could Be Insulin Resistance Syndrome

Gerald Reaven, MD, Professor Emeritus, Stanford University School of Medicine, Palo Alto, CA.

Daniel Einhorn, MD, Medical Director, Scripps/Whittier Diabetes Institute, and Associate Clinical Professor of Medicine, University of California at San Diego School of Medicine.

Omega Silva, MD, Past President, American Medical Women's Association, Alexandria, VA.

Did you know that there's a good chance you have *insulin resistance syndrome?* Experts suspect that as many as 1 in 3 Americans has it.

Your doctor may suspect you have the condition if you have abnormalities in your glucose and lipid (blood fats) metabolism, are obese, and have high blood pressure. Because insulin resistance seems to be a factor that connects those symptoms, that cluster of problems has come to be known as insulin resistance syndrome.

But the good news, they say, is that staying fit and shedding excess pounds can greatly reduce the chances that insulin resistance will lead to illness.

Even modest reductions in body weight—5% to 10%—and regular physical activity can sharply improve the outlook for people with abnormal insulin sensitivity, says Dr. Gerald Reaven, a Stanford University diabetes expert, who is acknowledged as the father of insulin resistance syndrome, which he had initially dubbed *Syndrome X.*

The prevalence of the syndrome in this country increased 61% in a decade, thanks to an equally stunning rise in obesity.

However, roughly 20% of people with the condition aren't overweight at all, Reaven says. So doctors who only look for the problem in their heavier patients may be missing a lot of cases. Identifying people with insulin resistance is especially important because it is a risk factor for heart disease.

THE SIGNS

High levels of blood fats called *triglycerides,* and low concentrations of high-density lipoprotein (HDL), the so-called "good" cholesterol are possible indications of syndrome X. (Many people with insulin resistance syndrome may have normal levels of LDL, the "bad" form of cholesterol.) A family history of diabetes and heart disease may also indicate a predisposition for syndrome X.

"If you are a person at risk, you should know your cholesterol values. If you have one or more of these abnormalities, you most likely have insulin resistance syndrome," says Dr. Daniel Einhorn, medical director of the Scripps/Whittier Diabetes Institute in La Jolla, California.

Doctors should also be alert to the condition in patients older than 40 years, as well as those whose body fat is distributed chiefly around their abdomen. Women with a history of diabetes during pregnancy (*gestational diabetes*) or a disorder called *polycystic ovary syndrome* have a high risk of insulin insensitivity, too.

Dr. Omega Silva, past president of the American Medical Women's Association, called insulin resistance a "public health epidemic that needs to be prevented rather than treated."

info For more on insulin resistance syndrome, look at the Web site for the American Association of Clinical Endocrinologists, *www. aace.com.*

Diabetes Risk May Be Connected To Your Thighbone

Keiko Asao, MD, MPH, researcher, Johns Hopkins University, Baltimore, MD.

Russell Luepker, MD, MS, Cardiologist, head, Epidemiology, School of Public Health, University of Minnesota, Minneapolis.

March 7, 2003, presentation, American Heart Association Annual Conference, Miami, FL.

Tall women may have a leg up when it comes to risk for diabetes, say researchers at Johns Hopkins University. Researchers there say the longer your thigh, the lower your risk may be for developing diabetes.

"I don't want to make people with short legs worry too much," says Dr. Keiko Asao, a Hopkins researcher and lead author of the study. However, factors affecting early growth (such as the length of your thigh) may contribute to the development of a blood sugar problem later in life, she says. Of course, leg length is just one clue and does not predict with any certainty that someone with shorter legs will develop diabetes, she adds.

Measuring from the groin to the kneecap, the average upper-leg length in Asao's study was 40.2 centimeters (15.8 inches) for those with normal glucose tolerance. For each centimeter less of upper-leg length, white women were 19% more likely to have diabetes and Hispanic women were 13% more likely to have diabetes. Glucose is the form of sugar in the blood, and is the main source of fuel for the body.

Although Asao and her colleagues studied both men and women, after adjusting for other risk factors, the inverse association remained significant only for white and Hispanic women.

EARLIER STUDIES

This study is not the first to look at leg length and disease risk. At least 2 British studies have also found a link between shorter total leg length and glucose problems. However, the Asao study is thought to be the first to focus on upper leg length. "Our study confirms their findings," Asao says.

Dr. Russell Luepker, a cardiologist and head of epidemiology at the University of Minnesota School of Public Health, says, "There is a body of literature that says tall people do better" in terms of certain disease risk.

Of the Asao study, he says, "I think it's interesting." These days, with increasing numbers of Americans being diagnosed with diabetes, "any insight into what may be underlying it may be helpful," he says.

On the other hand, Luepker adds, "Height is in no small part genetically controlled. I wouldn't lie awake nights worrying about this."

If you have impaired glucose tolerance, you can take steps to reduce the risk of getting Type 2 diabetes. The American Diabetes Association suggests talking with your doctor about changing your diet, getting more exercise, and losing weight if necessary.

info For information on how diabetes can affect your risk of stroke and heart attack, visit The Heart of Diabetes Web site at *www.s2mw.com/heartofdiabetes.*

High Blood Sugar Shrinks Your Brain

Francine R. Kaufman, MD, President, American Diabetes Association, and head, Division of Endocrinology, Children's Hospital, Los Angeles, CA.
Antonio Convit, MD, Associate Professor, Psychiatry, New York University School of Medicine.
February 3, 2003, *Proceedings of the National Academy of Sciences.*

When your blood sugar levels rise to abnormal levels, you're not just courting diabetes, researchers say. Your memory may suffer and your brain may actually shrink.

The study gives sedentary, fast food–loving Americans yet another reason to get off the couch and eat more healthfully, says lead author Dr. Antonio Convit, medical director for the Center for Brain Health at New York University School of Medicine. Those who exercise regularly and eat well generally have healthier blood sugar levels.

In the study, Convit and his colleagues evaluated 30 adults between the ages of 53 and 89 years. None of them were diabetic, but some had a condition called *impaired glucose tolerance,* or *prediabetes,* in which blood sugar levels are higher than normal.

The participants all received glucose intravenously and the researchers measured how quickly the sugar moved to tissue, an indication of glucose tolerance. Then they tested the participants' ability to recall short paragraphs and implemented other tests that involved thinking. The researchers also performed brain scans with magnetic resonance imaging (MRI).

Those with the lowest scores on the mental tests had the poorest glucose tolerance. They also had a smaller *hippocampus,* a key area in the brain for learning and recent memory.

Researchers suggest that the inability of the hippocampus to absorb enough glucose for fuel may eventually damage it and cause the hippocampus to fail. Convit says that people with diabetes typically have more memory problems than others. For years, "we have had hints about people with impaired glucose tolerance also having memory problems." His study shows that people who are not diabetic, but who just have mild glucose intolerance, may also have memory problems.

Dr. Francine Kaufman, the president of the American Diabetes Association, calls the new research "obviously intriguing," and agrees with Convit that the findings emphasize the importance of healthful eating and regular exercise.

■ ■ ■ ■

Risk Factors for Diabetes

Approximately 16 million Americans between the ages of 40 and 74 years have prediabetes, according to the National Institute of Diabetes and Digestive and Kidney Diseases.

Adults older than 45 years should ask their primary physicians about getting evaluated for glucose tolerance. Those younger than 45 years should also ask about a glucose evaluation if they are at high risk for developing diabetes. *High-risk factors include...*

- **Having given birth to a baby who weighed more than 9 pounds at birth.**
- **Obesity.**
- **High blood pressure.**
- **High blood cholesterol or triglycerides.**
- **Having blood relatives with diabetes.**

"Don't depend on mall screenings for diabetes," Kaufman warns. "They are often inaccurate." Ask your doctor for the best glucose test for you, she suggests.

What Did Your Grandpa Eat? Uncanny Risk Factor For Diabetes

Gunnar Kaati, MD, Associate Professor, Social Medicine, Umeå University, Umeå, Sweden.

Marcus Pembrey, MD, Geneticist, University College London, England.

What was on your grandfather's dinner table when he was a child may actually have something to do with whether you're a candidate for diabetes.

People from Sweden whose paternal grandfathers enjoyed a surplus of food in their early childhood had higher death rates from diabetes, according to research at Umeå University in Umeå, Sweden.

One conclusion from the study is that a surplus of food leads to overeating, which could cause changes in the genes carried by sperm. The altered genes are then passed from generation to generation.

Proving this theory is likely to be very difficult, however, because there are so many variables to consider. But the results could have important implications for the prevention of diabetes.

Previous research had indicated that food scarcity before puberty for a young boy corresponded to longer lives for his grandchildren. An abundance of food had the opposite effect.

The study suggests that some kind of imprint mechanism on the genes is involved.

"Nutrition affects ovaries and testes from the moment they form during fetal life through maturity," says Dr. Marcus Pembrey, of University College London.

THE STUDY

Survival statistics for groups of people born in 1890, 1905, and 1920 in an isolated community in northern Sweden were correlated with historical information on annual harvests, food prices, and other factors.

The grandchildren of men who had plenty of food during the slow-growth period of their childhoods were 4 times more likely to die of diabetes, says Dr. Gunnar Kaati, lead author of the study and an associate professor of social medicine at Umeå University.

When the paternal grandfather lived through a famine during this same prepubescent period, the grandchildren were less likely to die of diabetes, a disease often caused by being overweight.

■ ■ ■ ■

Diabetes Symptoms

The American Diabetes Association reports that diabetes often goes undiagnosed because many of its symptoms seem harmless. Early detection and treatment of diabetes can decrease the chances of developing complications from the disease. *Some symptoms of diabetes include...*

- **Frequent urination.**
- **Excessive thirst.**
- **Extreme hunger.**
- **Unusual weight loss.**
- **Increased fatigue.**
- **Irritability.**
- **Blurry vision.**

info If you have one or more of these symptoms, see your doctor right away. You can also take the American Diabetes Association's online quiz at *www.diabetes.org* to find out if you are at risk for diabetes.

Delicious News for Diabetics: Control Your Symptoms With Food

Simon R. Heller, MD, Clinical Sciences Centre, Northern General Hospital, Sheffield, England.

Francine R. Kaufman, MD, President, American Diabetes Association, and head, Division of Endocrinology, Children's Hospital, Los Angeles, CA.

October 5, 2002, *British Medical Journal.*

With some basic training in math and carbohydrate counting, people with Type 1 diabetes can follow a more flexible eating plan without losing control of their glucose levels or their quality of life. That's the conclusion of a study appearing in the *British Medical Journal* that tested the Dose Adjustment for Normal Eating program among patients in the United Kingdom.

"We know that insulin and food have to be matched, and once you do that you allow the patient to be in the driver's seat in figuring out what they want to eat and then how much insulin they need to cover it," says Dr. Francine Kaufman, president of the American Diabetes Association.

Approximately 1.5 million people in the United States suffer from Type 1 diabetes, which occurs when insulin-producing cells in the pancreas stop working. These people must inject insulin to survive. Without adequate amounts of insulin, blood glucose levels can soar. Over the long term, diabetes can lead to blindness, kidney failure, and amputation.

The Dose Adjustment for Normal Eating course taught patients how to adjust their insulin to match their food intake, rather than the other way around—the traditional treatment for Type 1 diabetes.

"The essential elements are carbohydrate counting and the skills to adjust your insulin to achieve a near-normal glucose level," says Dr. Simon Heller, co-lead author of the study.

WORTH THE EFFORT

After 6 months in the study, the people who had participated in the dose adjustment program had improved glucose control and quality of life, the researchers found.

To eat more flexibly, most patients had to inject insulin and monitor their blood glucose levels more often, procedures that can be cumbersome. But despite more shots per day and more monitoring, they had a very positive feeling about their diabetes and felt much more in control. "We were very surprised. That was the thing that blew us away," Heller says. "People felt much, much better about having diabetes and more like other people."

Although the short-term results are heartening, it remains to be seen what the long-term outcome will be, Heller says. However, researchers in Düsseldorf, Germany, found that the results were sustained over a period of 3 years, which, Heller says, "is quite remarkable."

info To find out more about carbohydrate counting and how it can help you manage your blood sugar, visit the Joslin Diabetes Center's Web site at *www.joslin.harvard.edu.*

■ ■ ■ ■

How to Count Carbs at Breakfast

The Joslin Diabetes Center has developed a method for counting carbohydrates that allows people with Type 1 diabetes to plan their meals.

The key is to choose whatever foods you want as long as the total carbohydrates are no more than 45 grams. *Here's an example in selecting breakfast...*

Food	Amount	Carbohydrate Grams
1% fat milk	1 cup	12
Bran Chex	⅔ cup	23
Frosted Flakes	¾ cup	26
Raisin Bran	¾ cup	28

Food	Amount	Carbohydrate Grams
Bread/toast	1 slice	15
Sugar, white table	1 teaspoon	4
Pancakes—4"	2	15
Low-fat granola	½ cup	30
Yogurt, fruited	1 cup	40
Yogurt, fruit with NutraSweet fruit juice	1 cup	19
Fruit juice	½ cup	15
Banana	½	15
Pancake syrup	2 tablespoons	30
Light pancake sugar free syrup	2 tablespoons	4

SAMPLE BREAKFAST

Food	Carbohydrate Grams
Fruit yogurt (with NutraSweet)	19
Cinnamon-sugar toast—1 slice with 1 teaspoon sugar and 1 teaspoon margarine	19
Milk, ½ cup	6
Carbohydrate total—44	

Diabetic? Here's How to Tell If You're at Risk for Heart Disease

Trevor J. Orchard, MD, Professor and Acting Chairman, Epidemiology, University of Pittsburgh Graduate School of Public Health, PA.

Nathaniel G. Clark, MD, RD, National Vice President, Clinical Affairs, American Diabetes Association, Alexandria, VA.

May 2003, *Diabetes Care*.

Some people with Type 1 diabetes may have a lower risk for heart disease than previously thought, according to a group of Pittsburgh researchers.

Their study found that traditional blood sugar control might have little influence over the development of heart disease in Type 1 diabetics. Instead, insulin resistance—the hallmark of Type 2 diabetes—is a better indicator of who's going to get heart disease among Type 1 diabetics.

"We suspect that insulin resistance occurs in those with Type 1 diabetes in the same way as it does in those with Type 2, essentially giving these individuals 'double diabetes' and greatly increasing their risk of heart disease," says Dr. Trevor J. Orchard, a professor in the department of epidemiology at the University of Pittsburgh Graduate School of Public Health.

It might mean that those Type 1 diabetics without insulin resistance are at a lower risk of heart disease than once believed, Orchard says.

And although those with insulin resistance may be at higher risk, medications and lifestyle changes can boost the body's ability to use insulin.

BREAKING FROM TRADITION

When trying to help diabetics control their risk of heart disease, doctors tend to focus on 3 factors—blood sugar level, blood pressure, and cholesterol. But it's unknown which is the most significant factor, or whether one matters more in one type of diabetes than the other, says Dr. Nathaniel G. Clark, national vice president of clinical affairs for the American Diabetes Association.

Orchard's study begins to get at that, he says. "I think the most important finding is that these researchers looked at the traditional risk factors, and what they found was that blood sugar wasn't terribly helpful in predicting who gets heart disease," Clark says. "There were other factors that were much more important." Namely, insulin resistance.

Orchard and his colleagues examined 658 Type 1 diabetics over a 10-year period and found that those with the highest levels of insulin resistance were the most likely to have a cardiovascular event. This information is important because if patients know they are likely to develop heart disease, they can take precautions to prevent it.

■ ■ ■ ■

An Overview of Diabetes

There are 2 types of diabetes—Type 1 and Type 2. In many ways they are very different, Orchard says.

Type 1, most often thought of as a disease that strikes in childhood, occurs when the body attacks and destroys its own insulin-producing beta cells.

Type 1, the less common form of the illness, accounts for 5% to 10% of the 17 million people in the United States with diabetes, according to the American Diabetes Association. Type 1 diabetics need daily insulin injections to survive.

In Type 2 diabetes, the pancreas is usually still producing insulin, but the cells of the liver, muscles, and fatty tissues develop a resistance to it. Type 2 can often be controlled with weight loss, diet, and exercise.

Niacin Lowers Heart Attack Risk in Diabetics

Michael Davidson, MD, Director, Preventive Cardiology, Rush Medical College, Chicago, IL.

November 20, 2002, presentation, American Heart Association Meeting, Chicago, IL.

October 24, 2002, *New England Journal of Medicine.*

Niacin supplements can cut the chance of a second heart attack in half in people who have diabetes or milder blood sugar problems, according to a Baltimore study. Although the B-3 vitamin complex called niacin nudges blood sugar higher, researchers say it more than overcomes that effect by suppressing dangerous blood fats that promote heart attacks.

The study also found that diabetics—who are at a sharply increased risk of cardiovascular diseases—seem to derive more heart protection from niacin than people without the disease. Dr. Michael Davidson, director of preventive cardiology at Rush Medical College in Chicago, said the findings indicate that the benefits outweigh the risks of the increased glucose levels.

Niacin's method of lowering heart attack risk is similar to that of other drugs, including aspirin, statins, other treatments that cut cholesterol, and beta-blockers, experts said.

THE STUDY

Led by Paul Canner of the Maryland Medical Research Institute in Baltimore, the study was funded by Kos Pharmaceuticals, which makes a slow-release prescription version of niacin called Niaspan. The study used an immediate-release form of niacin, which is also found in fortified cereals, as well as in grains, meats, and nuts.

Canner and his colleagues found that niacin reduced the risk of a second, nonfatal heart attack by 28% in people without diabetes, and by 54% in those with the disease. The trends for overall mortality were similar.

Cardiovascular disease is the leading killer of diabetics, who face 2 to 4 times the normal risk of heart attacks as a result of their condition.

■ ■ ■ ■

Sources of Niacin

Elson M. Haas, MD, author of *Staying Healthy with Nutrition: The Complete Guide to Diet and Nutritional Medicine* provides information about niacin. *Following are some important facts…*

• **Only small to moderate amounts of vitamin B-3 occur in foods as pure niacin;** other forms of niacin are converted from the amino acid *tryptophan.*

• **The best sources of vitamin B-3 are liver and other organ meats,** poultry, fish and peanuts, all of which have both niacin and tryptophan.

• **Yeast,** dried beans and peas, wheat germ, whole grains, avocados, dates, figs, and prunes are fairly good sources of niacin.

• **Milk and eggs are good** because of their levels of tryptophan.

Niacin isn't without side effects. The most common is flushing and itching in the face and neck, which can be severe in some people.

Super Infection Fighter for Diabetics

Thomas Barringer, MD, Director, Research in Family Medicine, Carolinas Medical Center, Charlotte, NC.

Wafaie Fawzi, MBBS, DrPH, Associate Professor, International Nutrition and Epidemiology, Harvard School of Public Health, Boston, MA.

March 4, 2003, *Annals of Internal Medicine.*

Can multivitamins really reduce your chances of getting an infection? Probably not, if you're healthy. But if you have Type 2 diabetes, that's another story, says a North Carolina researcher.

For his study, Dr. Thomas Barringer, director of research in the family medicine department at Carolinas Medical Center in Charlotte, North Carolina, set out to determine whether people who take vitamin and mineral supplements have fewer infections and feel healthier than people who don't take supplements. Approximately 40% of US adults take a vitamin supplement regularly, he says, yet previous research has found little evidence to show that it helps prevent illness.

What they found was that the rate of respiratory and gastrointestinal infection for healthy people who took a multivitamin was similar to the rate of infection for those who did not. But among the 51 people in the study who had Type 2 diabetes, only 17% in the multivitamin group came down with an illness during the yearlong study, while a whopping 94% of those taking only a placebo got sick.

People with Type 2 diabetes are at risk for vitamin and mineral deficiency and are at higher risk for certain types of infection, Barringer says.

But there was no benefit to taking supplements in the nondiabetic group, he adds.

IF YOU DON'T HAVE DIABETES, SHOULD YOU THROW AWAY YOUR VITAMINS?

Wafaie Fawzi, an associate professor of international nutrition and epidemiology at the Harvard School of Public Health, says it's too soon to give up on multivitamins. They're relatively inexpensive and there's little risk to taking them, says Fawzi, who wrote a commentary about the study.

"The study provides preliminary evidence that micronutrients may be important for reducing the risk of infections among adults in the US, especially those at higher risk, such as people with diabetes," he says. "The evidence is not conclusive in that regard and further trials are warranted."

Although the reduction in infections among people with diabetes sounds dramatic, it's possible not all diabetics would need a multivitamin, Barringer says.

The diabetics in the study were from a lower socioeconomic group than the nondiabetics, he says. People who have less education and are poorer are more likely to have nutritional deficiencies.

Barringer said he had wanted to conduct his vitamin test on people aged 65 years and older because the elderly can also be prone to minor nutritional deficiencies. But he couldn't find enough people willing to take part in the study.

"They were all taking multivitamins already, and nobody was willing to stop taking them for a year," Barringer says.

Amazing Advances in Diabetic Monitors

Francine R. Kaufman, MD, President, American Diabetes Association, and head, Division of Endocrinology, Children's Hospital, Los Angeles, CA,

Gerald Bernstein, MD, Past President, American Diabetes Association, and Endocrinologist, New York, NY.

Advancements in glucose monitoring devices have simplified the process of keeping blood sugar levels under control, even for children.

Approximately 1.5 million people in the United States suffering from Type 1 diabetes must inject insulin to keep their blood glucose levels under control. Poorly controlled glucose levels raise the risk of long-term complications, such as blindness, kidney problems, and amputation.

The traditional monitoring devices all operate on the same premise: You obtain a drop of blood, place it on the test strip, and let the monitor read the results.

Dr. Gerald Bernstein, a New York City endocrinologist and past president of the American Diabetes Association, says one of the new devices allows the patient to use a very small amount of blood—a "micro" drop is often enough. And with some monitors, the results come up in 5 seconds.

Many adults and children with diabetes test their blood sugar levels several times a day, and the quicker results add up, Bernstein says. "Seven or eight years ago, you needed a big drop of blood and 45 to 60 seconds [to get a reading]," Bernstein says.

Some monitors take blood from the forearm, such as the LifeScan OneTouch UltraSystem. This device is promoted by blues legend B.B. King, who must save his fingertips for picking his guitar. This system gives results in 5 seconds.

Another development is the GlucoWatch, a wristwatch-like glucose monitoring device. The watch extracts fluid through the skin and then measures the glucose in the fluid, according to the US Food and Drug Administration. Once the device has been warmed up and calibrated via a finger-stick blood test, it can provide up to 6 painless measurements every hour for 13 hours.

WHAT'S NEXT IN GLUCOSE MONITORING?

"The next biggest advance is continuous glucose monitoring," says Dr. Francine Kaufman, president of the American Diabetes Association and head of the Division of Endocrinology at Children's Hospital in Los Angeles.

She says it would be a significant advance if diabetics had some way to know what their blood sugar levels are at all times, and to be alerted to an impending change. Intermittent testing does not provide the complete picture, particularly at night, when blood sugar levels can drop.

There is a monitoring system for doctors called the Medtronic MiniMed Continuous Glucose Monitoring System that collects electrical signals from a glucose sensor every 5 minutes, converts the signals to glucose values, and stores them, providing up to 864 readings in 3 days. A consumer version of the device is in the works. It will allow patients to set a high or low threshold for blood glucose, so that an alarm will sound when the threshold is crossed.

7

Drug News

The Antibiotic Trap: Why They're Making Us Sicker

here are 2 troubling trends in the use of antibiotics—doctors are still handing out too many prescriptions for them, and prescribing patterns vary greatly throughout the country, researchers say.

A study shows that doctors are writing prescriptions for antibiotics to treat colds and other viral conditions for which the drugs are useless. And doctors in the Northeast and South are more likely than those in the West to be prescribing the newer, more potent "broad-spectrum" versions.

Broad-spectrum antibiotics, such as Cipro, are popular because they kill a wide variety of bacteria, compared with older "narrow-spectrum" drugs, such as early versions of penicillin. The broad-spectrum medicines are also preferred because they are new and, therefore, perceived by some as better, the study says.

Antibiotics work only against bacteria, not viruses. Using them for a common cold promotes the development of bacteria that are antibiotic-resistant, and it inflates health-care costs. In fact, the US government estimates that nearly half of antibiotic prescriptions are unnecessary, and the US Food and Drug Administration says all antibiotics must now carry warnings that overuse reduces their effectiveness.

The study analyzed data on almost 2000 adults collected over 3 years as part of the National Ambulatory Medical Care Survey (NAMCS). These adults had seen their doctors when they had common colds and other upper respiratory tract infections, such as sinusitis,

Michael Steinman, MD, Fellow, Geriatrics, San Francisco VA Medical Center, CA.

Marc Gillespie, PhD, Professor, Department of Pharmaceutical Sciences, St. John's University, Jamaica, NY.

February 12, 2003, *Journal of the American Medical Association*.

bronchitis, earaches, and sore throats that may, or may not, have required antibiotics.

According to the study authors, the common cold and acute bronchitis do not require antibiotics. Ear infections and acute sinusitis may respond to the drugs. Even when there is a benefit, however, broad-spectrum drugs are not necessarily the best choice.

Internal medicine specialists were substantially more likely to choose the broad-spectrum agents, and most of the antibiotic regimens prescribed by internists in the Northeast and South were broad-spectrum.

PATIENTS WANT ANTIBIOTICS, DOCTORS GIVE IN

Marc Gillespie, a professor in the department of pharmaceutical sciences at St. John's University in New York City, says the use of broad-spectrum antibiotics "points to a practice of doing things sooner rather than later. Unfortunately, that's always a struggle between the patient and the doctor. The patient really wants to walk away with an immediate solution."

Certainly more patient and physician education is needed, says Dr. Michael Steinman, lead author of the study and a fellow in geriatrics at the San Francisco VA Medical Center. Continuing improvements in the ability to diagnose viral infections may also brighten the picture, especially when it comes to demanding patients.

"A diagnosis is better than no diagnosis," Steinman says. If patients leave the doctor's office knowing that they have a viral infection that antibiotics won't help, they may be more accepting of the fact that they're going home empty-handed, Steinman says.

info If you'd like to know more about how and why bacteria can become resistant to antibiotics, visit the US Food and Drug Administration's Web site at *www.fda.gov.* "Antibiotic Resistance" is listed in the Hot Topics section. The Alliance for the Prudent Use of Antibiotics (APUA) at *www.tufts.edu/med/apua* may also provide some helpful information.

Overusing 2 Antibiotics Will Make Them Useless!

Marc Lipsitch, DPhil, Assistant Professor, Epidemiology, Harvard School of Public Health, Boston, MA.
Philip Tierno, PhD, Director, Microbiology and Immunology, New York University Medical Center, and author, *The Secret Life of Germs.*
March 10, 2003, *Nature Medicine.*

By July 2004, approximately two-thirds of the common strains of the bacteria that cause infections ranging from middle ear problems to meningitis may be resistant to both penicillin and erythromycin in some parts of the United States.

At least that's what Harvard University researchers believe.

The scientists used a formula to predict how certain antibiotic-resistant strains of *Streptococcus pneumoniae* would develop.

THE PROBLEM IS OVERUSE

Overall, they found that more than 40% of *S pneumoniae* would be resistant to penicillin and erythromycin if current usage trends continue. The problem exists mainly because antibiotics are used when they shouldn't be; that is, to fight common colds and other viral infections.

S pneumoniae are responsible for most ear infections, sinus infections, pneumonia, meningitis, and blood infections. These bacteria are not, however, responsible for strep throat.

MISUSE WIDESPREAD

How antibiotics are used and misused has led to growing resistance, and the more use and misuse there is, the more resistance you'll have in your local area, says study author Marc Lipsitch, an assistant professor of epidemiology at the Harvard School of Public Health.

The study looked at 8 different types of *S pneumoniae,* the ones most commonly resistant to antibiotics, and studied their effect in different parts of the country.

One of the first things the researchers noticed was a wide variation in the amount of resistance between the sites. For example, almost 15% of the strains in New York were resistant to penicillin; in Minnesota, that number jumped to more than 30%; in Georgia, it was more than 50%; and in Tennessee nearly 80% of the strains were resistant to penicillin.

Lipsitch says differences in antibiotic use were probably to blame for the geographic variations in resistance.

Next, they tried to predict how rapidly these strains would mutate into antibiotic-resistant strains.

PREDICTING THE MUTATIONS

If no changes occur in the way people take antibiotics, more than 40% of the strains studied at all of the sites will be resistant to both penicillin and erythromycin by the summer of 2004. In some parts of the country, that number could soar to 65% or higher.

TROUBLE AHEAD?

Does this mean we're doomed to a future of antibiotic-resistant superbugs? Maybe not, says Dr. Philip Tierno, head of microbiology and immunology at New York University Medical Center and author of *The Secret Life of Germs.* Tierno likens this study to the classic Charles Dickens tale *A Christmas Carol.*

"It's a vision of what the future could be," says Tierno, who says there's still time to change.

"Don't petition your doctor for unnecessary antibiotics," he suggests, adding that of the 90 million antibiotic prescriptions written each year, approximately 60 million aren't necessary.

However, Tierno says resistance will always be a problem because bacteria are constantly adapting. Humans have to be smarter, he says, which is why we need to continue developing new drugs and using vaccines whenever they're available.

info To learn more about antibiotic resistance, visit the National Institute of Allergy and Infectious Diseases at *www.niaid. nih.gov.*

Beware: Prescription Drugs That Cause Heart Problems

Lesley Curtis, PhD, Research Associate, Duke Clinical Research Institute, Duke University, Durham, NC.
Joe Selby, MD, MPH, Director, Division of Research, Kaiser Permanente Northern California, Oakland.
February 5, 2003, *American Journal of Medicine.*

Don't look now, but that combination of medications you're taking may have potentially deadly side effects... but then again, they may be perfectly safe.

Those are the conflicting messages of a study that examines how many people get prescriptions for drugs that could work together to create havoc in the heart.

Many drug combinations have the potential to disrupt the heart's rhythm and cause a condition known as *torsade de pointes*—a specific type of abnormally fast heartbeat. In some cases, especially among susceptible people, the condition could make the heart thrash uncontrollably and lead to death.

"The next step that's really crucial is for us to better understand what the real risks are associated with these drugs," says study co-author Lesley Curtis, a research associate at Duke University's Clinical Research Institute.

The antibiotics *clarithromycin, levofloxacin,* and *erythromycin,* and the antidepressants Prozac (*fluoxetine*) and Zoloft (*sertraline*) are common drugs that, when combined with other drugs, could cause this condition, says Dr. Joe Selby, director of research for the Kaiser Permanente Health Plan in Northern California.

Medical reference books let doctors know that the drugs could potentially lengthen the "QT interval," the time between beats when the heart reboots itself electronically, Selby says.

WHAT THE RESEARCHERS LOOKED AT

To find out how often patients were prescribed the drugs, Curtis and colleagues examined statistics about prescriptions compiled by a pharmaceutical benefits company for nearly 5 million people.

The researchers found that 23% of the patients received prescriptions for at least 1 of 50 drugs that could cause irregular heartbeats. Approximately 10% of them received at least 2 potentially risky drugs or 1 drug that could cause the condition and another that could relieve it.

Half of the potentially troublesome prescriptions were for antidepressants, and 64% of all the patients who got the antidepressant prescriptions were women, who are more likely to suffer from depression.

It's possible that many of the doctors who prescribe the drugs know about the possible side effects and consider the potential benefits worth the risk, Selby says. "We can't tell whether these [prescriptions] are mistakes or conscious decisions," he says.

According to Curtis, patients who are currently taking the drugs with potential side effects should talk to their doctors if they are concerned.

"The message should not be to stop taking your drugs," she says.

Medication Mishaps: How to Be Sure You Get the Right Rx!

David Bates, MD, Chief, Division of General Medicine, Brigham and Women's Hospital, Boston, MA.

Jay Brooks, MD, Chief, Hematology/Oncology, Ochsner Clinic, Baton Rouge, LA.

July 16, 2002, *Annals of Internal Medicine*.

It was every patient's nightmare. A 68-year-old, nondiabetic woman who had just had elective bypass surgery was given *insulin* instead of the anticoagulant *heparin* to flush her arteries. The insulin sent the woman's blood sugar plummeting. She fell into a coma and died 7 weeks later.

Medication mistakes like this one are fairly common in hospitals, says an article published in the *Annals of Internal Medicine*, but the majority are not life-threatening.

Although the process for dispensing drugs varies widely, not only between facilities but also within them, errors can occur at any of a number of points, the article says.

In many hospitals, prescriptions are handwritten by the doctor, and typed into a computer by a clerical worker who may or may not have trouble reading the handwriting. The typed information is sent to the pharmacy, where a technician begins the process of dispensing.

"If it's a pill, that's pretty simple," says Dr. Jay Brooks, chief of hematology/oncology at the Ochsner Clinic in Baton Rouge. "But if it's a mixture in a bag of fluids, it's more complicated because you have the actual mixing, then the proper labeling, then it has to go back to the floor," where you assume that the nurse or other staff member who actually gives the medicine does so correctly.

In the case of the 68-year-old bypass patient, several factors contributed to the fatal error, including a failure to store the drugs properly—the heparin and insulin vials were on top of a medication cart.

Apparently, mistaking heparin and insulin is common. "Both of these drugs are used frequently, the vials they're kept in look somewhat similar, and the medications are often not kept in secure places because it's more expedient," says Dr. David Bates, lead author of the study and the chief of general internal medicine at Brigham and Women's Hospital in Boston.

CHECKS AND BALANCES

Most hospitals have many checks to prevent such errors. Often the nurse on the floor will double-check what the clerk typed in the computer. The pharmacist might consult the doctor if a request seems strange. If Brooks is writing an out-of-the-ordinary prescription, he will often attach the journal article that explains the request or he'll call the pharmacist directly.

The article in the *Annals of Internal Medicine* identified some steps that might have prevented the mistake, including revamping how drugs are given.

For example, when Brooks uses heparin and the pain medication *lidocaine* in bone marrow procedures, he insists on the following procedure—the medical technologist picks up a vial, looks at the label, faces the label toward the doctor, and says the drug name out loud.

A number of hospitals have started using bar coding similar to supermarkets, Bates says. Unfortunately, drug makers do not routinely provide drugs with bar codes, so the hospitals and clinics must add the code themselves, at considerable expense.

"The single most beneficial change in terms of medication process is to get physicians to order medications using the computer, so that the orders can be checked for allergies and other problems," Bates says.

info For more information, visit the Agency for Healthcare Research and Quality at *www.ahrq.gov/qual* and click on "Medical Errors & Patient Safety."

FDA Warning: Be Careful Where You Buy These Drugs

Jason Brodsky, spokesman, US Food and Drug Administration, Rockville, MD.
Edgar Lichstein, MD, Chairman, Department of Medicine, Maimonides Medical Center, Brooklyn, NY.
December 9, 2002, US Food and Drug Administration news release.

The US Food and Drug Administration (FDA) has toughened its regulations on illegal imports of 10 prescription medications—ranging from a potent acne therapy to the abortion pill—that require stricter-than-usual physician supervision.

The FDA is also urging patients to avoid buying the compounds over the Internet.

Using FDA-approved products without adequate controls or monitoring, or using versions of these products not approved by FDA, raises the risk of serious health consequences, Dr. Mark McClellan, the agency's commissioner, says in a statement.

FDA spokesman Jason Brodsky says the agency doesn't know of anyone who has been harmed by taking illegally imported

drugs on the list. However, he adds that it's very unlikely that patients would report that they acquired their drugs illegally.

THE LIST

The FDA's list contains medications that require patient consent forms, physician monitoring, or other prescription controls because of safety concerns.

● **Accutane** (isotretinoin), used to treat severe acne.

● **Actiq** (fentanyl citrate), a powerful pain killer for cancer patients.

● **Clozaril** (clozapine), an anti-psychotic drug for severe schizophrenia.

● **Lotronex** (alosetron hydrochloride), for women with irritable bowel syndrome.

● **Mifiprex** (mifepristone or RU-486), the abortion pill.

● **Thalomid** (thalidomide), used to treat leprosy.

● **Tikosyn** (dofetilide), a drug that helps control abnormal heart rhythms.

● **Tracleer** (bosentan), for treating severe pulmonary arterial hypertension.

● **Trovan** (trovafloxacin mesylate or alatrofloxacin mesylate injection), an antibiotic used in hospitals.

● **Xyrem** (sodium oxybate), a treatment for sudden weakness in people with narcolepsy. This drug is similar to GHB, an illegal substance also known as the "date rape" drug.

Dr. Edgar Lichstein, chairman of medicine at Maimonides Medical Center, in Brooklyn, NY, says buying prescription drugs over the Internet without a doctor's help is a "very bad idea." Not only do consumers face serious side effects, Lichstein says, but they're not equipped to determine how those medications will react with other drugs they take.

info For more on the danger of buying medication online, try the National Association of Boards of Pharmacy at *www.nabp.net*.

Powerful Painkiller Works Better Than Morphine— And It's Safer, Too!

Robin L. Polt, PhD, Professor, Chemistry, University of Arizona, Tucson.
March 24, 2003, presentation, American Chemical Society Annual Meeting, New Orleans, LA.

When soldiers were wounded during the war in Iraq, medical personnel immediately tried to reduce their pain. But powerful pain medications like morphine can have lethal side effects for wounded servicemen and servicewomen.

Researchers from the University of Arizona and the University of New England in Biddeford, Maine, developed a pain-relieving medication that doesn't cause those potentially deadly reactions.

"What we've found in mice and rats is that these drugs are 2 to 3 times the potency of morphine and seem to be devoid of side effects," says one of the researchers, Robin L. Polt, professor of chemistry at the University of Arizona in Tucson.

In battlefield situations, Polt says, morphine can be deadly for wounded soldiers who have lost a lot of blood. He explains that because of the blood loss, morphine injected at the wound site tends to stay there. Because it doesn't circulate through the bloodstream, it doesn't give pain relief, and so more morphine is injected. Later, when a soldier receives a blood transfusion and normal blood circulation is restored, all of that morphine is finally released into the system and can cause a toxic reaction, Polt explains.

So Polt and his colleagues set out to make a painkiller that wouldn't create these problems.

Polt says that in the 1970s, scientists discovered natural painkilling peptides in the brain, known as enkephalins. They work by binding to the same pain receptors in the brain that morphine does. Initial excitement over the discovery quickly died down, however, when researchers realized that the synthetic drug couldn't pass through the blood–brain barrier that stops toxins from reaching the brain.

BREAKTHROUGH

Polt and his colleagues discovered a way to trick the body to allow man-made enkephalins to enter the brain. By attaching a simple glucose molecule to the drug, they were able to get the medication to pass through the blood–brain barrier and seek out the pain receptors in the brain.

Polt says the compound worked on mice and rats without causing narcotic-like side effects.

"These drugs are more remarkable for what they don't do," he says, pointing out they didn't cause the euphoria that morphine does and seemed to be "devoid of side effects."

However, human clinical trials are still in the planning stage. Scientists are waiting to see the results of these trials before drawing further conclusions on how useful this treatment will be.

What's most exciting about this work, says Polt, is that it could pave the way for more effective drugs in the future.

"There are approximately 250 peptides that the brain produces. If this process works for even a fraction of those, it could open up a way to make whole new classes of drugs," explains Polt. "It will lead to much better drugs than we have today with fewer side effects."

New Clot Blockers Offer Key Advantages Over Older Therapies

Charles Francis, MD, Professor, Medicine, University of Rochester Medical Center, Rochester, NY.
Sam Schulman, MD, PhD, Associate Professor, Medicine, Karolinska Institute, Stockholm, Sweden.
Sandor Shapiro, MD, Research Professor, Physiology, Jefferson Medical College, Philadelphia, PA.
October 30, 2003, *New England Journal of Medicine*.

The new generation of blood thinners is holding its own against the old guard. In fact, these medications may offer equal, if not better, protection against clots, and they have fewer complications.

Recent studies suggest that 2 of the new drugs prevent blood clots as well as or possibly better than *warfarin* or *heparin*, the current standards of care. Patients on the new drugs also don't seem to suffer more bouts of serious bleeding, a major concern with blood-thinning medications.

Dr. Charles Francis, a clotting expert at the University of Rochester in New York, says the success of the drugs reflects the growing knowledge of how blood coagulates.

"The agents that we've been dealing with for 50 years were general anticoagulants that were discovered almost by chance. These new agents are based on what we know of biochemistry, the structure of clotting proteins" and other facets of the clotting process, says Francis, who helped conduct 1 of the new studies.

Warfarin, which was first developed as a rat poison in 1948, and heparin have been the anticlotting agents of choice for 5 decades. Each drug is highly effective. But if warfarin, also known as Coumadin, and heparin are blunt instruments, the 2 new drugs, *fondaparinux* and *ximelagatran*, are honed scalpels.

Ximelagatran takes the most direct path, interfering with the protein *thrombin*, which is considered the blood's chief clotting molecule.

Fondaparinux disrupts an enzyme that's crucial for making thrombin. Fondaparinux, or Arixtra, developed by Sanofi-Synthelabo Inc. and Organon International, has won approval from the US Food and Drug Administration and European regulators. Ximelagatran, developed by AstraZeneca as Exanta, was still waiting for approval late in 2003.

The studies were funded by the drug companies whose products were tested.

The new drugs have an important advantage—their highly specific mechanism of action avoids the need for frequent lab tests and dose tinkering that warfarin and certain versions of heparin demand, experts say.

Warfarin, which can be taken orally, interacts with a wide variety of other medications and even foods in ways that can harm patients. It's also slow to take effect and must be stopped several days before surgery to prevent excessive bleeding in the operating room.

Heparin, which must be injected, can trigger severe immune reactions in some patients and causes more bleeding problems than warfarin. Patients on either blood thinner must be carefully watched, and even small dosage errors can lead to potentially deadly complications.

Dr. Sandor Shapiro, a blood specialist at Jefferson Medical College in Philadelphia, says the new drugs "look very interesting," although much more research is needed to fully understand their risks and benefits. "It would really be a revolution to have an oral anticoagulant available that acts directly on thrombin," adds Shapiro.

A key area of future research, Shapiro says, is to see how well the new drugs, especially thrombin inhibitors, are tolerated over time. Long-term use of the medications could have harmful effects, but only time will tell.

Anti-Nicotine Drug May Help You Kick 2 Habits

May 14, 2003, *Alcoholism: Clinical and Experimental Research 2003* news release.

A drug called *mecamylamine*—an FDA-approved prescription drug, typically used by people who are trying to quit smoking—appears to also reduce the euphoric effects of alcohol and decrease the desire to drink, say researchers at the University of Chicago.

Mecamylamine blocks the effects of nicotine in the brain, reducing the pleasurable effects of smoking. Researchers have long suspected that the same mechanism in the brain that responds to nicotine may also be involved in the response to alcohol.

The study included 14 male and 13 female nonsmoking social drinkers who took part in 6 laboratory sessions. At the start of each session, the volunteers received either a placebo or 1 of

2 doses of mecamylamine (7.5-milligram or 15-milligram capsules). That was followed 2 hours later by either an alcoholic or placebo beverage. Measurements were then taken of the volunteers' stimulation and euphoria levels, along with heart rate, blood pressure, and other physical markers.

The subjects reported that mecamylamine lessened "the stimulant and euphoric effects of alcohol and reduced the self-reported desire to consume additional alcoholic beverages." Additional study is needed, but researchers believe that the drug may have the same effect on those who drink as it does on those who smoke—it may reduce the desire for more.

"Our findings extend previous observations made in animals that alcohol produces its mood-altering effects, in part, through actions on the nicotinic receptor system," says corresponding author Harriet de Wit, an associate professor of psychiatry at the University of Chicago, in a news release.

"These findings also fit nicely with observations that alcohol users are often also smokers, and smokers tend to drink more than nonsmokers," de Wit says.

■ ■ ■ ■

Is There a Problem?

If you've ever wondered whether your own drinking might be a problem, or are worried about someone else's drinking, the National Institute on Alcohol Abuse and Alcoholism (*www.niaaa.nih.gov*) can help. *Here are 4 questions to ask yourself or someone you care about...*

• **Have you ever felt you should cut down on your drinking?**

• **Have people annoyed you by criticizing your drinking?**

• **Have you ever felt bad or guilty about your drinking?**

• **Have you ever had a drink first thing in the morning to steady your nerves or to get rid of a hangover?**

One "yes" suggests a possible alcohol problem. More than one "yes" means it is highly likely that a problem exists. If you think that you or someone you know might have an alcohol problem, it is important to see a doctor or other health-care provider right away.

info For more information on alcoholism, take a look at the National Institutes of Health MEDLINEplus health information page at *www.nlm.nih.gov/medlineplus/alcoholism.html.*

Viagra at 'Half'-Price

Carmen Reitano, Founder and President, Three Chestnuts Technologies Inc., Newburyport, MA.
Ira Sharlip, MD, President, Sexual Medicine Society of North America, and Urologist, San Francisco, CA.
US Patent and Trademark Office, Alexandria, VA.

Each diamond-shaped Viagra pill costs the same (almost $10) whether you get the 25-milligram (mg), 50-mg, or 100-mg version. This flat-pricing strategy has led many in the older-than-50 crowd to buy the larger pill and try to break it up into smaller pieces.

The patient should take the dose the doctor recommends, says Dr. Ira Sharlip, president of the Sexual Medicine Society of North America. "But I can tell you it's common practice for physicians to recommend a dose of 50 mg and write a prescription for a 100-mg tablet."

Carmen Reitano, 71, an inventor and Viagra user, was involved in a conversation about the difficulties of splitting a Viagra pill.

"It explodes," complained one man.

"You cut it with a knife and it splits apart with such fury it bounces off the wall," said another.

Reitano had never tried splitting his Viagra pills, but he decided to give it a try. He went home, took out the kitchen knife and tried to cut open one of his Viagra pills. Nothing happened. He went at it with an X-acto knife blade. Nothing. A hammer. Still, nothing.

"It's not flat. It's awkward to hold. There's no scoring on the covering," Reitano discovered. So, to help the many frustrated Viagra users, Reitano designed the V2 Pill Splitter, for which he was awarded a patent.

The V2 Pill Splitter can be purchased directly from Reitano's Web site, *www.v2pillsplitter.com* for $24.95, plus shipping and handling.

Pfizer, which manufactures Viagra, did not specifically comment, but recommends against pill-splitting on its Web site.

Two New Drugs That May Last Longer Than Viagra

Andrew McCullough, MD, Professor, Urology, and Director, Sexual Health Program, and Director, Male Infertility and Microsurgery Program, New York University Medical Center.

Natan Bar–Chama, MD, Assistant Professor, and Director, Male Reproductive Health, Mount Sinai Medical Center, New York, NY.

Two drug companies have developed medications for erectile dysfunction that are longer lasting than Pfizer's Viagra (*sildenafil citrate*).

Cialis (*tadalafil*), by Eli Lilly, has been approved for European distribution and Levitra (*vardenafil*), by Bayer, is already on the market.

Doctors warn, however, that if Viagra isn't effective for a man, chances are he may not do well on either of the new medications.

"All 3 drugs work pretty much the same way," says Dr. Andrew McCullough, director of the sexual health and male infertility and microsurgery programs at New York University Medical Center. He conducted clinical trials on all 3 drugs.

All 3 work by inhibiting an enzyme known as *phosphodiesterase 5* (PDE-5). As a result, following sexual stimulation, the smooth muscles of the penis are able to relax and widen, allowing more blood flow to enter and an erection to occur.

The big difference between the medications is how long they remain active in the bloodstream—and for some men that could prove an important detail.

LASTS LONGER

In clinical trials, Levitra and Cialis remained active in the body longer than Viagra. They allow for a longer period in which a man can have an erection, according to Dr. Natan Bar–Chama, the director of male reproductive health at the Mount Sinai School of Medicine in New York City.

According to the drug's manufacturers, Cialis remains active for a full 24 hours, with 59% of men reporting effects for up to 36 hours. Levitra has a similar time profile.

The effects of Viagra last 3 to 4 hours—although some men have reported benefits lasting up to 12 hours. The absorption of Viagra is also inhibited by food, which is not the case for the other 2 drugs.

Bar–Chama says the larger window of opportunity that Cialis and Levitra allow for spontaneous sex, along with slight differences in the individual formulations, may give some men who could not perform well on Viagra a new chance to succeed.

Viagra came under fire when isolated reports linked it to adverse cardiac events in men. The connection was never proved—and the latest studies show it may actually have beneficial effects on blood flow. But Viagra is still not recommended for men using medications containing nitrate—drugs normally prescribed to treat chest pains and angina.

Because both Cialis and Levitra work in much the same way as Viagra, they are likely to carry the same precautions. All 3 drugs also share similar common side effects, including headaches (14%) and heartburn (9%).

■ ■ ■ ■

Treatments for Impotence Aren't All Medicinal

The Erectile Dysfunction Institute is an umbrella organization that coordinates efforts to find cures for male impotence. *They describe the various treatments available for erectile dysfunction as follows...*

●**Drug therapy.** Drugs work to increase blood flow to the penis. Viagra is one of the major impotence treatments today. Levitra was also approved in 2003. Other drugs with similar phosphodiesterase (PDE-5) inhibitors are in clinical trials and will likely be marketed in the future. Some drugs may work on the mental or nerve-transmitting part of impotence, which helps the brain communicate to the penis.

●**Penile implants.** A surgeon places a small, saline-filled medical device that recreates the erectile function. The device transfers fluid to the penis when an erection is desired. The device is totally concealed. This procedure has one of the highest patient satisfaction rates of all impotence treatments.

●**Vacuum erection device.** The man puts a plastic tube over his penis and creates a vacuum by pumping the air out. The vacuum draws blood to his penis. This makes it erect. He then places an elastic band around the base of his penis to maintain blood in the penis and keep it firm.

●**Injection therapy.** The man injects medication into the side of his penis. The medication makes the blood vessels widen. As blood vessels widen or "dilate," blood flow increases to create an erection.

●**Urethral suppository.** The man inserts a soft pellet of medication into his urethra. His penis absorbs the medication. Blood flow increases, creating an erection (similar to injection therapy but without the needle).

●**Psychotherapy.** Whether ED has a physical cause or not, a man may benefit from therapy that teaches him how to reduce his anxiety about sex.

Amazing! Common Cholesterol Drug Controls MS Symptoms

Timothy Vollmer, MD, Chairman, Neurology, Barrow Neurological Institute, Phoenix, AZ.

Patricia O'Looney, PhD, Director, Biomedical Research Programs, National Multiple Sclerosis Society, New York, NY.

April 1, 2003, presentation, American Academy of Neurology Annual Meeting, Honolulu, HI.

Zocor, a commonly prescribed cholesterol medication, may slow progression of the degenerative nerve disease multiple sclerosis (MS).

The drug appears to inhibit enzymes that play a role in the development of inflammatory lesions in the central nervous system and seems to halt the recurrence of symptoms in the most common type of MS, say researchers from Yale University and the Barrow Neurological Institute in Phoenix.

"The greatest benefit is that the drug only targets areas of the immune system directly related to MS, so it doesn't affect the overall immune response that occurs with other treatments," says neurologist and study author Dr. Timothy Vollmer.

Currently, the only accepted treatment for MS is *interferon,* an injectable drug that halts symptoms, but suppresses a good portion of overall immune function and can have serious side effects.

Although the research on *simvastatin* (the generic name for Zocor) is promising, some experts caution against putting too much hope in the preliminary data.

Patricia O'Looney, director of Biomedical Research Programs for the National Multiple Sclerosis Society says more research is needed, and she does not recommend that MS patients take cholesterol medications unless they're undergoing treatment for high cholesterol.

Vollmer, chairman of neurology at the Barrow Neurological Institute, agrees, but feels confident of the study results. He notes that in patients with normal cholesterol levels the drug caused no further decreases. Also, the safety profile seems good because so many people have used the drug over a long period for high cholesterol.

Simvastatin is not free of side effects. In patients using this drug for cholesterol control, there is an increased risk of gastrointestinal upset, heartburn, and headaches. In rare instances, simvastatin can lead to severe muscle weakness and damage.

■ ■ ■ ■

What Is Multiple Sclerosis?

More information about MS is available at the National Multiple Sclerosis Society (*www.nmss.org*). *Following is a brief explanation of the disease…*

●**MS is a degenerative nerve disease that affects approximately 250,000 Americans,** mostly women.

●**The disease is characterized by lesions in the brain and the spinal cord.** MS attacks the *myelin sheath*—a thin coating that covers nerves and helps relay messages of movement and sensation from the body to the brain.

●**The most common form of MS is called relapsing–remitting,** which is characterized by symptoms or attacks that are followed by periods of partial or complete regression for weeks, months, or even years.

Combination Drug Therapy May Fortify Aging Bones

Susan Greenspan, MD, Professor, Medicine, and Director, Osteoporosis Prevention and Treatment Center, University of Pittsburgh School of Medicine, PA.

May 21, 2003, *Journal of the American Medical Association.*

A new study reports that hormone therapy used in tandem with the drug *alendronate* boosts bone mineral density in older women better than either therapy alone.

Bone mineral density is a key indicator of whether a person suffers from osteoporosis.

"For women who start out with very low bone density or…women who have failed on a single therapy, this would be a good option if the primary problem was osteoporosis," says study author Dr. Susan Greenspan.

Osteoporosis is the continuous thinning of bone tissue, making bones more susceptible to fracture. The condition is most common in women older than 50 years, and is largely a result of reduced estrogen.

The Women's Health Initiative (WHI), a long-term study designed partly to assess the risks and benefits of postmenopausal hormone therapy, found an increase in heart attacks, strokes, blood clots, and breast cancer in women taking hormone replacement therapy (HRT), but a decrease in colorectal cancer and hip fractures. HRT may also decrease the risk for Type 2 diabetes.

THIS STUDY WAS MORE SPECIFIC

The first difference between the WHI and this study, Greenspan says, are that "the findings from the WHI included women aged 79 and younger; we included older women in our study. The other difference is that [the WHI] was designed to look at general prevention and ours looked at prevention and treatment for osteoporosis. It was specific."

HRT has a general effect throughout the body. Alendronate has a more specific effect. It sits on top of the bones, where it's absorbed by cells called osteoblasts, which are responsible for eating away at the bone.

The researchers analyzed data on 373 women, 65 to 90 years old, 34% of whom had osteoporosis. The rest had low bone mass, a precursor of osteoporosis.

After 3 years, special radiographs called DXA scans revealed that bone mineral density was significantly higher in women treated with the combination therapy than with just a single therapy, with mean increases of 5.9% at the hip, 10.4% at the anterior lumbar spine (front view), and 11.8% at the lateral lumbar spine (side view).

CHOICE OF THERAPY IS AN INDIVIDUAL ONE

"The main results of this study can help answer the question of whether the potential risk of hormone treatment is worth the estimated 8% reduction in fracture risk when combination therapy is used compared with alendronate alone," the study authors write. Greenspan says doctors will have to weigh the risks and benefits of HRT for each individual patient.

The study showed the combination of HRT and alendronate was effective and safe in older women with low bone-density measures, the researchers say.

info For more on osteoporosis, visit the National Osteoporosis Foundation at *www.nof.org* or the National Institute of Arthritis and Musculoskeletal and Skin Diseases at *www.niams.nih.gov* and click on "Health Information."

■ ■ ■ ■

New Osteoporosis Drug Shows Good Results

Teriparatide, an osteoporosis drug approved by the US Food and Drug Administration late in 2002, appears to be particularly effective in postmenopausal women.

According to the FDA, the drug is for the treatment of osteoporosis in postmenopausal women who are at high risk for bone fracture.

Teriparatide is the first approved agent for the treatment of osteoporosis that stimulates new bone formation. It is administered by injection once a day in the thigh or abdomen.

Clinical trials also demonstrated that teriparatide reduced the risk of vertebral and non-vertebral fractures in postmenopausal women. The effects of teriparatide on fracture risk have not been studied in men.

Most side effects reported in association with teriparatide in clinical trials were mild and included nausea, dizziness, and leg cramps. During the clinical trials, 7.1% of patients receiving the drug discontinued it early due to adverse events, compared with 5.6% of patients receiving.

Teriparatide should not be used by persons with hypercalcemia, pregnant or nursing women or anyone who has ever been diagnosed with bone cancer or other cancers that have spread to the bones. Because the effects of long-term treatment with teriparatide are not known at this time, therapy for more than 2 years is not recommended. Children and adolescents and people with Paget's disease of the bone should not be treated with teriparatide.

Teriparatide is manufactured by Eli Lilly and Company of Indianapolis, Indiana, and is marketed under the trade name Forteo.

Safer, Cheaper Way to Get Rid of Lyme Disease

Gary P. Wormser, MD, Chief, Infectious Diseases, New York Medical College and Westchester Medical Center, Valhalla, NY.

May 6, 2003, *Annals of Internal Medicine.*

Patients with early-stage Lyme disease are recovering with just half the amount of antibiotics usually prescribed, says an infectious diseases doctor in New York.

Most doctors prescribe 21 days of *doxycycline* for early Lyme disease, and that, says lead researcher Dr. Gary P. Wormser, is overkill. Taking the antibiotic doxycycline for 10 days has proved just as effective for the tick-borne disease, if taken when a rash first appears, he says.

Shorter courses are equally effective, safer, less expensive, and less likely to promote bacterial resistance to antibiotics, Wormser says.

Wormser and his fellow researchers focused on 180 people with early Lyme disease and divided the patients into 3 groups.

One group received *doxycycline* for 20 days; a second group got 10 days of the antibiotic. A third group got one intravenous dose of another antibiotic, *ceftriaxone,* and 10 days of doxycycline.

After 20 days, approximately two-thirds of the patients in all 3 groups had complete recovery from Lyme disease, and more than 80% had fully recovered after 30 months. Researchers found no significant difference in responses among the 3 groups.

The length of antibiotic treatment for Lyme disease has been growing longer in recent years, Wormser says, despite a lack of evidence showing that longer treatment is necessary or beneficial.

Lyme disease is an acute inflammatory disease, caused by a bite from an infected deer tick and characterized by a skin rash, joint inflammation, and flu-like symptoms. If untreated, it can lead to serious illness, such as painful arthritis or neurological problems.

Treating Lyme disease with antibiotics for a longer period than necessary is particularly worrisome because of the risk of building antibiotic-resistant bacteria, Wormser says.

"Shorter courses of treatment may be less likely to promote the emergence of resistant bacteria that can endanger the entire community," he says. "In this day and age, any unnecessary use of antibiotics in the community or hospital setting is to be avoided. That's a big deal."

■ ■ ■ ■

Lyme Disease Symptoms

According to the American Lyme Disease Foundation (*www.aldf.com*), there are several common symptoms seen in the early stages of Lyme disease. *They are...*

- **Solid red or bull's-eye rash,** usually at site of bite.
- **Swelling of lymph glands** near tick bite.
- **Generalized achiness.**
- **Headache.**

EARLY DISSEMINATED STAGE

- **Two or more rashes not at site of bite.**
- **Migrating pains in joints/tendons.**
- **Headache.**
- **Stiff, aching neck.**
- **Facial palsy** (facial paralysis similar to Bell's palsy).
- **Tingling or numbness in extremities.**
- **Multiple enlarged lymph glands.**
- **Abnormal pulse.**
- **Sore throat.**
- **Changes in vision.**
- **Fever of 100° to 102° F.**
- **Severe fatigue.**

If you think you have the symptoms of Lyme disease, you should see your physician immediately. The rash, which may occur in up to 90% of the reported cases, is a specific feature of the disease, and treatment should begin immediately, the foundation says.

Finally! A New Drug That May Cure Psoriasis

Darrell Rigel, MD, Clinical Professor, Dermatology, New York University Medical Center.

Mark Lebwohl, MD, Professor and Chairman, Department of Dermatology, Mount Sinai School of Medicine, New York, NY, and Principal Investigator on Amevive.

A revolutionary new drug called Amevive (*alefacept*) offers new hope to almost 2 million Americans who suffer from severe psoriasis—an autoimmune disease that attacks the skin.

Equally important, Amevive is the first of what will ultimately be 4 new psoriasis treatment options, experts say. All of them fall into a relatively new category of drugs known as biologics.

We're really just seeing the very beginning of a whole new set of drugs, says Dr. Darrell Rigel, a professor of dermatology at New York University Medical Center.

Biologics are primarily derived from living cells. Unlike traditional drugs—which are usually a compilation of chemicals—biologics are, by and large, composed of human or animal proteins. They help the body help itself, reinforcing healthy communication between cells and intervening when that communication goes awry, which occurs in all autoimmune diseases.

GETTING AT THE ROOT

Amevive is the first treatment to address the problem at the root and treat the disease, not just the symptoms, of psoriasis, says Dr. Mark Lebwohl, chairman of dermatology at the Mount Sinai School of Medicine in New York City.

With psoriasis, that means targeting the overproduction of skin cells. Normally, skin cells die and are replaced by new ones every 30 days. Psoriasis, however, triggers an overreaction by the immune system that causes cellular communications to jam, forcing the skin cell production switch to stick in the "on" position.

As a result, the body turns out batches of new skin cells at 10 times the normal rate. That cell overload builds up on the surface of the skin, resulting in the characteristic red, raised, scaly patches that can make psoriasis a painful—as well as disfiguring—disease.

Amevive not only prevents the overstimulation of skin cell production, it attacks and destroys the defective immune cells that started the problem, Lebwohl says.

Until recently, treatments were limited.

"One choice is *methotrexate,* a potentially deadly chemotherapy drug which, while killing the bad cells, also wipes out the bone marrow, and with long-term use scars the liver," Lebwohl says.

Another choice is the drug *cyclosporin,* which can damage the kidneys, Lebwohl says.

A third alternative is light therapy. Although treatments work, they must be given often and over a long period of time, and light exposure has been linked to skin cancer, experts say.

Also, as soon as methotrexate or cyclosporin treatment is stopped, the symptoms return, Lebwohl says.

With Amevive, however, 12 weeks of treatment relieved symptoms for 7 months or longer; 24 weeks of treatment relieved symptoms for more than 1 year.

AMEVIVE'S DRAWBACKS

One downside is the cost, which could run as high as $20,000 a year. By comparison, methotrexate and light therapy cost approximately $2000 for a year of treatments, while cyclosporin costs approximately $9000 annually.

In addition, because Amevive temporarily dampens the immune system, it can increase the risk of infection or even malignancy.

info For more information, visit the National Psoriasis Foundation at *www.psoriasis.org* or the National Library of Medicine at *www.nlm.nih.gov*.

Hepatitis C Patients May Need Antidepressants

Peter Hauser, MD, Associate Director, Northwest Hepatitis C Resource Center, Portland Veterans Administration Medical Center, OR.

George Nikias, MD, Medical Director, Hepatitis Treatment Center, Hackensack University Medical Center, NJ.

November 2002, *Molecular Psychiatry*.

The drug that is the best treatment for hepatitis C, *interferon*, causes severe depression in many patients, say researchers. But this effect of interferon therapy can be countered with antidepressants.

One of 3 patients with the life-threatening liver disease became severely depressed after several months of interferon therapy and stopped taking their medication. When given an antidepressant, nearly all of those who were depressed improved enough to continue their treatment.

Many hepatitis C patients are depressed to the point where they stop their treatment on their own without seeing a physician, or their doctor will stop the interferon, says Dr. Peter Hauser, lead author of the study and associate director of the Northwest Hepatitis C Resource Center at the Portland Veterans Administration (VA) Medical Center. "But if they don't stay on the medicine, they don't have the chance to be treated."

THE BEST TREATMENT

Interferon therapy, combined with an antiviral agent called *ribavirin,* is now the most effective treatment for the disease, which is caused by the hepatitis C virus. Approximately 4 million Americans are infected with hepatitis C, says Hauser. It inflames the liver, interfering with its function, which can lead to cirrhosis and liver cancer, according to consumer information published by the Mayo Clinic.

There is no vaccine to prevent hepatitis C, and the interferon/ribavirin therapy can help up to 80% of those diagnosed with the disease, Hauser says. That's why it's so important that the side effect of depression not stop people from continuing the treatment, he adds.

"If we don't treat the side effects, we won't succeed with treating the disease," he says.

RAISING THE AWARENESS

Screening for depression among hepatitis C patients is very necessary, says Dr. George Nikias, medical director of the Hepatitis Treatment Center at Hackensack University Medical Center. "We need to raise the awareness that depression is very common, but also very treatable."

In Hauser's study, 13 of the 39 patients on interferon therapy developed major depression after approximately 3 months of treatment. Hauser and his colleagues treated those patients with a *selective serotonin reuptake inhibitor* (SSRI) called Celexa. Within approximately 6 weeks, 11 of the patients were no longer depressed. An SSRI was chosen, Hauser says, because interferon seems to deplete serotonin, a body chemical related to mood.

DEPRESSION THRESHOLD

Hauser found it significant that the depression occurred about the same time for all the patients.

"There seems to be a threshold effect. The patient will be fine for 2 or 3 months, but once the depression starts, there is a rapid escalation in its onset, often in a 2-week period," he says. Doctors should probably monitor patients for depression every 2 weeks, or no less often than every 4 weeks, he adds.

Beware! Kidney Drugs That Cover Up More Serious Problems

Ravindra L. Mehta, MD, Professor of Medicine, University of California, San Diego.

Darracott Vaughan, MD, Professor of Urology, Weill Cornell Medical Center, New York, NY.

November 27, 2002, *Journal of the American Medical Association.*

Giving diuretic drugs to people with acute kidney disease can hide signs of potentially fatal kidney failure, say California researchers.

These drugs increase the patient's urine output and that might mislead the doctor into thinking that truly drastic measures, like dialysis, are needed, says a group led by Dr. Ravindra L. Mehta, professor of medicine at the University of California at San Diego.

After studying 550 patients with acute kidney failure, the researchers found that the death rate for those given diuretics was nearly 80% higher than for those not given the drugs.

Doctors often don't recognize acute kidney failure, and the longer it goes unrecognized, the more likely the patient is to have kidney damage or even die, Mehta says. "Depending on diuretics to augment urinary output can cloud the issue."

DIAGNOSIS NOT EASY

Acute kidney failure is not always easy to detect, and even small changes in how the kidneys are working can lead to a bad outcome, Mehta says. The higher death rate was most notable in patients who had only a small response to the diuretics, he says.

"Our study suggests that if you don't get a good response, you shouldn't push it," he adds.

An editorial by Dr. Norbert Lameire and others at University Hospital in Ghent, Belgium, calls Mehta's work "timely and important" because the use of diuretics to increase urinary output for patients in intensive care units is still relatively common.

Until a solid clinical trial can show whether critically ill patients are harmed by diuretics, routinely giving the drugs to these patients should be discouraged, the editorial says.

HOPES DASHED

The study results are "very disappointing" because it reports that one of the things we thought would help doesn't, says Dr. Darracott Vaughan, a professor of urology at Weill Cornell Medical Center in New York and a past president of the American Urological Association.

Despite all efforts, we still have high damage and death rates with acute renal failure, he adds. "What is truly needed is basic research in understanding acute renal failure. We need to start all over again and see what will work."

info You can learn about your kidneys, how they work and how they fail, from the National Institute of Diabetes & Digestive & Kidney Diseases at *www.niddk.nih.gov* or the National Kidney Foundation at *www.kidney.org.*

Warning: Crohn's Drug Can Lose Its Effectiveness

Paul Rutgeerts, MD, PhD, Professor, Medicine, University of Leuven, Belgium.

Steven Field, MD, Clinical Assistant Professor, Medicine, New York University School of Medicine.

February 13, 2003, *New England Journal of Medicine*.

Researchers have discovered that almost two-thirds of patients who take the drug *infliximab* for Crohn's disease produce antibodies to the drug that erode its effectiveness.

Crohn's is an autoimmune disease that causes inflammation of the intestines, which in turn can cause pain and make the intestines empty frequently, resulting in diarrhea.

Infliximab, which is sold under the brand name Remicade, was approved in 1998 to treat people with Crohn's who weren't responding to first-line treatments.

When the drug works, it really works. "It's the best we have," says Dr. Paul Rutgeerts, senior author of the study and a professor of medicine at the University of Leuven in Belgium. The problem is that because infliximab is produced partly from mouse tissue, the body sometimes mounts an immune response and develops antibodies to attack the drug.

Dr. Steven Field, a clinical assistant professor of medicine at New York University School of Medicine, says that when the body makes antibodies to the drug "it causes side effects and limits its effectiveness."

Scientists are working on developing Crohn's drugs that aren't made with mouse tissue.

THE STUDY

Researchers looked at 125 patients with Crohn's disease in Europe who were given infliximab when the patient had relapsed, which is the only application it is approved for in Europe.

Antibodies were found in 61% of the study subjects. When concentrations exceeded a certain threshold, the drug didn't last as long in the body and there was also a higher risk of side effects called "infusion reactions."

These infusion reactions—an allergic reaction to the drug that includes shortness of breath and lightheadedness—also appeared to be an indicator of antibody formation.

Thirty-seven percent of patients had a higher concentration of antibodies against infliximab and these patients had all sorts of problems. They also had shortened response duration, Rutgeerts says. "At 4 weeks after infusion, almost no drug is left in circulation."

WHEN AND HOW OFTEN

The issue of how often to administer infliximab has been the subject of some controversy. Although a regular schedule admittedly helps suppress antibodies, physicians do not know how long patients should take the drug.

■ ■ ■ ■

Who's at Risk?

The Crohn's & Colitis Foundation of America (*www.ccfa.org*) has information on inflammatory bowel disease. *Following are some statistics...*

- **There are approximately 1 million Americans with inflammatory bowel disease.**

- **Men and women appear to be affected equally.**

- **Crohn's disease may occur in people of all ages,** but it is primarily a disease of the young adult.

- **Most cases are diagnosed before age 30,** although a much smaller number of patients may develop the disease between the ages of 50 and 70.

- **The disease can occur in young children,** or in people who are in their 70s or older.

■ ■ ■ ■

Crohn's Disease Symptoms Are Clearly Defined

Sometimes, Crohn's disease and irritable bowel syndrome are confused. *The National Institutes of Health describes the symptoms of Crohn's disease...*

•**Diarrhea.** Recurrent diarrhea is an important symptom. Bleeding is not as common as in ulcerative colitis, but can occur.

•**Constipation.** Constipation in Crohn's disease is usually a symptom of obstruction in the small intestine.

•**Abdominal symptoms.** The hallmark symptom is recurrent episodes of pain in the lower right part of the abdomen or above the pubic bone. This pain is often preceded by and relieved by defecation. Bloating, nausea, and vomiting may also occur. Intestinal pain may also be an indication of a serious condition, such as an abscess, or a perforation of the intestinal wall.

•**Fever.** Usually low-grade. Spiking fever and chills indicates complications.

•**Loss of appetite and weight loss.** Usually, but not always. Typical weight loss is 10% to 20% of normal.

•**Abnormal defecation.** Increased frequency, a feeling of incomplete evacuation, and tenesmus (a painful urge for a bowel movement even if the rectum is empty). Can occur in active stages.

•**Anal ulcers and fistulas.** Fistulas and ulcers around the anus may be early symptoms of Crohn's disease.

•**Neurologic or psychiatric symptoms** may be early signs of Crohn's disease when they are accompanied by gastrointestinal problems.

8

Emotional Well-Being

When it Comes to Health, Put Your Stock in Bonds

Good friends, a great spouse, close brothers and sisters—studies suggest that any of these nurturing relationships can be every bit as healthy for you as eating the right food and getting plenty of exercise.

"There is pretty compelling research evidence that having a confidant, someone to whom you can unburden yourself, is very important," says Linda Waite, a University of Chicago sociologist. "We don't know whether the nature of your confidant matters, or whether it just matters that you have someone to talk to, like a sister, a mother, or a spouse," Waite adds.

Adds Columbia University psychologist Matthew Silvan, "Some kind of open communication is very beneficial, and you don't necessarily have to be married. Some people have very strong social networks outside of marriage."

RESEARCH CONFIRMS THE THEORY

Medical studies show the benefits of positive relationships, the feeling of being "connected" to others. For instance, scientists at the University of Toronto studied a group of 103 men and women with early signs of high blood pressure.

Those who said they were happily married had an 8% drop in the size of their left ventricular mass in their heart over the 3-year study period. On the other hand, those who said their marriages were weak had, on average, a 6.2% increase in the size of their left ventricular mass. An increase in left ventricular mass is often associated with high blood pressure.

And if you're lonely, it can add stress to your heart. Students in an Ohio State University study who said they were lonely had

Linda Waite, PhD, Lucy Flower Professor in Urban Sociology, Department of Sociology, University of Chicago, IL.

Matthew Silvan, PhD, Assistant Clinical Professor, Psychiatry, Columbia University, New York, NY.

113

more constricted heart arteries and a less efficiently working heart than those who weren't lonely. Over time, constricted heart arteries, a condition called vascular resistance, increases the risk for heart disease.

Perhaps the most telling sign of the importance of intimacy is how many people yearn for it, Silvan says.

"Wanting emotional support is one of the biggest reasons—if not the major reason—people go into therapy," he says. "They are either having trouble in a relationship or can't have a relationship and want one."

info To learn more about the healing power of relationships, you can read an article by Robert B. Simmonds, PhD, at *www.emo tionalwellness.com/intimacy.htm.*

A Positive Attitude Could Save Your Life

Alan J. Christensen, PhD, Professor, Psychology and Internal Medicine, University of Iowa, Iowa City.
Joyce Gonin, MD, Associate Professor, Medicine, Georgetown University Hospital, Washington, DC.
July 2002, *Health.*

If you have a serious chronic illness, a pessimistic personality could actually shorten your life, according to a study by scientists at the University of Iowa, Iowa City. These researchers found that patients with chronic kidney disease who were prone to excessive worry and general anxiety were nearly 40% more likely to die over a 4-year period than the average patient.

"We have confirmed what many people have speculated—that there is a link between personality style and physical health," said Alan J. Christensen, a professor of psychology and internal medicine at the university, and lead author of the study.

Many previous studies on personality and health have been based on such variables as self-reported symptoms and visits to the doctor. However, the data for this study was based on mortality rates.

THE STUDY

The study evaluated a standard personality assessment administered to 174 men and women with an average age of 56 years. They were followed up for 2 to 5 years, with an average follow-up period of 4 years. Forty-nine of the patients died during this time.

The researchers found that those who had scored high on the neurotic assessment were 37.5% more likely to have died over the 4 years than the average patient. Those who received high marks for conscientiousness, which indicates a diligence and willingness to take on challenges, were 36.4% less likely to die over the 4-year period than the average patients.

IN THE MOOD

Dr. Joyce Gonin, who treats patients with chronic kidney disease at Georgetown University Hospital in Washington, DC, says, "It is very clear that the mood of the patient will indicate if the patient will comply with the medication and treatment. All too frequently, patients become depressed and skip their dialysis session.

"The more motivated a patient is, the more educated he or she becomes about the disease, the more control there is over the illness, and the less likely it is you will see preventable complications," she said. "You can't deal with the chronically ill patient without taking into account the psychosocial factors."

■ ■ ■ ■

Aging Well

The National Institutes of Health's National Institute on Aging (*www.nia.nih.gov/news*) lists keeping a positive attitude as one of the keys to healthy living. *Some others are…*

● **Maintain contact with family and friends,** and stay active through work, recreation, and community.

● **Do things that make you happy.**

● **Eat a balanced diet.**

● **Exercise regularly.**

● **Get regular check-ups.**

You May Need a Vacation After Your Vacation

Roger Cadieux, MD, Clinical Professor, Psychiatry, Penn State University College of Medicine, Hershey, PA. June 2002, *Gallup Poll.*

If you felt worn out before your vacation, wait until you get back! A Gallup Organization survey of 1000 adult vacationers found that more than half—54%—came home feeling tired. Almost 1 in 5 said they were "very tired" or even "exhausted" upon their return.

"Even though this is somewhat disturbing information, it's something most of us have pretty much felt has been there all along. It just hadn't been documented," says Dr. Roger Cadieux, a clinical professor of psychiatry at Penn State University's College of Medicine.

The culprit seems to be poor sleep before and during the holiday.

The preparation time just before the vacation seemed to be the most stressful period. According to the survey, 56% of respondents packed the night before or the day of the trip. Almost 1 in 3 people went to bed at least 2 hours later than usual because they were still trying to get ready, while slightly more than half said they woke up earlier than normal.

Thirty-six percent of those who were employed said they worked harder or stayed at the office later than usual in the days just before the vacation. About 25% said the increased job stress caused them to lose sleep.

SLEEPLESS ON VACATION

The disruptions to sleep continued while they were away from home, with many vacationers staying up later and waking up earlier than normal.

Ten percent had trouble sleeping on vacation. Most often, this seemed to be due to unfamiliar or noisy surroundings, as well as by uncomfortable beds or accommodations. About one-fifth attributed their sleep deprivation to medical conditions including indigestion, and 9% said they were worrying about work, financial, or family problems. Women were approximately twice as likely as men to have sleep problems while on vacation.

■ ■ ■ ■

10 Tips to Help You Really Relax On Vacation

If you want to have a truly relaxing vacation, you will probably need to focus on a few things before you leave and while you're on your trip. *Following are a few suggestions...*

● **If you've already got a sleep problem,** a vacation is not going to solve it. Have a heart-to-heart with your doctor and try to resolve the problem before going way.

● **Don't pack at the last minute.**

● **Try to get several good nights of sleep before you leave.**

● **Make traveling part of the vacation.** Instead of trying to cover 600 miles into a single day, drive 200 miles and take in the sites as you go.

● **Don't arrive at your destination stressed out.** Make sure that your family has books, games, or music to amuse them en route.

● **If you're flying, bring a blindfold and earplugs to block out distractions.**

● **Choose a destination in line with what you want to accomplish.** Egypt may be a good place if you want to see the world, but not if you just want to relax.

● **Don't try to accomplish too much in too short a period of time.**

● **Make sure your accommodations are conducive to a good night's rest.** Request a room away from the elevator and the ice machine.

● **Eat and drink moderately and,** in particular, avoid drinking too much alcohol because this can disrupt sleep cycles.

info For information on sleep and sleep disorders, visit the National Sleep Foundation at *www.sleepfoundation.org.* And the National Safety Council offers suggestions on avoiding driver fatigue at *www.nsc.org/library/facts* and click on "Driver Fatigue."

Lowering Your Blood Pressure Makes You Smarter...

Ian Deary, PhD, Professor, Psychology, University of Edinburgh, Scotland.

Mitchell I. Clionsky, PhD, Director, Neuro-Psychology Associates, Springfield, MA, and spokesman, American Psychological Association.

Robert A. Felberg, MD, Director, Stroke Clinic, Ochsner Clinic Foundation, New Orleans, LA.

March 2003, *Psychology and Aging.*

High blood pressure may take its toll on mental functions, as well as on the heart. Scottish researchers found that high blood pressure appears to increase brain tissue loss more rapidly than the normal aging process.

THE STUDY

Psychologists at the universities of Aberdeen and Edinburgh sought out elderly people who as 11-year-olds had their thinking power measured in the Scottish Mental Survey of 1932. When they were 78 years old, 83 of the survivors were given new tests of cognitive function and they underwent magnetic resonance imaging (MRI) of their brains.

Tests of nonverbal reasoning, memory and learning, processing speed, and executive function were then administered. Researchers found that the more white matter a person had, the lower their scores were.

High blood pressure is known to increase the formation of white matter, says Ian Deary, the University of Edinburgh psychologist who led the study.

It's normal for white matter to appear as the brain ages, says Mitchell I. Clionsky, a spokesman for the American Psychological Association, which is why older people are slower to solve problems and are not as attentive.

But in the worst case, a severe loss of brain cells that causes the appearance of white matter—an indication of brain cell loss seen by MRI—can cause a dementia resembling Alzheimer's disease, Clionsky says.

CONCLUSIONS

Dr. Robert A. Felberg, director of the stroke clinic at the Ochsner Clinic Foundation, says

the study shows that the mental changes that occur during a person's lifetime are not inevitable. There are some risk factors that can be modified.

Those risk factors closely parallel the ones for heart disease, but there are differences, Felberg says. Both heart disease and the loss of mental acuity are blood vessel diseases, but one is of the heart and the other is of the brain. "Cholesterol makes a big difference to the blood vessels of the heart, but the vessels of the brain are extremely sensitive to blood pressure."

info Advice on keeping blood pressure under control can be found at the National Heart, Lung, and Blood Institute's Web site at *www.nhlbi.nih.gov.*

Research Proves It: We Really Do Get Better With Age!

Sanjay Srivastava, PhD, Research Scholar, Stanford University, Palo Alto, CA.

Paul T. Costa, Jr., PhD, Chief, Laboratory of Personality and Cognition, National Institute on Aging, National Institutes of Health, Baltimore, MD.

May 2003, *Journal of Personality and Social Psychology.*

You've heard the saying, "You're not getting older, you're getting better." But did you know that theory has actually been supported by a research study?

People do change, and often for the better, suggests a study that questions the traditional thinking that says little change occurs after age 30.

"It wouldn't be fair to say everyone will get better with age," says Sanjay Srivastava, a research scholar at Stanford University in California who completed the project while at the University of California, Berkeley. "But, on average, [with age] people are becoming more responsible, better at keeping commitments, warmer, more nurturing, and more affectionate."

The finding that personality is more flexible than some experts think flies in the face of their so-called "plaster theory," which holds that the 5 main personality traits are genetically programmed, and little change occurs once you reach early adulthood. Those 5 traits are conscientiousness, agreeableness, neuroticism, openness, and extraversion.

AN INTERNET SURVEY

Srivastava and his colleagues recruited their sample participants—132,515 men and women aged 21 to 60 years—on the Internet, and asked them to supply their age and answer a personality inventory.

WHAT THE RESEARCHERS FOUND

• **Conscientiousness,** a trait that involves being organized and disciplined, increased throughout the age range studied, particularly in the decade of the 20s.

• **Agreeableness,** defined as being warm and generous toward others and able to see others' good qualities, went up throughout the age range studied but increased most during the 30s.

• **Neuroticism,** defined as being a worrier and emotionally unstable, declined with age for women but not men.

• **Openness** to new experiences declined slightly for both sexes with age.

• **Extraversion**—being gregarious and enthusiastic—declined for women but not for men.

Srivastava says he's interested in how the changes he observed might be linked to environmental factors and life experiences.

But he wonders: Are the personality changes preparing us for the environmental changes? Or do the environmental changes drive the personality changes?

UNIMPRESSED

A proponent of the plaster theory, Paul T. Costa, Jr., chief of the National Institute on Aging's Laboratory of Personality and Cognition, isn't impressed.

The study is a kind of snapshot at a given point in time, Costa says, but the only way to determine actual personality changes is to follow people over time.

He remains skeptical that major personality changes occur with age. "You don't find an individual who's an introvert at 35 becoming extremely extroverted at 55 or 45," he says. "What we do see are very modest changes."

info If you'd like to learn more about personality, visit the National Institute of Mental Health Web page at *www.nimh.nih. gov/publicat/baschap2.cfm* and click on "Personality Psychology."

Job Stress Doubles Heart Risks

Mika Kivimaki, PhD, Senior Researcher, Psychology, Finnish Institute of Occupational Health, Helsinki, Finland.
Paul J. Rosch, MD, President, American Institute of Stress, Yonkers, NY.
C. David Jenkins, PhD, Professor, Preventive Medicine, University of North Carolina, Chapel Hill.
October 19, 2002, *British Medical Journal.*

If you have a stressful job, you might want to consider updating your résumé and looking for a workplace that offers a more relaxing environment.

A Finnish study shows that workplace stress more than doubles the risk of death from heart attack, stroke, and other cardiovascular conditions. Although it's not an especially startling revelation, it was the first study to use both of the accepted models to gauge workplace stress for the same group of workers.

One model measures stress by the amount of control a worker has, says Mika Kivimaki, a senior researcher in psychology at the Finnish Institute of Occupational Health.

"The second [model] describes the effort put in at work and the reward you receive," Kivimaki adds. "Stress emerges when high physical or mental effort is combined with low reward—monetary or psychological."

Kivimaki was lead author of the study, published in the *British Medical Journal.* The study traces its roots to 1973, when it enlisted more than 800 healthy workers at a metal industry factory in Finland. The researchers followed the workers for more than 25 years.

After adjustment for age and sex, employees with high job strain, a combination of high demands at work and low job control, had slightly more than double cardiovascular mortality risk compared with their colleagues with low job strain, the researchers found.

"It is a well-known fact that if you already have heart disease, stress is a contributory factor to cardiovascular risk," Kivimaki says. "This study found increased risk for workers who had no cardiovascular disease at baseline."

Monitoring your health, eating well, and exercising regularly are ways to ward off stress, but getting a job that matches your personality is also important, says Dr. Paul J. Rosch, president of the American Institute of Stress.

"Some people thrive on the fast-lane, pressure-cooker work that destroys most of us," he says. "That same individual will feel stress doing assembly-line work. It's not the job; it's the job-individual interaction. The idea is to find some way to get a better sense of control over activities."

■ ■ ■ ■

Creating Worker-Friendly Environments

There's just so much that a worker can do to relieve on-the-job stress, says C. David Jenkins, a spokesman for the American Psychological Association. "It seems that a lack of control is more important than the work burden itself," he says.

Management often grumbles about such studies, but Jenkins, a professor of preventive medicine at the University of North Carolina School of Public Health, says the burden is on the occupational medical people and managers to provide more flexibility in working conditions. "The workplace has to be made more worker-friendly."

Jenkins says management could improve the effort–reward balance. *Here are his suggestions on how to do that...*

- •Raise salaries.
- •Provide more prestige.
- •Provide more praise.
- •Express appreciation to workers who don't feel adequately rewarded.

info For more information about job stress, visit the American Psychological Association Web site at *www.apa.org.*

Rooting for The Home Team Is Good for Your Heart

Frederic Berthier, MD, Department of Public Health and Medical Information, Nice Teaching Hospital, France.
Robert Kloner, MD, PhD, Director of Research, The Heart Institute, Good Samaritan Hospital, and Professor, Medicine, Cardiovascular Division, University of Southern California, Los Angeles.
April 2003, *Heart.*

Watching your favorite sports team win a big match may be good for your heart.

During the 1998 World Cup soccer finals, a study found that significantly fewer French men died from heart attacks than in the days before or after the final game. France defeated Brazil to win the World Cup that year.

Study author Dr. Frederic Berthier, from the Department of Public Health and Medical Information at Nice Teaching Hospital in France, says the researchers aren't sure why the World Cup would affect the death rate from heart attacks. They suspect it may be because of the euphoria created by the win.

Berthier also says there are typically lower rates of deaths from heart attacks on Sundays, and the final game took place on a Sunday.

This was the first study to show a reduction in heart-attack mortality after your favorite team wins, says Dr. Robert Kloner, director of research at The Heart Institute of Good Samaritan Hospital in Los Angeles.

Previous studies have suggested that during tense sporting events, especially with do-or-die situations like overtime, there was an increase in acute heart attacks.

Kloner notes there was a 25% increase in hospital admissions for heart attacks in England when that country lost a World Cup match to Argentina in a penalty-kick shootout.

If your team is the winning team, Kloner says it may cause relaxation and a decrease in stress levels, which may be why there are fewer heart-attack deaths.

So, if you have heart disease and you get overly excited while you're watching sports, you may want to talk to your doctor about it. Kloner says that if watching your favorite team brings on any kind of chest pain, you should talk with your doctor immediately.

THE STUDY

Berthier and his colleagues looked at mortality statistics from all over France for June through July 1997 and 1998. The researchers compared the death rates on the day of the World Cup final to that of 5 days before the match and 5 days after, as well as for the same time period in the preceding year.

On the day of the World Cup final, 23 men died from heart attacks, compared with an average of 33 per day during the 5 days before and after the event. Only 18 women died from heart attacks on the day of the World Cup final compared with an average of 28 in the days before and after the final match.

info For tips on recognizing and preventing heart attacks, visit the American Academy of Family Physicians at *www.aafp.org*.

Is Brain Stimulation the Best Treatment for OCD?

Ali R. Rezai, MD, head, Section for Stereotactic and Functional Restorative Neurosurgery, Codirector, Center for Functional and Restorative Neuroscience, and Associate Professor, Department of Neurosurgery, The Cleveland Clinic Foundation, OH.

April 29, 2003, presentation, American Association of Neurological Surgeons Annual Meeting, San Diego, CA.

People with *obsessive-compulsive disorder,* or OCD, are tormented by their own repetitive, nagging thoughts, and for many there's no treatment that offers relief.

But an experimental procedure may provide at least some improvement for patients with severe OCD, letting them return to work and some semblance of routine.

However, the treatment, spearheaded by a Cleveland Clinic Foundation neurosurgeon, produces significant side effects, prompting some questions about the therapy's efficacy.

The study tested deep brain stimulation as a possible treatment for OCD. Because an estimated 20% of OCD patients don't respond to drug or behavioral therapies, the researchers hoped to find a new way of treating the condition.

THE OCD LOOP

Those with OCD feel as though their brain gets snagged on a particular thought or impulse and it keeps playing the same message over and over again. For example, some people can't resist the nagging desire to wash their hands several times an hour, while others may constantly check the stove to make sure they haven't left it on. Patients with OCD are unable to control their intrusive thoughts and sometimes require institutionalization, the researchers say.

The researchers worked with 15 severely disabled OCD patients who'd been on prolonged medication and behavioral therapy. The subjects included 7 men and 8 women from Europe and the United States who were, on average, 14 years old when they were struck by OCD.

Each patient received deep brain stimulators—electronic devices that work like pacemakers—that were implanted into a fiber bundle located at the front of the brain. A deep brain stimulator quiets activity in 2 regions of the brain where OCD patients appear to have abnormal activity, the researchers say.

After receiving the therapy, the patients experienced a 54% improvement in quality-of-life scores, and several were able to return to work.

THE PROS AND CONS

Some of the specific benefits of the treatment included mood elevation, anxiety reduction, decreased OCD symptoms, and increased alertness. But some subjects also experienced depression, memory flashbacks, nausea, vomiting, visual blurring, and abnormal heart rhythms, among other side effects, the researchers say.

But lead researcher Dr. Ali Rezai of the Cleveland Clinic Foundation says the side effects can be controlled by changing the dosage of electricity to the stimulator.

"Deep brain stimulation has the advantage of being reversible and adjustable. These [side effects] are not chronic and can be eliminated," he says.

Rezai agrees that a longer-term study is needed before his team embarks on a larger clinical trial. "The results are encouraging but we need more follow-up before we enroll more patients."

info For information on OCD and related disorders, visit *www.ocfoundation.org*, an educational and self-help group in Connecticut.

Give Unto Others, and You'll Live Longer

Stephanie Brown, Psychologist, Institute for Social Research, University of Michigan, Ann Arbor.

Shelley Taylor, Professor, Psychology, University of California at Los Angeles, and author of *The Tending Instinct: How Nurturing Is Essential to Who We Are and How We Live*.

They say it's better to give than to receive, and researchers now have proof that the adage has more than a grain of truth in it.

Engaging in even a scant amount of altruistic behavior will make you live longer, say researchers at the University of Michigan, who looked at more than 400 older couples for 5 years.

Those who helped someone else even only once a year were up to 60% less likely to die than those who helped no one at all during the previous year, says lead author Stephanie Brown, a psychologist at the University of Michigan's Institute for Social Research in Ann Arbor. Although many would have died anyway, Brown explains, the researchers considered whether the person was a giver and took other factors, such as health, into account. From that, they figured the givers' likelihood of dying early.

The men in the study were at least 65 years old, and the women were at least 49 years old. Approximately 1 in 4 did not help anyone else in the previous year and also didn't make their spouse feel loved and cared for, Brown says.

KINDNESS FREELY GIVEN

The helping acts ranged from assisting faraway family members to babysitting for grandchildren, Brown says. No one was paid.

Another longevity factor: Husbands and wives who made each other feel loved and cared for lived longer than those who denied others their emotional support.

Researchers started out with the idea that helping others would be healthy, but even they were surprised by how strong the effect seemed to be, Brown admits.

WHY KINDNESS HELPS

Although no one knows for sure how the act of being helpful and kind to others adds years to your life, there are some theories, Brown says.

Giving to others may create positive feelings and buffer heart disease problems, she suggests: "We know stress is harmful."

The next step: Find out exactly why givers live longer and have better health.

Shelley Taylor, a professor of psychology at UCLA and author of *The Tending Instinct: How Nurturing Is Essential to Who We Are and How We Live*, says that helping others can relieve your stress. She recalls her own father saying he would die only when he couldn't be helpful anymore. "Just knowing someone else needs you can be gratifying," she says.

info To find out more about the benefits of giving, visit Health Canada at *www.hc-sc.gc.ca*.

■ ■ ■ ■

How You Really Benefit From Helping

According to Rebecca Shannonhouse, editor of *Bottom Line/Health,* volunteers get a healthy "helper's high."

Researchers have found that volunteers must have face-to-face contact with those they help in order to experience what's known as a "helper's high." That's the stress-reducing, endorphin-driven feeling of well-being that occurs when people help others. In fact, this type of personal contact can reduce depression, fatigue, and, in some cases, the intensity and duration of chronic pain.

"Volunteers who help strangers regularly for about 4 hours a month are *10 times* more likely to feel healthy than once-a-year helpers —or those who simply stuff envelopes, donate clothes, or do another activity without personal contact," explains Allan Luks, executive director of Big Brothers Big Sisters of New York City and author of *The Healing Power of Doing Good* (iUniverse).

Luks' advice for getting started as a volunteer is…

●**Work with people with whom you have a special affinity.** If you come from a family of immigrants, for example, work with immigrants yourself. If you've overcome a serious illness, help people with the same condition.

●**Investigate local opportunities.** To find volunteer opportunities in your area, consult the Web sites *www.volunteermatch.org* and *www.helping.org.* Or check the *Yellow Pages* for listings under "Social Service Organizations."

■ ■ ■ ■

Give to Charity With Care

On the other hand, if you prefer to give monetary donations to charity, try to use your head.

According to the Council of Better Business Bureaus (CBBB), more than 80% of the money raised by charities in the United States comes from individuals. *To help donors make wise giving decisions, the CBBB offers the following advice…*

●**Never give cash.** Always make contributions by check and make your check payable to the charity, not to the individual collecting the donation.

●**Keep records of your donations** (receipts, canceled checks, and bank statements) to document your charitable giving at tax time. Although the value of your time as a volunteer is not deductible, out-of-pocket expenses (including transportation costs) directly related to your volunteer service to a charity are deductible.

●**Don't be fooled by names that look impressive** or that closely resemble the name of a well-known organization.

●**Check out the organization** with the local charity registration office (usually a division of the state attorney general's office) and with your Better Business Bureau.

MAIL APPEALS

●**Fund-raising appeals received in the mail should clearly identify the charity** and describe its programs in clear and specific language. Beware of appeals that bring tears to your eyes but tell you nothing about the charity or what it's doing about the problem it describes so well.

●**Appeals should not be disguised** as bills or invoices. It is illegal to mail a bill, invoice, or statement of account due that is in fact an appeal for funds, unless it bears a clear and noticeable disclaimer stating that it is an appeal and that you are under no obligation to pay unless you accept the offer.

●**It is against the law to demand payment for unordered merchandise.** If unordered items, such as key rings, stamps, greeting cards, or pens, are enclosed with an appeal letter, you are under no obligation to pay for or return the merchandise. If payment is requested, inform your local BBB.

●**If an appeal includes sweepstakes promotions,** the mailing piece must disclose that you do not have to contribute to be eligible for the prizes offered. To require a contribution would make the sweepstakes a lottery through the mail, which is illegal to operate.

TELEPHONE, DOOR-TO-DOOR, AND STREET SOLICITATIONS

When you are approached for a contribution of time or your money, ask questions, and don't give a donation until you're satisfied with the answers. Charities with nothing to hide will encourage your interest. Be wary of their reluctance or inability to answer questions.

• **Ask for the charity's full name and address.** Demand identification from the solicitor.

• **Ask if your contribution is tax-deductible.** Contributions to tax-exempt organizations are not always tax-deductible.

• **Ask if the charity is licensed by state and local authorities.** Registration or licensing is required by most states and many communities. However, bear in mind that registration in and of itself does not imply an endorsement by the state or local government.

• **Don't succumb to pressure to give money on the spot** or allow a "runner" to pick up a contribution; the charity that needs your money today will welcome it just as much tomorrow.

• **Watch out for statements such as "all proceeds will go to the charity."** This can mean that the money left after expenses, such as the cost of written materials and fund-raising efforts, will go to the charity.

• **When you're asked to buy candy, magazines, cards, or tickets** to a dinner or show to benefit a charity, ask what the charity's share will be. You cannot deduct the full amount paid for any such items because the IRS considers only the part above the fair-market value to be a charitable contribution. *Example:* If you pay $10 for a box of candy that normally sells for $8, only $2 can be claimed as a charitable donation.

• **Call your local BBB if a fund-raiser uses pressure tactics** such as intimidation, threats, or repeated and harassing calls or visits. Such tactics violate the CBBB's recommended Standards for Charitable Solicitations.

info The Better Business Bureau has more information about how to determine if a charity is worthwhile on its Web site at *www.give.org/standards/newcbbbstds.asp.*

Stuck in the Same Old Routine? Don't Worry, It's Good for You!

Barbara Fiese, PhD, Associate Professor, Psychology, Syracuse University, NY.

Irene Goldenberg, Family Therapist, University of California at Los Angeles.

December 2002, *Journal of Family Psychology.*

Many Americans regularly engage in routines and rituals, and these practices improve their mental and physical health and sense of belonging, according to an analysis of 50 years of research.

Routine events, such as dinners together as a family, provide comfort simply by being events people can count on, says study author Barbara Fiese, associate professor of psychology at Syracuse University in New York.

Children flourish when they can predict things in their life, such as family dinners or regular bedtimes, the study found. "Even a short period of time has a positive effect. It's related to physical health in infants and children, and academic performance in elementary children," Fiese says.

Rituals, on the other hand, are symbolic practices people perform that help define who they are. The meaningful, symbolic parts of rituals seem to help emotional development and satisfaction with family relationships. When rituals are continued during times of stress, such as a death or divorce, they lessen the negative impact.

"It seems that at points of transition, such as school or marriage, rituals can increase one's sense of security," she says.

Irene Goldenberg, a family therapist at the University of California, Los Angeles, says that therapists routinely advise people to create rituals. "They represent an order and a sense of logic. They make the family more of a unit and tend to make it clear what the values are in the family."

info To learn more about the value of rituals to family life, visit ChildCareAware at *http://childcareaware.org/en/dailyparent/ vol5* or read more from the Kansas State University Agricultural Experiment Station and Cooperative Extension Service at *www.oznet. ksu.edu.*

■ ■ ■ ■

What Family Rituals Have the Most Value?

Family traditions and rituals can be positive forces from the earliest age.

The American Academy of Pediatrics recommends the book, *Caring for Your School-Age Child: Ages 5-12* (Bantam Books, 1999) to look at ways that establishing regular practices within the family can create strong ties and interdependence.

Here are some rituals that many families have made parts of their lives…

IMPORTANT CONVERSATIONS

Communication between parents and children should be a top family priority. Set aside time to talk, discussing the day's and the week's activities, really listening to one another.

Some families establish a weekly time for a family meeting. When everyone is present, family issues, relationships, plans, and experiences are discussed, and everyone from the youngest to the oldest gets a chance to be heard and to participate.

RECREATION AND CULTURAL ACTIVITIES

Family recreation is an important way to strengthen the family. Sports (participation and spectator), games, movies and walks in the park are good ways to increase cohesiveness and reduce stress.

Cultural activities can be valuable too. Visits to museums, libraries, plays, musicals and concerts can expand the family's horizons and deepen appreciation for the arts.

SHOPPING

Shopping trips can provide regular opportunities for parents and children to spend time together. Whether you are grocery shopping or buying birthday gifts, these excursions can be fun and exciting for youngsters in middle childhood. Let your children make lists, find items in the store, carry the bags to the car and unpack them once you return home. Allowing your child some choices and assigning some meaningful responsibilities can help build his self-confidence.

READING AND SINGING ALOUD

Reading and singing aloud as a family promotes feelings of closeness and an appreciation for music and books. Parents should find out what stories their children like to read, and what music they like to listen to. It is lots of fun to take turns reading aloud, and to let the children hear the stories and songs you enjoyed when you were growing up.

HOLIDAY TRADITIONS

These are another source of fun family activities. By learning about the history, significance, and rituals of a particular holiday, children will feel a greater sense of involvement in the holiday preparations and celebrations.

SPIRITUAL PURSUITS

For many families, religion plays an important role in providing a moral tradition, a set of values and a network of friends and neighbors who can provide support. Attending services is something family members can do together.

You do not necessarily need to go to a church, synagogue, or other place of worship regularly, however, to share moral values with your children and help them develop a sense of their history and the continuity of the family. Many families develop a strong spiritual life without the formal structure of organized religion.

Heart Problems Possible In Patients Recovering From Depression

Andrew Broadley, MD, Specialist Registrar, Cardiology, Torbay Hospital, Torquay, Devon, United Kingdom, and Clinical Research Fellow, University of Wales College of Medicine.

Philip Strike, MD, Clinical Research Fellow, University College London.

Stephen E. Kimmel, MD, Assistant Professor, Medicine and Epidemiology, University of Pennsylvania, Philadelphia.

November 2002, *Heart*.

You may be aware that medical studies have found a link between depression and heart disease. But a British study suggests that even patients who have been treated successfully for depression can still have problems that lead to cardiac dysfunction.

The study showed that people who had overcome bad bouts of depression still had arteries that did not expand normally when large amounts of blood were forced through them. The problem is known as "endothelial dysfunction." It is the same abnormality that is found in smokers, those with high blood pressure, high cholesterol, and diabetes–all of which are conditions that significantly predispose someone to heart disease.

"This failure to dilate in response to increased flow is associated with the development of coronary artery disease, which is the number one cause of angina and heart attacks," says study author Dr. Andrew Broadley, specialist registrar in cardiology at Torbay Hospital in Devon, United Kingdom.

In the recent study, researchers compared 10 healthy people with 12 people who had been treated for depression and had remained stable on their normal medications for a minimum of 3 months. When blood was forced through the artery of the arm, the cells in the lining of the arteries of healthy participants produced nitric oxide. This substance causes muscle layers to relax and the arteries to expand. The effect was much less noticeable in people being treated for depression.

It is not known what causes this abnormality, Broadley says. Although the dysfunction may be due to the depression itself, its cause could also be a result of the antidepressants the subjects were taking, or even a combination of both, he says. There are still many unanswered questions, Broadley admits, and having endothelial dysfunction does not mean that someone is sure to develop heart disease.

But clearly, the elevation of mood in successfully treated patients with depression did not reverse the abnormality in their arteries, Dr. Philip Strike, a clinical research fellow at University College London, wrote in an accompanying editorial in *Heart*.

SURPRISE FINDING

The researchers suspected an abnormality would be found among treated patients that would demonstrate a possible predisposition to heart disease, but the type of abnormality was not what they expected, Broadley says.

Dr. Stephen E. Kimmel, an assistant professor of medicine and epidemiology at the University of Pennsylvania, says that the bottom line of this study is that "we're not sure endothelial function is the only mechanism that increases cardiac risk in depressed patients."

Kimmel said he would like to see research that compares the arterial function in depressed patients with that of those treated for depression to determine whose dysfunction is more severe. It may be worse in untreated patients, he says.

■ ■ ■ ■

How Do You Know If You're Depressed?

Just as with other illnesses, depression comes in different types and degrees, according to The National Institute of Mental Health.

Major depression is manifested by a combination of symptoms that interfere with the ability to work, study, sleep, eat, and enjoy once pleasurable activities. Such a disabling episode of depression may occur only once but more commonly occurs several times in a lifetime.

A less severe type of depression, *dysthymia*, involves long-term, chronic symptoms that do not disable, but keep one from functioning well or from feeling good. Many people with dysthymia also experience major depressive episodes at some time in their lives.

Not everyone who is depressed or manic experiences every symptom. Some people experience a few symptoms, some many. Severity of symptoms varies with individuals and also varies over time.

DEPRESSION SYMPTOMS

- **Persistent sad,** anxious, or "empty" mood.
- **Feelings of hopelessness,** pessimism.
- **Feelings of guilt,** worthlessness, and/or helplessness.
- **Loss of interest or pleasure** in hobbies and activities that were once enjoyed, including sex.
- **Decreased energy,** fatigue, being "slowed down."
- **Difficulty concentrating,** remembering, making decisions.
- **Insomnia,** early-morning awakening, or oversleeping.
- **Appetite and/or weight loss** or overeating and weight gain.
- **Thoughts of death or suicide;** suicide attempts.
- **Restlessness,** irritability.
- **Persistent physical symptoms** that do not respond to treatment, such as headaches, digestive disorders, and chronic pain.

Another type of depression is *bipolar disorder,* also called *manic–depressive illness.* Not nearly as prevalent as other forms of depressive disorders, bipolar disorder is characterized by cycling mood changes—severe highs (mania) and lows (depression). Sometimes the mood switches are dramatic and rapid, but most often they are gradual. When in the depressed cycle, an individual can have any or all of the symptoms of a depressive disorder. When in the manic cycle, the individual may be overactive, over talkative, and have a great deal of energy. Mania often affects thinking, judgment, and social behavior in ways that cause serious problems and embarrassment.

For example, the individual in a manic phase may feel elated, full of grand schemes that might range from unwise business decisions to romantic sprees. Mania, left untreated, may worsen to a psychotic state.

MANIA SYMPTOMS

- **Abnormal or excessive elation.**
- **Unusual irritability.**
- **Decreased need for sleep.**
- **Grandiose notions.**
- **Increased talking.**
- **Racing thoughts.**
- **Increased sexual desire.**
- **Markedly increased energy.**
- **Poor judgment.**
- **Inappropriate social behavior.**

info You can learn more about depression from The National Institute of Mental Health at *www.nimh.nih.gov/publicat/depression.cfm*.

Stress Hikes Autoimmune Risk in Veterans

Joseph Boscarino, PhD, MPH, Senior Scientist, Division of Health and Science Policy, New York Academy of Medicine.

Suzanne Mazzeo, PhD, Assistant Professor, Psychology, Virginia Commonwealth University, Richmond.

Len Selfon, Director, Veterans Benefits, Vietnam Veterans of America, Silver Spring, MD.

March 8, 2003, American Psychosomatic Society Meeting, Phoenix, AZ.

The psychological and physical toll of war on veterans' health may be more serious than previously thought.

The impact of what they saw and did on the battlefield has long been known to cause some emotional harm, but researchers now believe that combat veterans are experiencing a wide range of health problems that may cause serious—possibly fatal—damage to their immune systems.

According to a new study, veterans who experience post-traumatic stress disorder (PTSD) are more likely to suffer from a host of autoimmune diseases that include rheumatoid arthritis, multiple sclerosis, and Graves' disease. PTSD is a common illness among combat veterans, with up to 1 in 3 experiencing the disorder. Symptoms of PTSD include flashbacks, nightmares, anxiety, and hyper-arousal.

Researchers from the New York Academy of Medicine examined the 20-year medical histories of nearly 2000 men who served in the US Army during the Vietnam War. The findings build on previous research that has shown combat exposure has both physical and mental health consequences that can be long lasting and debilitating.

SICK OF WAR

The study found that more than 50 men had PTSD, but more than 100 had PTSD coupled with another psychiatric disorder such as schizophrenia, depression, paranoia, or hysteria, indicating that Vietnam veterans often suffer from multiple mental illnesses.

Also, approximately 1 in 5 of those with PTSD had an autoimmune disease. Veterans with PTSD and a secondary mental diagnosis had the highest rates of autoimmune disease—they were 3 times more likely to develop an autoimmune disease than veterans without the extra illness.

"Autoimmune diseases are relatively rare, but they're very devastating. When you look at the PTSD group, it tends to jump out at you—you wonder where is this coming from?" says the study's lead author, Joseph Boscarino, senior scientist at the academy's Division of Health and Science Policy.

This study is still another that shows that stress caused by trauma is linked to poorer health, says Suzanne Mazzeo, a professor of psychology at Virginia Commonwealth University.

UNDERCOUNTED DISEASE?

Boscarino says that because the data used in the study are now 15 years old, the prevalence of autoimmune disease among PTSD-positive veterans would be much higher if the follow-up exams were done today.

Boscarino's findings are good news for Vietnam veterans who often struggle to receive benefits and health-care coverage for disorders that aren't obviously connected to their military service, says Len Selfon, director of Veterans Benefits for the Vietnam Veterans of America. Research on the link between psychological illnesses, such as PTSD, and physical illness is murky, he says.

The US Department of Veterans Affairs weighs epidemiological and clinical evidence to decide which medical conditions should be covered by their insurance, Selfon says.

This study helps show a medical connection between PTSD and autoimmune problems that may encourage the Department of Veterans Affairs to apply health-care coverage to these disorders, he says.

"This study is going to be helpful clinically for people being treated for PTSD and autoimmune disease. For the purposes of veterans receiving health care and benefits, it's important to link these disorders," Selfon says.

info To learn more about autoimmune diseases, check with the National Institute of Allergy and Infectious Diseases at *www.niaid.nih.gov.*

New Relief for Anxiety Sufferers!

Gregory J. Quirk, PhD, Assistant Professor, Physiology, Ponce School of Medicine, Ponce, Puerto Rico.

James L. Olds, PhD, Director, Krasnow Institute for Advanced Study, George Mason University, Fairfax, VA.

November 7, 2002, *Nature.*

If the response in rats is any indication, researchers believe they have made a discovery that could eventually help people with anxiety and *post-traumatic stress disorder* (PTSD).

Like humans, rats learn to be scared of events or things that they relate to pain. But when researchers electrically stimulated a part of the brain, the rats "forgot" they were afraid, according to study coauthor Gregory Quirk, an assistant professor of physiology at the Ponce School of Medicine in Puerto Rico. "We've fooled the brain into thinking that it's safe."

When faced with something frightening, rats will freeze and their heart rates and blood pressures go up—a classic fight-or-flight response, Quirk said. It's a hard-wired way that organisms deal with danger. That's true across many species—people, rats, birds, and lizards, he added.

In his study, Quirk taught rats to associate an audio tone with a mild shock to their feet. They froze each time they heard the tone. Then the researchers tried to make the rats forget about their fear by playing the tone without administering the shock. The rats lost their fear of the tone after it had been played many times without a shock, but as soon as the tone was followed by a shock again—even after a lot of time had gone by—the fear and freezing response came right back, Quirk said.

The rats did a better job of forgetting their fear—and not reacting to the tone—when researchers electrically stimulated a part of the brain that's associated with learning that something is no longer scary.

HOW IT COULD HELP

The findings could help people who can't learn to stop being afraid, such as those who suffer from post-traumatic stress disorder, he said. "In the current therapies, you find what the person is afraid of, and keep showing it to them again and again to extinguish their fear. But with time, the fear response slowly recovers, and that's a problem," he explained.

The proposed brain stimulation may be too broad to work effectively in humans, said James L. Olds, a neuroscientist and director of the Krasnow Institute for Advanced Study at George Mason University. It would turn on too many nerve cells in an important part of the brain, he said. But the findings are still remarkable and provide much insight into how the brain works, he said.

info For more information on post-traumatic stress disorder (PTSD), visit the National Center for PTSD at *www.ncptsd.org*. If you would like to know more about anxiety, go to the Anxiety Disorders Association of America Web site at *www.adaa.org*.

■ ■ ■ ■

What You Can Do to Fight Anxiety Disorders

The US National Institute of Mental Health (NIMH) estimates that anxiety disorders affect more than 19 million Americans, making them as a group the most common mental illness in America. But anxiety disorders are subdivided into many different categories. *Here's how the NIMH breaks down the disease, its symptoms and its treatment...*

●**Panic Disorder.** Repeated episodes of intense fear that strike often and without warning. Physical symptoms include chest pain, heart palpitations, shortness of breath, dizziness, abdominal distress, feelings of unreality, and fear of dying.

●**Obsessive–Compulsive Disorder.** Repeated, unwanted thoughts or compulsive behaviors that seem impossible to stop or control.

●**Post-Traumatic Stress Disorder.** Persistent symptoms that occur after experiencing or witnessing a traumatic event such as rape or other criminal assault, war, child abuse, natural or human-caused disasters, or crashes. Nightmares, flashbacks, numbing of emotions, depression, and feeling angry, irritable or distracted and being easily startled are common. Family members of victims can also develop this disorder.

●**Phobias.** Two major types of phobias are social phobia and specific phobia. People with social phobia have an overwhelming and disabling fear of scrutiny, embarrassment, or humiliation in social situations, which leads to avoidance of many potentially pleasurable and meaningful activities. People with specific phobia experience extreme, disabling, and irrational fear of something that poses little or no actual danger; the fear leads to avoidance of objects or situations and can cause people to limit their lives unnecessarily.

● **Generalized Anxiety Disorder.** Constant, exaggerated worrisome thoughts and tension about everyday routine life events and activities, lasting at least six months. Almost always anticipating the worst even though there is little reason to expect it; accompanied by physical symptoms, such as fatigue, trembling, muscle tension, headache, or nausea.

WHAT ARE EFFECTIVE TREATMENTS?

Treatments have been largely developed through research conducted by NIMH and other institutions. They help many people with anxiety disorders and often combine medication and specific types of psychotherapy.

A number of medications that were originally approved for treating depression have been found to be effective for anxiety disorders as well. Some of the antidepressants are called *selective serotonin reuptake inhibitors* (SSRIs). Other antianxiety medications include drugs called benzodiazepines and beta-blockers. If one medication is not effective, others can be tried. New medications are currently under development to treat anxiety symptoms.

Two clinically proven effective forms of psychotherapy used to treat anxiety disorders are behavioral therapy and cognitive-behavioral therapy. Behavioral therapy focuses on changing specific actions and uses several techniques to stop unwanted behaviors. In addition to the behavioral therapy techniques, cognitive-behavioral therapy teaches patients to understand and change their thinking patterns so they can react differently to the situations that cause them anxiety.

info The US Food and Drug Administration provides information on the latest medicines available to combat phobias at *www. fda.gov/fdac/features/1997/297_bump.html.*

Breast Implants Linked To Higher Suicide Rates

David L. Feldman, MD, Director, Plastic Surgery, Maimonides Medical Center, Brooklyn, NY.
James Wells, MD, President, American Society of Plastic Surgeons, Arlington Heights, IL.
Veronica Cornelia Maria Koot, MD, PhD, Clinician, University Medical Center, Utrecht, The Netherlands.
March 8, 2003, *British Medical Journal.*

Does having surgically enhanced breasts make women happier? *Consider this:* In one study, researchers found that Swedish women with breast implants were 50% more likely to commit suicide than women without them.

The study showed that deaths of women with breast implants were higher than expected in the categories of suicide and lung cancer due to smoking. The authors suggested the extra deaths might be attributable to underlying psychiatric problems, something that plastic surgeons are generally on guard for. Dr. Veronica Koot, one of the study's authors and a clinician at the University Medical Center in Utrecht, The Netherlands, said that "very low self-esteem" might be to blame.

"This is not the first study to suggest that suicide rates might be higher [in women who have had breast enlargement surgery]," says Dr. David L. Feldman, director of plastic surgery at Maimonides Medical Center in Brooklyn, New York. "Women are deluded into thinking that having larger breasts will change their life. It won't. It'll change their breasts."

A DIFFERENT VIEWPOINT

Not everyone agrees that the suicides can be linked to the breast implants. "That just doesn't compute with the information that we have in this country," says Dr. James Wells, president of the American Society of Plastic Surgeons. "We don't know that we have a cause-and-effect relationship."

Part of the problem, Wells suggests, is inherent in looking at people from 2 different societies; in this case, the United States and Sweden.

Wells estimates that US plastic surgeons turn away clients roughly 2% to 5% of the time.

"There's an evaluation process by the physicians to try to identify those patients who seem a little unstable. Their job history isn't stable, they're bouncing from relationship to relationship," he says. "We need to spend time listening to the patient. Surgeons have a responsibility to say no as much as they have a responsibility to say yes."

EVALUATING THE PATIENTS

Koot agreed that different screening procedures could account for a difference in risk, depending on the country.

The most common woman seeking breast augmentation in the US is happily married and has several children, Wells says. "She is looking to reverse what pregnancy did in terms of her breasts and appearance," he says.

Still, identifying the "right" person can be as much art as science. "We try to avoid operating on somebody who has a propensity for suicide, but this is a tough call and some people will slip through the cracks," Feldman says. "It does point out our obligation to do a full evaluation and not just rush a person off to the operating room."

info The American Society of Plastic Surgeons at *www.plasticsurgery.org* and The American Society for Aesthetic Plastic Surgery at *http://surgery.org* provide extensive overviews for women thinking about breast enlargement.

Some Video Games Are Good for You!

Catherine L. Harris, PhD, Assistant Professor, Psychology, Boston University, MA.
Laurent Itti, PhD, Assistant Professor of Computer Science, University of Southern California, Los Angeles.
May 29, 2003, *Nature*.

You might lament the endless hours of video games your children play, but researchers suggest their obsession can lead to more than high scores and sore thumbs.

Playing action-rich video games like car racing and shoot-'em-ups can improve visual perception and allow people to focus on many tasks at once. Such training helps them play the game at hand, and it might also give them an edge in real-world situations, such as driving a car in traffic, experts say.

"It's certainly wonderful to be able to focus on multiple things at once," says Catherine Harris, an assistant professor of psychology at Boston University who has studied video games and perception. "The video-game generation is going to be very resilient under distraction."

Video games might also be gender equalizers, Harris adds, helping girls trim certain perceptual leads boys now hold. "Typically, girls do have poorer use of spatial relations than boys do, but if girls could be encouraged to play more video games maybe that could change," she says.

In the latest study, Daphne Bavelier of the University of Rochester's Center for Visual Science and a colleague looked at the effects of action video-game habits in a group of young adults. Players had logged at least 4 hours a week at their sets while nonplayers had little, and ideally no, experience with the games.

Not surprisingly, players performed better than nonplayers on tests of visual attention in fields directly engaged by the video games. They tracked 30% more items, and did so faster. They were also more adept at locating a specific object in a field of clutter.

BETTER AT SWITCHING TASKS

But they also did better in areas beyond what the games "trained." They had less "attentional blink"—a lag in perception that occurs when processing multiple tasks—and were better able to switch tasks.

Of course, it's possible that video-game players by nature have better visual abilities than other people. So the researchers had a group of nonplayers train on a war game for 1 hour a day. After 10 days, they outscored a group of people who'd played Tetris—a rather simple but highly addictive shape game—on 3 measures of visual attention.

Laurent Itti, a perception expert at the University of Southern California in Los Angeles, says part of why people improve at playing video games or in doing other tasks that drench the senses is that they learn to sort out what's important and what's irrelevant.

"The naive observer will have his or her attention attracted to anything that's flashy," he says. "The trained observer will know that only a few [stimuli] are the ones to care about if you want to win at the game."

Important Update: Why Depression Can Strike Again

Helen Mayberg, MD, Professor, Psychiatry and Neurology, University of Toronto, Canada.

November 2002, *American Journal of Psychiatry*.

October 31, 2002, University of Pittsburgh news release.

People who have suffered one depressive episode may believe that they will suffer another. Researchers, in identifying what could be a depression trait marker in the brain, can support the logic behind that thinking.

"Depression is not a single event for many people, and each episode, if you're lucky, can be treated and you can be well. But depressed patients know that they are at risk for more episodes," says Dr. Helen Mayberg, lead author of the "trait marker" study and a professor of psychiatry and neurology at the University of Toronto. "The question is, what about your brain seems to be the area of vulnerability?"

Although it has already been proven that the brains of depressed people work in different ways than those of healthy people, Mayberg's study looked at people who had either recovered from their depression or who had been treated for it. What she and her colleagues found is that even when people recover, their brains still do not function normally.

In the trait marker study, researchers asked 25 women to remember an extremely sad experience in their lives, then scanned their brains with *positron emission tomography*, or PET, while the women recalled the event.

Ten of the participants had recovered from a major depressive episode (9 were on medication and 1 was not); 7 were in the throes of depression (only 1 was on medication), and 8 were healthy women who had no personal or family history of depression.

The scans, which measure blood flow, showed that the brains of the depressed women and those recovering from depression experienced different changes from the brains of the healthy participants.

"Under that emotional stressor, the recovered patients looked like the worst depressed patients," Mayberg says. "When we stressed healthy subjects' brains, we didn't see any decrease in brain activity."

Whether the differences in brain function are a cause or effect of a previous episode of depression remains unknown.

■ ■ ■ ■

Practical Help From a Psychiatrist

Dr. Carol Saltz, an assistant professor of psychiatry at New York Presbyterian Hospital and a psychoanalyst in private practice in New York City, offers this advice…

●**Get help if you suffer from depression**—even if you've had it for only a few weeks. One in 10 Americans suffers from depression. However, most of those people never seek help because they're embarrassed…or they wait so long that the depression becomes resistant to treatment. If you feel symptoms, such as difficulty sleeping, loss of appetite, difficulty concentrating or hopelessness, for more than two weeks, see a mental-health professional. If you have thoughts of harming yourself, seek help immediately.

●**Look for negative patterns in your life.** Don't spend another year making the same bad decisions…sabotaging work success…or failing at relationships.

Break the cycle by reviewing all aspects of your life—family, friends, work, leisure, etc. If things are going poorly, ask yourself why. Look for behaviors that may be setting you back. It's the first step to finding healthier ways to live your life.

• **Acknowledge that you're not perfect.** We all experience anger, frustration and anxiety from time to time. You'll suffer more if you believe that these and other "negative" emotions are somehow abnormal.

When things don't go smoothly, regroup and move forward…and remember to appreciate the good things in your life, such as your health or loving relationships. It's impossible to be happy when your expectations are too high.

Remember, There Are Lots of Ways to Improve Your Memory

Eleanor Maguire, PhD, Neuropsychologist, The Institute of Neurology, London, England.
December 2002, *Nature Neuroscience.*

If you are having trouble remembering things and think there's nothing you can do about it, take heart. There are ways to improve your memory.

"Although more research is needed, it may be that we all have the neural capacity to improve our memories," says Eleanor Maguire, a neuropsychologist at the Institute of Neurology in London, and the lead author of the study.

Maguire and her colleagues tested 10 people with remarkable ability to remember things, along with 10 people of comparable backgrounds who were not known for their memory skills.

All 20 underwent 2 to 3 hours of testing, including general intelligence exams, as well as structural and functional brain imaging. The researchers found that those with superior memories weren't more intelligent than those with average memories. Nor did they have any obvious brain differences, such as more gray matter from years spent challenging themselves mentally.

Using magnetic resonance imaging (MRI), the researchers discovered that those with superior memories used certain parts of their brains more than the control subjects did.

But they didn't perform exceptionally well in all areas of memory, however. Snowflake patterns, for instance, were remembered equally well by both groups. And when it came to remembering faces, those with superior memories only scored slightly better than the control group. It was only in the area of remembering numbers that those known for their memory skills excelled.

MEMORY ACES USE MNEMONIC TECHNIQUES

The people with better memories reported using *mnemonic* techniques—specific memory strategies—to remember things. One common mnemonic technique is to picture things you want to remember and imagine they are along a path that is familiar, such as a walk through your house. Mentally walking that path and seeing each thing helps you remember.

Many of the most effective mnemonics include imagery or involve processing something more deeply so that it forms associations and has a better chance of being remembered.

■ ■ ■ ■

Memory Tricks

The Middle Tennessee State University (*www. mtsu.edu*) in Murfreesboro has several suggestions on how to improve your memory. *They are…*

• **Intent to remember.** This has a lot to do with whether you remember something. A key factor to remembering is having the attitude that you will remember.

• **Recitation.** Saying ideas aloud and in your own words is probably the most powerful tool you have to transfer information from short-term to long-term memory.

• **Mental visualization.** Another powerful memory principle is making a mental picture of what needs to be remembered. By visualizing, you use an entirely different part of the brain than you did by reading or listening.

• **Association.** Memory is increased when facts that need to be learned are associated with something familiar to you.

9

Family Health

New Blood Pressure Guidelines Put More People at Risk

Some 45 million Americans who had previously thought they had normal blood pressure have a condition called "prehypertension," according to revised guidelines issued by United States health officials.

Probably the biggest change from the Joint National Committee on Prevention, Detection, Evaluation, and Treatment of High Blood Pressure is a new classification for hypertension, or high blood pressure. *The revised guidelines are as follows...*

•**Normal.** Any blood pressure reading lower than 120/80.

•**Prehypertension.** Any reading between 120/80 and 139/89. Previously this range was considered normal.

•**Stage 1 hypertension.** Any reading between 140/90 and 159/99.

•**Stage 2 hypertension.** A blood pressure reading of 160/100 and higher.

The new guidelines recommend that patients with Stage 1 or Stage 2 hypertension take 2 medications from the beginning of their treatment, rather than starting with 1 and waiting to see what happens before adding another drug.

"For the first time, they are quite strongly recommending that treatment of hypertension start with a combination of 2 drugs if the baseline blood pressure is at least 160/100," says Dr. Michael A. Weber, professor of medicine at State University of New York Downstate Medical Center in New York City, and past president of the American Society of Hypertension.

Thomas D. Giles, MD, Professor, Medicine, Louisiana State University Health Sciences Center, New Orleans.

Michael A. Weber, MD, Professor, Medicine, State University of New York Downstate Medical Center.

May 21, 2003, *Journal of the American Medical Association.*

May 2003, *American Journal of Hypertension.*

"The patients are almost certainly going to need 2 drugs anyway. So why not start that way and get there more quickly?"

DISPUTED RECOMMENDATION

One recommendation in the new guidelines troubles some experts. The guidelines suggest that the first-line treatment for individuals who don't need the 2-drug therapy should be the less expensive thiazide-type diuretics (except for people with certain high-risk conditions, such as diabetes or renal complications).

This recommendation was written because of the results of the Antihypertensive and Lipid Lowering Treatment to Prevent Heart Attack Trial, published in 2002.

"There was an enormous amount of controversy over that trial," says Dr. Thomas D. Giles, professor of medicine at Louisiana State University Health Sciences Center, in New Orleans.

INSURANCE IMPLICATIONS

But just because the guidelines have been issued doesn't mean doctors are compelled to follow them. Critics aren't worried so much about what doctors will do; they're worried about what health plans and patients might do.

"What we are a bit concerned about is that some of the health plans and insurance plans that are very anxious to save money will say they're not going to cover the other [more expensive] treatments or they'll cover them, but we have to write a justification," Weber says. "It's such a pain in the neck for doctors to jump through all those hoops. Many of them will just give in and go the path of least resistance [and follow the guidelines]."

PREVENTING HIGH BLOOD PRESSURE

You can take steps to prevent high blood pressure by maintaining a healthy weight; being physically active; following a healthy eating plan that emphasizes fruits and vegetables; choosing and preparing foods with less salt and sodium; and limiting alcohol intake.

info For more on high blood pressure, visit the American Society of Hypertension at *www.ash-us.org*.

Lower Your Risk for Heart Failure by 25%!

Donald Lloyd–Jones, MD, researcher, Framingham Heart Study, Framingham, MA, and instructor, Harvard Medical School, Boston, MA.

November 5, 2002, *Circulation.*

Researchers found that Americans have approximately a 1 in 5 chance of developing congestive heart failure during middle and late adulthood. For those with high blood pressure, the lifetime risk was twice as great.

Reducing the national systolic blood pressure—the top number in a reading—could lower rates of heart failure by at least 25%, experts say. Among patients with hypertension, a drop in systolic pressure can cut the risk of heart failure in half.

Normal blood pressure is now considered to be less than 120/80.

Many experts have called heart failure an epidemic in this country. The disease affects approximately 4.8 million Americans and kills almost 290,000 a year.

Drugs, such as diuretics, that help the body shed water can provide short-term relief for heart failure patients, as can other drugs that make the heart's job easier. However, the disease has no cure and even patients who have heart transplants don't have a normal life expectancy.

"We want people to understand the risk that they face and use that [information] for prevention," says Dr. Donald Lloyd–Jones, coauthor of the study. To avoid high blood pressure eat a low-salt diet, exercise regularly, and don't smoke.

■ ■ ■ ■

Dealing With Heart Failure

The Heart Failure Society of America (*www. hfsa.org*) urges patients to follow a treatment plan developed by a doctor or nurse. *The plan may include recommendations to...*

- **Take your medicines** as directed.

- **Weigh yourself every day** to see if you are retaining fluid.

- **Follow a low-sodium diet.**

- **Monitor your symptoms every day.**

- **Avoid alcohol** or drink sparingly.

- **Get vaccinations,** such as flu shots, on a regular basis.

- **Get regular physical activity.**

- **Quit smoking.**

- **Control your body weight** if you are overweight or have diabetes.

info For more on heart failure, visit the National Heart, Lung, and Blood Institute's Web site at *www.nhlbi.nih.gov.*

Erectile Dysfunction Could Be a Sign of Other Health Problems

Andrew McCullough, MD, Director, Sexual Health Program and Director, Male Fertility and Microsurgery Program, New York University Medical Center, and Assistant Professor, New York University School of Medicine.

Natan Bar–Chama, MD, Director, Male Reproductive Medicine and Surgery, Mount Sinai Medical Center, New York, NY.

The time may come when you can't blame stress or too much wine. You're going to have to admit your problem—to yourself and to your doctor.

Erectile dysfunction (ED)—the inability to have an erection or sustain one long enough for sexual intercourse—regularly affects approximately 30 million American men.

Once believed to be a rite of passage into the senior years, chronic ED is now showing up in men as young as 40 years, experts say.

"It's an important barometer of a man's overall health—particularly the health of the blood vessels. So if a man is at risk for any type of vascular disease, he is also at risk for ED, regardless of his age," says Dr. Andrew McCullough, director of the Sexual Health Program and director of the Male Fertility and Microsurgery Program at New York University Medical Center.

FORCE OF BLOOD

For an erection to occur, brain signals combine with local stimulation to relax a pair of muscles that run the length of the penis. This relaxation lets blood flow from nearby vessels into 2 tissue-filled chambers, also located inside the organ.

The blood's pressure makes the penis expand, creating an erection.

The process reverses when the muscles in the penis contract, usually following orgasm. This stops any more blood from flowing into the chambers, while simultaneously opening vascular ports that let blood drain back into the nearby vessels, McCullough explains.

Experts once thought ED was largely the result of psychological problems, but this is often not the case, particularly in men older than 40 years.

Physical conditions, including high blood pressure, high cholesterol, obesity, and diabetes, are often major causes, experts say.

"Frequently, erectile dysfunction is the first sign of these problems, and it can show up long before any typical symptoms develop," says Dr. Natan Bar–Chama, director of male reproductive medicine and surgery at Mount Sinai Medical Center in New York City.

Catching these conditions in their early stages can often have a remarkable effect on ED, he says.

SIMPLE STEPS TO BOOST VIRILITY

Simply lowering cholesterol or blood pressure—often through diet and exercise—can boost virility, says Bar–Chama. The same is true, he says, of losing weight and cutting back on cigarettes and alcohol.

But there are stumbling blocks. "Men have a problem asking physicians about ED. And doctors don't ask their patients if ED is a problem often enough," Bar–Chama says. Fewer than 2 men in 10 ever seek medical treatment—or even mention the problem to their doctor.

Treatments can include drugs like Viagra or mechanical devices that help bring blood into the penis and keep it there long enough to have an erection. But don't try anything on your own.

Both Bar–Chama and McCullough warn men against taking ED drugs without first receiving a physical examination, including important blood tests.

"You should never attempt to treat chronic ED on your own," McCullough says.

info To learn more, visit the American Foundation for Urologic Disease at *www. afud.org* or the National Library of Medicine at *www.nlm.nih.gov.*

This Blood Test Could Save Your Life

Dan Fisher, MD, Cardiologist, New York University Medical Center, and Clinical Assistant Professor, New York University School of Medicine.
November 12, 2002, *Circulation.*

A cheap and simple blood test may help predict who's more likely to live through an episode of heart trouble, say researchers.

"They're hoping that with a simple blood test, you can predict how well people are going to do after they have presented to the hospital with chest pain," says Dr. Dan Fisher, a clinical assistant professor at New York University School of Medicine in New York City.

"It's exciting to have something else to help determine patient management, especially if it's a simple blood marker, something you can check to see if you're at high risk or low risk," he adds.

HOW IT WORKS

Levels of a hormone called BNP are high in people with damaged hearts. When the pressure in the heart goes up (or when certain other conditions exist), BNP is released into the bloodstream where it helps get rid of excess sodium through urination.

The blood test measures the levels of a fragment of BNP. BNP itself can predict the future heart health of people who have had heart attacks or angina. But measuring this fragment of the hormone seems to provide an even better guide.

The blood test doesn't provide a diagnosis, but it does help doctors decide if the heart is responsible for shortness of breath. "If you've had a heart attack or it's angina, this helps determine how likely this person is to get into trouble, regardless of the specific diagnoses," Fisher says.

If a patient with a high likelihood of dying is identified through his/her BNP fragment levels, doctors can introduce more aggressive measures to save him.

"You may manage [patients] differently. You may get more aggressive with someone who has a high level," Fisher says. "This will help to risk-stratify and identify who needs to get an angiogram or some kind of intervention, as opposed to, 'Well, we'll treat you with medicines.'"

The few hospitals in the United States that have the test available are using it, Fisher says. "We're still waiting to get more widespread availability in emergency rooms and hospitals," he adds.

info Visit the American Heart Association at *www.americanheart.org* for more information on angina and heart attacks.

Are You Snoring Your Way to Heart Disease?

Yuksel Peker, MD, PhD, Consultant Internist and Pulmonologist, Sahlgrenska University Hospital, Gothenburg, Sweden.

Glenn Gomes, MD, Pulmonologist and Medical Director, Sleep Disorders Center, Ochsner Clinic Foundation, Baton Rouge, LA.

S noring caused by sleep apnea isn't just a nuisance—it can dramatically increase your risk of developing cardiovascular disease, according to one study. The good news is that with treatment, the risk drops.

People with sleep apnea—independent of age, body mass index, blood pressure, or smoking—have 5 times the risk of developing cardiovascular disease, says study author Dr. Yuksel Peker.

Peker, a pulmonologist at Sahlgrenska University Hospital in Gothenburg, Sweden, says he suspects the increased risk comes from the intermittent periods of low oxygen supply, which stresses the body.

THE STUDY

Researchers recruited 182 middle-aged men to observe them over a 7-year period. Sixty of the men were diagnosed with obstructive sleep apnea. None had any other known health problems when the study began.

After 7 years, 22 of the 60 men with sleep apnea had developed some form of cardiovascular disease, including high blood pressure, heart disease, and stroke. By contrast, only 8 of the 122 who didn't have sleep apnea had developed cardiovascular disease by the end of the study.

The researchers also found that treatment for sleep apnea was an effective way to reduce cardiovascular risk.

Out of the 38 men with sleep apnea and no cardiovascular disease, 16 were considered effectively treated. Only 1 man in that group developed cardiovascular disease.

But the 22 men who were "incompletely" treated for sleep apnea developed some form of cardiovascular disease, the study reports. "Incompletely" treated means they may not have followed the therapy suggested by the doctors.

Dr. Glenn Gomes, medical director of the Sleep Disorders Clinic at the Ochsner Foundation Clinic in Baton Rouge, Louisiana, says the study further illustrates the need for people who suspect they have sleep apnea to get properly diagnosed and then seek treatment.

Almost 25% of middle-aged American men and 9% of women have sleep apnea. These people stop breathing frequently while they sleep. Because their sleep is interrupted many times, they're often excessively tired during the day.

Some of the risk factors for sleep apnea are being male, being overweight, and being older than 40 years, according to the American Sleep Apnea Association.

■ ■ ■ ■

Sleep Apnea Treatments

People with sleep apnea can use a variety of treatments to try to correct the problem. *A few options are...*

- **Surgery.**
- **Oral devices** that keep the airway open.
- **A mask that patients wear during sleep** that blows air into the nose, keeping the airway open and unobstructed.

Antidepressant May Ease Sleep Apnea

David Carley, PhD, Professor, Medicine, Pharmacology and Bioengineering, and Director, Research, University of Illinois Center for Sleep and Ventilatory Disorders, Chicago, IL.

Eric M. Genden, MD, Associate Professor, Otolaryngology, and Director, Program for Sleep Disorders, Mount Sinai Hospital, New York, NY.

June 5, 2003, presentation, Associated Professional Sleep Societies, Chicago, IL.

An antidepressant taken an hour before bedtime may sharply reduce your sleep interruption if you have sleep apnea, a small study in Chicago found.

The antidepressant *mirtazapine* cut in half the number of times breathing stopped or slowed during sleep and reduced the number of times sleep was disrupted by 28% among study participants, according to David Carley and Dr. Miodrag Radulovacki, researchers at the University of Illinois at Chicago who led the study.

This small study was the first to use the antidepressant to treat humans for sleep apnea, says Carley, director of research at the University of Illinois at Chicago Center for Sleep and Ventilatory Disorders.

Mirtazapine, sold under the brand name Remeron, is approved by the US Food and Drug Administration only for the treatment of depression, Carley says.

"There is no [known effective drug] therapy for sleep apnea, so the concept of treating it with drugs is very attractive. But a study that small is very limited and no firm conclusions can be drawn," says Dr. Eric M. Genden, surgical director of the Program for Sleep Disorders at the Mount Sinai Hospital in New York City.

WHAT IS SLEEP APNEA?

Sleep apnea is a disorder characterized by brief interruptions of breathing during sleep—as many as 60 interruptions an hour. According to the National Institutes of Health, approximately 18 million Americans suffer from the disorder. Signs of sleep apnea include heavy snoring, disruption of sleep, lapses in breathing, and daytime sleepiness.

Current therapy (called *continuous positive airway pressure,* or CPAP) for sleep apnea consists of a nose mask that is attached to an air blower, which keeps pressure on the air passages so they remain open.

"The mask is difficult to tolerate over a long period of time, so compliance rates drop approximately 50% over the long run, and that's a problem," Carley says. "An equally effective but easier to tolerate treatment like a drug would be a major step forward."

■ ■ ■ ■

Other Treatment Options

According to the National Institute of Neurological Disorders and Stroke (NINDS) (*www.ninds.nih.gov*), treatment for mild cases of obstructive sleep apnea often consists of using methods to avoid sleeping on one's back. For people with significant nasal congestion, a decongestant therapy may be prescribed. Patients with obstructive and central apnea should avoid central nervous system depressants, such as alcoholic beverages, sedatives, and narcotics. Weight loss and diet control are encouraged for overweight patients.

Research Reveals New Causes of Sleep Apnea

Susan Redline, MD, PhD, Professor, Pediatrics, Rainbow Babies and Children's Hospital, Case Western Reserve University, Cleveland, OH.
Eric Genden, MD, Associate Professor, Otolaryngology, Head and Neck Surgery, and Surgical Director, Program for Sleep-Disordered Breathing, Mount Sinai School of Medicine, New York, NY.

May 7, 2003, *Journal of the American Medical Association.*

More people than previously thought—as many as 16%—will suffer from mild to moderately severe sleep-disordered breathing, including sleep apnea, during their lives. Researchers have found that the condition may be exacerbated by such surprising factors as high cholesterol levels and menopause in women.

"We estimate that approximately 7% of people will develop sleep apnea over 5 years," says Dr. Susan Redline, senior author of the study. The rate will vary greatly, she says, depending on age, weight, cholesterol level, and other factors.

Sleep apnea occurs when complete or partial obstruction of the airway leads to snoring, interrupted sleep and tiredness during the day. The obstruction is usually caused when the soft tissue in the back of the throat collapses during sleep.

People who have this disorder stop breathing for a few seconds every couple of minutes, which puts a tremendous amount of stress on the cardiovascular and pulmonary systems.

"I have patients who are 35 years old in complete heart failure," says Dr. Eric Genden, surgical director of the program for sleep-disordered breathing at Mount Sinai School of Medicine in New York City.

There are many successful treatments, ranging from wearing a mask that blows air past the obstruction to different types of surgeries.

WHO'S SUSCEPTIBLE

Researchers found that overweight people, middle-aged men, older women, and anyone with cardiovascular risk factors are at a greater risk of sleep apnea. High cholesterol levels and more fat in the middle of the body also increase the likelihood of problems.

The other surprising finding was that the probability of a man developing sleep apnea compared with the probability of a woman developing sleep apnea varied with age. Thirty-year-old men were 5 times more likely than women to develop the disorder. Men and women at age 60 had virtually the same rates of sleep apnea.

"Part of it might relate to how men and women put on fat and how that may change at different ages," Redline noted. It may also have to do with hormonal changes as a woman approaches and goes through menopause, she says.

The high incidence of sleep apnea found in this study also means everyone should be aware of the disorder, even if they don't suffer from it now.

Sleep Apnea Helper Also Fights GERD

J. Barry O'Connor, MD, Assistant Professor, Medicine, Division of Gastroenterology, Duke University Medical Center, Durham, NC.

Ali Serdar Karakurum, MD, Chief, Division of Gastroenterology, Nassau University Medical Center, East Meadow, NY.

January 13, 2003, *Archives of Internal Medicine*.

A commonly used treatment for obstructive sleep apnea does more than help sufferers get a good night's rest. It also reduces the symptoms of *gastroesophageal reflux disease* (GERD).

Researchers at Duke University followed more than 300 patients with obstructive sleep apnea for 7 years and found that 62% also suffered from nighttime symptoms of gastroesophageal reflux. Those who used their *continuous positive airway pressure* (CPAP) machines saw major improvements in their reflux symptoms.

PRESSURE HELPS

"CPAP elevates the pressure on the esophagus and keeps acid from coming back up,"

says study author Dr. J. Barry O'Connor, an assistant professor of medicine in the division of gastroenterology at Duke University Medical Center.

Sleep apnea is a common disorder, affecting up to 12 million people in the United States, according to the American Sleep Apnea Association. In obstructive sleep apnea, the soft tissue in the back of the throat relaxes and closes the airway. Because people can't breathe when this happens, they wake up numerous times during the night, though they might not even be aware of it. One of the most effective treatments for sleep apnea is a CPAP machine.

Gastroesophageal reflux is also a widespread disorder, affecting as many as 1 in 5 Americans at least once a week, according to the study. Reflux occurs when acid from the stomach backs up into the esophagus, causing heartburn. Symptoms often occur at night.

NOT PRACTICAL

"For patients who need CPAP anyway, they're killing two birds with one stone," says Dr. Ali Serdar Karakurum, chief of the division of gastroenterology at Nassau University Medical Center in East Meadow, New York. However, Karakurum adds, CPAP wouldn't be practical for most patients with reflux, since hoses from the machine are attached to the face during sleep. "The device is cumbersome and uncomfortable." And there are other, easier ways to manage reflux symptoms.

First, is lifestyle modification. Karakurum recommends avoiding tomatoes, citrus fruits, mint, coffee and other caffeinated products, high-fat foods, and tobacco. He also says eating more frequent, smaller meals helps. Losing weight helps lessen symptoms of both reflux and sleep apnea.

If lifestyle modifications don't work for your reflux symptoms, Karakurum says, there are also effective over-the-counter and prescription medications available.

info For more information on obstructive sleep apnea, go to the American Sleep Apnea Association at *www.sleepapnea.org*.

Acid Reflux— The Disease That Gets You While You Sleep!

William C. Orr, PhD, Professor, Physiology, University of Oklahoma Health Sciences Center, and President, Lynn Health Science Institute, Oklahoma City, OK.

October 21, 2002, presentation, American College of Gastroenterology Annual Meeting, Seattle, WA.

Acid reflux is bad enough during the day. But did you know that it can do most of its damage while you sleep?

The condition, known as *gastroesophageal reflux disease* (GERD), is the return of the stomach's contents—including the acidic stomach juices—to the esophagus.

If GERD goes untreated, it can lead to serious health problems, such as *esophagitis,* which can cause bleeding or ulcers in the esophagus. Some people also develop a condition called *Barrett's esophagus,* which is severe damage to the lining of the esophagus. This condition may be a precursor to esophageal cancer, according to the National Institute of Diabetes & Digestive & Kidney Diseases.

Sixty percent of the estimated 15 million Americans who have heartburn experience acid reflux at night, when their bodies are least prepared to deal with it, says William C. Orr, a professor of physiology at the University of Oklahoma Health Sciences Center.

Orr says that lying flat during sleep lets stomach acid collect in the esophagus, and prevents a natural flushing of the system via swallowing or salivating.

"If you have acid reflux during sleep, you have double trouble," he says. "Not only do you wake up at night and have trouble sleeping, but it's also much more risky. If the acid dwells in the esophagus, it may spill over into the lungs and create breathing problems."

In a research study, Orr and other researchers from the Lynn Health Science Institute in Oklahoma City compared the sleep habits of healthy people with patients who reported having heartburn at least 4 days a week and being awakened by heartburn at least 1 night a week. Those with heartburn had much more trouble sleeping, and felt drained during the day, Orr says.

"If you wake up from sleep with acid in your mouth at least once a week, you have a problem and you should see your doctor," Orr says.

Experts say that if you have heartburn, particularly at night, you should avoid eating heavy meals close to bedtime and elevate your head during sleep.

■ ■ ■ ■

Symptoms of GERD

Chronic heartburn is the most common symptom of GERD. Acid regurgitation is another common symptom. There are many less common symptoms also associated with GERD. *According to the International Foundation for Functional Gastrointestinal Disorders (www.aboutgerd.org), these symptoms may include...*

- **Belching.**
- **Difficulty or pain when swallowing.**
- **Waterbrash** (sudden excess of saliva).
- **Dysphagia** (the sensation of food sticking in the esophagus).
- **Chronic sore throat.**
- **Laryngitis.**
- **Inflammation of the gums.**
- **Erosion of the enamel of the teeth.**
- **Chronic irritation in the throat.**
- **Hoarseness in the morning.**
- **A sour taste.**
- **Bad breath.**

info For more information on stomach disorders, visit the American Gastroenterological Association online at *www.gastro.org/public.html.*

Smallpox Vaccines: Are They Safe Enough For You?

Edward H. Kaplan, PhD, Professor, Public Health, Yale University, New Haven, CT.

John Neff, MD, Professor, Pediatrics, University of Washington School of Medicine, Seattle.

ABC News, New York, NY.

Centers for Disease Control and Prevention, Atlanta, GA.

Deciding whether to get a smallpox vaccination seems to have taken a back seat for the time being. But the uncertainty of world events could put it back in the forefront at any time.

If you're confused about whether to get a smallpox vaccination, it's no wonder—even the experts don't agree whether it's necessary if no outbreak has occurred.

The smallpox vaccine is effective against the virus, but it can lead to deadly complications in approximately 1 in every 1 million people who receive it. Another 10 to 15 vaccinated people per million suffer serious side effects, such as severe rashes.

More than 10 million military personnel and health workers were scheduled to receive the vaccine through 2003, and the rest of the nation has the option of getting vaccinated. The government has left it up to individuals to decide whether to be inoculated, putting them in the position of having to weigh the risk of a smallpox attack against the low odds of suffering a serious or deadly side effect from the vaccine.

Ironically, the more people who opt for the vaccination, the more prudent waiting becomes, because those who do get the vaccine serve as a buffer for the rest.

VACCINATION PLANS

The Centers for Disease Control and Prevention reviewed smallpox vaccination plans from 49 states and 4 cities. Vaccines will be available at thousands of health care facilities and hundreds of clinics nationwide.

Health officials have stockpiled enough doses of the vaccine to immunize the entire country. Approximately 60% of the US population was born before routine smallpox vaccination ended.

"I would not personally consider that I am protected even though I had a shot as a child," says Edward Kaplan, an expert in smallpox vaccination, working at Yale University. But, he adds, people who have already been immunized are probably less likely to suffer side effects the second time around.

Pregnant women, people with HIV or AIDS, and those with certain skin conditions should not be given the smallpox vaccine in a pre-attack inoculation program. Inoculating them during an outbreak would depend on the scope and severity of the attack, Kaplan says.

Kaplan also believes that a voluntary vaccination system for the public is the right approach. But the decision to get inoculated will require careful thinking and cost-benefit analysis.

FINDING THE RIGHT PLAN

Kaplan says some states have considered a strategy of "ring vaccination," which controls an outbreak by vaccinating and monitoring a ring of people around each infected individual. The idea is to form a buffer of immune people to prevent the spread of the disease. That approach, he says, makes him nervous.

"If I was in a state where that was the agreed-upon policy, I would think very hard about getting vaccinated on a voluntary basis," he adds, saying he prefers mass inoculations.

Not every expert agrees with choosing to be vaccinated. Dr. John Neff, a pediatrician at the University of Washington who has studied smallpox, says the public doesn't need to be vaccinated before an outbreak.

"I think that the potential risk from an adverse event [from the vaccination] is higher than the risk of getting and dying from smallpox," Neff says.

info Visit the Centers for Disease Control and Prevention's Emergency Preparedness & Response Web site at *www.bt.cdc.gov.* Click on "Smallpox."

Flu Vaccine
You Simply Sniff for
Years of Protection

Laszlo Otvos, Jr., PhD, Associate Professor, Chemistry, Wistar Institute, Philadelphia, PA.

James C. King, MD, Professor, Pediatrics, University of Maryland School of Medicine, Baltimore.

June 2, 2003, *Vaccine.*

Flu shots are seen as a necessary evil by many who trudge to the doctor's office every year for that protective shot in the arm. But researchers are saying they're working on a flu vaccine that doesn't hurt and could last for several flu seasons.

A prototype vaccine, developed by researchers at the Wistar Institute in Philadelphia, was delivered in the form of a nasal spray and worked well in animal studies. Even better, the spray targets a protein within the flu virus that doesn't mutate as often as other proteins.

"Current vaccines target two proteins [within the flu virus] that mutate frequently," which is why public health officials constantly have to update the vaccine, says Laszlo Otvos, Jr., an associate professor of chemistry at the Wistar Institute. But the Wistar researchers focused instead on a more stable protein that mutates less frequently.

THE MICE REMAINED HEALTHY

The experimental vaccine, in nasal spray form, was given to mice 2 times. After they received it, a steep rise in antibodies was found in blood samples, and the mice resisted replication of the virus in their respiratory tracts.

Those mice that got the vaccine had much less of the virus in their respiratory tracts than those that didn't get it, Otvos says.

Every year, approximately 114,000 people in the United States are hospitalized with influenza, a viral respiratory infection, according to the Centers for Disease Control and Prevention (CDC) in Atlanta. Approximately 20,000 people die because of it, most of them elderly. Although the flu vaccine is not 100%

effective, if you do become infected after getting a flu shot, you're likely to be far less sick than without it, the CDC says.

WE'LL HAVE TO WAIT A BIT

Of the new vaccine, Dr. James C. King, a professor of pediatrics at the University of Maryland School of Medicine, says, "The idea is wonderful." His own research focuses on live, intranasal vaccines, but he says it will be several years before any will be ready for human consumption.

If it all bears out, Otvos says, the flu vaccine may become a once-in-a-lifetime preventive measure.

info For the facts about flu shots, see the CDC's National Immunization Program Web site at *www.cdc.gov/nip/flu.* For information on the flu virus, check the US Food and Drug Administration Web site at *www.fda.gov/ cber/flu/flu.htm.*

Breathe Easy. Good News
For Frequent Fliers

Jessica Nutik Zitter, MD, MPH, University of California, San Francisco.

Morton Lippmann, PhD, Professor and Program Director, Human Exposure and Health Effects, NIEHS Center, Department of Environmental Medicine, New York University School of Medicine.

Noal May, PhD, Industrial Hygienist, Civil Aerospace Medical Institute, Federal Aviation Administration, Oklahoma City, OK.

July 24, 2002, *Journal of the American Medical Association.*

Breathe easier, frequent fliers. Your risk of catching a cold while traveling is no greater on newer airplanes that recirculate cabin air than on older ones that pumped in fresh air from the outside, according to a study in the *Journal of the American Medical Association.*

Modern jets recycle approximately half their cabin air as a way to reduce the strain on their engines and improve gas mileage. Many older planes, though increasingly obsolete, use 100% compressed fresh air to ventilate the seating area.

Some studies have indicated that poorly ventilated spaces—such as airplanes and office buildings—can increase the risk of germ and virus transmission. Although airplanes that recirculate cabin air have fine filters to trap pathogens, experts have wondered if this system might put passengers at risk of disease by steeping them in other people's breath.

To answer that question, a research team led by Dr. Jessica Nutik Zitter, formerly an assistant clinical professor of medicine at the University of California, San Francisco, compared the rates of colds and other respiratory ailments in 1100 airplane passengers traveling between San Francisco and Denver in 1999. Slightly more than half flew in new jets with air-recycling systems.

Within a week of their trip, 19% of the group that had flown on a new plane complained of a cold, compared with 21% of the other passengers—not a meaningful difference, the researchers say. Rates of runny nose and cold together were 3% for both groups.

Zitter says the 3% jibes with the rates of colds in the general population at that time of year (January through April). However, she adds, that doesn't necessarily mean that flying carries zero risk of airway infections.

The duration of travel may play a role. The flight from San Francisco to Denver is approximately 2.5 hours; longer trips may present more of an infection risk, Zitter says.

Morton Lippmann, an environmental medicine expert at New York University School of Medicine, calls the findings not really surprising. In newer planes, infectious agents are not recirculated because the filters nab them, says Lippmann, chairman of a National Academy of Sciences panel that has looked at cabin air-quality issues.

Passengers may actually feel more comfortable flying on newer planes because the recycled air is moister than the fresh, dry air in older cabins. (Thank your fellow travelers' perspiration and exhaled vapor for that.) As a

result, skin and mucus membranes stay better hydrated in flight.

NEARNESS COUNTS

Air quality on planes can, and has, become an issue when the ventilation systems fail. Still, for the typical passenger, the biggest risk of catching an illness is if the person in the neighboring seat is sick, Lippmann says.

Noal May, an industrial hygienist at the Federal Aviation Administration's Civil Aerospace Medical Institute in Oklahoma City, says traveling by air is no more risky than other forms of public transportation, such as buses or trains.

However, "if you're sitting right next to the [sick] individual, your chances of catching something are much greater," May says.

info For more information, visit the Web site of the Federal Aviation Administration's Office of Aerospace Medicine at *www. cami.jccbi.gov.*

Whooping Cough: How to Keep Your Family Safe Now

Kristine M. Bisgard, MD, National Immunization Program, Centers for Disease Control and Prevention, Atlanta, GA.

,Carol J. Baker, MD, Professor, Pediatrics, Baylor College of Medicine, Houston, TX.

July 19, 2002, *Morbidity and Mortality Weekly Report.*

The once-feared *pertussis* bacteria that causes whooping cough is claiming more lives, and although the death rate is still very low, health officials say its resurgence should be taken as a warning.

"We have noticed an increase in deaths and an increase in cases in infants younger than 4 months of age, and that's likely indicating an increase in circulating bacteria," says Dr. Kristine Bisgard, an epidemiologist at the Centers for Disease Control and Prevention.

Starting at 2 months of age, children should receive 3 doses of the pertussis vaccine—DTaP, which also prevents diphtheria and tetanus—by the time they're 6 months old. The DTaP vaccine is among the most widely administered inoculations, with better than 90% coverage in children, Bisgard says. Still, the incidence of pertussis has increased.

The pertussis bacteria can be killed with antibiotics, but in some cases the attack is so strong that by the time whooping cough is diagnosed, even drugs can't control it.

Because the vaccine isn't 100% effective and because immunity to pertussis wanes over time, partially immune adolescents and adults are vulnerable to generally mild cases. These mild cases can be hard to distinguish from other respiratory ailments, such as a regular cold. As a result, people usually don't seek treatment. They then become reservoirs of infection. Pertussis spreads through respiratory droplets expelled in coughs, and, to a lesser extent, in secretions left on shared drinking glasses.

Bisgard says parents should keep young infants away from people with newly developed coughs. Pediatricians should consider whooping cough a potential threat to their youngest patients, she adds.

Dr. Carol J. Baker, a pediatrician at Baylor College of Medicine in Houston, says doctors also need to be on the lookout for pertussis in older children and adolescents.

"This is where we're beginning to see a lot more disease and a lot more concern," she says.

Baker says scientists are now investigating whether giving older children an additional inoculation against pertussis to restore their immunity might help quash the infection.

■ ■ ■ ■

More About Whooping Cough

Whooping cough is not as common as it once was. *Here's how to recognize it...*

•**Symptoms appear from 6 to 21 days after exposure** to the bacteria. On average, symptoms appear between 7 and 10 days after exposure.

•**The disease starts with cold symptoms**—runny nose and cough. Sometime in the first 2 weeks, episodes of severe cough develop and that cough can last 1 to 2 months.

The person may look and feel fairly healthy between these episodes.

•**During bouts of cough, the lips and nails may turn blue** due to a lack of air. Vomiting may occur after severe coughing spells.

•**During the severe coughing stage, seizures or even death can occur,** particularly in an infant.

•**Immunized school children and adults have milder symptoms** than young children.

•**Cases can occur in adults** because protection from the vaccine lasts only 5 to 10 years.

Drinking and Driving— Even One Drink Is Not Safe

Maurice Dennis, PhD, Director, Center for Alcohol and Drug Education Studies, Texas A&M University, College Station.

James Fell, member, Board of Directors, Mothers Against Drunk Driving (MADD), and Director, Traffic Safety and Enforcement Programs, Pacific Institute for Research and Evaluation, both in Calverton, MD.

Although most people think a glass of wine or a beer is safe, experts say drinking even significantly less than the legal limit can seriously impair your ability to drive.

Impairment can begin at much lower levels than the 0.08% blood-alcohol concentration—the legal limit in most states, says Maurice Dennis, director of the Center for Alcohol and Drug Education Studies at Texas A&M University.

"People think, 'If the legal limit is 0.08%, it's okay if I'm at 0.07999%,'" says Dennis, but a study he led suggests differently. "We saw losses [in driving skill] even at 0.04%."

Usually, imbibing a bit and driving is not a problem, Dennis notes. It's when "something out of the ordinary happens [on the road]," he says. "You've taken away the edge."

Under normal circumstances, all is fine. But one day, you may have had a few, get behind the wheel, and be behind someone who suddenly slams on the brakes, leaving you to either brake or swerve into another lane where there may be a pedestrian or another car.

In Dennis' experiment, when a driving emergency arose, those who had just a beer or 2 tended to make poor decisions, he says.

Dennis says he believes the blood-alcohol level at which one is legally not allowed to drive should be 0.05%.

Some impairment in judgment definitely exists at a level of 0.04%, agrees James Fell, who is on the national board of directors of Mothers Against Drunk Driving (MADD). On average, a small woman will have a blood-alcohol concentration of 0.04% after just 1 or 1½ beers. For a 150-pound man, it's closer to 2 beers.

"We're not prohibitionists," Fell says. But "if you're going to drink, make sure someone else drives for you."

■ ■ ■ ■

Common Myths About Drinking

The University of Oklahoma Police Department says nothing sobers up a drinker except time. *Some misconceptions about drinking...*

● **Drinking coffee** will help make a person more sober.

● **Eating certain foods** before an evening of heavy drinking will help keep you sober.

● **Eating a big meal** before drinking prevents a person from becoming drunk.

● **Splashing cold water on a person's face** or taking a cold shower helps him/her sober up.

● **Running around the block a few times** sobers a person.

What's your limit? The University of Oklahoma Police Department has an online blood-alcohol content calculator at *www.ou. edu/oupd/drug.htm.*

Alcoholism Answers: The Drink Link May Be All in the Taste Buds

Henry R. Kranzler, MD, Professor, Psychiatry, University of Connecticut Health Center, Farmington.

Fulton T. Crews, PhD, Professor, Pharmacology and Psychiatry, and Director, Bowles Center for Alcohol Studies, University of North Carolina, Chapel Hill.

June 2003, *Alcoholism: Clinical and Experimental Research.*

The answer to whether offspring of alcoholic fathers will suffer the same fate as their parent may lie on the tongues of the children.

Although alcoholism appears to run in families, many children of alcoholic parents don't develop the disease. Rather, how the offspring of alcoholic fathers experience sour or salty tastes may be what determines whether they become addicted to alcohol, say researchers.

Previous studies have established a link between an affinity for sweet tastes and alcohol addiction. This is the first large-scale effort to show that one's perception of sour and salty tastes may also play a role in predicting the development of the disease.

The researchers sought to replicate the intriguing findings of a Polish study, which showed that sons of alcoholic fathers tended to find salty and sour tastes more unpalatable than sons of nonalcoholic fathers.

TASTE TELLS

In this study, the researchers recruited 112 nonalcoholic men and women. After interviewing them about their family, the researchers learned that 45 had fathers who were alcoholics, while the remaining 67 had no paternal history of the disease.

Each of the participants tasted a series of salty and sour solutions in varying concentrations and rated each for intensity and pleasantness. The researchers found the subjects' reaction to the tastes mirrored the results of the Polish study.

"We replicated the Polish findings very closely in a different country, with males and females, and with a sample size that was 3 times larger," says Dr. Henry R. Kranzler, coauthor of the study and a professor of psychiatry at the University of Connecticut Health Center.

"Taste preferences may influence not the initial exposure, but subsequent exposures. If you experience something that isn't pleasurable, you're less likely to repeat it," Kranzler says.

TWO POSSIBLE ASSOCIATIONS

First, the results could indicate that people with a family history of alcoholism who possess certain taste characteristics are protected from alcoholism. Those with an enhanced sensitivity to salty and sour flavors are put off by the taste of alcohol.

The other possibility is that people with a paternal history of alcoholism may inherit genetic alterations in taste characteristics that put them at an increased risk for alcoholism.

"A taste trait may be related to the amount of risk of becoming an alcoholic. This would greatly benefit prevention–intervention efforts," says Fulton T. Crews, professor of pharmacology and psychiatry, and director of the Center for Alcohol Studies at the University of North Carolina at Chapel Hill.

info Learn more about alcoholism from the National Institute on Alcohol Abuse and Alcoholism at *www.niaaa.nih.gov* and the American Council on Alcoholism at *www.aca-usa.org*.

Epilepsy Drug Helps Alcoholics Stop Drinking

Bankole A. Johnson, MD, PhD, Professor, Psychiatry and Pharmacology, Deputy Chairman, Research, and Director, South Texas Addiction Research and Technology Center, University of Texas Health Science Center, San Antonio.

Robert Malcolm, MD, Associate Dean, Professor, Psychiatry and Family Medicine, Center for Drug and Alcohol Programs, Medical University of South Carolina, Charleston.

May 17, 2003, *The Lancet*.

In what could be a breakthrough in the treatment of alcoholism, researchers say an antiseizure drug dramatically reduced drinking among alcoholics.

Alcoholics who took *topiramate* were 6 times as likely as those who took a placebo to abstain from drinking for at least 4 consecutive weeks during a 12-week study, say researchers at the University of Texas Health Science Center in San Antonio. Topiramate is a drug that the US Food and Drug Administration approved for the treatment of epileptic and other seizures.

The study also found that those who took the placebo were 4 times as likely as those who took topiramate to drink heavily for 28 consecutive days.

MAY BE MOST EFFECTIVE

The dramatic results suggest that the drug may be more effective than any others currently being used to treat alcoholics, said lead researcher Dr. Bankole A. Johnson.

"The critical factor here is not only were all [of the study subjects] heavily dependent on alcohol, but they were all still drinking heavily," says Johnson, a professor of psychiatry and pharmacology and director of the Health Science Center's South Texas Addiction Research and Technology Center.

Researchers defined drinking heavily as more than 5 drinks per day for men and more than 4 for women.

Johnson says existing drugs for alcoholism—*antabuse,* which makes patients sick if they drink, and *naltrexone,* which blocks the pleasure sensations from alcohol—are designed mainly to prevent a relapse among alcoholics who stop drinking.

Topiramate helps alcoholics quit by blocking the "high" from alcohol while reducing withdrawal symptoms and cravings, Johnson says.

FUTURE USE

The Texas researchers' findings generated considerable excitement among experts on alcoholism. Dr. Robert Malcolm, associate dean and a professor of psychiatry and family medicine at the Center for Drug and Alcohol Programs at the Medical University of South Carolina, says topiramate could change the direction of alcohol treatment.

If further research with more subjects bears out the study's findings, Malcolm predicts that topiramate will become a drug that could be prescribed by primary care doctors, without the need for extensive counseling.

Lifesaving Questions You Should Always Ask Your Pharmacist

Suzy Cohen, RPh, CPh, Pharmacist, a nationally syndicated pharmaceutical columnist, and spokeswoman, National Association of Chain Drug Stores, Alexandria, VA.

Charles Fetrow, PharmD, Clinical Specialist, Pharmacy, University of Pittsburgh Medical Center–Passavant Hospital, PA.

National Association of Chain Drug Stores telephone survey.

The pharmacist isn't just the person who dumps pills into bottles. He or she is also the professional who can tell you about drug side effects and if any combination of drugs you're taking may interact badly.

The problem? According to a survey, people aren't asking their pharmacists enough questions and therefore, may be endangering their health.

A survey of 1001 people aged 18 years and older found that, although the large majority of them had a basic knowledge of the medicines they took, only half asked their pharmacists about possible side effects, and only one-fifth asked if their medicine was safe to take with over-the-counter medicines or herbal treatments. Pharmacists, who are licensed by their states, spend 5 to 6 years in training and are well versed in how drugs work in the body and how they interact with each other.

Problems ranging from drowsiness to dangerous combinations of over-the-counter and prescribed medicines can be avoided if a patient talks to the pharmacist, says Suzy Cohen, spokeswoman for the National Association of Chain Drug Stores, the group that created the survey.

"For instance, people should ask their pharmacist about the use of nonsteroidals, such as ibuprofen, which can lead to gastrointestinal problems like bleeding and can also elevate blood pressure, especially when combined with prescribed medications," she says.

TALKING TO THE PHARMACIST

For the survey, respondents were asked about getting prescription drugs, how much they talked to their pharmacists about their medications, and about the kinds of questions they asked their pharmacists.

The scores on the survey were the highest when people were questioned about taking their medicines. When asked if they took their medicine exactly as recommended, the average score was 84 out of a possible 100. The average score was 86 when respondents were asked if they knew why they were taking the medicine.

However, the score dropped to an average of 53 when people were asked whether they had questioned their doctor or pharmacist about precautions they should take when they took the medicine. The score dropped even further, to 41, when they were questioned as to whether they had asked anything further about their drugs.

"People think that because herbal treatments and vitamins are natural, they aren't drugs. They think, 'Why should I bother someone about them?'" says C.W. Fetrow, a clinical specialist in pharmacy at the University of Pittsburgh Medical Center. "But there are a lot of interactions between drugs and herbal treatments, and people should absolutely ask."

Women aged 35 to 54 years had the overall highest score (65). This meant they were the best informed and most willing to ask questions of the pharmacist. Both men and women younger than 35 years had the lowest overall score (53).

info Take a quiz to find out how smart you are about taking your prescription medicine at Pharmacy Care Quiz at *www.get rxhealthy.com*. Drug interactions can be found at *www.arthritis.com*. Search under "Drugs" for a direct link.

■ ■ ■ ■

What You Should Know About Prescription Medicine

The answers to this short quiz prepared by St. Mary's Hospital at San Rafael, California, might surprise you.

1. What percentage of people taking prescription medicine *don't* take it exactly as prescribed?

☐ 10%–30%

☐ 20%–40%

☐ 30%–50%

2. The best place to store medication is the bathroom cabinet...

☐ True

☐ False

3. If a pill is hard to swallow, you can crush it and mix it with food or juice...

☐ True

☐ False

ANSWERS

1. According to the Food and Drug Administration (FDA), between 30% and 50% of people do not take their medicine exactly as prescribed.

2. The bathroom cabinet is where many of us keep medicine. But the bathroom is the place most likely to be hot and humid due to constant baths and showers. The American Pharmaceutical Association (APA) advises consumers to use a cool, dry cabinet in a different room, one that's out of direct sunlight. Ideal storage is a place that can be locked and/or is out of children's reach.

3. The APA advises people not to chew, crush, or break any capsules or tablets unless instructed to do so by your doctor or pharmacist, since some long-acting medications are absorbed too quickly when this is done.

Ignorance Is *Not* Bliss: The Scary Truth About OTCs

Marc Siegel, MD, Clinical Assistant Professor, Medicine, New York University Medical Center.
Rebecca Burkholder, Director, Health Policy, National Consumer League, Washington, DC.

A headache. A backache. A bout of tennis elbow. If you're like most Americans, you frequently turn to an over-the-counter (OTC) pain reliever to get you through these types of ailments.

"I think many people believe that because something is sold over the counter they can take it as much as they need to, they can use it without checking with their doctor, and that, basically, it's harmless medication. And none of these things is true," says New York University internist Dr. Marc Siegel.

What you might not realize is how easy it is to abuse these drugs—and the alarming consequences of doing so.

This is particularly true if the medications you are reaching for are *nonsteroidal anti-inflammatory drugs* (NSAIDs), such as ibuprofen or naproxen, which are among the most popular over-the-counter drugs on the market.

LESS POWERFUL PRESCRIPTION DRUGS

What most people don't know is that many over-the-counter medications, particularly NSAIDs, are actually prescription drugs packaged in much less potent doses.

But if you take more than you should for longer than intended, you might reach prescription levels. "And when you do, you are playing with some potentially very dangerous drugs," Siegel says.

It can happen easily. In a survey of more than 4200 adults, released by the National Consumer League, researchers found that of the 84% of Americans who acknowledged taking pain relievers in the previous year, more than half also admitted they had knowingly taken more than the recommended dose, and many reported they had simply ignored label information.

"People read the label and they think, 'Oh, this doesn't apply to me—I'm healthy. This warning is only for people who have stomach problems or kidney problems,' so they ignore the warnings," says Rebecca Burkholder, director of health policy for the National Consumer League.

OVERLAPPING DRUGS

Another problem: Many over-the-counter drugs contain the same pain medications.

"Often, people are not aware that a drug contains the same pain ingredient as another drug they are already taking, so they end up taking more than they realize," Burkholder says.

According to the survey, nearly half of the people who took an over-the-counter pain reliever thought it was safe to take an over-the-counter cold or flu medication. More than 30% believed it was safe to take an over-the-counter painkiller while taking a prescription drug. And 20% thought it was okay to drink alcohol when taking over-the-counter painkillers. None of the above combinations is safe.

info For more information, visit The National Consumers League Web site at *www.nclnet.org.*

The Unexpected Danger Of Insurance Copays

Dana Goldman, PhD, Director, Health Economics, and Geoffrey Joyce, PhD, Economist, RAND Health, Santa Monica, CA.
October 9, 2002, *Journal of the American Medical Association.*

W hen your health plan or supplemental insurance program raises your co-payment for prescription drugs, you may spend a bit more and take fewer pills. How that affects a person's health isn't known.

Insurance plans reap nearly all the initial cost savings from the reduction in spending on drugs, but the individual eventually sees the benefit in the form of lower premiums, researchers say.

"It's quite surprising that small changes in copayments can actually save plans so much money," says study coauthor Dana Goldman, director of health economics at RAND, a research group.

Consumer drug spending is the fastest-growing segment of the health-care economy, rising more than 17% between 1999 and 2000. For private insurers, the increase was even greater, approaching 20%. Not surprisingly, businesses that provide health insurance for their workers have been struggling to contain these runaway costs. One approach has been to control the drug benefits they offer, either by requiring employees to purchase cheaper generic drugs whenever possible or by graduating the copayments for prescriptions.

LAYERED PLANS HELP REDUCE COSTS

Researchers found that doubling the copay (for example, from $5 to $10) slashed spending on drugs from $678 to $455 per member. Plans that required people to buy generic drugs when available also drove down costs significantly, the researchers found.

"I think injecting some price sensitivity is a good thing," says Geoffrey Joyce, a RAND economist and coauthor of the study. "Paying a $5 copay regardless of the cost of a drug doesn't send the right message to consumers."

On the other hand, Joyce says, most health plans are more sensitive to cost than to how effective the drug might be. Their decisions are often based on the discount they get from the company that sells a particular drug.

DO HIGHER COSTS EQUAL MORE ILLNESS?

As copayments climbed, the number of prescriptions filled dropped by more than 30%, from roughly 12 to 9 per year per person, the RAND study found.

The RAND researchers did not study whether people who were forced to pay more for their prescriptions stopped taking them and suffered ill health as a result.

"Will there be these adverse health consequences because people are cutting back too much? That's the next question for us," Gold-man says.

info If you'd like to know more about how your health-care dollar is spent, take a look at a consumer's guide to health insurance at the Georgetown University Health Policy Institute's Web site at *www.healthinsurance info.net.*

Hospitals' Hidden Killers: Blood Clots

Samuel Goldhaber, MD, Cochairman, Council for Leadership on Thrombosis (CLOT) Awareness and Management, and Director, Venous Thromboembolism Research Group, Brigham and Women's Hospital, and Associate Professor, Medicine, Harvard University Medical School, Boston, MA.

Steven Deitelzweig, MD, Section Head, Hospital-Based Internal Medicine, Ochsner Clinic Foundation, New Orleans, LA.

Doctors at the Ochsner Clinic Foundation in New Orleans have started a campaign against 2 conditions that are responsible for 10% of all hospital deaths each year.

One of these conditions is *deep vein thrombosis* (DVT), which occurs when a blood clot forms in the leg and blocks the flow of blood. This can lead to potentially life-threatening pulmonary embolisms, which are caused when a clot breaks free, travels upward through the body, and lodges in a lung. If the clot is large enough, it can cause sudden death.

Approximately 600,000 Americans develop pulmonary embolisms every year, and 200,000 people die from them. The American College of Chest Physicians says it may be the most preventable cause of hospital death.

ADDRESSING THE PROBLEM

Dr. Steven Deitelzweig, Ochsner's section head of hospital-based internal medicine, says no one appeared to be taking the lead to solve the problem, so he is spearheading the initiative at his clinic to raise the public profile of the problem.

Another group of medical experts has formed the Council for Leadership on Thrombosis (CLOT) Awareness and Management, which is sponsoring free screening programs at 185 hospitals nationwide. It has also established the Clot Alert Resource Center, which includes a Web site that provides information and services.

WHO'S AT RISK?

People hospitalized for long periods of time are particularly at risk because blood can collect in their legs and increase the probability of a clot forming. Air travelers can also be prone to the condition because of the long hours spent cramped in a seat, experts say.

Those with cancer, chronic heart or respiratory failure, and an inherited or acquired predisposition to clotting and varicose veins also have an increased risk. So do people who are obese, as well as women who are pregnant or are using birth control pills or hormone replacement therapy.

Symptoms of DVT can include leg pain, swelling, tenderness, discoloration or redness. Often, though, there are no symptoms. Dr. Samuel Goldhaber, cochairman of CLOT, says the conditions are difficult to diagnose.

WHAT CAN BE DONE

Deitelzweig and his colleagues have developed a clinical assessment tool to help identify people at risk for DVT. The various risk factors—obesity, heart failure, infections, lung problems, prolonged immobility—are put on a grid. Everyone admitted to the hospital is assessed and put in a category of low, medium, or high risk.

People with 2 risk factors get treated with nonpharmacological devices, such as compression stockings. If a person has at least 3 risk factors, or 2 risk factors and a history of stroke or cancer, they get at least 1 blood-thinning drug.

info For more information on the Council for Leadership on Thrombosis, visit Thrombosis Online at *www.thrombosisonline. com* or call 800-CLOT-FREE.

Simple Way to Make Gallbladder Surgery 71% Safer!

David R. Flum, MD, MPH, Professor, Surgery, University of Washington, Seattle.

Mark A. Talamini, MD, Director, Minimally Invasive Surgery, Johns Hopkins School of Medicine, Baltimore, MD.

April 2, 2003, *Journal of the American Medical Association*.

Gallbladder surgery has become so routine that it can often be done without having to stay overnight in the hospital. But mistakes can happen during the procedure. To avoid mistakes, such as cutting a bile duct, some researchers recommend something called *cholangiography*—an injection of a contrast dye, which helps surgeons identify the duct.

When a surgeon accidentally cuts into the bile duct, it almost always requires a second operation to fix it, says Dr. David Flum, study author and a professor of surgery at the University of Washington in Seattle. Sometimes 2 or 3 operations are needed, he says.

In his search through data on more than 1.5 million Medicare patients, Flum found that there had been a bile-duct injury during approximately 1 in every 200 operations.

"Even after controlling for important patient-level and surgeon-level factors, we found that the adjusted relative risk of common bile-duct injuries was 71% higher when cholangiography was not used," the report says. Flum says routine use of cholangiography can cut the risk of that complication by nearly half.

NOT EVERYONE AGREES

There has been a running controversy for decades about whether all gallbladder patients should have cholangiography, says Dr. Mark A. Talamini, director of minimally invasive surgery at Johns Hopkins School of Medicine.

Flum contends the issue has been settled by his and other large-scale analyses of surgical data, but Talamini isn't convinced. It's possible,

Talamini says, that the surgeons who do routine cholangiography are those who do more operations and therefore, are more skilled at avoiding mistakes. Or maybe many bile-duct injuries were recognized and repaired during the removal operation, so they don't show up in Flum's data, he says.

Talamini and his colleagues reserve cholangiography for selected patients.

■ ■ ■ ■

Symptoms of Gallstones

According to the National Institute of Diabetes & Digestive & Kidney Diseases, symptoms of gallstones are often called a "gallstone attack" because they occur suddenly. *A typical attack can cause...*

● **Steady pain in the upper abdomen** that increases rapidly and lasts from 30 minutes to several hours.

● **Pain in the back between the shoulder blades.**

● **Pain under the right shoulder.**

● **Nausea or vomiting.**

● **Abdominal bloating.**

● **Recurring intolerance of fatty foods.**

People who experience the above as well as any of the following symptoms should see a doctor right away...

● **Sweating.**

● **Chills.**

● **Low-grade fever.**

● **Yellowish color of the skin** or whites of the eyes.

● **Clay-colored stools.**

Many people with gallstones have no symptoms and do not need treatment.

info You can learn more about the gallbladder and its problems from the American Gastroenterological Association at *www.gastro.org*.

Strokes: Not Unusual
In Kids

Donna Ferriero, MD, Chief, Child Neurology, University of California Children's Hospital, San Francisco.

Keith A. Siller, MD, Neurologist and Stroke Specialist, New York University Medical Center.

Strokes aren't generally associated with children, but researchers have found youngsters can also have strokes…and they probably occur more often than even doctors realize.

Studies indicate that strokes are seriously under-recognized, and much more research is needed on the causes and treatment of stroke in children.

If you're worried something might be wrong with your child or grandchild—for example, if the child uses only one hand to do everything —you should have him/her evaluated by a pediatric neurologist.

"Trust your judgment if you feel something isn't right," advises Dr. Donna Ferriero, the chief of child neurology at the University of California, San Francisco.

As many as 1 in 4000 newborns has a stroke, and the rate could be as high as 7 in every 100,000 young people up to 20 years old. Each year, approximately 250 children die from stroke, which occurs when the blood supply to any part of the brain is interrupted. Although these numbers indicate that pediatric stroke is quite rare, it is almost twice as common in children as brain tumors.

The problem often goes undiagnosed because a stroke doesn't always cause the same symptoms in children as it does in adults. Even when it does, it's hard to determine whether a 2-year-old's speech is garbled or whether a toddler is having trouble walking. In newborns, it's even more difficult to diagnose because if they can't move one side of their body, it's not very noticeable—at least not immediately.

Another reason stroke can go undetected in children is because they have a remarkable ability to recover from one. Dr. Keith A. Siller, a stroke specialist at New York University

Medical Center, says children can often compensate for the injured area.

One bright note in the research is that the death rate from stroke among children is down dramatically. Between 1979 and 1999, such deaths dropped 58%, Ferriero says.

RISK FACTORS

The studies were able to identify several risk factors for stroke in children. As in adults, being African-American is a risk factor for stroke in children. And it appears that boys are slightly more at risk than girls. Other risk factors are dehydration, bacterial infections, heart disease, chicken pox, or blood clotting disorders.

info For more information on stroke in children, visit The Cleveland Clinic Health System at *www.clevelandclinic.org*.

Concussions Can
Lead to Depression

Kevin Guskiewicz, PhD, ATC, Research Director, Center for the Study of Retired Athletes, Associate Professor and Director, Sports Medicine Research Laboratory, University of North Carolina, Chapel Hill.

Gary Pace, PhD, Clinical Director, May Center for Education and Neurorehabilitation, May Institute, Brockton, MA.

April 28, 2003, presentation, American Association of Neurological Surgeons Annual Meeting, San Diego, CA.

The young football player in your family who suffers multiple concussions may have a much greater risk of clinical depression later in life, according to a study conducted at the University of North Carolina.

The study results raise questions about the long-term impact of concussions for athletes.

Researchers from the Center for the Study of Retired Athletes at the University of North Carolina surveyed 2488 retired National Football League (NFL) players. Those who had 3 or more concussions in their professional careers were nearly 3 times as likely to suffer clinical depression as those who had no concussions, the study found.

Study author Kevin Guskiewicz says it's unclear why repeated concussions increase the likelihood of depression.

Earlier research, including a study at the University of Pittsburgh Medical Center, suggested that athletes who return to play before fully recovering from a concussion increase the risk of much more serious, perhaps even permanent, brain damage.

Although the study focused on NFL players, researchers say the findings could also apply to many others who suffer concussions. In organized football for all age groups in the United States, as many as 240,000 players a year may suffer concussions, the US Centers for Disease Control and Prevention says.

SOURCE OF DEPRESSION

Gary Pace, clinical director of the May Center for Education and Neurorehabilitation at the May Institute in Brockton, Massachusetts, says concussions can cause subtle problems in concentration, motor skills, and memory, making reading, sports, and many other activities difficult. Not being able to do the things they once enjoyed could contribute to the athletes' depression.

Determining whether depressed victims of multiple concussions are less responsive to antidepressants than other people could help distinguish whether the depression stems at least partly from the loss of abilities, he says.

Pace says the findings underscore the dangers of concussion, which could be greater in youngsters with still-developing brains.

"The message for parents," Pace says, "is that you have to take any kind of concussion very, very seriously."

■ ■ ■ ■

Signs of Concussion

According to the American Academy of Family Physicians (*www.aafp.org*), a concussion is an injury to the brain usually caused by a blow to the head. Most of the time it doesn't involve a loss of consciousness. *Signs include...*

- **Headache.**
- **Vision disturbance.**
- **Dizziness.**
- **Loss of balance.**
- **Confusion.**
- **Memory loss (amnesia).**
- **Ringing ears.**
- **Difficulty concentrating.**
- **Nausea.**

Food-Borne Illnesses May Cause Death Up to One Year Later

Kare Molbak, MD, PhD, Senior Medical Officer, Department of Epidemiology, Statens Serum Institute, Copenhagen, Denmark.
James Nataro, MD, PhD, Professor, Pediatrics, Medicine and Microbiology, University of Maryland School of Medicine, Baltimore.
Philip Tierno, MD, PhD, Director, Clinical Microbiology and Diagnostic Immunology, New York University Medical Center, and author, *The Secret Life of Germs* and *Protect Yourself Against Bioterrorism*.
February 15, 2003, *British Medical Journal*.

More people may be dying of food-borne illnesses than experts originally thought, and they may be dying even a year after the first sign of the infection.

People who get food-borne infections may also have severe illnesses or otherwise poor health, but the scientists took that into account and still wound up with an increased death rate, says Dr. Kare Molbak, the senior author of the study and a senior medical officer with the department of epidemiology at Statens Serum Institute in Copenhagen, Denmark.

To their surprise, the scientists found that some of the bacteria carried a risk of death even 1 year after the acute phase of the infection, Molbak adds.

The US Centers for Disease Control and Prevention estimates that food-borne diseases cause 76 million illnesses and 5200 deaths each year.

Molbak's study looked at 4 bacteria that cause food-borne illness—*salmonella, campylobacter, yersinia enterocolitica*, and *shigella*

—in almost 50,000 Danish people and compared them with almost 500,000 people from the general population.

More than half of those in the food-borne-illness group were infected with salmonella, one-third with campylobacter, less than 10% with yersinia enterocolitica, and 3.4% with shigella.

Each of the bacteria can cause diarrhea, cramping, abdominal pain, and fever. Most cases resolve on their own, but some patients need care and even hospitalization.

As a group, the people with a food-borne infection had a 3.1 times higher death rate than the people in the control group.

The death rate among those who contracted a strain of salmonella called salmonella dublin was 12 times higher than for the control patients. For the other types of salmonella, campylobacter, and yersinia enterocolitica, mortality was approximately 2 to 3 times higher.

MORE EXPLANATIONS

There can be a number of explanations for the higher death rates, Molbak says. Some of the patients may have had a relapse of the infection even though it appeared to have cleared.

Dr. Philip Tierno, director of clinical microbiology and immunology at New York University Medical Center says, "When you understand how these agents cause disease in an individual, you realize that the lymph system is involved, and your immune system obviously is involved. Maybe an allergic reaction might even occur."

Dr. James Nataro, a professor of pediatrics, medicine and microbiology at the University of Maryland School of Medicine in Baltimore, is not so sure.

It's plausible that if you get diarrhea from one of these organisms, you may face a higher risk of death for 6 months to a year, he says. "That negative impact could make you susceptible to other unrelated diseases. But are we ready to accept the conclusions based on these data? I think we're very far from it," he adds.

It's possible that a single as-of-yet undiscovered factor contributed both to the person contracting a food-borne bacteria and later dying, Nataro says.

info The Centers for Disease Control and Prevention at *www.cdc.gov* has information on salmonella, campylobacter, shigella, and yersinia enterocolitica.

■ ■ ■ ■

The 'Golden Rules' to Combat Food-Borne Illnesses

The partnership for Food Safety Education —a coalition of US government and business organizations—offers the following advice to "Fight BAC!" against food-borne bacteria…

●**Clean.** Simple as it sounds, washing everything, including hands, with soap and water is one of the most effective bacteria busters. The Centers for Disease Control and Prevention estimates that proper hand washing could eliminate nearly half of all cases of food-borne illness. Selecting the right tools can also help.

A University of Arizona study found that the average used kitchen sponge harbors some 7.2 billion bacteria.

Don't forget to use a clean towel to wipe clean hands. A recent Fight BAC! study showed that 1 in 5 Americans uses a dirty towel to wipe clean hands. Consider paper towels and nonporous cutting boards to eliminate some favorite germ breeding grounds.

●**Separate.** Cross-contamination is how bacteria spread from one food to another. It's especially important to keep raw meats and their juices away from ready-to-eat food. *Example:* Never bring in the barbecued burgers on the same platter that was used to transport the raw patties to the grill.

●**Cook.** Experts agree that harmful bacteria can't take the heat. Cooking food to safe internal temperatures can kill potentially harmful bacteria and make the food safe to eat. A food thermometer takes the guesswork out of safely cooking meat. When using the microwave, rotating and stirring dishes can help avoid potential cold spots that could also harbor bacteria. Liquid leftovers such as soups and gravies should be reheated to a boil; other leftovers, reheated to 165 degrees F.

●**Chill.** Don't leave the casserole on the counter. Refrigerate foods within 2 hours to keep bacteria from multiplying. Divide food into shallow containers. A packed fridge doesn't allow cooling air to circulate. Finally, make sure the refrigerator is at 40 degrees and the freezer is at 0 degrees Fahrenheit. Nearly 25% of consumers' refrigerators are not kept cold enough.

Blue Blood Doesn't Work Any Better Than Red

John N. Lavis, MD, PhD, Associate Professor, Clinical Epidemiology and Biostatistics, Faculty of Health Sciences, McMaster University, Hamilton, Ontario, Canada.

May 2003, *American Journal of Public Health*.

Here's some sobering news for the upper crust of British society—fancy titles don't provide the same life-extending benefits as boatloads of money do.

In a study of dead aristocrats going back to the 1500s, researchers found that dukes didn't live longer than marquesses, earls, and viscounts, even though dukes stand at the top of the social ladder known as the *peerage*.

"Being at the top of the social hierarchy doesn't appear to confer a significant advantage [in terms of longevity]," says study co-author Dr. John N. Lavis, an associate professor at McMaster University in Canada. "We were surprised."

The researchers wanted to examine how wealth and social status combine to affect life span, Lavis said. "We know from many, many studies that there's a link between socioeconomic status and health. Poor people live shorter, less healthy lives. But we keep saying socioeconomic status is important without being able to disentangle how much is social and how much is economic."

Lavis and his colleagues decided to turn to Britain's peerage, a system that has placed aristocrats into a rigid hierarchy for some 5 centuries.

WHAT'S IN A TITLE?

The British king or queen awards the titles to men—and only rarely to women—who have provided service to the crown or can boast of a great accomplishment, Lavis explains. The titles are typically handed down to first-born sons. Dukes are at the top of the hierarchy, followed by marquesses, earls, viscounts, Scottish lords of parliament, and baronets (who aren't officially part of the peerage).

The titles don't necessarily mean the holders are wealthy. "We can't say for certainty that they're all rich," Lavis says. "Some [families] have held the titles for centuries and may have lost their wealth. But on average, this tends to be a very wealthy group."

The researchers examined the birth and death records of 9529 male aristocrats from a reference book called *Burke's Peerage and Baronetage*. Female aristocrats were left out because there were only 87 of them.

NO DIFFERENCE IN LIFE SPAN

When they adjusted the life spans of the aristocrats for the century of their birth, the researchers found no statistically significant difference between the life spans of the various types of aristocrats. Those who were named by the king or queen didn't live any longer than their peers who got their titles by inheriting them.

"We found no link between social status and health," Lavis says. In general, he adds, it appears that "someone's economic position is more important than someone's social position."

info Curious about how the aristocracy of Great Britain and Ireland developed? Visit the Web site of Burke's Peerage & Gentry at *www.burkes-peerage.net*.

Family History Helps Predict Risk of Prostate Cancer

Harry Ostrer, MD, Professor, Pediatrics, Pathology and Medicine, New York University School of Medicine.

Durado Brooks, MD, Director, Prostate and Colorectal Cancer, American Cancer Society, Atlanta, GA.

April 1, 2003, *Cancer*, online edition.

Researchers have found that men who have a first-degree relative (father, brother, or son) with prostate cancer have a greater risk of getting the cancer compared with the general population.

A review of 33 previously published studies found that men who had brothers with prostate cancer are 3.3 times more likely to get the disease than the general population. Those whose father had been diagnosed with prostate cancer have a 2.1 times greater risk of getting it.

Dr. Harry Ostrer, a professor of pediatrics, pathology, and medicine at the New York University School of Medicine and coauthor of the analysis, says the link may be due to shared genes or environmental exposure.

OTHER FINDINGS

The study also found that men who have a second-degree relative (uncle, grandparent, cousin) with prostate cancer have a 1.6 times greater risk of getting it.

The greater the number of first-degree relatives with prostate cancer, researchers found, the greater the risk of getting the disease. And, the younger the age at which a family member is diagnosed, the greater the risk for other family members.

Dr. Durado Brooks, director of prostate and colorectal cancer for the American Cancer Society, says the analysis has quantified the risk more clearly.

The report may help men decide when and if to go for screening, Brooks says. Men who know they are at higher risk than the general population may decide to undergo screening tests earlier.

Men at average risk should begin screening at age 50; those at high risk should begin screening at age 45, Brooks says.

Screening includes a digital rectal exam and a blood test to detect *prostate-specific antigen* (PSA), a substance that may rise in the presence of prostate cancer.

■ ■ ■ ■

A Common Affliction

In the United States, prostate cancer is the most common malignancy among men, not including skin cancers.

According to American Cancer Society projections, more than 220,000 men are expected to receive a diagnosis of prostate cancer in 2003, and 28,900 deaths are expected from the disease.

The prostate, a walnut-sized gland located in front of the rectum and beneath the bladder, contains cells that produce some of the seminal fluid.

In addition to family history, another risk factor for prostate cancer is advancing age; 70 years is the average age at diagnosis.

Can a Change in Lifestyle Prevent Prostate Cancer?

Dean Ornish, MD, Director, Preventive Medicine Research Institute, Sausalito, CA.

B. Jay Brooks, MD, Chief of Oncology/Hematology, Ochsner Clinic, Baton Rouge, LA.

April 28, 2003, American Urological Association Annual Meeting, Chicago, IL.

You can reverse the progress of prostate cancer by changing your lifestyle, a leading proponent of alternative medicine says.

It's a claim met with interested skepticism by medical experts.

Dr. Dean Ornish, founder and director of the Preventive Medicine Research Institute in Sausalito, California, has been preaching lifestyle change as a way to reverse heart disease for years, in medical journals and in his 5 best-selling books.

His prescription calls for a low-fat vegan diet supplemented with soy and antioxidants, moderate aerobic exercise, stress management, and psychosocial group support. Ornish says this regimen lowered levels of *prostate-specific antigen* (PSA), a marker of the cancer, in a 1-year study.

The study included 87 men diagnosed with prostate cancer at an early stage—a stage when doctors often choose to do nothing while they check on the progress of the tumor (called "watchful waiting"). In the study, 41 of the men were assigned to follow the Ornish regimen carefully, under supervision. The others were allowed to try the regimen if they chose, with no supervision.

At the end of 3 months, PSA levels dropped by 5% in the group following the supervised regimen, but rose by 1% in the other group, Ornish says.

After 1 year, PSA levels were down by 3% in the supervised group, up 7% in the control group.

The regimen must be followed precisely to achieve its full results, Ornish says. Most of the men in the control group tried to follow the regimen, with middling success. Their PSA levels rose, but not as much as they would have had they not adopted some of the measures, he maintains.

STUDY'S SCOPE DRAWS CRITICISM

The study's reliance on PSA levels, however, is seen as a problem by Dr. B. Jay Brooks, chief of hematology/oncology at the Ochsner Clinic in Baton Rouge, Louisiana.

"This was an extremely small study, and the end point was a rise in PSA, which is not necessarily related to the progress of the cancer," Brooks says. "The difference between the experimental group and the control group was extremely small and barely reached statistical significance."

It is "an interesting concept," Brooks adds, "but this needs to be expanded to a larger group of patients and followed for a long period of time, perhaps 5 years. If it were me or any of my patients, I would certainly not rely on a change in lifestyle to affect a proven diagnosis [of cancer]."

According to the American Cancer Society (*www.cancer.org*), diet can lower your risk of getting prostate cancer in the first place. You may be able to lower your risk by eating less fat and more vegetables, fruits, and grains.

■ ■ ■ ■

Other Prostate Conditions That Should Concern You

While prostate cancer is the worst possible result of an abnormal prostate gland, an enlarged prostate can also result in another troublesome condition known as *benign prostatic hyperplasia* (BPH).

According to the National Institutes of Health, BPH is common in older men. Over time, an enlarged prostate may block the urethra, making it hard to urinate. It may cause dribbling after urination or a frequent urge to urinate, especially at night. Your doctor will conduct a rectal exam to diagnose BPH. The doctor also may look at your urethra, prostate, and bladder.

Treatment choices for BPH include…

●**Watchful waiting.** If the symptoms are not troubling, your doctor may suggest waiting before starting any treatment. In that case, you will need regular checkups to make sure the condition does not get worse.

●**Alpha-blockers** (some generic names are doxasozin, terazosin) are medicines that can relax muscles near the prostate and ease symptoms. Side effects may include headaches, dizziness, or feeling tired or lightheaded.

●**Finasteride (Proscar)** acts on the male hormone (testosterone) to shrink the prostate. Side effects of this medication can include diminished interest in sex and problems with erection or ejaculation.

●**Surgery** also can relieve symptoms. But surgery can cause complications and it does not protect against prostate cancer.

Talk with your doctor about this treatment choice. Regular checkups are important even for men who have had BPH surgery.

DNA Test Helps Fight Prostate Cancer

Donald C. Malins, PhD, DSc, Principal Scientist and Director, Biochemical Oncology Program, Pacific Northwest Research Institute, Seattle, WA.

Durado Brooks, MD, Director, Prostate and Colorectal Cancer Programs, American Cancer Society, Atlanta, GA.

April 14–18, 2003, *Proceedings of the National Academy of Sciences.*

A DNA test could give doctors a "heads-up" to monitor certain male patients more closely to detect early-stage prostate cancer or its spread to other parts of the body. The test also appears to flag which men are likely to develop the disease, according to Seattle researchers.

Doctors often miss the spread of prostate cancer to other parts of the body because the migrating cancer cells can be difficult to detect. The test could help doctors adjust treatment to fight off the spreading cancer before it kills the patient, said lead investigator Donald C. Malins, principal scientist at the Pacific Northwest Research Institute.

Prostate cancer is the most commonly diagnosed cancer among men in the United States. It kills approximately 30,000 each year, according to the National Prostate Cancer Coalition. Although prostate cancer is easily treatable in its early stages, the disease is not diagnosed in many men until it's too late.

Malins and his colleagues tested 49 men, some of whom suffered from prostate cancer, by examining prostate tissue samples using a DNA test they developed.

Samples in 40% of the healthy men older than 55 years showed signs of damage to the DNA of the prostate. The damage was similar to that in the men who actually had prostate cancer, suggesting that the healthy men could have problems down the line.

The researchers also discovered that their DNA test could predict which prostate cancer tumors would spread to other parts of the body.

Dr. Durado Brooks, director of prostate and colorectal cancers at the American Cancer Society, said the DNA test shows promise. "A tool like this could be very helpful in providing a clearer idea about who needs to be treated more aggressively for the possibility of metastasis [spread of cancer] or who needs to be followed closely," he said.

But Brooks added that more research needs to be done to confirm that the DNA test works. Even if someone is found to be at risk, there's no guaranteed way to prevent prostate cancer, he said.

GETTING SCREENED

The National Prostate Cancer Coalition (*www.pcacoalition.org*) recommends screenings for all men older than 50 years and for men older than 40 years who have a family history of prostate cancer or who are African–American.

Remarkable Finding: Ordinary Aspirin Helps Prevent Colorectal Cancer!

Thomas F. Imperiale, MD, Professor, Medicine, Indiana University School of Medicine, Indianapolis.

E. Robert Greenberg, MD, Professor, Medicine, Dartmouth College, Hanover, NH.

March 6, 2003, *New England Journal of Medicine.*

For colorectal health, the best thing you can do is be appropriately screened for cancer. But if you've already had colorectal cancer or have a history of intestinal polyps, 2 studies offer hope that an aspirin a day can reduce the risk of developing polyps in the future.

In one study, done at 36 cancer centers, researchers looked at 635 patients with a history of colon cancer. After 1 year, 17% of those who had taken an aspirin daily had developed polyps, but 27% of those who had taken only a placebo developed polyps.

A second study, led by doctors at the Dartmouth–Hitchcock Medical Center, had similar results, but with an interesting twist—the incidence of polyps in those who took a smaller dose of aspirin daily, 81 milligrams (mg), was lower than that of participants who took 1 adult aspirin of 325 mg. The incidence of polyps was highest in people who took only a placebo.

It's not exactly clear why aspirin prevents the formation of intestinal polyps, says Dr. Thomas F. Imperiale, professor of medicine at Indiana University School of Medicine. But aspirin inhibits the action of an enzyme called *cyclooxygenase-2* (cox-2), Imperiale says, and high levels of that enzyme are found in colon cancers. Cox-2 is believed to increase cancerous cell growth and invasion, he says.

ASPIRIN NO SUBSTITUTE FOR REGULAR CHECKUPS

"These studies say that aspirin can reduce the risk of recurrent polyps, but they don't say anything else," Imperiale says. Most of all, the studies "do not say that people should take aspirin instead of the recommended steps for prevention of colorectal cancer," he says.

The real importance of the study is scientific, says Dr. E. Robert Greenberg, professor of medicine at Dartmouth. "It gives us a better understanding of the factors that might be involved in causing cancer."

However, "if someone is considering taking aspirin to prevent heart disease, this might be one piece of information that pushes him off the fence," Greenberg says.

The American Cancer Society estimates that more than 147,000 cases of colorectal cancer will be diagnosed this year in the United States, and that it will cause more than 57,000 deaths. The society recommends yearly stool examinations and digital rectal examinations for people older than 40 years, sigmoidoscopies at age 50 and every 3 to 5 years after that, and colonoscopies at age 35 to 40 for those with a close relative diagnosed with colorectal cancer at an early age.

info You can learn more about measures to prevent colorectal cancer from the Memorial Sloan–Kettering Cancer Center at *www.mskcc.org* or the National Cancer Institute at *www.cancer.gov*.

Mammograms Still the Best Way to Detect Breast Cancer Early

Susan K. Boolbol, MD, Breast Surgeon, Cancer Center, Beth Israel Medical Center, New York, NY.
October 7, 2002, presentation, American Society for Therapeutic Radiology and Oncology Annual Meeting, New Orleans, LA.

A study presented to the American Society for Therapeutic Radiology and Oncology found that women older than 40 years who get routine mammographies are more likely to have their breast cancer caught in its earliest and most treatable stage.

"I think that screening mammograms help us to detect breast cancers at an earlier stage," says Dr. Susan K. Boolbol, a breast surgeon at Beth Israel Medical Center's Cancer Center in New York City.

The issue has sparked controversy ever since Danish researchers, publishing in *The Lancet*, questioned whether early detection actually reduced death rates.

SAVING LIVES

"The controversy dealt with whether we are saving lives, and it's difficult to extrapolate that information," Boolbol says. "We do know that the death rate from breast cancer has decreased slightly over the past several years. Can we attribute that to mammograms alone? No, we cannot. It's a variety of things."

Similarly, scientists are arguing about whether some breast cancers could be left untreated without the patient dying. Again, the answer is unclear. "That very well may be true, but we do not know which ones. So, as physicians dealing with breast cancer every day, every breast cancer we detect, we treat," Boolbol adds.

THE STUDY

Researchers found that women who were screened at least once a year were most likely to have a diagnosis of breast cancer that has not spread, compared with women who were screened less often. Because of the smaller tumor size, these women were also more likely to be given the option of breast-conservation therapy, as opposed to a mastectomy.

Before mammograms were used for screening purposes, approximately 5% of breast cancers were detected at the earliest stage. Now that number hovers around 25%, a huge increase. "The survival rate for women with the earliest stage of breast cancer is higher than 98%," Boolbol says. "So why not pick it up at this stage?"

The American Cancer Society suggests that women 40 years of age and older get annual mammograms.

info For information on breast cancer, visit the Susan G. Komen Breast Cancer Foundation at *www.komen.org*.

Smoking Increases Breast Cancer Risk 70%

Pierre R. Band, PhD, Senior Medical Epidemiologist, Health Canada, Quebec.

October 5, 2002, *The Lancet*.

Although smoking has always been associated with lung cancer, there's been little research showing a cause-and-effect relationship between smoking and breast cancer. But a recent Canadian study indicates that girls in their early teens who start smoking around the time they get their first periods appear to have a greater risk for developing breast cancer later in life.

Women who did not start to smoke until after the birth of their first child and who had gained weight since their late teen years, however, seem to have a lower risk of developing the disease than women who don't smoke.

Confused? According to the researchers, whose work was published in *The Lancet*, those apparently conflicting effects involve the interaction among carcinogens in cigarette smoke, breast cells, and estrogen. Breast tissue is most sensitive to the cancer-causing effect of carcinogens around the time of puberty, when breast cells have not fully developed and are

dividing rapidly, says Pierre R. Band of Health Canada, lead author of the report.

Yet for women who have gone through menopause, smoking reduces the estrogen activity that can stimulate the growth of cancer cells.

One striking statistic that emerged from the study was that women who had not yet gone into menopause and who started smoking within 5 years of the onset of menstruation had a 70% higher risk of breast cancer than nonsmokers. By contrast, the risk of breast cancer for postmenopausal women who started to smoke after a first pregnancy was only half that of nonsmokers.

Those results suggest strategies for studying different aspects of breast cancer, Band says. One focus of research should be the "window of susceptibility" to cancer-causing agents, he says. Women who start smoking early in life should be the target population for studies looking at the effects of cancer-causing agents, while the effects of hormones, and the drugs that influence their action, should be studied in women who have gone through menopause.

"The public health message is that our observations reinforce the importance of smoking prevention, especially in early adolescence," Band says.

Smoking May Lower Fertility in Women *and* Men!

Andrew McCullough, MD, Director, Sexual Health Program and Director, Male Infertility and Microsurgery Program, New York University Medical Center, and Assistant Professor, Clinical Urology, New York University School of Medicine.

Michael Stahler, PhD, Director, In Vitro Fertilization Laboratories, William Beaumont Hospital, Royal Oak, MI.

July 2, 2002, Abstract, Annual Conference of the European Society of Human Reproduction and Embryology, Vienna, Austria.

If you or your partner smokes, and you're thinking about trying to have a baby by in vitro fertilization (IVF), you might want to make quitting smoking the top priority.

Women who smoke cigarettes are much less likely to conceive using IVF or intracytoplasmic sperm injection (ICSI) than women who do not smoke. And new research has found that the odds of getting pregnant also drop if a woman's partner smokes.

"[This research] supports what we have felt in the infertility world for a long time—that there is an association between male infertility and smoking," says Dr. Andrew McCullough, director of the Sexual Health, Male Infertility and Microsurgery Programs at New York University Medical Center.

HOW IT'S DONE

To perform IVF, doctors give a woman high doses of hormones to induce ovulation. The woman's eggs are harvested and placed in a petri dish with the man's sperm. If all goes well, the sperm will fertilize the eggs to create embryos. The embryos are then implanted in the woman.

ICSI is similar, except the egg and the sperm aren't just left in the dish. Scientists manually fertilize the eggs by taking a single sperm and injecting it into the egg. Success rates for the procedure vary and depend on such factors as maternal age, how many eggs are retrieved and the health of the eggs and sperm.

Among the 301 couples recruited by the Institute for Reproductive Medicine at the University of Münster in Germany, 139 men and 77 women were smokers.

For couples receiving ICSI, 38% of the women with nonsmoking partners became pregnant compared with 22% of the women with smoking partners. For the IVF group, only 18% of the women with smoking partners became pregnant compared with 32% of the women with nonsmoking partners.

McCullough and Michael Stahler, director of In Vitro Fertilization Laboratories at William Beaumont Hospital in Royal Oak, Michigan, both recommend that men avoid illicit drugs, tobacco, and excessive drinking when trying to conceive. Both point out that the use of steroids can have a serious impact on fertility.

McCullough also cautions against repeated hot whirlpool baths, which may subject the scrotum to temperatures high enough to temporarily reduce sperm production. And Stahler adds that excessive caffeine use probably also hampers sperm function.

■ ■ ■ ■

More Reasons to Quit

The Advanced Fertility Center of Chicago (*www.advancedfertility.com*) explains some of the adverse effects of tobacco smoking on fertility. *They are...*

● **Tobacco smoke contains many toxic substances.**

● **A study done on mice showed that nicotine had disruptive effects on egg maturation,** ovulation rates, and fertilization rates. The study also showed more chromosomal abnormalities in the eggs exposed to nicotine.

● **Ovarian reserve and egg quality are reduced** in women who smoke.

● **Smokers have lower numbers of follicles** when stimulated for IVF.

● **Smokers have lower numbers of eggs** retrieved with IVF.

● **Smokers have lower rates of fertilization** with IVF.

● **Smokers have increased rates of miscarriage** with IVF pregnancies.

If you or your partner smoke, quit. And if you're planning on using IVF to get pregnant, quit even sooner. You'll improve your chances of having a successful pregnancy.

The Virus That Could Cause Multiple Sclerosis

Alberto Ascherio, MD, DrPH, Associate Professor, Epidemiology, Harvard School of Public Health, Boston, MA.

Timothy J. Coetzee, PhD, Director, Research Training Programs, National Multiple Sclerosis Society, New York, NY.

March 26, 2003, *Journal of the American Medical Association.*

Researchers may be closer to determining if there is a link between the Epstein–Barr virus (EBV) and multiple sclerosis (MS).

Dr. Alberto Ascherio, an associate professor of epidemiology at the Harvard School of Public Health has worked to establish that link for the past few years. The link is not yet proved, says the lead author of the study, but combined with previous studies, it does provide evidence to support a causal relationship.

Ascherio speculates that the MS link is due to an underlying genetic predisposition. In some individuals, he says, the virus somehow triggers an attack by the immune system on *myelin,* the protective covering of nerve fibers, causing problems ranging from numbness and tingling to paralysis.

Timothy J. Coetzee, director of research training programs for the National Multiple Sclerosis Society, says that no causal relationship has yet been established between an infectious agent and MS. But if an agent were identified, he says, it would help with the process of devising a treatment. "If it is a viral agent, you could think about antivirals. If it is a bacterium, you could think about antibiotics."

THE RESEARCH

The study is by far the largest ever done, drawing on blood samples taken from more than 3 million US military personnel between 1988 and 2000.

Lynn I. Levin, of the Walter Reed Army Institute of Research, and colleagues at the Army Physical Disability Agency looked at antibodies to the Epstein–Barr virus in 83 people granted disability because of MS and in people without the disease. Epstein–Barr antibodies were consistently higher in those with MS, and the risk of developing MS was 34 times higher among those with the highest levels of antibodies to the virus, the report says.

THE VIRUS

According to the Centers for Disease Control and Prevention, EBV is a member of the herpesvirus family and one of the most common human viruses.

In the United States, as many as 95% of adults between the ages of 35 and 40 years have been infected with EBV at some time in their lives.

Many children become infected with EBV, and these infections usually either cause no symptoms or are indistinguishable from the other mild, brief illnesses of childhood. When infection with EBV occurs during adolescence or young adulthood, it causes infectious mononucleosis 35% to 50% of the time.

info For information about MS, consult the National Multiple Sclerosis Society Web site at *www.nmss.org.*

Surprising New Treatment For Crohn's Disease

Brian Dieckgraefe, MD, PhD, Assistant Professor, Medicine, Washington University School of Medicine, St. Louis, MO.

Ali Serdar Karakurum, MD, Chief, Division of Gastroenterology, Nassau University Medical Center, East Meadow, NY.

November 9, 2002, *The Lancet.*

By turning conventional wisdom on its head, researchers at Washington University in St. Louis may have identified a new drug for Crohn's disease, a chronic disease of the gastrointestinal system.

Instead of keeping the immune system in check like most therapies used for this disease, these scientists boosted a certain part of the immune system and saw improvements in nearly all of the patients they studied.

"The current thinking would predict that anything that stimulates the immune system would make it worse," says Dr. Brian Dieckgraefe, first author of the study. "Our therapy is the opposite of what everybody else is doing." As he puts it, they put gas on the fire, with surprising results.

Crohn's disease affects approximately 500,000 Americans. "It's an immune response against some unknown stimulus, and the inflammation [of the intestines] causes tremendous amounts of damage," Dieckgraefe says. "It's a terrible disease." It typically starts when a person is in his/her 20s, though children can have it, as well.

NO DRUG IS A PERFECT FIT

"Crohn's disease is very complex, and for decades we have not been able to find an excellent therapy," says Dr. Ali Serdar Karakurum, chief of the gastroenterology division at Nassau University Medical Center in East Meadow, New York. Part of the reason is that no one knows exactly what causes Crohn's, he adds.

Dieckgraefe and his coauthor, Dr. Joshua R. Korzenik of Barnes–Jewish Hospital, also in St. Louis, did their study after seeing improvements in people who had genetic diseases with symptoms very much like those of Crohn's.

BEFORE AND AFTER

Most strikingly, they noticed that after 1991, when children with immune-deficient diseases were using a drug called Leukine, none of them developed Crohn's disease. Crohn's sometimes results in people with autoimmune deficient diseases.

"After 1991, we couldn't identify a single kid who had developed Crohn's disease. The drug [which stimulates the immune system] may either delay its onset or block it," Dieckgraefe says.

They tested the drug in 15 patients, and after getting shots daily for 8 weeks, almost all greatly improved and more than half went into remission. "That's quite impressive," Karakurum says.

Because they suppress the immune system, drugs typically given for Crohn's disease can pave the way for life-threatening infections and can make it hard for the body to recognize cancer cells. Leukine doesn't have these problems. "It is a natural protein produced in the body. It's not some unusual molecule that's been cooked up in a laboratory," Dieckgraefe says.

Dieckgraefe and Korzenik have licensed the technology to Berlex Laboratories, which has started a large-scale trial.

info For more on Crohn's disease, visit the Crohn's & Colitis Foundation of America at *www.ccfa.org* or the National Institute of Diabetes & Digestive & Kidney Diseases at *www.niddk.nih.gov.*

Are Your Kidneys Damaged? You May Not Know It

Josef Coresh, MD, PhD, Associate Professor, Epidemiology, Medicine and Biostatistics, Johns Hopkins Bloomberg School of Public Health, Baltimore, MD.

Tom Hostetter, MD, Director, National Kidney Disease Education Program, National Institutes of Health, Bethesda, MD.

January 2003, *American Journal of Kidney Diseases.*

Kidney disease is even more widespread than previously believed; so much so that researchers have considerably increased their estimates of how many people are affected by it. Nearly 8 million Americans have lost more than half of their kidney function, and another 11 million adults periodically have protein in their urine, one of the first signs that kidney disease is developing.

"We are now recognizing that moderate and severe kidney disease is quite common," says Dr. Josef Coresh, lead author of the study and an associate professor of epidemiology, medicine and biostatistics at Johns Hopkins Bloomberg School of Public Health.

ESTABLISHING A SYSTEM

There has never been a standardized method for classifying kidney functions, Coresh says. And because of this, it's been difficult to determine who has kidney problems and who doesn't.

To begin the process, Coresh and his colleagues analyzed health data from more than 15,000 people. Then a committee of experts convened by the National Kidney Foundation came up with a set of guidelines that defined kidney disease. *Following are the 5 stages of kidney disease…*

●**5.9 million Americans are at Stage 1**— normal kidney function but protein in the urine on 2 occasions.

●**5.3 million people are at Stage 2**— mildly decreased kidney function and protein in the urine on at least 2 occasions.

●**7.6 million people are at Stage 3**—kidneys filter less than half the amount filtered by a healthy young adult. (Approximately 1 in 5 adults older than 65 years is at Stage 3.)

●**Approximately 400,000 people are at Stage 4 and 300,000 are at Stage 5**—2 stages that occur when the kidneys have lost nearly all of their function.

DETECTION IS KEY

One of the obstacles in detecting kidney disease at its earliest stages is that there are few, if any, symptoms, according to Dr. Tom Hostetter, director of the National Institutes of Health's National Kidney Disease Education Program.

Early symptoms may include some fatigue or anemia, but nothing specific to the kidney, Coresh says. Diabetes and high blood pressure are often the causes of kidney disease, he adds.

A crucial task is teaching laboratories how to better interpret kidney function tests, Hostetter says.

info For more information on kidneys, visit the National Kidney Foundation at *www.kidney.org.*

Get the Lead Out And Keep Your Kidneys Healthy

Kun–Ying Pan, MD, Nephrologist, Chang Gung Memorial Hospital, Taipei, Taiwan.

Philip A. Marsden, MD, Nephrologist and Professor, Medicine, St. Michael's Hospital and University of Toronto, Ontario, Canada.

January 23, 2003, *New England Journal of Medicine.*

Anyone suffering from progressively worsening kidney disease of unknown cause should have his/her lead levels checked, a Taiwanese researcher says.

That's because there's a direct relationship between elevated lead levels in the body and chronic kidney disease. A study found that lower levels of lead can slow the disease's progression and improve kidney function.

Patients given injections designed to help their bodies expel lead molecules in the blood showed significant improvement in kidney function, as well as reduced lead levels.

"So if we look at the body lead [levels], we may provide another way to slow the progression of renal disease," says researcher Dr. Kun-Ying Pan, a kidney specialist in Taipei. "And that means a lot because it can reduce the time someone needs to be on dialysis treatment."

The Taiwanese study went so far as to assert that the therapy could improve kidney function enough to delay the need for dialysis by approximately 3 years. And, the study says, the therapy's expense would amount to a fraction of the cost of dialysis.

27-MONTH STUDY

The study focused on 64 patients with chronic renal insufficiency and lead levels at the high end of the normal range. None of the patients had diabetes, the leading cause of kidney failure in the United States.

Of the 64 patients, 32 received chelation therapy—injections of EDTA (ethylene diamine tetra-acetic acid), a synthetic amino acid, over a 27-month period. The EDTA binds to the molecules of lead in the blood, and both are expelled from the body in the urine. These patients showed decreased lead levels and improved kidney function.

For the 32 patients in the control group, who received placebo injections during the same period, lead levels increased and kidney function continued to deteriorate.

Dr. Philip Marsden, a professor of medicine at the University of Toronto and St. Michael's Hospital, says the study shows that those with chronic kidney disease are particularly susceptible to lead exposure. The research should provide hope for those patients with kidney disease and elevated lead levels, he said.

"It's not academic; it's a practical matter that can save their kidneys," Marsden said.

Marsden noted that the study failed to prove that simply reducing lead levels improved kidney function. He says some effect of the injections, other than lead reduction, could have improved kidney function.

Johns Hopkins Bloomberg School of Public Health estimates that nearly 8 million Americans, or 4% of adults, have lost more than half of their kidney function. Another 11 million adults, or 6%, have the persistent presence of protein in their urine, one of the first signs that kidney disease is developing.

info You can learn more about kidney disease from the American Association of Kidney Patients Web site at *www.aakp.org*.

The 'Ouch' Gene—The Reason Some Only Whimper While Others Wail!

Charles Argoff, MD, Director, Cohn Pain Management Center, Syosset, NY, and Assistant Professor, Neurology, New York University School of Medicine.

February 21, 2003, *Science*.

If you whine over a paper cut or moan over a stubbed toe, blame your genes. A new study published in *Science* indicates that the difference between a wimp and a tough guy (or girl) is due, in part, to a tiny variation of a single gene.

In a related study, also in *Science*, researchers found out how nerve cells form "memories" of past pain. The research could help explain why some people have chronic pain, even after the cause of it is gone.

"We know as clinicians that there are certain individuals who, given the same exposure to pain, experience it chronically and forever, while there are those who get over the pain quickly," says Dr. Charles Argoff, director of the Cohn Pain Management Center and an assistant professor of neurology at New York University School of Medicine.

info For help coping with pain, check out the American Pain Foundation at *www.painfoundation.org* or the American Chronic Pain Association at *www.theacpa.org*.

Good News for People With Lyme Disease

Nancy Shadick, MD, Rheumatologist, Brigham and Women's Hospital, and Assistant Professor, Medicine, Harvard Medical School, Boston, MA.

Eugene Shapiro, MD, Professor, Pediatrics, Epidemiology and Investigative Medicine, Yale University School of Medicine, New Haven, CT.

December 21, 1999, *Annals of Internal Medicine*.

October 28, 2002, presentation, American College of Rheumatology Annual Scientific Meeting, New Orleans, LA.

Joint pain, chills, fever, fatigue, stiff neck, facial palsy, headache, confusion—these are all symptoms of Lyme disease. The good news for those suffering from the disease, however, is that their quality of life will probably improve over time. So say researchers who did a follow-up on the Nantucket Lyme Disease Cohort study.

"On average, 12 years after [getting the] infection, we found no impairment of quality-of-life measures. Subjects did still complain of memory and fatigue problems, but it was not reflected in functional status," says Dr. Nancy Shadick, lead author of the study.

The results are not surprising to other experts in the field.

"There are a number of other studies now that have looked at long-term outcomes," says Dr. Eugene Shapiro, a professor of pediatrics, epidemiology and investigative medicine at Yale University School of Medicine, "and, for the most part, people who have had Lyme disease are no different than those who didn't in terms of long-term outcomes."

WHEN AND WHERE THE STUDY BEGAN

In 1993, Shadick and her team started assembling a group of approximately 350 people from Nantucket Island, off the coast of Massachusetts. Half had previously had Lyme disease and half hadn't. The prevalence of Lyme disease on Nantucket is approximately 14.3%, one of the highest reported incidences of the illness in the country.

Twelve years after the initial infection, physical exams and neurological tests exposed no differences in the 2 groups of study participants.

Quality-of-life measurements had improved in the Lyme disease group and were found to be no different than those of people who had not been sick.

No one is quite sure what to make of the continued complaints of fatigue and memory difficulties. "I think the explanation is, in part, because of all the publicity about Lyme disease," Shapiro says. "There's a certain bias. Once you're labeled as having Lyme disease, you're more likely to notice and/or report any given symptom."

info For more information about Lyme disease, visit the American Lyme Disease Foundation Web site at *www.aldf.com.*

Best-Ever Bug Repellent: DEET

Mark Fradin, MD, Clinical Associate Professor, University of North Carolina School of Medicine, Chapel Hill.

Jonathan Day, mosquito expert, Medical Entomology Lab, University of Florida, Vero Beach.

Richard Pollack, PhD, Instructor, Tropical Public Health, Harvard School of Public Health, Boston, MA.

Joseph Conlon, technical advisor, American Mosquito Control Association, Orange Park, FL.

July 4, 2002, *New England Journal of Medicine.*

If you want to keep mosquitoes off you, bug repellants with DEET are the best way to go. The smell may be bad, but the bug's bite is worse.

A United States government study compared 16 products that boast bug-banishing properties—from citronella oil to soy-based formulations. The study found that those with DEET typically kept the bugs off the longest. Only the soy-based formulation came close to the synthetic chemical, which the researchers say has an undeserved reputation for being harmful to people. Citronella, spiked cosmetics, and wristbands didn't fend off mosquitoes very long, if at all, according to findings published in the *New England Journal of Medicine.*

STUDY CONFIRMS POWER OF DEET

Dr. Mark Fradin, a dermatologist and lead author of the study, and Jonathan Day, a mosquito expert at the University of Florida's medical entomology lab in Vero Beach, tested the repellents on the arms of 15 people.

To simulate nature and to avoid stacking the deck against weaker repellents, the cage contained only 10 mosquitoes at a time, as opposed to the hundreds that are often in these "arm-in-cage" tests.

Deep Woods OFF!, which contains 23.8% DEET by volume, prevented the first bite the longest—beating the other products by an average of 5 hours. The 2 runners-up also contained DEET, in strengths of 20% and 6.65%.

The only non-DEET product in the top 5 was HOMS Bite Blocker for Kids, which contains 2% soy oil and worked for an average of a little longer than 90 minutes.

IT'S SAFE IF USED CORRECTLY

In high concentrations, DEET can irritate mucus membranes in the eyes and nose. Even so, after 8 billion applications on humans, there have been fewer than 50 documented cases of serious illness from using the repellent.

"I have yet to see anything that holds a candle to DEET. It's the product that I would use," says Richard Pollack, a Harvard University tropical disease specialist and coauthor of an editorial accompanying the journal article.

Joseph Conlon, technical advisor for the American Mosquito Control Association, says many herbal extracts, such as clove oil and spearmint oil, work at high concentrations. But at those concentrations, they're harmful to your skin, as well as to the mosquitoes. Companies sell products that contain tiny amounts of the active ingredient, and advertise that they work even though they're unlikely to keep insects at bay.

Raspy Voice: 6 Ways To Become a Smooth Talker

Julie Barkmeier, PhD, Assistant Professor, Speech and Hearing Sciences, University of Arizona, Tucson.

Joseph C. Stemple, PhD, Director, Blaine Block Institute for Voice Analysis and Rehabilitation, Dayton, OH.

Imagine Demi Moore and Clint Eastwood having an animated conversation. Do you think their voices are sexy? Voice disorder specialists say they have a problem. They speculate that nodules on Moore's vocal folds and a stiffness of Eastwood's larynx could be causing the raspy, whispery quality of their voices.

Voice disorders are a common but under-treated problem, experts say. Approximately 3% to 9% of the United States population has a voice disorder, according to the American Speech–Language–Hearing Association. And about 70% of people older than 48 years develop problems with their voices because of aging.

"People really don't think much about how they speak until there's something wrong," says Joseph Stemple, director of the Blaine Block Institute for Voice Analysis and Rehabilitation in Dayton, Ohio.

The people most susceptible to voice disorders are those who use their voices the most —teachers, actors, singers, salespeople, receptionists, and telemarketers, Stemple says.

WHAT IS A VOICE DISORDER?

"Anything that impairs your voice enough that you have to modify how you function, whether it's not talking on the phone or having to work hard to make your voice sound normal" is considered a voice disorder, says Julie Barkmeier, an assistant professor of speech and hearing sciences at the University of Arizona.

Laryngitis is a transient voice disorder that just about everyone gets at some point, but other voice disorders are more serious.

Some voice disorders are psychological. Some people lose their voices entirely because of extreme stress and anxiety, Stemple says.

There are neurological voice disorders, as well. One is *spasmonic dystonia,* which occurs when the vocal cords spasm uncontrollably, leading to choked and strangled-sounding speech. Spasmonic dystonia can be treated with Botox, the same muscle-paralyzing toxin that's used to erase wrinkles, Stemple says.

Laryngeal cancer, or cancer of the larynx, can also cause a change in your voice quality. If you have a pronounced change in your voice that persists for 2 weeks or more, you should get checked out by your doctor, Barkmeier says.

■ ■ ■ ■

Voice Disorders Are Preventable

Specialists encourage you to take care of your voice by practicing good voice hygiene.

"A lot of people could avoid problems if there was information out there about good vocal hygiene," Barkmeier says. "We know using the voice—especially improperly—for long periods of time can cause a breakdown of the voice over time." *Here are some tips on protecting your voice...*

●**Don't yell or talk loudly over background noise.** Speak at a comfortable pitch and volume.

●**Don't cough or clear your throat frequently.**

●**Stay well hydrated.** Drinks lots of water and reduce your caffeine intake.

●**Don't smoke.** It can irritate the vocal folds.

●**Before speaking, take a deep breath.** Lack of air can strain the muscles of your larynx.

●**Give your voice a rest.**

info For more information on voice problems, visit the American Speech–Language–Hearing Association Web site at *www.asha.org* or the Center for Voice Disorders at the Wake Forest University Baptist Medical Center Web site at *www.bgsm.edu/voice.*

10

Heart Disease

New Guidelines for Heart Attack Prevention

If you're more than 20 years old, you should be checked routinely for those harbingers of heart trouble—high cholesterol, abnormal blood sugar levels, and high blood pressure. The American Heart Association (AHA) has updated its screening guidelines to reflect what researchers increasingly know to be true—although cardiovascular disease may be the leading killer of older Americans, its foundations are often laid in youth.

That's not all the AHA is recommending. Everyone over 40 should learn his or her 10-year risk for getting heart and vessel disease, which causes heart attacks, strokes, and other life-threatening ailments. And they should reduce these risks with exercise, a low-fat diet, smoking cessation, and, if necessary, by taking drugs that can lower cholesterol and blood pressure.

"We have to start preventing heart attacks in the first place rather than treating them after they've occurred," says Dr. Thomas Pearson, chief of cardiology at the University of Rochester Medical Center and chairman of the AHA panel that drew up the guidelines.

Heart disease kills approximately 950,000 Americans each year, according to the Centers for Disease Control and Prevention.

Although Americans' risk of dying from heart attacks has dropped in the last decade, our rate of heart attacks seems to have stayed the same, Pearson says. One reason is the rise in Type 2 diabetes, a major cause of cardiovascular illness. Type 2 is the most common form of diabetes and can often be controlled through diet and exercise.

Thomas Pearson, MD, PhD, MPH, Professor, Chairman, Department of Community and Preventive Medicine, University of Rochester Medical Center, Rochester, NY.

Larry Chinitz, MD, Associate Professor, Departments of Medicine (Cardiology) and Cardiac Catheterization, New York University School of Medicine.

July 16, 2002, *Circulation*.

Beginning at the age of 20 years, adults should be screened for cardiovascular disease. This includes evaluating family history, as well as taking a general lifestyle profile, at every physical exam to assess smoking status, exercise habits, diet, and other risks.

Doctors should also record blood pressure, pulse, body mass index, and pattern of weight distribution at each office visit, or at least every 2 years. Blood fats and blood sugar content should be measured every 2 years for those who have risk factors for heart disease and every 5 years in those patients without risk factors.

THE 10-YEAR RISK

The guidelines call for doctors to prepare a 10-year projection of the heart disease risk at least every 5 years for people age 40 years and older. Elements of this equation can include total "good" and "bad" cholesterol, age, sex, and the presence of diabetes. People should also be tested for blood fat problems beginning at age 20.

"You can have a little bit of high blood pressure, a little bit of high cholesterol, and a little bit of smoking, and your risk can be as much as that of a patient who has had a heart attack," Pearson said.

Even young, otherwise healthy people with high cholesterol are at sharply higher risk of heart trouble as they age, experts say.

But cardiologists typically don't see patients until they are older and their heart problems are well established; primary care doctors do. So the recommendations are mainly aimed at these physicians. Treatment recommendations can range from low-dose aspirin therapy to blood thinners.

"If you could get a general doctor to know the guidelines and screen young patients, that would be a big change," says Dr. Larry Chinitz, a heart expert at New York University in New York City.

info For more information, visit the National Heart, Lung, and Blood Institute at *www.nhlbi.nih.gov/chd.*

Cholesterol-Lowering Drug Saves Heart Transplant Patients

Sean Pinney, MD, Attending Cardiologist, Columbia Presbyterian Medical Center, New York, NY.

Edward M. Geltman, MD, Professor, Medicine, Washington University School of Medicine, St. Louis, MO.

December 10, 2002, *Circulation.*

Giving heart transplant recipients a cholesterol-lowering statin drug greatly improves their chances of long-term survival, German cardiologists report.

After 8 years, nearly all of the transplant patients who were given simvastatin, marketed in the United States as Zocor, were still alive, while just more than half of the patients who got standard medical treatment for the first 4 years were still alive, says a report by the heart transplant team at the Munich-Bogenhausen hospital.

The entire study was planned to run 8 years, but the difference in survival rates, and in the condition of the patients' arteries, was so clear after 4 years that all patients were given simvastatin at that time, the report says.

In particular, the statin treatment prevented the thickening of the coronary artery that would gradually choke off blood flow. It also reduced life-threatening transplant rejection episodes.

The German study provides convincing evidence for a practice that has become common in most American heart transplant centers, says Dr. Sean Pinney, an attending cardiologist in the Columbia-Presbyterian Medical Center in New York City and a member of the center's heart transplant team.

All the patients in his center and in some other hospitals are treated with statins, Pinney says. The study bolsters the use of statins in heart transplant patients, reinforcing their role in preventing artery disease, he adds.

ANOTHER ANGLE

Dr. Edward M. Geltman, professor of medicine at Washington University in St. Louis and director of the heart failure program at

Barnes Jewish Hospital there, says the reduction in severe rejection episodes could also be an important result.

By themselves, statins are not known to affect the immune system. However, that might change in the presence of cyclosporine A, which is given to transplant patients to prevent the immune system from reacting against the transplanted tissue, Geltman says.

"Our assumption is that it works not entirely by lowering cholesterol but by reducing the number of inflammatory episodes," he says. "It could be due to the way the liver detoxifies cyclosporine, a metabolic pathway in which there is an interaction with the statin. That has been shown for two different statins, simvastatin and pravastatin."

Whatever the reason, the high survival rate in the German study is outstanding and way beyond the US national average, Geltman says.

info Get information about heart transplantation from the American Heart Association at *www.americanheart.org*, which also has information on statins and other cholesterol-lowering drugs.

Common Virus May Cause Heart Disease: Are You at Risk?

Marek Smieja, MD, PhD, Assistant Professor, Department of Pathology and Molecular Medicine, McMaster University, Hamilton, Ontario, Canada.
Richard C. Pasternak, MD, Associate Professor, Medicine, Harvard Medical School, Boston, MA.
December 24, 2002, *Circulation*.

A relatively common virus known as *cytomegalovirus*, or CMV, appears to be a predictor of a person's susceptibility to heart attack or heart disease. What makes the finding even more interesting is that researchers weren't looking for this virus when they made the discovery.

The scientists were seeking antibodies—evidence of infection—in blood samples from people with heart disease or stroke, and the primary target was *Chlamydia pneumoniae*, which causes lung disease, says Dr. Marek Smieja, an assistant professor in the department of pathology and molecular medicine at McMaster University in Canada.

But *C pneumoniae* turned out to be no more of a predictor of heart disease than two viruses the researchers were using as controls. What the tests did demonstrate, however, was that the risk of heart attack or stroke increased by 24% for people with antibodies to cytomegalovirus, or CMV—a member of the virus family that includes chicken pox and Epstein–Barr. CMV is relatively common, striking between 50% and 85% of people by the time they reach age 40.

MORE ILLNESSES, GREATER RISK

The study also found that people infected with CMV, *C pneumoniae*, and the 2 control viruses were 41% more likely to suffer a heart attack or stroke or die of cardiovascular disease than those infected with 1 or no viruses.

"Perhaps not 1 infection but total exposure to viruses does increase the risk," Smieja says. "The concept of measuring a person for total exposure to infection is alive and well."

From a research point of view, that's true, says Dr. Richard C. Pasternak, an associate professor of medicine at Harvard Medical School and a spokesman for the American Heart Association. But in medical practice, he says, there isn't much point in taking such measurements.

"There are 3 plausible ways an infectious agent could be related to heart disease," Pasternak says. "It could cause the problem. It could facilitate development of the problem by amplifying the effect of other risk factors. Or it could be an aftereffect of the problem, weakening people so they are at higher risk. This is an excellent study, but it doesn't get us closer to understanding which of the 3 is true."

info The Yale-New Haven Hospital offers an excellent explanation to help you understand a heart disease diagnosis at *www.ynhh.org/cardiac/diagnosis*.

The Gene That Could Protect You From Heart Attacks and Stroke

David Schwartz, MD, MPH, Director, Center for Environmental Genomics, Duke University Medical Center, Durham, NC.

July 18, 2002, *New England Journal of Medicine*.

Researchers have identified an infection-fighting genetic variant that may also help protect against heart attack and stroke. The variant could be used not only as a screening test, but also as the basis for a new kind of protective cardiovascular therapy, says Dr. David Schwartz. Schwartz is the director of the Center for Environmental Genomics at Duke University Medical Center and lead author of an article in the *New England Journal of Medicine*.

The genetic variant in question is not the kind of genetic trait most researchers would associate with cardiovascular disease, because it's a form of a gene involved with the immune system's defenses against infection. However, its identification adds to a growing body of evidence that inflammation, including the kind caused when the body fights an infection, plays a major role in heart attack and stroke.

The idea is that molecules and cells that attack bacteria and viruses also attack the tissue that lines the arteries, inflaming the tissue, and stimulating atherosclerosis—the formation of the clotty deposits called plaque that can block an artery and eventually cause a heart attack or stroke.

ZEROING IN

Schwartz and his colleagues zeroed in on a genetic variant of proteins called "toll-like receptors," which are found on the surface of immune system cells and on the cells lining airways and blood vessels. The Duke researchers set out to learn whether people with this genetic variant, which reduces receptor signaling and diminishes the inflammatory response, have a decreased risk of atherosclerosis (hardening of the arteries).

As part of the 5-year follow-up of an Italian study, the researchers screened 810 people for the genetic variant. They collected information on their immunologic status and took ultrasound pictures of the major arteries in the patients' necks. The results showed that 55 participants had the genetic variant. Blood tests showed those individuals had lower levels of inflammatory immune cells and molecules. And the ultrasound pictures showed the same 55 had significantly less atherosclerosis.

A SCREENING TOOL?

"There are 2 potential ways, and possibly a third, to use this information," Schwartz says. "First, it could be used to screen individuals to see whether they are protected against atherosclerosis.

"Second, it is a novel mechanism that one could manipulate in a variety of different ways to affect the risk of developing atherosclerosis.

"Third, by identifying a mechanism that causes atherosclerosis, it opens the possibility of combination therapy, such as treating high cholesterol levels in conjunction with altering the activity of the receptor," he adds.

New Discovery That May Shield You From Heart Failure

Peter Mohler, PhD, Postdoctoral Fellow, and Vann Bennett, MD, Professor, Cell Biology, Duke University Medical School, Durham, NC.

February 6, 2003, *Nature*.

A genetic defect that makes the heart stand still for a crucial moment appears to be involved in a number of unexplained sudden deaths, researchers say.

The defect has been identified in a French family in which sudden cardiac death is common, and it could also be involved in many other diseases, says study author Peter Mohler, a Howard Hughes Medical Institute postdoctoral fellow at Duke University Medical Center.

The defect is a mutation of a gene that codes for a protein called *ankyrin-B,* which plays an important role in the complex series of electrical and chemical events that govern the heartbeat.

In the "fairly small population of French people," the mutation has led to a family history of sudden death, Mohler says.

"They have been dying sudden deaths for centuries, as early as the age of 19," he says. "One of them died while running up a hill. Another died while being awakened suddenly."

THE RESEARCH

Using a specially bred strain of mice, the Duke researchers are exploring the implications of their discovery.

"We hope to understand more about the cellular pathway that this protein uses for targeting the ion channels of the heart," says Dr. Vann Bennett, professor of cell biology at Duke and leader of the research team.

There is a prospect of using the discovery to improve heart treatment, he says, because the researchers found that the mutation lowered intracellular levels of calcium.

"This can be very bad. If we could raise calcium levels in a controlled way, the heart could actually be stronger, so this would be a way of helping heart failure," Bennett says.

The researchers are also looking into its possible role in other diseases. Ankyrin-B is found in many tissues and organs, and very little is known about it.

It appears to have an important role in the pancreas, where insulin is produced, and mice with the genetic abnormality develop a mild form of diabetes, Mohler says.

The experiments could have implications for disorders of other organs that have excitable membranes like those in the heart, he says. These include the nervous system and the linings of the lungs and kidneys.

24-Hour Blood Pressure Monitoring Is Better Than Doctor's Office Reading

Denis Clement, MD, PhD, Professor, Cardiology, Ghent University Hospital, Ghent, Belgium.

Daniel C. Fisher, MD, Cardiologist, New York University Medical Center.

June 12, 2003, *New England Journal of Medicine.*

If you're currently being treated for hypertension, monitoring your blood pressure for 24 hours may more accurately assess your risk for cardiovascular disease than occasional readings in your doctor's office, a European study shows.

Patients whose average 24-hour systolic blood pressure was high were nearly twice as likely to have a heart attack or stroke as patients with a lower 24-hour systolic blood pressure, says one of the study's authors, Dr. Denis Clement, a professor of cardiology at Ghent University Hospital, Ghent, Belgium. This was true even if they had had a normal blood pressure reading at the doctor's office.

Blood pressure is a measure of the force your blood exerts on your blood vessel walls as it travels through them. The top number, the systolic pressure, is a measure of the force of blood pumping as the heart contracts. The bottom number, or diastolic, is a measure of blood pressure when the heart is at rest.

Blood pressure readings can be affected by a number of things, including what you've eaten or how you're feeling. For example, many people have higher-than-normal blood pressure readings at the doctor's office because they're anxious about being there.

If your blood pressure readings are higher than 140/90 on 2 separate occasions, you have high blood pressure, also called *hypertension.* People with blood pressure readings between 120/80 and 139/89 are considered *prehypertensive.* Lower numbers are considered normal.

Having high blood pressure puts you at risk for heart disease, stroke, and kidney disease. Fifty million people in the United States have high blood pressure, according to the National Heart, Lung, and Blood Institute.

DOUBLE THE RISK

For the European study, the researchers enrolled nearly 2000 people who were being treated for high blood pressure. Their average age was approximately 56 years.

All of the study volunteers underwent 24-hour blood pressure monitoring, including while they slept.

After 5 years, the researchers reviewed the medical files of all volunteers to assess how accurate the 24-hour monitoring had been in predicting cardiovascular problems. During that time, 157 people had a heart attack or stroke. The risk was double for those with high blood pressure.

The authors of the study aren't sure whether their findings would apply to people who don't already have high blood pressure. But they suggest making 24-hour ambulatory blood pressure readings standard care for people with diagnosed hypertension.

Dr. Daniel C. Fisher, a cardiologist at New York University Medical Center, says that although 24-hour monitoring isn't something he routinely does, there probably is a role for it.

"Your blood pressure is not a fixed number," he says. "It varies throughout the day."

The Right Time to Read Your Stress Test

Michael S. Lauer, MD, Director, Clinical Testing, Department of Cardiovascular Medicine, The Cleveland Clinic, OH.

Richard A. Stein, MD, Professor, Clinical Medicine, Weill Cornell Medical Center, New York, NY, and spokesman, American Heart Association.

February 27, 2003, *New England Journal of Medicine.*

When you go for a stress test, physicians typically focus on the printout from the electrocardiogram that is done while you are walking on the treadmill.

But did you know that how your heart behaves in the minutes after you stop could tell your doctor more than the test itself?

How much and how fast the heart rate recovers, and whether there are abnormal heartbeats after exercise, are far stronger indicators of risk for heart disease than what happens during the test, says Dr. Michael S. Lauer, lead author of a paper on the study and director of clinical testing in cardiovascular medicine at the Cleveland Clinic.

Researchers looked at almost 30,000 patients who took exercise tests at The Cleveland Clinic, either because they had coronary artery disease or were suspected of having it. As is customary, the testers kept the heart monitor on for a few minutes after the person left the treadmill. Centers do that "just to be sure that the patient is not in trouble," Lauer notes.

In the trial, the researchers looked closely at the results of heart monitoring, recording abnormal heartbeats and how fast the heart rate returned to normal. Then they looked at the number of cardiovascular deaths in the group, and how those deaths were related to how the heart behaved after exercise.

EVERY MINUTE REALLY DOES COUNT

As expected, occurrence of abnormal heartbeats during exercise increased the risk of death over the next 5 years; the death rate for patients who had those abnormalities was 9%, compared with 5% for those who didn't.

However, the occurrence of abnormal heartbeats in the minutes after testing was an even stronger indicator of risk. Eleven percent of the patients with those abnormalities died in the follow-up period.

"This is a very important finding in terms of being able to assess the risk of patients," says Dr. Richard A. Stein, a spokesman for the American Heart Association.

Cardiologists won't stop looking at what happens during exercise, Stein adds, but they will start paying more attention to the minutes after exercise as well.

It remains to be seen how the finding will be integrated into medical practice, Stein says. Cardiologists may concentrate even more on controlling the known risk factors in patients whose after-exercise electrocardiograms are abnormal.

MRIs Can Detect Heart Attacks Before They Happen

W. Gregory Hundley, MD, Associate Professor, Internal Medicine and Radiology, Wake Forest University School of Medicine, Winston–Salem, NC.

Gerald Pohost, MD, Chief, Cardiovascular Medicine, Keck School of Medicine, University of Southern California, Los Angeles.

October 15, 2002, *Circulation*.

Magnetic resonance imaging (MRI) has been used for peering at the body's organs, but scientists say it can also tell whether chest pain is a harbinger of a future heart attack.

An MRI scan creates 3-dimensional images and can predict the odds of a heart attack or heart-related death in people with chest symptoms, even after accounting for risk factors such as high blood pressure, smoking, and diabetes. Intriguingly, the authors of a new study said, the device can even pinpoint reduced blood flow to the apex of the heart, a particular signal of trouble.

"With the MRI, the pictures are clearer, and the spatial resolution is higher" than with conventional noninvasive heart imaging, said Dr. W. Gregory Hundley, a radiologist at Wake Forest University School of Medicine in Winston–Salem, North Carolina, and leader of the research team.

Doctors generally create an image of the heart using ultrasound technology. That test is cheap and portable, but it doesn't work very well on obese people or on smokers. In fact, up to 20% of patients have pictures that are difficult to read.

TESTING THE MRI

Hundley's group gave MRI "stress tests" to 279 people with cardiovascular disease and poor sound wave images. To simulate the effects of exercise, doctors gave the patients drugs that make the heart beat faster.

People whose blood flow was reduced by 40% or more had 4 times the risk of a heart attack or heart-related death over the next 2 years than those with normal results.

Hundley's group was the first to take pictures of damage to the apex—the top of the heart. People who had such damage were 6 times more likely than those without injury to suffer more heart attacks or to die of cardiovascular illness.

Dr. Gerald Pohost, chief of cardiovascular medicine at the University of Southern California's Keck School of Medicine in Los Angeles and an MRI advocate, acknowledges that the scan costs more than other heart imaging tools. "But it has great potential to do a lot of things," Pohost said, from generating 3-dimensional pictures of the pump to observing how it processes energy.

Unfortunately, MRI is not for everyone. The machines don't function properly in the presence of metal plates, pacemakers, or defibrillators, so some people can't undergo the test.

Tell Your Doctor to Focus On Your Heart Rate— Not the Rhythm!

Robert O. Bonow, MD, Professor, Medicine, Northwestern University, Evanston, IL, and President, American Heart Association (2002–03), Dallas, TX.

Rodney H. Falk, MD, Professor, Medicine, Boston University School of Medicine, MA.

December 5, 2002, *New England Journal of Medicine*.

Two major studies have found that it is often better to focus on the heart's rate rather than its rhythm, even when the rhythm is abnormal and potentially dangerous.

Overly aggressive efforts to restore the normal rhythm of the atria, the upper chamber of the heart, can sometimes be damaging, and even fatal, the researchers found.

The studies will go a long way toward settling a controversy about how aggressive a doctor should be in trying to maintain regular rhythm, says Dr. Robert O. Bonow, a professor of medicine at Northwestern University and president of the American Heart Association.

Bonow says a cardiologist should still make an initial effort to restore normal atrial rhythm. If that doesn't work, the next treatment for patients with no underlying condition, such as valve disease or heart failure, would be "a simple approach to restoring normal heart rate," he says.

SIDE EFFECTS CAN BE DEADLY

The problem with an aggressive effort that concentrates on atrial rhythm is that many of the drugs used for that purpose can have serious side effects, says Dr. Rodney H. Falk, a professor of medicine at Boston University School of Medicine.

In some cases the drugs can cause weakness of the heart muscle; in a small percentage of cases, they can provoke a rhythm disturbance in the ventricle, the lower chambers of the heart. "There is a small chance that they might kill the patient," Falk says.

Medications designed to restore the normal rate of beating of the ventricles, which can go higher than 100 beats a minute because of atrial fibrillation, have fewer side effects and are easier to manage, Falk and Bonow say. Atrial fibrillation, the most common heart rhythm abnormality, is a condition that affects an estimated 2 million Americans. It occurs when the atria begin to beat irregularly, rather than beat rhythmically. Its incidence increases with age; it occurs in at least 6% of people aged 80 years and older.

THE STUDIES

The American Atrial Fibrillation Follow-up Investigation of Rhythm Management (AFFIRM) study enrolled 4060 patients, whose average age was just younger than 70 years. Over a period of 5 years, the death rate for those given rhythm-control medication was 23.8%, compared with 21.3% for those given medication aimed at controlling the rate at which their ventricles beat.

"More patients in the rhythm-control group than in the rate-control group were hospitalized, and there were more adverse drug affects in the rhythm-control group as well," a report on the study says.

A European study got comparable results for the 522 patients it enrolled. "Rate control is not inferior to rhythm control for the prevention of death and mortality," according to a report on the study.

Lifesaving Drug Even Your Cardiologist May Not Know About!

Sergio Pinski, MD, Section Head, Cardiac Pacing and Electrophysiology, Department of Cardiology, Cleveland Clinic Florida, Weston, FL.

Daniel C. Fisher, MD, Cardiologist, New York University Medical Center.

February 12, 2003, *Journal of the American Medical Association.*

At least one beta-blocker may dramatically reduce your chances of dying from congestive heart failure. But this drug won't increase the risk of serious side effects.

That is the finding of a multinational study of the beta-blocker *carvedilol*. Researchers described a 35% decrease in patient risk of death compared with that of volunteers who took a placebo. The medication didn't increase the risks of such side effects as fluid retention and worsening heart failure.

More than 5 million Americans have been diagnosed with congestive heart failure and more than 550,000 are newly diagnosed each year, according to the American Heart Association. Your lifetime risk of developing heart failure is approximately 1 in 5, says Dr. Sergio

Pinski, section head of cardiac pacing and electrophysiology at the Cleveland Clinic Florida.

Dr. Daniel C. Fisher, a cardiologist at New York University Medical Center, says this study provides reassurance to doctors who might be reluctant to prescribe beta-blockers for their heart-failure patients.

"Because beta-blockers slow the heart rate and lower blood pressure, it seems counterintuitive that they would work in heart failure patients. But what we're learning is that you can give beta-blockers and these patients benefit," says Fisher.

Pinski echoes that sentiment, saying that many doctors who went to medical school 20 or 30 years ago were taught not to prescribe beta-blockers for heart failure.

A BETA-BLOCKER THAT MEASURES UP

With many drugs, including carvedilol, doctors must carefully tweak the dosage to its most useful level so that effects can be measured. If you start with too high a dose, there is a greater risk of side effects.

For this study, researchers from Australia, Canada, Switzerland, Poland, England, Germany, and the United States conducted a randomized, placebo-controlled study at 334 hospitals in 21 countries. The study included 2289 volunteers who had symptoms of heart failure, but who were not retaining excessive fluid. To be included in the study, the participants' hearts had to be pumping at less than 25% of what is considered normal.

Study participants either received carvedilol or a placebo. More than 1100 volunteers were started on carvedilol doses twice a day and received increasing amounts. The benefits of carvedilol treatment started to become apparent as early as 2 to 3 weeks after the start of treatment. Fewer people in the carvedilol group died or were hospitalized than in the placebo group, and there was no statistically significant increase in serious side effects.

Pinski says that it's unclear whether these results would be similar for other beta-blockers, but that carvedilol has been used in people with different types of heart failure and has had consistently positive results.

■ ■ ■ ■

Signs of Heart Failure

According to the American Heart Association (*www.americanheart.org*), there are several common signs and symptoms of heart failure. *They are...*

- **Shortness of breath.**
- **Persistent coughing or wheezing.**
- **Buildup of excess fluids in body tissues** (swollen feet or ankles, for example).
- **Fatigue.**
- **Lack of appetite,** nausea.
- **Confusion,** impaired thinking.
- **Increased heart rate,** palpitations.

Some Drugs Can Work As Well as Surgery Against Angina

Stephen Siegel, MD, Assistant Clinical Professor, Cardiology, New York University Medical Center.

John Reilly, MD, Interventional Cardiologist, Ochsner Clinic Foundation, New Orleans, LA.

March 5, 2003, *Journal of the American Medical Association.*

A study by researchers in Switzerland found that surgery and medication both significantly improve quality of life and help prevent further heart problems, including fatal heart attacks, in elderly patients with angina.

However, both have drawbacks and neither treatment is clearly more effective than the other for treating angina, a recurring pain or discomfort in the chest that occurs when a part of the heart isn't getting enough blood. And, after 1 year, the quality of life outcome and survival rates of both treatments will be similar, the authors say.

Previous research has shown younger angina patients do well when they are treated with an invasive procedure, such as bypass surgery or angiogram (in which the blocked area is opened with a balloon or stent), according to the study.

But few studies have looked specifically at angina patients aged 75 years and older. Doctors tend to avoid invasive procedures in the elderly because of fears that their advanced age could put them at higher risk of death, explains Dr. Stephen Siegel, a cardiologist at New York University Medical Center.

THE STUDY

The Swiss researchers divided 282 angina patients, aged 75 to 91 years, into 2 groups. One group was treated with medications, such as aspirin, beta blockers, ACE inhibitors, and nitrates, and the other group underwent an invasive procedure.

The study found that both groups had an improved quality of life 1 year later.

EACH STRATEGY HAD SHORTCOMINGS

After 6 months, the group that had received the invasive procedure had a slightly higher death rate. At 1 year, however, the death rate was nearly identical.

Members of the medication-only group had particular problems that included an increased likelihood that they'd be hospitalized for recurring angina symptoms.

Between 6 months and 1 year, almost half the patients treated with medications alone had a "major adverse cardiac event," including death, nonfatal heart attack, or hospitalization for angina symptoms, compared with only 19% of those who underwent an invasive procedure.

Cardiologists who treat angina are generally divided into 2 camps—those who favor aggressive invasive treatments, and those who favor a more conservative, wait-and-see approach.

Siegel, who describes himself as on the conservative side, says the Swiss study provides new evidence that older patients can be treated safely and successfully with invasive procedures.

Dr. John Reilly, an interventional cardiologist at the Ochsner Clinic Foundation in New Orleans, says it's important to remember the 2 strategies aren't mutually exclusive. Angina patients treated with an invasive procedure should also be prescribed medicines to keep their angina at bay.

Both doctors believe the bottom line is that each patient must be evaluated individually. A patient's age, medical history, and angina severity all have to be taken into consideration.

Acetaminophen May Protect Diseased Hearts

Gary Merrill, PhD, Department of Cell Biology and Neuroscience, Rutgers University, Piscataway, NJ.

The pain reliever found in such over-the-counter products as Tylenol may do more than ease your aches and pains—it may also keep your heart healthy. Acetaminophen can help the heart muscle recover faster from periods of low blood flow, known as ischemic attacks, which typically occur in people with heart disease, say researchers at Rutgers University.

"Acetaminophen-treated hearts recovered more rapidly and completely in terms of function than placebo-treated hearts did," says lead researcher Gary Merrill, a professor in the department of cell biology and neuroscience at Rutgers.

Ischemia is the result of reduced blood flow to an area of the body. In cardiac ischemia, blood flow to the heart is reduced, usually because of narrowed arteries. These periods of reduced blood flow can cause pain, but often do not. As many as 4 million Americans have cardiac ischemia and don't know it, according to the American Heart Association.

PRESERVING THE HEART

Using animal models, including guinea pigs, Merrill and his colleagues studied how acetaminophen affects the heart after a period of ischemia. They used a dosage that would be considered high, but not toxic, for humans, Merrill says.

The researchers found acetaminophen acted directly on the heart and helped to preserve heart function, says Merrill. The researchers believe this effect comes from the antioxidant properties in acetaminophen.

"Acetaminophen appears to have a fairly broad spectrum of action against multiple oxidants," Merrill says.

Their findings were published in the *American Journal of Physiology*.

However, Merrill cautions not to change your acetaminophen intake on the basis of these studies because the results still need to be duplicated in humans.

Merrill's work was supported, in part, by grants from McNeil Consumer and Specialty Pharmaceuticals, the makers of Tylenol.

info To learn more about acetaminophen and its side effects, visit the Community Health Care Medical Library & Patient Education at *www.chclibrary.org*.

Common Anti-Inflammatory Drugs Reverse Heart Disease

Frank Ruschitzka, MD, Assistant Professor, Medicine, University Hospital, Zurich, Switzerland.
American Heart Association Web site.
January 13, 2003, *Circulation*.

Take heart! Discoveries that can help in the treatment of heart disease are being made every day.

Among them: Evidence that cardiovascular disease is at least in part an inflammatory condition. This news comes from a Swiss study, which shows that an anti-inflammatory drug benefits heart patients.

In the study, a group led by Dr. Frank Ruschitzka, an assistant professor of medicine at the University Hospital in Zurich, gave the anti-inflammatory drug *celecoxib*—you may know it as Celebrex—to some of the patients. Celecoxib is a *cyclooxygenase-2* (cox-2) inhibitor, a member of a family of drugs that are potent anti-inflammatory agents.

All the patients in the study had severe heart disease. Some of the patients took celecoxib

while the rest were given a placebo. After 2 weeks, the 2 groups switched treatments. Over the course of the study, researchers measured factors important in heart disease, including how well the cells lining the heart's blood vessels function, the levels of molecules associated with inflammation, and LDL cholesterol levels (the "bad" cholesterol that clogs arteries).

For the patients who took celecoxib, the drug helped expand their arteries, lower their LDL cholesterol levels, and improve the beneficial effect of nitric oxide, a gas that helps expand blood vessels, the report says.

Although the study was small—only 14 patients—the results are clinically significant, Ruschitzka says. "This is the first study to show that this regimen improves function," he says. But despite the promising findings, "I would be cautious about giving recommendations to physicians on the basis of such a small trial." He says the results warrant a large-scale clinical trial to test the drug's use in heart disease.

Celecoxib was used in the study because not all cox-2 inhibitors would produce the same results, Ruschitzka says. "Studies in rodents point to some differences between the drugs," he says.

The American Heart Association says the warning signs of inflammation deserve attention—along with more traditional risk factors, such as cholesterol levels—when trying to determine a person's risk of heart disease and stroke.

■ ■ ■ ■

Risk Factors for Heart Disease

According to the American Heart Association, some risk factors can be modified, treated, or controlled, and some can't. The more risk factors you have, the greater your chance of developing coronary heart disease.

What you can't change...

●**Increasing age.**

●**Gender.** Men have a greater risk of heart attack than women do.

●**Heredity.**

Factors you can control...

● **Tobacco smoke.** Cigarette smoking acts with other risk factors to greatly increase the risk for coronary heart disease. People who smoke cigars or pipes seem to have a higher risk, but their risk isn't as great as that of cigarette smokers.

● **High blood cholesterol.**

● **High blood pressure.** High blood pressure increases the heart's workload, causing the heart to thicken and become stiffer.

● **Physical inactivity.**

● **Obesity and overweight.** People who have excess body fat—especially if a lot of it is at the waist—are more likely to develop heart disease and stroke even if they have no other risk factors.

● **Diabetes mellitus.** Diabetes seriously increases your risk of developing cardiovascular disease.

Warning for Heart Patients: Aspirin and Ibuprofen Don't Mix!

Thomas M. MacDonald, MD, Medicines Monitoring Unit, Department of Clinical Pharmacology and Therapeutics, Ninewells Hospital and Medical School, University of Dundee, Scotland.

Garret FitzGerald, MD, Chairman, Pharmacology Department, University of Pennsylvania, Philadelphia.

February 15, 2003, *The Lancet.*

Ibuprofen, a common over-the-counter painkiller, could kill heart patients who combine it with aspirin.

A study in the United Kingdom found that people with heart disease who took aspirin and ibuprofen had much higher death rates than those who took another aspirin–painkiller combination or just aspirin itself.

Frequent treatment with ibuprofen "might chronically prevent the good effects of aspirin," said study coauthor Dr. Thomas M. MacDonald, a professor of clinical pharmacology at Ninewells Hospital and Medical School in Dundee, Scotland. Ibuprofen is sold under brand names such as Advil, Motrin-IB, Ibuprin, and Nuprin in the United States.

The good news is that other painkillers, such as acetaminophen (Tylenol), seem not to create health problems when taken with aspirin, MacDonald said.

ASPIRIN IS STILL GOOD

The study doesn't dispute the beneficial uses of aspirin, which makes blood less "sticky" and less likely to form obstructions in arteries. For these reasons, aspirin appears to reduce the risk of heart attack and stroke, MacDonald said. Doctors often advise heart patients, as well as healthy people, to take small doses of aspirin each day.

Although aspirin reduces pain from inflammation as well as helping the heart, aspirin doesn't work well against other types of pain and soreness. Some people turn to ibuprofen, which combats back pain, arthritis, and general muscular aches and pains, MacDonald said.

But a previous small American study suggested that ibuprofen may interfere with the blood-thinning properties of aspirin. Even when patients took ibuprofen throughout the day and aspirin only in the morning, the ibuprofen appeared to make aspirin less beneficial.

MacDonald said he and his colleagues wanted to expand on the results of the American study by examining death rates. They looked at more than 7000 heart disease patients who were discharged from hospitals and took low doses of aspirin.

The 187 patients who took both aspirin and ibuprofen were about twice as likely to die of any cause as patients who just took aspirin. The group that took both also had a 75% increase in their risk of dying from heart disease.

THE DOUBLE WHAMMY

Taken together, the two drugs have many more side effects than either alone, MacDonald said. "There is more risk of bleeding with the combination. It's a double whammy—not so much benefit and more risk of side effects."

Patients who took aspirin and the painkiller dicloflenec, known as Cataflam or Voltaren, didn't suffer higher death rates. Neither did people who took aspirin along with a non-steroidal anti-inflammatory drug (NSAID) other than ibuprofen.

"Broadly, it appears a choice other than ibuprofen would seem desirable," said Dr. Garret FitzGerald, coauthor of a previous study of the aspirin–ibuprofen combo. He is chairman of the pharmacology department at the University of Pennsylvania. Heart patients should ask for their doctor's advice if they want to take an NSAID in addition to aspirin, he added.

But patients who take ibuprofen with aspirin very occasionally shouldn't be at risk, he said.

info Learn about a variety of painkillers at the Mayo Clinic Web site at *www.mayo clinic.com.*

Protect Yourself: Common Heart Drug May Cause Heart Failure

Harlan M. Krumholz, MD, Professor, Medicine, Yale University School of Medicine, New Haven, CT.

Randall C. Starling, MD, Heart Transplant Surgeon, The Cleveland Clinic, OH.

February 19, 2003, *Journal of the American Medical Association.*

When it comes to using the drug *digitalis* to treat heart failure in men, less is more.

The drug, used to improve the heart's pumping action, displays toxic effects when found at higher levels in the bloodstream, according to a Yale University study.

Digitalis, derived from the foxglove plant, has been used to treat heart conditions for centuries, but the US Food and Drug Administration approved its use against heart failure only after the Digitalis Investigation Group trial was completed in the 1990s.

The Yale report, derived from an analysis of the data from that trial, found that men with higher blood levels of digoxin—a purified form of digitalis—had a greater risk of death than those with lower levels of the drug in their blood.

The report "has the potential for really affecting practice," says Dr. Harlan Krumholz, a professor of medicine at the Yale School of Medicine and senior author of the study. "If there is a beneficial effect of digitalis, it appears at levels in the blood that are lower than what is typically seen."

Krumholz led an earlier study on digitalis that found that it might do more harm than good in women.

Some experts on heart failure have reached a consensus that blood levels of digoxin should be low, Krumholz says, but "I know from clinical experience and talking to people and reading the literature that generally there is not an emphasis on getting digoxin levels low. This is evidence that we should be treating at lower levels."

DEATH RATES IN THE STUDY

In the Yale analysis, men with the lowest blood levels of digoxin had a 6.3% lower risk of death than those getting a placebo. There was no reduction in risk for men in the middle range, and an 11.8% higher death rate for those men with the highest blood levels, compared with those getting a placebo.

It's important to note that the study looked at blood levels, not at the doses given to patients, Krumholz says. The same dose can produce different blood levels, depending on patient characteristics, he says. For example, an older man with reduced kidney function could have a higher level of digoxin in his blood than a younger person given the same dose.

"Everything that Dr. Krumholz says makes sense," says Dr. Randall C. Starling, director of heart transplant services at The Cleveland Clinic. "This has added additional information and understanding on the dose-response level, as well as breaking it down to looking at all kinds of patients."

Blood levels are so important that patients with heart failure who are taking digitalis should have periodic blood tests, Krumholz says.

■ ■ ■ ■

The Pros and Cons of Digitalis

Digitalis is used to treat congestive heart failure (CHF) and heart rhythm problems. In people with CHF, it can increase blood flow throughout the body and decrease swelling in hands and ankles. *Among its side effects, according to the Texas Heart Institute (www.tmc.edu/thi/digimeds.html), are...*

●**Irregular heartbeat causing dizziness,** palpitations, shortness of breath, sweating, or fainting.

●**Hallucinations,** confusion, depression.

●**Unusual fatigue or weakness.**

●**Eyesight trouble.**

●**Upset stomach,** loss of appetite.

●**Erectile dysfunction.**

●**Breast enlargement in men.**

Beyond Magnesium: Best New Treatments for Heart Attack Patients

Elliott Antman, MD, Director, Coronary Care Unit, Brigham and Women's Hospital, Boston, MA.
Chris White, MD, Chairman, Department of Cardiology, Ochsner Clinic Foundation, New Orleans, LA.
October 14, 2002, *The Lancet.*

Once hailed as an easy and inexpensive way of improving the odds of surviving a heart attack, magnesium is no longer routinely given to ailing patients.

Known to calm the heart muscle, magnesium was commonly given to heart attack victims in the 1970s to treat the arrhythmias that force the heart to beat wildly before it finally gives out. At that time, studies showed that magnesium reduced short-term mortality by as much as half.

But a later study showed magnesium given intravenously to heart attack victims had little effect. Researchers gave 3113 heart attack patients magnesium sulfate intravenously for the first 24 hours after they were hospitalized.

Another 3100 patients received a placebo. The study results showed no difference in the death rate over the next 30 days.

With newer treatments now in use, says Dr. Elliott Antman, director of the coronary care unit at Brigham and Women's Hospital in Boston and the lead author of the study, it's possible that the beneficial effects of magnesium have been superseded. The treatments now in use weren't widely available until the 1990s.

ADVANCES IN TREATMENT

Doctors can attempt to minimize the damage of a heart attack in 2 ways, explains Dr. Chris White, chairman of the department of cardiology at Ochsner Clinic Foundation in New Orleans.

The first way to minimize damage is by calming the heart, making it work less so it requires less oxygen. That's how doctors treated heart attacks prior to the 1990s, with treatments like magnesium, White says.

The other method—which has been the focus of much research for at least 15 years— is increasing the amount of oxygen to heart tissue. One way to do that is to use clot-busting drugs that limit damage to the heart muscle by dissolving the clots that block arteries. The other is angioplasty, in which a catheter is threaded through an artery to improve blood flow in a narrowed vessel.

Aspirin, which interferes with blood clotting, can help keep arteries open in people who've had a heart attack. And ACE inhibitors block an enzyme in the body that helps cause blood vessels to tighten.

■ ■ ■ ■

Heart Attack Warning Signs

According to the American Heart Association, there are some warning signs that can mean a heart attack is happening. *They include...*

●**Chest discomfort.** Most heart attacks involve discomfort in the center of the chest that lasts more than a few minutes, or that goes away and comes back. It can feel like uncomfortable pressure, squeezing, fullness, or pain.

●**Discomfort in other areas of the upper body.** Symptoms can include pain or discomfort in 1 arm or both arms, as well as in the back, neck, jaw, or stomach.

●**Shortness of breath.** This feeling often comes along with chest discomfort. But it can occur before the chest discomfort.

●**Other signs.** These may include breaking out in a cold sweat, nausea, or lightheadedness.

If someone you're with has chest discomfort, especially with 1 or more of the other signs, don't wait to call for help. Call 911…and get to a hospital right away.

Heart Attack May Signal More Serious Problems

Gilles Rioufol, MD, PhD, Associate Professor, Hemodynamics, Hospices Civils de Lyon, France.

E. Murat Tuzcu, MD, Director, Intravascular Ultrasound Laboratory, The Cleveland Clinic, OH.

July 23, 2002, *Circulation.*

If you've had a heart attack, your arteries may still be carrying more of the same kinds of fatty deposits that caused the attack in the first place. This conclusion is more evidence that the body's response to inflammation plays a role in future heart attacks, and that an attack is an indication of trouble throughout the arterial system and not just a localized event, say researchers.

Circulation reports that doctors at the Hospices Civils de Lyon in France used an advanced technique called *intravascular ultrasound* to get 3-dimensional views of the 3 major coronary arteries of 24 patients in the month after they had heart attacks. The doctors found that the arteries of 80% of the patients still had the same sort of lesions that had caused their heart attacks in the first place.

The lesions are unstable fatty deposits (called plaques) in the artery walls that are likely to rupture. A stable plaque might not be a problem. But if an unstable one ruptures, the body responds with an inflammatory process that includes, among other activities, the formation of blood clots that can block an artery, causing a heart attack.

A heart attack is a sign of overall coronary instability, which is called acute coronary syndrome, says Dr. Gilles Rioufol, lead author of the study and an associate professor in the hemodynamics department at the French hospital.

Because the researchers found so many unstable plaques, treating only the lesion is not enough, he says. "It is an argument to treat and check all inflammation in patients."

PREDICTING TROUBLE

Being able to predict which lesions would rupture would have tremendous potential for heart attack prevention, says an accompanying editorial by cardiologists at The Cleveland Clinic. But doctors need a more practical test than the intravascular ultrasound used in the French study. This test was a 10-minute procedure in which a probe was threaded into a coronary artery.

"When a heart attack patient comes to the hospital, generally you find that 1 site in a blood vessel suffers severe narrowing because a plaque has ruptured. For many years, we have been convinced that there are a number of similar sites in the arteries. The implication is that acute coronary syndrome is a systemic disease of the arteries," says Dr. E. Murat Tuzcu, director of intravascular ultrasound at The Cleveland Clinic and coauthor of the accompanying editorial.

Believing the disease is systemic means that the treatment of a heart attack should be "very aggressive," using cholesterol-lowering drugs, clot preventers, such as aspirin, and other heart medications, Tuzcu says. The ideal treatment for the long-term, he says, would be to find and treat the other unstable plaques before they rupture.

That would require easy detection of those plaques, however. "It would be nice if we had a relatively simple tool that we could put into a coronary artery or, better yet, some way to look into the coronary arteries, find the other plaques, and treat them accordingly," Tuzcu says. "Unfortunately, what we have not is not ready for prime time."

CPR and Defibrillation Pump Up Heart Attack Survival Rates

Lars Wik, MD, PhD, Ulleval University Hospital, Oslo, Norway.

March 19, 2003, *Journal of the American Medical Association.*

Should your heart stop, quick administration of an electric shock is usually the best medical treatment, but a Norwegian study found that the combination of *cardiopulmonary resuscitation* (CPR) and electric shock works best for patients when emergency response is delayed.

CPR—the combination of chest compressions and rescue breathing—plus the electric shock called *defibrillation* increased survival rates, but only when the emergency response time to ventricular fibrillation, a heart-stopping condition, was 5 minutes or longer, reports a group led by Dr. Lars Wik of the Ulleval University Hospital in Oslo.

The chance of survival is notoriously low when the heart begins to fibrillate—writhing uselessly instead of pumping blood to the body. Minutes count. The standard emergency treatment is defibrillation, a shock to restore normal heartbeat. In this study, some patients were given CPR, as well.

Overall, there was no significant difference in the 1-year survival rate for patients who immediately received defibrillation only and those who also got CPR. But there was a significant difference in the same survival rate when treatments started more than 5 minutes after the problem was reported—20% of those getting the combined therapy survived, compared with 4% of those getting defibrillation only.

A CHANGE IN APPROACH

Although the study says these results require confirmation in additional randomized trials, it has changed the way some paramedics respond to all reports of ventricular fibrillation, Wik says. "Five minutes is probably not the cutoff time," he says. "We have

introduced the CPR-first strategy for all cardiac arrest patients."

The higher rate of survival "may be due to improvement of the blood oxygenation and metabolites around the heart," Wik says.

The Norwegian trial was prompted, in part, by results of an earlier study by a group led by Dr. Leonard A. Cobb of the University of Washington School of Medicine. In that study, adding CPR to defibrillation increased survival from 24% to 30%, with the increase concentrated in patients for whom treatment was started 4 minutes or later after the first report. However, that study was not conducted under the "gold standard" rules for medical research, with patients selected at random to receive one treatment or the other.

Dr. Terence D. Valenzuela, of the University of Arizona department of emergency medicine, says the Norwegian study has "potential clinical importance" because its results "are remarkably similar to those reported by Cobb." But more carefully controlled studies are needed before the CPR-plus-defibrillation treatment can be widely adopted, Valenzuela says.

Have Open-Heart Surgery Without Opening Your Chest

Michael Argenziano, MD, Director, Robotic Cardiac Surgery, Columbia–Presbyterian Medical Center, New York, NY.

November 19, 2002, presentation, American Heart Association Scientific Sessions, Chicago, IL.

Your next heart surgeon may be a robot. Well, not exactly; but instead of standing over you wielding a scalpel, the surgeon will be sitting at a console, manipulating controls to manage robotic arms that repair a damaged portion of your heart.

And the surgery will be done in a less invasive way. Instead of making a foot-long incision in the chest, as is often required for heart surgery, the surgeon will work through 4 small holes that keep the damage to your body to a minimum.

"This is open-heart surgery without opening the chest," says Dr. Michael Argenziano, director of robotic surgery at Columbia–Presbyterian Medical Center in New York City.

Argenziano has used Intuitive Surgical's da Vinci System, which is increasingly available at medical centers in the United States and around the world.

The system costs $1 million, but Argenziano says it is clearly worth it. "We were able to perform the operation with all the benefits we expected," he says. "There was minimum pain postoperatively and the patients went home a few days earlier than they expected."

European surgeons are ahead of Americans in use of the system because the US Food and Drug Administration has stricter requirements for approval, Argenziano says. The 15 successful operations he did to repair atrial septal defects—in which there is an unwanted opening between the 2 upper chambers of the heart—are among the results submitted to the FDA to get approval for routine use of the robotic system for that operation.

The FDA has approved the use of the da Vinci System for repair of the mitral valve, which controls the flow of blood between the 2 left chambers of the heart, and its use in bypass surgery could be next.

BENEFITS OF ROBOTIC SURGERY

A benefit for the surgeon is that he or she can sit down during what can be a 4-hour procedure, although "we're used to being on our feet," Argenziano says. He's more interested in the benefits for the patient.

The robotic procedures did take longer than conventional surgery; the heart had to be stopped for an average of 34 minutes, compared with 20 minutes. The reason might be the need for the surgeon to learn how to use the new system, Argenziano says. The average stay in the intensive care unit after surgery was 18 hours, the same as for traditional surgery, but patients did get to go home much sooner.

The benefits of the robotic cardiac surgery include…

●**Instruments can be manipulated with more accuracy than fingers.**

●**Magnified images of the surgery site** are finer than the view available to the surgeon's own eye.

●**Pencil-sized instruments are minimally invasive,** and they allow for a shorter recovery time.

"Instead of being in the hospital for 7 to 10 days, the patient is there for 3 days," Argenziano says. "Instead of a recovery time of 6 to 12 weeks, it is 2 to 4 weeks. This is definitely part of the future."

info More information about robotic surgery can be found at the Columbia University Department of Surgery Web site at *www.columbiasurgery.org/divisions/cardiac/robot.html.*

Statins Save Heart Surgery Patients

Deepak L. Bhatt, MD, Interventional Cardiologist, The Cleveland Clinic Foundation, OH.

Albert W. Chan, MD, MSc, FACC, Associate Director, Catheterization Laboratory, Ochsner Clinic Foundation, New Orleans, LA.

David A. Meyerson, MD, Cardiologist, Johns Hopkins Hospital, Baltimore, MD, and spokesman, American Heart Association, Dallas, TX.

April 8, 2003, *Circulation.*

Taking cholesterol-lowering drugs before you have surgery aimed at opening clogged arteries reduces death, heart attacks, and further artery blockages—at least, if you have high inflammation levels, say researchers at The Cleveland Clinic.

For a year, the researchers followed up approximately 1500 patients who had undergone a procedure to open a blocked artery. The procedures included balloon angioplasty, in which a balloon is threaded into a clogged artery and inflated to improve blood flow, and use of a stent, a wire mesh tube inserted to hold open an artery.

Those patients with the highest levels of a protein that signals inflammation of blood vessels had the greatest benefit from the statins, the study found.

One in 4 of the patients had high levels of this protein, called high-sensitivity C-reactive protein (hsCRP).

Among the patients with elevated levels of hsCRP, those who took statins before surgery had a 40% lower rate of death, heart attack, and need for more artery-opening procedures 1 year later, compared with those who did not take statins.

EASY CHANGE MAKES BIG DIFFERENCE

"It's remarkable that this really easy intervention seemed to make such a big difference," says study co-author Dr. Deepak L. Bhatt, interventional cardiologist at The Cleveland Clinic Foundation.

Dr. Albert W. Chan, the lead investigator in the study, says statins seem to have an effect apart from their cholesterol-lowering function among those with high inflammation levels. So, the findings suggest that levels of hsCRP may be important in deciding how to treat heart patients, regardless of their cholesterol levels.

"This may actually further change our concept of using cholesterol level as the only target for adjusting the dose or starting someone on statins," Chan says.

GUIDE FOR THE FUTURE?

Chan, who was at The Cleveland Clinic at the time of the study but now is associate director of the Catheterization Laboratory at the Ochsner Clinic Foundation in New Orleans, says the findings, if confirmed by a larger study, could be important to guiding therapy in the future.

He says the study did not determine when statin treatment should begin. Other research has shown statins lowered hsCRP levels within 2 weeks, the study says.

Dr. David A. Meyerson, a cardiologist at Johns Hopkins Hospital and a spokesman for the American Heart Association, says, "The study affirms our continued belief that the statins represent a group of invaluable medications in the treatment of coronary heart disease and provide these benefits through a mechanism of action beyond cholesterol-lowering qualities."

Cholesterol-Lowering Statins: Are They Really Worth It?

Richard C. Pasternak, MD, Director, Preventive Cardiology, Massachusetts General Hospital, and Associate Professor, Medicine, Harvard Medical School, Boston.

Barry Davis, MD, PhD, Director, ALLHAT Clinical Trial Center, and Professor, Biometry, University of Texas School of Public Health, Houston.

Joshua S. Benner, PharmD, ScD, Director, Health Economics, Epinomics Research, Alexandria, VA.

December 18, 2002, *Journal of the American Medical Association*.

Statins really do lower cholesterol, but that doesn't automatically mean a lower risk of heart problems or death compared with conventional therapy to lower blood fat, say researchers.

Still, experts say the results don't undermine the broad utility of statins, which are among the most widely prescribed drugs on the planet. Rather, the study suggests doctors need to do a better job of keeping patients on the medications if they expect the same performance produced by rigorous clinical trials.

This is not a blemish on statins, according to Dr. Richard C. Pasternak, a Harvard University cardiologist who wrote an editorial accompanying the study. "It's more a blemish on our ability to maintain best practice."

STATIN'S STATUS

In previous studies statins have led to marked reductions in total cholesterol and the LDL, or the "bad," form of blood fat. However, those trials have been in tightly controlled settings that don't necessarily reflect the real world. They also typically involved people with high or extremely high cholesterol.

The latest study involved more than 10,000 people with moderately high cholesterol, high blood pressure under control with medication, and at least one risk factor for heart disease, such as Type 2 diabetes.

Half the patients got *pravastatin* (Bristol-Myers Squibb's Pravachol); the rest received the usual prescription of lifestyle changes, such as a low-fat diet and exercise. Nearly one-third of those in the latter group switched to pravastatin during the 8-year study.

After 4 years, people taking the statin drug saw their total cholesterol drop by approximately twice as much as those in the other group.

However, the gap between the 2 groups for total cholesterol was less than half the average of 8 other large studies comparing statins with other therapies.

The number of deaths in each group was essentially identical, as were the rates of non-fatal heart attacks and deadly artery trouble.

"The [clinical] trials provide a compelling case for statin use, but in the real world it doesn't appear that patients are getting the full benefit that the trials suggest," says Joshua S. Benner, director of health economics at Epinomics Research, a Virginia-based consulting firm.

STATINS STILL WORK

Even so, Dr. Barry Davis, a coauthor of the paper, still believes the benefits of statins are clear and probably understated in the study.

Statins can, in the big picture, lower cardiovascular problems and death, especially from heart attacks, he says.

Davis, who ran the latest study at the University of Texas–Houston Health Science Center, explains that the benefits of the drug were obscured by patients switching out of the usual care group and into the statin arm of the study. That migration was prompted by the evidence of the drug's ability to prevent cardiovascular deaths made public during the late 1990s. If no one had switched, they probably would have seen a difference in death rates, he says.

info You can learn more about statins at the Heart Information Network at *www. heartinfo.org.*

Aspirin—Cheap, Safe Way to Save Bypass Patients

Dennis Mangano, MD, PhD, Chief Executive Officer, Ischemia Research and Education Foundation, San Francisco, CA.

Eric Topol, MD, Chairman, Cardiovascular Medicine, The Cleveland Clinic Foundation, OH.

October 24, 2002, *New England Journal of Medicine.*

A recent study challenges the long-held belief that aspirin should not be used after coronary bypass surgery because it increases the risk of excess bleeding.

The new research finds aspirin therapy should be standard treatment immediately following cardiac surgery because it dramatically decreases the rate of death and complications following the procedure.

"Aspirin [after cardiac bypass surgery] could prevent 9000 deaths a year and more than 25,000 complications in the US," says Dr. Dennis Mangano, chief executive officer of the Ischemia Research and Education Foundation in San Francisco.

"Aspirin had a very dramatic result, and it's cost-effective and safe," Mangano says.

SIGNIFICANT SAVINGS PREDICTED

He adds that aspirin therapy could save as many as 500,000 days of hospitalization and a whopping $1.5 billion. Worldwide, he says that 27,000 lives could be spared and more than 50,000 complications could be avoided by giving aspirin soon after cardiac bypass surgery.

More than 12 million Americans have coronary heart disease, according to the American Heart Association. Coronary bypass surgery is one treatment for the disease and every year in the United States nearly 1 million people undergo the procedure, the study reports.

In bypass surgery, surgeons literally create a detour around a blocked artery. They do this by taking a blood vessel from another part of the body, using it to create a new route for blood to get to the heart.

Although this procedure can reduce symptoms, 15% of patients experience complications that can involve not only the heart, but also the brain, the kidneys, and even the intestines. Traditionally, little could be done to prevent these complications.

THE STUDY

For this study, some 3000 patients received varying doses of aspirin—from 80 milligrams to 650 milligrams—within 48 hours of their surgery, while 2000 other patients did not.

The results were "striking," says Dr. Eric Topol, chairman of cardiovascular medicine at The Cleveland Clinic Foundation and author of an accompanying editorial.

Patients receiving aspirin therapy had 33% less risk of dying compared with those who weren't given the drug. The risk of complications was reduced by approximately 40%, according to the study. And aspirin didn't cause more bleeding, Mangano says.

A MAJOR CHANGE FORESEEN

Topol says this study will likely usher in "a sweeping change in treatment after cardiac surgery." He also says aspirin may be useful in preventing complications in other types of surgery, as well, but it would need to be studied separately before any changes in treatment could be recommended.

Topol says if you're going in for cardiac bypass surgery, be sure to discuss the use of aspirin immediately after surgery with your doctor. Don't, however, initiate aspirin therapy on your own.

info For more information on the benefits of aspirin, visit *www.yourfamilys health.com*. To read about coronary bypass surgery, visit the Mayo Clinic Web site at *www.mayoclinic.com*.

Improved Angioplasty Cuts Need for Further Surgery

Patrick L. Whitlow, MD, Director, Interventional Cardiology, The Cleveland Clinic Foundation, OH.

October 16, 2001, *Circulation*.

October 14, 2002, American Heart Association news release.

When angioplasty is performed, a balloon-tipped catheter is inserted into a narrowed artery. The balloon is then inflated to widen the vessel. When angioplasty was first introduced, the procedure often wasn't successful enough and surgery still had to be performed. But the need for an operation after angioplasty has been greatly reduced, according to a study published in *Circulation: The Journal of the American Heart Association*.

The reason: Surgeons have become much more adept in performing angioplasty, and the instruments used are much more sophisticated.

BYPASS SURGERY DOWN

The study was conducted by a team led by Dr. Patrick L. Whitlow, director of interventional cardiology at The Cleveland Clinic Foundation in Cleveland. More than 18,500 angioplasty cases were examined, covering a period from 1992 to 2000.

"We found a significant decline in the prevalence of emergency bypass surgery, from 1.5% in 1992 to 0.14% in 2000," Whitlow says. "The data suggest that the overall safety of angioplasty has dramatically improved in the last decade."

In addition to more experienced doctors and better technology, the researchers say that new anticlotting drugs have made angioplasty more effective. They also found that women, people with complex blockages, and those having angioplasty because of a heart attack were more likely to need emergency heart bypass surgery.

info For more information on the latest developments in angioplasty, check out MEDLINEplus, a service of the National Library of Medicine and the National Institutes of Health, at *www.nlm.nih.gov.*

The Safest Time of Day For Angioplasty

Felix Zijlstra, MD, PhD, Cardiologist, Weezenlanden Hospital, Zwolle, the Netherlands.

Frederick A. Spencer, MD, Associate Professor, Medicine, University of Massachusetts Medical School, Worcester.

June 18, 2003, *Journal of the American College of Cardiology.*

If you have a heart attack and receive an angioplasty late at night, your odds of a successful recovery are substantially reduced compared with those who have a heart attack during the day, say researchers.

Heart attack patients "showed a difference in outcome depending on whether they were treated during the day or during the night," says Dr. Felix Zijlstra, a cardiologist at Weezenlanden Hospital in Zwolle, the Netherlands.

Zijlstra and his colleagues found patients treated during off-hours, 6 PM to 8 AM, were more likely to die within 30 days. Of the 1702 patients studied, approximately 2% of those treated during the day had died within 30 days after their heart attack, compared with more than 4% of those treated during the night.

When the researchers looked at the success rates of angioplasties, the procedure used to open blocked coronary arteries, they found the procedure failed in approximately 4% of patients treated during the day compared with close to 7% of patients treated at night.

Zijlstra speculates this difference is due to the variations in our body clock, known as circadian rhythms. "There is evidence that everything in our body is related to circadian patterns," Zijlstra says. Neural hormonal shifts during the day may affect how well blood flow to the coronary artery is restored during angioplasty, he adds.

TIME MAY NOT BE THE FACTOR

However, there is an argument as to whether the difference in outcome is due to the patient or the doctor, Zijlstra notes. In their study, all the doctors who performed angioplasties were senior cardiologists with many years of experience. And all patients were treated within the same time from the onset of their heart attack.

"We can never exclude the possibility that a sleepy cardiologist may make a wrong decision, but it is not very likely," Zijlstra says.

He adds that "it is important to be aware that patients treated during off-hours may have worse outcomes." These patients may need more stabilizing drugs or additional blood-thinning medications, Zijlstra says.

BIOLOGY IS NOT DESTINY

Dr. Frederick A. Spencer and Dr. Richard C. Becker from the University of Massachusetts Medical School, the authors of an accompanying editorial, do not completely agree that a biological basis accounts for the differences in outcomes.

Spencer, an associate professor of medicine, believes the differences are more a function of the health-care system itself. "The system clearly has differences day to night that have not been well explored," he says. A physician who is performing angioplasties round the clock simply is not as good at 3 AM, he adds.

There should be day and night teams and required rest periods for doctors performing angioplasties, he says. "Physicians are people, too, and we have to pay attention to sleep deprivation. But if we want to optimize health care, it's not going to come cheap."

Best Way to Clean Out Your Arteries and Drop Plaque by Over 30%

Matthew Budoff, MD, FACC, Director, Electron Beam CT Laboratory, Research and Education Institute, Harbor–UCLA Medical Center, Torrance, CA.

Victor Goh, MD, Consultant Cardiologist, Electron Beam Center, Matilda International Hospital, Hong Kong.

June 8, 2003, presentation, Second Asia Pacific Scientific Forum, American Heart Association, Honolulu, HI.

We've all heard how dangerous plaque can be when it builds up in our arteries, but did you know that a combination of cholesterol-lowering drugs and healthy lifestyle changes can reduce that plaque by one-third?

Researchers verified the plaque reduction during a 12-year study with the use of electron beam CT scans. These special types of CT scans take rapid pictures of the heart to determine levels of calcium deposits on cholesterol plaque in the arteries. This plaque can lead to artery blockages and heart attacks.

"This test provides us with the ability to track plaque over time and to demonstrate that lifestyle modification does impart a benefit by reducing atherosclerosis or plaque," Dr. Matthew Budoff says.

Budoff is director of the Electron Beam CT Laboratory at the Research and Education Institute at Harbor–UCLA Medical Center in Torrance, California, and a co-author of the study.

He and Dr. Victor Goh, a consultant cardiologist at the Electron Beam Center at Matilda International Hospital in Hong Kong, followed 102 people at high risk for heart disease, performing electron beam CT scans at the beginning of the study in 1990 and then again in 2001 and 2002.

THE STUDY

All patients were prescribed statins—such as Lipitor or Zocor—to lower cholesterol, and instructed to eat better, exercise more, and control their weight.

At the second scan, 33 patients had reductions in their calcification scores, and these were patients who hadn't slacked off on lifestyle changes and medication use, Budoff says. "The majority of the 69 other patients had a small increase and a minority had a significant increase," says Budoff. "The results are quite dramatic."

The researchers also tracked all 102 patients for heart disease problems and found only one patient had had a heart attack, and it was not fatal. There were 2 strokes and no deaths.

The message, says Budoff, is that "it's very important to maintain the [statin use and lifestyle changes] because there is a long-term benefit as we showed in our study."

New Treatment Could Cure Clogged Blood Vessels

Hiroya Masaki, MD, PhD, Kansai Medical University, Moriguchi, Japan.

Richard Nesto, MD, Associate Professor, Medicine, Harvard Medical School, and Chairman, Cardiovascular Medicine, Lahey Clinic Medical Center, Boston, MA.

November 18, 2002, presentation, American Heart Association Scientific Sessions Meeting, Chicago, IL.

Poor blood circulation in the legs can lead to amputation. But researchers say they can prevent such drastic measures with an injection of a patient's own bone marrow.

A Japanese research team reports that the marrow injections help new blood vessels form in legs that have clogged arteries. The technique is effective and appears to be safe, with no serious side effects or complications, says Dr. Hiroya Masaki of Kansai Medical University in Moriguchi, Japan.

In peripheral artery disease, deposits build up along the walls of the arteries and reduce blood circulation, especially to the legs and feet. People with the disease have a higher risk of death from stroke and heart attack. The condition can be painful and, in later stages, it can lead to a marked reduction of blood flow and even gangrene, which can necessitate the amputation of a limb.

Conventional treatments include medication to prevent blood from clotting or angioplasty, in which a deflated balloon is passed into the narrowed vessel and then inflated to open the vessel up. Surgery can also be done to bypass the diseased vessel portion or to cut out the fatty deposits.

A DIFFERENT APPROACH

The Japanese researchers tried something different. They took bone marrow cells from the patients' hip bones, and then injected either their marrow or a placebo into their diseased calf muscles. In the study, patients who were injected with their marrow cells had a "striking" increase in new formation of vessels, thereby improving blood flow, the researchers found. New vessel formation was much less in those who got the placebo injections.

"It's interesting that they used the person's own bone marrow cells," says Dr. Richard Nesto, chairman of cardiovascular medicine at Lahey Clinic Medical Center in Boston and a spokesman for the American Heart Association. The technique seems safe and effective,

Nesto says. Once perfected, he adds, it would seem feasible the treatment could be done as a simple outpatient procedure.

■ ■ ■ ■

Are You at Risk?

According to the American Heart Association (*www.americanheart.org*), you may be at higher risk for peripheral artery disease if you are in a particular category. *The categories are as follows...*

●**You're older than 50 years,** with a history of smoking or diabetes.

●**You're older than 70 years.**

●**You have high blood pressure or an unhealthy cholesterol level.**

Most people with peripheral artery disease don't have any symptoms, so if one of these categories describes you, the American Heart Association recommends that you talk to your doctor to learn more about it.

11

Natural Remedies

The 'Magic Bean' That Lowers Your Cholesterol

When it comes to maintaining cardiovascular health, any soy is good soy. Researchers have found that both high- and low-isoflavone soy significantly improve cholesterol profiles in men and women.

Isoflavones are plant estrogens found in soy. They're being investigated for their health value, and scientists believe there is reason to be optimistic. "We're building up complement diets, which contain a combination of…recognized cholesterol-lowering foods," says Dr. David Jenkins, lead author of a recent study and a professor of medicine and nutritional sciences at the University of Toronto and St. Michael's Hospital. Jenkins's data adds credence to the belief that soy isoflavones contain a number of cardiovascular benefits. The goal, he says, is to develop a diet that may one day

replace the drugs some people take to control their cholesterol.

In addition to soy, some of the other cholesterol-lowering foods in what Jenkins calls his "portfolio diet" are oats, barley, and nuts (especially almonds).

SOY PRODUCTS EATEN BY STUDY GROUP

Jenkins's study, published in the *American Journal of Clinical Nutrition*, involved 23 men and 18 postmenopausal women, all of whom had elevated cholesterol levels. The participants were put on 3 successive 1-month diets—1 control diet with no soy, 1 soy-based diet high in isoflavones, and another soy-based diet low in isoflavones.

The soy protein sources used in this study were foods that could easily be obtained and

David Jenkins, MD, PhD, Professor, Medicine and Nutritional Sciences, University of Toronto and St. Michael's Hospital, Ontario, Canada.

Nieca Goldberg, MD, Chief, Cardiac Rehabilitation and Prevention Center, Lenox Hill Hospital, and Assistant Clinical Professor, Medicine, New York University School of Medicine.

August 2002, *American Journal of Clinical Nutrition*.

eaten by the general public—soy milk, soy yogurt, soy dogs, soy links, and soy burgers, Jenkins says. In the end, no major differences were found between the 2 soy protein diets with regard to their beneficial effect on blood lipids.

Studies show that people need to eat more than 25 grams of soy—the equivalent of 4 cups of soy milk—each day to reduce their LDL, or "bad," cholesterol, says Dr. Nieca Goldberg, author of *Women Are Not Small Men—Life-Saving Strategies for Preventing and Healing Heart Disease in Women.*

■ ■ ■ ■

Cholesterol Testing

According to the National Heart, Lung, and Blood Institute, if you're 20 years or older you should have your cholesterol measured at least once every 5 years. It's best to have a blood test called a "lipoprotein profile." This type of blood test is performed after a 9- to 12-hour fast. *It will give you helpful information about your...*

- **Total cholesterol.**

- **LDL ("bad") cholesterol**—the main source of cholesterol buildup and blockage in your arteries.

- **HDL ("good") cholesterol,** which helps prevent cholesterol from building up in your arteries.

- **Triglycerides**—another form of fat in your blood.

The Institute says the best reading for total cholesterol is one that is less than 200 milligrams per deciliter (mg/dL); 200 to 239 mg/dL is considered borderline high, and anything above 240 is high.

info More information can be found at the National Heart, Lung, and Blood Institute's Web site at *www.nhlbi.nih.gov.* You can also find information on cholesterol at the American Heart Association's Web site at *www.americanheart.org.*

The Very Best Wine for Heart Health

Ulrich Forstermann, MD, PhD, head, Department of Pharmacology, Johannes Gutenberg University, Mainz, Germany.

Robert Vogel, MD, Professor, Medicine, University of Maryland Hospital, Baltimore.

February 5, 2003, *Journal of the American College of Cardiology.*

Red wine can protect blood vessels from clotting and from plaque buildup. But a recent study shows that all red wines are not created equal. German researchers say wines from their country probably are not as good at reducing the risk of heart disease as are wines from France.

"French wines are richer in flavonoids, polyphenols, and phytoalexins than are the German wines tested in this study," explains lead author Dr. Ulrich Forstermann, head of pharmacology at Johannes Gutenberg University in Mainz. These ingredients stimulate the enzyme activity and have the potential to protect against *atherosclerosis* or hardening of the arteries, Forstermann says.

But French wines probably aren't the only ones that would have this beneficial effect. Any wine rich in flavonoids and other heart-healthy compounds would probably produce similar findings, he says. There are red wines from Italy, California, and South Africa that also fit the bill.

The reason some wines are so rich in these substances comes from the way they are grown, and especially the soil they are grown in, he adds.

THE RESEARCH

To find out whether alcohol could increase the amount of the enzymes available in the body to combat heart disease, Forstermann and his team cultured cells from human umbilical cords and then exposed them to 6 French red wines, 3 German red wines, and pure alcohol or nothing as controls.

The researchers found that some of the French wines caused the enzyme activity to quadruple, while the German wines prompted little change. Pure alcohol had no effect.

The researchers also tested to see if the way the wine was fermented had any effect—it didn't. Wine matured in oak barrels or steel tanks showed the same effects.

CONFLICTING STUDIES

Dr. Robert Vogel, a professor of medicine at the University of Maryland Hospital, questioned the relevance of the study, but said it points out why there have been so many conflicting studies on the benefits of red wine.

Studies done in America have tended to show little difference between red wine and other forms of alcohol in protecting heart health, while many European studies have found that red wine is superior.

Vogel notes, however, that 1 or 2 drinks a day will probably help prevent heart disease for people older than 40 years.

Forstermann agrees. "One or two glasses of red wine in the evening are good for you. Besides the relaxing, calming, and stress-reducing effect of a moderate dose of alcohol, good red wines contain compounds with protective effects on the cardiovascular system."

■ ■ ■ ■

The Health Benefits of Red Wine

According to the Yale–New Haven Hospital, research has indicated that moderate intake of alcohol improves cardiovascular health.

Harvard researchers include moderate alcohol consumption as one of the "8 proven ways to reduce coronary heart disease risk." However, research has suggested that red wine is the most beneficial to your heart health.

The cardio-protective effect has been attributed to antioxidants present in the skin and seeds of red grapes. *Scientists believe the antioxidants, called flavonoids, reduce the risk of coronary heart disease by...*

●**Reducing the production of low-density lipoprotein** (LDL) cholesterol (also known as the "bad" cholesterol).

●**Boosting high-density lipoprotein** (HDL) cholesterol (the "good" cholesterol).

●**Reducing blood clotting.**

Cranberry Juice Cuts Risk of Heart Disease by 40%

Joe Vinson, PhD, Professor, Chemistry, University of Scranton, PA.

Jyni Holland, MS, RD, Clinical Nutritionist, New York University School of Medicine.

March 24, 2003, study presentation, American Chemical Society Annual Meeting, New Orleans, LA.

Three glasses of cranberry juice just might keep the cardiologist at bay. That's the finding of a small study by researchers at the University of Scranton. The research suggests that nutrients in cranberry juice can reduce the risk of heart disease—in some cases, up to 40%—mostly by increasing levels of HDL, the "good" cholesterol. The juice also more than doubled the blood levels of antioxidant nutrients—those nutrients that protect the heart by blocking certain types of cell damage.

But before you stock up on cranberry juice, consider this: Those who drank cranberry juice sweetened with corn syrup—the kind you find on most supermarket shelves—experienced a rise in triglycerides, which are dangerous to the heart, says Joe Vinson, the researcher who presented the findings. Vinson's research was fully funded by the Cranberry Institute.

Although Vinson suggests the solution is to drink your juice artificially sweetened, not all nutritionists agree that's the best advice. Jyni Holland, a nutritionist at New York University School of Medicine, says the best thing is to eat a variety of whole fresh fruits and vegetables since, in their natural form with nothing added, these foods have heart-healthy qualities and don't have side effects.

MORE MAKES THE DIFFERENCE

The 90-day study also found that the more cranberry juice you drink, the more protection you have. For those who had just one 8-ounce serving daily, Vinson says there was little health benefit. Significant differences in both antioxidant levels and HDL cholesterol were not seen until 2 to 3 glasses of juice were consumed daily.

The research involved just 19 people, all with cholesterol levels well above the normal level of 200 milligrams per deciliter. None were taking cholesterol medication.

Ten of the participants drank artificially sweetened cranberry juice, while the rest of the participants drank juice sweetened with corn syrup.

During the first month, each person drank one glass of juice per day. The second month they drank 2 glasses a day, and the third month 3 glasses daily. At the end of each month, Vinson measured their levels of total cholesterol, HDL, triglycerides, and antioxidants.

THREE A DAY

"After one month there was no change in any of the participants. At 2 servings a day, triglyceride levels rose marginally, but only in those drinking cranberry juice sweetened with corn syrup," says Vinson.

However, antioxidant levels more than doubled at 2 glasses daily; when 3 glasses a day were consumed, the antioxidant levels climbed to 121% in both types of juices.

What's more, the HDL, or "good" cholesterol, of those drinking 3 glasses of either juice per day jumped up by 10%.

That translates to an estimated 40% drop in heart disease, Vinson says.

But important to note, says Holland, is that the study was not a controlled trial, and there was virtually no attention paid to any changes in the participants' diet or exercise regimens. Moreover, she notes, they were not questioned as to any lifestyle or other changes that could have affected the study outcome.

info Go to *http://chef2chef.com* and type in "cranberry" to find out how to make your own cranberry juice and other ways to use cranberries.

Fish Oil Blocks 'Mischief-Makers' In the Heart

Alexander Leaf, MD, Jackson Professor of Clinical Medicine Emeritus, Harvard Medical School, and former Chief, Medicine, Massachusetts General Hospital, Boston.

J. Anthony Gomes, MD, Professor, Medicine, and Director, Cardiac Electrophysiology and Electrocardiography, Mount Sinai School of Medicine, New York, NY.

June 3, 2003, *Circulation.*

Including 2 servings of oily fish in your diet every week could prevent sudden cardiac death. Scientists have known for years that regularly eating fish such as salmon, tuna, or bluefish is beneficial, and a recent study on the hearts of rats shows one reason why.

The research showed that fatty acids in this type of fish are stored in individual heart cells and serve to prevent irregular heart rhythms (also known as arrhythmias) by working through the heart's calcium and sodium channels.

Sudden cardiac death is the cause of at least 250,000 deaths each year in the United States alone, says the American Heart Association. As its name implies, this type of death occurs unexpectedly and in people who may or may not have diagnosed heart disease. Most cardiac arrests occur as a result of life-threatening arrhythmias.

YOU NEED FATS TO FUNCTION

The body requires 2 types of polyunsaturated fatty acids to function. Both must come from the diet, because the body does not produce them. The American Heart Association recommends that to get those fats, healthy adults eat at least 2 servings of fish per week, especially fish high in fatty acids, such as mackerel, lake trout, herring, sardines, albacore tuna, and salmon.

When a person has a heart attack, the cells in the area that is no longer receiving blood tend to die. There remain a few cells in the peripheral area between the dead cells and the remaining normal heart muscle, which become "mischief-makers," says Dr. Alexander Leaf, lead author of the study. The mischief-makers can shoot off an electrical signal that causes an irregular contraction of the heart, producing arrhythmia, he says.

HOW THE FISH OIL GOES TO WORK

The study on the hearts of rats showed that fatty acids eliminate the mischief-makers and preserve the organ's normal electrical activity. The benefit takes place quickly, Leaf says, and it takes just a small amount of the right fatty acids.

Although they believe the research is interesting, other experts call for studies in humans.

"I do not think what they've said is very conclusive. There is no prospective, double-blind study that shows the efficacy in the prevention of sudden death," says Dr. J. Anthony Gomes, professor of medicine and director of cardiac electrophysiology and electrocardiography at the Mount Sinai School of Medicine in New York City.

Can Folic Acid Protect Your Heart?

David Wald, MBBS, Specialist Registrar, Cardiology, Southampton General Hospital, England.

American Heart Association, Dallas, TX.

November 23, 2002, *British Medical Journal.*

Although British research indicates that high doses of folic acid can protect the heart, the American Heart Association (AHA) is recommending against it. Dr. David Wald, a specialist registrar in cardiology at Southampton General Hospital in England, says taking folic acid can reduce the risk of heart disease by 16%, stroke by 24%, and deep-vein blockages by 25%.

Wald says high blood levels of the amino acid homocysteine are a clear and present danger to the arteries, and people should be taking folic acid to reduce the risk caused by elevated homocysteine levels.

That view is in sharp contrast to the AHA position: "We don't recommend widespread use of folic acid and B vitamin supplements to reduce the risk of heart disease and stroke."

The AHA and other authorities say that a cause-and-effect relationship between high homocysteine levels and heart risk has not yet been established.

THE STUDY

Wald's warning is based on a survey of more than 100 studies on the association between homocysteine and cardiovascular disease. Those studies show that "homocysteine is a cause of cardiovascular disease, such as heart attack and stroke," Wald says.

He says that some of his earlier work indicates that taking 800 micrograms (mcg) a day of folic acid will effectively reduce the risk caused by elevated levels of homocysteine. B vitamins can also help, he says, but "their effect is much more modest. Folic acid is far and away more effective."

DAILY INTAKE

The US Food and Drug Administration limits the amount of folic acid in nutritional supplements to 400 mcg, the recommended daily allowance, so a doctor's prescription is necessary for preparations containing higher amounts.

Bread and other grain products are fortified with folic acid in the United States to reduce the risk of the birth defect spina bifida. Folic acid is also found in beans and peas, nuts, orange juice, green leafy vegetables, and liver.

But Wald says the folic acid levels in foods, even those that are fortified, are not enough to provide optimum protection against heart disease and stroke, and he recommends widespread use of supplements.

"All people stand to benefit from taking folic acid, but the people who will benefit the most are those who already have cardiovascular disease, those who have had a heart attack, a stroke, or deep-vein thrombosis," Wald says. "And the risk increases after age 55, and we are advising all people to take folic acid after that age."

■■■■

Where to Find Folic Acid

According to the Spina Bifida Association of America, there are 2 forms of folic acid (also called folate)—synthetic and natural. Our bodies absorb the synthetic form of folic acid more easily than the natural form.

The synthetic form is found in…

- **Multivitamins.**
- **Fortified bread and grain products,** like breakfast cereals.
- **Folic acid prescriptions.**

Natural folic acid is found in…

- **Leafy green vegetables,** such as broccoli and spinach.
- **Some fruits and juices,** such as orange juice.

Warning: Vitamin E, Beta-Carotene May Make Heart Disease Worse

Marc Penn, MD, PhD, Director, Experimental Animal Laboratory, and Associate Director, Cardiovascular Medicine Fellowship, Departments of Cardiovascular Medicine and Cell Biology, The Cleveland Clinic Foundation, OH.
Dan Fisher, MD, Cardiologist and Assistant Professor, Medicine, New York University Medical Center.
June 14, 2003, *The Lancet.*

Supplements containing vitamin E or beta-carotene (a form of vitamin A) don't protect the heart, according to researchers who analyzed 15 major studies including nearly 220,000 people. The research analyzed 7 major randomized trials on vitamin E and 8 on beta-carotene.

"We found these supplements did not offer any benefits in relation to all-cause mortality, or even decrease the risk of death from stroke or heart disease," says study author Dr. Marc Penn, a cardiologist at the Cleveland Clinic Foundation.

In the case of beta-carotene, Penn says the risk of death was slightly higher for those using the supplements.

Based on the findings, Penn strongly suggests all trials on beta-carotene stop immediately and that the use of vitamin E for cardiovascular protection be discontinued. And patients at high risk for cardiovascular disease or death, he said, should not be included in any future trials involving vitamin E.

"What we believed to be true in the 1980s concerning the protective effects of antioxidant supplements simply did not hold up to scientific scrutiny," said New York University cardiologist Dr. Dan Fisher. "Clearly, supplements of vitamin E and beta-carotene are not part of the solution."

Penn and Fisher agree that antioxidants will play some future role in protection from cardiovascular disease, but their role isn't clear. "And more important, we don't know what kind of supplementation, if any, is going to provide that protection," he said.

Earlier findings on their effectiveness were misinterpreted, Penn said, because the participants in the studies were not randomized.

"What those patient questionnaires really told us was that vitamin E was a marker for people who took better care of their bodies. Overall, people who took vitamin E exercised more, ate better, and reduced stress. And those were the real reasons their risk of cardiovascular disease was lower, not the use of the supplements," Penn says.

'Open Sesame'—Oil That Drops Blood Pressure Dramatically

April 28, 2003, presentation, Scientific Meeting of the Inter-American Society of Hypertension, San Antonio, TX.
April 2003, American Heart Association news release.

Using sesame oil instead of other cooking oils helps reduce high blood pressure and lower the amount of medication required to control high blood pressure, according to a study by researchers in India.

The study looked at the effect of sesame oil on 328 people with hypertension who were taking 10 to 30 milligrams (mg) a day of the calcium channel blocker *nifedipine,* which lowers blood pressure by relaxing arterial membranes.

The average age of the people in the study was 58 years, and they had moderate to severe long-term hypertension but no history of stroke or heart disease.

They consumed an average of 35 grams of sesame oil a day for 60 days. Their blood pressure was measured at the start of the study, every 15 days during the study, and on day 60.

The study found that by using sesame oil as their sole cooking oil, participants lowered their blood pressure readings from an average 166/101 to 134/84.6.

The average dose of nifedipine taken by the study participants was reduced from 22.7 mg per day to 7.45 mg per day by the end of the study.

■ ■ ■ ■

What Do the Blood Pressure Numbers Mean?

The American Heart Association says that in blood pressure readings, the top (*systolic*) number represents the pressure while the heart is beating and the bottom (*diastolic*) number represents the pressure when the heart is resting between beats. The association says normal blood pressure should be below 120/80.

Everyday Disease Fighter In Your Breadbox!

Thomas Hofmann, PhD, Professor and Director, Institute for Food Chemistry, University of Muenster, Germany.

Samantha Heller, MS, RD, Senior Clinical Nutritionist, New York University Medical Center.

November 6, 2002, *Journal of Agricultural and Food Chemistry.*

The next time your child peels the crust off a piece of bread, you may want to think twice before throwing the scraps away—they may be rich in disease-fighting antioxidants. German researchers have discovered that during the baking of bread, an antioxidant called *pronyl-lysine* is created, especially in the crust.

Antioxidants are healthful compounds found in many foods and are believed to help fight cancer and other diseases, according to the American Dietetic Association.

Thomas Hofmann, a professor and head of the Institute for Food Chemistry at the University of Muenster, and his colleagues used a sourdough bread mixture that contained rye and wheat flour, and discovered the antioxidant after baking. The antioxidant had not been present in the flour used to make the bread.

The antioxidant is created during a chemical reaction among amino acids, starch, and sugars in the bread. This reaction causes the crust to have a darker color than the rest of the bread, Hofmann says.

The same antioxidant is found in malt and beer. Higher quantities are found in dark bread and dark beer, Hofmann says, as well as in bread stuffing widely used for holiday meals.

Once the scientists identified the antioxidant, they tested it on human intestinal cells in the lab and found that it increased the amount of enzymes that are believed to play a role in the prevention of some cancers.

THE NEXT STEP

The next step in the research is to learn whether the antioxidant is absorbed into the blood during digestion, where it might be able to help fight disease, says Samantha Heller, a senior clinical nutritionist at New York University Medical Center in New York City. The researchers are conducting animal tests to see whether this occurs.

Either way, bread can be part of a healthy diet, Heller adds. The fiber found in whole grain breads, fruits, and vegetables is a known disease fighter and it helps keep you feeling full.

■ ■ ■ ■

Beware of Too Much of a Good Thing

Just how much antioxidant-containing substance is too much?

While acknowledging evidence that some vitamins—A, C, D, E—and the elements zinc and selenium contain antioxidants that could fight off cancer and heart disease, the American Heart Association does not recommend using antioxidant vitamin supplements until more complete data are available.

The organization continues to recommend eating a variety of foods from all the basic food groups every day. *This includes...*

- **Six or more servings of breads,** cereals, pasta, and starchy vegetables.

- **Five servings of fruits and vegetables.**

- **Two to 4 servings of fat-free milk** and low-fat dairy products.

- **Up to 6 cooked ounces of lean meat,** fish, and poultry.

Meanwhile, the US Preventive Services Task Force, a government-sponsored research and advisory group, issued a report that says, "There is little reason to discourage people from taking vitamin supplements. Patients should be reminded that taking vitamins does not replace the need to eat a healthy diet."

The panel, which reviewed 38 published studies, cautioned consumers against using megadoses of vitamins in the hopes that if a little is good, a lot is better. "Some vitamins, such as A and D, may be harmful in higher doses. Therefore, doses greatly exceeding the recommended dietary allowance (RDA) or adequate intake (AI) should be taken with care," the report says.

■ ■ ■ ■

Best Antioxidant Vitamins

The most well known antioxidants are vitamins C and E, which many researchers believe help fight disease. To take advantage of their benefits, choose foods that are rich in these substances.

Vitamin C can be found in citrus fruits, strawberries, sweet peppers, broccoli, and potatoes.

Vitamin E can be found in vegetable oils, salad dressings, margarine, wheat germ, whole-grain products, seeds, nuts, and peanut butter.

info To learn more about antioxidants, visit the American Dietetic Association on the Internet at *www.eatright.org*.

Take a Bite Out of This: Sauerkraut Fights Cancer

Leonard Bjeldanes, PhD, Professor, Food Toxicology, University of California, Berkeley.

Eeva–Liisa Ryhanen, PhD, Research Manager, MTT Agrifood Research Finland, Jokioinen.

Yeong Ju, PhD, Researcher, University of Illinois, Urbana–Champaign.

One of the more unlikely foods that helps to prevent cancer is a favorite topping for hot dogs—sauerkraut. The cabbage in sauerkraut comes from the same vegetable family as broccoli and brussels sprouts, which are known for their ability to ward off breast, lung, and colon cancer.

"The cancer rates come down as much as 40% when you go from low consumption of these vegetables to high consumption," says Leonard Bjeldanes, a professor of food toxicology with the University of California at Berkeley.

And the fermentation process used to make the Eastern European creation appears to unlock even stronger anticarcinogenic elements, according to Eeva–Liisa Ryhanen, one of the authors of a study at MTT Agrifood Research Finland in Jokioinen, Finland. Ryhanen says the fermented cabbage could be healthier than raw or cooked cabbage, especially for fighting cancer.

Although Bjeldanes agrees that fermentation assists in breaking down the glucosinolates in cabbage, fermented foods aren't necessarily better, he says. Pickles and yogurt, for example, don't appear to prevent cancer.

THE STUDIES

In Finland, researchers analyzed cabbage before and after fermentation to see how the elements had changed. They found the glucosinolates in cabbage dissolved into a class of enzymes that have been shown in prior studies to prevent cancer, Ryhanen says.

Another researcher, though, found major differences between the sauerkraut sold in Poland and the sauerkraut sold in the United States. The American variety had fewer cancer-fighting elements than its overseas cousin, says Yeong Ju, a researcher with the University of Illinois.

"The fermentation process can make a big difference in potency," she says.

POTENCY MATTERS

Mostly, the difference between the 2 cultures is how much cabbage and sauerkraut they eat. Ju had earlier compared the incidence of breast cancer among Polish women and Polish immigrants in Michigan. The immigrants were 4 to 5 times more likely to develop cancer than were the women who stayed in Poland.

The Polish women eat much more cabbage and sauerkraut, which inhibits estrogen, thereby slowing down the development of the cancer, Ju says.

For the Finnish researchers, the next step is to improve the fermentation process so more beneficial enzymes are released, Ryhanen says. Besides its anticancer agents, sauerkraut has antibacterial qualities and acids that help the body digest the cabbage.

info To learn about how eating vegetables helps prevent cancer, visit the National Cancer Institute's Web site at *www.cancer.gov*. The US government's guidelines on eating vegetables are available at NCI's Cancer Control & Population Sciences Web site at *http:// cancercontrol.cancer.gov*.

Ex-Smokers: Selenium May Reduce Your Risk of Bladder Cancer

Samantha Heller, MS, RD, Senior Clinical Nutritionist, New York University Medical Center.
November 2002, *Cancer Epidemiology, Biomarkers and Prevention*.

If you're a former smoker and want to protect yourself against bladder cancer, you might want to include selenium-rich foods in your diet.

Researchers say the selenium effect doesn't hold true for current smokers or those who have never smoked. They theorize that this is because those who have never smoked have not exposed their bodies to the same oxidative stress that former smokers have. In addition, current smokers are overwhelming any positive effects from selenium with the toxic chemicals found in tobacco. The researchers also found that higher selenium levels only seemed to affect invasive forms of bladder cancer.

Selenium is an essential trace mineral and antioxidant that helps keep the immune system and the thyroid gland working properly. It is found in plant foods, meat, fish, cereal, dairy products, eggs, and some nuts, particularly Brazil nuts. The selenium content of food varies, depending on how much selenium is present in the soil where the food is grown.

Selenium deficiency is unusual in the United States, but not so in other parts of the world. In places such as China and Russia, where the selenium content of the soil is low, selenium deficiency is more common. The recommended daily intake of selenium is approximately 55 micrograms (mcg). Doses higher than 400 mcg daily could lead to side effects such as gastrointestinal problems, hair loss, and mild nerve damage, according to the National Institutes of Health.

SUPPLEMENTS ARE NOT THE ANSWER

Nutritionist Samantha Heller of New York University Medical Center says that if you want to prevent bladder and other cancers, supplementing with selenium isn't the answer.

"All healthy things work together as a team," Heller explains. So, if you supplement with selenium and a couple of other vitamins, you could still be missing out on essential nutrients. "It's like trying to play in the World Series without a pitcher or a third baseman," she adds.

The key, she says, is keeping everything in balance. That means stop smoking and start eating a balanced diet that includes lots of vegetables, nuts, and legumes, Heller says.

The authors of the study conclude that more research needs to be done, and they don't recommend taking selenium supplements until more conclusive proof of their benefits is available.

info For more information on bladder cancer, visit the National Cancer Institute's Web site at *www.cancer.gov/cancerinfo/wyn tk/bladder.*

Block Prostate and Breast Cancer With Broccoli

Durado Brooks, MD, Director, Prostate and Colorectal Cancers, American Cancer Society, Atlanta, GA.

Gary Firestone, PhD, Professor, Molecular and Cell Biology, University of California, Berkeley.

Satya Narayan, PhD, Associate Professor, Anatomy and Cell Biology, University of Florida, Gainesville.

June 6, 2003, *Journal of Biological Chemistry.*

Men who eat lots of vegetables seem more likely to avoid prostate cancer, but researchers now think a chemical in broccoli and cauliflower could help doctors treat the disease, too.

No one has tested the chemical on humans yet, however, and it may take years to turn it into a usable drug.

Prostate cancer rates are lower in countries where people eat plenty of fruits and vegetables, although the exact link between diet and the disease isn't clear, according to Dr. Durado Brooks, director of prostate and colorectal cancers for the American Cancer Society.

Researchers at the University of California at Berkeley investigated the cancer-fighting effects of chemicals in cruciferous vegetables such as broccoli, cauliflower, kale, brussels sprouts, and cabbage.

They found that a chemical that is a by-product of eating cruciferous vegetables appeared to prevent the growth of breast cancer cells. Then they found that prostate cancer cells treated with the chemical grew 70% slower than untreated cells.

The chemical appears to prevent cancer cells from receiving signals from the hormone testosterone, says study coauthor Gary Firestone, a professor of molecular and cell biology at the University of California at Berkeley. That, in turn, prevents the cells from growing.

The traditional hormone therapy for prostate cancer patients is designed to prevent testosterone from getting to the cells in the first place.

It's possible that the chemical could be used in combination with hormone therapy, Firestone says, to moderate the side effects of lowering testosterone levels.

However, Brooks says, hormone treatment is much less common than other prostate cancer treatments. Surgery and radiation are the usual treatments.

EASY AND INEXPENSIVE PROTECTION

Producing drugs from the vegetables may be easy and inexpensive, he adds. "There's a lot of broccoli and cabbage, and you should be able to obtain a lot of this chemical at a very cheap price."

Research into chemicals derived from vegetables may be more important in terms of prevention, says Satya Narayan, an associate professor of anatomy and cell biology at the University of Florida.

But it's still not clear how many vegetables men would need to eat to protect themselves from getting prostate cancer in the first place.

■ ■ ■ ■

Fighting Cancer With Vegetables

Vegetables and fruit can be an important part of a healthy diet. *According to the University of Minnesota Cancer Center...*

• **Eating 5 or more servings of fruit and vegetables every day** may help reduce the risk of cancer, heart disease, and other potentially life-threatening diseases.

• **People who eat 5 servings of vegetables a day have half the risk** of developing cancer as those who eat only 1 or 2 servings a day.

• **Some experts estimate that more than one-third of the 500,000 cancer deaths each year could be prevented** by eating a diet rich in fruits and vegetables.

info Learn more about prostate cancer by visiting the National Prostate Cancer Coalition at *www.4npcc.org.*

Tea and Soy Punch Out Prostate Cancer

Jin–Rong Zhou, PhD, Assistant Professor, Surgery, Harvard Medical School, and Director, Nutrition/Metabolism Laboratory, Beth Israel Deaconess Medical Center, both in Boston, MA.

Jyni Holland, MS, RD, Clinical Nutritionist, New York University Medical Center.

February 2003, *Journal of Nutrition.*

Tea and soy—2 foods that many scientists believe reduce the risk of breast cancer in women—may also protect men from prostate cancer. That's the conclusion of a Harvard University study that looked at the power of tea and soy to inhibit the growth of prostate tumors in mice.

Unlike other studies that examined the foods' individual effects on tumor growth, this research focused on the power that came from the combined effect of tea and soy.

"I think the most important finding is that consumption of both soy and tea has a synergistic effect," says study author Jin–Rong

Zhou, adding that each appears to reinforce the power of the other to fight cancer.

Zhou says he got the idea to test the soy–tea combination when statistical data showed that China had one of the lowest prostate cancer risk profiles in the world. Sensing that diet may play a key role, he dissected Chinese food habits and looked at what the men were eating most.

Although a number of foods made the list, Zhou says tea and soy jumped out, mostly because previous studies showed they might possess anticancer properties.

Zhou and his colleagues put their theory to the test on 16 mice, each genetically engineered to grow tumors in the prostate region. All the mice ate a diet of protein, carbohydrates, vitamins, and minerals, and some were also fed daily doses of soy compound in varying amounts. Infusions of both black and green tea were given to all the mice to drink.

At the end of the study, the mice were examined for not only the presence of prostate tumors, but also the size of the tumors, their rate of growth, and how much the disease had spread. These figures were then analyzed in regard to soy and tea consumption.

WHAT THE RESEARCHERS FOUND

Individually, the soy compound, and the black and green tea reduced the rate at which tumors developed. When tumors did grow, they were smaller when either tea or soy was consumed.

However, when taken together, the tea–soy combination was even more powerful, not only at inhibiting tumor growth, but also at reducing the weight of any tumors that did develop, as well as controlling the spread of cancer to nearby lymph nodes. The soy and green tea combination also reduced hormone concentrations linked to prostate cancer.

THE BOTTOM LINE

Alone, and especially together, tea and soy exhibited powerful effects against prostate cancer, the study says.

For Jyni Holland, a clinical nutritionist at New York University Medical Center, the research holds promise, but she doesn't think men should flood their diet with tea or soy just yet.

"Keep in mind that it was a mouse study, and many promising animal results never translate to human success," says Holland.

At the same time, she says that since both tea and soy have been shown in other studies to yield many important health benefits, adding them to your diet in moderation could have positive results.

■■■■

Is Drinking Tea Really Beneficial? Yes!

Research studies indicate that drinking tea may protect against cancer, heart disease, and stroke. The Medical College of Wisconsin has some answers to the most frequently asked questions about the benefits of drinking 1 or 2 cups of tea a day. *They are...*

• **Does it make a difference if a person chooses black versus green tea?** Although most studies have looked at green tea, black tea has also been studied. Both contain antioxidants called *polyphenols,* but with different chemical structures. Both types of tea have the same benefits.

• **Does decaffeinated tea have the same health benefits?** Decaffeinated tea contains fewer polyphenols, so it might not have the same health benefits. Instant powdered tea loses polyphenols in processing, so brewed tea is recommended.

• **Can I take a supplement containing green tea extract instead of drinking tea?** Research has been completed on tea, but not on tea extracts. There is no evidence that extracts or pills will have the same health benefits as drinking tea.

• **I like herbal tea. Can it be substituted for green or black tea?** Most herbal teas are a blend of leaves, flowers, and roots from plants, so they are not real tea. However, some herbal teas may have other health benefits.

• **Will drinking tea interfere with iron absorption?** The flavonoids in tea partially reduce the absorption of *non-heme iron* (iron from plant sources). The negative effect on iron absorption can be partially counteracted by using lemon in your tea. There is no loss of iron absorption from *heme iron* (iron from animal sources).

Pekoe Boo! How a Cup of Tea Scares Away Bacterial Infections

Jack F. Bukowski, MD, PhD, Assistant Professor, Medicine, Harvard Medical School, and Staff Rheumatologist, Brigham and Women's Hospital, both in Boston, MA.

Jeffrey B. Blumberg, PhD, Professor of Nutrition and Director, Antioxidants Research Laboratory, Associate Director, Jean Mayer USDA Human Nutrition Research Center on Aging, Tufts University, Boston, MA.

April 21–25, 2003, *Proceedings of the National Academy of Sciences.*

Drinking tea may help prime your immune system and enable you to more easily fight off bacterial infections, say researchers.

Their study adds to the growing list of health benefits researchers have attributed to tea. Previous research has found that the drink can help ward off heart disease and cancer, probably because of its abundance of antioxidants.

Some teas may fight infection, however, because they contain a substance called *L-theanine*, which is broken down into a group of chemicals called *alkylamine antigens*. Antigens produce antibodies that fight infections.

The researchers studied the effects of these antigens on *gamma-delta T-cells,* one of the immune system's infection fighters.

The study was small, cautions the lead author, Dr. Jack F. Bukowski, an assistant professor of medicine at Harvard Medical School and staff rheumatologist at Brigham and Women's Hospital in Boston. And although his team proved that tea drinkers produced more disease-fighting chemicals than coffee drinkers, the researchers did not track whether the tea drinkers actually had fewer infections.

EXPOSING THE CELLS

His team first did work in the laboratory, exposing some human gamma-delta T-cells to an alkylamine antigen but not exposing others. Then they exposed the cells to bacteria, simulating an infection. The cells exposed to the antigen produced a lot of interferon, an infection fighter, in the first 24 hours, Bukowski says, while those not exposed did not produce it.

The study also proved that these cells have a memory, he says, and can recognize bacteria the next time and fight them.

Next, Bukowski and his team asked 11 people to drink 5 to 6 cups of black tea every day, and another 10 people to drink the same quantity of instant coffee. The subjects did this for either 2 or 4 weeks.

The researchers tested the blood of the coffee and tea drinkers by exposing it to bacteria in the lab. Tea drinkers made 5 times more interferon after they started drinking tea, Bukowski says. The coffee drinkers showed no enhanced production of interferon.

But not all teas contain L-theanine, Bukowski cautions. Green, black, oolong, and pekoe teas do, he says.

If the research bears out, tea drinking may protect against skin infections caused by bacteria, bacterial pneumonias, and food poisoning, among other ailments, Bukowski says.

PRIMING THE RESPONSE

Another expert who has researched tea and its antioxidant benefits says the study results make sense.

"These compounds may prime our immune cells so that when they see [bacteria] they are better able to respond," says Jeffrey B. Blumberg. He is a professor and director of the Antioxidants Research Laboratory and associate director at the Jean Mayer USDA Human Nutrition Research Center on Aging at Tufts University in Boston.

Blumberg notes, however, that the study was preliminary and more research is needed.

info For more on tea, visit *www.teausa. com*. For more on the immune system, see the National Institute of Allergy and Infectious Diseases at *www.niaid.nih.gov.*

Drink Tea to Banish Bad Breath

Milton Schiffenbauer, PhD, Professor, Biology, Pace University, New York, NY.

Jon Richter, DMD, PhD, Director, Richter Center for the Treatment of Bad Breath Disorders, Philadelphia, PA.

May 20, 2003, presentations, American Society for Microbiology, Washington, DC.

A cup of tea has been said to be a good tonic for frazzled nerves, but did you know that it may also sweeten a mouthful of bad breath?

Two recent studies suggest that regular tea drinking can stave off those unsociable mouth odors.

Researchers at the University of Illinois at Chicago found the popular beverage contains compounds called *polyphenols* that halt the growth of odor-causing bacteria. Those bacteria thrive in the back of the tongue and in the deep recesses of your gums.

Polyphenols appear to hit *halitosis*—the medical term for bad breath—with a one–two punch by preventing the growth of the bacteria and then blocking their ability to produce sulfur compounds, the study suggests.

PUTTING TEA TO THE TEST

The researchers tested the drink's odor-fighting powers by incubating tea polyphenols with 3 species of bacteria associated with bad breath for 48 hours.

Using a range of concentrations typically found in black tea (16 to 250 micrograms per milliliter), they found the polyphenols inhibited the growth of bacteria. Moreover, at even lower concentrations, the polyphenols cut the formation of hydrogen sulfide, the smell-producing culprit, by 30%.

A second study, by Pace University researchers, found that green tea extract also shows microbe-fighting properties that protect the mouth from disease-causing bacteria and viruses.

"Many toothpastes don't fight viruses. But when we add green tea, it's an amazing result —I get a 90% destruction of viruses," says study author Milton Schiffenbauer, a microbiologist and professor at Pace University in New York City.

Both studies are preliminary and have not been tested outside of the laboratory environment—a fact that Dr. Jon Richter, director of the Richter Center for the Treatment of Bad Breath Disorders, says is a major weakness of the research.

TAKE IT OUTSIDE

"You can put just about anything on a petri dish with bacteria and show a decrease in growth. If they really want to see how these tea products affect bad breath they ought to take patients with bad breath and see if their condition gets better after drinking tea and run the study with control patients," Richter says.

info Learn about the causes and treatments for dragon breath from the American Dental Association at *www.ada.org/public/topics/alpha* or the University of Manitoba at *www.umanitoba.ca/outreach/wisdomtooth*. Click on "Bad Breath."

Echinacea Questioned As Cold-Fighter

Bruce Barrett, MD, PhD, Assistant Professor, Family Medicine, University of Wisconsin–Madison.
James Dillard, MD, Assistant Clinical Professor, Columbia University College of Physicians and Surgeons, New York, NY.
December 17, 2002, *Annals of Internal Medicine.*

Echinacea, the well-known herb used as a popular cold treatment, isn't very effective in shortening the duration of the common cold or the severity of its symptoms, according to researchers from the University of Wisconsin.

But they acknowledge that more research is needed before they can recommend that cold sufferers shelve their echinacea.

SOME DISAGREE WITH STUDY

Advocates of the herb suspect it increases the activity of the immune system, helping it to fight off a cold.

Despite the study results showing no benefit to the herbal treatment, the lead author, Dr. Bruce Barrett, an assistant professor of family medicine, says he's not ready to give up on echinacea—a favorite of North American Plains Indians who used it often for medicinal purposes.

THE STUDY

The researchers gave the herb or a placebo, in capsule form, to 142 otherwise healthy college students who had just come down with colds. Without knowing whether they were getting the herb or the placebo, the students took the pills for up to 10 days.

No differences were found in the severity of symptoms, such as cough, nasal congestion, fever and aches, or in the duration of the cold. In each student, the cold symptoms lasted 2 to 10 days.

Among the limitations of his study, Barrett says, was the type of herb used. He used a mixture of herb and root, which has not previously been tested. He says it may be ineffective because of a low bioavailability—the degree to which the mixture can be used by the body for its intended purposes.

LIQUID FORM MAY HELP

If you are going to try an herbal remedy, Dr. James Dillard, assistant clinical professor at Columbia University College of Physicians and Surgeons in New York City, recommends that the liquid form—called a *tincture*—of echinacea be used.

"There have been many studies to show echinacea works, but many people don't take it the right way, which is why they don't always get results," Dillard says.

Using echinacea daily as a preventive won't help because it begins losing its effectiveness after about 10 days, experts say. Instead, "take 1 large dose at the first symptom of a cold and you can cut the duration significantly," Dillard suggests.

Exposed! Echinacea Supplements That Don't Contain Echinacea

Christine Gilroy, MD, Assistant Professor, University of Colorado Health Sciences Center, Denver.

Henry Anhalt, DO, Director, Pediatric Endocrinology, Infants and Children's Hospital of Brooklyn at Maimonides Medical Center, Brooklyn, NY.

March 24, 2003, *Archives of Internal Medicine.*

Versions of the herbal remedy echinacea sold over-the-counter as a cold-fighter and immune booster differ widely in their contents, and the labels often don't reflect what's inside the bottle.

One study found that only 7% of their sample met all 4 of the government's labeling requirements.

The authors bought 59 different echinacea products from Denver–area retailers over 2 days during August, 2000. Six of the products (10%) contained no measurable echinacea, and labeling matched contents in only 52%. Of the 21 "standardized" preparations, only 43% met the quality standard described on the label.

Herbal medicines are big business. In 1997, Americans spent $5.1 billion on the products, almost 4 times as much as they spent in 1990. Echinacea accounts for 10% of total sales.

DIFFERENT TYPES, DIFFERENT EFFECTS

The researchers say that many consumers apparently don't realize that there are actually 3 different types of echinacea with 3 different effects.

Studies have shown that *echinacea purpurea* may help with symptoms of the common cold. *Echinacea pallida root* extract may decrease the duration of common cold symptoms. And there's debate about the efficacy of *echinacea angustifolia*.

The issue of "standardization," a term used on the labels of many herbal preparations, is also something that may confuse consumers. It is supposed to indicate that the particular herb is comparable with other preparations of the same herb.

Dr. Christine Gilroy, the lead author of the study and an assistant professor at the University of Colorado Health Sciences Center in Denver, however, is skeptical. She says it's a marketing ploy for quality.

The study showed that the standardized preparations did tend to have better compliance than the nonstandardized preparations. And, she says, the store-brand labels tended to do a better job of documenting what was in the product.

LACK OF REGULATION FOR HERBAL PRODUCTS

There are no federal rules or regulations for the distribution of herbs, making it difficult for consumers to distinguish between effective and ineffective herbal preparations. It is also difficult to determine which products are safe and which may be potentially harmful.

Greater regulation is needed, according to Dr. Henry Anhalt, the director of pediatric endocrinology at Infants and Children's Hospital of Brooklyn at Maimonides Medical Center. "Let's make sure the consumer is being protected," he says.

"This perception that health food stores are out there for the benefit of the public alone has got to stop. You may die by getting poorly controlled stuff or you may be paying for stuff and not getting what you paid for," he adds.

info If you'd like to know about echinacea, visit the Herb Research Foundation at *www.herbs.org/greenpapers/echinacea.html.*

■ ■ ■ ■

Just What Is Echinacea?

Echinacea purpurea is a purple coneflower found in North America and long believed to have curative powers for colds, flu, and a number of other minor ailments. Clinical research indicates that, indeed, echinacea extracts may be able to help fight respiratory infections.

The Institute for Complementary and Alternative Medicine, part of the University of Medicine and Dentistry of New Jersey, offers information about echinacea. *Following are its uses and the precautions you should take...*

•Applications. Echinacea purpurea may be effective in the treatment of colds, influenza-like symptoms, and respiratory and lower urinary tract infections. The current scientific literature, however, does not suggest a benefit for long-term use for the prevention of colds or influenzas.

•Cautions. Echinacea is not advisable for use during pregnancy. It is not recommended for people undergoing chemotherapy, those with diabetes, or those with autoimmune diseases, such as multiple sclerosis, AIDS, collagen disease, leukosis, and tuberculosis. Supplemental echinacea is not advisable for individuals who are allergic to the daisy flower family (Asteraceae).

Staggering Lack of Information on 'Dietary Supplements' Can Lead to Death

Susan Smolinske, PharmD, Managing Director, Regional Poison Control Center, Children's Hospital of Michigan, Detroit.

John Hathcock, PhD, Vice President, Nutritional and Regulatory Science, Council for Responsible Nutrition, Washington, DC.

Lewis Kohl, DO, Chairman, Emergency Medicine, Long Island College Hospital, Brooklyn, NY.

US Food and Drug Administration, Washington, DC.

January 11, 2003, *The Lancet*.

Consumers have suffered heart attacks, seizures, liver failure, and even death after taking various dietary supplements, and the authors of a recent research study are calling for more regulation of the substances and for a better system of monitoring harmful reactions.

Dietary supplements—in the form of botanicals, herbal remedies, minerals, vitamins, and "cultural remedies," such as Asian herbal prescription medicines—are unregulated by the United States government. And according to the researchers' study, some 29,000 such products are now sold in the US.

These products do not have to be tested before hitting the stores, and the US Food and Drug Administration (FDA) only monitors problems post-marketing. What's more, monitoring is done only on a voluntary basis, says an FDA official who spoke on the condition of anonymity. If a problem is reported, it's up to the FDA to prove there really is a problem.

Manufacturers of pharmaceutical drugs, by contrast, must report all potential side effects to the FDA before a drug is sold to consumers.

The study also notes there is no all-encompassing register of supplement names and ingredients, further hindering efforts to monitor health effects.

STUDY RESULTS

Eleven poison control centers throughout the United States supplied information on what kinds of ill effects people were reporting, and researchers found nearly 500 cases where negative events seemed to be linked to dietary supplements.

Only slightly more than 1 in 3 of the dietary supplements reported to the poison control centers were listed in the commercial information database routinely used by the centers' staffs.

One-third of the events recorded were linked to outcomes such as heart attacks, coma, bleeding, seizures, and even 4 deaths, the study authors say. People using more than one supplement tended to have worse symptoms, as did people who were older or who had been using the supplements over longer periods of time.

A surveillance system for supplements, such as the one already in place for drugs, would be ideal, says Susan Smolinske, a co-author of the study and managing director of the Children's Hospital of Michigan Regional Poison Control Center in Detroit.

STUDY IS 'FLAWED'

But John Hathcock, vice president of nutritional and regulatory science for the Council for Responsible Nutrition, says the study finds no casual relationship between supplement use and sickness.

"These are spontaneous reports coming from all sources," he says. He believes there's no good way of telling whether these reports have any substance with regard to adverse effects. "That, in a nutshell, is a great weakness of the study."

Issues of interactions, dosages, concentrations, and ingredients are often not spelled out with dietary supplements, says Dr. Lewis Kohl, chairman of emergency medicine at Long Island College Hospital in Brooklyn. However, some of these substances may actually help people—it's just a question of which ones and at what dose.

info For more on dietary supplements, visit the National Institutes of Health's Office of Dietary Supplements at *http://dietary-supplements.info.nih.gov*. For the supplement industry perspective, try the Council for Responsible Nutrition at *www.crnusa.org*.

Hum Your Way to Sinus Relief

Jon Lundberg, MD, PhD, Associate Professor, Physiology and Pharmacology, Karolinska Institute, Stockholm, Sweden.

Eddie Weitzberg, MD, PhD, Associate Professor, Anesthesiology and Intensive Care, Karolinska Hospital, Stockholm, Sweden.

July 2002, *American Journal of Respiratory and Critical Care Medicine*.

Could it be possible to avert sinus headaches just by humming a little? Swedish scientists have found that humming increases ventilation in the sinuses, raising the prospect that daily "tune-ing" might reduce the risk of sinusitis in patients who are susceptible to upper respiratory infections.

"Since humming increases sinus ventilation dramatically, we speculate that daily periods of humming could be helpful in preventing sinusitis in certain patients where bad ventilation is a part of the disease process," says Dr. Jon Lundberg, one of the study authors

and an associate professor of physiology and pharmacology at the Karolinska Institute in Stockholm. The findings, published in the *American Journal of Respiratory and Critical Care Medicine*, may also lead to a more accurate way to diagnose sinusitis.

Approximately 14% of the United States population suffers from this condition, which involves inflammation of one of the sinus cavities —usually from upper respiratory infections.

■ ■ ■ ■

Sinusitis Symptoms

The National Institute of Allergy and Infectious Diseases (*www.niaid.nih.gov*) Web site says that the location of your sinus pain depends on which sinus is affected. *Some of the more common sites of pain and related symptoms are…*

•**A headache when you wake up in the morning** is typical of a sinus problem.

•**Pain when your forehead is touched** may indicate that your frontal sinuses are inflamed.

•**Infection in the maxillary sinuses can cause your upper jaw and teeth to ache** and your cheeks to become tender to the touch.

Most people with sinusitis, however, have pain or tenderness in several locations, and their symptoms usually do not clearly indicate which sinuses are inflamed.

In addition, the mucus draining from the *sphenoids* or other sinuses down the back of your throat (postnasal drip) can cause you to have a sore throat. Not everyone with these symptoms, however, has sinusitis.

Dr. Eddie Weitzberg, lead author of the study and an associate professor in the department of anesthesiology and intensive care at Karolinska Hospital, likens the sinuses to a basement that constantly needs to be ventilated.

Humming just might be one of the simplest diagnostic tools available.

"Measuring nitric oxide during humming could be a measurement of the size of the holes from the sinus to the nose [ostia], and that could be of great interest to ear–nose–throat doctors, because one of the main promoters of sinusitis is narrow ostia," Weitzberg says.

How Do You Get Rid Of Warts? Duct Tape!

Dean R. Focht III, MD, Fellow, Department of Pediatric Gastroenterology and Nutrition, Cincinnati Children's Hospital Medical Center, OH.

October 2002, *Archives of Pediatrics and Adolescent Medicine.*

Next time your child has a wart, consider heading to Home Depot before hitting the pharmacy.

That's because do-it-all duct tape appears to be the best bet for getting rid of the pesky lesions, according to a study by Washington researchers.

The common wart, or *Verruca vulgaris*, occurs in up to 10% of children and less often in adults. The standard treatment is to freeze the wart with drops of liquid nitrogen. This procedure can work, but it can result in repeated, painful applications that can sometimes lead to blisters and infections. Also, previous research found that medical freezing (called *cryotherapy*) worked no better than the active ingredient in Compound W.

"When we started the study, we were just hoping to find some type of method less threatening to kids that would work as well," says Dr. Dean R. Focht III, who led the study while at Madigan Army Medical Center in Tacoma, Washington.

A GOOD IRRITANT

The researchers believe that covering warts with duct tape creates an area of localized irritation. Since warts are essentially benign viral tumors, drawing the attention of the immune system to the site of the wart can suppress the microbes and allow the lesions to heal.

Focht, now a gastric disease fellow at Cincinnati Children's Hospital Medical Center in Ohio, and his colleagues compared duct tape treatment with freezing in 61 children and young adults, aged 3 to 22 years, with warts on their hands, feet, and other body parts.

Roughly half the group received cryotherapy every 2 to 3 weeks for a maximum of 6 treatments. The rest had their warts patched with duct tape.

By study's end, 85% of the patients in the tape group got rid of their warts, compared with 60% of those who received cryotherapy. Nearly 75% of the taped warts were gone within 4 weeks.

Some children who had tape over only one wart, had other warts disappear, too. That jibes with the theory that the tape rallies the immune system and routs the viral infection all over the body, Focht says.

info For more on warts, visit the Cincinnati Children's Hospital at *www.cincinnati childrens.org.*

The Best Remedy for Fighting Anthrax

Tareg Bey, MD, PhD, Associate Clinical Professor, University of California–Irvine, Orange.

Andrew Cannons, PhD, Scientific Director, Center for Biological Defense, University of South Florida, Tampa.

Nammalwar Sriranganathan, DVM, PhD, Associate Professor, Microbiology, Virginia Polytechnic Institute and State University, Blacksburg.

March 12, 2003, *Journal of the American Medical Association.*

Washing your hands with plain old soap and water may be the best way to rid yourself of anthrax spores, if you've been exposed to the bacteria.

The next best method was a very diluted *chlorhexidine gluconate* preparation. This solution is a common mouth rinse often prescribed by dentists. An alcohol wipe didn't get rid of any of the anthrax spores, say researchers.

This research brings home the importance of the right protective gear and clothing—in this case, gloves and the right choice of disinfectant—for people who come into contact with anthrax, says Dr. Tareg Bey, associate clinical professor at the University of California at Irvine and 1 of only approximately 200 board-certified medical toxicologists in the United States.

WASH BEFORE AND AFTER

People likely to come in contact with the bacteria, such as health care workers, should wear gloves and wash their hands both before and after contact with surfaces or sores that might be contaminated, say researchers.

The researchers decided to test these recommendations using spores of different bacteria, *Bacillus atrophaeus*, as a stand-in for anthrax.

It's a pretty good substitute and is used in other experiments, says Andrew Cannons, scientific director of the University of South Florida Center for Biological Defense in Tampa. The results would approximate how anthrax would behave.

If anything, he adds, *B atrophaeus* may be slightly hardier, and therefore more difficult to wash away, than its infamous cousin.

For the study, healthy adults washed their hands in 3 ways: Using an ethyl alcohol rub, using a diluted chlorhexidine gluconate preparation, and using an antibacterial towel that released liquid bleach. Ordinary soap was used as a control.

Washing with the chlorhexidine preparation and the soap and water for 10, 30, or 60 seconds eliminated the bacteria. The bleach-containing towels worked better the longer they were used. The ethyl alcohol rub didn't work at all.

"We're talking about a mechanical thing. Washing your hands under a tap is going to remove spores," Cannons says. "If you wipe with an antibacterial wipe, the spores will stay."

DON'T SCRUB

However, Dr. Nammalwar Sriranganathan, an associate professor of microbiology at Virginia Tech in Blacksburg, cautions that you should not scrub yourself when washing. "When you scrub your hands, it will cause minor abrasions, and the organism can enter."

According to the authors, this study is the first direct evidence supporting the recommendations from the Centers for Disease Control

that health care workers should wear gloves when touching potentially contaminated surfaces and that they should also wash their hands with soap and water after removing the gloves.

info For more on anthrax, visit the University of Wisconsin–Madison Web site at *www.news.wisc.edu/anthrax.*

■ ■ ■ ■

What You Need to Know About Anthrax

Before the autumn of 2001, anthrax was most commonly known as an ailment found in livestock. But after anthrax spores began showing up in envelopes mailed to media organizations and politicians, public awareness and safety concerns increased.

The Centers for Disease Control and Prevention offers an anthrax information page (*www. bt.cdc.gov/agent/anthrax/needtoknow.asp*) that answers the most commonly asked questions.

WHAT IS ANTHRAX?

Anthrax is a serious disease caused by *Bacillus anthracis,* a bacterium that forms spores. A spore is a cell that is dormant, but that may come to life under the right conditions. There are 3 types of anthrax—cutaneous (skin), inhalation, and gastrointestinal.

HOW DO YOU GET IT?

Anthrax is not known to spread from one person to another. Humans can become infected with anthrax by handling products from infected animals or by breathing in anthrax spores from infected animal products (wool, for example). People can become infected with gastrointestinal anthrax by eating undercooked meat from infected animals.

ANTHRAX AS A WEAPON

Anthrax also can be used as a weapon. That's what occurred in the United States in 2001 when anthrax was deliberately spread through the postal system in contaminated letters. The result was 22 cases of anthrax infection and 5 deaths.

TREATMENT

In most cases, early treatment with antibiotics can cure cutaneous anthrax. Even if left untreated, 80% of cutaneous anthrax cases are not fatal. Gastrointestinal anthrax is more serious, and between 25% and 50% of cases lead to death. Inhalation anthrax is much more severe. In 2001, about half of the cases of inhalation anthrax ended in death.

WHAT ARE THE SYMPTOMS?

The warning signs of anthrax depend on the type of the disease.

- **Cutaneous.** The first symptom is a small sore that develops into a blister. This blister then develops into a skin ulcer with a black area in the center. The sore, blister, and ulcer do not hurt.

- **Gastrointestinal.** The first symptoms are nausea, loss of appetite, bloody diarrhea, and fever, followed by intense stomach pain.

- **Inhalation.** The first symptoms of inhalation anthrax resemble cold or flu symptoms, and can include a sore throat, mild fever, and muscle aches. Later symptoms include cough, chest discomfort, and shortness of breath, tiredness, and muscle aches.

Caution: Do not assume that anyone with cold or flu symptoms has inhalation anthrax.

Help Alkaline Burns With Vinegar

Stephen M. Milner, MD, Director, Regional Burn Center, Memorial Medical Center, Springfield, IL.
Peter Grossman, MD, Associate Director, Grossman Burn Center, Sherman Oaks Hospital, Sherman Oaks, CA.
May 2003, *Plastic and Reconstructive Surgery.*

If you drop an open bottle of liquid cleaning solvent on the floor and the substance splashes, burning the skin on your arms and torso, what should you do?

For burns caused by alkaline substances commonly found in household cleaning products, traditional first aid calls for rinsing the area with plenty of water. But an Illinois study shows that water followed by vinegar may neutralize these burns faster than water alone, reducing damage to the skin and tissue.

The lead author of the study says he is not suggesting that anyone with such a burn forgo rinsing with copious amounts of water.

"I would still say if you get an alkaline burn, you should still wash it under the tap or shower as a first-line measure," says Dr. Stephen M. Milner, director of the Regional Burn Center at Memorial Medical Center in Springfield, Illinois. "I think it's important to wash it off for as long as you possibly can, about 20 minutes or longer. Adding vinegar [after the rinse with water] might be good."

SHORTER TREATMENT PERIODS

In a study of rats, Milner and his colleagues looked at skin burns treated with water alone and those treated with water plus *acetic acid,* similar to household vinegar. Animals treated with the acetic acid had a shorter treatment period and their skin pH—a measure of how acidic or alkaline it was—returned to normal more quickly.

"Most cleaning supplies [found around the home] contain alkali," Milner says. Each year, alkaline agents are responsible for more than 15,000 skin burns in the United States, he says.

Another expert calls the study interesting. "It piques my interest and merits further investigation," says Dr. Peter Grossman, associate director of the Grossman Burn Center at Sherman Oaks Hospital in Sherman Oaks, California.

Milner cautions that his study looked only at skin burns, not burns to the eyes or internal organs, so he cannot say whether vinegar or other types of acetic acid might help heal those types of injuries.

■ ■ ■ ■

Burn Treatments

In case of burns, The National Safety Council (*www.nsc.org*) advises that you immediately run cool water over the injured skin until the area is pain-free both in and out of water. Wash minor first- and second-degree burns with mild soap, and apply an antibiotic ointment. Leave blisters intact. Cover a second-degree burn with a clean bandage and keep it dry.

- **First-degree burns** are red and very sensitive to touch. These burns involve minimal tissue damage and they affect the outer layer of skin, causing pain, redness, and swelling. Sunburn is a good example of a first-degree burn.

- **Second-degree burns** are more serious than first-degree burns because a deeper layer of skin is burned. They can more easily become infected. Also, if the burn affects more than 10% of your skin, you may go into shock because large quantities of fluid are lost from the burned area.

- **Third-degree burns** involve the deepest layer of skin and cause charring of the skin or a translucent white color. These burn areas may be numb, but the person may complain of pain. This pain is usually because of second-degree burns. Healing from third-degree burns is very slow because the skin tissue and structures have been destroyed. Third-degree burns usually result in extensive scarring.

It's important to get immediate treatment for third-degree burns, second-degree burns that cover a large area of the body, or burns on the face, neck, hands, feet, or genitals.

Important Discovery For Folks With Eczema

Richard Gallo, MD, PhD, Chief, Dermatology, Veterans Affairs San Diego Healthcare System, CA.
October 10, 2002, *New England Journal of Medicine.*

The recurring infections suffered by people with the most common form of eczema—*atopic dermatitis*—are caused by the failure of a defense system that works as a natural antibiotic.

Atopic dermatitis is an inherited disease that affects approximately 3% of Americans and is most common in childhood. The condition causes infections to occur over and over again because skin cells don't produce

natural antibiotic compounds called *cathelicidins* and *beta-defensins*, according to a report published in the *New England Journal of Medicine.*

Researchers showed that the antimicrobial molecules work together to kill a bacterium known as Staphylococcus aureus, a common cause of skin infections. When they compared skin samples from 8 patients with various skin conditions, those with atopic dermatitis showed no elevation in the defense molecules. "Our finding that these natural peptide antibiotics are deficient in patients may explain why they get infections," says Dr. Richard Gallo, chief of dermatology with the Veterans Affairs San Diego Healthcare System.

"This gives us greater insight into the disease and might make clinicians more cognizant of the risk of infection for these patients," Gallo says. "We hope that within 5 years or so it will lead to a more rational design of antibiotic replacements for these patients."

info For information about atopic dermatitis, go to the American Academy of Dermatology at *www.aad.org* or the National Institute of Arthritis and Musculoskeletal and Skin Diseases at *www.niams.nih.gov.*

■ ■ ■ ■

How Do You Know If You Have Eczema?

Symptoms of eczema vary from person to person. The most common symptoms are dry, itchy skin; cracks behind the ears; and rashes on the cheeks, arms, and legs. Scratching and rubbing in response to the itching worsen the inflammation that is characteristic of this disease. *Here's how the Federal Citizen Information Center at the US General Services Administration describes eczema symptoms...*

- **Thick, leathery skin,** known as *lichenification,* that results from constant scratching and rubbing.

- **Small raised bumps,** or *papules,* that may open when scratched, and then become crusty and infected.

•**Dry, rectangular scales on the skin,** a condition known as *ichthyosis.*

•**Small, rough bumps,** known as *keratosis pilaris,* generally on the face, upper arms, and thighs.

•**Hyperlinear palms,** which have increased number of skin creases.

•**Red, raised bumps,** known as *hives,* often appear after exposure to an allergen, at the beginning of flare-ups, or after exercise or a hot bath.

•**Cheilitis**—an inflammation of the skin on and around the lips.

•**Atopic pleat**—an extra fold of skin that develops under the eye.

•**Hyperpigmented eyelids** that have become darker in color from inflammation or hay fever.

Check with your physician if you have any of the above symptoms, especially if they don't disappear within a week.

The American Academy of Dermatology (*www.aad.org*) warns patients not to scratch skin ailments, and suggests using lotions and creams, including nonprescription corticosteroids, to keep skin moist. More severe cases of eczema may require prescription corticosteroids or light therapy.

Soy Compound May Relieve Menopause Symptoms Without the Side Effects

Samantha Heller, MS, RD, Senior Clinical Nutritionist, New York University Medical Center.

April 26–30, 2003, presentations, American College of Obstetricians and Gynecologists Annual Meeting, New Orleans, LA.

A soy-based compound promises to rival estrogen by relieving hot flashes and building bone mass in menopausal women without many of the troubling side effects associated with traditional hormone replacement therapy.

A group of Israeli researchers announced the findings, which were based on a 12-month study that involved patients, laboratory cell lines, and animals.

"The conflicting data on hormone replacement therapy (HRT) has led to an intensive search for alternative treatments," reports Dr. Benjamin Chayen, on behalf of his colleagues at the Sheba Medical Center in Tel-Hashomer, Israel, where the research was conducted. That led the scientists to the soy compound known as Tofupill.

Among the 37 women who used the soy supplement, 75% reported relief from hot flashes. Tests showed they also experienced a measurable increase in bone density—up to 4% in the spine and 2.9% in the neck.

In laboratory tests, the researchers found the soy compound had no negative effects on breast cancer cell lines, indicating it may not share estrogen's ability to stimulate tumor growth. And in rat studies, the soy appeared to stimulate growth of skeletal tissue without stimulating cell growth in the uterus, as estrogen therapy can do.

A BIT OF A LEAP?

Although experts say the results are promising, New York University nutritionist Samantha Heller believes the research makes too many "leaps of faith" about issues that remain unproven.

"It is not appropriate to extrapolate data gathered on rats and in vitro directly to humans and suggest that there is little concern regarding short- and long-term effects of supplementation," Heller says.

She also points to conflicting evidence regarding the safety and efficacy of soy supplementation in women. "I would exercise caution with soy supplementation until more research is done," she says. "But including soy products in your diet may still confer many health benefits."

info For more about the women's health topics that are making news, visit ObGyn Net at *www.obgyn.net/women/women.asp.* Visit *www.soyfoods.com* for a free downloadable booklet that contains complete nutritional information about the health benefits of soy, dozens of recipes, and hints for how to add soy to your diet.

Natural Hormones: Best Choice for Easing Menopause

Robert D. Langer, MD, MPH, Professor, Family and Preventive Medicine, University of California, San Diego, School of Medicine.

Philip Sarrel, MD, Emeritus Professor, Obstetrics and Gynecology and Psychiatry, Yale University School of Medicine, New Haven, CT.

November 2002, *Journal of Obstetrics and Gynecology.*

Women approaching menopause often struggle with the question of whether to use hormone replacement therapy (HRT) to ease menopausal symptoms. Although long-term use has been called into question by recent studies that link the combination of estrogen and progestin to an increased risk of breast cancer, heart disease, and stroke, long-term use can also reduce the risk of osteoporosis. There is no one-size-fits-all answer, but there is lots of information available to help guide the decision.

For example, researchers have found that women who take natural progesterone have far less bleeding than women who take a synthetic version of the same hormone. Not only does this vastly improve the quality of life for menopausal women, it may also have far-reaching implications for the future of HRT.

In a recent study, researchers used a natural *micronized progesterone* (MP) which is essentially the same as the hormone a woman makes before menopause, says author Dr. Robert D. Langer, a professor of family and preventive medicine at the University of California, San Diego, School of Medicine. "It is chemically identical in all respects."

A synthetic version of progesterone, known as MPA, had to be discontinued when researchers discovered that women taking it had a higher incidence of breast cancer, heart attack, and stroke. The synthetic hormone, 35 times stronger than natural progesterone, essentially nullified the beneficial effects provided by the estrogen. So far, all indications are that natural progesterone would not have the same negative effect.

LESS BLEEDING MEANS FEWER SURPRISES

The results of Langer's study showed that the women taking natural progesterone had fewer days of bleeding and less intense bleeding than did women taking traditional MPA. The MP was also equally good in protecting against endometrial cancer.

"It's a quality-of-life issue," says Dr. Philip Sarrel, professor emeritus of obstetrics and gynecology and psychiatry at Yale University School of Medicine. No woman wants the hassle of "unscheduled bleeding," he says, and that's the problem they are trying to avoid. "It really is an issue of what is going to work best in the life of a woman."

Natural MP is the only type of progesterone Sarrel uses in his practice. "I have patients who cannot tolerate MPA. Within 2 to 3 days of starting, they get flushes or chest pains or irritability or angry outbursts, all of which are adverse affects of too much progestin," he says. "With MP, it's really minimized. It's not perfect, but it's a lot better from an everyday clinical practice point of view."

■ ■ ■ ■

More Than Hot Flashes

Most women will experience menopause by age 50, but it can occur earlier or later, depending on individual hormone patterns. There may be both physical and psychological symptoms during menopause. Symptoms may occur for a few weeks, a few months, or sometimes for several years. Individual symptoms may be sporadic or they may occur regularly.

Perimenopause, a condition that signals the beginning of menopause, has symptoms of its own. According to the women's research Web site, Project Aware (*www.project-aware.org*), some clinicians maintain that perimenopause can last for as long as 5 to 15 years, often starting between 35 and 45 years.

Most premenopausal women experience changes in their menstrual cycle. When estrogen levels begin to drop, the follicular phase of the cycle may be shortened, and this can shorten the total cycle from 28–30 days to 24–26 days, resulting in more frequent periods.

On the other hand, some women begin having longer cycles because they are not ovulating as frequently. Additionally, the fluctuating estrogen levels can produce a host of disturbing symptoms—hot flashes, increasing vaginal dryness, sleep problems, mood swings, and breast tenderness.

SYMPTOMS COMMON DURING MENOPAUSE

According to the University of Michigan Health System, there are several signs that menopause has started. *They are...*

- **Irregular menstrual periods.**
- **Hot flashes.**
- **Night sweats.**
- **Disturbed sleep patterns.**
- **Vaginal dryness** and shrinkage of genital tissues, sometimes resulting in discomfort or pain during sexual intercourse.
- **Dry skin.**
- **More frequent urination** or leakage of urine (urinary incontinence).
- **More frequent minor vaginal and urinary tract infections.**
- **Fatigue.**

There are also psychological symptoms that may signal the start of menopause. These symptoms are often exacerbated by other midlife concerns. *These psychological symptoms may include...*

- **Anxiety.**
- **Depression.**
- **Tearfulness, irritability.**
- **Less desire for sex.**
- **Lack of concentration.**
- **More trouble remembering things.**

Increasing Your Sex Drive—With Light!

Daniel Kripke, MD, Professor, Psychiatry, University of California, San Diego.
Ronald Swerdloff, MD, Professor, Medicine, Chief, Division of Endocrinology, Department of Medicine, Harbor UCLA Medical Center, University of California at Los Angeles Medical School, Torrance.
April 24, 2003, *Neuroscience Letters.*

Ultra-bright lamps may boost the body's ability to produce sex hormones, particularly for men, say researchers who studied the effects of light therapy on mood.

The importance of the finding is not fully established, but it's possible that light therapy could one day be used to control ovulation in women or treat people who take antidepressants and find themselves with low sex drives, the researchers say.

"It's a very promising lead," says study co-author Dr. Daniel Kripke, a professor of psychiatry at the University of California at San Diego. Light therapy is natural and could be a safe way to accomplish some important health goals, he says.

Researchers have known for decades that exposure to light affects the way animals live. Changes in the light from the sun, for example, set off hibernation in some mammals. Seasonal changes in light also control reproduction in rats and mice; they only mate during warmer months, Kripke says.

THE HUMAN FACTOR

Researchers are still working to understand how exposure to light affects humans. Kripke and colleagues discovered 2 decades ago that light therapy—shining powerful lamps at people's eyes—affects mood. Light therapy has become a common treatment for seasonal affective disorder, a type of depression that strikes when days grow shorter.

In his study, Kripke enlisted 11 healthy men, aged 19 to 30 years, to test whether light affects the body levels of luteinizing hormone, which is produced by the pituitary gland and also leads to the release of other hormones, such as testosterone in men. The men woke at 5 AM for 5 days and spent an hour in front of a light box giving off 1000 lux, much more brightness than typical indoor lighting. Later, they spent 5 days in front of a light box that only gave out 10 lux.

The result: Body levels of luteinizing hormone grew by nearly 70% while the men were exposed to the higher levels of light.

The researchers didn't look at women because the rapidly cycling hormones in their bodies would make it difficult to study the effect, Kripke says. However, luteinizing hormone does affect ovulation, he adds, and "we think light is potentially a very promising treatment for women who have ovulatory problems or long and irregular menstrual cycles."

TESTOSTERONE INCREASE?

Light therapy could also boost testosterone in men, potentially increasing sexual potency and muscle mass, he says. Researchers, however, did not monitor testosterone levels in the men.

A hormone expert cautioned that research is still needed. The study was small, and it's not clear whether the changes in the level of the hormone are significant enough to actually cause changes in the body, says Dr. Ronald Swerdloff, chief of the division of endocrinology at Harbor UCLA Medical Center, part of the University of California at Los Angeles School of Medicine.

info For more information, visit the Society for Light Treatment & Biological Rhythms at *www.websciences.org/sltbr*.

Light May Be Right Therapy For Methanol Poisoning

Janis Eells, PhD, Associate Professor, Pharmacology and Toxicology, Medical College of Wisconsin, Milwaukee.
March 2003, *Proceedings of the National Academy of Sciences*.

A simple light therapy may be able to prevent blindness from methanol poisoning, researchers say.

In a study at the Medical College of Wisconsin, researchers used a red light operating at near infrared levels to prevent cell damage to the eyes of rats who were exposed to methanol poisoning.

Methanol is used in antifreeze, windshield wiper fluid, and other liquids. Poisonings typically occur among children who drink it accidentally, or adults trying to commit suicide, says study author Janis Eells, an associate professor of pharmacology at the Medical College of Wisconsin.

Without treatment, it can cause blindness, even death. It's difficult for doctors to diagnose because symptoms don't appear for several days after ingestion and they mimic other disorders. With prompt treatment—say within a day—most people recover without lingering effects.

Eells says animals treated with a light-emitting diode (LED) were protected and did much better than the animals not treated with the LED.

Because methanol poisoning is rare, Eells says the real benefit from this work may be in treating other diseases, like macular degeneration or glaucoma, that cause damage to the cells in the eyes similar to that done by methanol poisoning.

Methanol causes blindness by attacking the mitochondria in the retina and optic nerve and disrupting their ability to supply cells with power. Mitochondria provide cells with the energy they need to function. The LED light treatment works by stimulating the mitochondria, Eells explains.

"The LED light had protected the rats. It appears to be preventing damage," says Eells, adding that subsequent studies have also shown the LED light can reverse damage that's already been done.

The researchers saw no adverse side effects from the LED treatment. Eells says she expects that results would be similar in humans because the changes that occur in rats with methanol poisoning are similar to the changes that happen in humans.

■ ■ ■ ■

Potential Poisons in the Home

According to the National Capital Poison Center, there are several especially hazardous household items. *They are...*

- **Antifreeze.**
- **Windshield washer solutions.**
- **Drain cleaners.**
- **Toilet bowl cleaners.**
- **Insecticides.**
- **Artificial nail polish removers.**
- **Topical anesthetics** (for example, products that may be used for sunburn pain).
- **Medicines,** medicines, medicines.

Buy small quantities of these items. Discard unneeded extras. Make sure they are always out of the reach of children.

info Visit the National Capital Poison Center at *www.poison.org* for tips on what to do if a poisoning has occurred.

■ ■ ■ ■

Know Where the Dangerous Substances Are in Your House

Patricia Clinton, a clinical assistant professor at the University of Iowa College of Nursing and a pediatric nurse practitioner, has some suggestions for keeping dangerous substances out of the reach of children.

"Storing medicines in a small suitcase kept on the top shelf of a closet is a good idea," Clinton says.

Medications and chemicals should also be kept in their original containers. Children have swallowed chemicals, such as paint thinner, thinking they were beverages because they were kept in plastic milk cartons or glass juice bottles, Clinton says.

Even more important is reacting quickly if a poison has been taken. Clinton says that *syrup of ipecac,* a chemical that induces vomiting, should be kept in all households. But never take or administer it before calling poison control. Parents need to make sure that the vomiting won't cause more harm than good. Clinton notes that if the substance ingested is lye-based, inducing vomiting could burn the child's throat. If an oil-based substance is vomited, it could result in a form of pneumonia that is difficult to treat.

WHERE ARE THE POISONS AT YOUR HOUSE?

The University of Utah's Poison Control Center has a list of the most common household poisons. *They are...*

- **Garage/Storage Area**
  - Paint thinner/remover.
  - Gas, oil, antifreeze.
  - Pesticides.
  - Lye.
  - Car care items—wax, solvent, upholstery cleaner.
- **Kitchen**
  - Cleaning solutions.
  - Tarnish removers.
  - Disinfectants.
  - Drugs.
- **Bedroom**
  - Drugs.
  - Perfumes.
  - Cosmetics.
- **Bathroom**
  - Drugs.
  - Cleaning solutions.
  - Disinfectants.
  - Drain cleaner.

info The Utah Poison Control Center Hotline 800-222-1222 is available 24 hours a day, every day. Their Web site is *http://uuhsc.utah.edu/poison.*

Fructose Intolerant? The Real Reason You May Have Gas

Peter Beyer, Associate Professor, Department of Dietetics and Nutrition, University of Kansas Medical Center.

October 21, 2002, report to the American College of Gastroenterology 67th Annual Scientific Meeting, Seattle, WA.

October 21, 2002, American College of Gastroenterology news release.

Fructose, the simple sugar that's found in honey, fruits, and some soft drinks, may be to blame for unexplained stomach ailments such as cramps, gas, and diarrhea.

This sugar, which is now commercially produced, is the main sweetener used in all sorts of food products, from soft drinks to yogurt. The problem is that some people lack the ability to absorb fructose properly.

A group of researchers at the University of Kansas Medical Center believe this type of sugar is responsible for a host of common gastrointestinal complaints, and they urge doctors to use fructose breath tests as a diagnostic tool for unexplained abdominal maladies.

Their study, presented at the American College of Gastroenterology's Annual Scientific Meeting in Seattle, suggests that fructose malabsorption affects a significant number of healthy adults.

Gastric woes arise when the fructose travels down the digestive tract into the colon, where some bacteria use the sugar as a food source and consequently flourish. In the process, hydrogen gas is released and may cause pain, bloating, and diarrhea.

During their research, the investigators fed their subjects 25 grams of fructose—the equivalent of a 12-ounce can of soda sweetened with high-fructose corn syrup—and then gathered breath samples. Testing revealed an abnormal level of hydrogen gas in almost 50% of the participants. On another occasion, after the subjects had dined on 50 grams of fructose, approximately 75% of them exhaled high levels of hydrogen. If the sugar had been digested normally, the gas would be absent from their breath.

"When given levels of fructose commonly consumed in the Western diet, a significant number of our subjects had both objective and subjective evidence of fructose malabsorption, meaning that the breath analysis showed hydrogen in excess of 20 parts per million, and they had symptoms such as gas and diarrhea," says Peter Beyer, of the University of Kansas Medical Centers' Dietetics and Nutrition Department.

He believes physicians should add breath analysis for fructose intolerance to their diagnostic test reservoir.

"If a patient is found to be fructose intolerant and symptomatic, the doctor may recommend a low-fructose diet," says Beyer. "But in severe cases, antibiotic therapy may be required to provide relief."

info The National Institute of Diabetes & Digestive & Kidney Diseases at *www. niddk.nih.gov* has more information about sugar and its role in stomach ailments.

∎ ∎ ∎ ∎

'Natural' Can Still Be Painful

A number of "natural" substances can cause gastrointestinal problems, according to the National Institute of Diabetes & Digestive & Kidney Diseases. Natural sugars, starches, and fiber may make some people uncomfortable.

SUGARS

The sugars that cause gas are raffinose, lactose, fructose, and sorbitol.

●**Raffinose.** Beans contain large amounts of this complex sugar. Smaller amounts are found in cabbage, brussels sprouts, broccoli, asparagus, other vegetables, and whole grains.

●**Lactose.** Lactose is the natural sugar in milk, milk products (such as cheese and ice cream), and processed foods (such as bread, cereal, and salad dressing). Many adults, particularly of African, Native American, or Asian background, have low levels of the enzyme needed to digest lactose. As people age, their enzyme levels decrease, and over time they may experience increasing amounts of gas after eating foods containing lactose.

●**Fructose.** Fructose is naturally present in onions, artichokes, pears, and wheat. It is also used as a sweetener in some soft drinks and fruit drinks.

●**Sorbitol.** Sorbitol is a sugar found naturally in fruits, including apples, pears, peaches, and prunes. It is also used as an artificial sweetener in many dietetic foods and sugar-free candies and gums.

STARCHES

Most starches, including potatoes, corn, noodles, and wheat, produce gas as they are broken down in the large intestine. Rice is the only starch that does not cause gas.

FIBER

Many foods contain soluble and insoluble fiber. Soluble fiber dissolves easily in water, and takes on a soft, gel-like texture in the intestines. Found in oat bran, beans, peas, and most fruits, soluble fiber is not broken down until it reaches the large intestine, where digestion causes gas.

Insoluble fiber, on the other hand, passes through the intestines essentially unchanged and produces little gas. Wheat bran and some vegetables contain this kind of fiber.

Surgery Discovery: Potato Powder Stems Bleeding

Mark H. Ereth, MD, Associate Professor, Anesthesiology, Mayo Clinic, Rochester, MN.
October 15, 2002, presentation, American Society of Anesthesiologists Annual Meeting, Orlando, FL.

The humble spud may stand poised for a major medical breakthrough. A patented starchy powder made from potatoes appears to clot blood instantly. That could come in handy during surgeries and emergency procedures and also reduce the number of blood transfusions, say researchers at the Mayo Clinic.

"It works like a sponge for water molecules in the blood, allowing the platelets to clot almost immediately," says lead researcher Dr. Mark H. Ereth, an associate professor of anesthesiology at the Mayo Clinic.

APPROVED IN THE US

The powder, approved for most surgical uses in the United States, Canada, and Europe, sidesteps problems associated with other clotting agents. It is cheaper and cleaner than clotting agents made from human and cow plasma, and it avoids the risks of disease and allergic reaction, Ereth says.

In their study, the researchers made 2 tiny incisions in the arms of 30 people. One incision was treated with the potato powder; the other was left to clot on its own. The untreated cut took almost 6 minutes to reach *hemostasis* (blood clotting), while 77% of the cuts treated with the powder stopped bleeding immediately.

"In the other 23% of cases, the clotting was rapid, but there was a little bit of oozing afterward," Ereth says.

ELIMINATING COMPLICATIONS?

The powder, which is made of purified potato starch processed to produce tiny, absorbent particles, can help surgeons avoid blood transfusions by preventing excessive bleeding. It's particularly useful for paramedics or combat doctors who must stabilize massive wounds to prevent shock and other complications from a major loss of blood, Ereth says.

All of that from a potato.

12

Nutrition, Diet & Fitness

Love It or Hate It, Atkins Diet Brings Results

You might not find much middle ground when it comes to professional opinions about the well-known Atkins Diet. Researchers and physicians either condemn it or sing its praises.

Nevertheless, 2 studies suggest the popular weight-loss plan is more effective than a traditional low-fat diet at helping people shed unwanted pounds.

What's more, the Atkins approach—which encourages consumption of high-fat and high-protein foods, such as meat and dairy products and discourages consumption of carbohydrates—doesn't boost cholesterol levels, as you might expect, the studies say.

"The results are very surprising and at the same time very preliminary," says Gary D. Foster, clinical director of the University of Pennsylvania's Weight and Eating Disorders

Program and leader of one of the studies. "The take-home message is that this diet deserves further study."

The results, says a spokeswoman for the Atkins Center in New York City, are confirmation of the views of the late Dr. Robert Atkins.

The study, led by Foster, enrolled 63 obese men and women whose average weight was 216 pounds. Some were given a copy of Atkins' New Diet Revolution, and were asked to follow that diet, which emphasizes fat and protein intake and limits carbohydrates. Others were given instructions about a conventional weight-loss diet—1200 to 1500 calories a day for women, 1500 calories a day for men, composed of 60% carbohydrates, 25% fat, and 15% protein.

After 3 months, the average weight loss was 14.7 pounds in the Atkins group and 5.8

Gary D. Foster, PhD, Clinical Director, Weight and Eating Disorders Program, University of Pennsylvania, Philadelphia.

David L. Katz, MD, Director, Yale–Griffin Prevention Research Center, Yale School of Medicine, New Haven, CT.

May 22, 2003, *New England Journal of Medicine*.

pounds in the conventional group. At 6 months, weight loss averaged 15.2 pounds in the Atkins group and 6.9 pounds in the conventional group. At 1 year, average weight loss was 9.5 pounds in the Atkins group and 5.4 pounds in the conventional group—a statistically insignificant difference, the study says.

A parallel study conducted by researchers at Washington University in St. Louis showed essentially similar results.

CRITIC FINDS FLAWS

A critic of the Atkins diet, Dr. David L. Katz, director of the Yale–Griffin Prevention Research Center at the Yale School of Medicine, says the studies were not "blinded," meaning participants knew what their role was. "If you know that you are testing something new, that is exciting, and it introduces a very important bias," Katz says.

Also, the dropout rate was high—43% in the conventional group, and 39% in the Atkins group. That could have skewed the results, he adds. And the researchers never measured calorie intake, Katz points out. Since the Atkins group participants were told to cut back on carbohydrates, "it was almost inevitable that they had lower calorie intake," he says.

info You can get the argument in favor of the Atkins diet from the Atkins Center for Complementary Medicine at *http://atkins. com* and one against it from the Physicians Committee for Responsible Medicine at *www. atkinsdietalert.org.*

A 'Sensible Solution' To the High-Protein Diet

Donald K. Layman, PhD, Professor, Nutrition, University of Illinois at Urbana–Champaign.
Althea Zanecosky, RD, spokeswoman, American Dietetic Association, Chicago, IL.
February 2003, *Journal of Nutrition.*

If you are trying to slim down, you are faced with a choice. Are you better off eating a big bowl of pasta or a grilled steak with a couple of veggies on the side?

You might be surprised to learn that the meat dish wins, according to University of Illinois research that found a diet moderately high in protein and low in carbohydrates helps you lose weight while maintaining muscle mass.

That may sound like the famous Atkins Diet, which advocates cutting out virtually all carbohydrates. Instead, this diet calls for a less drastic shift—laying off refined grain products such as bread, pasta, cereal, and snack foods, while increasing the intake of lean meat, poultry, and low-fat dairy products.

Study author Donald K. Layman, a professor of nutrition at the University of Illinois at Urbana–Champaign, calls his diet the "Sensible Solution."

Layman and his colleagues put 24 overweight women aged 45 to 56 years on a diet of 1700 calories a day.

One group followed the US Department of Agriculture's Food Guide Pyramid, eating a diet that was high in carbohydrates from bread, rice, pasta, and cereal sources and low in protein from animal products, including meat, poultry, eggs, cheese, and milk.

The other group ate more protein and fewer carbs—about 10 ounces of meat a day (much of it beef) and 3 servings of low-fat milk or cheese.

After 10 weeks, both sets of women lost approximately the same amount of weight, about 16 pounds. However, the women on the higher-protein diet lost more fat and less muscle.

REVERSING A TREND

During the carbohydrate craze of the 1980s and 1990s, Americans were told that dietary fat was bad for your heart and caused weight gain, Layman says.

"We became obsessed with fat in our diet, and we were told that animal products are high in fat," Layman says. "So we decreased our consumption of high-quality proteins and increased our consumption of refined grain products. But this hasn't resulted in a decrease in obesity. And it's pretty hard to make a case that our overall nutrition is better."

In the study, the women on the high-protein diet consumed, on average, approximately 170 grams of carbohydrates per day, well within the accepted nutritional guidelines, says Althea Zanecosky, a Philadelphia-based spokeswoman for the American Dietetic Association.

The Atkins Diet, by comparison, recommends approximately 30 grams of carbs per day, while the average American is eating approximately 300 grams per day, according to Layman.

Layman attributes his results, in part, to *leucine,* an amino acid that previous research has shown regulates muscle. Meat, poultry, fish, eggs, and dairy products are rich in leucine, he says.

EVERYTHING IN MODERATION

None of this should give you carte blanche to start stuffing yourself with high-fat pepperoni, sausage, or fast-food burgers.

"I'm in no way saying fat is a freebie," Layman says.

Zanecosky says nutrition experts are beginning to again emphasize the importance of lean meat and low-fat dairy products in a healthy diet.

Still, she says, the bottom line is limiting your calories by reducing portion size. Remember, she adds, all of the women in Layman's study were restricted to 1700 calories a day and they all lost weight.

Heart-Healthy Diet Doubles Your Weight Loss

Bonnie Brehm, PhD, RD, Assistant Professor, College of Nursing, University of Cincinnati, OH.

Evelyn Tribole, RD, Dietitian, Irvine, CA.

April 2003, *Journal of Clinical Endocrinology & Metabolism.*

Less fat, more carbohydrates? Fewer carbs, more fat? Which diet is better? If you're healthy but very heavy and considering a weight-loss diet, it might help to know that you can lose twice as much weight on a low-carb diet as you would on a low-fat

diet, and you won't compromise your cardiovascular health, researchers say.

Study author Bonnie Brehm, an assistant professor in the College of Nursing at the University of Cincinnati, says the results surprised her. Because low-carbohydrate plans include a high percentage of calories from fat and protein, "we had hypothesized that this [low-carb plan] would harm cardiovascular health." The researchers also said they believed the low-fat group would lose more weight and body fat.

In fact, after 6 months, the 22 women on the low-carb plan averaged an 18.7-pound loss, while the 20 women on the low-fat plan averaged an 8.5-pound loss.

Both groups also showed improvement in markers of cardiovascular health, such as blood pressure, blood lipids, and blood cholesterol levels, Brehm says. The women ranged in age from 29 to 58 years, but most were in their 40s. Their body mass index (BMI) ranged from 29.5 to more than 37. A person with a BMI of 30 or above is considered obese.

Average calorie intake was similar for both groups—1302 a day for the low-carb group and 1247 for the low-fat group.

Brehm isn't sure why the low-carb group lost more weight. The women agreed they would not change their exercise habits during the study.

"I told them, if you are a couch potato today [at the start of the study], you must remain a couch potato for 6 months," Brehm says. "If you walk 4 times a week, continue."

ONE DIETITIAN DISAGREES

Another dietary expert familiar with the study says she wouldn't advise women to go the low-carbohydrate route to lose weight.

"The study only lasted 6 months," says Evelyn Tribole, a dietitian and author of numerous nutrition books, including *Intuitive Eating.*

"When you go on such a low-carb diet, there's not much food left to select from," she says. And exercising for an hour or 90 minutes at a stretch may be more difficult on such a diet, she says, because the body depends on carbohydrates for energy.

The Low-Carb Effect on Your Kidneys

Eric L. Knight, MD, MPH, Physician Researcher, Brigham and Women's Hospital and Massachusetts General Hospital, Boston.

March 18, 2003, *Annals of Internal Medicine.*

With so many high-protein, low-carbohydrate diets on the market, you might like to know how well your body metabolizes all that protein. Researchers have found that where the kidneys are concerned, there's good news and there's bad news.

If your kidneys are healthy, you can eat a high-protein diet with no adverse affects. But if you have even mild kidney problems, lots of protein—particularly nondairy animal protein—can speed the decline of your kidney function, says Dr. Eric Knight, a researcher at Brigham and Women's Hospital and Massachusetts General Hospital in Boston.

Patients with chronic kidney disease are often put on low-protein diets to decrease the workload of the kidneys and slow progression of the disease. After the body uses the protein from food, a waste product called urea is made and excreted by the kidneys. If kidneys aren't working well, the excess urea may build up, so decreasing protein intake is often suggested.

However, the question of whether high protein intake affects those with milder disease or no disease has received less attention.

"I think we are the first to study the impact of protein intake on kidney function in those with normal kidney function and mild kidney dysfunction," Knight says.

THE STUDY

Knight's team evaluated 1624 women, of whom 25% had mild kidney problems.

After 11 years, researchers found no association between high protein intake and worsening kidney function in women who had started the study with healthy kidneys. But for those whose kidneys were mildly inefficient, the women with the highest protein intake were "3.5 times more likely to have a significant decline in kidney function," Knight says. Animal protein in particular was associated with worsening kidney function.

THE DOCTOR CAUTIONS

"Those with pre-existing kidney disease should get advice from their doctors before starting a diet high in protein," Knight says. And since mild kidney problems usually are not accompanied by symptoms, people might not be aware that their kidneys are ailing, he adds. A blood test can help determine the status of your kidneys.

■ ■ ■ ■

Warning Signs of Kidney Trouble

The National Kidney Foundation has come up with a list of warning signs of kidney and urinary tract diseases. *They are...*

- **High blood pressure.**

- **Blood and/or protein in the urine.**

- **A creatinine blood level greater than 1.2 for women and 1.4 for men.** Creatinine is a waste product removed from the blood by healthy kidneys. In kidney diseases, creatinine levels in the blood may increase. Creatinine levels vary with age, race, and body size. A lower value may be a sign of kidney disease in children.

- **More frequent urination,** particularly at night.

- **Difficult or painful urination.**

- **Puffiness around eyes,** swelling of hands and feet, especially in children.

info You can get more information about having your kidney function tested, and also find special diets, which can help reduce the kidneys' workload, on the National Kidney Foundation's Web site, *www.kidney.org.*

Small Change: The Easiest Way to Lose Weight Without Changing Your Life!

Jeffrey Friedman, MD, PhD, head, Laboratory of Molecular Genetics, Rockefeller University, New York, NY.

James Hill, PhD, Researcher, University of Colorado Health Sciences Center, Denver.

Adam Drewnowski, PhD, spokesman, American Dietetic Association, and Director, Center for Public Health Nutrition, University of Washington, Seattle.

February 7, 2003, *Science.*

Researchers are still trying to determine whether it is genetics or a growing affinity for fast food and a sedentary lifestyle that is behind the growing number of obese Americans.

Dr. Jeffrey Friedman, head of the laboratory of molecular genetics at Rockefeller University in New York City, argues that the tendency toward obesity is rooted in evolution. According to Dr. Friedman, early survival meant being able to withstand periods of famine. Therefore, individuals who were able to store fat well had a better chance of surviving. And now, many Americans can thank (or curse) their ancestors for their battles with weight. Friedman adds that eating is a powerful, primal drive, one that wins out over the desire to be thin in people predisposed to obesity.

"The feeling of hunger is intense and, if not as potent as the drive to breathe, is probably no less powerful than the drive to drink when one is thirsty," Friedman says. "This is the feeling the obese must resist after they have lost a significant amount of weight."

ANOTHER OPINION

Although Friedman's published remarks argue that genetics is the primary determinant for obesity, an article by James Hill, a researcher at the University of Colorado Health Sciences Center in Denver, points to a different culprit—the environment.

For contemporary Americans, adults and children, that means super-sized portions, calorie-dense fast food, hours in front of a video screen, too little exercise, and too much to eat.

EVEN A SLIGHT ADJUSTMENT CAN HELP

Hill has proposed a simple solution to halt the creeping weight gain: Eat 100 fewer calories a day. That's equal to the calories in a cookie or 3 bites of a fast-food burger.

It takes just a slight energy imbalance to cause a gradual increase in weight, Hill says. Say you ate just 50 more calories every day than you burned during physical activity. That means 5 extra pounds in a year.

"We believe that what we've been doing isn't working," Hill says. "Trying to tell people to get out and change their whole lives isn't helping. We have to stimulate people to think differently about this."

Adam Drewnowski, a spokesman for the American Dietetic Association and director of the Center for Public Health Nutrition at the University of Washington in Seattle, says he believes the environmental argument more than Friedman's genetic argument, because genetics doesn't explain why minorities, the poor, and people with little education have the highest rates of obesity.

"In the last 20 years, as obesity has doubled and tripled, the genetic pool has remained the same," he says.

It will be lifestyle changes, not medical interventions, that will ultimately stem the tide of obesity in this country, Drewnowski says. "It all comes back to this issue of eating less and exercising more. The Romans used to say, 'To avoid corpulence, eat less and take physical activities.' After 2000 years of research, we've come back to the same conclusion."

He favors Hill's 100-calorie-a-day approach. "It's simple. It's easy," Drewnowski says. "What he's saying is that you don't have to make drastic changes."

Win at Weight Loss— With a Good Attitude

Fred Kuchler, PhD, Researcher, Economic Research Service, US Department of Agriculture, Washington, DC.

Edward Abramson, PhD, Professor, Psychology, California State University, Chico.

Although genetics may play a role, attitude can be everything if you're a woman trying to maintain your weight. Research has found that women who believe that their weight is under their control are thinner than women who think the extra pounds are predetermined by their genetic makeup.

A weight loss expert who has studied the causes of overeating says the research result about attitude bears out his experience with people trying to lose weight.

"I think that attitude is very important," says Edward Abramson, professor of psychology at California State University, Chico, and author of several weight-control books.

He says the feeling of being in control is critical to any weight loss program. "You need the sense of being able to have an impact based on your behavior."

"Although it is true there are some women who will never be petite, they can be more healthy and feel better about their bodies if they take control of their weight," Abramson says.

THE STUDY

Fred Kuchler and Biing–Hwan Lin, researchers with the US Department of Agriculture's Economic Research Service, used data from 2 government surveys that polled 5274 men and women.

The aim was to find which diet and lifestyle choices mattered for weight control and whether the choices varied by sex. The analysis was meant to help those who design weight-maintenance programs.

The studies linked several habits to effective weight control, including getting regular exercise and eating breakfast daily. Then they asked both men and women to tell whether they agreed with this statement: "Some people are born to be fat, others thin; there is nothing I can do." They called it the "gene theory."

When they correlated the response to the statement with the person's body mass index —a measure of height to weight to assess optimal weight—they found that women who disagreed with the gene theory tended to have a lower body mass index.

■ ■ ■ ■

Sensible Weight Maintenance

According to the US Food and Drug Administration (FDA), losing weight may not be effortless, but it doesn't have to be complicated.

To achieve long-term results, avoid quick-fix schemes and complex regimens. Focus instead on making modest changes to your life's daily routine. A balanced, healthy diet and sensible, regular exercise are the keys to maintaining your ideal weight.

Although nutrition science is constantly evolving, there are some generally accepted guidelines for losing weight. *Following are a few of those guidelines…*

●**Consult with your doctor,** a dietitian, or other qualified health professional to determine your ideal healthy body weight.

●**Eat smaller portions** and choose from a variety of foods.

●**Load up on foods that are naturally high in fiber**—fruits, vegetables, legumes, and whole grains.

●**Limit portions of foods that are high in fat**—dairy products such as cheese, butter, and whole milk; red meat; cakes and pastries.

●**Exercise at least 3 times a week.**

info For information on people who have lost weight and kept it off, see the National Weight Control Registry at *www. lifespan.org/services/bmed/wt_loss/nwcr.*

Online Dieting—It Works!

Gladys Block, PhD, Professor, Epidemiology, and Director, Public Health Nutrition Program, University of California, Berkeley.

February 22, 2003, presentation, American College of Preventive Medicine meeting, San Diego, CA.

You've heard about Internet dating services, but what about an Internet diet service? That's right, the next message to hit your E-mail in-box could be just the thing to help you lose that extra pound or 2, by teaching you the facts about food that you need to know if you want to lose weight.

An experimental online nutrition improvement program sent weekly tips via E-mail about how to make small improvements in your diet, along with nutrition information, to 84 people who worked for the same company. Nearly 70 of the 84 participants tried to make changes in their diets, and 90% of those succeeded, says Gladys Block, a professor of epidemiology at the University of California, Berkeley.

It was a 12-week program, and it took approximately 10 minutes to read each message, Block says. Participation was voluntary, and participants were asked whether they would like to work on cutting their intake of dietary fat or boosting their intake of fruits and vegetables.

TAILORED MESSAGES

The messages were tailored to each person's lifestyle, taking into account their eating habits, whether the participants cooked at home or dined out and whether they had kids to feed. "We didn't tell someone how to get fast food that's lower in fat if they mostly ate at home," Block said. "And if they had kids at home, we didn't recommend some weird vegetable that their kids would turn up their noses at."

"Every week, the messages would include a brief fact, and our hope was that it would be kind of an intriguing fact," Block says. "There was also nutrition and health information every week. We told them, for instance, what saturated fat is, what a serving [size] of fruits and vegetables is. Every week there was a set of three or four tips, things they could do in the area they were working on."

A WEEKLY PROMISE

Participants were asked each week to promise to do something simple in the coming week to make a positive dietary change—remembering to take a piece of fruit to work or trying a vegetarian meal to cut down on fat, for example.

"Our whole purpose was not to radically change their lives, but to move them in the right direction," Block says.

At the end of the 12 weeks, the participants reported on their own progress. Most said they had learned something about their eating habits and even more said they read at least half the E-mail messages and would recommend the package to others. More than half said they had talked to someone else about improving their diet after reading the messages.

Block says this program can be used by companies that hope to help their employees improve their eating habits.

■ ■ ■ ■

Be Careful When Surfing the Net For Diets

More than 15,000 Internet sites offer information and/or products that promise to benefit your health or help you lose weight. While many sites are legitimate and helpful, many others have been shown to be outright frauds. Consumers should exercise caution when using the Web for health information. *Healthfinder, the US government's search engine for credible health sites, suggests the following sites as reputable sources for diet and nutrition information…*

•**Delicious Decisions.** The American Heart Association's Nutrition Web site. *www.delicious decisions.org.*

•**Aim for a Healthy Weight!** Information for Health Professionals. *www.nhlbi.nih.gov/ health/public/heart/obesity/lose_wt/profmats.htm.*

- **Quick-Weight-Loss or Fad Diets.** The American Heart Association. *www.american heart.org/presenter.jhtml?identifier=4584.*

- **FDA.** Frequently asked questions about food, nutrition, and cosmetics. *www.cfsan. fda.gov/~dms/qa-top.html.*

- **What I Need to Know About Eating and Diabetes.** *http://diabetes.niddk.nih. gov/dm/pubs/eating_ez/index.htm.*

- **Information from Your Family Doctor.** *http://familydoctor.org/cgibin/familydoc.pl?op =search&query=Men.*

- **National Health Survey.** *www.healthsur vey.org/cgi-bin/WebObjects/Project.*

- ***www.navigator.tufts.edu/weight*** will lead you to the Nutrition Navigator of Tufts University's distinguished School of Nutrition Science and Policy. The Navigator rates the quality of Web sites offering diet and nutritional information.

Good News: French Fries Don't Cause Cancer

Lorelei Mucci, PhD, Researcher, Harvard School of Public Health, Boston, MA.

January 28, 2003, *British Journal of Cancer.*

French fry lovers can relax for now. The most recent research indicates that *acrylamide,* a substance found in various cooked and fried foods, does not raise the risk of certain cancers in humans.

Acrylamide raised alarm bells when an earlier study found high amounts of it in fried foods. The authors called acrylamide a likely carcinogen and "a serious problem." They weren't sure, however, how serious a problem it was in humans.

The International Agency for Research on Cancer (IARC) added acrylamide to its list of probable human carcinogens in the 1980s, says Lorelei Mucci, lead author of the new study, which she completed while a doctoral student

at the Harvard School of Public Health and the Karolinska Institute in Stockholm, Sweden. But that decision was based largely on animal and laboratory—not human—studies.

"We weren't surprised at the results of our study," says Mucci. "We had theorized that doses in foods were low enough that the body could detoxify them," she adds.

THE FRENCH FRY FACTOR

Acrylamide forms during the cooking process. It is part of the reaction between amino acids and sugars when high-starch foods are heated to high temperatures.

The brouhaha first erupted when unexpectedly high levels of the substance were found in foods such as french fries, potato chips, cereals, and bread. And the US Food and Drug Administration found that acrylamide levels varied wildly even in different packages of the same brand of potato chips.

In her study, Mucci and her colleagues in Sweden and Boston looked at the diets of nearly 1000 people with bladder, bowel, or kidney cancer and approximately 500 healthy people to see if they could find a link between foods high in acrylamide and cancer.

GOOD FOR YOU?

The result: There was no increased risk for these cancers, even in those who ate the most acrylamide. Moreover, there was a reduced risk for large bowel cancer, possibly explained by the fact that many of the foods containing acrylamide are cereals high in fiber.

The research doesn't necessarily mean acrylamide is safe. But if acrylamide is cancerous, the 3 types of cancer studied are the kinds you would expect to see because of the way acrylamide is detoxified in the body, Mucci says.

info For more on acrylamide in food, visit the Joint Institute for Food Safety and Applied Nutrition (JIFSAN) at *http://acryla mide-food.org* or the US Food and Drug Administration at *www.fda.gov.*

The Upside to Being Overweight: Heart Attack Survival

Kristin Newby, MD, Associate Professor, Medicine, Duke University Medical Center, Durham, NC.

Terrence J. Sacchi, MD, Chief, Cardiology, Long Island College Hospital, Brooklyn Heights, NY.

Eric Eisenstein, Assistant Research Professor, Medicine, Duke Clinical Research Institute, Durham, NC.

April 1, 2003, presentation, American College of Cardiology Scientific Sessions, Chicago, IL.

You know that being obese is bad for you. And no one should misconstrue the following information as an excuse for being fat. But there may be a short-term silver lining to all the fat that Americans typically accumulate.

Much to their surprise, scientists at Duke University Medical Center found that overweight and obese individuals actually have better 1-year survival rates following a heart attack than people whose weight is within a healthier range.

Not so surprisingly, the researchers also determined the United States had the highest combined rate of obese and very obese people, while Asia had the highest percentage of healthy-weight people.

One of the ironies in these findings is that being heavy is a risk factor for coronary artery disease, and may have been what helped land these patients in the hospital in the first place.

THE STUDY

Dr. Kristin Newby, coauthor of the study and an associate professor of medicine at Duke University Medical Center, had initially hypothesized with her colleagues that overweight and obese people would have higher mortality rates in the first year following a heart attack. But the results of the study showed that the opposite was true.

To test the hypothesis, the researchers looked at data already collected for 2 related international trials and divided the 15,904 participants into 4 groups according to their body mass index (BMI)—normal (18.5–25), overweight (25–29.9), obese (30–34.9), and very obese (higher than 35).

One year after a heart attack, individuals in the obese group had the lowest death rate (2.2%), followed by those classified as very obese (2.6%), overweight (2.7%), and, finally, normal bringing up the rear (4.3%).

Normal-weight participants also had the highest death rate after 90 days, and a similar pattern was evident even at 30 days.

AGE VS. GIRTH

The results may have more to do with the age of the people studied than their girth, says Dr. Terrence J. Sacchi, chief of cardiology at Long Island College Hospital in Brooklyn Heights, New York. "It seems that the patients in the overweight and obese group were younger, and also they were treated more aggressively," he says.

"When adjusted for confounders, the findings still held up in overweight and obese people, but not in the very obese group," says Eric Eisenstein, Newby's coauthor and an assistant research professor at the Duke Clinical Research Institute. "Even after adjusting for all those factors, we still found that at 1 year the overweight and obese groups had a lower hazard of death than the normal people and the very obese people."

RESULTS NOT AN INDICATOR OF LONG-TERM SURVIVAL

One thing to keep in mind is that this study looked only at intermediate-term survival, not long-term survival. "I don't think anyone is advocating remaining obese," Sacchi says. "It is associated with multiple risk factors."

info For a handy online calculator that quickly computes your BMI, visit the National Heart, Lung, and Blood Institute at *http://nhlbisupport.com/bmi/bmicalc.htm.*

Weight Loss Helps Fight Eye Disease

Johanna M. Seddon, MD, SM, Massachusetts Eye and Ear Infirmary, Associate Professor, Ophthalmology, Harvard Medical School, and Associate Professor, Epidemiology, Harvard School of Public Health, Boston, MA.

Robert Cykiert, MD, Clinical Associate Professor, ophthalmology, New York University School of Medicine.

June 2003, *Archives of Ophthalmology.*

Watching your weight might also have a powerful impact on the progression of *age-related macular degeneration* (AMD), a disease that affects some 1.7 million Americans and is a major cause of blindness for seniors.

Researchers evaluated the progression of the disease and found that certain factors—most notably body mass index and exercise—can play a role in how quickly the progression occurs, says study author Dr. Johanna M. Seddon of the Massachusetts Eye and Ear Infirmary.

The findings are important because those factors can be modified and controlled.

"Right now, we know that some of the same risk factors for heart disease—smoking, obesity, and lack of exercise—also affect the progression of AMD," Seddon says.

AMD develops when the high concentration of light-sensing cells in the central portion of the retina—the macula—malfunction or begin to lose function.

Initially, there is a decrease in central vision and inability to see fine detail; eventually, it destroys sight completely.

Ophthalmologist Dr. Robert Cykiert says the study is important for patients with AMD because taking steps to slow down the progression of the disease is the only tool patients have to preserve their eyesight.

Cykiert, a clinical associate professor of ophthalmology at New York University School of Medicine, says, "I would tell any overweight patients at risk for AMD, or with AMD, that it's probably a good idea to lose some weight, particularly since obesity is associated with so many other diseases."

THE FINDINGS

Patients in the study with a high body mass index—those considered overweight to obese—experienced the fastest AMD disease progression, nearly twice as fast as those with a lower body mass index.

And those with a higher waist circumference—indicating a greater amount of weight in the midsection—had a twofold increase in risk for the progression of AMD.

On a more positive note, those who participated in a regular exercise program saw a reduction in disease progression—up to 25% for those who engaged in vigorous activity 3 times a week or more.

■ ■ ■ ■

Who's Affected by Macular Degeneration?

Macular degeneration affects many older Americans. *Following are some facts about the disease...*

•**One in 6 Americans between the ages of 55 and 64 years,** 1 in 4 between the ages of 64 and 74 years, and 1 in 3 older than 75 years will be affected.

•**Each year 1.2 million of the estimated 12 million people with AMD will suffer severe central vision loss.**

•**Each year 200,000 individuals will lose all central vision in one or both eyes.**

info To learn more about AMD and find a quick eye test you can perform at home, visit the Macular Degeneration Foundation at *www.eyesight.org.*

Eat Less, Live Longer, Grow Younger!

George S. Roth, PhD, Senior Guest Scientist, and E. Jeffrey Mettler, MD, Medical Officer, Clinical Research Branch, National Institute on Aging, Baltimore, MD.

August 2, 2002, *Science.*

If you want to live longer, you should probably eat less. So says George S. Roth, a senior guest scientist at the National Institute on Aging (NIA).

"We've known for 70 years that if you feed rats and mice less, they live longer and are healthier," says Roth. "But until 1987, that had not been tested in an animal living more than 15 years. So, we started the first monkey trial." That trial, now in its fifteenth year, is showing that monkeys who eat 30% less food than normal are healthier and seem to be aging more slowly. Scientists have reported that the longer-living monkeys have lower body temperature, lower insulin levels, and higher levels of an adrenal gland hormone, DHEAS. The same appears to be true in humans.

"We wanted to see how the results that show up clearly in the animal model translate to humans," says Dr. E. Jeffrey Mettler, a medical officer in the NIA clinical research branch who leads the Baltimore study. What they found in the humans was what has been found in the monkeys—lower levels of insulin, lower body temperature, and higher DHEAS levels are associated with longer lives.

But the results are so tentative and the link with calorie intake so indirect that the most Mettler will say is that "there is some evidence that the idea might not be totally wrong."

What's clear, he adds, is that the results support the well-accepted view that "being overweight is not healthy"—a critical fact because studies show that 60% of Americans are overweight.

And Roth says that although monkeys—and maybe humans, too—benefit from calorie restriction, he acknowledges that most people would be unwilling or unable to reduce their calorie intake by 30%. The average American man consumes between 2100 and 3000 calories a day, and because women weigh less, their intake is 25% lower.

In the past, people have used diet pills to restrict their caloric intake. One type of diet pill mimics the effects of caloric restriction without having to diet, Roth says. The drug inhibits *lipase*—an enzyme that breaks down fat in the intestines—so it decreases the amount of fat your body absorbs from food by 30%. This results in a lower calorie intake. But all that undigested fat can make sudden, unwelcome appearances in the form of diarrhea.

The hunt is on for a molecule that would have that effect without being dangerous.

"We think we will be able to find other natural compounds that do the same thing," Roth says. "There are many compounds that can be screened."

Caution: Most diet pills fall under the FDA category of dietary supplements, so their sale and use are entirely unregulated. If you're really serious about taking weight-loss pills, work with a medical professional to develop a treatment plan using FDA-approved drugs that fits your needs.

■ ■ ■ ■

A Weighty Subject

Until the perfect diet pill comes along, it's up to you to maintain a healthy weight. You might find it interesting to read about the Obesity Education Initiative at the National Heart, Lung, and Blood Institute's Web site at *www.nhlbi.nih.gov/about/oei. The NHLBI offers these tips for making healthier meals...*

● **Make a meatloaf with lean ground turkey.**

● **Make tacos with skinless chicken breast.**

● **Cool soups and gravies and skim off fat** before reheating them.

● **Try salsa on a baked potato** instead of butter.

●**Make a spicy baked fish** by seasoning with green pepper, onion, garlic, oregano, lemon, or cilantro.

●**Eat fruit for dessert,** instead of cake.

■ ■ ■ ■

How Do You Eat Less?

Believe it or not, there are ways to cut down on the amount of food you eat at each meal. *The following advice is from a New York Presbyterian Hospital publication...*

●**Limit TV and video games to less than 2 hours per day.** When we sit, we burn fewer calories, we're less likely to exercise, and we're more likely to feel hungry, even when we're not.

●**Don't eat while watching TV.** When people watch TV, they often don't realize how much they are eating or when they are full.

●**Are you hungry or just bored?** Often, we eat because we're bored rather than hungry. If you're just bored, try to distract yourself—go for a walk, talk to a friend, do some sit-ups. If that doesn't work, try eating a light, healthy snack.

●**Eat slowly.** Put your fork down after every bite. The slower you eat, the more likely you'll recognize when you're full.

●**Eat from a small plate.** Believe it or not, this makes portions look bigger, so you'll probably eat less.

●**Limit the amount of chips and sweets in the house.** The less they're around, the less you'll eat them. Instead, keep healthy snacks readily available.

●**Exercise, exercise, exercise.** When we exercise, metabolism increases and we burn more calories. We feel less hungry, bored, or stressed. Exercise can mean walking, doing sit-ups or jumping jacks, or dancing for at least 15 minutes. Also, try taking the stairs instead of the elevator.

Eat Fish for Mental Fitness

Ellen Drexler, MD, Associate Attending Neurologist, Maimonides Medical Center, Brooklyn, NY.

Pascale Barberger–Gateau, MD, PhD, Senior Lecturer, University Victor Segalen Bordeaux, Bordeaux, France.

For years, doctors have advised people to eat fish instead of red meat to cut down on their intake of cholesterol. Now, researchers say eating fish may be as good for the brain as it is for the heart.

Elderly people who eat fish or other seafood at least once a week have a lower risk of developing dementia, including Alzheimer's disease, according to researchers at the University Victor Segalen Bordeaux in France.

The polyunsaturated fatty acids found in fish have been studied for their possible role in preventing dementia, and there is also some evidence that they may help coronary artery disease. Dr. Pascale Barberger–Gateau, lead author of the recent study, says the risk of dementia decreased with the frequency of fish consumption. Fish that are especially rich in the beneficial fatty acids include mackerel, salmon, sardines, and tuna.

Researchers say the fatty acids in fish oils may reduce inflammation in the brain or they may be involved in regeneration of nerve cells, both of which may contribute to less incidence of dementia.

Seafood consumption tends to be higher among people who have more education, raising the possibility that educational level may play a role, as well. A relationship between higher educational levels and lower rates of dementia has already been noted.

One theory is that people with more education acquire healthy dietary habits when they are very young.

The role of polyunsaturated fatty acids is still far from certain. "Are we going to tell all our patients to run out and eat fish every night?" says Dr. Ellen Drexler, associate attending neurologist at Maimonides Medical

Center in Brooklyn, New York. "I don't think so. It may just be correlations with other good health habits, though there is some biological plausibility."

THE STUDY

The study looked at data from 1674 people 68 years and older who were in a large aging study conducted in 75 parishes in southwestern France. None of the participants had dementia at the start of the study.

The researchers recorded the frequency with which the participants ate meat and fish, then grouped the responses into categories. The participants were checked at 2, 5, and 7 years.

After 7 years, the researchers found that people who ate more fish or other seafood—at least once a week—had a decreased incidence of dementia. They found no relationship between meat consumption and risk of developing dementia.

info Check out the American Geriatrics Society at *www.americangeriatrics.org* for more information about dementia.

■ ■ ■ ■

Easy and Healthy Ways to Prepare Fish

Cooking fish on an outdoor grill takes some talent and a bit of finesse. *An organization called Fish4Fun (www.fish4fun. com) offers the following tips for grilling fish...*

●**Use a hinged wire grill basket** to cook whole fish, such as snapper, trout, or salmon. The basket also works well for fillets of tender fish such as perch, snapper, catfish, or flounder.

●**Firm fish, such as tuna, salmon, or shark, can be cooked directly on the grill,** if handled carefully.

●**Skewer small shellfish,** such as shrimp or scallops, on metal or water-soaked wooden skewers or cook them in a grill basket.

●**Grill fillets over medium to medium-low heat.**

●**Turn fish only once.** (Flipping back and forth will cause fish to break apart.)

●**If you use a marinade, allow the fish to soak up the flavor for at least 30 minutes.** Refrigerate while soaking in marinade.

●**If you plan to use the marinade as an extra sauce** on top of cooked fish or seafood, boil the marinade liquid by itself for at least 5 minutes to cook out any bacteria that may remain from when the fish was soaking.

●**To grill shellfish in the shell,** such as oysters, mussels, and clams, place them directly on the hottest part of the grill. They're done when the shell opens. If any shells don't open after about 5 minutes, discard them.

Delicious Mediterranean Diet Defeats Arthritis

Clifton O. Bingham, III, MD, Director, Seligman Center for Advanced Therapeutics, Hospital for Joint Diseases, New York, NY.
Lars Skoldstam, MD, PhD, Department of Medicine, Kalmar County Hospital, Kalmar, Sweden.
March 2003, *Annals of the Rheumatic Diseases.*

A Mediterranean diet high in olive oil, cooked vegetables, and fish may ease your symptoms of rheumatoid arthritis.

A Swedish study of 51 people found that those who followed this eating regimen had less inflammation and were more active at the end of 3 months.

Outside experts, however, say this study is far from the final word on the subject.

"The design is flawed and the results are, at best, modest," says Dr. Clifton O. Bingham, III, director of the Seligman Center for Advanced Therapeutics at the Hospital for Joint Diseases in New York City. "The results are statistically significant, but it's not clear that any are clinically significant."

Rheumatoid arthritis is an autoimmune disorder that involves inflammation to the lining of the joints.

Previous research has shown a link between fish oil—which has anti-inflammatory properties—and the treatment of rheumatoid arthritis,

Bingham says. However, the amounts required are so high that they have little relevance to a person's daily diet.

ELEMENTS OF THE DIET

The Swedish study looked specifically at the Cretan Mediterranean diet, which includes copious amounts of fruit, vegetables, cereals, legumes, poultry, and fish. Red meat and high-fat dairy products are kept to a minimum and olive and canola oils are the primary sources of fat.

Fifty-one participants with stable but active rheumatoid arthritis were randomly assigned to either the Cretan diet or to a typical Western diet for 3 months.

For the first 3 weeks, participants ate lunch and dinner at the clinic's cafeteria. They were then provided with instructions and recipes and left to prepare their own meals.

Little change was seen before the 6-week mark. By the end of 12 weeks, physical function, vitality, and various other measures had improved in the Mediterranean-diet group but not in the control group. People in the treatment group also lost an average of 6.6 pounds.

"A general idea of mine is that the Mediterranean diet is palatable and should be easy for most patients to accept, even as a lifelong eating plan," says Dr. Lars Skoldstam, lead author of the study.

The researchers speculate that olive oil can be metabolized into agents with anti-inflammatory effects and that olive oil also has antioxidant properties. Vegetables are also rich in natural antioxidants, which help control inflammation, Skoldstam says.

DRAWBACKS OF THE STUDY

Unfortunately, flaws in the study design cast doubt on the relevance of the findings. In addition to being an extremely small sample, the treatment group was not under any supervision beyond the 3-week mark. "These are both fatal flaws in interpreting the data," Bingham says. "As a researcher, you don't know what the participants are eating unless you actually control all of the food yourself."

The effects seen in the study are "nowhere near the results obtained with currently available medications to treat rheumatoid arthritis,"

Bingham says. "Diet should never be seen as the sole therapy for this disease but, rather, as an adjunct to medication."

info The American Heart Association at *www.americanheart.org* provides information on the Mediterranean diet.

■ ■ ■ ■

What Is the Mediterranean Diet?

While it is generally acknowledged that the Mediterranean diet is regional, there doesn't seem to be one country that can lay claim to its components. Here's what the American Heart Association has to say.

At least 16 countries border the Mediterranean Sea. Diets vary between these countries and also between various regions within a country. Many differences in culture, ethnic background, religion, economy, and agriculture result in different diets. *But the common Mediterranean diet has these characteristics…*

●**High consumption of fruits,** vegetables, bread and other cereals, potatoes, beans, nuts, and seeds.

●**Olive oil is an important monounsaturated fat source.**

●**Dairy products, fish, and poultry are consumed in low to moderate amounts,** and little red meat is eaten.

●**Eggs are consumed 0 to 4 times a week.**

●**Wine is consumed in low to moderate amounts.**

Mediterranean diets are often close to the American Heart Association's dietary guidelines, but they don't follow them exactly. In general, the Mediterranean diets contain a relatively high percentage of calories from fat. This contributes to the increasing obesity in these countries, which is becoming a concern.

People who follow a Mediterranean diet eat less saturated fat than those who eat an average American diet. In fact, the saturated fat consumption for those eating a Mediterranean diet is well within our dietary guidelines. More than half the fat calories in a Mediterranean diet come from monounsaturated fats (mainly from olive oil). Monounsaturated fat doesn't raise cholesterol levels as saturated fat does.

The incidence of heart disease in Mediterranean countries is lower than in the United States. Death rates are lower, too. The lower rate of heart disease may not be entirely due to the diet. Lifestyle factors (such as more physical activity and extended social support systems) may also play a part.

Research Proves High-Fiber Diets Lower Colon Cancer Risk by 27%

Sheila A. Bingham, PhD, head, Diet and Cancer Group, Dunn Human Nutrition Unit, UK Medical Research Council, Cambridge, England.

Ulrike Peters, PhD, MPH, Nutrition and Epidemiology Research Fellow, Divisions of Cancer Epidemiology and Genetics, National Cancer Institute, Rockville, MD.

M. Robert Cooper, MD, Professor Emeritus, Hematology and Oncology, Wake Forest University Baptist Medical Center, Winston–Salem, NC.

May 3, 2003, *The Lancet.*

Eat your vegetables because they're good for you. You've probably heard that since you were a child.

Studies over the years have gone back and forth on just how good they are for you. But 2 studies in Europe and the United States have swung the pendulum back in support of the medical advice that a high-fiber diet—one that includes lots of plant foods—sharply reduces the risk of colon cancer.

In the European study, which the researchers called the largest ever on the relationship between diet and cancer, the scientists tracked more than 500,000 people in 10 countries.

Those who ate the most fiber, an average of 36.4 grams a day, had a 27% lower risk of the polyps than those who ate the least fiber, averaging 12.6 grams a day, the study found. Polyps are precursors to colon cancer. The correlation proved strongest for colon cancer and was not statistically relevant for rectal cancer, the study says.

"The most interesting thing is, it does actually confirm all the other studies" that were done before the one study that found no relationship between high-fiber diets and cancer, says Sheila A. Bingham, the lead author of the European study. Bingham heads the diet and cancer group at the UK Medical Research Council's Dunn Human Nutrition Unit in Cambridge, England.

The US study focused on 37,600 people, about 3600 of whom had nonmalignant polyps. Based on surveys, researchers divided the people into 5 groups, according to their fiber consumption.

"You really can see the risk [of colon cancer] is going down when the fiber is increasing; it's a very strong trend," says Ulrike Peters, a researcher at the National Cancer Institute and the lead author of the US study.

ANOTHER POINT OF VIEW

But Dr. M. Robert Cooper, the principal investigator in the earlier trial, says he stands by its findings that a high-fiber diet doesn't protect against colon cancer.

"We need to go on to something that's more significant than fiber," Cooper says, calling for more emphasis on screening for colon cancer.

■ ■ ■ ■

Easy Ways to Add Fiber

Looking for ways to get more fiber into your diet? *The American Cancer Society (www.cancer.org) offers these suggestions...*

•**Keep mixed nuts and vegetable juice boxes handy.**

•**Keep a bowl full of fresh veggies and fruits** on your kitchen counter.

•**Fruits packaged in their own juice,** frozen fruits and vegetables, and low-sodium canned vegetables provide the same healthful benefits as fresh produce.

•**Dried fruits** are snacks that you can take anywhere.

Acne Not Just in Young, And Certain Foods May Indeed Be the Cause

Loren Cordain, PhD, Professor, Health and Exercise Science, Colorado State University, Fort Collins.
Ted Daly, MD, Dermatologist, Nassau University Medical Center, East Meadow, NY.
Harry Saperstein, MD, Director, Pediatric Dermatology, Cedars–Sinai Medical Center, and Associate Professor, Medicine and Pediatrics, University of California, Los Angeles.
December 2002, *Archives of Dermatology*.

The standard Western diet of refined sugars and starches may be more to blame for the high rates of acne than you'd think.

That's the belief of researchers who suspect that highly processed foods, such as breads, cereals, chocolate, and pizza, cause the body to produce high levels of insulin, which in turn leads to an excess of male hormones. Excess male hormones cause an overproduction of *sebum*—the greasy stuff that blocks your pores—and the result is acne.

"Acne can be psychologically devastating to a teen," says study author Loren Cordain, a professor of health and exercise science at Colorado State University.

More important, he adds, acne is just a small part of a larger health problem. The typical Western diet probably also contributes to heart disease and other ailments.

NOT JUST TEENS

Nearly all teens in Western societies have acne; approximately half of those older than 25 years have it, and for Westerners in middle age, 12% of women and 3% of men still suffer from acne.

The researchers studied 2 pimple-free populations—1 from New Guinea and the other from Paraguay. These people live without electricity or running water and eat a decidedly non-Western diet. They eat only foods they can hunt, gather, or grow.

"There was a startling lack of acne," Cordain says, and it wasn't a one-time effect. Even after 2 years of study, the researchers never saw a single case of acne among the Paraguay tribe.

Previous research had shown that when tribespeople such as those studied adopt a Western lifestyle, acne follows. So genetics weren't to blame.

That left diet, the only known environmental factor that could cause the excess of insulin, male hormones, and overproduction of sebum seen in Western civilization.

OTHERS NOT SO SURE

"If processed foods cause acne, why don't little kids and the elderly have acne?" asks Dr. Ted Daly, a dermatologist at Nassau University Medical Center in East Meadow, New York. Daly says he also finds it hard to believe that of the people studied by Cordain's group, the researchers couldn't find one pimple or blackhead. If that's the case, Daly says, there is no proof that there isn't a genetic basis, or something else in the environment that accounts for their clear skin.

Dr. Harry Saperstein, director of pediatric dermatology at Cedars–Sinai Medical Center in Los Angeles, says the Cordain theory is interesting but still hasn't been proven.

Cordain recommends a diet that won't raise insulin levels. Bread, potatoes, many cereals, and candy all raise those levels, while fruits, vegetables, and bran products raise them much less. He advocates a diet that's approximately one-third protein (from lean meat and fish), one-third fat, and one-third complex carbohydrates, such as fruits and vegetables.

Daly says if you want to reduce acne outbreaks, keep your skin clean and use a benzoyl peroxide wash or cream daily.

info For more information, visit the National Institute of Arthritis and Musculoskeletal and Skin Diseases at *www.niams.nih.gov* or the American Academy of Dermatology at *www.aad.org*.

Eating Breakfast Lowers Your Disease Risk by 50%

Linda Van Horn, PhD, Professor, Preventive Medicine, Northwestern University, Chicago, IL.

Alice H. Lichtenstein, DSc, Professor, Nutrition, Tufts University, Boston, MA.

March 6, 2003, presentation, American Heart Association's Annual Conference, Miami, FL.

Sugar-laden cereals and high-fat muffins in the morning may not be ideal fare, but eating anything for breakfast seems healthier than skipping the first meal of the day, researchers report.

For 8 years, researchers tested study participants for insulin resistance and assessed them for obesity and abnormal glucose levels, elevated blood pressure, and elevated lipid values. Researchers also took into account physical activity, smoking, age, and sex.

Although the best results were achieved by those who ate whole-grain cereals and other nutritious breakfast items, "eating breakfast at all was preferential to not eating," says Linda Van Horn, a professor of preventive medicine at Northwestern University and one of the authors of the study.

Breakfast eaters are up to 55% less likely than their non-breakfasting counterparts to develop problems such as diabetes or obesity, the study suggests.

THE RESULTS

Alice H. Lichtenstein, a professor of nutrition at Tufts University in Boston, says the study supplies interesting information, but "we need to know a lot more about dietary patterns."

She would like to see more detailed monitoring of what the people in the study ate and their actual glucose levels. Still, there is an assumption, which this study seems to confirm, that eating in the morning prevents binge eating later in the day. "People have been told for years that you're better starting off your day with breakfast," Lichtenstein says.

The wise will heed this advice, which is easy and makes a difference, Van Horn concludes. "One simple thing you can do to cut heart disease risk in half is eat breakfast," she says.

Dangerous Belly Fat Builds Quickly in Couch Potatoes

William E. Kraus, MD, Cardiologist, Associate Professor, Duke University Medical Center, Durham, NC.

Gerald F. Fletcher, MD, Professor, Medicine, and Director, Preventive Cardiology, Mayo Clinic, Jacksonville, FL, and spokesman, American Heart Association.

May 28, 2003, presentations, American College of Sports Medicine Annual Meeting, San Francisco, CA.

A sedentary lifestyle can lead to a build-up of dangerous levels of fat deep within your belly, increasing your risk of heart disease and other conditions.

That's the conclusion of Duke University Medical Center researchers who say this "visceral fat" accumulates deep in the body around organs at a faster rate than subcutaneous fat, which lies under the skin.

On the upside, the researchers found that months of regular, moderate exercise can prevent the build-up of visceral fat, while vigorous exercise can significantly reduce levels of such fat.

Researchers followed 170 overweight men and women aged 40 to 65 years for approximately 8 months. The researchers divided participants into 4 groups.

One group did no exercise. The other 3 groups were classified according to a weekly exercise regimen equivalent to approximately 11 miles of walking, 11 miles of jogging, or 17 miles of jogging.

Lack of any exercise led to significant increases in visceral fat, the researchers found. "This finding emphasizes the high cost of continued physical inactivity for sedentary, overweight adults," they wrote.

Dr. William E. Kraus, a cardiologist and associate professor at Duke University Medical Center, who led the exercise trial, offers simple advice to counter the buildup of visceral fat.

"Get out and do something; don't sit," says Kraus. "Being sedentary is very bad for your health."

TROUBLESOME EFFECTS OF INACTIVITY

It's even worse than researchers had previously realized, adds Kraus. "The most striking result was how bad the sedentary people got over 8 months," he says.

Dr. Gerald F. Fletcher, a professor of medicine and director of preventive cardiology at the Mayo Clinic in Jacksonville, Florida, says the study illustrates well the "vicious syndrome" that results from visceral abdominal fat.

Fletcher, also a spokesman for the American Heart Association, says visceral fat buildup increases the risk of high blood pressure, blood clotting, elevated levels of "bad" cholesterol, and insulin resistance, a precursor to diabetes.

EXERCISE IS THE KEY FOR ALL AGES

Fletcher stresses the importance of exercise to prevent the intestinal fat buildup, noting that more than two-thirds of Americans are overweight.

"I'm just hoping this study will motivate our obese public to do things we've been preaching for years," Fletcher says. "We looked at all the ways to treat [visceral fat buildup], and the best way is physical activity."

Even elderly patients who had been sedentary can benefit greatly from moderate exercise, he says.

info Get recommendations for getting the greatest benefit from physical activity in your daily life and keep track of your progress at the American Heart Association's fitness Web site *www.justmove.org*.

Lose Belly Fat and Save Your Life

Arthur Agatston, MD, Cardiologist and Associate Professor, Medicine, University of Miami School of Medicine, FL, and Consultant, National Institutes of Health Clinical Trials Committee, Bethesda, MD. He is author of *The South Beach Diet*. *www.southbeachdiet.com*.
July 1, 2003, *Bottom Line/Health*.

Diet is the key to reducing visceral fat—specifically, a diet that contains little or no refined carbohydrates.

The carbohydrates that dominate the typical American diet—white bread, pasta, cereal, snack foods, cakes, cookies, candies, etc.—are stripped of fiber during processing. These foods are quickly digested and absorbed as glucose, the form that sugar takes in the bloodstream.

The body must produce ever-increasing amounts of insulin to remove excess glucose and fat from the blood. Elevated levels of insulin promote fat storage in the abdomen.

High insulin levels end up removing too much glucose from the blood. The resulting low blood sugar, called *reactive hypoglycemia*, triggers food cravings. The more you give in to the cravings, the more weight you gain.

Here is a 3-phase plan that reduces insulin resistance and food cravings without dramatic calorie reductions. People typically lose 8 to 13 pounds in the first 2 weeks and 1 to 2 pounds a week thereafter.

PHASE 1

For 14 days, eat all the lean meat, chicken, turkey, and seafood you want. Eliminate refined carbohydrates—bread, pasta, rice, baked goods, candy, and alcohol.

Eliminating these foods for 14 days reduces cravings for carbohydrates and helps normalize glucose levels.

Fruits and root vegetables, such as carrots and potatoes, should be avoided in this phase. You can have as much as you want of other vegetables.

You also can have mono- and polyunsaturated fats, such as olive and canola oils. These satisfy appetite, reduce food cravings, and help lower levels of harmful triglycerides and

LDL ("bad") cholesterol—key risk factors in people with large stores of visceral fat.

Nuts also are allowed. They are filling and contain mainly monounsaturated fats. Nuts are high in calories, so limit yourself to about 15 almonds or cashews, 30 pistachios, or 12 peanuts (technically a legume) daily.

Don't worry about overeating. Eat until you're satisfied—you'll still lose weight. Most of the weight loss that occurs during this phase will come from your midsection.

PHASE 2

During week 3, you can reintroduce refined carbohydrates into your diet. Your body will respond more normally to insulin's effects. You can allow yourself a small serving of bread, pasta, potatoes, or rice twice a day. Cookies, cakes, candy, alcohol, and snack foods, such as potato chips, still should be avoided.

Other Phase 2 strategies...

●**Eat fish at least twice a week.** The omega-3 fatty acids in fish have been shown to reduce heart attack and stroke risk. Salmon, mackerel, and herring are particularly rich in omega-3s.

●**Eat a high-protein breakfast.** Morning protein suppresses food cravings and promotes weight loss. People who skip breakfast experience morning drops in blood glucose that trigger cravings. They also tend to eat more calories during the day.

Try an omelette with cheese or vegetables, such as asparagus or broccoli, or have Canadian bacon, turkey bacon, low-fat cottage cheese, or farmer cheese.

●**Snack when you're hungry.** Always try to keep some food in your stomach. It is the best way to prevent sudden food cravings.

Rather than grabbing fast foods that are high in glucose-raising carbohydrates, try cheese sticks or a serving of sugar-free yogurt.

PHASE 3

This is the maintenance phase of the diet. Once you have reached your desired weight, continue to limit refined carbohydrates to keep food cravings under control, minimize insulin resistance, and maintain low levels of visceral fat.

Easiest Way to Lose Weight and Get Healthy!

Colleen Doyle, MS, RN, Director, Nutrition and Physical Activity, American Cancer Society, Atlanta, GA.

Anne McTiernan, MD, Director, Prevention Studies Clinic, Fred Hutchinson Cancer Research Center, Seattle, WA.

Too many Americans are overweight. That's the conclusion of the American Cancer Society (ACS), which estimates that as many as 180,000 Americans each year will die of cancers related to obesity and lack of activity. Overweight people are particularly at risk for colon and breast cancer, researchers say. Overweight people also tend to produce more insulin, which promotes the growth of tumors.

Facing an epidemic of obesity, ACS is calling on governments, schools, and businesses to help promote exercise and healthy living in communities.

"The environment in which we live—where we work, where we play, where we hang out —has really become a barrier in terms of making choices," says Colleen Doyle, director of nutrition and physical activity for ACS. "We need walking paths, bike lanes, buses that have racks for bikes."

Although ACS urges communities to get involved, individuals can still make choices that lead to healthier living, such as eating better and exercising more.

That means eating at least 5 servings a day of fruit and vegetables and getting moderate exercise for 30 minutes a day, 5 days a week.

For women, exercise reduces the level of estrogen, a hormone linked to breast cancer. Even after menopause, exercise reduces the estrogen level and the risk of breast cancer, says Dr. Anne McTiernan, director of the Prevention Studies Clinic at the Fred Hutchinson Cancer Research Center in Seattle, and author of *Breast Fitness: An Optimal Exercise and Health Plan for Reducing Your Risk of Breast Cancer.*

WHAT KIND OF EXERCISE IS BEST?

"Any type of activity is beneficial," says Doyle. "Obviously, if you're a couch potato, you're not going to get up and start running five miles a day. But something is better than nothing. Walking, swimming, raking the leaves, throwing the ball with your kid, dancing, gardening—everything counts," she says.

People older than 30 years or those with health problems should consult their doctor before beginning an exercise program.

If you're pressed for time, you don't have to do all the exercise at once. Three 10-minute sessions throughout the day may provide the same benefit as a single 30-minute session.

If you're not sure how much you can do or how far to push yourself, you may want to work with a personal trainer, McTiernan says.

info You may also want to read the revised guidelines on nutrition and physical activity for cancer prevention from the American Cancer Society at *www.cancer.org*. Type in "Nutrition" in the search box, for a complete description of the ACS's recommendations for nutrition, exercise, and lifestyle changes.

■ ■ ■ ■

How to Start an Exercise Program

Starting an exercise program is the first step toward healthier living. *Here are some suggestions from the American Academy of Orthopaedic Surgeons...*

START SLOWLY

•**Your goal is to set an exercise habit you enjoy.** Make sure your first activity sessions are fun and not tiring. Give your body a chance to get used to it.

ESTABLISH A REASONABLE SCHEDULE

•**Set a weekly exercise schedule that includes days off.** For example, you might exercise every other day, with 3 days off each week.

•**Start with a program of moderate physical activity**—30 minutes a day. Keep it interesting with a balanced program of different activities, such as walking, bicycle riding, swimming, or working in the garden.

•**If 30 minutes of activity is too difficult or you don't have enough time,** break it up into shorter intervals. For instance, walk for 15 minutes in the morning and work in the garden for 15 minutes later in the day.

STICK WITH IT

•**Focus on working toward your goals gradually.** Consider tracking your progress with a simple chart, perhaps listing the number of minutes you exercise each day.

•**Don't stop your fitness program.** The benefits begin to diminish in 2 weeks and disappear in 2 to 8 months.

•**Congratulate yourself** for each accomplishment. Your progress will develop into a pattern through which you'll work up to higher levels of exertion over time.

Tired of the Gym? Do Some Housework

Joel Press, MD, Physiatrist, Center for Spine, Sports & Occupational Rehabilitation, Chicago, IL.

Richard A. Stein, MD, Professor, Medicine, State University of New York Health Sciences Center, and spokesman, American Heart Association.

If you don't have the time or the money for a workout at the gym, you may be able to get the same healthy benefits with a simple regimen of daily household chores.

The American Academy of Physical Medicine and Rehabilitation says ordinary housework can be turned into stretching, toning, and strengthening exercises. These functional fitness exercises can increase flexibility, strengthen muscles, and minimize injuries and back problems. And they're more practical than lifting weights or using gym equipment.

"What we try to do is make the exercise program simulate what a person actually does in his life, to make it functional," says Dr. Joel Press, a physiatrist at the Center for Spine, Sports & Occupational Rehabilitation in Chicago.

Press, who designed the program, said the activities could be as simple as balancing on one leg while you brush your teeth or sweeping the kitchen floor with deliberate strokes.

Dr. Richard A. Stein, a professor of medicine at the State University of New York Health Sciences Center and a spokesman for the American Heart Association, agrees that heavy house-cleaning activities, such as mopping and vacuuming, can be good aerobic exercise.

"People need to look for the household activities that occur more than once a week and last between 10 and 30 minutes," Stein says. "There needs to be a fair amount of body movement, and it needs to cause you a fair amount of fatigue, as it would with exercise."

■ ■ ■ ■

Exercise While You Clean the House!

Here are some exercises that you can do at home and still accomplish your housework. *Why not consider...*

●**Laundry Toss.** Stand about 10 to 15 feet away from the washing machine with the laundry basket about waist high on your left side and the washing machine on your right. Pick up pieces of the dirty laundry and, while turning at the hips; pitch the laundry into the open washer. This exercise can strengthen abdominal, lower back, and hip muscles.

●**Unload and Lift.** As you remove dishes from the dishwasher, turn your body from side to side so your torso twists while you reach to put the clean dishes away. Press recommends putting away one dish or piece of silverware at a time for maximum stretching.

●**Rake and Twist.** Whether you're raking leaves or sweeping, take long, steady strokes, turning at your hips as you rake or sweep toward your body. Make sure you do this exercise sweeping both from left to right and from right to left.

●**Standing Side Stretch.** Grab the nearest weighty object—anything from a carton of milk to a briefcase—and hold it in one hand while standing up straight with your feet slightly more than a shoulder's width apart. Then slowly bend at the waist, straight to the side, lowering the hand with the weighted object down your side as far as it will go, and holding it for a count of 15 or 20 seconds. Repeat on the other side.

info For more on exercise at home, visit the American Physical Therapy Association at *www.apta.org.*

Harder Exercise May Be Better for Your Heart

Dan Fisher, MD, Cardiologist, Clinical Assistant Professor, Department of Medicine, New York University Medical Center.

Jeffrey Borer, MD, Cardiologist, Harriman Professor of Cardiovascular Medicine, Weill Medical College, Cornell University, and Chief, Division of Cardiovascular Pathophysiology, New York–Presbyterian Hospital, New York, NY.

April 15, 2003, *Heart.*

The more vigorous your workout, the better it is for your heart, according to a study of 2000 men who died of cardiac-related ailments.

Research conducted at Belfast University in Northern Ireland found that those who participated in the most aggressive physical activity lived the longest.

The level of activity was significant, but the total number of calories expended while exercising was not. Men who regularly expended energy equal to 9 minutes of jogging or 7 minutes of stair climbing lived longer than those who walked or did ballroom dancing for 90 minutes.

Some American doctors say that although more strenuous exercise may be better, lighter exercise has value, as well.

"While this study emphasizes the benefits of heavy exercise over lighter activity, it does not prove that lighter exercise has no value," says New York University cardiologist Dr. Dan Fisher, who did not participate in the research. "And we should not take this finding to mean that only heavy exercise is good for the heart."

Fisher says any level of activity is better than no activity, with many studies illustrating that moderate workouts done on a regular basis have important heart-healthy benefits— a tenet also endorsed by the American Heart Association and others.

Cardiologist Dr. Jeffrey Borer agrees, saying any exercise is good for the heart.

The study shows that exercise does reduce the risk of cardiac events and cardiac deaths and the benefits seem related to the intensity rather than the duration of the exercise, says Borer, chief of the Division of Cardiovascular Pathophysiology at New York–Presbyterian Hospital.

However, says Borer, it's not possible to draw conclusions concerning the benefits of less vigorous exercise—or to infer that less vigorous exercise isn't worthwhile.

RECOMMENDATIONS

"Although this study demonstrates you might get more benefits from heavy exercise, any level of activity has important health benefits, including reducing cholesterol, blood sugar, and blood pressure levels, all of which benefit the heart," says Fisher.

He also cautions against engaging in strenuous exercise without proper conditioning.

"The message you *don't* want to take away from this study is that you should jump from a sedentary lifestyle into heavy exercise. This won't help your heart and it might even cause you harm," says Fisher.

Instead, Fisher and Borer say, get your doctor's advice on the best exercises for your fitness level and gradually expand your workout regimen as your strength increases.

Morning Exercise May Increase Infection Risk

July 29, 2002, *British Journal of Sports Medicine* news release.
American Council on Exercise Web site.

If you like to start your day with an invigorating run or swim, you may be exposing your body to greater risk of an infection.

Research has shown that moderate exercise gives your body's immune system a boost. But the time of day you exercise may be a factor in your immune system's ability to do its job.

THE STUDY

After studying 14 competitive male swimmers—with an average age of 18 years—British researchers concluded that early morning exercise may increase a person's susceptibility to infection. The swimmers did the 400-meter crawl 5 times, with a 1-minute rest between each swim. They did this for 2 days at 6 AM and 6 PM each day.

Samples of spit were taken from the swimmers before and after each swim to measure their saliva for levels of *cortisol*, a stress hormone that suppresses the immune system.

The study found the swimmers' cortisol levels were higher before exercise in the morning than before their evening exercise. The levels were significantly higher after the swimming sessions.

The researchers from Britain's Brunel University and the University of Luton also checked the swimmers' saliva for IgA secretory rate. IgA helps defend the body from infections in the nose and mouth.

The IgA secretory rate was significantly reduced by both the morning and evening swims. The rate was lower before the morning swims.

The findings were reported in the *British Journal of Sports Medicine*.

THE INTERPRETATION

The authors say their findings indicate that a person's body clock has a considerable impact on the immune system. They suggest it's best to do your exercise or training in the evening when you have lower levels of cortisol and a higher rate of saliva flow, which also helps protect against infections.

People returning to exercise and training after an illness or injury should avoid early-morning workouts, the authors advise. The same is true for athletes who have higher stress levels because of an upcoming competition and for those training at high altitudes. Both of those situations can affect the immune system.

TIMING ISN'T EVERYTHING

Studies have consistently shown that exercise later in the day produces better performance and more power, the council says. Muscles are warmer and more flexible, perceived exertion is low, reaction time is quicker, strength is at its peak, and resting heart rate and blood pressure are lower than earlier in the day.

However, if you feel good beginning your day with exercise, stick with it. Everyone agrees that exercise at any time is better than no exercise at all. In fact, people who exercise in the morning are more successful at making it a habit. If your schedule favors an early workout, emphasize stretching and a good warm-up to ensure that your body is ready for action.

info The American Council on Exercise (ACE) has more insight into exercise and the immune system on its Web site at *www.acefitness.org.*

Trans Fatty Acid Content Makes Its Way Onto US Food Labels

Cindy Moore, MS, RD, spokeswoman, American Dietetic Association, and Director, Nutrition Therapy, The Cleveland Clinic Foundation, OH.
November 15, 2002, US Food and Drug Administration Federal Register.

Just as most Americans are finally digesting the nutrition labels appearing on all processed foods, the US Food and Drug Administration (FDA) sits poised to add another term on the back of your favorite box of cookies or package of lunch meat.

That term is "trans fatty acid." The FDA has announced that manufacturers must start including this information on food labels by 2006.

"This is a good thing, because it will provide consumers with more information about the foods they are [eating] so they can make better food choices," says Cindy Moore, director of nutrition therapy at the Cleveland Clinic Foundation, and a spokeswoman for the American Dietetic Association.

Trans fatty acids, or TFAs, are a type of saturated fat that occurs naturally in small amounts in foods, such as beef and dairy products.

But trans fatty acids can also be the end result of a manufacturing process that turns healthy liquid fats—such as vegetable oil—into unhealthy solid fats needed to produce many foods, particularly baked goods and snacks. As such, they show up in a wide variety of products you commonly eat.

"If you eat any commercially prepared foods, particularly baked goods, chances are you are getting a fair amount of TFAs in your diet," Moore says.

This matters, she adds, because studies show that TFAs can increase some specific health risks—particularly the risk of heart disease.

"The higher your intake of trans fatty acids, the higher your ratio of LDL ("bad") cholesterol to HDL ("good") cholesterol. And that plays out in terms of the risk for heart disease," Moore says.

But it's not only your heart that can suffer. Studies show that high levels of TFAs can also increase your risk of Type 2 diabetes.

In fact, all things being equal, the negative effects of TFAs on your health are even greater than those of the much-ballyhooed saturated fats—the traditionally bad, "heart-hurting" fats found in butter and cream.

HOW MUCH IS TOO MUCH?

According to the National Institute of Medicine, no level of TFAs is considered safe.

But because TFAs are present in so many foods, the institute's report also concluded that without significant changes in your diet, it may be difficult to eliminate TFAs completely.

The suggested compromise: Strive to keep TFA levels as low as possible. And in this respect, the new labels can help.

In the meantime, Moore says you can still make smarter food choices by reducing your intake of any foods that list "partially hydrogenated oils" in their ingredients list.

Toxic Vitamins: Are You Taking Too Much of a 'Good' Thing?

Jyni Holland, MS, RD, Clinical Nutritionist, New York University Medical Center.

Laurie Tansman, MS, RD, CDN, Clinical Nutritionist, Mount Sinai Medical Center, New York, NY.

In our quest to fight colds, build muscle, or have smoother skin, some of us believe that taking extra doses of vitamins and minerals is the best way to go. But taking large doses of any one supplement can do us more harm than good, experts say.

"Unless you are suffering from a severe deficiency, if you have a disease or disorder that is causing you to be nutrient-deficient, the most you are going to need is a high-quality multivitamin supplement, to be taken as insurance, and not used as your main source of nutrients," says Laurie Tansman, a clinical nutritionist at Mount Sinai Medical Center in New York.

Most people won't get into trouble taking a high-potency multivitamin. But problems can occur, experts say, when you start playing around with individual doses—even when recommended by some diet and fitness programs.

VITAMINS

Vitamins A, D, and E are among those causing the most concern because they are fat-soluble, can be stored for long periods of time in the body—mostly in the liver—and a cumulative buildup can occur, turning your vitamin regimen from healthy to toxic.

• **Vitamin D is one of the most toxic supplements,** and in very large amounts can lead to liver and kidney failure, says Jyni Holland, a clinical nutritionist at New York University Medical Center.

• **Take too much vitamin A and you could end up with hair loss,** nausea, vomiting, and significant joint pain. And there is evidence to show that too much vitamin A may cause birth defects, so it is recommended that pregnant women take no more than what comes in their prenatal vitamins.

• **Too much vitamin E can thin the blood so much it could lead to internal hemorrhaging,** particularly if you are taking any blood-thinning medication for a cardiac or hypertension problem.

• **Vitamin K has the reverse effect—causing blood to clot.** But it, too, can cause problems when used by those taking blood-thinning drugs.

• **The B vitamins and vitamin C are water-soluble and therefore don't build up in tissues and rarely reach toxic levels** on their own. They are considered relatively safe, even in high doses—unless you are also taking iron supplements. Because vitamin C enhances iron absorption, taking large doses of both could increase your risk of a toxic reaction. In very high levels, vitamin B-6 has been associated with neurological symptoms such as nerve tingling, while vitamin B-3—also known as niacin—could be a problem if you suffer from heart disease.

MINERALS

• **Calcium has been linked to the formation of kidney stones** and can be packed with vitamin D, which helps the body absorb calcium. "If you are megadosing on calcium, you may also be megadosing on vitamin D and setting yourself up for some toxic reactions without even realizing you are doing so," Tansman says.

• **Iron supplements are commonly used by menstruating women,** and are also sometimes used by body builders and athletes seeking to fight fatigue. "What most people don't realize is iron is an oxidant. And when it's exposed to oxygen inside the body, it becomes a free radical," Holland says. Free radicals cause an oxidation process that eventually damages cells and can increase the risk of certain diseases, including cancer.

Both Holland and Tansman agree that overdosing on supplements can be easier than you think, and that the best way to get all the nutrients you need is to take 1 multivitamin daily and eat plenty of vitamin-rich foods.

The Multivitamin Myth: Not All of Them Pack The Same Punch

James Dillard, MD, Medical Director, Complementary and Alternative Medicine, Oxford Health Plans, and Clinical Medical Advisor, Rosenthal Center for Complementary and Alternative Medicine, Columbia University, and Assistant Clinical Professor, Columbia University College of Physicians and Surgeons, New York, NY.

Samantha Heller, MS, RD, Nutritionist, New York University Medical Center.

More is not better when it comes to the ingredients in your vitamin supplement. When a multivitamin pill is packed with extra nutrients or herbs along with vitamins and minerals, it's not the bargain you think it is, says Dr. James Dillard, a clinical medical advisor at the Rosenthal Center for Complementary and Alternative Medicine at Columbia University.

Why? A tablet or capsule can only hold so much, and the more ingredients in a single pill, the less of each ingredient you can have; sometimes pills have so little of each nutrient, they are hardly worth taking, he says.

That can hurt if you think you're protecting yourself, especially if you're a woman who needs extra calcium, says registered dietician Samantha Heller.

"Calcium should always be taken as a separate supplement, as they simply can't fit all a woman's needs into 1 multivitamin pill," says Heller, a nutritionist at New York University Medical Center.

TOO MUCH OF A GOOD THING

Vitamin supplements with nutrient levels that soar above the recommended daily amounts (RDA) can also cause problems, increasing the risk of such side effects as diarrhea and nausea, Heller says. Too much vitamin A and D, for example, can be toxic, she says.

A vitamin supplement can even make you feel ill. According to Dillard, nuances in the way vitamins are made, or even the source of the nutrients themselves, can affect the way you react to any specific supplement. That can result in everything from dizziness to headaches, fatigue, hives, or other allergic reactions.

"If you take a vitamin supplement and don't feel well, switch brands," Dillard says.

But which brand should you take? Many experts say the bigger, more experienced companies are more likely to give you a higher-quality product.

"The bigger companies that do nothing but manufacture vitamins simply can't afford to give you an inferior product," Dillard says. "And I don't know if that can be said for lesser known, or private-label companies, like supermarkets that package their own brand of supplements."

Also important is a product with no sugars, starches, binders, or fillers.

THE DISSOLVE FACTOR

Another key concern is getting the nutrients into your bloodstream, a goal that's often defeated when supplements have a hard-shell coating.

"If we X-ray someone's stomach, we can often see dark shadows indicating undissolved vitamin pills," Dillard says.

Look for products that carry the US Pharmacopeia seal of approval, usually noted as "USP Approved" on the label. This means the product was tested by a government agency and will dissolve in a minimum amount of time.

Here's a home test suggested by Dillard to see how well your vitamin dissolves: Mix equal parts water and vinegar in a glass and drop in your vitamin pill. Within 40 minutes, it should be well on its way to being dissolved. If it's not, he says, it's probably going to pass through your body undigested.

Finally, always check the expiration date before buying a vitamin supplement. If you don't find one, don't buy the product.

■ ■ ■ ■

For Multivitamin Veracity, Check for the USP Seal

There are literally thousands of unregulated products marketed under the category "dietary supplement." These include the vitamins and multivitamins available everywhere from supermarkets to health food stores to drug stores to Internet sites.

So, how do you know which ones are worth buying? More importantly, how do you know which ones are going to help you and not cause harm?

Because multivitamin content isn't regulated by the United States government, consumers must rely on other sources for verification. The best source may be the US Pharmacopeia (*www.usp.org*), a nonprofit agency that's been operating since 1820.

USP has developed 5 testing standards that must be met to earn approval from its Dietary Supplement Verification Program (DSVP). *To earn a "USP Verified" seal for its label, the product must...*

1. Contain the ingredients listed on the label.

2. Have the declared amount and strength of ingredients.

3. Break down easily in stomach fluids so the body can effectively absorb the nutrients in the supplement.

4. Have been screened for harmful contaminants, such as heavy metals, microbes, and pesticides.

5. Have been manufactured in safe, sanitary, and controlled conditions.

Sticks and Stones May Break Your Bones, But So Can Vitamin A

Loren Wissner Greene, MD, Clinical Associate Professor of Medicine and Codirector, Bone Density Unit, New York University School of Medicine.

Karl Michaelsson, MD, Department of Surgical Sciences, Section of Orthopedics, University Hospital Uppsala, Sweden.

January 23, 2003, *New England Journal of Medicine*.

Too much vitamin A can increase your risk for bone fracture, according to a 30-year research study.

Swedish men with the highest levels of vitamin A in their blood also had a higher risk of breaking their bones than men who had lower levels of the vitamin.

Vitamin A, or *retinol,* is found in fish, liver, kidneys, and various dairy products. Although our bodies also convert some of the nutrients in fruits and vegetables into retinol, many countries fortify dairy foods—such as milk—with extra vitamin A and D, giving us yet more of the nutrient. In Sweden, for instance, margarine and low-fat dairy products are pumped with these extra vitamins.

The Swedish study, which looked at more than 2000 middle-aged men for a span of 30 years, found 7 times as many fractures in the men with the highest amounts of vitamin A in their blood than in those with the lowest amounts. Those with the highest amounts were also nearly 2.5 times more likely to break a hip than were men who had moderate amounts of vitamin A. Interestingly, the dietary intake of vitamin A in Scandinavia is up to 6 times as high as in southern Europe, the study authors say.

WATCH YOUR INTAKE

So what does this mean when it comes to eating fish, liver, vitamin A-fortified milk, and, of course, taking our daily multivitamins?

The short answer is that vitamin A supplementation and fortification might not be such a good idea in the industrialized world.

The long answer really depends on who you are. Black and Mexican–American children have been shown to have lower retinol levels than white children. Men older than 30 years and women older than 50 years have relatively high levels of the vitamin.

"The results can't be translated into [specific] dietary intake levels of vitamin A," says Dr. Karl Michaelsson, lead author of the study. Despite the absence of precise numbers, Michaelsson believes "it can be recommended to lower the amount of retinol in multivitamin tablets and the amount fortified in foods, mainly margarine and low-fat milk products."

"I would say that most people should not be ingesting vitamin A supplements and, beyond that, when you take a multivitamin, you should watch the amount in the supplement," advises Dr. Loren Wissner Greene, codirector of the bone density unit at New York University School of Medicine in New York City.

13

Pain Treatments

Women Cope Better With Pain

Studies show that women may be better able to cope with pain than men—at least during certain periods of their lives, according to Dr. James N. Dillard, author of *The Chronic Pain Solution.*

The key to coping may be estrogen. Produced by the ovaries in peak amounts during the reproductive years, the hormone's influence may extend far beyond a woman's reproductive tract and reach to the pain centers of the brain.

Estrogen plays an important role in the individual response to pain, says Dr. Jon-Kar Zubieta, a neuroscientist at the University of Michigan who has published several studies investigating links between sex hormones and pain tolerance.

One of the ways estrogen helps women cope with pain, he says, is by increasing the availability of *endorphins*—brain chemicals that help dampen the pain response.

When estrogen levels are high, there's an increased number of areas in the brain where endorphins can be stored, waiting to flood the body with the chemicals capable of overriding pain signals.

"That's one reason why women can get through the pain of childbirth—right before they give birth, their estrogen levels are soaring, so their ability to cope with pain is expanded," Zubieta says.

The studies also show the level of pain protection may drop dramatically the closer a woman gets to menopause as her estrogen levels plummet. Dillard says that may be one

James N. Dillard, MD, DC, CAc, Assistant Clinical Professor, Columbia University College of Physicians and Surgeons, Clinical Adviser, Columbia's Rosenthal Center for Complementary and Alternative Medicine, and Director, Complementary Medicine Services, University Pain Center, New York, NY.

Jon-Kar Zubieta, MD, PhD, Lead Researcher, Neuroscientist and Director, Psychiatry Division, University of Michigan Depression Center, Ann Arbor.

reason why so many women begin to feel more aches and pains as they enter midlife.

Studies at the University of Massachusetts also revealed that women might have more muscle endurance during exercise than men, thanks again to estrogen, which works to reduce soreness and pain after exertion.

CONDITIONING

But when it comes to perceiving pain, it's not just hormones that matter. Dillard, an assistant clinical professor at Columbia University College of Physicians and Surgeons in New York City, says social and cultural conditioning matters, as well.

Because women are preconditioned to at least some degree of monthly menstrual pain, not to mention a pretty hefty level of discomfort during childbirth, Dillard suspects they may react with less alarm when other types of pain occur. And this, he says, may make a big difference when it comes time to have that tooth pulled.

If a woman is accustomed to pain, Dillard says, she will be more tolerant because she is less alarmed by the pain signals.

info For more information on chronic pain, visit the National Foundation for the Treatment of Pain at *www.paincare.org*.

Do MRIs Lead to Unnecessary Surgery?

Richard Deyo, MD, MPH, Professor, Medicine and Health Services, University of Washington, Seattle.

Jeffrey G. Jarvik, MD, MPH, Associate Professor, Radiology and Neurosurgery, University of Washington, Seattle.

Nortin Hadler, MD, Professor, Medicine and Microbiology/Immunology, University of North Carolina, Chapel Hill.

June 4, 2003, *Journal of the American Medical Association*.

Patients and doctors may prefer high-tech spine scans over X-rays, but getting a sharper picture doesn't necessarily create a better outcome for people with low back pain.

That's the conclusion of a study that acknowledges that rapid magnetic resonance imaging (MRI) tests may provide physicians with a faster, clearer view of the anatomy than an X-ray, but that MRI is much more likely to lead to disc surgery—a procedure that has limited value to all but a few people with low back pain.

The study looked at a relatively new form of MRI called rapid MRI, which is similar to the conventional imaging test but takes only a fraction of the time. It provides detailed pictures of the anatomy that X-rays can't match.

The study followed 380 men and women with low back pain. Half underwent rapid MRI as a first resort, while the rest had more conservative spinal X-rays to detect the cause of their discomfort.

After 1 year, the 2 groups were equally likely to report continued back disability, back pain, and other measures of distress. That suggests the group that got rapid MRI wasn't receiving more finely tuned treatment, says study coauthor Dr. Richard Deyo.

However, those who had the MRI test were 2.5 times more likely to have undergone spinal surgery to correct a problem than those in the X-ray group—10 people versus 4.

Dr. Jeffrey Jarvik, a neurosurgeon at the University of Washington and lead author of the study, says he was somewhat surprised by the results. "I really thought the rapid [MRI] might in fact improve patient outcomes, or at least there might not be the suggestion that it was a more expensive alternative."

LEARN TO LIVE WITH BACK PAIN

Dr. Nortin Hadler says back surgery should be consigned to the waste bin of medical procedures. "There's absolutely no evidence that it works," says Hadler, a professor of medicine at the University of North Carolina and author of an editorial accompanying the journal article. "It ought to be a vanishingly rare procedure."

Hadler, who is wary of the perpetual "medicalization" of minor complaints, says most Americans experience major back pain at least once a year and almost every adult has some spine abnormalities. "Once you show someone that anomaly on the MRI it grows in his or her mind, and it's hard to think that it's not meaningful," he says.

Botox Takes Another Wrinkle Out of Low Back Pain

Todd Schlifstein, MD, Associate Professor, Medicine, New York University Medical Center.

March 20–23, 2003, Presentations, American Pain Society Annual Conference, Chicago, IL.

Botox first made headlines as a controversial wrinkle treatment, but the drug has quickly made a statement in other areas of health care. Doctors in the United States and Europe say it can be used to treat low back pain, sciatica, and even some forms of neck discomfort.

According to rehabilitation physician Todd Schlifstein, Botox offers an important option, particularly for people who may not respond to traditional care.

"It's not for everybody or for every type of pain, but when it's used appropriately, it can offer relief, even when other treatments have failed," says Schlifstein, a rehabilitation physician at New York University Medical Center.

A LITTLE HISTORY

Botox is the brand name of a naturally occurring substance known as *botulinum toxin type A*. The toxin itself is related to botulism, a form of food poisoning that occurs when meat or other foods develop bacteria known as *Clostridium botulinum*. Doctors had long known that in severe cases of botulism, paralysis results. They later learned that in controlled amounts, this same toxin can be used to control contractions in patients suffering from diseases linked to severe muscle spasms, such as multiple sclerosis (MS).

However, during tests on patients with MS, doctors discovered something more. When Botox was injected into facial muscle spasms, wrinkles began to relax—and seemed to disappear. Not long thereafter, an antiaging cosmetic treatment was born.

Soon after that, experimentation involving lower back pain began, and Schlifstein says the results are promising for many patients.

"If the back pain is the result of spasms deep within the muscles, Botox, used in controlled amounts, can offer relief lasting at least 3 months—and sometimes permanently—from a single treatment," says Dr. Schlifstein.

SUPPORTING EVIDENCE

Researchers from the A&A Pain Institute of St. Louis, and from The Neurological Research Center in Bennington, Vermont, and doctors from Burnley General Hospital in England all treated patients with low back pain or sciatica. All of the 12 patients in each of the 3 studies had tried traditional treatments, including steroid injections, physical therapy, or in some cases, surgery, without success. After having Botox injected into their back muscles, all 12 patients reported at least a 50% reduction in pain and a few said their pain was gone completely. None reported significant side effects, although in 1 study some patients reported the return of a little pain after approximately 3 months. The patients being treated for the pain of sciatica also reported increased hip movement and flexibility. Botox is also being used to treat neck pain and migraine.

info If you'd like to know more about how the botulinum toxin can heal or harm, visit the US Food and Drug Administration's Web site at *www.fda.gov*.

Powerful Drugs That Relieve Back Pain

J.D. Bartleson, MD, Neurologist, Mayo Clinic, Rochester, MN.

John Giglio, Executive Director, American Pain Foundation, Baltimore, MD.

October 2002, *Pain Medicine*.

It's a mistake to ignore the potential value of opioids as powerful pain relievers for such chronic conditions as lower back and musculoskeletal pain, according to a study at the Mayo Clinic.

There is evidence that opioids such as *morphine, oxycodone,* and *fentanyl* can help and should be the treatment of choice for some patients, says Dr. J.D. Bartleson, a Mayo Clinic neurologist and lead author of the study.

Doctors and pharmacists have tended to avoid prescribing them, patients are afraid of becoming addicted to them, and government officials are concerned about their abuse.

"The prejudice against the use of analgesic opioids is unfortunate," Bartleson said. He says that they can provide significant relief for patients experiencing severe pain and that physicians and patients should be considering them more often than they do now.

With carefully monitored use, opioids could provide a better alternative for some patients than back surgery and other painkillers, Bartleson said. "Fewer than half of all back surgeries are successful in relieving chronic back pain," he noted. "Other medicines for pain—including aspirin and acetaminophen—can cause permanent adverse effects. Opioids have been demonstrated to provide pain relief, without long-term side effects."

FINDINGS SUPPORTED

John Giglio, executive director of the American Pain Foundation, agrees. He said the recent controversy over the illegal recreational use of the opioid OxyContin has further muddied the waters over the benefits of this entire class of prescription medications.

"There is mounting evidence that physicians are being deterred from using opioid drugs for patients in pain, not only because of the bad publicity about certain medications, but also because they are concerned they will be investigated by the US Drug Enforcement Agency if they prescribe them," Giglio says.

Chronic back pain is only one of the conditions for which negative publicity has overshadowed opioids' legitimate and proven medical benefit, he said. Even in the treatment of serious malignant conditions, doctors

and patients tend to shy away from the powerful drugs. Giglio and Bartleson agree that additional, longer-term and better-designed studies are needed to study how opioids can be best used in medical care.

Although Bartleson now counts himself among the believers in the benefits of opioids in the treatment of chronic back pain, he doesn't advocate their use for every patient. Opioids aren't for everyone, he cautions, and physicians must determine the best treatment for each patient.

■ ■ ■ ■

Pain Care Bill of Rights

The American Pain Foundation wants every heath care consumer to be advised of their rights. *They are...*

●**The right to have your report of pain taken seriously** and to be treated with dignity and respect by doctors, nurses, pharmacists, and other health care professionals.

●**The right to have your pain thoroughly assessed and promptly treated.**

●**The right to be informed by your doctor about what may be causing your pain,** possible treatments, and the benefits, risks, and costs of each.

●**The right to participate actively in decisions about how to manage your pain.**

●**The right to have your pain reassessed regularly** and your treatment adjusted if your pain has not been eased.

●**The right to be referred to a pain specialist** if your pain persists.

●**The right to get clear and prompt answers to your questions,** the right to take time to make decisions, and the right to refuse a particular type of treatment.

Although not always required by law, these are the rights you should expect—and, if necessary, demand—during the care of your pain.

Driving for Hours Won't Harm Your Back

Michele Crites–Battié, PhD, Professor, Department of Physical Therapy, University of Alberta, Edmonton, Canada.

October 14, 2002, *The Lancet*, online edition.

The next time you feel sore after a long day spent in the car, rest assured that your rattled bones are fine. Many drivers suffer from back problems, especially those who, like truckers, spend hours on the road each day. Some people suspect the physical stresses of driving—including the never ending vibration of the vehicle in motion—cause the spine to deteriorate faster and displace discs.

But Michele Crites–Battié, a professor of physical therapy at the University of Alberta in Canada, says her study of identical twins shows that people who drive for a living don't permanently damage their backs by driving.

THE STUDY

In the study, Crites–Battié and her colleagues examined a Finnish study of identical male twins and found 45 pairs in which one twin drove for a living and the other did not. Using magnetic resonance imaging (MRI), the researchers studied whether the spines of the drivers were any different from those of their twins.

"They engaged in tractor driving, bus and truck driving, and transport and heavy equipment operation," Crites–Battié says. "To our surprise, there was no apparent detrimental effect on the [spinal] discs, and there was not even a hint of greater degeneration in the spine of drivers versus nondrivers. We found no indication of a negative effect."

Crites–Battié cautions, however, that the pain complaints of drivers can still be legitimate, even if driving doesn't change the physical state of the spine.

"We're almost all prone to back problems to some degree, and driving may exacerbate symptoms," she says.

info For information about taking care of your back, visit the American Academy of Orthopaedic Surgeons at *www.aaos.org*.

■ ■ ■ ■

The Key to Avoiding Injury

According to the American Physical Therapy Association (*www.apta.org*), the key to avoiding back injury lies in minimizing the risk inherent in any activity. *They recommend applying the following principles…*

- **Work on your posture.** Don't slouch. Maintain the natural "arch" in your lower back whether standing or sitting.

- **Lift with your legs.** Don't bend over the object; bend your legs and keep your back straight. And most importantly, don't twist as you lift!

- **Sit with care.** Lumbar support and periodic breaks to move around are essential.

- **Control your weight.** Being overweight, especially if you have a "pot belly," puts added stress on your lower back.

- **Take breaks.** When you're on the road, stop frequently and get out and walk. When driving, position yourself so that your knees are slightly bent and your back is arched.

Fishing Can Be a 'High Injury' Sport

Keith Robert Berend, MD, Division of Orthopaedic Surgery, Duke University Medical Center, Durham, NC.

Spring 2002, *Journal of the Southern Orthopaedic Association*.

What do fishing and tennis have in common? Some of the same ailments caused by repetitive motion, such as "tennis elbow" are experienced by both fishermen and tennis players.

Fly-fishermen, in particular, are developing their own set of health problems that may end up keeping them away from their favorite casting spots, according to one orthopedic surgeon.

Dr. Keith Robert Berend, a fly-fisherman himself, says doctors are seeing more cases of of "fly-fishing elbow," "stooper's back" and "caster's shoulder." Berend is affiliated with the Duke University Medical Center's Division of Orthopaedic Surgery. He said he became interested in fishing injuries while spending time at lakes and hearing complaints from other fishermen.

"I thought there was something here. My father is an avid fly-fisherman and has back pain. I spend the off-months in the fly shop, drinking coffee and listening to people talk about their ailments," he says.

Fly-fishermen typically make several practice casts before actually hurling the fly into the water. That can put a strain on the body. To check on the prevalence of injuries among fly-fishermen, Berend surveyed 131 fishermen.

Fifty-nine percent of the fly-fishermen reported lower back pain. Saltwater fishermen had the highest rates of shoulder and elbow pain (31%), while trout fishermen were most likely to report wrist pain (31%).

"It's a repetitive-motion sport that loads the body's upper extremities and the trunk, much like other sports," Berend says. "People need to train to do this sport, just like if you're going to play golf or tennis. You need to engage in stretching and conditioning exercises year-round."

Fly-fishermen need to stay in shape to avoid muscle aches and pain, Berend adds.

■ ■ ■ ■

Exercises to Strengthen Your Back

The American Academy of Orthopaedic Surgeons suggests a gradual back-strengthening exercise program. *Here are some exercises to make your back stronger…*

INITIAL EXERCISES

●**Ankle Pumps.** Lie on your back. Move your ankles up and down. Repeat 10 times.

●**Heel Slides.** Lie on your back. Slowly bend and straighten your knee. Repeat 10 times.

●**Abdominal Contraction.** Lie on your back with knees bent and hands resting below your ribs. Tighten the abdominal muscles to squeeze ribs down toward back. Be sure not to hold your breath. Hold for 5 seconds. Relax. Repeat 10 times.

●**Heel Raises.** Stand with your weight even on both feet. Slowly raise heels up and down. Repeat 10 times.

●**Straight Leg Raises.** Lie on your back with 1 leg straight and 1 knee bent. Tighten your abdominal muscles to stabilize your lower back. Slowly lift your leg straight up about 6 to 12 inches. Hold 1 to 5 seconds. Lower leg slowly. Repeat 10 times.

INTERMEDIATE EXERCISES

●**Single Knee-to-Chest Stretch.** Lie on your back with both knees bent. Hold your thigh behind the knee and bring 1 knee up to the chest. Hold for 20 seconds. Relax. Repeat 5 times on each side.

●**Wall Squats.** Stand with your back leaning against the wall. Walk your feet 12 inches in front of you. Keep abdominal muscles tight while slowly bending both knees 45 degrees. Hold for 5 seconds. Slowly return to upright position. Repeat 10 times.

●**Hamstring Stretch.** Lie on your back with legs bent. Hold 1 thigh behind the knee. Slowly straighten the knee until a stretch is felt in back of thigh. Hold for 20 seconds. Relax. Repeat 5 times on each side.

ADVANCED EXERCISES

●**Hip Flexor Stretch.** Lie on your back on the edge of a bed, holding your knees to your chest. Slowly lower 1 leg down, keeping the knee bent, until a stretch is felt across top of the hip/thigh. Hold for 20 seconds. Relax. Repeat 5 times on each side.

●**Piriformis Stretch.** Lie on your back with both knees bent. Cross 1 leg on top of the other. Pull the opposite knee to the chest until a stretch is felt in the buttock/hip area. Hold for 20 seconds. Relax. Repeat 5 times on each side.

AEROBIC EXERCISES

Keep your spine in a neutral position, stabilizing it with your abdominal muscles, so you protect the lower back during aerobic exercise.

●**Stationary bike** for 20 to 30 minutes.

●**Treadmill** for 20 to 30 minutes.

Supplement That Relieves Joint Pain

John H. Klippel, MD, Medical Director, Arthritis Foundation, Atlanta, GA.

Sicy H. Lee, MD, Clinical Assistant Professor, Medicine, Hospital for Joint Diseases, New York, NY.

Arthritis is a word we're all familiar with, but did you know that in approximately 15 years 1 in every 5 of us will have it? It's true, according to estimates from the Arthritis Foundation and the US Centers for Disease Control and Prevention.

The baby boomers are getting older, says Dr. John H. Klippel, medical director of the Arthritis Foundation. "People are living longer. We're an aging society."

Arthritis is actually an umbrella term for more than 100 different conditions ranging from lupus to carpal tunnel syndrome to rheumatoid arthritis. Approximately 43 million Americans suffer from some form of arthritis, making it the nation's leading cause of disability.

Osteoarthritis, a condition in which the cushioning cartilage between bones wears away, is the most common form of the disease, accounting for about 30 million cases, according to the American Academy of Orthopaedic Surgeons. The incidence of osteoarthritis increases significantly as people age. And because there is no cure, doctors say the best they can do is manage its painful symptoms.

"Standard therapy is very limited because we don't have an established regimen of halting the disease," says Dr. Sicy H. Lee, a clinical assistant professor of medicine at the Hospital for Joint Diseases in New York City. "We emphasize slowing down the progression of the disease and making the patient more comfortable and more functional."

MEDICATIONS CAN HELP

Several medications are available to help treat the symptoms of osteoarthritis. These include over-the-counter drugs as well as the recently introduced *cox-2 inhibitors,* for which you need a prescription. There have also been advances with artificial joint fluids that are injected into the knee.

Dietary supplements to help arthritis sufferers are also moving closer to the mainstream. *Glucosamine* and *condroitin* have received particular attention. "There's increasing evidence that not only do they relieve the signs and symptoms of arthritis but may actually protect the cartilage and prevent damage to the cartilage," Klippel says.

For some people who have arthritis severe enough to impede their ability to get around or even get out of a chair, surgery to replace damaged joints may become an option.

PREVENTION IS KEY

"Osteoarthritis is not inevitable," Klippel says. Attention to physical fitness and maintaining the proper weight can prevent the onset of the disease or stem its progression.

"Given the size of the problem, the public is going to have to realize quickly the importance of staying fit and keeping weight under control if they are going to prevent osteoarthritis," Klippel says.

info To get more information on arthritis and what to do about it, visit the Arthritis Foundation at *www.arthritis.org* or the Centers for Disease Control and Prevention at *www.cdc.gov/nccdphp/arthritis.*

■ ■ ■ ■

Osteoarthritis Can Begin in the Teen Years

While most cases of osteoarthritis are discovered during midlife or later, it's actually possible to trace the development of many cases to adolescence or young adulthood.

The Harvard Medical School Family Health Guide cites a Johns Hopkins study, which followed a group of 1337 (mostly white male) medical students for an average of 36 years. Participants who had sustained a knee injury in adolescence or young adulthood (the average age at the time of injury was 16) were 3 times more likely to suffer from knee osteoarthritis by middle age as those who hadn't had an injury.

The Family Health Guide cautions parents of adolescents and young adults who have experienced a traumatic knee injury to be aware of ways they can try to prevent osteoarthritis. These methods include using the proper sports equipment correctly and under safe conditions, temporarily modifying high-impact exercise, and, in the future, perhaps early intervention drug therapy.

The Painkiller That Backfires for Arthritis Sufferers

Elham Rahme, PhD, Assistant Professor, Medicine and Scientific Researcher, Research Institute of the McGill University Health Centre, Montreal, Quebec, Canada.

John Klippel, MD, Medical Director, Arthritis Foundation, Atlanta, GA.

November 2002, *Arthritis and Rheumatism.*

Acetaminophen is often a first line of treatment for arthritis because it is believed to have fewer side effects than other painkillers. But Canadian researchers have shown that in high doses, acetaminophen is just as likely to cause gastrointestinal (GI) problems, such as upset stomach and ulcers, as *nonsteroidal anti-inflammatory drugs* (NSAIDs), such as ibuprofen or naproxen.

"Physicians need to know that if they are increasing the dose of acetaminophen rather than switching to another medication because they think they will see less GI events, they should look at other options," says one of the study's authors, Elham Rahme, an assistant professor of medicine at the Research Institute of the McGill University Health Centre in Montreal. And, she adds, patients shouldn't increase their dose of acetaminophen without first consulting their doctor.

Arthritis affects as many as 1 in 3 American adults, according to the Arthritis Foundation, and acetaminophen—the active ingredient in Tylenol, among others—is frequently recommended to manage the pain associated with this disorder.

HIGHER DOSE, GREATER RISK

After studying almost 50,000 arthritis patients, half of whom were taking acetaminophen, "we saw that there really is a difference," Rahme says. "At the low dose of acetaminophen, GI events are much lower than in the NSAID group, but when you go to 2600 milligrams (mg) a day and higher, there were similar rates of GI events."

Rahme said the rate of stomach and intestinal troubles almost doubled between the lowest dose (less than 650 mg per day) of acetaminophen and the highest dose (more than 3250 mg daily). The researchers started to see side effects at the equivalent of 8 regular-strength or 5 extra-strength tablets a day.

Rahme says there are some limitations to the study. For example, there may have been a slight bias toward having GI problems because the patients included in the study were older and often on more than one medication. Many had already been on either acetaminophen or NSAID therapy. Rahme says the researchers tried to control for these variables and still saw more GI problems in patients on high doses of acetaminophen.

Dr. John Klippel, medical director of the Arthritis Foundation, wasn't surprised by the results of this study, but says that acetaminophen will probably remain the first line of treatment for many patients because it's cost-effective and still considered quite safe in low doses.

He cautions that consumers should check the label of any over-the-counter medication they are taking to be sure they're not getting extra doses of acetaminophen. "Acetaminophen is probably the most widely used analgesic in the world, and it's contained in a lot of cold and headache preparations, " Klippel says.

For managing pain, the Arthritis Foundation recommends taking control, keeping a positive attitude, not focusing on the pain, and practicing positive self-talk.

Osteoarthritis Sufferers Pay a 'Stiff' Price for Not Exercising

Martin P.M. Steultjens, PhD, Netherlands Institute of Health Services Research, Utrecht.

Joel Press, MD, Medical Director, Center for Spine, Sports and Occupational Rehabilitation of the Rehabilitation Institute of Chicago, IL.

July 2002, *Arthritis and Rheumatism.*

A study by Dutch researchers has found that people with osteoarthritis of the knee must follow a workable exercise plan to stave off potentially severe muscle deterioration. This research is the first to document that muscles weakened from inactivity increase the disability suffered by those with osteoarthritis of the knee.

"It's sort of a downward spiral. As people feel more pain, they exercise less, which in the long term leads to muscle weakness and even more disability," says Martin P.M. Steultjens, a scientist with the Netherlands Institute of Health Services Research in Utrecht and lead author of the study.

Osteoarthritis afflicts an estimated 21 million Americans, mostly after age 45. Women are more commonly affected than men, according to the Arthritis Foundation.

THE STUDY

Steultjens and his colleagues found that approximately 25% of the patients' disabilities could be traced to a lack of physical activity that weakened their muscles, causing their joints to become less stable and less able to bear their weight.

The result: They were more disabled than they would have been if they had maintained their muscle strength.

"This study shows the association between pain and disability. In the early stages of osteoarthritis, patients have pain and, afraid to have pain again, they become inactive," Steultjens said. People should be encouraged to keep up some kind of activity even while suffering from osteoarthritis.

THE EXERCISES

Exercising with osteoarthritis is possible as long as you tailor the program to each patient, according to Dr. Joel Press, medical director of the Center for Spine, Sports and Occupational Rehabilitation of the Rehabilitation Institute of Chicago.

"You have to be a little creative, and look at each person differently to find exercises he or she can tolerate and that don't increase the pain," he says.

Example: If you have trouble walking, try swimming or a stationary bicycle—both keep weight off the joints.

info Information about diagnosing and treating osteoarthritis can be found at the Johns Hopkins University Web site at *www.hopkins-arthritis.com.*

Osteoarthritis 'Points' to Heart Disease

Mikko Haara, MD, University of Kuopio, Kuopio, Finland.

February 2003, *Annals of the Rheumatic Diseases.*

Got arthritis in one finger? That could point to trouble beyond just a stiff digit, according to new research.

Finnish researchers were surprised to discover an association between osteoarthritis in only a single finger joint in men and the likelihood that they will die of cardiovascular disease.

Women with osteoarthritis in the fingers aren't home free by any means, the study also found. They had a modestly higher risk of dying from heart disease if they had arthritis in one finger or in symmetrical joints, the Finns reported.

A team led by Dr. Mikko Haara, a researcher at the University of Kuopio in Finland, looked at a population sample of 8000 Finns, aged 30 years and older, and took hand X-rays of 3595 subjects. The subjects were gathered from 1977 to 1989. By the end of 1994, 897 had died.

Then Haara's team looked at causes of death and whether the subjects had arthritis.

Men with symmetrical arthritis of the fingers weren't at increased risk of dying from heart disease, but those with arthritis in a single finger joint were 42% more likely to die of heart disease.

By contrast, women were at increased risk whether they had a single digit involved or symmetrical joints, with a 25% higher risk for symmetrical joints with arthritis and 26% for a single joint.

Exactly why this occurs isn't known, Haara says. But "even if the mechanism remains unclear, it is well known that body mass index" is tied to both osteoarthritis and cardiovascular disease. More than half the participants were overweight.

If you already have arthritis, he says, ask your doctor about medication and nondrug options, like a moderate exercise program.

■ ■ ■ ■

Exercises to Combat Osteoarthritis

The National Institute of Arthritis and Musculoskeletal and Skin Diseases (*www.niams.nih.gov*) suggests exercises that may help fight osteoarthritis. *They are...*

•**Range-of-motion exercises** (for example, dance) help maintain normal joint movement and relieve stiffness. This type of exercise helps maintain or increase flexibility.

•**Strengthening exercises** (for example, weight training) help keep or increase muscle strength. Strong muscles help support and protect joints that are affected by arthritis.

•**Aerobic or endurance exercises** (for example, bicycle riding) improve cardiovascular fitness, help control weight, and improve overall function. Weight control can be important to people who have arthritis because extra weight puts extra pressure on many joints. Some studies show that aerobic exercise can reduce inflammation in some joints.

Ask your doctor or physical therapist for specific guidelines on exercising.

Rheumatoid Arthritis Patients Have a Clue to Best Treatment

Theodore Pincus, MD, Professor, Medicine, Division of Rheumatology/Immunology, Vanderbilt University Medical Center, Nashville, TN.

Steven B. Abramson, MD, Director, Rheumatology, New York University Medical Center and the Hospital for Joint Diseases, and Professor, New York University School of Medicine.

April 2003, *Arthritis and Rheumatism.*

What's the best way for doctors to know if an arthritis medication is working? Ask the patient.

That's the simple conclusion of a multicenter study that compared the effectiveness of a patient questionnaire with a laundry list of clinical observations and tests.

"Oftentimes, it's the most simple things in medicine that produce the best results," says Dr. Theodore Pincus, lead author of the study on the subject.

Although there's no universally accepted system of assessing a patient's response to treatments for rheumatoid arthritis, the most accepted method is one established by the American College of Rheumatology (ACR) for use during drug trials.

Known as the ACR20, it involves laboratory tests and detailed observations of a patient's condition, including joint size and degree of swelling.

GOOD IN THE LAB, NOT SO GOOD IN THE FIELD

As good as the system can be, it is complicated, costly, and time-consuming, and, doctors say, in many respects has little relevance in a clinical setting.

"The more complicated things get in assessing a patient's condition, the more room for error there is, particularly when the examination involves multiple joint measurements," says Pincus, a professor of medicine at Vanderbilt University in Nashville.

The solution, Pincus says, may lie in a 1-page questionnaire filled out by the patients themselves. The questions, adapted from the ACR20, focus on signs that predict how well a drug is working—including a patient's well-being, level of pain, and quality of life.

"We ask a patient, 'Can you turn on the faucet? How hard is it to open a door knob? Can you get in and out of your car?' The answers to these kinds of questions are much more meaningful when it comes to figuring out how this patient is really doing," says Pincus.

CREATING A STANDARD

For Dr. Steven B. Abramson, the study's results are a step forward.

"The ACR20 is an excellent criteria, but it really was not developed for clinical use, so it's not really that useful in a clinical setting," says Abramson, director of rheumatology at New York University Medical Center.

By streamlining the criteria and allowing for a standardized system of assessing a patient, Abramson believes the questionnaire holds great promise for more efficient—and maybe less costly—care.

"It would also be a big help in, for example, justifying to insurance companies why a particular patient may need a more expensive drug. The questionnaire would make it easy to show what works and what doesn't," Abramson says.

The study looked at nearly 500 people with rheumatoid arthritis. They were divided into 3 groups—2 groups took arthritis drugs and 1 group took a placebo. Their progress was monitored using either the ACR20 system or the questionnaire.

The result: The questionnaire was as accurate as the ACR20 in predicting how well the medications worked. And it worked equally well at pinpointing quality of life issues.

info To learn more about diagnosing and treating rheumatoid arthritis, visit the the National Institutes of Health at *www.nlm. nih.gov.*

Women With Rheumatoid Arthritis Need to Take Special Care of Their Hearts

Daniel H. Solomon, MD, MPH, Clinical Rheumatologist, Assistant Professor, Harvard Medical School, Brigham and Women's Hospital, Boston, MA.

Elizabeth Ross, MD, Cardiologist, Washington, DC, and National Spokeswoman, American Heart Association.

March 11, 2003, *Circulation.*

Researchers have found that women with rheumatoid arthritis face a much greater risk of heart attacks than women who do not have rheumatoid arthritis.

Rheumatoid arthritis, or RA, is an autoimmune disease in which the body's immune system attacks healthy joint tissue, causing inflammation and then joint damage. The disease affects 2.1 million Americans; approximately 1.5 million of them are women.

Between 1976 and 1996, researchers tracked more than 114,000 women, including 527 with rheumatoid arthritis. The study found that those with RA were twice as likely to have heart attacks as women without RA, and women who had the disease for at least 10 years faced 3 times the risk of heart attacks.

Researchers from the Brigham and Women's Hospital in Boston took into account known risk factors for heart attacks, such as age, smoking, hypertension, diabetes, and high cholesterol when they conducted their analysis.

Dr. Daniel H. Solomon, a clinical rheumatologist and assistant professor at Brigham and Women's, said the findings should influence treatment of patients with RA.

Brigham researchers plan to study whether such steps as cholesterol-lowering treatment, blood-pressure medication, and regular low doses of aspirin for RA patients would reduce the risk of heart attack.

Solomon said other studies have linked RA and increased rates of heart disease because the inflammation is believed to contribute to fatty build-up in the blood vessels, which can cause heart attacks.

Further research could help determine whether anti-inflammatory drugs for RA also reduce the risk of heart disease.

REASONS UNKNOWN

Dr. Elizabeth Ross, a cardiologist based in Washington, DC, said the study shows that RA increases the risk of heart attacks, but the reason remains unclear.

"Maybe RA is one of those disorders where we need to be more aggressive in prevention and treatment of heart disease," said Ross, who is a national spokeswoman for the American Heart Association.

Although she thinks there could be other factors, Ross said the study reinforces the need to focus on such known risk factors for heart disease as blood pressure, smoking, diet, and exercise.

■ ■ ■ ■

Symptoms of Rheumatoid Arthritis

According to the Arthritis Foundation, symptoms of RA include inflammation of joints, swelling of the joints, difficulty moving, and pain. *Other symptoms include...*

- **Loss of appetite.**
- **Fever.**
- **Loss of energy.**
- **Anemia.**
- **Occasional rheumatoid nodules** (lumps of tissue under the skin).

Two-Drug Combo Brings More Relief for Rheumatoid Arthritis Sufferers

Joel Kremer, MD, Professor, Medicine, The Center for Rheumatology, Albany Medical Center, Albany, NY.
John H. Klippel, MD, Medical Director, Arthritis Foundation, Atlanta, GA.
November 5, 2002, *Annals of Internal Medicine*.

A mix of 2 drugs that had not previously been tested together has proven to be an effective treatment for sufferers of rheumatoid arthritis.

Patients who take the drug *methotrexate*, considered the gold standard of treatment, may find more relief by combining it with a drug called *leflunomide*, according to a study of 263 patients in the United States and Canada.

Typically, half of all patients who take methotrexate find it "not totally effective" at relieving the debilitating disease's symptoms, says Dr. Joel Kremer, professor of medicine at The Center for Rheumatology in Albany, New York, and author of the study. "A significant proportion of patients had good outcomes when leflunomide was added."

Rheumatoid arthritis is an autoimmune disease in which joints become inflamed, resulting in swelling and pain. The slow disintegration of the joint may eventually lead to immobility. According to the Arthritis Foundation, 2.1 million Americans suffer symptoms.

The researchers conducted a 24-week trial at 20 centers in the US and Canada that included 263 people with rheumatoid arthritis. The study was supported by a grant from Aventis Pharmaceuticals, the manufacturer of leflunomide.

All participants were given methotrexate. Half the volunteers also received leflunomide; the rest received a placebo.

At the end of the 24 weeks, almost half of those receiving leflunomide achieved at least a 20% improvement in their symptoms, as defined by the American College of Rheumatology criteria. Only 19.5% of the placebo group achieved the same improvement.

Many patients taking leflunomide had significantly greater relief of symptoms. The doses of leflunomide varied, depending on the patient's tolerance of the drug and relief of symptoms.

RISKS OF COMBINED-DRUG THERAPY

There are many unpleasant side effects associated with each drug. But the main concern was that the risk of liver toxicity—a serious side effect associated with both drugs—would be heightened by combining them. Only 3 patients on the combined therapy dropped out of the study because of problems with their liver function tests, Kremer said.

There's always a concern about side effects when 2 drugs are combined for the first time, reports Dr. John H. Klippel, medical director of the Arthritis Foundation. "You may see new side effects you wouldn't see with either drug alone," he said. "This study does teach us that combining 2 drugs with risks of liver problems doesn't increase the risk."

Klippel laments the fact that, with all the treatments presently available for rheumatoid arthritis, "true remission and complete absence of symptoms is very rare." For years, people have taken methotrexate alone, so it's good to find other drugs, such as leflunomide, that work well with it, he believes.

"The optimal therapy for rheumatoid arthritis is continually changing. I think combination therapy represents an important advance for the treatment of people with rheumatoid arthritis," he says.

Migraine Sufferers Can Get Pain Relief Right Now

Cormac O'Donovan, MD, Assistant Professor, Neurology, Wake Forest University School of Medicine, Winston–Salem, NC.

Seymour Diamond, MD, Executive Chairman, National Headache Foundation, and Director, Diamond Headache Clinic, Chicago, IL.

April 2003, *Headache*.

Approximately 30 million Americans suffer from migraines, and up to half of all migraines are never diagnosed, experts say. Migraines produce intense, throbbing pain—typically on one side of the head —in addition to nausea and sensitivity to light and sound.

But many migraine sufferers take too many addictive medications that only give them short-term relief, instead of using newer drugs that work better, say researchers from Wake Forest University School of Medicine.

Their recent study results indicate that migraine patients often don't get the best treatments for the debilitating ailment because they see primary care physicians, not specialists, who are much more likely to prescribe the newer medications.

"The most striking finding was [that] the most habit-forming drugs were used in large degrees," says Dr. Cormac O'Donovan, the senior author of the study.

O'Donovan, an assistant professor of neurology at Wake Forest, has important advice for migraine sufferers who are relying on addictive drugs—reevaluate your medications if they're habit-forming.

These drugs only give temporary relief and increase the risks of addiction and severe "rebound" headaches when a patient stops taking them, he says.

PRIMARY DOC IS (MOSTLY) FIRST STOP

The Wake Forest researchers based their conclusions on nearly a decade of data from a large, ongoing survey of physicians. More than 7 in 10 migraine sufferers who sought treatment saw primary care physicians, while fewer than 2 in 10 saw neurologists, according to the data.

And the primary care physicians prescribed addictive drugs more than 3 times as often as *triptans,* which first hit the market in 1993 as a breakthrough in migraine treatment. Triptans mimic the neurotransmitter *serotonin* (the level of serotonin drops off during migraines) and soothe the inflammation of nerve endings in the brain.

RAISING AWARENESS

Most migraine sufferers will never see a specialist, so better treatment will depend largely on more awareness of options among primary care doctors, O'Donovan says.

"We need to get the primary care physicians on board," he says. "There's not enough familiarity with [the newer treatments]."

Dr. Seymour Diamond, executive chairman of the National Headache Foundation, agrees.

"There's a great majority of migraine sufferers still taking pain medicine" instead of more effective alternatives, Diamond says.

Too often, that's because of rushed appointments with a primary care doctor, Diamond says.

"Typically, a patient comes in and says, 'I have a headache,' and the doctor will write a prescription for a painkiller, sedative, or tranquilizer. Headache is probably one of the most common disorders—and probably one of the most mistreated," he adds.

Doctors should do a complete physical exam on headache patients and ask about the pain, its frequency and location, other symptoms, and possible contributing factors, Diamond says.

info For more on migraines and their treatments, visit the Migraine Awareness Group: A National Understanding for Migraineurs (MAGNUM) at *www.migraines.org* or the National Institute of Neurological Disorders and Stroke (NINDS) at *www.ninds.nih.gov.*

■ ■ ■ ■

Know What Type of Headache You Have

Your head may hurt, but it may hurt for a number of different reasons, according to The National Institutes of Health. Here are some ways to determine what type of headache you have and some suggestions on how to treat it.

Headaches are usually caused by either muscle contraction (tension headache) or vascular problems (migraine headache or cluster headache). Some headaches, however, are caused by a combination of these 2.

Here are headache signs that signal a potentially serious problem...

•**Involves sudden, violent pain** (could indicate an aneurysm).

•**Gets worse over time** and includes other symptoms, such as...

  •Speech changes.
  •Visual changes.
  •Personality changes.

•**Awakens you from sleep** (could indicate a brain tumor).

•**Includes nausea, vomiting, fever, and a stiff neck** (could indicate meningitis).

TENSION HEADACHES

A tension headache is a common headache pattern that may or may not be associated with psychosocial stressors. *Tension headaches are characterized by the following...*

•**Pain usually felt in the back of the head and neck,** and usually not one-sided.

•**Pain that lasts for weeks or months** with only brief periods of relief, although it may fluctuate in severity.

•**Attacks that begin at any time of the day.**

•**Pain that can be described as a "tight band,"** pressing, but rarely throbbing, and never accompanied by fever.

MIGRAINE HEADACHES

Migraine headaches are often preceded by fatigue, depression, and visual disturbance (light flash or loss of peripheral vision). *Migraine headaches are characterized by the following properties...*

•**Pain that is characteristically only on one side at a time,** but may involve the entire head.

•**Pain that is throbbing in nature** and usually develops in the morning and gradually becomes worse after an hour or so.

•**Attacks that may occur as often as every few days or weeks** or as seldom as months apart. Migraines often continue for hours, but rarely last longer than a day or 2.

•**Pain that may be aggravated by stress, alcohol, or certain foods** (such as chocolate) and is frequently accompanied by nausea and vomiting, and relieved by sleep.

CLUSTER HEADACHES

Cluster headaches are a variation of migraine headaches and are far less common. They occur mostly in men, while typical migraines are more common in women. *Cluster headaches are characterized by pain that...*

•**Is often situated behind an eye** (usually the same eye).

•**Comes on very suddenly** and without warning.

•**Peaks within 5 to 10 minutes** and disappears in less than an hour.

•**Is often triggered by alcohol.**

●**Will awaken you from sleep,** and will occur several times a day for weeks and then stop.

SINUS HEADACHES

Inflamed sinuses (acute sinusitis or chronic sinusitis) can also cause headaches. *Sinus headaches are characterized by the following...*

●**Pain that usually begins during or after a bad cold,** particularly if you have a postnasal drip.

●**Pain that it is localized to one specific area of the face or head.**

●**Pain that is worse in the morning,** before mucus has had an opportunity to drain.

●**Pain that it is made worse by coughing,** sneezing, or sudden movements of the head.

●**Pain that it is aggravated by alcohol,** sudden temperature changes, and going from a warm room out into the cold (during cold seasons).

TEMPORAL ARTERITIS

Temporal arteritis occurs mostly in people over the age of 50 years. *These headaches are characterized by the following...*

●**Pain that is aggravated by chewing.**

●**Impaired vision.**

●**Aches and pains** all over the body.

●**The presence of a fever.**

●**Weight loss.**

●**Elevated blood ESR** (erythrocyte sedimentation rate).

●**May progress to loss of vision.**

New Relief for Migraine Sufferers

Lisa K. Mannix, MD, Neurologist, Cincinnati, OH, and Member, Board of Directors, National Headache Foundation, Chicago, IL.
April 2003, *Headache.*

Not long ago, migraine sufferers headed for darkened bedrooms to wait out the pain. Or they downed powerful painkillers that, for some, led to addiction. And doctors didn't offer much help. Many dismissed the headaches as psychological ailments.

Migraines produce intense, throbbing pain, typically on one side of the head, sometimes accompanied by nausea and sensitivity to light and sound.

But a huge advance in the treatment of migraines came in 1993 when the first triptan medication hit the market. *Sumitriptan,* also known as Imitrex, mimics the neurotransmitter serotonin, the levels of which drop off during migraines.

Then 6 more triptans hit the market. Like other classes of drugs, such as antidepressants and antibiotics, different triptans might work for some people, but not others. So more choices mean more hope for migraine sufferers.

Other treatments which appear to help prevent migraines or reduce their frequency and severity include Botox—better known for its ability to smooth away facial wrinkles—as well as beta blockers and calcium-channel blockers, both used to treat high blood pressure and coronary artery disease, experts say. Antiseizure medications, used to treat epilepsy and bipolar disorders, also show promise for their ability to prevent migraines.

MANY DON'T KNOW ABOUT NEWER TREATMENTS

Many migraine sufferers remain unaware of the triptans and other newer treatments, including the preventive drugs, experts say. This ignorance stems in part from earlier, failed treatment for migraine sufferers, their relatives, or acquaintances, says Dr. Lisa K. Mannix, a neurologist and member of the National Headache Foundation's board of directors.

"People may not come back to the medical system because they may not realize we have better drugs," she says. "People say, 'I went 10 or 15 years ago and got side effects and [the treatment] didn't work.' Or they say, 'It didn't work for my mom, so why should it work for me?'"

Mannix says that approximately 25% of migraine patients could benefit from preventive medications, such as antiseizure drugs, but only 5% take them. "So there's some serious undertreatment going on here," she says.

Besides medication, practical steps such as eating and sleeping well, exercising regularly, and reducing stress can help fight migraines, specialists say. *The Mayo Clinic also suggests that migraine sufferers...*

• **Keep a diary,** which can help you identify migraine triggers.

• **Avoid trigger foods.**

• **Try muscle relaxation exercises** and techniques.

• **Quit smoking.**

But for persistent migraines, Mannix says, "The big thing is you don't have to suffer. We've sort of unraveled some of the mystery, and there's a lot of good treatment available."

info For more on migraines and their treatment, visit the Mayo Clinic at *www. mayoclinic.com.*

5 Steps to Migraine Relief

Eric Wall, MD, MPH, Portland, OR.
November 19, 2002, *Annals of Internal Medicine.*

When doctors asked patients which ailment they wanted to know the most about, headaches topped the list. In response, the 2 largest groups of primary care physicians in the United States developed a set of guidelines for the prevention and treatment of migraines. Their recommendation? Aspirin or ibuprofen should be the first line of therapy.

According to the guidelines, 28 million Americans suffer from these severe, recurring headaches, representing 18% of all women and 6.5% of all men. Approximately half of these people have not been given a diagnosis or remain undertreated.

"These guidelines are really evidence-based, which means they were crafted only after a really rigorous review of the medical literature," says Dr. Eric Wall, a family physician from Portland, Oregon, who represented the American Academy of Family Physicians in the development of the guidelines. "We really had to hammer it out."

The guidelines may be more conservative than many people would like, Wall concedes, but they are a reflection of the available literature.

"Some people will say they don't go far enough, that they don't address new treatments, new therapies," he says. "The guidelines are fairly conservative in their recommendations but, unfortunately, that really reflects the state of the science right now."

A multidisciplinary team from the American College of Physicians–American Society of Internal Medicine and the American Academy of Family Physicians joined forces to help people who suffer from migraines. *Their recommendations are...*

• **The first line of therapy should be nonsteroidal anti-inflammatory drugs** (NSAIDs), with the most reliable appearing to be over-the-counter aspirin and ibuprofen. There is no proof that acetaminophen on its own is effective for migraines.

• **If these drugs don't work, patients and physicians should then move on** to drugs specifically developed for migraines, such as triptans or DHE nasal spray.

• **If patients have nausea or vomiting,** non-oral remedies should be tried first. Nausea and vomiting should also be treated directly.

• **People who have repeated migraines should be evaluated for possible preventive therapy.** Generally, good candidates for preventive measures are patients who have at least 2 migraines that last at least 3 days each month; those who fail to respond to migraine treatment; or those who use medication more than twice a week.

• **Migraine sufferers should be actively involved in formulating their own treatment plan,** the guidelines say. And they should chart their headaches and identify and avoid such triggers as alcohol, chocolate, caffeine, foods containing additives (MSG, tyramine, or nitrates), sleep loss, stress, and perfumes.

Anti-Headache Diet Keeps You Pain-Free

David Marks, Former Medical Director, New England Center for Headache, Stamford, CT, and coauthor of *The Headache Prevention Cookbook—Eating Right to Prevent Migraines and Other Headaches.*
August 2003, *Bottom Line/Health.*

R ed wine and other alcoholic beverages are notorious headache triggers. But several other less-obvious foods and beverages can also cause problems.

Eliminating these foods from your diet can often provide relief and allow you to reduce or stop your use of headache medications.*

Important: Tell your doctor about your diet plans, so he/she can help monitor your progress and adjust your headache treatment accordingly.

Here's how to get started...

IDENTIFY YOUR FOOD TRIGGERS

Dozens of foods can cause migraines and other headaches, but most people are bothered by only a few. To identify the foods that affect you, avoid *all* potential triggers (see the following list) for 2 weeks. If your headaches are in fact food-related, you will observe an improvement.

REINTRODUCE PROHIBITED FOODS

After the 2-week period, resume eating 1 food from the prohibited list each week. If you experience no change, the food is not a headache trigger for you. If your headaches return or worsen, the reintroduced food is probably a trigger and should be permanently eliminated from your diet.

FOODS TO AVOID

• **All alcoholic beverages,** including cooking sherry.

• **All cheeses,** except for American, ricotta, cottage, Velveeta, and cream cheese.

*See your doctor immediately if your headache is worse or "different" than usual...comes on rapidly and severely...first occurs after age 50...and/or is accompanied by neurological symptoms, such as paralysis, slurred speech, or loss of consciousness. These symptoms may indicate an aneurysm, brain tumor, stroke, or some other serious problem.

• **Any food containing monosodium glutamate (MSG) or preservatives,** including those found in canned soups.

• **All seeds and nuts.**

• **All chocolate, carob, and licorice.**

• **Bacon, hot dogs, pepperoni, sausage, salami, bologna, ham,** and all canned, cured, or processed meat products.

• **Pickles, chili peppers, and olives.**

• **Nonorganic dried fruits,** such as raisins, dates, and apricots.

• **Soy sauce, olive oil, and vinegar,** except for white and cider.

• **All artificial sweeteners,** including those found in diet sodas.

• **Non-dry mustard, ketchup, and mayonnaise.**

• **All beans,** including lima, string, garbanzos, and lentils.

• **Whole milk, sour cream, buttermilk, whipped cream, and ice cream.**

FOODS TO LIMIT

• **Tomatoes and onions** (½ cup each per day).

• **Oranges, grapefruits, tangerines, lemons and limes** (½ cup each per day).

• **Bananas** (½ banana per day).

• **Skim-milk yogurt** (½ cup per day).

• **Caffeinated drinks** (16 ounces per day).

Zzzz! Snoring May Cause Headaches!

Jeanetta Rains, PhD, Director, Center for Sleep Evaluation, Elliot Hospital, Manchester, NH, and Adjunct Assistant Professor of Psychiatry, Dartmouth Medical School, Lebanon, NH.
Ann Scher, PhD, Epidemiologist, National Institute on Aging, Bethesda, MD.
April 22, 2003, *Neurology.*

P eople who have headaches every day might actually be bringing them on during the night—by snoring, a research study says.

The study compared the snoring habits of 206 people between the ages of 18 and 65 years who had chronic daily headaches with 507 people who had occasional headaches.

Participants were asked how often they snored—a behavior that's difficult to measure because the subjects are asleep when it occurs—and how often and how severely they experienced headaches.

Because the study relied on self-reported data, the accuracy of the findings may have been compromised. But the researchers took pains to statistically control their results for factors that might confuse the relationship between snoring and headaches. After rigorously separating out confounding factors such as sex, age, and marital status, they found that the relationship between headaches and snoring remained strong.

"These findings point to habitual snoring as a risk factor [for chronic headache] even when they statistically controlled for other known risks for chronic headache and sleep-disordered breathing," says Jeanetta Rains, director of the Center for Sleep Evaluation at Elliot Hospital in Manchester, New Hampshire, and adjunct assistant professor of psychiatry at Dartmouth Medical School.

WHICH CAME FIRST— THE HEADACHE OR THE SNORING?

One crucial question remains unanswered by the study, however: Does the snoring cause the headache or does the headache cause snoring?

Snoring—which occurs when restricted airflow vibrates against the soft tissue of the airway—can cause a drop in the amount of oxygen in the body, resulting in a throbbing headache. But medications used to alleviate headache pain can also disturb sleep and promote snoring.

"We can't really say what the causative relationship is because we assessed the snoring at the same time as we assessed the headaches," says lead author Ann Scher, an epidemiologist at the National Institute on Aging. "Both explanations are reasonable."

To tease out this precise relationship, the researchers said they have to conduct a clinical trial that will examine how treating snoring symptoms affects chronic headaches.

Such a study would require snoring patients to adopt lifestyle changes, such as losing weight, decreasing alcohol consumption, and avoiding sleeping on their backs to curb their snoring behavior.

"Those individuals who wake up with a headache almost every morning should be asked about snoring," says Rains.

info You can find out more about headaches from the American Council for Headache Education (*www.achenet.org*). The American Sleep Apnea Association (*www. sleepapnea.org*) provides information about how snoring may be affecting your daytime activities.

Fast Relief for Fibromyalgia—Aerobics

July 25, 2002, *British Medical Journal.*

Aerobic exercise appears to be a simple and effective treatment for people with fibromyalgia, a condition that includes chronic muscular pain and unexplained joint tenderness.

To test that theory, a group of British researchers recruited 132 people with fibromyalgia and assigned them to either aerobic exercise classes or relaxation classes. The classes were held twice a week for 12 weeks. The class instructors were personal trainers with no special experience in training people with medical problems.

After 3 months, more of the people taking aerobic exercise classes rated themselves as feeling "much better" or "very much better" than did those taking the relaxation classes. Those benefits were the same or improved after a year, the study says.

The authors say that the findings, which appear in the *British Medical Journal*, show the benefits of aerobic exercise for people with fibromyalgia and that the exercise doesn't require specially trained instructors.

However, they also say high dropout rates can be a problem in exercise treatment programs; this issue still needs to be studied.

WHAT IS FIBROMYALGIA?

The American College of Rheumatology estimates that 3 to 6 million Americans, primarily women of childbearing age, are affected by fibromyalgia. Fibromyalgia is a chronic disorder characterized by widespread musculoskeletal pain, fatigue, and multiple "trigger points." These are the precise, localized areas (particularly the neck, spine, shoulders, and hips) where tenderness occurs. People with this syndrome may also experience sleep disturbances, morning stiffness, irritable bowel syndrome, anxiety, and other symptoms.

WHAT CAUSES IT?

Although the cause is unknown, researchers have several theories about causes or triggers of the disorder. Some scientists believe that the syndrome may be caused by an injury or trauma. This injury may affect the central nervous system. Fibromyalgia may be associated with changes in muscle metabolism, such as decreased blood flow, causing fatigue and decreased strength. Others believe an infectious agent may trigger the syndrome, but no such agent has been identified.

HOW IS IT DIAGNOSED?

Fibromyalgia is difficult to diagnose because many of the symptoms mimic those of other disorders. The physician reviews the patient's medical history and makes a diagnosis of fibromyalgia on the basis of a history of chronic widespread pain that persists for more than 3 months. The American College of Rheumatology has developed criteria for fibromyalgia that physicians can use in diagnosing the disorder. A person is considered to have fibromyalgia if he or she has widespread pain in combination with tenderness in at least 11 of 18 specific trigger point sites.

HOW IS IT TREATED?

Treatment requires a comprehensive approach. The physician, physical therapist, and patient may all play an active role in the management of fibromyalgia. Studies, like the one above, have shown that aerobic exercise, such as swimming and walking, improves muscle fitness and reduces muscle pain and tenderness. Heat and massage may also give short-term relief. Antidepressant medications may help elevate mood, improve quality of sleep, and relax muscles. Patients with fibromyalgia may benefit from a combination of exercise, medication, physical therapy, and relaxation.

New Hope for Transplant Patients

Karl Beutner, MD, PhD, Associate Clinical Professor, Dermatology, University of California, San Francisco. July 4, 2002, *New England Journal of Medicine.*

The same vaccine that keeps children from getting chicken pox can lessen the pain of shingles in adults who have had a bone marrow transplant or have otherwise suppressed immune systems.

Approximately 1 in 5 persons who contract chicken pox will eventually suffer a bout of *shingles,* although no one knows exactly why the virus shows up again in this form. Shingles, also known as *herpes zoster,* commonly plagues transplant patients during the year following the procedure as a consequence of immunosuppressing drugs given to prevent organ rejection. It also shows up in other people who have weakened immune systems.

Shingles initially strikes at nerve endings of the skin, leading to severe pain and a rash. However, in people with weakened immunity, the virus can affect internal organs, too.

Shingles could be fatal for these patients; it's "at the very least miserable," says Dr. Karl Beutner, a dermatologist at the University of California at San Francisco. The fact that boosting immunity helps prevent shingles supports the theory that the virus stays dormant in the nervous system and awakens when the body's defenses falter, Beutner adds.

THE FINDINGS

A report on the findings of Dr. Ann Arvin, an infection expert at Stanford University School of Medicine, and her colleagues appeared in the *New England Journal of Medicine.*

Arvin's group used a weakened version of the chicken pox vaccine on 53 transplant patients. The vaccine was administered once before the transplant operation and 3 times afterward over a period of months.

The results: Only 13% of the patients who received the vaccine developed shingles, compared with 30% who weren't inoculated.

info For more on shingles, visit the American Academy of Dermatology at *www.aad.org/pamphlets*. Click on "Herpes Zoster" under the heading Viral Disease Topics.

Better Way to Repair Hernias

Celia M. Divino, MD, Director, Minimally Invasive Surgery, Maimonides Medical Center, Brooklyn, NY.
David L. Stoker, MD, Consultant Surgeon and Director, Surgery, North Middlesex University Hospital, London, England.
May 10, 2003, *British Medical Journal*.

Repairing hernias with laparoscopic surgery results in far fewer complications than conventional surgery does.

Five years after a hernia operation, study patients who'd had a laparoscopic procedure reported less pain or discomfort than those who had undergone conventional repair.

The findings challenge the recommendations of the National Institute for Clinical Excellence in Britain, which has recommended that conventional "open repair" surgery be favored over other methods. And the data will almost certainly add momentum to a trend favoring laparoscopy for this type of procedure, says Dr. Celia M. Divino, director of minimally invasive surgery at Maimonides Medical Center.

Laparoscopic surgery involves making only a small incision, then placing a tiny video camera inside the abdominal cavity to guide the surgeon. Traditional surgery to repair inguinal hernias—when part of the intestine bulges through muscles in the groin area—has involved repairing the opening in the muscle wall. Sometimes the area is also reinforced with a mesh patch.

TRADITIONAL SURGERY STILL STANDARD

"Open repair is still standard for several reasons," Divino says. "Open repair is usually done under local anesthesia. Laparoscopy is done under general [in which the patient is unconscious], so you have to choose your patients carefully because not everybody is a candidate for general anesthesia."

In the United Kingdom, says Dr. David L. Stoker, study author and a director of surgery at North Middlesex University Hospital in London, 95% of the approximately 100,000 hernia repairs done every year are still open repair. Hernia repair is considered an intermediate-grade surgery—not major surgery, but not like having a tooth pulled, either. "They're very important because there are so many of them. Hernia mainly affects working men, so economically it's a very important operation. It's important to get people back to work," Stoker says.

Stoker and his colleagues randomly assigned patients to either open hernia repair or laparoscopic surgery at 2 London hospitals. At the end of 5 years, they reviewed the progress of 242 patients, 120 of whom had had open repair and 122 of whom had had the laparoscopic procedure.

Nearly half the patients in the open repair group had complications, compared with only 11% in the laparoscopic group. Only patients in the open repair group experienced serious complications. Recurrence rates were nearly identical for both groups.

info For more on hernia and hernia repair, visit the National Digestive Diseases Information Clearinghouse at *www.digestive.niddk.nih.gov* and click on "Digestive Diseases" or visit the British Hernia Centre at *www.hernia.org*.

■ ■ ■ ■

The Most Common Types of Hernias

A hernia occurs when part of an organ (usually the intestine) protrudes through a weak point or tear in the thin muscular wall that holds the abdominal organs in place. *The*

National Institutes of Health's MedlinePLUS archive lists the most common types of hernias...

INGUINAL HERNIA

An *inguinal* hernia is when a loop of intestine enters the inguinal canal, a tubular passage through the lower layers of the abdominal wall. Usually, there is no apparent cause of a hernia, although they are sometimes associated with heavy lifting.

In men, a hernia can develop in the groin near the scrotum. A direct inguinal hernia creates a bulge in the groin area, and an indirect hernia descends into the scrotum. Inguinal hernias occur less often in women than men.

A family history of hernias increases the risk. Those with cystic fibrosis and undescended testicles are also more susceptible to inguinal hernias.

Symptoms of inguinal hernias...

●**Groin discomfort or groin pain** aggravated by bending or lifting.

●**A tender groin lump or scrotum lump.**

●**A bulge or lump** can usually be seen in children.

HIATAL HERNIA

A *hiatal hernia* occurs when a portion of the stomach protrudes upward into the chest through an opening in the diaphragm (the sheet of muscle used in breathing that separates the chest from the abdomen).

The cause is unknown, but hiatal hernias may be the result of a weakening of the supporting tissue. Increasing age, obesity, and smoking seem to be risk factors in adults. Children with this condition usually have it present at birth (congenital). It is usually associated with gastroesophageal reflux in infants.

Hiatal hernias are very common, especially in people over 50 years old. This condition can cause regurgitation of gastric acid from the stomach into the esophagus.

Symptoms of hiatal hernia...

●**Heartburn,** which gets worse when bending over or lying down.

●**Difficulty swallowing.**

●**Chest pain.**

●**Belching.**

Note: Frequently there are no symptoms.

DIAPHRAGMATIC HERNIA

A congenital *diaphragmatic hernia* is an abnormal opening in the diaphragm that allows part of the abdominal organs to migrate into the chest cavity. This occurs before birth.

A diaphragmatic hernia is caused by the improper fusion of structures during fetal development. The abdominal organs such as the stomach, small intestine, spleen, part of the liver, and the kidney appear in the chest cavity. The lung tissue on the affected side is thus not allowed to completely develop. Respiratory distress usually develops shortly after the baby is born because of ineffective movement of the diaphragm and crowding of the lung tissue which causes collapse. The reason why this occurs is not known.

Symptoms of diaphragmatic hernia...

●**Severe breathing difficulty.**

●**Bluish coloration of the skin** due to lack of oxygen.

●**Fast breathing.**

●**Asymmetry of the chest wall.**

●**Fast heart rate.**

INCISIONAL HERNIA

Incisions (from a previous surgery, for example) can leave the muscles weak in an area, and a hernia can form at the incision site. Incisional hernias may not appear until after straining, heavy lifting, or a prolonged period of coughing.

WHEN TO GET HELP

Seek appropriate care for chronic coughs or for constipation if you have a hernia. Straining associated with these conditions causes the intestines to protrude further into the hernia.

Call your health care provider if...

●**A hernia becomes progressively larger, discolored, or painful.**

●**A person with a hernia develops fever,** vomiting, abnormal appearance of the hernia, or if the hernia is painful or tender. A strangulated hernia (one in which the blood supply is lost to the organs that protrude through the hernia) is a medical emergency!

14

Research News

6 New Lifesaving Discoveries for Heart Patients

Heart pacemakers, in their original form, were actually outside of the patient's body. Currently, pacemaker devices are surgically implanted in the patient's body and they may last as long as 7 to 10 years.

And, now, a pacemaker is approximately the size of 3 silver dollars.

Advances like the improved pacemaker have caused dramatic decreases in the death rates from heart disease and stroke. Nevertheless, heart disease remains the number 1 killer in the United States. *Here are some of the more exciting fields of research, areas that hold promise for slashing the number of deaths from this disease even more in the future…*

• **Drug-eluting stents may be the next big thing in cardiology.** Stents are routinely used to prop open arteries that have been cleared by angioplasty. But they also provoke inflammation and scarring, which can cause the artery to close again. The new stents are coated with a drug that fights the inflammation and scarring. A large US trial demonstrated a 75% reduction in the restenosis, or renarrowing, of the vessel.

"It's looking like in many, many cases these will be as durable as surgery. That's big," says Dr. Jeffrey W. Moses, chief of interventional cardiology at Lenox Hill Heart and Vascular Institute in New York City.

• **Pharmaceuticals continue to be developed at a rapid pace.** Dozens of companies are working on more than 100 new medicines

Jeffrey W. Moses, MD, Chief, Interventional Cardiology, Lenox Hill Heart and Vascular Institute, New York, NY.

Richard A. Stein, MD, Spokesman, American Heart Association, and Professor, Clinical Medicine, Weill Cornell School of Medicine, and Chief, Cardiology, Brooklyn Hospital Center, NY.

to prevent or treat heart disease and its cousin, stroke.

"We're building a knowledge base but we're also learning a lot of pragmatic things, like inexpensive drugs that can do what expensive drugs do," says Dr. Richard A. Stein, a spokesman for the American Heart Association and chief of cardiology at Brooklyn Hospital Center in New York City.

● **Genetic studies will provide a lot of the big excitement in the coming years.** "We're beginning to understand how [genes] relate to disease, and we're looking at them as possible targets, either through genetic manipulation or through altering their means of expressing themselves," Stein says.

● **Technology is making possible advances from defibrillators in homes and airports to hand-held,** portable electrocardiogram (EKG) machines. Microprocessors may one day allow the opening of arteries from the inside without the worry of them closing up again.

● **Muscle cells may soon be grown in the laboratory,** then injected back into a patient's heart through the coronary arteries. This would regenerate the damaged heart of people who have had heart failure.

NO MORE SURGERY?

● **Open-heart surgery could eventually be a thing of the past,** thanks to innovations such as the drug-eluting stent and the ability to repair or replace valves without opening the chest. Bypasses are now being done without the heart-lung machine, and robotic arms can do precise stitching through tiny holes.

THE LAST FRONTIER

Scientific breakthroughs will help people immeasurably in the future. But there's one frontier that may be the toughest to conquer.

"We're not any better at getting people to eat right, and all of science will not overcome a terribly unhealthy lifestyle," says Dr. Stein of the American Heart Association. "One of the things I look forward to is behavioral therapy being able to assist folks."

Manmade Arteries Will Save Thousands of Bypass Patients

Chris Counter, PhD, Assistant Professor, Pharmacology and Cancer Biology, Duke University School of Medicine, Durham, NC.

Augustus O. Grant, MD, 2003–04 President, American Heart Association, and Professor, Medicine, Duke University School of Medicine, Durham, NC.
June 6, 2003, *EMBO Reports*.

By finding a way to keep smooth muscle cells dividing indefinitely, scientists have managed to fashion the first-ever human arteries from non-embryonic tissue in a laboratory. Eventually, these engineered human arteries may be available for routine use in coronary artery bypass surgery.

"We took a task that was previously thought to be impossible and now put it in the realm of the possible," says Chris Counter, co-senior author of a paper detailing the discovery.

Dr. Augustus O. Grant, of the American Heart Association and a professor of medicine at Duke University School of Medicine, praised the work and said it was a big step in heart research.

The majority of coronary artery bypass grafting in the United States uses blood vessels that have been harvested from somewhere else on the patient's body, usually from the legs. But each year, some 100,000 people who need small-vessel grafts can't get them because their own veins are unsuitable.

One major obstacle has been the fact that smooth muscle cells, which form the outer wall of the vessels, have not survived long enough in culture to be able to develop a sturdy artery. The authors of the study borrowed from cancer biology to find a solution.

Each cell chromosome has a section called a *telomere*. Each time a cell divides, the telomere shortens until, after a certain number of divisions, the telomere becomes so short it sends a signal to the cell to stop dividing—the biological equivalent of planned obsolescence.

Researchers inserted a gene to shut off the signal that tells the cell to stop dividing, which made the cells live longer. Longer-living cells meant the scientists had time to construct their arteries.

RESEARCH CONTINUES

The authors estimate that it could take as long as a decade before these arteries are in routine use in operating rooms.

More long-term studies are needed to show the durability of these vessels. Scientists also want to make the entire vessel out of one person's cells several times. Counter says his group has already repeated the accomplishment with cells from one person.

The researchers also want to make sure the signal can be turned on again. "We want to erase all signs that we manipulated the cells before it goes back into the patient," Counter says.

ABOUT CORONARY BYPASS SURGERY

According to the Texas Heart Institute, bypass surgery is the most common type of heart surgery. More than 300,000 people have successful bypass surgery in the United States each year.

Arteries can become clogged over time by the buildup of fatty plaque. Bypass surgery improves the blood flow to the heart with a new route, or bypass, around a section of clogged or diseased artery.

Lifesaving Test Predicts Heart Trouble in the 'Healthy'

Patrick G. O'Malley, MD, MPH, Chief, Division of General and Internal Medicine, Walter Reed Army Medical Center, Washington, DC.

May 13, 2003, *Circulation.*

Put to the test, an imaging process called *electron beam computed tomography* (EBCT or EBT) warned of future cardiovascular trouble in healthy, seemingly trouble-free individuals.

"Half of deaths due to heart disease occur in people with no symptoms," Dr. George T. Kondos, who was head of the team that did the test, says in a statement. "And one-third of people with heart disease don't have any of the traditional risk factors—diabetes, high blood pressure, high cholesterol, family history, or peripheral vascular disease. Those individuals would go undetected by traditional screening methods."

EBCT detects a different source of trouble —calcium deposits in artery walls that can eventually be blocked, causing a heart attack or stroke. It is a fast form of X-ray imaging technology that can be done in a few minutes.

More than 5600 men and women were given the test by Kondos, who is an associate professor of medicine at the University of Illinois College of Medicine in Chicago. The participants were divided into 4 groups, depending on the extent of calcium deposits found by an EBCT scan.

Over the next $3\frac{1}{2}$ years, men in the highest quarter of calcium scores were 2.3 times more likely to die or have a heart attack and 10.1 times more likely to have bypass surgery or artery-clearing angioplasty than those in the lowest quarter, the report says. There were no comparable figures on deaths and heart attacks for women, because few of them occurred, but the incidence of bypass surgery or angioplasty was 3.6 times higher for those in the highest quarter compared with those in the lowest.

STUDY HELPS RESOLVE RUNNING DEBATE

"This is an important advance in the study of this technology," says Dr. Patrick G. O'Malley, an EBCT expert and chief of the division of general and internal medicine at Walter Reed Army Medical Center in Washington, DC.

The research helps resolve a running debate on EBCT's effectiveness. "It is an open question whether it can predict over and above the conventional risk factors," O'Malley says.

O'Malley led a study showing that EBCT readings must be followed up by doctors to make sure people with high scores pay careful attention to the conventional risk factors to prevent heart attack and stroke.

Whether EBCT is cost-effective is a question that still must be answered.

Soon to Come...Surefire Way to Treat Heart Failure

David A. Kass, MD, Professor, Medicine and Biomedical Engineering, Johns Hopkins Medical Institutions, Baltimore, MD.

Martin Feelisch, PhD, Professor, Physiology, Louisiana State University Health Science Center, Shreveport.

April 14–18, 2003, *Proceedings of the National Academy of Sciences.*

According to researchers at Johns Hopkins Medical Institutions, a new kind of drug may provide all the benefits of nitroglycerine in treating heart failure, but none of its deficiencies.

Nitroglycerine works by releasing a chemical called nitric oxide in the body. Although it does help a weakened heart get blood to the body by widening blood vessels, it has its downside. It blunts the system that powers the heart's contractions. "It's like having your foot on the brake when you're driving," explains Dr. David A. Kass, a professor of medicine and biomedical engineering at Johns Hopkins. The new compound doesn't have that defect.

Kass talked with Dr. David Wink, a researcher at the National Cancer Institute, who had been doing some work with nitroxyl anion, a molecule of nitric oxide with one electron added. Wink's work indicated that nitroxyl anion might damage the heart, but Kass and Wink thought it looked interesting enough to warrant a closer look. "I handed it to one of my postdoctoral students, a little like a fishing expedition," Kass says.

Lab work showed that nitroxyl anion not only widens blood vessels, but strengthens the force of the heart's contractions. Dr. Nazareno Paolocci, a scientist in Kass's group, took over, pushing the studies to see whether that effect could be put to medical use.

PROMISING RESEARCH

There is great promise in the research, says Martin Feelisch, a professor of physiology at the Louisiana State University Health Sciences Center. "What is new here is the appreciation that a very primitive molecule, nitric oxide with just one electron more, has completely different properties."

The compound used in the study "is not the breakthrough drug that will make it through to clinical trials," Feelisch says. "But the trial does show that with this principle, it is possible to come up with a new pharmacological way to improve the contractability of the heart."

Kass's laboratory has developed "a completely new nitroxyl anion donor that is almost 100 percent effective" and could eventually result in a simple pill for people with heart failure.

Nicotine Vaccine May Help Smokers Kick The Habit

Kim D. Janda, PhD, Professor, Chemistry, The Scripps Research Institute, La Jolla, CA.

June 18, 2003, *Journal of the American Chemical Society.*

A nicotine vaccine shows promise in ending nicotine addiction and helping smokers kick the habit, researchers say.

The vaccine allows the immune system to provide potent antibodies to remove nicotine from the body before it reaches the brain, says lead researcher Kim D. Janda, a professor of chemistry at The Scripps Research Institute in La Jolla, California.

The vaccine could act as a crutch for people trying to stop smoking by preventing nicotine from reaching the brain, Janda says.

Janda's team had already developed a successful cocaine vaccine, but when they first developed a nicotine vaccine, the researchers found it wasn't very effective.

Janda says the researchers didn't understand why the early nicotine vaccine was ineffective, since the nicotine and cocaine molecules are similar. When they went back and looked more closely, they found the cocaine molecule was restricted in its movement but the nicotine molecule wasn't.

FURTHER STUDY NEEDED

The next step in the development of this new vaccine is to do more studies; it has only been tested in mice and rats. Once the researchers have more evidence that the vaccine is safe, it will be ready for clinical human trials.

The vaccine is designed to help smokers during the critical first 90 days of smoking cessation, when many relapse. The vaccine has been tested in 2 forms. The active form requires that people receive boosters, which would be effective for several months; in its passive form people would be given the antibodies, which last for a few weeks.

■ ■ ■ ■

About Nicotine

The National Institute on Drug Abuse (*www.nida.nih.gov*) has information on nicotine. *The facts...*

●**Nicotine is the drug in tobacco that causes addiction.**

●**Nicotine is one of the most heavily used addictive drugs in the United States.**

●**Smoking is a major cause of stroke,** heart attack, and lung cancer, all of which are leading causes of death in the US.

●**Nicotine taken in by cigarette or cigar smoking takes only seconds to reach the brain** but has a direct effect on the body for up to 30 minutes.

●**With regular use of tobacco,** levels of nicotine accumulate in the body during the day and persist overnight. Thus, daily smokers or chewers are exposed to the effects of nicotine for 24 hours each day.

Researchers Find Gene That May Halt Spread Of Cancer

Dan Theodorescu, MD, PhD, Professor, Urology and Molecular Physiology, University of Virginia Health System, Charlottesville.
Duane Superneau, MD, Chief, Medical Genetics, Ochsner Clinic Foundation, New Orleans, LA.
November 15, 2002, *Cancer Research*.

Imagine the ability to slow or even stop the spread of aggressive forms of cancer. Scientists are working on it after identifying a gene that may have that effect in some cancer cells.

The gene is missing or present in low levels in invasive, spreading cancer, according to a study by researchers at the University of Virginia. The gene's absence may point to the cancer's potential to spread, says Dr. Dan Theodorescu, a professor of urology and molecular physiology at the university. This finding could lead to new tests to help doctors determine the best way to treat individual cancers, and eventually could lead to gene therapy to treat aggressive cancers.

Cancer can develop only when the body's functions go awry. Normally, human cells grow to replace old, dying cells. If new cells form when the body doesn't need them and older cells don't die off, a tumor develops from all those extra cells. Some tumors are benign and generally don't cause problems. Others are malignant and can invade and damage other cells, traveling to other parts of the body.

To isolate the gene in question, Theodorescu and his team compared 2 types of bladder cancer—1 aggressive and invasive, the other localized and nonspreading. They found that people with the aggressive form of cancer had low levels of a gene known as RhoGDI2.

UNDER THE MICROSCOPE

The researchers also examined tumors from prostate, lung, breast, colorectal, gastroesophageal, kidney, liver, ovarian, and pancreatic cancers to see if they would find reduced levels of the RhoGDI2 gene in these cancers—and they did.

Theodorescu says it could be possible to develop a test to look for levels of the gene in tumors,. which would let doctors treat their patients more accurately and effectively. For example, someone with low levels of RhoGDI2 might be a good candidate for chemotherapy, since it is likely the tumor will be more aggressive. After more research, it might be possible to replace the gene in cancer patients so their cancer doesn't spread, he says.

Dr. Duane Superneau, chief of medical genetics at the Ochsner Clinic Foundation in New Orleans, says the gene could act as a marker for the early detection of aggressive cancer. He points out that the gene doesn't appear to affect the growth of the tumor, but the tumor wouldn't spread. That means cancer patients would still need to have surgery to have the tumor removed, but might not need chemotherapy afterward because the cancer cells wouldn't have spread to other sites in the body.

info The National Cancer Institute's Web site, *www.cancer.gov,* has comprehensive resources and support on cancers and how genetics plays a role in the disease.

Experimental Drug Shrinks Liver Tumors

Jean-Francois Geschwind, MD, Associate Professor of Medicine and Radiology, and Director, Interventional Radiology, Johns Hopkins Medical Institutions, Baltimore, MD.

Peter Pedersen, PhD, Professor, Biological Chemistry, Johns Hopkins School of Medicine, Baltimore, MD.

July 15, 2002, *Cancer Research.*

A sugar-derived chemical saps energy-thirsty liver cancer cells, starving them while apparently leaving healthy cells alone, say Johns Hopkins University scientists. The chemical, *3-bromopyruvate*, destroys liver cancer and also shrinks tumors that have spread from that organ into the lungs, say the

researchers. The substance is related to a molecule that occurs naturally in the breakdown of sugar.

The researchers have only tested the chemical on rabbits and say they have to make sure the drug doesn't harm normal tissue before they test it on humans. However, if it is benign, it might one day be a therapy for other forms of tumors, as well.

Liver cancer, which has been linked to the hepatitis B virus, strikes approximately 16,600 Americans a year and accounts for roughly 1% of tumor deaths in the United States.

Approximately half of all patients can be cured. However, for those with inoperable liver cancer, or metastatic tumors that have spread from the colon, surviving for a year is a feat.

HOW THE TUMOR FEEDS

A unique feature of liver tumors is that while they draw their nutrients from an artery, the organ itself is fed separately by the portal vein. In theory, it's possible to target cancerous cells by injecting drugs directly into arterial blood, yet do minimal damage to the surrounding organ.

The researchers in the study, which appeared in *Cancer Research*, attempted such a strategy.

Led by radiologist Dr. Jean-Francois Geschwind, the scientists gave injections of 3-bromopyruvate to rabbits with liver cancer.

The chemical drains cells of their energy in 2 ways…

●**By suppressing their ability to use glucose for fuel,** and

●**By hindering internal power plants** called *mitochondria* from making the energy molecule *adenosine triphosphate* (ATP).

Because cancer cells need glucose to support their frenetic growth, a drug that selectively destroys tissues that demand sugar will work to kill the tumors.

Indeed, a single injection of the drug into the artery supplying the tumors led to "dramatic" shrinkage of the masses, Geschwind says. "By being able to thread a catheter and get close to the tumor, we can deliver agents in much higher concentrations directly to the tumor. You can really kill the tumor that way," he adds.

HEALTHY CELLS WERE SPARED

"We would have expected some collateral damage, but in this case the specificity of the drug and the method of administering it made a perfect marriage," Geschwind says.

Some of the rabbits developed liver cancer nodules in their lungs. So the researchers then injected 3-bromopyruvate directly into their bloodstream through a vessel in their ears. Again, the tumors shrank markedly, but the animals appeared otherwise unscathed, says Peter Pedersen, a Johns Hopkins biochemist and a coauthor of the study.

"We didn't find problems with toxicity, but we don't know what the long-term [outlook] is," Pedersen says. The treatment was gentler on normal cells than a current therapy for liver cancer called chemoembolization, in which doctors inject drugs into the tumors while using an oil solution to block off the artery that feeds them.

info To learn more about liver cancer, check out the American Liver Foundation at *www.liverfoundation.org.*

Scientists May Soon Help The Liver to Heal Itself

Adrian M. Di Bisceglie, MD, Chairman, American Liver Foundation's Hepatitis Council, New York.

Leonard I. Zon, MD, Professor, Pediatrics, Children's Hospital and Harvard Medical School, Boston, MA.

Napoleone Ferrara, MD, Senior Investigator, Genentech Inc., San Francisco, CA.

February 7, 2003, *Science.*

Your liver has the unique ability to regenerate itself, and scientists hope that by examining how that happens they can help the millions of people suffering from cirrhosis, liver cancer, and chronic hepatitis.

"You can take three-quarters of somebody's liver, and within 2 weeks it grows back to its original size," says Dr. Adrian Di Bisceglie,

chairman of the American Liver Foundation's Hepatitis Council. "It's really a marvel."

Needless to say, scientists have studied this phenomenon with great interest and have, in fact, identified various growth factors that contribute to the process.

Researchers at Genentech Inc. have discovered an additional pathway that plays a part in liver growth.

After injecting toxin into laboratory mice to damage their livers, the researchers observed that the injured cells released a growth hormone that sent commands to nearby endothelial cells, which line the blood vessels. The endothelial cells then responded by releasing growth factors that, in turn, caused the liver cells to multiply, thus helping the liver to regenerate.

"It's an intimate communication between the cell populations," says Dr. Leonard I. Zon, a professor of pediatrics at Children's Hospital and Harvard Medical School in Boston.

Scientists had known that liver cells could tell endothelial cells to multiply, but the second half of the process was a surprise, Zon says.

In another experiment, the researchers neutralized the growth hormone and then induced liver damage. They found that neutralizing the growth hormone either before or after inducing damage greatly increased liver cell death. This strongly suggests that the growth hormone has a role in protecting the liver.

The goal: Enhancing the liver's healing qualities.

Scientists hope to learn how to stimulate the liver's internal mechanism for taking care of itself.

"This could have beneficial effects in liver damage whether due to drugs, alcohol, or perhaps viral hepatitis," says Dr. Napoleone Ferrara, senior author of the study and a senior investigator at Genentech in San Francisco.

Sometime in the distant future, this could be used not only to prevent liver disease—say, immediately after someone has been exposed to a toxin—but to try to rejuvenate the liver after damage has already occurred, Zon says.

The discoveries are exciting but aren't likely to translate into tangible gains anytime soon.

"There's a big gap between this and actual real treatment," Di Bisceglie notes.

■ ■ ■ ■

Signs of Liver Trouble

The American Liver Foundation (*www.liver foundation.org*) has information on all aspects of liver health. *Here are the 5 signs of liver trouble...*

- **Yellow discoloration of the skin or eyes.**

- **Abdominal swelling** or severe abdominal pain.

- **Prolonged itching of the skin.**

- **Very dark urine or pale stools,** or the passage of bloody or tar-like stools.

- **Chronic fatigue,** nausea, or loss of appetite.

If you experience any of these symptoms, contact your doctor.

New Hepatitis B Drug Blocks Liver Damage, With Fewer Side Effects

Patrick Marcellin, MD, Hopital Beaujon, Clichy, France.

Hari Conjeevaram, MD, Assistant Professor, Medicine, University of Michigan School of Medicine, Ann Arbor.

February 27, 2003, *New England Journal of Medicine.*

A drug already approved by the US Food and Drug Administration shows promise in halting liver damage in people with chronic hepatitis B without the side effects of the current treatments.

The FDA approved *adefovir dipivoxil* in 2002, but studies supporting its effectiveness had not been fully published, says Dr. Patrick Marcellin, lead author of 1 of 2 studies on the drug.

The 2 existing drugs used in the treatment of chronic hepatitis B both have drawbacks. *Interferon alfa* has side effects like flu-like symptoms and depression. And *lamivudine* can generate a mutation in the virus, making it resistant to the drug.

Adefovir dipivoxil was originally developed to treat HIV and appears to sidestep both these problems.

"The main advantage of adefovir is that you don't see the mutations in the virus that you see with lamivudine," said Dr. Hari Conjeevaram, an assistant professor of medicine at the University of Michigan School of Medicine.

In the first year, approximately 15% to 25% of patients with hepatitis B develop resistance to lamivudine, Conjeevaram says, with the number increasing each year thereafter if the medication is continued.

THE STUDIES

The first study looked at 185 patients with the type of hepatitis B that is inactive and does not need to be treated ("negative"). Each patient was randomly assigned to receive either 10 milligrams adefovir or a placebo once a day for 48 weeks.

Liver biopsies at the end of the study period revealed that 64% of adefovir patients showed improvement in the condition of their liver, compared with only 33% of patients in the placebo group. In addition, levels of hepatitis B virus in the blood were reduced to undetectable amounts in 51% of the patients receiving adefovir.

The second study looked at 515 patients with the "positive" form of the disease. This type of hepatitis B is active and needs to be treated. Each patient was randomly assigned to receive 10 milligrams adefovir, 30 milligrams adefovir, or a placebo for 48 weeks.

At 48 weeks, 53% of patients receiving the 10-milligram dose, 59% of those taking 30 milligrams, and 25% of the placebo group showed improvements in their liver function. Virus levels dropped 21% in the 10-milligram group and 39% in the 30-milligram group.

Most important, neither study showed the virus was becoming resistant to the drug, and there were negligible side effects.

■ ■ ■ ■

What You Should Know About Hepatitis B

The Hepatitis B Foundation Web site (*www.hepb.org*) can tell you more about this disease. *Here are the highlights...*

•**Hepatitis B is the most common serious liver infection in the world.** It is caused by the hepatitis B virus (HBV), which attacks liver cells and can lead to liver failure, cirrhosis (scarring), or cancer of the liver.

•**The virus is transmitted through contact with blood** and bodily fluids that contain blood.

•**Most people are able to fight off an HBV infection** and clear the virus from their blood. However, 5% to 10% of adults, 30% to 50% of children, and 90% of babies will not get rid of the virus and will develop a chronic infection.

•**Chronically infected people can pass the virus to others** and are at increased risk for liver problems later in life.

•**HBV is 100 times more infectious than the AIDS virus.** Yet hepatitis B can be prevented with a safe and effective vaccine. All sex partners, family, and close household members of a chronically infected person should be screened and vaccinated. For those who are chronically infected with HBV, the vaccine is of no use.

Scientists Discover a Protein That Grows Hair!

David Van Mater, MD, PhD candidate, Human Genetics Department, University of Michigan Medical School, Ann Arbor.

Andrzej Dlugosz, MD, Associate Professor of Dermatology, University of Michigan Medical School, Ann Arbor.

May 15, 2003, *Genes & Development*.

David Van Mater was trying to grow tumors, but ended up growing hair instead. His discovery could be good news for people struggling with certain types of hair loss.

Van Mater, a University of Michigan graduate student, was researching the activities of a protein called *beta-catenin* in mice as part of an investigation into colon cancer.

The researchers wanted to see if they could induce tumors by activating beta-catenin, and get rid of the tumors by turning off the protein. They applied a chemical called 4-OHT, which activates beta-catenin, to shaved areas on the backs of lab mice.

SURPRISING FINDINGS

To their surprise, no tumors appeared, but they did see exaggerated growth of hair follicle cells along with other changes in the skin sections that seemed to indicate the hair was in its growth phase, rather than what would be consistent with the regrowth that usually occurs after shaving. Adult hair follicles go through a cycle consisting of periods of growth, regression, and rest.

Dr. Andrzej Dlugosz, an associate professor of dermatology at the University of Michigan Medical School, suggested turning on the beta-catenin for just a short period of time, instead of the longer period.

NORMAL GROWTH CYCLE

The scientists started over, applying 4-OHT once, instead of every day, and doing it during the follicles' resting stage. After 15 days, the mice had grown new hair that was exactly the same as the old hair, and went through the growth cycle as if it were normal.

To Van Mater, the most interesting aspect was that just by turning on the beta-catenin for a short period of time, the researchers were able to put in place the full complex series of events for hair to regenerate.

"The nice thing is that briefly turning on 1 molecule can activate the entire process, and it's a very complicated process," adds Dlugosz. But simply turning on the process is not enough to reverse male pattern baldness.

info For information about hair loss, visit the American Academy of Dermatology at *www.aad.org*.

■ ■ ■ ■

Myths About Hair Loss

The American Hair Loss Council (*www. ahlc.org*) can direct you to a hair-loss specialist in your area. *They have also compiled the most common myths about hair loss...*

●**Frequent shampooing** contributes to hair loss.

●**Hats and wigs** cause hair loss.

●**100 strokes with the hairbrush daily** will create healthier hair.

●**Permanent hair loss is caused by perms,** colors, and other cosmetic treatments.

●**Women are expected to develop significant hair loss** if they are healthy.

●**Shaving one's head will cause the hair to grow back thicker.**

●**Standing on one's head will stimulate hair growth.**

Important News for Vietnam Vets

Jeanne Mager Stellman, PhD, Professor, Clinical Public Health, Mailman School of Public Health, Columbia University, New York, NY.

Arnold Schecter, MD, Professor, Environmental Sciences, University of Texas–Houston School of Public Health, Dallas.

John Sommer, Executive Director, American Legion, Washington, DC.

April 17, 2003, *Nature*.

The American and South Vietnamese military forces sprayed much more Agent Orange over Vietnam than earlier estimates suggested.

A precise accounting of how much plant-killing chemicals were used during the war, and where, could help public health researchers better understand the impact of the cancer-causing chemical dioxin, which is contained in Agent Orange, says Jeanne Mager Stellman, a Columbia University chemist and leader of the study.

Earlier estimates reckoned that between 1962 and 1971, US-led forces sprayed 18 million gallons of Agent Orange in Vietnam. The Army also sprayed smaller quantities of other agents, including Pink, Blue, and Purple, to clear the lush region, which included Laos and Cambodia. The military deployed defoliants from airplanes, helicopters, boats, and backpacks.

The new research expands by about 1.82 million gallons the amount of Agent Orange and other defoliants used to thin the jungle. The estimate was gleaned from data from specific spraying missions; information that wasn't previously analyzed.

The researchers, who compared army mission logs and village resettlement activities, also estimate that more than 4 million Vietnamese men, women, and children probably were exposed to dioxin in the spraying. And roughly 2.7 million US soldiers served in Vietnam and Southeast Asia during the war years.

Dioxin persists in the environment and is still entering the food supply in Vietnam, says Dr. Arnold Schecter, an environmental health expert at the University of Texas–Houston School of Public Health.

John Sommer, executive director of the American Legion's office in Washington, DC, calls the work extremely important for Vietnam veterans because scientists now have a better idea of how much pesticide was used.

HEALTH EFFECTS OF DIOXINS

According to the US Environmental Protection Agency, exposure to dioxins at high enough doses may cause a number of adverse health effects.

The most common health effect in people exposed to large amounts of dioxin is chloracne, a severe skin disease with acne-like lesions that occur mainly on the face and upper body. Other effects include skin rashes, skin discoloration, excessive body hair, and possibly mild liver damage.

Several studies suggest that workers exposed to high levels of dioxins in the workplace over many years have an increased risk of cancer. Exposure to low levels of dioxins over long periods (or high level exposures at sensitive times) might result in reproductive or developmental effects.

info For more on Agent Orange and the Vietnam War, visit the Web sites for the American Legion at *www.legion.org* or the Vietnam Veterans of America at *www.vva.org*.

Gene Discovery May Lead to Better, Less Toxic Cancer Treatments

Richard Pestell, MD, PhD, Professor and Chairman, Department of Oncology, Georgetown University, Washington, DC.
May 2003, *Molecular Biology of the Cell.*

An American research team has uncovered a gene responsible for the spread of cancer through the body, a finding that may provide a new way to control the disease.

The discovery could lead to new, less toxic drug therapies for the disease. The strategy hinges on "knocking out" the cancer-spreading gene to halt the movement of cancer cells from the primary tumor site. That movement is what ultimately leads to the patient's death.

Although such a treatment would not eliminate a cancerous tumor, it would control the spread of the disease and prevent the cancer from attacking other parts of the body, says Dr. Richard Pestell, lead author and chairman of Georgetown University's department of oncology. Patients could then live normally with the cancer in place, much like those people who live with diabetes.

The gene is essential for the migration of cells. By blocking the action of the gene, it may be possible to control the cancer and manage the disease, according to Pestell. The work was done at the Albert Einstein College of Medicine, before Pestell worked at Georgetown.

Pestell's team was alerted that the cyclin D1 gene might play a role in metastasis after learning that patients with spreading cancer also had an over-expression of the gene.

Current therapies for cancer halt the disease's spread by impeding the cell division process (called proliferation), which causes hair loss and other side effects.

If the researchers can determine exactly how cell migration differs from cell proliferation, new therapies could focus on just the cells that migrate, which would eliminate many of the side effects of chemotherapy.

■ ■ ■ ■

How Cancer Spreads

Researchers have gathered a significant amount of information about the spread of cancer. *Here are some facts...*

●**Cancers do not spread in a completely random fashion.** Some parts of the body are more vulnerable than others.

●**When a certain type of cancer spreads to another part of the body,** it does not change its type.

●**The most common way for cancer to spread is through the lymphatic system.**

●**The lymph system has its own channels that circulate throughout the body,** similar to the veins and arteries of the blood stream.

●**Cancer can also metastasize through the bloodstream.** Cancer cells, like healthy cells, must have a blood supply to live so all cancer cells have access to the bloodstream.

New Drug Prevents and Treats Smallpox Infection

Karl Hostetler, MD, Professor of Medicine, University of California, San Diego, and Director, Endocrine and Metabolism Clinic, Veterans Affairs San Diego Healthcare System, CA.
Henry Shinefield, MD, Codirector, Kaiser Permanente Vaccine Study Center, Oakland, CA.
George Painter, PhD, President and Chief Executive Officer, Chimerix Inc., Research Triangle Park, NC.

A new drug is in the research pipeline that, one day, may prevent and treat smallpox in people who might die if they take the available vaccine.

And make no mistake—smallpox is still very high on the list of substances used by bioterrorists, according to the US Centers for Disease Control and Prevention in Atlanta. It's listed above botulism, plague anthrax, and nerve gas as a possible terrorism agent.

Ethics do not allow the drug to be fully tested on people unless there actually is a smallpox epidemic. But the drug protected mice from a virus similar to smallpox, and now researchers are preparing to try it out on monkeys.

PROTECTING THE WEAKEST

The drug could protect the many people—including AIDS patients, cancer patients, and those with skin infections—who can't be vaccinated against smallpox, says Dr. Karl Hostetler, a professor of medicine at the University of California at San Diego. The smallpox vaccine infects people with a virus that is similar to smallpox itself, which means that people with weakened immune systems may become ill or even die because they can't fight off the infection caused by the vaccine.

Drugs like *cidofovir*, which prevents viruses from reproducing, were used initially in the 1980s and 1990s to treat a devastating eye infection in AIDS patients. Although researchers aren't sure if cidofovir works on human smallpox, doctors are using it to treat people who get bad reactions from the smallpox vaccine, says Dr. Henry Shinefield, codirector of the Kaiser Permanente Vaccine Study Center.

MAJOR DRAWBACK

The problem is that the drug is available only in an intravenous form.

"The patient has to be hydrated prior to the drug administration; it has to be given slowly over a protracted period of time, and a patient has to be treated with another drug to protect the kidneys," Hostetler says. "There's a lot of fiddling around."

Hostetler and his colleagues are trying to create an oral form of the drug that wouldn't have as many side effects. It's always better to have an oral form, Shinefield says. You've got better control of the drug, and generally the tolerance is better.

According to the researchers, the findings of preliminary studies suggest that people could take several staggered doses each month to protect themselves from becoming infected in an outbreak.

Chimerix Inc., a company developing the oral forms of cidofovir, hopes within 2 years to test the drug on humans to see its side effects, said president and chief operating officer George Painter.

info For more information on smallpox, check out Stanford University's Web site at *www.stanford.edu*.

How Carbon Monoxide Could Save Your Life

Augustine Choi, MD, Professor, Medicine, University of Pittsburgh School of Medicine, PA.

Judith Alsop, PharmD, Director, Sacramento Division, California Poison Control System.

January 19, 2003, *Nature Medicine*.

You may know that carbon monoxide is a colorless, odorless gas that kills. But it's a lifesaver for rats and mice with heart disease, and researchers hope its healing powers will extend to humans.

Rats and mice exposed to carbon monoxide were more likely to recover from angioplasties and aorta transplants, according to a University of Pittsburgh study. The researchers suspect the gas prevents blood vessels from becoming blocked again right after surgery.

However, it may be some time before humans get the same carbon monoxide treatment.

"The trick is to find the optimal safe dose, and future studies have to focus on the concentration that will be required," says study co-author Dr. Augustine Choi, a professor of medicine at the University of Pittsburgh.

According to the American Heart Association, doctors perform an estimated 1 million angioplasties each year in the United States.

Typically, the procedure involves inserting a catheter into an artery, maneuvering it to the site of the blockage, and expanding the artery by inflating a small balloon. If all goes well, the balloon will deflate but the artery will stay open, reducing the risk of heart attack by improving blood flow.

However, arteries become blocked again in about one-third of patients, often requiring another angioplasty or a heart-bypass operation. In some cases, the angioplasty itself contributes to the blockage by causing inflammation in the artery, Choi explains.

The researchers found the blood vessels of the rodents were much more likely to stay clear if the animals were exposed to carbon monoxide before the surgeries. Approximately 1 hour of exposure in a chamber seemed to do the trick, Choi says.

The gas seems to prevent inflammation from forming, Choi explains. The researchers plan to test their treatment on pigs next, whose circulatory systems are more similar to those in humans.

CARBON MONOXIDE POSES SAFETY RISK

Choi acknowledges that tests on humans will raise concerns. Carbon monoxide is emitted by automobile exhaust, barbecue grills, woodstoves, and malfunctioning space heaters and furnaces. In large amounts, it can be deadly.

"If you're inhaling carbon monoxide, you aren't inhaling enough oxygen," says Judith Alsop, director of the Sacramento division of the California Poison Control System. "The 2 organs that need the most oxygen are your heart and brain, and they manifest the most injury."

Victims of carbon monoxide poisoning will feel dizzy, light-headed, and weak at first, Alsop says. Other symptoms include headaches, nausea, and vomiting.

Heart patients are especially susceptible to carbon monoxide poisoning because their bodies can't handle the stress, she says. Doctors treat the symptoms by administering oxygen.

Super Germs: Scientists Find the 'Bad Bacteria' Gene

Bruce Polsky, MD, Chief, Division of Infectious Diseases, St. Luke's–Roosevelt Hospital Center, New York, NY.

James Musser, MD, PhD, Chief, Laboratory of Human Bacterial Pathogenesis, Rocky Mountain Laboratories, NIAID, Hamilton, MN.

July 15, 2002, *Proceedings of the National Academy of Sciences.*

What is it that makes some strains of bacteria more vicious than others? The answer is in the genes—specifically, killer genes culled from resident viruses.

Scientists at the National Institute of Allergy and Infectious Diseases looked at the genetic information in a brutal strain of streptococcus bacteria and found that it contains a larger number of genes from viruses that inhabit bacteria.

The discovery is likely to lead to new ways of fighting a variety of serious infections, including strep throat, "flesh-eating" disease, scarlet fever, rheumatic fever, toxic shock syndrome, and kidney ailments, the researchers say. Infections with this strain of streptococcus have unusually high death rates, they say.

Other experts agree the work is significant, but wonder whether it will change available treatments.

"I think what this does is help explain how a more serious form of that same bacteria could emerge, but I don't think it changes our approach," says Dr. Bruce Polsky, chief of the division of infectious diseases at St. Luke's-Roosevelt Hospital Center in New York City.

Dr. James Musser, lead author of the study, says that bacteria have their own set of viruses, just as humans do, which can be passed on to different strains of the bacterium. In his study, the bacterial viruses account for a very large percentage—about 10%—of the entire chromosome. Each of the viruses carries the genetic information for a new toxin.

Musser likens the process to a warhead. He explains that by acquiring new viruses, the bacterium can quickly develop a new set of disease-causing characteristics, which is what he and his colleagues saw happen in their study. The bacterium took a bad pathogen and turned it into a really bad pathogen.

They say that they know exactly what goes on inside the pathogen and that they know what, at the molecular level, allowed the organism to emerge. "There are some very rational things to do now that we have the genome sequence that may lead to accelerated development of new diagnoses, new therapies, and control measures, and ultimately, we hope, vaccines."

info The National Institute of Allergy and Infectious Diseases has an excellent fact sheet on *streptococcus* at *www.niaid.nih. gov/factsheets/strep.htm.*

Newly Discovered Emphysema Gene May Mean Better Treatment

David G. Morris, MD, Assistant Professor, Medicine, University of California at San Francisco.

Anita B. Roberts, PhD, Chief, Laboratory of Cell Regulation and Carcinogenesis, National Cancer Institute, Bethesda, MD.

March 13, 2003, *Nature.*

In one of the more complicated biomedical research stories you will encounter, scientists at the University of California at San Francisco have identified a gene that can increase susceptibility to the crippling lung disease emphysema.

Dr. David G. Morris, an assistant professor of medicine at the university and leader of the group, can explain it all to you in about 10 minutes, if you are willing to follow a tangled tale of genes, enzymes, and proteins. And although the research was done with mice, it might lead to better treatment of emphysema in humans.

The gene in question is one whose activity affects growth factor-beta (TGF-beta), which the researchers already know is involved in

fibrosis, a lung disease in which tissue overgrows in the lungs. Emphysema is a completely different condition, in which there is slow degradation of lung tissue, specifically the tiny air sacs through which oxygen flows. The sacs swell and lose elasticity because of the steady destruction of a protein called elastin.

SMOKING AND GENETICS

Emphysema is most often caused by smoking. However, genetics also plays a role because most people who smoke for decades do not develop the disease—only 10% to 15% do. One genetic defect has already been identified, an absence of *alpha-1 antitrypsin*, a gene that keeps elastin from being destroyed.

What Morris has identified is a gene that is involved in both fibrosis and emphysema and whose activity affects the role of an enzyme called transforming growth factor-beta in a way that had not been imagined.

This particular gene had always been linked to fibrosis, Morris says. "This is a new way of looking at TGF-beta—that its absence leads to emphysema." The work opens doors to understanding emphysema in humans and learning why some people get it and others don't.

TESTS ON PEOPLE

A human study has already begun. Researchers at Harvard Medical School have assembled a group of patients and families in whom emphysema occurs early in life without an alpha-1 antitrypsin defect.

"This opens a whole series of things that people can look at," says Anita B. Roberts, chief of the laboratory of cell regulation and carcinogenesis at the National Cancer Institute, who wrote an editorial that appeared in *Nature.*

The work, adds Roberts, is "confusing, but exciting."

info To learn the simple facts about emphysema, consult the American Lung Association at *www.lungusa.org* or try a support group at *www.emphysema.net.*

Surgery That Works Better Than Drugs for Some Emphysema Patients

Steven Piantadosi, MD, PhD, Director, Biostatistics, Johns Hopkins Cancer Center, Baltimore, MD.
May 22, 2003, *New England Journal of Medicine*.

Surgery to help people with emphysema breathe easier can be better than drug treatment—but it's not for everyone—according to a comparison of the 2 therapies.

The costly operation, called lung-volume reduction surgery, works best for people with isolated areas of lung damage and whose ability to exercise is greatly impaired by their disease. For others, the procedure may be only modestly better than conventional care, and in 1 group—those with diffuse airway injury but relatively good exercise function—it seems to cause more harm than good, the study found.

"The study sharpens up our ability to tell who should get the surgery and who shouldn't," says study coauthor Dr. Steven Piantadosi, a statistics expert at Johns Hopkins University in Baltimore. Unfortunately, emphysema patients for whom the operation isn't warranted "are flying by the seat of their pants," Piantadosi says. "If it's not clearly indicated, it's probably not a good idea for them to be operated on."

Between 1 and 2 million Americans suffer from emphysema, a chronic and deadly lung condition most often caused by smoking. The disorder is marked by the gradual erosion of tiny airways, starving patients of oxygen and hobbling their ability to perform even the most minimal activities.

DO THE BENEFITS OUTWEIGH THE RISKS?

The National Emphysema Treatment Trial sought to learn whether the benefits of the lung surgery outweighed its potential risks. The trial included 1218 men and women with severe emphysema. All received "medical therapy," including drugs (such as steroids) to open their airways, as well as oxygen, encouragement to exercise, and other lung rehabilitation. In addition, half had lung volume reduction surgery.

For the average patient, the surgery led to an immediate improvement in lung function, which tapered off by 2 years after the procedure. Those in the other group saw their lung function continue to wane.

By the end of the study, death rates in the 2 groups were the same.

IT'S NOT FOR EVERYBODY

Surgery was most effective in people with localized lung damage and poor ability to exercise, halving the risk of death compared with medical management alone. That makes sense, experts say, because removing the injured tissue, ideally, will allow healthy airways to take over. Meanwhile, people with bad exercise capacity are more likely to die in the absence of treatment. For this group, even a small increase in the ability to move around improves their overall quality of life.

Lung volume reduction surgery was least effective in the group with widespread lung damage but good exercise ability. They had a higher risk of death compared with medical management only, yet reaped no benefits from the procedure.

info Learn about lung volume reduction surgery (LVRS) from the University of Maryland Medicine at *www.umm.edu/tho racic/lung_vol_redu.html* or the National Emphysema Treatment Trial (NETT) online at *www.nhlbi.nih.gov/health/prof/lung/nett*.

New Research May End West Nile Virus for Good

Dawn Wesson, PhD, Associate Professor, Tropical Medicine, Tulane School of Public Health and Tropical Medicine, New Orleans, LA.
Andrew Spielman, ScD, Professor, Tropical Public Health, Harvard School of Public Health, Boston, MA.
Mylène Weill, Lecturer, Molecular Biology, University of Montpellier II, France.
May 8, 2003, *Nature*.

French researchers believe they've found a way to help fight the mosquito-borne West Nile virus.

Mosquitoes that carry the deadly virus have formed a resistance to some insecticides, but the researchers say they've found a genetic solution to overcome it. The finding may contribute to new insecticides.

Experts are divided, however, on the implications of the findings.

"We've known that this type of resistance has occurred for a while now," says Dawn Wesson, an associate professor of tropical medicine at Tulane School of Public Health and Tropical Medicine in New Orleans. "The significance here is that they've identified the actual mutation that is responsible for that resistance."

Others believe the French researchers have overstated the significance of their findings.

"It does not address 2 major categories of insecticides that are now being used against mosquitoes," says Andrew Spielman, a professor of tropical public health at the Harvard School of Public Health. "They're talking about a mutation that doesn't relate to commonly used insecticides."

MUTATING MOSQUITOES

According to the study authors, mosquitoes that transmit malaria and West Nile virus developed insecticide resistance more than 25 years ago in Africa, the Americas, and Europe.

In normal mosquitoes, insecticides interfere with an enzyme that controls recharging of the insect's cells. The mosquito essentially ends up dying of overstimulation, Wesson says.

The genetic mutation basically lets the mosquito dodge the effects of 2 families of insecticides, organophosphates, and carbamates.

"The pesticide binds to the enzyme and inactivates it [in normal mosquitoes]," says study author Mylène Weill, a lecturer in molecular biology at the University of Montpellier II in France. "The mutation prevents the insecticide from binding to the enzyme."

The researchers found the mutation in 10 highly resistant strains of mosquitoes from Africa, the Caribbean, and Europe that carry West Nile virus, and in 1 other resistant African strain that carries malaria.

THE NEXT STEP

The question is whether this finding will translate into any new mosquito-control strategies; Spielman is doubtful.

Weill, however, is more hopeful. "We know now the target and the mutation, so we can produce a mutated form of the enzyme and select strains for new molecules that can be active in that," she says.

Scientists with the Centers for Disease Control and Prevention believe West Nile virus first arrived in the Western Hemisphere with an outbreak in New York City during the summer of 1999. The CDC (*www.cdc.gov*) has more information about West Nile virus.

info For more information on pesticides, visit the US Environmental Protection Agency at *www.epa.gov/pesticides.*

MS Sufferers: Is Interferon Worth the Side Effects and Cost?

Graziella Filippini, MD, Director, Epidemiology Unit, National Neurological Institute, Milan, Italy.

Arney Rosenblat, spokeswoman, National Multiple Sclerosis Society, New York, NY.

February 15, 2003, *The Lancet.*

Italian research has challenged the wide use of interferons over the long term to treat multiple sclerosis (MS).

"We found a modest benefit in the first year of treatment," says Dr. Graziella Filippini, director of the epidemiology unit of the National Neurological Institute in Milan. "There is not sufficient data to estimate the effect after the first year of treatment."

MS is a disease in which the body's immune system, for unknown reasons, attacks and destroys the tissue that forms a protective sheath around nerve cells. Approximately 85% of MS patients have the relapsing form of the condition, with flare-ups that cause symptoms ranging from numbness and tingling to paralysis.

The US Food and Drug Administration has approved 3 different forms of interferon, biologically engineered versions of a natural immune system molecule, to treat those flare-ups. However, widespread discussion continues about their true effectiveness, benefits, side effects, and costs.

PAST STUDIES PROVIDE INSIGHT

Filippini and her colleagues reviewed all the scientifically controlled studies of interferon treatment on patients with the relapsing form of MS done over a 10-year period. They picked out 7 trials including 1215 patients, 667 of whom were followed up for 1 year and 917 of whom were followed up for 2 years.

"Interferon seemed to reduce the number of patients who had exacerbations [flare-ups] during the first year of treatment, but results at 2 years' follow-up were not robust and were difficult to interpret because of the many dropouts," the researchers report.

Those results "do not give a reason to continue treatment after the first year," Filippini says.

Interferon treatment also causes significant side effects, such as fever, muscle pains, and headache, the review found. In one trial that studied quality of life, patients who received interferon reported consistently lower scores than those who got a placebo. Overall, medical problems, many affecting the blood, were more common in patients receiving interferon, and interferon's "acute toxic effects adversely affected quality of life," the report says.

SEEKING A MORE DEFINITIVE CONCLUSION

The case for or against interferon remains to be solved, Filippini says, adding: "We need a collaboration between the best neurological centers in the world to consider this problem."

Arney Rosenblat, a spokeswoman for the National Multiple Sclerosis Society, said the research came as a surprise and would require examination.

Meanwhile, she says, the American Academy of Neurology (*www.aan.com/professionals*) has guidelines that list interferon as an accepted treatment for MS.

info You can learn more about MS and its treatment from the National Multiple Sclerosis Society at *www.mss.org*.

Getting Closer To a Cure for Anxiety and Aggression

Evan Deneris, PhD, Associate Professor, Neuroscience, Case Western Reserve University, Cleveland, OH. January 23, 2003, *Neuron*.

Researchers at Case Western Reserve University in Cleveland believe the gene that regulates the production of serotonin also controls aggression and anxiety. Take away your serotonin and you may become frightened and downright mean, they say.

The researchers bred mice that produced no serotonin and then watched as the mice hid in corners and attacked any other mouse that came too close. The only difference between the mean-spirited mutants and normal mice was a single gene—Pet-1. That gene works in the brain by regulating the production of serotonin, a chemical (called a neurotransmitter) that is thought to influence emotion, learning, memory, and pain detection. People who don't have enough serotonin can suffer from such mood disorders as depression and anxiety.

A small number of the neurons have the ability to sprinkle serotonin to many different regions of the brain, which is why they have been implicated in so many brain processes and psychiatric disorders, says study author Evan Deneris, an associate professor of neuroscience at Case Western. "But we know extremely little about them. This is the first gene we've found to control this," he says.

The altered mice in the experiments grew up without serotonin. Although many of their behaviors, such as eating and moving, remained unaffected, the mice acted much more impulsively because the lack of serotonin clouded their judgment, Deneris says. He says he'd like to do the reverse in another experiment—add more Pet-1 genes to mice brains to boost their serotonin levels and find out whether that creates a more mellow mouse.

If adding more Pet-1 genes to mice creates a higher serotonin level and results in less aggression and anxiety, then the possibility exists that it may do the same for humans.

Understanding how genetics influences behavior has become "a major effort by the National Institute of Mental Health," Deneris says.

info To learn more about the genetics of mental disorders, visit the National Institute of Mental Health at *www.nimh.nih.gov/research/genetics.htm.*

Stem Cells Help 'Heal' Spinal Cord Injuries

Jean de Vellis, PhD, Editor-In-Chief of the *Journal of Neuroscience Research*, Professor of Neurobiology, and Director, Mental Retardation Research Center, University of California, Los Angeles.

Sandra Hill–Felberg, PhD, Research Instructor, Tulane University Department of Medicine, New Orleans, LA.

September 15, 2002, *Journal of Neuroscience Research.*

Japanese researchers have shown for the first time that when stem cells from an unborn rat were transplanted into the spinal cords of injured rats, the cells actually formed new connections with existing cells.

New connections, or synapses, mean the cells are being integrated into the normal circuitry of the spinal cord. In other words, the spinal cord is healing.

The result was improved motor capabilities in the injured rats, according to the study in the *Journal of Neuroscience Research*.

"The researchers showed that the transplanted cells connect with existing cells, and the existing cells reach out and connect with the transplants," says Jean de Vellis, a professor of neurobiology and director of the Mental Retardation Research Center at the University of California, Los Angeles. "That reciprocity has never been shown before."

Developing any treatments for humans with spinal-cord injuries is probably still years away, he adds.

HOPE ON THE HORIZON

"This is a very, very hopeful sign that we can achieve partial or even, eventually, full recovery of the spinal cord," says de Vellis, who also is editor-in-chief of the *Journal of Neuroscience Research*.

Because of their potential to develop into virtually any cell in the body, embryonic and fetal stem cells are the focus of much research. They've been tested, with some success, for their potential to replace cells destroyed in the brains of people with Parkinson's disease and epilepsy.

However, in many cases, the transplanted cells didn't make new connections, says Sandra Hill–Felberg, a research instructor at Tulane University's department of medicine.

"This paper showed you actually get synapses," Hill–Felberg says.

The team from Keio University School of Medicine in Japan took a 14-day-old rat fetus and extracted from it a type of stem cell that is programmed to develop into various kinds of nervous system cells.

From that tissue, the researchers grew enough cells to transplant into 450 rats—a feat in itself.

Previous stem cell research has been hampered because some cells that multiply under lab conditions look normal but they don't behave like normal cells when they are transplanted, de Vellis says.

HEALING THE INJURY

The Japanese researchers then injured the spinal cords of hundreds of female rats. Nine days later, the researchers injected stem cells near the injury site in some of the rats.

They waited 9 days because research has shown that's the time when the injury site is most hospitable to transplantation, de Vellis says. At that point, the body reaches its peak production of growth factor around the injury site, part of the body's attempt to heal itself.

Five weeks after the transplant, 13 of the 15 rats with transplants had enough agility to retrieve food pellets from cubbyholes. Only approximately half the rats without the transplants could do the same.

But more motor skill tests are needed to confirm the improvement, says Hill–Felberg.

info The National Spinal Cord Injury Association at *www.spinalcord.org* has more information about spinal cord injuries, or you can check out the Spinal Cord Injury Information Network at *www.spinalcord.uab.edu.*

Researchers Closer to Better Treatments For Malaria

Regina Rabinovich, MD, Director, Malaria Vaccine Initiative, Washington, DC.
October 3, 2002, *Nature.*
October 4, 2002, *Science.*

For more than 2000 years humans have sought a cure for malaria, a mosquito-borne illness that never goes away once it's inside your system. Malaria, which still kills more than 3 million people worldwide each year, causes chills, fever, nausea, and diarrhea. The disease can leave a person so weak that he or she can die—or die from some other infection.

Finally, a gene mapping of both the chief malaria parasite and the mosquito that most frequently transmits it to people in Africa may help doctors find better treatments and vaccines.

It will be a long process, but Dr. Regina Rabinovich, director of the Malaria Vaccine Initiative, says, "There's probably a shorter line" between the data and better treatments than there is between the data and better vaccines.

Scientists now have complete or virtually complete genetic portraits of all 3 players in the malaria triangle—the parasite that causes the disease, the mosquito that transmits it, and the human hosts they combine to infect.

Roughly half a billion people per year contract malaria, and one-third of its victims are young children and infants in Africa. Drugs can treat malaria, but the 3 most commonly used medicines are 50 to 2000 years old. Resistance to these treatments is a growing problem.

info You can get more information on Rabinovich's Malaria Vaccine Initiative on the Internet at *www.malariavaccine.org.*

Resistance to Breast Cancer Drug May Open Door for Other Treatments

Kimberly Blackwell, MD, Assistant Professor, Oncology, Duke Comprehensive Cancer Center, Durham, NC.
David Nathanson, MD, Oncologist, Henry Ford Health Center, Detroit, MI.
December 13, 2002, presentation, San Antonio Breast Cancer Symposium, TX.

Breast cancer patients who have developed a resistance to the drug *tamoxifen* may be able to use a replacement drug, if the recent research on mice can be duplicated with humans.

A large number of women treated for breast cancer with tamoxifen develop a resistance to the drug after several years. But research indicates that these women may become eligible for other cancer-fighting drugs they may have not been able to take before, such as Herceptin.

For now, the findings suggest that if a woman has become resistant to tamoxifen, she should be tested by her doctor to see if she can now receive Herceptin, according to Dr. Kimberly Blackwell, an assistant professor of oncology at Duke Comprehensive Cancer Center in Durham, North Carolina.

"I think it makes a lot of sense," said Dr. David Nathanson, an oncologist at Henry Ford Hospital in Detroit. He added he would like to see clinical research in humans, but it appears that when tamoxifen is no longer working, doctors may be able to use Herceptin.

Nathanson says if Herceptin becomes an option, it would be good news, but women should realize that even now when tamoxifen fails, physicians have a number of other medications they can try.

THE STUDY

The researchers studied 27 mice that were raised to develop human breast tumors in their hind flanks. Blackwell said that when the mice became resistant to tamoxifen, the tumor became altered.

Blackwell's study found that when a woman's tumors stopped responding to tamoxifen, her breast cells increased production of another growth-regulating receptor protein, called HER-2. After all of the tumors in the laboratory mice developed a resistance to tamoxifen, they became receptive to drugs that target the HER-2 receptor, such as Herceptin. If this is also true in women, Herceptin could be used once a tumor becomes resistant to tamoxifen to block the production of HER-2 and shrink the tumor. Approximately 75% of the women who were candidates for treatment with tamoxifen would not have benefited from this other class of drugs before their tumors changed.

Experimental Treatment Jolts Blood of Heart-Failure Patients

James B. Young, MD, Medical Director, Kaufman Center for Heart Failure, and Head, Heart Failure and Cardiac Transplant Medicine Section, The Cleveland Clinic, OH.

Clyde Yancy, MD, Associate Professor, Medicine, University of Texas Southwestern Medical Center, Dallas, and spokesman, American Heart Association.

Unconventional is one way to describe an experimental treatment to reduce the risk of death in patients with congestive heart failure. Researchers would take a vial of your blood…zap it with heat, radiation, and ozone gas…and then inject it back into your body.

It's called "immune-modulation therapy," an approach that tries to reduce the inflammation associated with heart failure by tricking your immune system.

The therapy yielded impressive results in a pilot trial of 73 patients with advanced heart failure. During the 6-month review, approximately half the patients received the experimental therapy; the other half received placebo. All the patients also received their normal medications.

Dr. James B. Young, head of the heart failure and cardiac transplant medicine section at the Cleveland Clinic, participated in the pilot study and is expected to serve as principal investigator in a broader 2000-person study.

"What we saw was a highly statistically significant reduction in death rates, as well as a statistically significant reduction in hospitalizations," Young says.

Noting that a few previous attempts to treat heart failure with anti-inflammation drugs have failed, Young says, "I entered the original pilot study pretty skeptical."

The results of the initial trial, however, persuaded him that immune-modulation therapy merited a large-scale test.

Nearly 5 million Americans suffer from congestive heart failure, which weakens the heart so it doesn't pump blood efficiently. Approximately half these patients die within 5 years of diagnosis.

IMMUNE-MODULATION THERAPY

In immune-modulation therapy, a vial of blood is drawn from the heart-failure patient, then exposed to 108-degree heat, radiation from ultraviolet light, and ozone gas. When the blood is injected back into the body, it alters the immune system and reduces inflammation.

In the expanded trial, patients will receive immune-modulation therapy for a year. As with the pilot, the therapy will be added to the patients' regular medications.

Young acknowledges the small sample size in the pilot study, and says judging the success of the procedure will have to await results of the larger test.

Dr. Clyde Yancy, an associate professor of medicine at the University of Texas Southwestern Medical Center, says immune-modulation therapy appears to be based on "sound science" and the preliminary test yielded encouraging results.

That said, he, too, cautions against concluding the therapy works based on the small pilot study. "We have many times before seen pilot trials not pan out in a larger study," says Yancy, a spokesman for the American Heart Association.

Yancy stresses that highly effective medications already exist for all but the most severely ill heart patients. Experts remain uncertain whether inflammation causes heart failure or is a symptom of the disease. The experimental therapy, he says, may help determine whether inflammation is the root cause of the disease.

info For more on heart failure, visit the American Heart Association at *www. americanheart*.org or the Heart Failure Society of America at *www.hfsa.org*.

Deafness Gene Discovery Another Step in Understanding Hearing Loss

David Kohrman, PhD, Assistant Professor, Otolaryngology and Human Genetics, University of Michigan Medical School, Ann Arbor.

Neil Segil, PhD, Scientist and Section Chief of Cell Cycle Growth and Differentiation, House Ear Institute, University of Southern California, Los Angeles.

Ed Wilcox, PhD, Staff Scientist, Laboratory of Molecular Genetics, National Institute on Deafness and Other Communication Disorders, National Institutes of Health, Bethesda, MD.

September 2002, *American Journal of Human Genetics.*

August 2002, *Human Molecular Genetics.*

Scientists have identified yet another deafness gene, bringing to 26 the number of genes known to play a role in deafness. However, how the scientists arrived at the discovery of the latest gene is novel.

First, a team from the University of Michigan identified the gene in mice, naming it the TMIE gene for transmembrane inner ear, which is the location of the protein encoded by the gene.

"Either the protein is not made [in the case of hearing loss], or it's made but is faulty," explains David Kohrman, an assistant professor

of otolaryngology and human genetics at the University of Michigan, who discovered the TMIE gene.

Next, he shared the information with a team from the University of Iowa and the National Institutes of Health, that had been studying families with inherited hearing loss. They had located the general area of the gene in these families, but information from the mouse research helped them zero in on the human gene.

The findings appear in 2 journals: The *American Journal of Human Genetics* and *Human Molecular Genetics.*

MANY FLAWS CREATE DEAFNESS

"Defects in lots of different genes cause deafness," says Kohrman, lead author of the paper published in *Human Molecular Genetics.*

The new gene is thought to play a role in how the ear's sensory hair cells work. These hair cells help turn external sounds into the electrical impulses that the brain can interpret.

Approximately 1 in 1000 infants has a profound hearing impairment, according to the National Institutes of Health. Half the cases are believed to be genetic in origin.

"Dr. Kohrman and his colleagues did a great job," says Neil Segil, a scientist at the House Ear Institute, a research and treatment facility in Los Angeles. "It's exactly the kind of synergy that can be expected when we invest in animal research, and coordinate it with human research. We can't do this kind of research in humans [that was done in mice to find the gene]."

HOW MANY MUTATIONS?

"The biggest question that is still outstanding is exactly how prevalent this mutation, or defective gene, is," Segil says.

"There is always some hope that as each new mutation is identified, it will represent a larger portion," Segil says. Eventually, he adds, treatments will be tailored to the genes involved in the particular case of hearing loss.

"There are probably over 100 genes that, when mutations occur, can cause deafness," Segil says.

The newly discovered gene is not the most common hearing-loss gene, says Ed Wilcox, a staff scientist at the National Institute on Deafness and Other Communication Disorders, part of the National Institutes of Health. He is also coauthor of the paper in the *American Journal of Human Genetics*.

"But it is certainly not a rare gene either," he says. "It is going to contribute to the understanding of the genetics of hearing loss."

info For more information, see the Deafness Research Foundation at *www.drf.org.* For information on communication options, visit the National Institute on Deafness and Other Communication Disorders at *www. nidcd.nih.gov.*

Scientists Harness Deadly Anthrax to Target Cancers

Stephen H. Leppla, PhD, and Thomas H. Bugge, PhD, Senior Investigators, National Institutes of Health, Bethesda, MD.

Arthur E. Frankel, MD, Professor, Cancer Biology and Medicine, Wake Forest University, Winston–Salem, NC.

January 13, 2003, *Proceedings of the National Academy of Sciences.*

Chances are you are all too familiar with the scare that anthrax struck into the hearts of Americans because of its potential use as a biological warfare agent. But despite that sinister side, scientists have found ways to turn the infectious and deadly anthrax into a cancer fighter.

Researchers from the National Institutes of Health have developed an engineered version of the anthrax toxin that has killed tumors in mice.

Tumor cells in humans contain high levels of a protein that can be targeted by the new anthrax treatment. Stephen Leppla and Thomas Bugge, both senior investigators at the National Institutes of Health, and their colleagues genetically altered the structure of the anthrax toxin so that it invades only cells that secrete that protein—known as *urokinase.*

In the lab, the new treatment worked well on skin tumors and lung and tissue cancers.

After 1 treatment, the toxin reduced tumor size by 65% to 92%, depending on the type of tumor. And 2 treatments eliminated 88% of connective tissue cancers and 17% of skin tumors. The tumor cells began to die just 12 hours after the first treatment.

Even better, the toxin did its work without damaging surrounding cells, a problem that often occurs with other cancer treatments.

A MAJOR ADVANCE IN THE FIELD

Targeting proteins with poison is not new. But the institute's innovation is that the toxin sent to the tumor cell is activated only if it finds the specific protein it is engineered to detect and invade. Leppla says his team hopes the approach will bear out as a way to target and kill tumor cells without causing damage to normal, surrounding cells.

"This is about the most sophisticated molecular biology discovery" in the field in many years, says Dr. Arthur Frankel, a professor of cancer biology and medicine at Wake Forest University in Winston–Salem, North Carolina.

The approach must be studied in humans to see if it works, and trials will take several years.

If the approach does bear out, it could help in many types of cancer, Frankel says, because the protein urokinase is present in many cancerous tumors.

Vampire Bat Saliva May Add Bite to Stroke Treatment

Robert L. Medcalf, PhD, Senior Research Fellow, Monash University Department of Medicine, Box Hill Hospital, Victoria, Australia.

Keith A. Siller, MD, Medical Director, New York University Comprehensive Stroke Care and Research Center.

January 10, 2003, *Stroke.*

An ischemic stroke happens when at least 1 blood clot blocks the supply of blood to the brain. Conventional treatments are only effective when administered up to 3 hours after the onset of stroke. But a substance taken from the saliva of vampire bats is effective when given up to 9 hours after onset, says study author Dr. Robert L. Medcalf, a senior research fellow at Monash University Department of Medicine at Box Hill Hospital in Victoria, Australia.

The study was done in mice, and it's not known how effective the treatment will be in humans. Moreover, some experts believe the emphasis on a longer time window obscures the necessity of treating stroke victims as quickly as possible.

"Even if this drug is better than the current one, you still need to get people treated very quickly," says Dr. Keith Siller, medical director of New York University's Comprehensive Stroke Care and Research Center. "You have a limited time window to restore blood to the brain and that window doesn't change, no matter what you give."

SALIVA HAS NATURAL CLOT-BUSTER

Conventional clot-busting agents are beneficial, but they affect the entire circulation system, whether a clot exists or not. They pose an increased risk of cerebral hemorrhage (bleeding in the brain) and may cause brain-cell death, the study's author says. Researchers have focused on refining these agents so that they target only the clot and do not injure blood vessels.

Scientists believe they may have a candidate in the new compound extracted from vampire bat saliva. The compound takes advantage of vampire feeding principles and tries to make them work in humans. When vampire bats bite their victims, they release a clot-dissolving substance that keeps the blood flowing long enough to suck a full meal. Without the clot-buster, the victim's blood would clot and dry up, leaving the bat hungry.

In this study, the compound appeared to become active only in the presence of fibrin, the "building blocks" of a clot. In fact, its clot-busting properties increase about 13,000-fold in the presence of fibrin, whereas a conventional agent increases by a factor of 72.

This is important because blood clots and, therefore, fibrin are not actually located in the brain, so the bat-saliva compound has no effect in this vulnerable region.

The next step is a test by some of the same investigators in human stroke patients in Europe, Asia, and Australia.

info For more information on ischemic stroke, visit the National Stroke Association at *www.stroke.org*.

The Gene That Stops Prostate Cancer From Spreading

Evan T. Keller, DVM, PhD, Assistant Professor, Comparative Medicine and Pathology, University of Michigan Medical School, Ann Arbor.

June 18, 2003, *Journal of the National Cancer Institute*.

A gene has been found that acts early to stop prostate cancer cells from spreading to other parts of the body, say researchers. The finding could help identify ways to control the spread of potentially deadly tumors, the University of Michigan researchers say.

This is important because the primary tumor of prostate cancer often doesn't kill—it's the spread of those cancerous cells that does.

Approximately 20 genes involved in the spread—or *metastasis*—of prostate cancer have already been identified. The new one—called RKIP, which produces the RKIP protein—is important because it serves as a kind of traffic cop. It acts early to stop cancer cells from leaving the prostate and entering the bloodstream and wreaking havoc, says the study.

"There is a metastatic cascade, in which the cells enter the blood vessels, then go into a target organ, then grow there," says study author Evan T. Keller, an assistant professor of comparative medicine and pathology at the University of Michigan Medical School.

STOPPING IT BEFORE IT STARTS

RKIP works at an early stage in the cascade. If you can block that stage, you could prevent the cascade, he explains.

The researchers' work with RKIP is also important because they've been able to identify a specific function of the gene, Keller says. Little progress has been made in figuring out what the other genes do that are involved in this metastasis.

The hope is the discovery will open the way for gene therapy or even drug therapy that will act on the RKIP gene and prevent the spread of the cancer, Keller says.

RUNNING ON FULL

The RKIP gene—the initials stand for Raf kinase inhibitor protein, which it makes— suppresses metastasis. Cancer cells that have a full quota of the RKIP gene are unlikely to metastasize. Those that have little or none of it do spread, Keller says.

After years of general lab work, the researchers made more specific measurements. One critical test used cancer cells taken from prostate cancer patients within hours of their death, when the fragile molecules involved in RKIP activity were still present. RKIP levels in 12 samples of nonmetastatic cancers were close to those of healthy cells. But no RKIP protein was found in any of the 22 samples of metastatic prostate cancer.

Then the researchers performed gene therapy, adding the RKIP gene to cells grown in the laboratory, then to mice with prostate cancer. Adding the gene reduced metastasis in cell cultures and the animals.

Keller and his colleagues are moving in several directions. One is to see whether the RKIP gene plays a role in metastasis of other cancers, such as breast, lung, and liver tumors.

"And we are trying to look at the mechanism of how this gene affects what the tumor is doing," Keller says.

info You can learn more about prostate cancer from the National Library of Medicine at *www.nlm.nih.gov.*

Cancer Drug Keeps Blood Vessels Open After Angioplasty

Lee Giorgi, MD, Consulting Cardiologist, Mid America Heart Institute, Saint Luke's Health System, Kansas City, MO.

Kenneth Kent, MD, PhD, Director, Cardiac Catheterization Laboratory, and Professor, Medicine, Georgetown University Hospital, Washington, DC.

April 17, 2003, *New England Journal of Medicine.*

Stents coated with the cancer drug Taxol, researchers say, keep arteries open longer than untreated devices.

Stents are the flexible metal scaffolds that prop open vessels after angioplasty to maintain blood flow to the heart. Renarrowing, or restenosis, of those vessels occurs in roughly 20% of patients, forcing doctors to repeat the costly procedure.

The study found that stents medicated with Taxol are much less likely to fail because the drug retards the growth of cells in the lining of the blood vessels where the stents are placed.

The research was funded by Cook Inc., a stent maker in Bloomington, Indiana. One of the authors also received speaking fees from Boston Scientific, another leading stent maker.

The US Food and Drug Administration has approved the use of a stent coated with the drug sirolimus, which has also been found to prevent restenosis.

CANCER DRUG MAY HELP HEART DISEASE

Taxol, or *paclitaxel*, is commonly used to treat advanced breast and ovarian cancers, as well as certain lung tumors and a form of cancer associated with AIDS. The drug is a synthetic version of a molecule found in the bark of the Pacific yew tree, whose anti-cancer properties were discovered in the early 1960s.

Previous research has found stents that release the drug appear to reduce the rate of restenosis, which typically occurs within the first 6 months after the procedure. The research shows a high dose of the drug works best.

Coated stents cost more to implant, but if they reduce the rate of restenosis they could save money in the long run. Some 850,000 Americans receive stents every year. One study found that drug-coated stents cost approximately $2000 more than conventional stents, but most of that is recovered through long-term savings.

STUDY RESULTS VS. REAL-WORLD USE

Dr. Lee Giorgi, an interventional cardiologist at the Mid America Heart Institute, part of Saint Luke's Health System in Kansas City, Missouri, says that while the data from clinical trials are impressive, it's likely their real-world performance will be somewhat weaker. Not only do trials typically include ideal patients, but the studies take place in heart centers with elite physicians, he says.

However, Dr. Kenneth Kent, director of the cardiac catheterization program at Georgetown University Hospital, says heart specialists also had a learning curve with conventional stents when they first appeared. Eventually, Kent says, the devices will be as familiar as the old models.

Commonly Used Weed Killer Chemical Mixes Up Sex Hormones

Tyrone Hayes, PhD, Associate Professor, Integrative Biology, University of California, Berkeley.

October 31, 2002, *Nature.*

Recent research has found that a chemical called *atrazine*, which is one of the world's most popular weed killers, scrambles the sexual development of certain frogs—turning males into hermaphrodites or creating other hormonal irregularities.

Atrazine is sprayed on the vast majority of crops in the United States and in other countries to control the spread of weeds. Apparently this herbicide spurs the African clawed tadpoles' male hormone testosterone to turn into the female hormone estrogen, say researchers.

SECOND SPECIES AFFECTED

In earlier research, California scientists found that atrazine exposure scrambled the hormones of a different species of male frogs. Tyrone Hayes, a biologist at the University of California, Berkeley, and leader of the research effort, says he expects that exposure to atrazine will also greatly reduce fertility in yet a third species.

The field-testing site was on Wyoming's North Platte River, in a county where atrazine was not sold or used significantly. However, the North Platte River is fed by streams rooted in Colorado that are tainted with the substance, the researchers say.

Hayes's group found that frogs living in areas contaminated with atrazine were more likely to have reproductive anomalies than those where the pesticide wasn't present.

They saw no hermaphroditic frogs where there was no atrazine, while sites with at least 0.2 parts per billion in water all had such creatures. In one area, nearly all the male frogs collected had abnormal reproductive organs.

The US Environmental Protection Agency (EPA) has been reviewing atrazine's safety.

The EPA has already determined that atrazine is unlikely to cause cancer in humans. However, the agency has found evidence that exposure to high amounts of atrazine may cause heart damage, eye trouble, muscle breakdown, weight loss, and other health problems. No research exists on what affect the chemical has on sex hormones in mammals.

American farmers use more than 76 million pounds of atrazine a year. This amount covers roughly three-quarters of all US farm acreage.

info For more on atrazine, visit the EPA at *www.epa.gov* or the University of Wisconsin at *www.uwsp.edu.*

Herbal Combo Shows Promise in Fighting Prostate Cancer

Aaron Katz, MD, director, Center for Holistic Urology, Columbia–Presbyterian Medical Center, and Associate Professor of Clinical Urology, Columbia University College of Physicians and Surgeons, New York, NY.

Howard Korman, MD, Urologist, William Beaumont Hospital, Royal Oak, MI.

December 13, 2002, presentation, Society of Urologic Oncology.

National Institutes of Health, Bethesda, MD.

An herbal formula sold under the brand name Zyflamend may offer new treatment and prevention options for patients with prostate cancer, say Columbia University researchers.

The formula, a combination of 10 different herbs, was used in lab experiments to suppress the growth of prostate cancer cells and it caused many cells to self-destruct, report the researchers.

"This is a natural product that contains herbs and spices and in our lab studies seems to have an effect on the cancer we looked at," says one of the study's authors, Dr. Aaron Katz, the director of the Center for Holistic Urology at Columbia–Presbyterian Medical Center in New York City. "The compound needs future research on the clinical side, but it holds potential for reducing PSA [prostate-specific antigen] levels."

Prostate cancer is the most common cancer in men, except for skin cancer. More than 189,000 men are diagnosed with this form of cancer every year, according to the American Cancer Society.

HERBAL RECIPE

Zyflamend is made with a combination of turmeric, ginger, holy basil, hu zhang, Chinese goldthread, barberry, oregano, rosemary, green tea, and Chinese skullcap.

The researchers added Zyflamend to prostate cancer cells in lab cultures. They also tested the effects of curcumin, a compound from the spice turmeric. Curcumin is believed to have an anti-inflammatory effect that could reduce the growth of prostate cancer.

They found that Zyflamend reduced the growth of prostate cancer cells and induced cell death, and that curcumin alone did not produce these effects.

Dr. Howard Korman, a urologist and prostate cancer specialist at William Beaumont Hospital in Royal Oak, Michigan, says the results are exciting.

"Some of our most effective medicines come from plants," says Korman, "and these results are interesting and hopeful."

A NOTE OF CAUTION

However, he warns, "It's a big step to go from the lab to people."

Katz says the researchers are hopeful the therapy will work as well in people as it does in the lab, and they plan on conducting clinical trials in the future.

If it works as they hope, Katz says the herbal formula could be used as preventative therapy because it has no significant side effects. He says it could also, perhaps, be used as a treatment for men with small tumors who don't want to undergo surgery or radiation.

info The American Cancer Society at *www. cancer.org* offers tips that may help to prevent prostate cancer.

15

Stroke Prevention

The Only Aspirin Dose That Actually Prevents Stroke

Baby aspirin and coated aspirin might not be sufficient to prevent strokes, according to research performed at several major stroke centers.

People at risk for a stroke who take baby aspirin (also known as low-dose aspirin) were less likely to reap its blood-thinning benefits than those taking an adult-sized pill. The same was true of those who took coated aspirin compared with the uncoated kind, say researchers.

This research could have major implications because it could lead to the idea of aspirin as a dose-adjusted medication, says Dr. Mark Alberts, lead author of the study and director of the stroke program at Northwestern Memorial Hospital in Chicago. In other words, instead of a one-size-fits-all approach, he says, doctors would measure the effect of the dose and see if the patient needs a different dose.

THE ACCEPTED DOSE

Right now, doctors believe that 50 to 325 milligrams (mg) of aspirin may help prevent ischemic stroke, says Dr. Marshall Keilson, associate director of neurology at Maimonides Medical Center in Brooklyn, New York. *Ischemic* strokes are the most common type of stroke and occur when blood flow in an artery to the brain is pinched off, usually because of clotting. Aspirin thins the blood and prevents clots from forming.

Keilson says doctors use low doses of aspirin because they feel it reduces such complications as gastrointestinal upset and bleeding.

Mark Alberts, MD, Director, Stroke Program, Northwestern Memorial Hospital, Chicago, IL.

Marshall Keilson, MD, Associate Director of Neurology, Maimonides Medical Center, Brooklyn, NY.

Dan Fisher, MD, Cardiologist, New York University Medical Center.

February 14, 2003, presentation, American Stroke Association conference, Phoenix, AZ.

Many patients taking aspirin are still having strokes and, for that matter, heart attacks (aspirin is also thought to prevent some heart attacks). "Those episodes are indicating that the low doses that are commonly being used —around 81 mg—may not be adequate for stroke prevention," Keilson says.

In his study, Alberts and his coauthors measured how effective different doses and formulations of aspirin were at thinning blood in patients who had cerebrovascular disease.

WHAT WORKS BEST

More than half of the patients taking 81 mg a day did not have an anticlotting effect, which was significant, Alberts says. Of those taking coated aspirin, more than 60% did not have an anticlotting effect. But only 28% of the people taking 325 mg of uncoated aspirin did not have an anticlotting effect. In other words, higher doses and uncoated formulations seemed to work better. But, there's a long way to go before these early results become routinely recommended.

The study measured only thinning of the blood, not whether a person had another stroke. "We want to see if this is predictive of clinical results, which is the holy grail of research," Alberts says.

Keilson agrees. "Sometimes things that are done in a laboratory don't carry over in people," he says, adding that a large trial with thousands of patients is needed.

Risk factors overlap, says Dr. Dan Fisher, a cardiologist with New York University Medical Center in New York City. "We're still trying to find the right time to use aspirin. The guidelines are not perfect. We don't have clear answers."

info For more on the different types of stroke, visit the National Stroke Association at *www.stroke.org*. The association also has information on current guidelines for the use of aspirin in preventing strokes and heart attacks.

A Shot a Day Helps Keep Strokes Away

Kristi Reynolds, graduate research student, Tulane University School of Public Health and Tropical Medicine, New Orleans, LA.

Robert H. Eckel, MD, Professor, Medicine, University of Colorado Health Sciences Center, Denver, and Chairman, American Heart Association's Scientific Council on Nutrition, Physical Activity and Metabolism.

February 5, 2003, *Journal of the American Medical Association*.

Drinking more than 5 shots of hard liquor a day increases your risk of stroke by more than 60%, compared with those who don't drink at all. But lighter drinking—1 shot a day—may actually reduce the risk by 20%.

Researchers at the Tulane University School of Public Health and Tropical Medicine gathered 122 studies that examined the health benefits and hazards of alcohol, and analyzed 35 that focused on drinking and stroke.

Compared with nondrinkers, heavy drinkers had a 69% greater risk of *ischemic* stroke, the kind that occurs when a clot blocks blood flow to part of the brain. And the heavy drinkers had approximately double the risk of hemorrhagic stroke, which happens when a blood vessel in the brain bursts.

Those who consumed less than 1 shot a day, however, reduced their risk of ischemic stroke by 20%, and those who drank 2 or 3 shots a day had a 28% reduction, according to the study. (One shot is 1 oz of 100-proof spirits or 1.5 oz of 80-proof spirits, the amount of alcohol in one 12-oz beer or 4 oz of wine.)

Lead author Kristi Reynolds, a graduate research student at Tulane, says the analysis was done because there have been conflicting results from studies about the relationship between drinking alcohol and stroke risk. The report clarifies alcohol's benefits and risks.

Dr. Robert H. Eckel, a professor of medicine at the University of Colorado Health Sciences Center and chairman of the American Heart Association's scientific council on nutrition, physical activity, and metabolism, says the association is aware of the potential benefits, as well as the potential dangers, of drinking.

"If you look at alcohol as a drug, the potential adverse effects would be sufficient enough to limit its use," Eckel said.

The American Heart Association does not encourage any abstainer to take up drinking because of its possible beneficial effects. "We encourage adults to discuss the use of alcohol with their physicians," Eckel said.

info To learn more about stroke, visit the National Institute of Neurological Disorders and Stroke at *www.ninds.nih.gov*.

More Great Reasons for Men to Lose Weight

Tobias Kurth, MD, Brigham and Women's Hospital, Boston, MA.
S. Goya Wannamethee, PhD, Royal Free and University College Medical School, London, England.
December 9, 2002, *Archives of Internal Medicine*.

If you're worried about the risks of losing weight late in life, don't be. Two separate studies give insights into the dangers and myths of weight gain and weight loss for older men.

The first study adds stroke to the list of primary risks from obesity. "This should give [men] another reason to stay lean," says the lead author of this study, Dr. Tobias Kurth, with Brigham and Women's Hospital in Boston.

Kurth and a team of doctors associated with Harvard Medical School looked at the health records of more than 20,000 male doctors, ages 40 to 84 years. The participants reported information from 1982 to 1995 as part of the Physicians' Health Study.

STROKE RISK

In the United States, the number of overweight people is rapidly increasing. The researchers found that obesity was a major risk factor for stroke.

Obesity has long been associated with heart disease, the leading cause of death in the US. But obesity hasn't been clearly tied to stroke, the third-leading killer, because prior studies were too small, Kurth says.

"We should view obesity as a primary risk factor and not a potential, secondary risk factor," Kurth says.

In fact, the size of the study allowed Kurth to devise a simple formula showing how adding pounds increases the risk of stroke. For most men, an increase in weight of 7 to 8 pounds results in a 6% increase in the risk of stroke, he says.

To more accurately track how weight gain affects risk for stroke, men should calculate their body mass index (BMI), which shows the relationship between weight and height. According to the World Health Organization, a BMI of less than 25 is normal, 25 to 30 is overweight, and more than 30 is obese. According to Kurth, every 1-point increase in BMI increases stroke risk by 6%.

ROLLER COASTER WEIGHT

The second study concludes that middle-aged and elderly men shouldn't fear the weight fluctuation that often results from healthy dieting.

Doctors had worried that losing weight and weight "cycling"—gaining and losing weight through dieting—was unhealthy for men. But a long-term British study of more than 5600 middle-aged men concludes that this kind of thinking is a barrier to managing obesity.

Although the study found that men who experienced sustained weight loss or weight fluctuation were more likely to die than those who stayed about the same weight, the culprit wasn't weight cycling, it was a pre-existing condition, says lead author S. Goya Wannamethee, of the Royal Free and University College Medical School in London.

"Many of the earlier studies did not adequately take pre-existing disease or smoking into account," Wannamethee says.

info To calculate your BMI, visit the Centers for Disease Control and Prevention at *www.cdc.gov*. For assistance in losing weight, check the American Obesity Association at *www.obesity.org*.

■ ■ ■ ■

Are You a Candidate for a Stroke?

The National Stroke Association's prevention guidelines can help you determine if you're at risk for having a stroke. *Following are their stroke prevention guidelines...*

●**Know your blood pressure.** If it is elevated, work with your doctor to keep it under control. High blood pressure is a leading cause of stroke. Have your blood pressure checked at least once each year—more often if you have a history of high blood pressure. Consult your doctor if the top (*systolic*) number is higher than 135 or if the bottom (*diastolic*) number is more than 85.

●**Find out if you have atrial fibrillation** (also called AF). If you have AF, work with your doctor to manage it. Atrial fibrillation can cause blood to collect in the chambers of your heart. This blood can form clots and cause a stroke. Your doctor can detect AF by carefully checking your pulse.

●**If you smoke, stop.** Smoking doubles the risk of stroke. If you stop smoking today, your risk for stroke will begin to decrease.

●**If you drink alcohol, do so in moderation.** Drinking a glass of wine or beer or 1 drink each day may actually lower your risk of stroke (provided there is no other medical reason why you should avoid alcohol). Remember that alcohol is a drug—it can interact with other drugs you are taking. Alcohol is harmful if taken in large doses. If you don't drink, don't start.

●**Know your cholesterol number.** If it is high, work with your doctor to control it. Lowering your cholesterol may reduce your risk for stroke. High cholesterol can indirectly increase your stroke risk by putting you at a greater risk for heart disease—an important stroke risk factor. Often, high cholesterol can be controlled with diet and exercise; some individuals may require medication.

●**If you are diabetic, follow your doctor's recommendations carefully to control your diabetes.** Having diabetes puts you at an increased risk for stroke. Your doctor can prescribe a nutrition program, lifestyle changes, and medicine that can help control your diabetes.

●**Include exercise in your daily routine.** A brisk walk, swim, or other exercise for as little as 30 minutes a day can improve your health in many ways, and may reduce your risk for stroke.

●**Lower the sodium (salt) and fat in your diet.** By cutting down on sodium and fat, you may be able to lower your blood pressure and, most importantly, lower your risk for stroke.

●**Ask your doctor if you have circulation problems.** If so, work with your doctor to control them. Fatty deposits can block the arteries that carry blood from your heart to your brain. This kind of blockage can cause a stroke.

●**If you have any stroke symptoms, seek immediate medical attention.**

Reduce Your Risk of Stroke by Brushing Your Teeth

Kaumudi J. Joshipura, ScD, Associate Professor of Epidemiology, Harvard School of Public Health and Harvard School of Dental Medicine, Boston, MA.

Ralph L. Sacco, MD, Professor of Neurology and Epidemiology, Neurological Institute of Columbia University College of Physicians and Surgeons, New York, NY.

December 13, 2002, *Stroke*.

People who have periodontal disease and lose a lot of teeth are more likely to have a stroke...but why?

Kaumudi J. Joshipura, who found the link, says she can't explain the relationship.

"It is still a mystery," says Joshipura, who is an associate professor of epidemiology at the Harvard School of Public Health and the Harvard School of Dental Medicine.

It's true that her study, which looked at data on more than 40,000 men, did find that men with fewer teeth generally were older, drank more alcohol, were less physically active, and were more likely to smoke, all of which are risk factors for stroke.

But those common risk factors aren't enough to explain the relationship, Joshipura says.

PUZZLING LINK

Indeed, the analysis came up with one counterintuitive finding: The association between tooth loss and stroke was higher among nonsmokers than among smokers.

Other studies have tended to find a similar association, but they have been controversial, Joshipura says. One strength of her study, Joshipura says, is that it was made up largely of white professionals—dentists, veterinarians, pharmacists, optometrists, and so forth—who generally "behave properly" as far as health habits are concerned.

Over 12 years, there were 349 blood clot-induced strokes among the 40,000 men. Men who had fewer than 25 teeth when they entered the study were much more likely to have this kind of stroke than those with more than 25 teeth.

The risk went up as the number of teeth went down. In fact, men who had no more than 10 teeth when they came into the study were 66% more likely to have this kind of stroke.

The number of teeth lost during the study didn't have much of an effect on the risk of stroke—perhaps because tooth loss tended to be minor, and it takes many years for the effect of tooth loss to impact stroke risk, Joshipura says.

IS INFLAMMATION THE CULPRIT?

One theory that is gaining attention is that the infection related to periodontal disease and tooth loss causes inflammation that injures the arteries, says Dr. Ralph L. Sacco, professor of neurology and epidemiology at the Neurological Institute of Columbia University College of Physicians and Surgeons in New York City and a spokesman for the American Stroke Association.

"We have our own studies showing that tooth loss is related to carotid artery disease," Sacco says. The carotid artery is the main artery to the brain.

Sacco poses the question: Could chronic infection—showing up as periodontal disease—be related to hardening of the arteries?

At any rate, Sacco says, the relationship is "another good reason to brush your teeth."

info You can learn about periodontal disease and what to do about it from the American Academy of Periodontology at *www. perio.org.*

Behavior Key to Preventing Strokes in Young and Middle-Aged Adults

Joseph P. Broderick, MD, Chairman, Department of Neurology, University of Cincinnati, OH.

Thomas G. Brott, MD, Professor, Medicine, Mayo Medical School, Jacksonville, FL.

May 23, 2003, *Stroke.*

They're called *subarachnoid* strokes, and they're about as deadly as strokes come. They happen when a blood vessel ruptures just outside the brain.

They tend to strike young and middle-aged adults. Fifty-five thousand to 60,000 Americans suffer a subarachnoid hemorrhage each year, and 40% to 50% of them die.

Yet research shows these kinds of strokes can be prevented.

"Most subarachnoid hemorrhages in young and middle-aged people are preventable," says Dr. Joseph P. Broderick, chairman of the department of neurology at the University of Cincinnati. The key is a change in behavior.

To determine which behavior changes are most important, Broderick and his colleagues questioned 312 young and middle-aged men and women who had suffered these hemorrhages over a 5-year period. They asked about lifestyle and other factors that could be related to the risk of such strokes. Then the researchers compared the answers with those of 618 similar people who had not had a subarachnoid stroke.

THE RISK FACTORS FOR STROKE

One risk factor that stood out was family history. The risk was 3.8 times higher for people with a close relative who had had a subarachnoid stroke, compared with those without such a family history. Obviously, you can't change family history, the leading risk factor. So, for those with such a history, Broderick says, "it becomes more critical and more important to make lifestyle changes."

Another big culprit in these kinds of strokes, to no one's surprise, was smoking. Two-thirds of the stroke patients were smokers, compared with 30% of the healthy people.

"It should be emphasized that cigarette smoking is the most important modifiable risk factor," says Dr. Thomas G. Brott, a professor of medicine at the Mayo Medical School in Jacksonville, Florida, and a member of the research team.

Another common risk factor was one that's behind most cardiovascular disease—high blood pressure. People with the condition had 2.4 times the normal risk of subarachnoid hemorrhage.

A LESSER ROLE

Diabetes and high blood cholesterol, 2 other familiar cardiovascular risk factors, don't seem to play a role in subarachnoid hemorrhage, the study indicates, but drug use might. The numbers are small, but it's significant that 3 of the stroke patients reported cocaine use, while none of the healthy people did, Broderick says.

One unexpected finding was that the stroke risk was higher for thin people—a low body mass index (23 or lower) was associated with a 50% higher risk of subarachnoid hemorrhage. "The association was strongest among 4-pack-a-day smokers, so this might be an indirect effect of smoking," says Brott, noting that heavy smoking can keep people thin.

info To learn more about preventing a stroke, visit the American Heart Association at *www.americanheart.org*.

Zeroing in On the Real Cause of High Blood Pressure

David Roth, MD, Chief, Nephrology and Hypertension, University of Miami School of Medicine, Miami, FL.

Sheldon Greenberg, MD, Program Director, Nephrology, Maimonides Medical Center, Brooklyn, NY.

January 9, 2003, *New England Journal of Medicine*.

According to the Mayo Clinic, high blood pressure affects up to 50 million Americans, and the vast majority of these people have a condition called primary hypertension, for which no specific cause has ever been identified.

However, German researchers have recently found a possible cause for most of these cases of high blood pressure. They have obtained data to support a theory that people with fewer *nephrons*—or filtering units—in their kidneys are more susceptible to hypertension.

"This [study] dovetails into theories that have been proposed over the last decade or more suggesting that the concept of how many nephrons we're endowed with translates into the expression of disease, in this case hypertension and/or kidney disease," says Dr. David Roth, chief of nephrology at the University of Miami School of Medicine.

A TIME-CONSUMING COUNT

For the study, the researchers counted the number of nephrons in the kidneys of 20 middle-aged white patients who had died in accidents. Ten of these patients had documented hypertension and 10 did not.

Each kidney in a patient without hypertension had approximately 1.4 million nephrons; those with hypertension had approximately 700,000 nephrons each.

The difference in numbers is too great to ignore, experts say.

"If it was only 50,000, you'd say that's nothing," Roth said. "But double is a significant finding, even though the number of patients was small."

Although the results of this preliminary study seem startling, there is no way to know whether the number of nephrons led to the development of hypertension in the 10 patients, Roth says. More studies are necessary to determine a true cause-and-effect relationship.

"There's still probably a large number of people who don't have their blood pressure checked for years and have slow organ damage and dysfunction from undiagnosed hypertension," says Dr. Sheldon Greenberg, program director of nephrology at Maimonides Medical Center in Brooklyn, New York. "That's probably the more important aspect for the public."

info For more on hypertension, visit the American Society of Hypertension at *www.ash-us.org.*

Low-Cost Hypertension Drugs May Work Just as Well as Expensive Ones

Jackson T. Wright, Jr., MD, PhD, Professor, Medicine, Case Western Reserve University, Cleveland, OH.

Lawrence J. Appel, MD, MPH, Professor, Medicine, Johns Hopkins University, Baltimore, MD.

December 18, 2002, *Journal of the American Medical Association.*

You might expect newer, more advanced, and costlier medications for high blood pressure to be more effective than the older and less expensive *thiazide diuretics.* But a Cleveland study found that's not necessarily the case.

In an 8-year trial, the incidence of heart failure was lower and the risk of fatal heart disease or heart attacks was no greater for people who took a diuretic than for those who took the newer *calcium channel blockers* or *angiotensin-converting enzyme (ACE) inhibitors.*

The study may be the most comprehensive effort ever made to compare the effectiveness of different blood pressure drugs. *Here's how each drug works...*

• **Diuretics** lower blood pressure by increasing the passing of water and sodium.

• **Calcium channel blockers** widen blood vessels by relaxing the muscles around them.

• **ACE inhibitors** block the activity of an enzyme that makes arteries constrict.

Diuretics, by far the oldest drugs, are generally available as relatively inexpensive generics, while the calcium channel blockers and ACE inhibitors often are higher-priced, brand-name products.

The 50 to 60 million Americans who have been diagnosed with high blood pressure now spend an estimated $15.5 billion a year on drugs, the report says. A large proportion of patients need more than 1 drug, but the report says, "it is reasonable to infer that a diuretic be included in all multi-drug regimens."

A SAVINGS IN COST

A preliminary cost analysis showed that "if patients were switched from calcium channel blockers and ACE inhibitors to diuretics, the annual savings in direct costs would be between $250 and $600 per patient," says study leader Dr. Jackson T. Wright Jr., a professor of medicine at Case Western Reserve University. There would be other savings from a reduced need for hospitalizations, Wright adds.

Diuretics have fallen out of favor with many doctors because they have potentially dangerous side effects, such as raising blood cholesterol and sugar levels, causing concern that they might actually be increasing the risk of heart disease, says Dr. Lawrence J. Appel, a professor of medicine at Johns Hopkins University.

However, the study "provides strong evidence that they should be first-line therapy," he says.

info The National Heart, Lung and Blood Institute at *www.nhlbi.nih.gov/hbp* provides information on managing your blood pressure.

Genetics Doubles Your Risk of Stroke

Paula Jerrard–Dunne, MD, Clinical Research Fellow, St. George's Hospital Medical School, London, England.

Larry B. Goldstein, MD, Professor of Medicine, Duke University, Durham, NC.

April 25, 2003, *Stroke,* online issue.

Only approximately half of all strokes can be attributed to traditional risk factors. That leaves half unexplained, and researchers are beginning to make connections between the brain-damaging event and genetics.

Risk factors include high blood pressure, smoking, diabetes, and high cholesterol, says Dr. Paula Jerrard–Dunne, a clinical research fellow at St. George's Hospital Medical School in London and lead author of the study. "Not all people have these risk factors, and it is hard to explain why some people with risk factors go on to develop a stroke and others do not. That means that other factors, such as genetic predisposition, may also be important."

Practically speaking, says Dr. Larry B. Goldstein, a professor of medicine at Duke University School of Medicine, what this study says is that if you have a family member younger than 65 years who has had a stroke, you should speak to your doctor about risk factors and what you can do about them.

A number of studies have hinted strongly at a genetic factor in stroke risk, Goldstein says, but this study is particularly valuable because of its careful focus on 2 specific types of ischemic stroke, which are the kind that happen when a clot blocks a blood vessel. A clot can block a large vessel, causing potentially fatal, severe brain damage, or it can block a small blood vessel, causing problems that are not life-threatening, such as the loss of movement in a limb.

The British researchers selected 1000 people who had suffered ischemic strokes. Their average age was 65 years. They found that the large-vessel stroke patients were more than twice as likely to have an immediate family member who had suffered a stroke or heart attack at age 65 or younger. For small-vessel stroke patients, the risk was slightly lower, but still significant.

KNOW YOUR FAMILY HISTORY

Family history is much more important in young people because "in older people, the effects of blood pressure, smoking, poor diet, and so forth have had a longer time to cause damage to the blood vessels," Jerrard–Dunne says. For people who have strokes when they are relatively young, "we suspect that there might be an underlying genetic susceptibility which makes them much more sensitive to the effects of risk factors."

How to Tell If Someone Is Having a Stroke

Amy Hurwitz, medical student, University of North Carolina–Chapel Hill School of Medicine.

Robert Felberg, MD, Medical Director, Stroke Center, Ochsner Clinic Foundation Hospital, New Orleans, LA.

February 13, 2003, presentation, American Stroke Association Conference, Phoenix, AZ.

Can you tell if someone is having a stroke? Yes, say researchers. The odds are good that you can, even for a complete stranger, if you know how to spot the symptoms.

Even though treating stroke patients requires extensive training, people without training can easily learn to *detect* stroke symptoms, says study author Amy Hurwitz, a medical student at the University of North Carolina–Chapel Hill School of Medicine.

SPEED IS ESSENTIAL

A quick diagnosis is vital because a treatment is available for strokes caused by blood clots, but it only works if it's given within 3 hours of the onset of symptoms.

"Even a delay of 20 minutes can make a huge difference," says Dr. Robert Felberg, medical director of the stroke program at Ochsner Clinic Foundation Hospital in New Orleans. He says that, ideally, you should get to the hospital within the first hour after symptoms appear, because doctors need time to make the diagnosis and run a CT scan to confirm it before they can safely give the clot-busting stroke medication.

Every year, 600,000 Americans have a stroke, and 160,000 of them die, according to the American Stroke Association. Stroke is also the leading cause of long-term disability.

TESTING THE THEORY

For this study, the researchers chose 100 random visitors to the hospital and put them in a room in the emergency department where a stroke survivor and one of the researchers were waiting. The stroke survivors still had visible symptoms, such as arm weakness, facial weakness, or slurred speech.

The visitor learned how to give a 3-item exam used by doctors to assess stroke victims.

1. Look at the patient's smile to see if it is symmetrical.

2. Could the patient raise both arms and keep them raised?

3. Ask the patient to speak a standard phrase.

The volunteers were then asked to decide if the patient had performed normally or abnormally on the tests.

The visitors correctly gave the test nearly all of the time. In patients with facial weakness, they correctly identified that symptom approximately 70% of the time; arm weakness was correct in nearly all of the patients; and speech problems were found nearly 90% of the time.

"This is a great study that could have a lot of benefit," Felberg says. "The biggest problem we have is that 75% of the American population doesn't know what a stroke is." Often, he says, people will ignore their symptoms or try to "sleep them off," and by the time they seek treatment, it's too late.

Teaching people to look for facial or arm weakness or slurred speech would be a great first step, Felberg says.

One big problem with the diagnosis of stroke, says Hurwitz, is that no 1 symptom stands out, such as the chest pain or shortness of breath in heart attack victims.

Spotting Stroke Symptoms Quickly May Save Lives

An unexplained headache is only 1 of a number of symptoms that could indicate that a stroke is occurring. *The National Stroke Association describes several warning signs that may signal the onset of a stroke...*

●**Sudden numbness or weakness of face, arm, or leg,** especially on one side of the body.

●**Sudden confusion,** trouble speaking, or understanding.

●**Sudden trouble seeing** in one eye or both eyes.

●**Sudden trouble walking,** dizziness, loss of balance, or coordination.

●**Sudden severe headache** with no known cause.

Time is the most important element if someone exhibits any of these signs. Make the individual as comfortable as you can, and call 911 immediately. Remember the time when you first noticed the symptoms so you can tell the EMS aides. This information may help in determining what clot-busting drugs can be administered.

'Silent' Strokes May Cause Dementia

John P. Blass, MD, PhD, Professor, Neurology, Medicine and Neuroscience, Weill Cornell Medical College, New York, NY.
March 27, 2003, *New England Journal of Medicine.*

Even if a stroke causes few or no symptoms, affected people can suffer a mental decline similar to Alzheimer's disease, says a Dutch study.

Older people who suffer these "silent" brain obstructions are more likely to have dementia and a steeper decline in cognitive function than those who don't ever have a stroke, write epidemiologists at Erasmus Medical Center in

Rotterdam in a report that stops just short of saying these attacks actually cause this mental decline.

This research is the latest chapter in an evolution of medical thought about dementia that has gone on for more than a century, says Dr. John P. Blass, a professor of neurology, medicine and neuroscience at Weill Cornell College and author of an accompanying editorial.

CHANGING OPINIONS

For more than 100 years, scientists thought senior dementia was due to problems with blood vessels in the brain, Blass says. Approximately 35 years ago, that belief changed, and people thought there was a distinction between problems caused by blood vessel diseases and degenerative diseases. "In the last 10 or 15 years, the pendulum is swinging back toward a midpoint." Blood vessel disease is being recognized as a risk factor for dementia, he adds.

The Danish results come from studying more than 1000 people between the ages of 60 and 90 years who were free of dementia when the study began.

Dementia developed in 30 people during the almost 4-year study, and the presence of silent brain infarcts more than doubled the risk of dementia, the researchers report. The increased risk was seen only in people who had suffered infarcts at the beginning of the study and had more infarcts over the following years.

Possible explanations: A stroke may speed the progress of dementia in someone with Alzheimer's disease; or, perhaps obstructions trigger the development of the plaques and nerve tangles that are seen in Alzheimer's disease.

MORE QUESTIONS

The study leaves several questions unanswered, Blass says, adding that a large multicenter trial is needed.

Such a study would indicate what to do about clinically normal people who have had a silent infarct, Blass says. "The possible clinical implication is that these people should be given baby aspirin or other medications to prevent further strokes," he says.

Sometimes these obstructions do cause symptoms, Blass says. "[If you have] weakness of an arm or leg or tingling of an arm or leg, something may be happening in the brain," he says, adding that you should see a doctor.

info To learn more about dementia, consult the National Library of Medicine at *www.nlm.nih.gov.*

Keeping Stroke Patients Awake Saves Lives

Steven Rudolph, MD, Stroke Neurologist and Director, Stroke Unit, Lenox Hill Hospital, New York, NY.

Alex Abou–Chebl, MD, Interventional Neurologist, The Cleveland Clinic Foundation, OH.

February 14, 2003, presentation, International Stroke Conference, Phoenix, AZ.

Researchers have found that opening the clogged brain arteries of stroke-prone patients while they are awake may reduce the risk of complications.

The operation has traditionally been performed while the patient is under general anesthesia. This can cause serious complications, in part because physicians can't assess the patient's status in the middle of the procedure.

The experimental therapy, similar to established treatments for heart disease, involves inserting a balloon into the blocked artery and inflating it to clear the pathway of obstacles. Later, physicians insert a *stent,* or a small prop, to hold the artery open.

When the procedure is done under local anesthesia, physicians can communicate with the patient and carefully alter the movement and pressure of the balloon if the patient displays adverse symptoms, says study author Dr. Alex Abou–Chebl, an interventional neurologist at the Cleveland Clinic Foundation.

Although patients experience some pain and discomfort under local anesthesia, Abou-Chebl says they tend to prefer the procedure because they are aware of what's occurring and they forgo the risks associated with general anesthesia, such as heart attack, brain damage, and even death.

THE STUDY

The Cleveland Clinic team studied the procedure in 11 patients who had a history of stroke or *transient ischemic attack* (TIA), a warning sign that causes stroke-like symptoms, but no permanent damage.

All were patients who did not respond to the standard preventive treatment for stroke —aspirin and blood-thinning drugs—and all elected to undergo the procedure.

Of the 11 subjects, 3 experienced serious complications associated with the procedure and 1 patient died from an adverse reaction to a drug.

At least 1 of the patients, however, may have been saved by the experimental procedure. The patient reported head pain during the operation, prompting the team of physicians to deflate the balloon.

"If we had not known that he had a headache, we would have inflated the balloon further, which might have ruptured the artery, and he could have died on the spot," Abou–Chebl says.

MORE RESEARCH NEEDED

Others say the study was too small and the results too mixed to warrant optimism about the technique.

"This doesn't prove that this is such a good idea. This just proves that you can do it," says Dr. Steven Rudolph, a stroke neurologist and director of Lenox Hill Hospital's Stroke Unit in New York City.

"It's much more useful to have people under anesthesia who can't move when you're trying to put something in a blood vessel that measures 1 millimeter across," he says.

Abou–Chebl agrees that a randomized controlled trial with larger numbers of patients is needed to confirm these findings.

Caffeine–Alcohol Combo Protects Against Stroke Brain Damage

James C. Grotta, MD, Director, Stroke Program, University of Texas–Houston Medical School.
Philip B. Gorelik, MD, Professor of Medicine, Rush–Presbyterian Medical Center, Chicago, IL.
April 10, 2003, *Stroke*.

What started as idle conjecture has produced a promising—and unconventional—treatment to prevent brain damage caused by a stroke.

Says Dr. James C. Grotta, director of the stroke program at the University of Texas–Houston Medical School, "One of my laboratory workers was musing about the fact that moderate or mild use of alcohol can be effective in reducing the effect of stroke. So we started fooling around with combinations of it with other things, flavonoids and vitamin C and so [on], and we stumbled on this."

"This" is a mixture that Grotta calls *caffeinol*. It consists of the amount of caffeine found in 1 or 2 cups of strong coffee and the amount of alcohol in 1 cocktail.

Brain damage in rats was reduced by 80% when caffeinol was given within 3 hours after a stroke.

POSSIBLE IN HUMANS

The first human trials have shown that the blood level of caffeinol that is effective in rats can be achieved in humans, and steps toward treatment of people have been taken.

In the study, some of the patients who got caffeinol were also being treated with a clot-busting drug that is often used for stroke. The combination appears safe, Grotta says. Although 1 patient did have bleeding within the brain, an independent safety officer concluded the hemorrhage was not related to caffeinol.

This indicates that caffeinol can be added to standard stroke treatment, Grotta says.

COMBO IS BETTER

"We think that the combination is more effective than any other drugs you look at in the laboratory, particularly for strokes that affect the *cortex,* the gray matter of the brain that controls language and other abilities," he says.

The next step, being tried now, is to combine caffeinol with the cooling of the body, a process that helps reduce stroke damage. The cooling is done by running cold liquid through a catheter inserted in the femoral vein, "like a refrigerator coil," Grotta explains.

That combination of treatments has been used safely in one patient, and it will be tried in 10 or 20 more to test safety, Grotta says.

IRISH COFFEE NOT THE ANSWER

But the caffeine–alcohol combination is for treatment, not prevention, Grotta says. "Anyone who thinks that having a cup of Irish coffee every day will help prevent stroke will find that it does not work," he says.

This appears to be the first time the idea of using either caffeine or alcohol to treat stroke has been proposed, says Dr. Philip B. Gorelik, professor of medicine at Rush–Presbyterian Medical Center in Chicago.

"These compounds have the potential for being useful neuroprotective agents in humans. [The researchers] are taking the appropriate steps to evaluate their concept," says Gorelik, a spokesman for the American Heart Association.

Catheters Put Some Heart Patients at Risk of Stroke

Heyder Omran, MD, Associate Professor, Cardiology, University of Bonn, Germany.

Stephen Ramee, Cardiologist, Ochsner Clinic Foundation, New Orleans, LA.

April 12, 2003, *The Lancet.*

Using catheters to diagnose *aortic-valve stenosis,* a particular type of heart disease, puts patients at an unnecessarily high risk of stroke, say researchers. Instead, these patients fared better when surgeons relied on echocardiograms, a noninvasive procedure.

"If you do a good echocardiogram, and you are confident about the results, I don't see a reason for doing the passage through the valve [with a catheter]," says Dr. Heyder Omran, lead author of the study and an associate professor of cardiology at the University of Bonn in Germany. "That will certainly expose the patient to the risk of stroke."

Aortic-valve stenosis is a narrowing, or obstruction, of the valve between the left ventricle of the heart and the aorta, a large artery that connects to it.

It is one of the most common forms of valvular disease, occurring in approximately 1 in every 2000 people, according to the American Heart Association. Its symptoms include fainting, chest pain, and shortness of breath after exercise. To fix the problem, surgeons replace the valve.

MEASURING THE DISEASE

There are 2 ways to diagnosis the degree of stenosis, or narrowing of the valve.

1. One procedure involves pushing a catheter through the diseased valve. The pressure differences between the heart chamber and the aorta reveal the extent of the disease.

2. The other way to diagnose stenosis is by echocardiogram, a test that uses sound waves to create a picture of the heart. The picture is more detailed than an X-ray, and there is no radiation exposure.

In most cases, using the echocardiogram alone is the way to go, Omran says. His study results showed that patients who had catheterization had a much higher rate of stroke.

QUESTIONING THE FINDINGS

But not everyone agrees. "Catheterization is used routinely to assess the valvular disease, and complications are rare," says Dr. Stephen Ramee, a cardiologist at the Ochsner Clinic Foundation in New Orleans.

Furthermore, he adds, magnetic resonance imaging (MRIs) are very, very sensitive and whatever lesions they are picking up might not matter.

But the most important reason for continuing to use catheterization, he says, is that echocardiograms are easily misread. Echocardiograms can make it appear as though the disease is more or less severe than it really is.

Any added risk of catheterization is far outweighed by the risk of doing unnecessary heart surgery, he says.

The key, he adds, is "to make the diagnosis correctly and to not send a patient to surgery if he or she doesn't need it."

Ramee says he uses the echocardiogram first. If that shows there's a problem, he uses catheterization. If both confirm the disease is severe enough to require treatment, then, and only then, will he do heart surgery.

Risky Surgery You May Not Need!

Ethan A. Halm, MD, MPH, Assistant Professor, Health Policy and Medicine, Mount Sinai School of Medicine, New York, NY.

Mark J. Alberts, MD, Professor, Neurology, Northwestern University, Chicago, IL.

May 9, 2003, *Stroke,* online edition.

If the artery-clearing operation known as a *carotid endarterectomy* is in your future, then have your doctor verify that it's necessary.

A New York physician's study found that more than 10% of the 130,000 procedures done in the United States every year would be better left undone because the potential risks outweigh the benefits.

But there's some good news, says study author Dr. Ethan A. Halm, an assistant professor of health policy and medicine at Mount Sinai School of Medicine in New York City. The number of inappropriate operations is down by two-thirds since the 1980s, and there are some ways to determine whether the operation is right for you.

A carotid endarterectomy is done to prevent a stroke. The surgeon removes plaque from the arteries leading to the brain. Plaque is formed by fatty deposits that could eventually block a blood vessel and damage part of the brain.

"This kind of surgery was very controversial in the 1970s and 1980s," Halm explains. "Enthusiasm for it dampened when a RAND Corporation [study] showed that the risk of patients dying was much higher than people

thought. Then the National Institutes of Health invested millions of dollars in controlled studies to clarify who benefits and who doesn't."

WHY SURGERY CAN BE WRONG FOR YOU

The 2 big reasons to call an operation inappropriate were the presence of other serious conditions in the patient or the fact that the carotid artery had not narrowed enough to warrant surgery, the guidelines say.

One striking finding was the unusually high rate of serious problems for patients who had both an *endarterectomy* and bypass surgery, a combination deemed necessary because fatty deposits were blocking both the carotid artery and blood vessels of the heart. More than 10% of those patients died or had a stroke within 30 days after the operation, the study found.

"The complication rate is quite high, and this combined procedure should not be done," says Dr. Mark J. Alberts, a professor of neurology at Northwestern University and director of its stroke program.

Inappropriate operations can be avoided if the patient is assessed "by a multidisciplinary team, not only the surgeon but also a neurologist and an internist or cardiologist," Alberts says.

SPEAK UP

Your voice should be heard, too, Halm says. "Patients need to ask their doctors if their mix of health problems is too risky for them to have the surgery."

Chiropractic Linked to Rare Incidents of Strokes

Wade S. Smith, MD, PhD, Associate Professor, Neurology, and Director, Neurovascular Service, University of California, San Francisco.

William Lauretti, DC, Bethesda, MD.

May 13, 2003, *Neurology.*

People who undergo manipulation or adjustment of the high spine put themselves at risk of ruptured arteries that can lead to strokes.

A study found that stroke patients with torn arteries in the neck were 6 times more likely to have been to a chiropractor for an adjustment in the preceding month than those whose strokes occurred for other reasons.

Splits, or dissections, of the neck arteries are believed to cause up to one-fifth of all strokes in people younger than 60 years, or approximately 2 to 3 cases per 100,000.

There is a strong association between neck manipulation and stroke, says study author Dr. Wade S. Smith, a neurologist at the University of California, San Francisco. "It's probably rare, but it's there."

But Smith and his colleagues stopped short of advising people not to go to chiropractors or undergo neck manipulations because the procedure probably accounts for fewer than 1 in 1 million strokes.

Neck pain often precedes a dissection, and it's a main reason people go to a chiropractor —raising the possibility that manipulations are unfairly blamed for the vessel damage.

One problem that did surface is that many chiropractors fail to warn their patients about the possible complication, and neurologists don't always consider the link, either.

Dr. William Lauretti, a chiropractor and a delegate to the American Chiropractic Association, says he and his colleagues don't usually address the risk because it's so low and, from their perspective, unproved.

Lauretti says the forces that spinal manipulation puts on the neck arteries are weaker than those that accompany normal movement of the head, and much less than required to stretch the vessel.

THE STUDY

Smith's group looked for the link between spinal manipulation and strokes in men and women younger than 60 years. They interviewed 51 people who had suffered either a major stroke or a *transient ischemic attack* (TIA)—a form of small stroke—following a split artery.

Seven of these patients said they'd been to a chiropractor the month before suffering their stroke. On the other hand, 3 of 100 men and women stroke patients who hadn't had a vessel rupture had seen a chiropractor recently.

But even after accounting for neck pain, the risk of dissection following spinal manipulation persisted. And more than half of the people who'd suffered a dissection after seeing a chiropractor said their neck pain had appeared or worsened during or after the spinal procedure.

■ ■ ■ ■

Factors That Increase Stroke Risk

According to the National Stroke Association, there are several factors that can raise the risk of stroke. *They are...*

●**Smoking** doubles stroke risk.

●**Excessive consumption of alcohol** is associated with stroke in a small number of research studies.

●**Excess weight** puts a strain on the entire circulatory system. It also makes people more likely to have other stroke risk factors such as high cholesterol, high blood pressure, and diabetes.

info For more on chiropractic care, visit the American Chiropractic Association at *www.amerchiro.org.*

16

Women's Health

Long-Term Hormone Replacement Therapy Does More Harm Than Good

 huge trial on the effectiveness of hormone replacement therapy (HRT) in fighting a number of ailments experienced by postmenopausal women was halted because it was dangerous to the participants. The study, which was to have run for 8 years, was stopped in July 2002 because researchers found that some of the drug combinations raised the risk of heart problems and breast cancer.

The clinical trial, sponsored by the Women's Health Initiative (WHI), used a combination of the hormones estrogen and progestin. The trial ran for 5.2 years before it was determined that women using the combination HRT (specifically, a product called Prempro) were more likely to have breast cancer, heart attack, stroke,

and blood clots, even though they were protected against osteoporosis and colon cancer.

New analyses, published in the *Annals of Internal Medicine* and the *Journal of the American Medical Association*, lend more support to the findings in the WHI study. The *Annals* review primarily addresses cardiovascular disease risk; the *JAMA* review also considers other potential effects of long-term HRT use, such as osteoporosis and colon cancer prevention, and includes the results of the WHI study in its analysis.

THE CONCLUSIONS

In both reviews, the researchers combed through medical literature from 1966 to 2001.

Heidi D. Nelson, MD, MPH, Associate Professor, Medicine and Associate Professor, Medical Informatics and Outcomes Research, Oregon Health & Science University, Portland, OR.

Linda L. Humphrey, MD, MPH, Associate Professor, Medicine, Oregon Health & Science University and Portland Veterans Affairs Medical Center, Portland, OR.

William Parker, MD, Gynecologist, UCLA Medical Center, Santa Monica, CA.

August 20, 2002, *Annals of Internal Medicine.*

August 21, 2002, *Journal of the American Medical Association.*

"For prevention of chronic conditions, there aren't a lot of reasons to take [combination HRT]," says Dr. Heidi D. Nelson, an author of the *JAMA* review and an associate professor of medicine and medical informatics and outcome research at the Oregon Health & Science University in Portland. She adds, "I want to make clear we were only looking at HRT for the prevention of chronic conditions," and not for short-term relief of hot flashes and other menopausal symptoms, which is what HRT is often used for.

The *Annals* review, led by Dr. Linda L. Humphrey, associate professor of medicine at Oregon Health & Science University and the Portland Veterans Affairs Medical Center, concludes that HRT has no benefit in the primary or secondary prevention of coronary heart disease.

NO HEART BENEFIT FOUND

"The thing that was so exciting a few years ago is that everyone thought [HRT] helped your heart," Nelson says. "Our review found no benefit for the heart. That takes a huge amount of the luster away from taking something long-term. It does help your bones. That's been consistent in all the studies. But there are other things you can do [to preserve bone density]. What really has changed over the past few years is the realization that there is more evidence for harm."

A woman's decision of whether to take HRT today for the prevention of chronic conditions, Nelson says, "is a different decision than it was before."

She is talking, she stresses, only about combination therapy using estrogen plus progestin. The arm of the WHI study evaluating estrogen-only, given to women who do not have a uterus, is continuing. (Women with an intact uterus are given combination therapy because taking estrogen alone raises the risk of endometrial cancer.)

Both researchers say some women may have quality-of-life reasons for continuing to take HRT for more than a few years. Some say they simply feel better on the therapy, have fewer mood swings, less vaginal dryness, and better libido.

CONSULT YOUR DOCTOR FIRST

The new analyses probably won't change the advice doctors are giving women on a case-by-case basis about HRT according to their individual risks, says Dr. William Parker, a gynecologist at Santa Monica–UCLA Medical Center who is very familiar with HRT research.

info For more on the Women's Health Initiative, visit its Web site, *www.whi.org* where you'll find information and updates on HRT research. You can also find a series of questions and answers about HRT prepared by the American College of Obstetricians and Gynecologists, at its Web site at *www.acog.org*.

'Designer Estrogens' Offer Alternative to HRT

Victor G. Vogel, MD, MHS, FACP, Professor, Medicine and Epidemiology, University of Pittsburgh School of Medicine, and Protocol Chairman, Study of Tamoxifen and Raloxifene, National Cancer Institute.

January 1, 2003, *Cancer*.

Physicians and women are showing renewed interest in medications known as *selective estrogen receptor modulators,* or SERMs. That's especially true since a recent major study linked conventional hormone replacement therapy (HRT) to unacceptable health risks.

SERMs, also called designer estrogens, offer an alternative to HRT. And they can eliminate one of the side effects of HRT—an increased risk of breast cancer—according to researchers from the University of Athens and the University of Patras, both in Greece.

HOW THEY ACT

SERMs block the actions of estrogen in breast tissue, and in certain other tissues, by filling up cells that serve as "estrogen receptors." Although the SERM medication fills in the receptor, it does not send messages to the cell to grow and divide, and thus reduces cancer risk. However, the SERM medicines do send estrogen-like signals when they fill up receptors in bone cells, thus helping to slow or prevent osteoporosis, the researchers say.

The most common SERMs are *tamoxifen* (Nolvadex), *toremifene* (Fareston), and *raloxifene* (Evista).

SERMs may be preferred over conventional HRT, the researchers write, because they mitigate the breast cancer risk but maintain the bone-protecting benefits of estrogen replacement therapy.

WHERE HRT WENT WRONG

A portion of the massive Women's Health Initiative, a study in which women were given estrogen and progestin, was halted when the overall health risks were found to exceed the benefits. Women taking combined HRT for 1 year had more coronary heart disease events, strokes, lung embolisms, and more invasive breast cancers than did women taking a placebo. Of the 10,000 women taking HRT, there were 6 fewer colon cancers and 5 fewer hip fractures. The estrogen-only arm of the trial is continuing.

SERMs are a promising alternative to conventional HRT, the researchers conclude. Taking a multidisciplinary approach will help doctors and women individualize therapy, depending on their needs and risks.

What this research shows us is that you do have options, says Dr. Victor G. Vogel, a professor of medicine and epidemiology at the University of Pittsburgh, who studies SERMs.

Like other experts, Vogel says women can take HRT on a short-term basis for relief of menopausal symptoms, such as hot flashes. The SERMs, as Vogel and the authors of the paper point out, do not help hot flashes and can actually increase them.

info You can find more information about SERMs on a breast cancer education Web site at *www.breastcancer.org* or from the American Cancer Society at *www.cancer.org*.

Stroke: The Newly Discovered Risk of Hormone Replacement Therapy

Sylvia Wassertheil–Smoller, PhD, Professor, Epidemiology and Social Medicine, and Head, Division of Epidemiology and Biostatistics, Albert Einstein College of Medicine, New York, NY.

Steven Goldstein, MD, Professor, Obstetrics and Gynecology, New York University School of Medicine.

February 14, 2003, presentation, American Stroke Association conference, Phoenix, AZ.

Not only won't combined hormone therapy protect a woman from heart disease, as was previously thought, but the estrogen–progestin combination may also increase a woman's risk of stroke, in some instances by as much as 70%.

And the increases are not limited to women with high blood pressure, which is a risk factor for stroke.

All groups of postmenopausal women had an increase in stroke, says study author Sylvia Wassertheil–Smoller, a professor of epidemiology and social medicine at Albert Einstein College of Medicine in New York City. This means healthy women, women with high blood pressure, younger women, and older women. "The use of the estrogen–progestin combination should not even be considered as a strategy for protecting a woman's health," she warns.

REMIXING THE DATA

Smoller's research is a re-analysis of data from the Women's Health Initiative, a study examining hormone replacement therapy. Although slated to last 8 years, part of the trial ended after 5 years when research showed combined hormone therapy appeared to increase health risks, particularly for cardiovascular disease. The estrogen-only arm of the study is continuing.

Smoller's analysis was devised to see whether the same links appeared in relation to stroke. The researchers looked at data on 8506 women aged 50 to 79 years, all of whom received the combined estrogen–progestin therapy. They compared the women with a like number of women who were not taking hormones.

Overall, researchers saw 133 strokes in the group taking the hormones, compared with 93 in the control group. Women aged 50 to 59 years who were taking hormones had the most dramatic increases—as much as 70% over those who didn't take hormones. Those aged 70 to 79 years had the least risk—only 26%.

The most surprising finding of all, Smoller says, was that even in women who had no history of heart or blood vessel disease, stroke rate climbed by 40% when the combined hormone therapy was used.

ANOTHER VIEW OF THE ANALYSIS

New York University gynecologist Dr. Steven Goldstein believes the analysis has serious flaws and its conclusions are premature. Among the most obvious problems, he says, is the lack of information concerning other risk factors for stroke, particularly in women with normal blood pressure.

The study can't say if these women had high cholesterol, if they smoked, if they were overweight—all factors that could have easily influenced the risk of stroke, irrespective of hormone use, Goldstein says.

He adds that it is impossible to link stroke to hormone use unless researchers can say that these other factors were not present.

"It is very unfair to women to draw conclusions that create fear without sufficient proof that there is even cause for alarm," he says.

According to the American Stroke Association, almost 100,000 women die of stroke each year. That figure is nearly twice the number of women who die from breast cancer.

info To learn more about this study, visit the Women's Health Initiative at *www.whi.org*. To learn more about stroke, check out the American Stroke Association Web site at *www.strokeassociation.org*.

Are Estrogen Patches Safer Than Pills?

Wanpen Vongpatanasin, MD, Assistant Professor, Medicine, University of Texas Southwestern Medical Center, Dallas.
Cynthia A. Stuenkel, MD, Associate Physician, Family and Preventive Medicine, University of California, San Diego.
April 16, 2003, *Journal of the American College of Cardiology*.

Estrogen replacement via a patch may be better than the pill variety. The estrogen patch doesn't raise blood levels of a protein associated with higher heart disease risk, a small study shows.

However, it's too soon to say the patch is a safer form of hormone therapy, says Dr. Wanpen Vongpatanasin, a cardiologist at the University of Texas Southwestern Medical Center.

The study included only 21 women and looked simply at a single marker of heart disease, but did not compare long-term effects of the different therapy forms.

One major study was halted after researchers found that the women taking oral hormone replacement therapy were at higher risk of heart disease and stroke than those not taking it. But researchers continue to analyze the health effects of hormone therapy to determine whether different formulations or delivery methods might carry fewer risks.

In her study, Vongpatanasin and her colleagues from the University of California at Davis Medical Center looked at levels of the participants' C-reactive protein—a marker of inflammation that predicts heart attack and heart disease—while they used the patch, pill, and placebo.

ESTROGEN LEVELS THE SAME, BUT C-REACTIVE PROTEIN AMOUNTS DIFFER

"The pills raised the C-reactive protein by more than twofold, whereas when the women were on the patch or on placebo, there was no change," Vongpatanasin says. But the blood levels of estrogen were similar with pill and patch.

Exactly why oral estrogen drives up the C-reactive protein is not known, Vongpatanasin says. "C-reactive protein is produced mainly by the liver," she explains. Oral estrogen is processed through the liver before circulating to other areas in the body, but estrogen delivered by patch enters the bloodstream directly.

The study is interesting, says Dr. Cynthia A. Stuenkel, an associate physician in family and preventive medicine at the University of California, San Diego, but it's not enough proof to say for sure that the patch has no risks. It has been reported previously that oral estrogen increases C-reactive protein and that the patch doesn't, "but this is the first head-to-head comparison."

However, C-reactive protein is simply a marker for heart disease. It's known that a high baseline level of C-reactive protein puts you in a higher risk category for heart disease. "But it remains to be proven whether an increase in C-reactive protein from taking oral estrogen is associated with an increased risk of heart disease," Stuenkel says.

info For more information on hormone therapy, visit the National Institutes of Health Web page at *www.nih.gov/PHTindex.htm*.

HRT Can Make Breast Cancer More Aggressive

Wulf H. Utian, MD, PhD, Professor Emeritus, Case Western Reserve University School of Medicine, and Executive Director, North American Menopause Society, both in Cleveland, OH.

August 9, 2003, *The Lancet*.

Hormone replacement therapy (HRT), initially thought to be the best way to help women combat menopause symptoms, and even help protect their hearts, may do none of that.

In fact, HRT may actually fuel a more aggressive breast cancer, according to a study of more than 1 million British women. Appropriately called the Million Women Study, it was conducted between 1996 and 2001 by Cancer Research UK, an epidemiology unit based in Oxford, England.

The 5-year study followed more British women, ages 50 to 64 years, who were either going through menopause or who had already gone through menopause. Approximately half had taken or were taking hormone supplements. These hormone supplements were either a combination of estrogen and progestin or just estrogen alone. Progestin is added to the combination therapy to avoid uterine cancers triggered that can be triggered by estrogen alone. Some were also taking a drug called tibolone, which is a precursor to estrogen, progestin, and other sex hormones. Tibolone is not sold in the United States.

Those women taking combination HRT had a higher risk of developing breast cancer *and* a greater risk of dying from the disease than women not using the therapy.

Previous studies, including the Women's Health Initiative (WHI) in the United States, have identified the link between breast tumors and HRT. But the British research is the first to suggest that the tumors caused by hormone supplements are more aggressive.

The new research was published in *The Lancet*, a British medical journal. The study found that the risk of breast cancer is magnified the longer women take HRT, but it also concluded that this risk fades with time after the therapy is stopped.

Over the last decade, the researchers estimate that use of HRT in the United Kingdom has led to 20,000 extra cases of breast cancer among women ages 50 to 64 years.

Reaction from the medical community has not been totally supportive. Dr. Wulf H. Utian, executive director of the North American Menopause Society, says that calls for women to stop taking hormone therapy are "radical" and equivalent to "shouting 'Fire!' in a crowded movie theater."

Doctors in the United States prescribe HRT for 2 reasons. One is to control menopausal symptoms that are associated with the loss of estrogen, such as hot flashes and vaginal dryness. The other reason HRT is prescribed is to prevent bone fractures from osteoporosis, another consequence of declining levels of the female sex hormone.

Until recently, many women had been taking HRT to prevent heart and circulatory diseases, based on the strength of previous studies that suggested such a benefit. But more recent evidence from 2 studies showed that the therapy doesn't help—and can even harm—the heart.

One study showed that HRT does not slow the progression of atherosclerosis—a buildup of fatty deposits in the arteries—in women who already have the condition. The second, part of the Women's Health Initiative, found that HRT poses the greatest risk of heart attack during the first year of use. Both studies appeared in the *New England Journal of Medicine*.

info For more on the Women's Health Initiative, visit the National Heart, Lung, and Blood Institute at *www.nhlbi.nih.gov/whi*.

Hormone Therapy May Reduce Alzheimer's Risk In Women

Susan M. Resnick, PhD, Investigator, Laboratory of Personality and Cognition, National Institute on Aging, Baltimore, MD.

John C.S. Breitner, MD, Professor and Head, Geriatric Psychiatry, University of Washington, and Director, Geriatric Research, Education and Clinical Center, VA Puget Sound Health Care System, Seattle, WA.

November 6, 2002, *Journal of the American Medical Association*.

Older women who used hormone therapy for at least 10 years are less likely to get Alzheimer's disease than those who never took hormones. But researchers are holding off on endorsing hormone replacement therapy—HRT—until more is learned about the health risks and benefits of the treatments.

Researchers concluded that the use of HRT is associated with a reduced risk of Alzheimer's disease later in life. Studies have shown that women appear to be at increased risk of Alzheimer's after age 80.

The researchers found no apparent benefit for current users, but did find a benefit for those who had used HRT for more than 10 years. Those who had used it previously for at least 10 years reduced their risk to the point where it became comparable with men's risk of getting Alzheimer's, which is lower, the researchers say.

The study concluded that women who used HRT had a 41% reduction in their risk of Alzheimer's than did those who never received the therapy. Those women who used it for more than 10 years had a 2.5 times lower incidence of the disease than nonusers. Almost all of the risk reduction was associated with former use of HRT, not current use, unless the women had used it for more than 10 years.

There may be a window of opportunity, around the time of menopause, when the depletion of a woman's level of estrogen may have the greatest harmful effects on the brain's neurons.

However, the researchers can't say for sure that the hormones are what helps ward off the disease. Women who decided to take hormone therapy may simply be more health-conscious, according to Dr. John C.S. Breitner, study coauthor and head of geriatric psychiatry at the University of Washington in Seattle.

CAUTION ADVISED

Although HRT might sound good to a woman fearful of getting the degenerative brain condition marked by severe memory loss, the study results are not, by themselves, a reason to sign on for long-term hormone therapy, says Breitner. "I wouldn't tell [a woman] to take HRT based on these data," he adds.

Another Alzheimer's expert, Susan M. Resnick, an investigator at the National Institute on Aging Laboratory of Personality and Cognition, says she would not recommend any treatment options because of this study.

Several other ongoing studies will help provide answers about HRT and Alzheimer's disease in coming years, she says.

Resnick acknowledges that waiting on the results of these and other studies can be frustrating for women faced with a decision about HRT now. However, she says, the risk/benefit profile of HRT may change with the new studies.

studies have shown that progesterone cream may be better tolerated by some women than the oral form of the hormone.

info To find out more about all kinds of women's health issues, visit The National Women's Health Information Center at *www.4women.gov.*

Lotions Smoothe Menopause Symptoms As Well as Medicines

Jennifer Landes, DO, Helene B. Leonetti, MD, and James N. Anasti, MD, St. Luke's Hospital, Bethlehem, PA.

April 26–30, 2003, presentations, American College of Obstetricians and Gynecologists Annual Meeting, New Orleans, LA.

Researchers from St. Luke's Hospital in Bethlehem, Pennsylvania, say that topical progesterone cream may be as effective as oral progesterone in treating menopause symptoms—while still protecting the uterus from precancerous cell growth.

The research involved 20 healthy menopausal women randomly assigned to daily use of either oral estrogen and progesterone, or oral estrogen and progesterone cream, for 6 months. The women then switched preparations for an additional 6 months of study.

To keep track of uterine health, each woman received an endometrial biopsy at the start of the study and again after each 6-month phase —that's important because topical progesterone cream had been thought less effective in maintaining a healthy uterine lining than the oral form.

The final result: Topical progesterone was as effective as the oral version in both the treatment of menopause symptoms and the protection of the uterine lining. The finding is significant, the researchers say, because earlier

Is It Menopause? Forget Blood Tests

Cynthia Krause, MD, Assistant Clinical Professor, Gynecology, Mount Sinai Medical Center, New York, NY.
February 19, 2003, *Journal of the American Medical Association.*

A combination of a woman's age, her menstrual history, and her symptoms may be the most reliable way to tell if she's in *perimenopause*—even more reliable than medical tests alone. That's the conclusion of a study published in the *Journal of the American Medical Association*. Calling perimenopause a condition of many factors that precedes menopause, the authors urge doctors to take a broader view of the criteria that make up this midlife condition.

"No one symptom or test is accurate enough by itself to rule in, or rule out, perimenopause," write the authors, a group of researchers from both Duke University and the Veterans Affairs Medical Center in Durham, North Carolina.

HORMONE TESTS SECONDARY

Moreover, they write, clinicians should consider both age and menstrual history as the primary indications of perimenopause, without relying on hormone tests to validate their findings.

For gynecologist Dr. Cynthia Krause, the study "preaches" what most doctors practice every day.

"Perimenopause isn't so much a specific time of life as much as it is a phase of life, with no clear-cut entry and no clear-cut exit, particularly one that can be marked by a test

311

result or even a group of symptoms," says Krause, an assistant clinical professor of gynecology at the Mount Sinai Medical Center in New York City.

Perimenopause describes the phase just before menopause, a time when a woman's reproductive function stops.

And it is actually during perimenopause that women experience the bulk of their menopausal symptoms, which can include hot flashes, bleeding irregularities, mood swings, and fatigue.

According to the study, most women enter perimenopause between the ages of 45 and 55 years, with most having symptoms around age 47. The most common age for menopause to begin is between 51 and 52.

The authors say their research shows that a woman's age is the most predictive sign of her menstrual status. The next most reliable sign includes her own assessment, usually based on such symptoms as hot flashes, night sweats, and vaginal dryness.

BLOOD TESTS NOT TOO USEFUL

The least effective means of diagnosing perimenopause, they say, are blood tests that measure levels of follicle-stimulating hormone (FSH), which can be high, or inhibin B, which can be low, as a woman gets older.

What is important, says Krause, is the possibility that perimenopausal symptoms could be caused by some other health problem.

"For example, irregular bleeding or even hot flashes are often signs of perimenopause, but they could also be the result of other problems," Krause says.

Using the multifactorial approach, she says, doctors are likely to come up with an accurate diagnosis.

The research was an analysis of 16 studies done between 1966 and 2001. In them, the authors found similar criteria kept cropping up as signs of perimenopause—age, plus symptoms that include hot flashes, night sweats, and vaginal dryness.

Although the authors point out that many doctors rely on blood tests—particularly FSH

—to determine a woman's reproductive status, at least in this analysis, the test results were not definitive.

info To learn more about perimenopause, visit the Mayo Clinic at *www.mayoclinic.com* or the North American Menopause Society at *www.menopause.org*.

What Can Make Hot Flashes Worse: Smoking and Weight Gain

Jodi Flaws, PhD, Associate Professor, Department of Epidemiology and Preventive Medicine, University of Maryland School of Medicine, Baltimore, MD.

Steven Goldstein, MD, Professor, Obstetrics and Gynecology, New York University School of Medicine.

February 2003, *Obstetrics and Gynecology*.

Women who are overweight, as well as those who smoke, have more frequent and more severe hot flashes than thinner women and nonsmokers, say scientists at the University of Maryland School of Medicine.

Their research bolsters the belief that lifestyle plays a major role in some symptoms of menopause. What doctors don't know is whether changing habits—such as quitting smoking or losing weight—will make a difference once the symptoms have begun.

The study was observational, not a cause-and-effect proof, says study author Jodi Flaws. Future research, she says, should show if stopping smoking or losing weight can reduce the severity of hot flashes once they have started.

For Dr. Steven Goldstein, the study is a win-win situation. "It adds to the body of evidence that quitting smoking and losing weight is not only good for your heart and good for your lungs, but it may also make you more comfortable," says Goldstein, a professor of obstetrics and gynecology at New York University School of Medicine.

SMOKING OR OVERWEIGHT—HOT FLASHES

Women who smoked had more than twice the incidence of hot flashes than women who didn't, the research showed. And the more a woman smoked, the more severe her hot flashes became.

Obese women were twice as likely to be troubled by hot flashes than women whose body mass index was 25 (an average-weight woman, 5'4" tall who weighs 145 pounds, for example).

If you can't quit smoking or give up your chips and dip, there's hope. A second study in the journal says that ultra-low doses of the anticonvulsion drug *gabapentin* may help control hot flashes, without any of the side effects now linked to hormone replacement therapy (HRT).

Here, researchers from the University of Rochester found that after just 3 months of gabapentin, women had approximately half the number and half the severity of hot flashes.

Some side effects: Sleepiness, dizziness, a rash, or mild swelling.

New Use for Aspirin: Fighting Leukemia

Julie Ross, PhD, Associate Professor, Pediatrics, University of Minnesota Cancer Center, Minneapolis.

Alan Kinniburgh, PhD, Vice President, Research, Leukemia and Lymphoma Society, White Plains, NY.

June 13, 2003, *Cancer Epidemiology, Biomarkers and Prevention.*

Postmenopausal women who take aspirin 2 or more times each week may lower their risk of developing leukemia by more than 50% compared with women who do not take the drug.

Although these research results are preliminary, this could signal yet another usage for the miracle drug that was invented more than a century ago and has already been shown to have a beneficial effect on colon cancer and heart disease.

"I was very excited about the findings because leukemia is one of those cancers that has a high fatality rate," says Julie Ross, senior author of the paper.

"It certainly is a teaser in the sense that there seems to be a 50% reduction in the incidence of leukemia," says Alan Kinniburgh, vice president of research at the Leukemia & Lymphoma Society. However, he adds that, "more studies are needed to see if this holds true."

LOWER RISK

The authors analyzed information on nearly 30,000 women who took part in the Iowa Women's Health Study, which looked at overall health, lifestyle, behaviors, and incidence of cancer.

The women detailed how often they took aspirin, other NSAIDs (nonsteroidal anti-inflammatory drugs, such as Advil), or arthritis medicine. None of the women had leukemia at the beginning of the study.

STRIKING RESULTS

Women who used aspirin at least 2 times a week had a more than 50% lower risk of developing leukemia than women who said they didn't take aspirin. Nevertheless, there are still many questions to be answered. For one thing, the researchers didn't know exactly how much aspirin the women were taking, or for how long.

Also, we don't know why aspirin might protect against this or any other type of cancer. "I have no idea what the mechanism might be," says Ross, an associate professor of pediatrics and a member of the University of Minnesota Cancer Center in Minneapolis.

Kinniburgh believes aspirin may have an effect on certain inflammatory processes taking place in leukemia.

info For more on adult leukemia, visit the Leukemia & Lymphoma Society Web site at *www.leukemia.org* or the National Cancer Institute Web site at *www.cancer.gov.*

Keep Your Blood Pressure Low— Especially During Menopause

Suzanne Oparil, MD, Professor of Medicine, and Director, Vascular Biology and Hypertension Program, University of Alabama at Birmingham.

Pamela Marcovitz, MD, Director, Ministrelli Women's Heart Center, William Beaumont Hospital, Royal Oak, MI.

July 24, 2002, conference, Sex Differences in Cardiovascular Health and Disease, sponsored by the Society for Women's Health Research and the University of Wisconsin School of Medicine, Madison.

Women tend to have lower blood pressure before they go through menopause, which suggests the possibility that female hormones play a role in keeping blood pressure low. Indeed, researchers have found that hormone replacement therapy in postmenopausal women may lower blood pressure, but the effect isn't significant.

"As far as treatment for high blood pressure in older women, they cannot rely on hormone replacement therapy," says Dr. Suzanne Oparil, a professor of medicine and the director of the Vascular Biology and Hypertension Program at the University of Alabama at Birmingham. "They must take antihypertensive medications, exercise, and keep their weight down."

THE EFFECT OF AGING

Blood pressure increases as women get older as part of the aging process, Oparil says. When women are younger, their arteries act like rubber bands. As they age, the arteries become more fibrous and behave more like ropes. As a result, there is more resistance within the arteries, so the heart has to pump harder to get the blood through. This, Oparil says, creates a higher systolic number—that's the top number on a blood pressure measurement.

Oparil adds that researchers are still trying to discover what effect estrogen has on blood pressure, if any. Some say that the rise in blood pressure after menopause may be coincidental. For example, many women gain weight after menopause, and Oparil says that some scientists believe the weight gain is what causes the higher blood pressure readings.

One thing researchers are sure of, however, is that high blood pressure is a serious problem for older women. If it goes undiagnosed, it puts women at risk for heart disease and stroke.

WHAT YOU NEED TO KNOW

First, Oparil says, women need to know what their numbers are. If the nurse or doctor doesn't tell you what your blood pressure is, ask. It should be lower than 140 over 90, and, according to Dr. Pamela Marcovitz, director of the Ministrelli Women's Heart Center at William Beaumont Hospital in Royal Oak, Michigan, the ideal blood pressure is approximately 125 over 80 or lower. If you've been diagnosed with high blood pressure, you will probably need to take medication, but changing your lifestyle can also help, she says.

■ ■ ■ ■

How to Control Your Blood Pressure

If you want to do all you can to keep your blood pressure under control, the National Heart, Lung, and Blood Institute (*www.nhlbi. nih.gov*) has some suggestions. *They are…*

●**Eat healthy foods,** including fruits, vegetables, and grains (such as beans, rice, corn tortillas, and pasta).

●**Eat less salt and sodium.** Most sodium is found in packaged foods. Read the labels to check the amount of sodium in 1 serving of a particular food. Use sodium-free seasonings in the food you cook at home.

●**Don't smoke.**

●**Be active.** *Make sure you move every day:* climb stairs, walk, dance, play golf, and so forth.

●**Lose weight if you are overweight.**

●**Limit alcohol consumption.**

Are Painkillers Raising Your Blood Pressure?

Gary C. Curhan, MD, ScD, Epidemiologist, Harvard Medical School and Harvard School of Public Health, Boston, MA.

Eric Eichhorn, MD, Medical Director, Cardiopulmonary Research Science and Technology Institute, Dallas, TX.

October 28, 2002, *Archives of Internal Medicine.*

New research suggests that young and middle-aged women who take painkillers such as Tylenol, Motrin, and Advil may be setting themselves up for significantly higher blood pressure, even if they don't already suffer from hypertension.

"Lots of people believe that these medications are completely safe because they're available over the counter," says study coauthor Dr. Gary C. Curhan, an epidemiologist at Harvard School of Public Health. "But we know that [they] can have multiple other effects. High blood pressure should be 1 more thing that people consider if they use these medications on a regular basis."

There are 3 main types of over-the-counter painkillers—aspirin, acetaminophen, and *nonsteroidal anti-inflammatory drugs* (NSAIDs), which include ibuprofen-based medications such as Advil and Motrin. Researchers have linked NSAIDs to high blood pressure, but previous studies only looked at people who already suffered from the condition, Curhan says.

In the new study, Curhan and his colleagues examined an ongoing study of 80,020 nurses, aged 31 to 50 years, who have been involved in the study since 1989. The nurses had no history of high blood pressure and these researchers studied their answers to a 1995 survey about their use of painkillers.

Approximately half the women took aspirin at least 1 day per month, and between 72% and 77% took NSAIDs or acetaminophen.

When various risk factors were taken into account, those who took acetaminophen at least 22 days per month had twice the risk of developing high blood pressure compared with those who took no drugs from that class. Those who took NSAIDs had an 86% higher risk. "I consider that pretty substantial," Curhan says.

Meanwhile, those who took aspirin were at no higher risk. NSAIDs and acetaminophen may interfere with the ability of blood vessels to remain dilated, Curhan explains. "If the blood vessels constrict, then the blood pressure can go up." Some experts liken blood vessels to a garden hose. If you squeeze the hose, the pressure inside will build.

There's another potential problem, Curhan adds. "[Constriction of blood vessels] can cause the body to retain sodium, and that can raise blood pressure."

Curhan said the study results still need to be confirmed by further research, which may shed light on how long it takes for painkiller use to affect blood pressure. "Nobody's done a study like this before," he says.

For now, women who take the painkillers should consider all the risks, Curhan says. "My hope is that they're not taking them for the wrong reasons. Lots of people take these for a variety of reasons, many of which don't have anything to do with what they're designed to do."

Dr. Eric Eichhorn, medical director of the Cardiopulmonary Research Science and Technology Institute in Dallas, says the design of the study doesn't account for other factors that could affect blood pressure in the women. "It's guilt by association," he says. "There are a whole lot of other factors that could be responsible." Moderate use of painkillers should still be all right, he says. "When used appropriately, they serve a very important function. My guess is that it's a continuum. If you take painkillers for a day or 2, that's probably fine. But if you take them all the time every day of the month, your chances of hypertension increase."

info Learn more about NSAIDs and how they work at *www.medinfo.co.uk/drugs/nsaids/html.*

Don't Let Your Doctor Ignore Your Risk of Heart Disease

Nieca Goldberg, MD, Cardiologist, Lenox Hill Hospital, New York, NY.

April 15, 2003, American Heart Association news release.

April 15, 2003, *Circulation*.

Doctors should pay the same attention to preventing sudden cardiac death in women as they do in men, a Harvard study urges.

Admittedly, the rate of sudden cardiac death is lower in women than in men, says Dr. Christine M. Albert, lead author of the study and assistant professor of medicine at Harvard Medical School. But there seems to be an assumption that the conventional risk factors for heart disease—such as smoking, high blood pressure, obesity, and diabetes—don't raise a warning flag for women as they do for men, she adds.

However, analyses of the Nurses' Health Study, which followed more than 121,000 women for 20 years, say otherwise.

"Our data suggest that coronary heart disease risk factors do indeed predict sudden coronary death in women, and therefore coronary heart disease risk factor intervention should affect risk of sudden cardiac death in women," the study says.

For 69% of the 244 women who suffered sudden deaths recorded in the study, death was the first sign of heart disease, Albert acknowledges. But almost every one of those women had a significant cardiac risk factor. For example, diabetes was associated with a 2.5 times higher risk and obesity was linked with a 1.6 times higher risk. Oddly, high blood cholesterol did not raise the risk significantly.

Smoking was the real killer. "The women who smoked 25 or more cigarettes a day had a 4-fold increased risk of sudden cardiac death," Albert says.

A genetic factor might be involved, particularly among women who die suddenly at a young age, Albert says. Family history was a risk factor if a woman had a parent who suffered sudden cardiac death before the age of 60 years.

IDENTIFYING AND TREATING RISK FACTORS

The report means that more emphasis should be placed on detecting and treating risk factors in women, says Dr. Nieca Goldberg, a cardiologist at Lenox Hill Hospital in New York City and a spokeswoman for the American Heart Association.

"It has been shortsighted in terms of the medical community ignoring symptoms detected in screening for a lot of women," Goldberg says. "Smoking, diabetes, and hypertension [high blood pressure] need to be screened for and aggressively treated."

info You can learn about sudden cardiac death and what can be done to prevent it from the American Heart Association at *www.americanheart.org*. You can also try the National Heart, Lung, and Blood Institute's Women's Heart Health Education Initiative at *http://hin.nhlbi.nih.gov/womencvd*.

The Vaccine That Blocks 50% of All Cervical Cancer

Carol L. Brown, MD, Assistant Attending Surgeon, Memorial Sloan–Kettering Cancer Center, New York, NY.

Carolyn D. Runowicz, MD, Vice Chairwoman, Department of Obstetrics and Gynecology, and Director, Gynecologic Oncology Research Program, St. Luke's Roosevelt Hospital Center, New York, NY.

November 21, 2002, *New England Journal of Medicine*.

A vaccine for the virus responsible for half of all cases of cervical cancer has a perfect success rate, researchers say. In fact, scientists say that if doctors are able to vaccinate women against 5 specific viruses before they become sexually active, it could reduce the number of deaths caused by cervical cancer by as much as 95%.

The viruses—varieties of the human papillomavirus, or HPV—have a clear link to cancer. Although most are easily fought off by the body, the remaining ones are responsible for about 98% to 99% of all cervical cancers, says Dr. Carol Brown, a gynecologic oncologist at Memorial Sloan-Kettering Cancer Center in New York City.

The variety for which the vaccine was created infects 20% of adults, and is also the strain most commonly linked to cervical cancer.

"The reason this study is exciting is because cervical cancer is happening in unscreened or infrequently screened women," says Dr. Carolyn Runowicz, director of the gynecologic oncology research program at St. Luke's Roosevelt Hospital Center in New York City.

STUDY WILL LEAD TO PREVENTION

This study opens the door to prevention, Runowicz says. There are 4500 deaths from cervical cancer in the United States every year, and they are primarily women who have not been screened, she says.

Although the study results have the potential to make big strides in cancer prevention, the study does have its limitations. A lot has to be done before a vaccine can be made commercially available, Brown says. More women need to be studied; physicians and patients need to know how long the protection will last and whether a booster will be needed. Another issue is that there are approximately 5 HPVs responsible for the majority of cervical cancers; this study looked at just one.

WHO IS AT RISK FOR HPV INFECTION?

According to the National Cervical Cancer Coalition, HPV infection is most common in women in their late teens and 20s. Because HPV is spread mainly through sexual contact, the risk increases with the number of sexual partners. Women who become sexually active at a young age, who have multiple sex partners, and whose sex partners have other partners are at increased risk.

■ ■ ■ ■
Where to Find Cancer Research

The National Cancer Institute maintains a Web site, *www.cancer.gov*, that provides education resources, including publications and fact sheets for cancer patients and their families. *It has also developed a computerized database designed to give patients access to...*

● **Treatment, supportive care, screening, and prevention.**

● **Information on most types of cancer.**

● **Descriptions of research studies,** also known as clinical trials, that are open for enrollment.

● **Information on organizations and physicians who specialize in cancer care.**

info You can find more about cervical cancer from the National Cervical Cancer Coalition at *www.nccc-online.org*.

Birth Control Pill Linked To Cervical Cancer

Amy Berrington, MD, Research Fellow, Cancer Research United Kingdom and University of Oxford, England.
Debbie Faslow, PhD, Director of Breast and Gynecological Cancer, American Cancer Society, Atlanta, GA.
April 5, 2003, *The Lancet*.

Women who use birth control pills increase their risk of cervical cancer the longer they take the contraceptive, a British study confirms.

The study was done to obtain more definite information about the risks that previous research has established. What the study provides, says Debbie Faslow, director of breast and gynecological cancer for the American Cancer Society, is more detail on the relationship between cervical cancer and birth control pills.

CRITICAL RISK FACTOR IDENTIFIED

The risk is directly related to the length of time women use hormonal contraceptives, as they are formally known. The cervical cancer risk is higher for women infected with the human papillomavirus (HPV), which is thought to be the major cause of cervical cancer. However, using the pill elevates the risk for women who are free of HPV, the researchers say.

That relationship holds even when many possible risk factors are taken into account, including number of sexual partners, use of cigarettes, and whether a woman has been screened for cervical cancer, says Dr. Amy Berrington, a research fellow at the Cancer Research United Kingdom Epidemiology Unit, a lead author of the report.

THE RISK DOUBLES AT 10 YEARS

Working with the French International Agency for Research on Cancer, the British epidemiologists reviewed data from 28 studies that included more than 12,500 women with cervical cancer. They found that the risk was increased by 10% in a woman who used the pill for fewer than 5 years (compared with women who never used it), 60% for those who used it for 5 to 9 years, and the risk was doubled after 10 or more years of use.

UNANSWERED QUESTIONS

The study clearly shows the increased risk associated with taking the birth control pill, but it does not establish a cause-and-effect relationship, says Berrington. Another question that researchers are still trying to answer is how long the increased risk lingers after a woman stops using the pill. The bottom line is that review of several studies shows the association between taking the pill and developing cervical cancer, but does not provide absolute proof.

Faslow, of the American Cancer Society, believes something else must be involved, because cervical cancer has nothing to do with hormones of the kind used in the pill. She suspects it might be related to the decreased use of condoms (condoms help prevent HPV infection), although the British study found that the use of such barrier contraceptives did not affect the result.

Obesity in Younger Women Nearly Doubles Risk of Colorectal Cancer

Paul D. Terry, Epidemiologist, Postdoctoral Fellow, National Institutes of Health, Chapel Hill, NC.
Thomas Fogel, MD, Radiation Oncologist, Ventura, CA, and spokesman, American Cancer Society.
August 2002, *Gut*.

If you're overweight, haven't reached menopause, and need another reason to drop a few pounds, consider this—obesity can almost double your risk of colorectal cancer.

A complex relationship involving insulin, an insulin-related molecule, and the hormone estrogen appears to be the link, says the study's lead author, Paul D. Terry, an epidemiologist and a postdoctoral fellow at the National Institutes of Health at Chapel Hill, North Carolina.

A LARGE SAMPLE

Data for the report come from the Canadian National Breast Screening Study, which involved nearly 90,000 women, all of whom were between the ages of 40 and 59 years when recruited for the study. Within approximately 10 years, 527 of the women were given a diagnosis of colorectal cancer.

THE RESULT

The incidence of colorectal cancer in obese premenopausal women was 88% higher than for slimmer premenopausal women. There was almost no difference in the incidence of colorectal cancer between thin and obese women after menopause.

THE THEORY

Excessive body fat often leads to increased levels of insulin. And excess insulin increases levels of another molecule, insulin-like growth factor-1, which has been associated with the development of colon cancer. In postmenopausal women, estrogen produced by fat tissue appears to offset the cancer-causing effect of insulin-like growth factor-1, Terry says.

As an epidemiologist, Terry says that he can't make recommendations about how obese women can reduce their cancer risk, but there is some obvious advice. "Obese younger women, and their doctors, should do everything in their power to get on a program of weight reduction."

The report should not affect the current recommendations for colorectal cancer screening for most people, says Dr. Thomas Fogel, a radiation oncologist and a spokesman for the American Cancer Society. Screening tests—a colonoscopy or, alternatively, fecal occult blood testing and a sigmoidoscopy—is recommended, starting at age 50.

■ ■ ■ ■

Other Ways to Reduce Your Risks Of Colorectal Cancer

The American Cancer Society has some suggestions on how to reduce your risk for colorectal cancer. *They are...*

•**People who have a history of colorectal cancer in their family** should check with their doctor for advice about tests that can find cancer early.

•**Follow the screening guidelines to help detect colon or rectal cancer.** When it is found and treated early, it can often be cured. Screening can also find precancerous polyps. Removing these polyps helps prevent some cancers.

•**Eat plenty of fruits, vegetables, and whole grain foods** and limit the amount of red meats you eat, especially those high in fat. Some studies suggest that taking a daily multivitamin containing folic acid or folate can lower colorectal cancer risk. Other studies suggest that getting more calcium by using supplements or eating low-fat dairy products can help.

•**Get some exercise.** Even small amounts of exercise on a regular basis can be helpful.

•**Some studies have shown that use of estrogen replacement therapy for women after menopause** may reduce the risk of colorectal cancer. You should talk to your doctor about the therapy's risks and benefits.

How to Control an Overactive Bladder

Jane Miller, MD, Associate Professor and Director of Female Urology, University of Washington Medical Center, Seattle.
April 2002, *Bottom Line/Health*.

Do you ever dash out of a room because of an urgent need to urinate? Do you sometimes experience urine leakage or wetting accidents (incontinence)? You're not alone. Problems with bladder control affect up to half of all people age 40 and older.

The culprit is often overactive bladder (OAB)—a condition marked by bladder contractions that trigger an intense urge to urinate.

Because the contractions can strike at any time, OAB can be much more frustrating than stress incontinence. That's urine leakage that is triggered by exercise, coughing, or sneezing.

To cope with OAB, many sufferers limit their activities outside the home—a practice that all too often leads to isolation...and depression.

OAB is often viewed as a female problem. However, new research shows that in the over-64 population, more men than women are afflicted.

Unfortunately, 7 out of 10 people who suffer from OAB are too embarrassed to discuss the condition with their doctors. That's a mistake. Serious conditions, including bladder cancer, diabetes, and neurological disease, can cause symptoms that mimic OAB.

Once a doctor has ruled out a serious medical problem, OAB symptoms can improve significantly with new prescription medications, behavioral approaches or, in difficult cases, surgery. With few exceptions, these treatments can be used by women and men.

IS A PILL ENOUGH?

For decades, doctors have prescribed *oxybutynin* (Ditropan) to help stop involuntary bladder contractions. It's an effective treatment. However, oxybutynin must be taken 3 times a day and can cause constipation and/or dry mouth.

Many patients get better results with newer OAB drugs, such as *tolterodine* (Detrol LA) and Ditropan XL, a timed-released formula of oxybutynin. Both are taken only once a day and produce significantly fewer side effects than the older drugs.

Detrol LA and Ditropan XL cost about $80 a month, compared with $20 a month for Ditropan.

If you start taking 1 of these drugs and you haven't seen improvement in 4 weeks, talk to your doctor about changing the dosage or adding a second medication. A combination of drugs is often more effective than relying on 1 alone.

CHANGING YOUR HABITS

Recent research shows that a combination of drugs and behavior changes proved more effective than either treatment alone. However, if an OAB sufferer prefers to avoid drugs altogether, behavioral modifications can sometimes help. *Effective strategies...*

•**Urinate on schedule.** People with OAB void 8 or more times a day. Many average 20 bathroom visits a day.

Helpful: Keep a voiding diary for 3 to 5 days. Write down when and how much you drink, eat and urinate. To measure urine, use an old measuring cup or ask your doctor for a container that fits into the toilet.

Using this technique, one of my patients realized that her too-frequent urination had a simple cause. She was drinking too much—8 ounces of fluid every hour—to combat dry mouth caused by another condition.

Not every case is so clear-cut. But a diary can help patients and doctors pinpoint patterns.

•**Train your bladder.** Weak pelvic floor muscles may hamper your ability to control your bladder. Kegel exercises performed regularly strengthen these muscles.

What to do: Tighten the same muscles you use to hold in urine or gas. Hold for 5 seconds. Begin with 10 Kegels twice a day. Increase by 10 Kegels a week, working up to 50 twice a day.

Helpful: To prevent leakage when you feel a strong urge to urinate, sit quietly and perform a Kegel exercise. This will stop the urge

long enough to give you time to get to the bathroom.

•**Limit caffeine, alcohol, acidic fruit juices, and spicy foods.** These tend to irritate the bladder and may aggravate OAB symptoms.

WHEN ALL ELSE FAILS

If medication and/or exercises don't provide enough relief, patients may opt for electrical stimulation to help tone the muscles that control the flow of urine through the urethra. For this procedure, a physical therapist inserts a small tampon-like probe into the vagina—or, for men, into the rectum. The probe is connected to a machine that provides low-level electrical stimulation.

A physical therapist trained in pelvic floor dysfunction should direct patients in this treatment.

Surgery is a last resort. A new technique involves implanting a device called InterStim in the skin overlying the buttocks. The device —about the size of 12 stacked credit cards— delivers a mild electrical current that stimulates the nerves linked to bladder control. This surgery typically costs more than $10,000. Many insurance companies will cover it.

info For more information on InterStim, contact the manufacturer at 800-328-0810 or online at *www.medtronic.com.*

Think Your Way to Total Bladder Control

Leslee L. Subak, MD, Associate Professor, Obstetrics and Gynecology, Women's Continence Center, University of California at San Francisco.
July 2002, *Obstetrics and Gynecology.*
National Kidney and Urologic Diseases Information Clearinghouse.

Many women with bladder-control problems never discover how easy it can be to regain control, and medication isn't always a necessity.

That's the conclusion of a study on urinary incontinence in women, showing that a simple form of behavioral therapy may be the best line of defense, especially for older women.

"What is really exciting about this study is that it empowers women by showing that they can take control of urinary incontinence, and that it can be done in a very simple and very inexpensive way," said study author Dr. Leslee L. Subak, an obstetrician-gynecologist at the University of California at San Francisco who specializes in treating urinary problems.

The research, published in *Obstetrics and Gynecology*, reveals how instruction on bladder control, along with professional support, reduced urinary incontinence episodes by up to 100% in some women, and by at least 50% in the majority of the study group.

THE CONDITION

Urinary incontinence is one of the most prevalent health conditions in women, affecting up to 50% of the postmenopausal age group. Some women experience incontinence daily, sometimes unable to control their bladder at all, day or night.

Although in most instances the problem doesn't signify a life-threatening condition, Subak said it has been cited as an enormous quality-of-life issue—and one that women often find difficult to discuss, even with their doctor.

THE THERAPY

Subak's study involved 76 women who underwent a series of discussions and exercise sessions. They were also asked to keep diaries on the frequency of their "bathroom habits." In subsequent support group meetings, the women discussed their diary entries and set new voiding schedules, increasing the time between trips to the bathroom. A control group of 76 women received no instructions and no support, but did keep a urinary diary.

The end result: After 6 weeks, the women in the support group experienced a 50% reduction in incontinence episodes, compared with a 15% reduction in the control group.

Exercises to strengthen or retrain pelvic muscles and sphincter muscles can also reduce or cure stress leakage, according to the National Kidney and Urologic Diseases Information Clearinghouse. Women of all ages can learn and practice these exercises, which are taught by a health-care professional.

info For more information, go to the National Kidney and Urologic Diseases Information Clearinghouse Web site at *http://kidney.niddk.nih.gov.*

■ ■ ■ ■

A Restful Night

According to Dr. Gary Lemack, assistant professor of urology at the University of Texas Southwestern Medical Center in Dallas, there are several ways to avoid nighttime bathroom visits. His advice, which appeared in *Bottom Line/Personal,* is to avoid bladder irritants, such as citrus fruits, spicy foods, and nicotine…and diuretic drinks, including anything containing caffeine or alcohol, for several hours before bedtime. Also, drink your last fluids of the day no later than 3 hours before bedtime. Most fluids will be in your bladder by the time you are ready for sleep, so you should be able to use the bathroom and then sleep through the night.

Simple Home Test for Yeast Infection— Cheap and Accurate

April 26–30, 2003, presentations, American College of Obstetricians and Gynecologists Annual Meeting, New Orleans, LA.

Doctors from the Robert Woods Johnson Medical School say that a simple self-test for a vaginal yeast infection may be as effective as doctor-generated tests in accurately diagnosing the problem.

In studies conducted on 143 women, researchers revealed that an easy, self-performed swab test that measures the acid level in the vagina (called a vaginal pH test) could accurately diagnose a yeast infection almost as often as a physician-generated test.

The researchers say vaginal pH testing by women may be a convenient way to determine the true cause of vaginal infections before buying an over-the-counter yeast treatment. This, they say, could reduce the rate of inaccurate self-diagnosis and subsequent incorrect use of antifungal medications—a problem that can sometimes lead to serious complications.

Vaginal pH test strips for use at home are available at most pharmacies.

info To find out more about these tests, look at the US Food and Drug Administration's Web site at *www.fda.gov/cdrh/oivd/homeuse-vaginal.html.*

■ ■ ■ ■

Another Viewpoint: A Physician Cautions About Self-Testing

Beware of diagnosing your own yeast infections, advises Dr. Daron Ferris, professor of obstetrics/gynecology and family medicine at the Medical College of Georgia in Augusta.

According to a recent finding published in *Bottom Line/Personal,* only about half of the women treating themselves with over-the-counter remedies actually had vaginal yeast infections. The rest had either another type of infection or no infection at all.

Problem: Left untreated, certain vaginal infections, such as trichomonas and bacterial vaginosis, can lead to infertility and make women more susceptible to the AIDS virus. Women experiencing vaginal itching, burning, or irritation should consult their physicians.

The Urinary Tract Disorder Many Doctors Misdiagnose

Victor Nitti, MD, Vice Chairman, Department of Urology, New York University School of Medicine.
Michael P. O'Leary, MD, MPH, Associate Professor, Surgery, Harvard Medical School, and Division of Urology, Brigham and Women's Hospital, Boston, MA.

It often begins as a urinary tract infection (UTI) with all-too-familiar symptoms—burning and pain while urinating, a constant urge to "go" up to 30 times a day, and pelvic pain as soon as your bladder becomes full.

But unlike a common UTI, which usually responds quickly to a round of antibiotics, for some people the symptoms never really go away.

The root of their problem may not be a UTI at all, but a condition known as *interstitial cystitis* (IC), a baffling urinary tract disorder that many doctors can easily miss.

"I've seen patients who'd gone from one doctor to another, believing they had a chronic urinary tract infection and they never could find the answer," says Dr. Victor Nitti, vice chairman of the department of urology at the New York University School of Medicine, and a specialist in treating interstitial cystitis.

IC is a chronic inflammatory condition that affects mostly women. Because symptoms include not only pain while urinating but also chronic pelvic and bladder pain, IC can interfere with everything from sitting comfortably in a chair to having intimate relations.

If the condition isn't diagnosed correctly, a person can quickly get caught up in a landslide of ineffective treatments, from muscle relaxants to tranquilizers and painkillers—and still not know what's really wrong, Nitti says.

ACIDIC FOODS ARE SUSPECT

Although no one is certain what causes IC —or what puts a person at increased risk— some theories link the problem to environmental allergies or, more likely, food sensitivities, particularly foods high in acid.

IC expert Dr. Michael P. O'Leary says foods such as tomatoes, chocolate, lemons, and other citrus fruits, and some spices can irritate a sensitive urinary tract, and eventually may cause the inflammation that is the hallmark of the disease.

THE TREATMENTS

For some women, relief is as close as an anti-inflammatory medication or even an anti-histamine, which are commonly used to treat allergies. Alone or in combination with dietary modifications, these drugs can often reduce symptoms dramatically, Nitti says.

When those treatments don't help, more potent medications can be prescribed, including a class of drugs known as anticholinergics — medicines that work directly on the nerve endings in the urinary tract, O'Leary says. In rare instances, there are also a number of surgical procedures that can help.

If you've been diagnosed with a UTI that repeatedly fails to respond to antibiotics, if you're plagued with continued bouts of UTI symptoms, or if you experience symptoms of a UTI but urine tests fail to reveal any bacteria, Nitti says consider a consultation with a urogynecologist—or any doctor who specializes in the diagnosis and treatment of IC.

info To learn more about interstitial cystitis, visit the Interstitial Cystitis Association at *www.ichelp.org.*

Study Links Miscarriages To Heart Disease Later On

Gordon C.S. Smith, MD, PhD, Professor, Obstetrics and Gynecology, Cambridge University, The Rosie Hospital, Cambridge, UK.

Robert M. Silver, MD, Associate Professor, Obstetrics and Gynecology, University of Utah School of Medicine, Salt Lake City.

February 22, 2003, *British Medical Journal.*

Three or more miscarriages before successfully giving birth may mean heart disease for a woman later in life, researchers say. During a study that looked at the maternity data for more than 120,000 women, researchers found that women who had repeatedly miscarried before the first live birth were more than twice as likely to develop heart disease as women who had never miscarried.

The researchers say that the women in the study who had between 1 and 3 miscarriages were almost 1.5 times more likely to have heart disease later in life.

THE RESEARCHERS' INTERPRETATIONS

The main implication of the study is that the same factors that can put a woman at risk for heart disease may also play a role in pregnancy complications, says study author Dr. Gordon C.S. Smith, a professor of obstetrics and gynecology at Cambridge University and the Rosie Hospital in Cambridge, England. For example, he says, certain antibodies are associated with both miscarriage and the risk of heart disease. And, he says, he and his colleagues think it unlikely that the women already had heart disease when they had their miscarriages.

"We know from family history studies that there are genes which predispose toward heart disease. There are also other acquired factors that can predispose toward heart disease. Our interpretation of these findings is that these same factors may also determine pregnancy complications," Smith says. If further study has the same results, heart disease risk assessment for women may one day include questions about her reproductive history, he adds.

Dr. Robert M. Silver, an associate professor of obstetrics and gynecology at the University of Utah School of Medicine, agrees, saying that the many medical conditions that predispose women to have a miscarriage can also predispose them to have heart disease.

Among those conditions, he says, are kidney disease and a predisposition to blood clots. Approximately 16% of pregnancies end in miscarriage, Silver says, and about 12% of those occur before week 12 of the pregnancy.

The strength of the study is that it was done on a very large number of patients, he says. One problem, though, is that the researchers did not control sufficiently for all the potential variables.

Women should not be alarmed, Silver says. Most miscarriages happen because of genetic problems with the pregnancy, not because of underlying health problems of the mother. "Most women who have miscarriages are not at increased risk for heart disease."

Whether or not you've ever miscarried, you can reduce your risk of heart disease, by not smoking; eating a healthy diet to maintain good cholesterol levels and manage your weight; increasing your physical activity if you tend to be sedentary; and, if you have diabetes, working with your doctor to keep it under control.

Antibiotics May Prevent Miscarriage And Early Delivery

Samuel Bender, MD, Clinical Assistant Professor, Obstetrics and Gynecology, New York University School of Medicine.

Sandra A. Carson, MD, Professor, Obstetrics and Gynecology, Baylor School of Medicine, Houston, TX.

March 22, 2003, *The Lancet.*

A British study found that screening women for bacterial vaginosis early in pregnancy and giving antibiotics to those with an infection mild enough to cause no symptoms reduces the likelihood of miscarriage and premature delivery.

The British researchers acknowledge that at least 2 other studies of the use of antibiotics for the prevention of miscarriage have produced negative results. However, "the type, dose, and route of antibiotic used might be important with respect to outcome."

These researchers screened 6102 women from 12 to 22 weeks' gestation who were making their first prenatal hospital visit. They found 494 women with symptom-free bacterial vaginosis and divided them into 2 groups. One group was given 300-milligram oral doses of the antibiotic *clindamycin* twice daily; the other group got a placebo.

A few women dropped out of the study, but the researchers say the clinical results were clear. "Women receiving clindamycin had significantly fewer miscarriages or preterm deliveries."

The benefits were seen especially in women with severe infections. The incidence of miscarriage and preterm delivery in those women was 5.4% for those who got the antibiotic, 35.7% for those who didn't.

A NUDGE TOWARD TREATMENT

It's a result that pushes obstetricians and gynecologists toward antibiotic treatment when bacterial vaginosis is found, says Dr. Samuel Bender, a clinical assistant professor of obstetrics and gynecology at New York University School of Medicine.

"There has been a lot of literature in the last decade or so going backward and forward on it," Bender says. "Some studies show that treatment makes a difference, some show it does not." One factor involved in the mixed results is that all the studies have used different antibiotics, different doses, and different routes of delivery, oral or vaginal, he says. Two negative studies that got a lot of attention in the field used a different drug called metronidazole, Bender adds.

This study, he says, "offers a compelling reason to treat patients with antibiotics, even in the absence of symptoms."

As for screening, says Dr. Sandra A. Carson, a professor of obstetrics and gynecology at the Baylor School of Medicine, "it's something we do all the time by getting a Pap smear," adding the advice of the American College of Obstetrics and Gynecology that "women should have a Pap smear every year." Her assessment is that the study "may mean that patients, even if asymptomatic, need to be treated."

info More information about vaginal infections is available from the National Women's Health Information Center at *www.4women.gov/faq* and the National Institute of Allergy and Infectious Diseases at *www.niaid.nih.gov/factsheets/stdvag.htm.*

New Research Says Women May Want to 'Scale' Back on Eating Fish

Susan Schober, PhD, Senior Epidemiologist, National Center for Health Statistics, US Centers for Disease Control and Prevention, Hyattsville, MD.

April 2, 2003, *Journal of the American Medical Association*.

Most of us have low levels of mercury in our blood, but approximately 8% of women in the United States have levels above what is considered safe by federal standards, according to a government study.

"Overall, mercury levels are low in the US population," says study author Susan Schober, a senior epidemiologist at the National Center for Health Statistics.

Fish consumption is a significant source of mercury exposure. Schober cautions that pregnant women and women who plan to become pregnant should follow the US Food and Drug Administration (FDA) guidelines on fish consumption, as well as any state and local advisories on the amount of fish that is safe to eat.

Besides fish, mercury exposure comes from coal burning, the incineration of medical waste, dental fillings, and the workplace.

Schober and her colleagues conducted physical examinations and took blood samples to test for mercury levels in 705 children between the ages of 1 and 5 years. They also tested 1709 women between the ages of 16 and 49 years. And they interviewed the study participants—or their parents—about their consumption of fish or shellfish during the previous 30 days.

Most of the women and children had acceptable levels of mercury in their blood. Women, on average, had 3 times the level of mercury in their blood that the children did. Mercury levels were almost 4 times as high in women who ate 3 or more servings of fish a week, compared with those who reported eating no fish.

WHICH FISH IS SAFE?

When mercury interacts with microbes in the water, it changes into methylmercury, a known neurotoxin. Methylmercury is particularly dangerous to developing fetuses, the study says. Methylmercury slows fetal and child development and causes irreversible deficits in brain function.

The FDA recommends that pregnant women avoid eating swordfish, shark, tilefish, and king mackerel altogether. Other fish and shellfish should be limited to no more than 12 ounces per week. The Canadian Food Inspection Agency adds fresh and frozen tuna to that list.

Schober is quick to point out that "fish is an important food that has a lot of nutritional benefits, so we certainly don't want people to be so concerned [about mercury] that they don't eat fish." In fact, she says, the American Heart Association recommends eating 2 servings of fish a week.

Some fish are probably safer than others, the study reports. Haddock, tilapia, salmon, cod, pollock, and sole appear to have lower levels of methylmercury, according to the study.

Schober says it's important to pay attention to local and state advisories, as well the FDA guidelines, because some areas of the country may have higher mercury pollution than others.

What Everyone Should Know About Lupus

Raphael DeHoratius, MD, Professor, Medicine and Director, Lupus Study Center, Jefferson Medical College, Thomas Jefferson University, Philadelphia, PA.

January 2003, *Bottom Line/Health*.

Lupus symptoms are often subtle and easily confused with those caused by other conditions. As a result, many sufferers don't get a proper diagnosis for up to 3 years. Most people think of lupus as a "women's disease." After age 50, women account for three-quarters of the cases of this potentially deadly disease.

Like diabetes, rheumatoid arthritis and other autoimmune diseases, lupus occurs when the immune system mistakenly targets the body's own tissues for destruction.

However, lupus is potentially more serious because it triggers the production of antibodies that damage tissue throughout the body, including the skin, joints, and red and white blood cells.

Lupus antibodies also combine with body antigens, such as DNA, to form *immune complexes.* These inflammatory molecules travel in the blood and lodge in the kidneys, heart, lungs or other organs.

Most lupus sufferers can live normal, active lives—if they get effective care. *Here are the facts you must know to protect yourself against this disease...*

•There are 3 types of lupus.

•Systemic lupus is the most serious form. It can damage virtually every part of the body, including the heart and kidneys. Symptoms include skin ulcers...joint pain...fatigue...fever ...digestive problems...and intense sensitivity to sunlight.

•Discoid lupus mainly affects the skin. During flare-ups, a thick, scaly rash appears on the face, hands or other areas exposed to sun. About 20% of people with discoid lupus also experience joint pain, fatigue, anemia, or other symptoms.

•Drug-induced lupus occurs when the immune system produces antibodies to medications. The most common culprits are the heart drug *procainamide* (Pronestyl) and the blood pressure drugs *hydralazine* (Apresoline) and *methyldopa* (Aldomet). Sulfa-based drugs, including the antibiotic *sulfisoxazole* (Gantrisin), may also trigger reactions. Drug-induced lupus disappears within a few weeks of discontinuing the medication.

•Lupus is difficult to diagnose. Lupus

symptoms resemble those caused by dozens of conditions, including the flu, arthritis, and even psychological stress.

Symptoms may disappear for weeks, months, or years, then emerge in a serious "flare-up." Some sufferers are sick for days. Others have symptoms for months.

If your doctor suspects lupus, he/she should order an antinuclear antibody (ANA) blood test. This detects the presence of antibodies that suggest a heightened immune response characteristic of lupus.

Caution: The ANA test falsely indicates lupus up to 30% of the time. A positive reading doesn't mean that you have lupus—just that you need additional tests, including the anti-double-stranded DNA and anti-Smith (anti-Sm) antibody blood tests. These tests cost more than the ANA but are much more reliable.

•Lupus cannot be cured with medication.

Drug treatments only control *complications,* such as kidney inflammation (nephritis) or swelling of the heart membrane (pericarditis).

Lupus sufferers may need 1 or more of the following...

•Nonsteroidal anti-inflammatory drugs (NSAIDs). Over-the-counter (OTC) NSAIDs, such as *ibuprofen* (Motrin) and *naproxen* (Aleve), as well as prescription NSAIDs, such as *diclofenac* (Voltaren), reduce joint and muscle pain.

About 90% of people with lupus take 1 or more of these drugs...but they can't be used in individuals with impaired kidney function.

Helpful: Prescription NSAIDs aren't necessarily more effective than OTC varieties, but they may be cheaper if your insurance policy covers prescription drugs.

•Antimalarial drugs. *Hydroxychloroquine* (Plaquenil) and *chloroquine* (Aralen) prevent flare-ups of common lupus symptoms—fatigue, skin rash, joint pain, etc. The drugs take up to 3 months to work.

Hint: To curb side effects, such as diarrhea, rash and vision problems, your doctor should advise gradually decreasing the frequency with which you take the drugs when lupus symptoms have been "quiet" for 6 months to 1 year.

•Corticosteroids. Anti-inflammatory drugs in this class include *prednisone* (Cortan) and *methylprednisolone* (Medrol). They're the best drugs for controlling flare-ups. But because of side effects—bone thinning, ulcers, weakened skin, cataracts, and increased risk for heart disease in women—they should be used only when there's serious inflammation in the heart, kidneys, or other organs.

Helpful: Prescription or OTC hydrocortisone creams are effective at controlling skin rash. If used for less than 2 weeks, they rarely cause side effects because only small amounts of the active ingredients actually pass into the bloodstream.

•Immunosuppressants. They reduce immune-system activity and can prevent damage to the kidneys and central nervous system. Given orally or intravenously, such drugs as *azathioprine* (Imuran), *cyclophosphamide* (Cytoxan), and *mycophenolate* (CellCept) curb the production and action of tissue-damaging immune cells...and allow lower corticosteroid doses.

•**Lupus patients can help curb flare-ups.** The key is to eat a balanced diet and get enough rest. *They should also...*

•Use adequate sun protection outdoors. Wear a long-sleeved shirt, long pants, and a broad-brimmed hat...and use sunscreen with a sun-protection factor (SPF) of at least 15. Exposure to sunshine can trigger flare-ups.

•Avoid alcohol. It can interact with lupus medications and possibly increase liver and kidney damage caused by the disease.

•Avoid smoking. It lowers resistance to infections and accentuates the damage lupus can cause to the heart and blood vessels.

•**Lupus should be treated by a rheumatologist.** Continue seeing the same doctor over time. You're more likely to get an accurate diagnosis and optimum care when your doctor is aware of *patterns* as well as individual symptoms.

info To locate a rheumatologist who specializes in lupus, contact the Lupus Foundation of America, 301-670-9292, *www.lupus.org*.

Health Resources

■ **Administration on Aging**
Washington, DC 20201
202-619-0724
www.aoa.gov

■ **Alzheimer's Association**
225 North Michigan Ave., Suite 1700
Chicago, IL 60601-7633
800-272-3900, 312-335-8700
www.alz.org

■ **American Academy of Allergy, Asthma & Immunology**
611 East Wells St.
Milwaukee, WI 53202
800-822-2762, 414-272-6071
www.aaaai.org

■ **American Academy of Dermatology**
PO Box 4014
Schaumburg, IL 60168-4014
847-330-0230
www.aad.org

■ **American Academy of Neurology**
1080 Montreal Ave.
Saint Paul, MN 55116
800-879-1960, 651-695-2717
www.aan.com

■ **American Board of Medical Specialties**
1007 Church St., Suite 404
Evanston, IL 60201-5913
847-491-9091
Board Certification Verification:
866-ASK-ABMS (275-2267)
www.abms.org

■ **American Cancer Society**
1599 Clifton Rd. NE
Atlanta, GA 30329

800-ACS-2345 (227-2345)
www.cancer.org

■ **American Chiropractic Association**
1701 Clarendon Blvd.
Arlington, VA 22209
800-986-4636
www.amerchiro.org

■ **American Chronic Pain Association (ACPA)**
PO Box 850
Rocklin, CA 95677
800-533-3231
www.theacpa.org

■ **American College of Obstetricians and Gynecologists**
PO Box 96920
Washington, DC 20090-6920
800-673-8444, 202-638-5577
www.acog.org

■ **The American College of Rheumatology**
1800 Century Place, Suite 250
Atlanta, GA 30345
404-633-3777
www.rheumatology.org

■ **American Council for Headache Education**
19 Mantua Rd.
Mt. Royal, NJ 08061
856-423-0258
www.achenet.org

■ **American Council on Alcoholism**
PO Box 25126
Arlington, VA 22202
703-248-9005
Alcoholism Treatment HelpLine: 800-527-5344
www.aca-usa.org

American Council on Exercise (ACE)
4851 Paramount Dr.
San Diego, CA 92123
800-825-3636, 858-279-8227
www.acefitness.org

American Dental Association
211 E. Chicago Ave.
Chicago, IL 60611
312-440-2500
www.ada.org

American Diabetes Association
National Call Center
1701 North Beauregard St.
Alexandria, VA 22311
800-DIABETES (342-2383)
www.diabetes.org

American Dietetic Association
120 South Riverside Plaza, Suite 2000
Chicago, IL 60606-6995
800-877-1600
www.eatright.org

American Foundation for Urologic Disease
1128 North Charles St.
Baltimore, MD 21201
800-242-2383, 410-468-1800
www.afud.org

American Gastroenterological Association
4930 Del Ray Ave.
Bethesda, MD 20814
301-654-2055
www.gastro.org

American Geriatrics Society
350 Fifth Ave., Suite 801
New York, NY 10118
212-308-1414
www.americangeriatrics.org

The American Heart Association
7272 Greenville Ave.
Dallas, TX 75231
800-AHA-USA-1 (242-8721), 301-223-2307
www.americanheart.org

American Liver Foundation
75 Maiden Lane, Suite 603
New York, NY 10038
800-GO-LIVER (465-4837), 212-668-1000
www.liverfoundation.org

The American Lung Association
61 Broadway, 6th Floor
New York, NY 10006
212-315-8700
www.lungusa.org

American Lyme Disease Foundation, Inc.
293 Route 100
Somers, NY 10589
914-277-6970
www.aldf.com

American Macular Degeneration Foundation
PO Box 515
Northampton, MA 01061-0515
888-MACULAR (622-8527), 413-268-7660
www.macular.org

American Pain Foundation
201 N. Charles St., Suite 710
Baltimore, MD 21201-4111
888-615-PAIN (7246)
www.painfoundation.org

American Physical Therapy Association
1111 North Fairfax St.
Alexandria, VA 22314-1488
800-999-APTA (2782), 703-684-APTA
TDD: 703-683-6748
www.apta.org

American Psychological Association
750 First St. NE
Washington, DC 20002-4242
800-374-2721, 202-336-5500
www.apa.org

American Sleep Apnea Association
1424 K St. NW, Suite 302
Washington, DC 20005
202-293-3650
www.sleepapnea.org

American Society of Hypertension
148 Madison Ave., 5th Floor
New York, NY 10016
212-696-9099
www.ash-us.org

American Society of Plastic Surgeons
444 E. Algonquin Rd.
Arlington Heights, IL 60005
888-4-PLASTIC (475-2784)
www.plasticsurgery.org

American Speech–Language–Hearing Association
10801 Rockville Pike
Rockville, MD 20852
800-498-2071, 800-638-8255
www.asha.org

American Stroke Association
7272 Greenville Ave.
Dallas TX 75231
888-4-STROKE (478-7653)
www.strokeassociation.org

- **Anxiety Disorders Association of America**
  8730 Georgia Ave., Suite 600
  Silver Spring, MD 20910
  240-485-1001
  www.adaa.org

- **Arthritis Foundation**
  PO Box 7669
  Atlanta, GA 30357-0669
  800-283-7800
  www.arthritis.org

- **Centers for Disease Control and Prevention**
  1600 Clifton Rd.
  Atlanta, GA 30333
  404-639-3311
  TTY: 404-639-3312
  Public Inquiries: 800-311-3435
  www.cdc.gov

- **Colorectal Cancer Network (CCNetwork)**
  PO Box 182
  Kensington, MD 20895-0182
  301-879-1500
  www.colorectal-cancer.net

- **Council for Responsible Nutrition**
  1828 L St. NW, Suite 900
  Washington, DC, 20036-5114
  202-776-7929
  www.crnusa.org

- **The Crohn's & Colitis Foundation of America**
  386 Park Ave. S, 17th Floor
  New York, NY 10016
  800-932-2423
  www.ccfa.org

- **Deafness Research Association**
  1050 17th St., Suite 701
  Washington, DC 20036
  202-289-5850
  www.drf.org

- **Endocrine Society**
  The Hormone Foundation
  8401 Connecticut Ave., Suite 900
  Chevy Chase, MD 20815-5817
  800-HORMONE (467-6663)
  www.hormone.org

- **Herb Research Foundation**
  4140 15th St.
  Boulder, CO 80304
  303-449-2265
  www.herbs.org

- **The Leukemia & Lymphoma Society**
  1311 Mamaroneck Ave.
  White Plains, NY 10605
  800-955-4572, 914-949-5213
  www.leukemia-lymphoma.org

- **The Melanoma International Foundation**
  3741 Walnut St., #448
  Philadelphia, PA 19104
  866-INFO-NMF (463-6663)
  www.nationalmelanoma.org

- **National Cancer Institute**
  6116 Executive Blvd., MSC8322, Suite 3036A
  Bethesda, MD 20892-8322
  800-4-CANCER (422-6237)
  TTY: 800-332-8615
  www.cancer.gov

- **National Capital Poison Center**
  3201 New Mexico Ave. NW, Suite 310
  Washington, DC 20016
  202-362-3867
  Emergency Line: 800-222-1222
  www.poison.org

- **National Headache Foundation**
  820 N. Orleans, Suite 217
  Chicago, IL 60610
  888-NHF-5552 (643-5552)
  www.headaches.org

- **National Institute of Allergy and Infectious Diseases (NIAID)**
  Building 31, Room 7A-50
  31 Center Dr., MSC 2520
  Bethesda, MD 20892-2520
  301-496-1886
  www.niaid.nih.gov

- **National Institute of Arthritis and Musculoskeletal and Skin Diseases**
  One AMS Circle
  Bethesda, MD 20892-3675
  877-22-NIAMS (226-4267), 301-495-4484
  TTY: 301-565-2966
  www.niams.nih.gov

- **National Institute of Diabetes & Digestive & Kidney Diseases**
  Building 31, Room 9A04
  Center Drive, MSC 2560
  Bethesda, MD 20892-2560
  301-496-3583
  www.niddk.nih.gov

- **National Institute of Mental Health (NIMH)**
  6001 Executive Blvd.
  MSC 9663, Room 8184
  Bethesda, MD 20892-9663
  866-615-NIMH (6464), 301-443-4513
  TTY: 301-443-8431
  www.nimh.nih.gov

- **National Institute of Neurological Disorders and Stroke**
  PO Box 5801
  Bethesda, MD 20824
  800-352-9424, 301-496-5751
  TTY: 301-468-5981
  www.ninds.nih.gov

- **National Institute on Aging**
  Building 31, Room 5C27
  31 Center Dr., MSC 2292
  Bethesda, MD 20892
  301-496-1752
  www.nia.nih.gov

- **National Institute on Alcohol Abuse and Alcoholism (NIAAA)**
  6000 Executive Blvd., Willco Building
  Bethesda, MD 20892-7003
  301-443-0796
  www.niaaa.nih.gov

- **National Kidney Foundation**
  30 East 33rd St., Suite 1100
  New York, NY 10016
  800-622-9010, 212-889-2210
  www.kidney.org

- **National Library of Medicine**
  8600 Rockville Pike
  Bethesda, MD 20894
  888-FIND-NLM (346-3656), 301-594-5983
  www.nlm.nih.gov

- **National Multiple Sclerosis Society**
  733 Third Ave.
  New York, NY 10017
  800-FIGHT-MS (344-4867)
  www.nmss.org

- **National Osteoporosis Foundation**
  1232 22nd St. NW
  Washington, DC 20037-1292
  202-223-2226
  www.nof.org

- **National Prostate Cancer Coalition**
  1154 15th St. NW
  Washington, DC 20005
  888-245-9455, 202-463-9455
  www.4npcc.org

- **The National Psoriasis Foundation**
  6600 SW 92nd Ave., Suite 300
  Portland, OR 97223-7195
  800-723-9166, 503-244-7404
  www.psoriasis.org

- **The National Safety Council**
  1121 Spring Lake Dr.
  Itasca, IL 60143-3201
  630-285-1121
  www.nsc.org

- **National Sleep Foundation**
  1522 K St. NW, Suite 500
  Washington, DC 20005
  202-347-3471
  www.sleepfoundation.org

- **National Spinal Cord Injury Association**
  6701 Democracy Blvd., Suite 300-9
  Bethesda, MD 20817
  800-962-9629
  www.spinalcord.org

- **National Stroke Association**
  9707 E. Easter Lane
  Englewood, CO 80112
  800-STROKES (787-6537), 303-649-9299
  www.stroke.org

- **The National Women's Health Information Center**
  8550 Arlington Blvd., Suite 300
  Fairfax, VA 22031
  800-994-WOMAN (9662)
  www.4woman.gov

- **Parkinson's Disease Foundation**
  710 West 168th St.
  New York, NY 10032-9982
  800-457-6676
  www.pdf.org

- **The Skin Cancer Foundation**
  245 Fifth Ave., Suite 1403
  New York, NY 10016
  800-SKIN-490 (754-6490)
  www.skincancer.org

- **The Susan G. Komen Breast Cancer Foundation**
  5005 LBJ Freeway, Suite 250
  Dallas, TX 75244
  972-855-1600
  www.komen.org

- **United Network for Organ Sharing**
  PO Box 2484
  Richmond, VA 23218
  804-782-4800
  www.unos.org

- **US Food and Drug Administration**
  5600 Fishers Lane
  Rockville MD 20857-0001
  888-INFO-FDA (463-6332)
  www.fda.gov

Index

sleep apnea and, 137–138
trans fatty acids as risk factor for,
240
types defined, 191
visceral fat and, 235, 236
Cholesterol-lowering drugs
Alzheimer's and, 36
heart transplant patients and,
168–169
to reduce heart surgery risk, 183–184
as treatment for atherosclerosis, 188
as treatment for multiple sclerosis,
105
risk of not taking, 4–5
Chronic pain, 164
Circadian rhythms, and effect on
angioplasty success, 187
Coenzyme Q-10, as treatment for
Parkinson's, 28
Coffee, and Parkinson's disease, 26
Cognitive-behavior therapy, for
anxiety disorders, 128
Cognitive functioning. *See*
Alzheimer's disease; Blood
pressure; Dementia; Memory
Cohort method (of determining
cancer survival rates), 63–64
Colds, echinacea for, 203
Colon (colorectal) cancer.
See also Cancer
aspirin to prevent, 157–158
beta-carotene and, 81–82
E. coli and, 74–75
hormone replacement therapy and,
305, 307
human growth hormones and,
71–72
IGF2 gene, 73
obesity and increased risk of, 236,
318–319
prevention measures, 82, 319
sigmoidoscopy, 75
survival rate, 64
Complementary therapies
for Parkinson's disease, 28
Computed axial tomography (CAT)
scans, 83
Concussions and depression in
children, 151–152
Condroitin, 250
Congestive heart failure. *See*
Cardiovascular disease
Continuous positive airway pressure
(CPAP), 137, 138
Corticosteroids, 43, 211
for lupus, 326
Cortisol, 239

Cosmetics, anti-aging, 22–23
Cox-2 inhibitors, 26, 177
Cranberry juice, 192–193
Crohn's disease, 111–112, 161–162
Cryotherapy for warts, 207

D

Daily Value (DV), 14
Deafness gene, 285–286
Deep-brain stimulation, 27–28
DEET in bug repellent, 165
Defibrillation and CPR, 182
Dementia. *See also* Alzheimer's
disease and benefits of alcohol
consumption, 9
fish to prevent, 229–230
high blood pressure and, 116
hormone replacement therapy and,
5–6
Parkinson's disease and, 23, 24–25
screening, 9–10
"silent stroke" and, 299–300
"walking test" for, 6–7
Depression
Alzheimer's and, 35–36
concussions in children and, 151–152
heart problems and, 124–125
recurrence of, 130–131
warning signs of, 125
"Designer estrogens," 306–307
Diabetes
breakfast and lowered risk of, 234
carbohydrate counting, 91–92
erectile dysfunction and, 134
gene research, 86, 90–91
glucose monitoring devices, 94–95
grandfather's diet and risk for, 90–91
impaired glucose tolerance, 89–90
insulin resistance and heart disease,
92
insulin resistance syndrome, 87–88
multivitamins and infection
resistance, 94
niacin and reduced heart attack risk,
93–94
pancreatic islet transplantation for
Type 1, 84–85, 85
risk factors for, 89–90, 235
stem cell research, 85
trans fatty acids as risk factor for,
240
transdifferentiation, 85–86
types defined, 85, 93
wine drinking by women and,
86–87
women's leg length, and risk of,
88–89

Diet. *See also* Diet, low-carbohydrate;
Diet, low-fat
acne, and role of, 233
Alzheimer's and, 33–34
eating less for longevity, 228–229
food triggers for headaches, 260
high blood pressure and, 133
Parkinson's disease and, 23, 24–25
pills, 228
"Sensible Solution" diet, 219–220
Diet, low-carbohydrate
Atkins Diet, 218–219
dangers of, 220, 221
to reduce visceral fat, 235–236
versus low-fat diet, 220
Diet, low-fat
and macular degeneration, 20
versus Atkins Diet, 218–219
versus low-fat diet, 220
Dietary supplements, dangers of,
205–206
Digital rectal exam (DRE), 69
Digitalis and heart failure, 179–180
Dioxin, 274–275
Diuretics, kidney disease and, 110
DNA test for prostrate cancer, 157
Dogs. *See* Pets
Dopamine, 23, 26, 28
Driving, long-distance
and damage to driver's back, 248
tips for avoiding injury, 248
Drugs
antibiotics, 96–97, 97–98
antidepressants, 109–110
antinicotine/antialcohol drug,
102–103
cholesterol-lowering, 4–5, 105–106
costs, 3–4, 297
for Crohn's disease, 111–112
for erectile dysfunction, 104–105
errors, 12–13, 99–100
heart problems and, 98–99
for hypertension, 297
illegal importing of, 100
for kidneys, 110
for Lyme disease, 107–108
for multiple sclerosis, 105–106
for osteoporosis, 106–107
painkillers, 101
for psoriasis, 108–109
side effects, 15
Viagra pill splitter, 103
Drusen, 19
Duct tape for warts, 207
Dwarfism and longevity, 3
Dysthymia, 124–125